Countries and Concepts

Countries and Concepts

Politics, Geography, Culture

Thirteenth Edition

Michael G. Roskin
Lycoming College

Boston   Columbus   Indianapolis   New York   San Francisco   Amsterdam
Cape Town   Dubai   London   Madrid   Milan   Munich   Paris   Montréal   Toronto   Delhi
Mexico City   São Paulo   Sydney   Hong Kong   Seoul   Singapore   Taipei   Tokyo

Publisher: Charlyce Jones-Owen
Project Manager: Rob DeGeorge
Editorial Assistant: Maureen Diana
Operations Specialist: Mary Ann Gloriande
Digital Studio Project Manager: Tina Gagliostro
Permissions Project Manager: Peggy Davis
Project Coordination, Text Design, and Electronic Page Makeup: Integra Software Services Pvt., Ltd
Cover Design: Lumina Datamatics, Inc.
Cover Image: Michael G. Roskin
Printer and Binder: RR Donnelley/Crawfordsville
Cover Printer: Phoenix Color Corp.

Acknowledgements of third party content appear on page xix, which constitutes an extension of this copyright page

Library of Congress Cataloging-in-Publication Data

Roskin, Michael G.,
    Countries and concepts : politics, geography, culture / Michael G. Roskin,
Lycoming College. — Thirteenth edition.
        pages   cm.
    ISBN 978-0-13-396308-3 — ISBN 0-13-396308-X   1. Comparative government.   I. Title.
    JF51.R54 2015
    320.3—dc23

                                                                    2014017552

10 9 8 7 6 5 4 3 2 1

                                                Student Edition:
                                                ISBN 10:   0-13-396308-X
                                                ISBN 13: 978-0-13-396308-3

                                                A La Carte Edition:
                                                ISBN 10:   0-13-395145-6
                                                ISBN 13: 978-0-13-395145-5

                                                Instructor's Review Copy:
                                                ISBN 10:   0-13-395147-2
                                                ISBN 13: 978-0-13-395147-9

Brief Contents

Detailed Contents

8 India 329

Preface

Some students see little point in comparative politics. It may be interesting, they say, but it has no applied use. Not true; it can be quite practical. One of the great questions of the early twenty-first century is whether China can turn democratic. Comparative politics can contribute strongly to this question and provide both practical and theoretical knowledge. Without any pat answers, we can show how other countries founded and maintain democracies. Comparativists cannot predict what will happen in China, but they can warn with both positive and negative examples.

Brazil's generals, for example, gradually "decompressed" their authoritarian system into stable democracy, demonstrating that such transitions are possible. Louis XVI, on the other hand, waited until too late to allow a National Assembly. The result was the French Revolution and instability ever since. Beijing has already assimilated the lesson of the Soviet collapse, namely, the Soviet tendency to petrify until the system cracked. China's leadership has been far more flexible, practicing an "adaptive authoritarianism" that gives way in the face of mass unrest.

The thirteenth edition of *Countries and Concepts* introduces such examples in new boxes, one per chapter, on what that country could teach China. At this point, of course, Beijing is in no mood to listen to outside advice, which it denounces as meddling in its internal affairs and aimed at overthrowing the regime. Some day, however, after having waited until too late, the Zhongnanhai may feel a sudden need for comparative suggestions on how to democratize. Until then, the "lessons" are just intellectual exercises to demonstrate the utility of comparative politics.

Countries and Concepts does not attempt to create young scholars out of college students. Rather, it sees comparative politics as an important but usually neglected grounding in citizenship that we should be making available to our young people. I agree with the late Morris Janowitz (in his 1983 *The Reconstruction of Patriotism: Education for Civic Consciousness*) that civic education has declined in the United States and that this poses dangers for democracy. Our students are often uninformed about the historical, political, economic, geographical, and moral aspects of democracy, and to expose them to professional-level abstractions in political science ignores their civic education and offers material that is largely meaningless to them. An undergraduate is not a miniature graduate student.

Accordingly, *Countries and Concepts* includes a good deal of fundamental vocabulary and concepts, buttressed by many examples. It is dedicated to Kant's injunction that concepts must never be separated from percepts. It is readable. Many students neglect assigned readings; with *Countries and Concepts,* they cannot make the excuse that the reading is long or boring.

Some reviewers note that *Countries and Concepts* contains values and criticisms. This is part of my purpose. The two go together; if you have no values, then you have no basis from which to criticize. Value-free instruction is probably impossible. If successful, it would produce value-free students, and that, I think, should not be the aim of the educational enterprise. If one knows something with the head but not with the heart, then one really does not know it at all.

Is *Countries and Concepts* too critical? It treats politics as a series of ongoing quarrels for which no very good solutions can be found. It casts a skeptical eye on all political systems and all solutions proposed for political problems. As such, the book is not out to "get" any one country. All political systems are flawed; none approaches perfection. Let us simply say so. *Countries and Concepts* rejects absurd theories of smoothly functioning systems or rational calculators that never break down or make mistakes. Put it this way: If we are critical of the workings of our own country's politics—and many, perhaps most, of us are—why should we abandon that critical spirit in looking at other lands?

New to This Edition

Instructor input and the rapid march of events prompted some changes in the thirteenth edition of *Countries and Concepts*.

Country updates include:

- *France*: Socialist François Hollande won the presidency in 2012 but became deeply unpopular.
- *Germany*: Angela Merkel was reelected chancellor in 2013, but without great enthusiasm.
- *Japan*: The Liberal Democrats returned to power under a nationalistic prime minister.
- *Russia*: Putin's third presidential term brought a deliberate crisis with Ukraine.
- *China*: A fifth generation of leaders took power in Beijing and instituted economic but not political reforms.
- *India*: The BJP and Modi, pledging economic growth, ousted the Congress Party in 2014.
- *Mexico*: PRI returned to the presidency but as a moderate and modern party.
- *Brazil*: Mass anger disrupted Brazil as its economy stalled.
- *Nigeria*: Violence among Northern Islamists shook an increasingly unstable Nigeria.
- *Iran*: A moderate cleric won the presidency in 2013 but liberalized little.

The current edition retains most of the previous changes. A general and abstract introductory chapter surveys the theory behind comparative politics, including the definition of democracy, the rise of states, and modernization theory. We retain Brazil, which appeared in earlier editions, as its growth from a shaky to a firm democracy shows that a country can modernize out of praetorianism. A "Why This Country Matters" section introduces every chapter. We also keep the shorter, one-chapter versions of our major systems—Britain, France, Germany, Russia, and China—to keep them closer in length to the other systems—Japan, India, Mexico, Brazil, Nigeria, and Iran—and easier to assign in the course of one semester.

Features

The thirteenth edition continues the loose theoretical approach of previous editions with the observation that politics, on the surface at least, is composed of a number of conflicts or quarrels. These quarrels, if observed over time, form patterns of some durability beyond the specific issues involved. What I call "patterns of interaction" are the relationships among politically relevant groups and individuals, what they call, in Russian, *kto-kovo*, who does what to whom. There are two general types of such patterns: (1) between elites and masses and (2) among and within elites.

Before we can appreciate these patterns, however, we must study the political culture of a particular country, which leads us to its political institutions and, ultimately, to its political history. This produces a fivefold division in the study of each country. We could start with a country's contemporary political quarrels and work backward, but it is probably better to begin with the underlying factors as a foundation from which to understand their impact on modern social conflict. This book goes from history to institutions to political culture to patterns of interaction to quarrels. This arrangement need not supplant other approaches. Instructors have had no trouble utilizing this book in connection with their preferred theoretical insights.

Also, political geography gets some of the attention it deserves. Instructors agree that ignorance of geography is widespread; the subject seems to have been dropped from most school curricula. *Countries and Concepts* tries to fill this gap by combining political with geographical material, and the two fields overlap.

The structure and purpose of *Countries and Concepts* continue as before. The book analyzes four European nations plus China at somewhat greater length and seven other nations a bit more briefly. I am willing to change this balance in subsequent editions, depending on instructor input. Should, for example, France and Germany shrink some more and India and Nigeria expand? The first part of the book (Chapters 2 through 5) deals with democracies, the second part (Chapters 6 and 7) with post-Communist Russia and China, and the third part (Chapters 8 through 12) with the developing areas.

Our greater coverage of the developing areas is called for by their economic growth and the shift of U.S. interest far beyond Europe. The emerging lands are simply too important, especially on the question of democracy. China, India, Mexico, Brazil, Nigeria, and Iran are not "representative" systems—What developing-area countries are?—but are interesting in their six different relationships to democracy: (1) the suppression of democracy in a rapidly industrializing China, (2) a durable if imperfect democracy in India, (3) democracy stabilizing in Mexico after a long period of one-party rule, (4) the establishment of democracy in Brazil, (5) the difficult founding of a stable democracy in coup-prone Nigeria, and (6) democracy smothered by an Islamic revolution in Iran. These six systems provide a counterpoint to the more settled systems of Europe and Japan. Instructors can and do omit some or all of these systems—for lack of time or to focus more closely on other countries—without breaking the continuity of the text.

The order of studying these countries is not fixed. I find four groupings convenient, each followed by an exam, to facilitate comparisons between countries with similar problems: (1) Britain and France, (2) Germany and Japan, (3) Russia and China, and (4) India, Mexico, Brazil, Nigeria, and Iran. The book may lend itself to other groupings. Some may want to compare China and India, the Asian giants on two very different developmental paths.

Also included are the chapter-opening learning objectives, which prime students for the main points, and the running marginal glossaries, which help students build their vocabularies as they read. The definitions here are those of a political scientist; in other contexts, one might find different definitions. Questions at the end of each chapter will help students review the concepts they've learned. The feature boxes still have poster-heads—Geography, Democracy, Personalities, Political Culture, Comparison, and, now, China Lessons—to give them greater focus and continuity.

Acknowledgments

I welcome your suggestions on any area of the book and its supplementary materials. Many have generously offered their comments, corrections, and criticism. Especially valuable were the comments of Julie Mazzei, Kent State University; Edward Schwerin, Florida Atlantic University; Yury Polsky, Westchester University; David Goldberg, College of DuPage; Timothy Schorn, College of South Dakota; Nina Barzachka, Mary Baldwin College; Philip Otterness, Warren Wilson College; Sam Hoff, Delaware State University; Elizabeth Nyman, University of Louisiana at Lafayette; Anne Marie Choup, University of Alabama, Huntsville; Gunther Hega, Western Michigan University; Jacqueline Gehring, Allegheny College; Danny Damron, Brigham Young University; Robert L. Youngblood, Arizona State University; Eleanor E. Zeff, Drake University; Christian Soe, California State University at Long Beach; Cheryl L. Brown, University of North Carolina at Charlotte; Karl W. Ryavec, University of Massachusetts at Amherst; Frank Myers, State University of New York at Stony

Brook; Ronald F. Bunn, University of Missouri at Columbia; Said A. Arjomand, State University of New York at Stony Brook; Larry Elowitz, Georgia College; Arend Lijphart, University of California at San Diego; Thomas P. Wolf, Indiana University, Southeast; Susan Matarese, University of Louisville; Hanns D. Jacobsen, Free University of Berlin (on Germany); Ko Shioya of *Bungei Shunju* (on Japan); Carol Nechemias, Penn State at Harrisburg; Marcia Weigle, Bowdoin College (on Russia); Lowell Dittmer, University of California at Berkeley; Richard Suttmeier, University of Oregon; Kenneth Lan and Morton Holbrook, United International College, Zhuhai, China; Bill K. P. Chou, University of Macau; Liu Lin, Jishi Li, and Chu Chengya, Shandong University; Dan O'Connell, Florida Atlantic University; Peter Muth (on China); Jim Coyle, Chapman University, and Lycoming colleague Mehrdad Madresehee (on Iran); John Peeler, Bucknell University; Stephen D. Morris, Middle Tennessee State University; and Niels de Terra (on Mexico); Robbins Burling, University of Michigan; Sumit Ganguly, Indiana University (on India); and Ed Dew, Fairfield University, for his suggestion to include geography. And to several professors in China—who must remain nameless—I say thanks and *Minzhu!* All errors, of course, are my own. Instructors may send professional comments and corrections to me at maxxumizer@gmail.com. I am grateful for suggestions for subsequent editions.

Michael G. Roskin

BREAK THROUGH
To learning reimagined

REVEL™

Educational technology designed for the way today's students read, think, and learn

When students are engaged deeply, they learn more effectively and perform better in their courses. This simple fact inspired the creation of REVEL: an immersive learning experience designed for the way today's students read, think, and learn. Built in collaboration with educators and students nationwide, REVEL is the newest, fully digital way to deliver respected Pearson content.

REVEL enlivens course content with media interactives and assessments— integrated directly within the authors' narrative—that provide opportunities for students to read about and practice course material in tandem. This immersive educational technology boosts student engagement, which leads to better understanding of concepts and improved performance throughout the course.

Learn more about REVEL
www.pearsonhighered.com/revel/

Supplements

Pearson is pleased to offer several resources to qualified adopters of *Countries and Concepts* and their students that will make teaching and learning from this book even more effective and enjoyable. Several of the supplements for this book are available at the Instructor Resource Center (IRC), an online hub that allows instructors to quickly download book-specific supplements. Please visit the IRC welcome page at www.pearsonhighered.com/irc to register for access.

Instructor's Manual/Test Bank

This resource includes learning objectives, chapter outlines, chapter summaries, lecture starters, discussion questions, activities, and teaching suggestions, as well as original multiple-choice, true/false, short answer, and essay questions for each chapter. Available exclusively on the IRC.

Pearson MyTest

This flexible, online test-generating software includes all questions found in the test bank, allowing instructors to create their own personalized exams. Instructors can also edit any of the existing test questions and even add new questions. Other special features of this program include random generation of test questions, creation of alternate versions of the same test, scrambling of question sequence, and test preview before printing. Available exclusively on the IRC.

PowerPoint® Presentation

Organized around a lecture outline, these multimedia presentations also include photos, figures, and tables from each chapter. Available exclusively on the IRC.

Longman Atlas of World Issues (0-205-78020-2)

From population and political systems to energy use and women's rights, the *Longman Atlas of World Issues* features full-color thematic maps that examine the forces shaping the world. Featuring maps from the latest edition of *The Penguin State of the World Atlas*, this excerpt includes critical thinking exercises to promote a deeper understanding of how geography affects many global issues.

Goode's World Atlas (0-321-65200-2)

First published by Rand McNally in 1923, *Goode's World Atlas* has set the standard for college reference atlases. It features hundreds of physical, political, and thematic maps as well as graphs, tables, and a pronouncing index.

Chapter 1
The Uses of Comparative Politics

Athens fell into paralysis in the fifth century BC and never recovered. Could it happen to current political systems?

Learning Objectives

1.1 Explain how comparative politics looks at the paralysis problem.

1.2 Contrast the terms *nation* and *state*.

1.3 Illustrate the impact a country's past has on its present politics.

1.4 List the main institutional structures most modern countries have.

1.5 Identify the most common social cleavages and explain how they influence political culture.

1.6 Describe how generalizations can lead to theory. Give examples.

1.7 Evaluate the importance of economics as a political quarrel.

The Paralysis Problem

1.1 Explain how comparative politics looks at the paralysis problem.

Much of the world faces what might be termed a "paralysis problem": governments stuck in situations they know are bad but blocked by opposing domestic forces from doing much about them. Related to the "double-bind" or "Catch-22" problem in which people know they must do something but are not allowed to, the paralysis problem afflicts most of the 11 countries in this book. Only Germany is in relatively good shape because of painful reforms carried out years earlier, but Germany too is paralyzed between bailing out feckless economies to the south or watching the eurozone—and perhaps the entire European Union—collapse. The U.S. Congress is so paralyzed, it can barely pass a budget.

Simultaneously, the democracies of the United States, European Union, and Japan are paralyzed over economic stagnation that potentially could damage their political systems. Torn between opposing interest groups and advice, no leaders dare upset large portions of their public with bold reforms. Our developing countries, although continuing to grow, face monumental corruption problems that undermine regime legitimacy. They keep promising to clean up but cannot fire large numbers of the corrupt officials they depend on to run the system. Eventually, some countries could reach a "tipping point" in which either disgruntled masses rise up or the military takes over.

comparative politics
Subfield of political science focused on interactions *within* other countries.

austerity
Government cutting expenditures to balance budget; economic belt-tightening.

authoritarian
Nondemocratic or dictatorial politics.

democracy
Political system of mass participation, competitive elections, and human and civil rights.

Here is where **comparative politics** is useful. It cannot predict, but it can warn. By comparing several countries it can discern patterns that specialized studies of one country cannot. Which governments apply **austerity** policies in the face of massive unemployment? Do their electorates react by voting them out? Are business, labor, and other interest groups so entrenched that they block needed reforms? How then may a government override them? Do ideological passions divide the country? How can **authoritarian** systems transition to **democracy**? These are some of the questions comparative politics attempts to answer with data and analyses.

Comparativists might look at revolutions in Tunisia, Egypt, Libya, Yemen, and Syria and note that none of the old regimes had much legitimacy; their people did not respect them. Second, most of their population was young, under 30, a "demographic bulge," many of them educated but unemployed or underemployed. Third, corruption, always a problem in these countries, got worse, probably related to economic growth. And fourth, the social media—Internet, cellphones, Twitter, and Facebook—spread worldwide just as these problems were boiling up. China seems have two of these four factors (the third and fourth). What, then, are China's chances for stability?

power
Ability of A to get B to do what A wants.

quarrels
As used here, important, long-term political issues.

Next, a comparativist might attempt to predict how revolutions will end up. Revolutions show a strong tendency to become chaotic and fall under a dictator. Few end well. To head off unhappy endings, a political scientist might suggest that the current regime carry out a gradual, peaceful transition aimed at eventual democracy. Unfortunately, by their very nature, authoritarian regimes reject advice to give up their wealth and **power**. Then, too late, when some incident has triggered a crisis, the frightened regime promises reforms. But its opponents sense weakness and demand the regime's ouster. Comparative politics offers the concepts, vocabulary, and case studies that can be useful, especially in tumultuous times.

Quarrels Over Time

There is no single, set way to compare countries. This book takes politics as a series of enduring **quarrels** that define the country's divisions and conflicts. A religious split or civil war long ago, for example, may influence party voting for centuries. Knowing a country's "quarrels over time" launches our analyses of a given political system. This book does not sell any one particular theory or methodology but uses a loose framework of five basic questions,

Democracy

Is Democracy Inevitable?

The long-term trend clearly favors democracy. From a handful of democracies after World War II, now perhaps half of the world's 193 nations are fully or partially democratic (see Defining Democracy box below for the Freedom House rankings). The human thirst for respect and dignity eventually weakens dictatorships. But it is also clear that democracy does not come easily or automatically, as Russia, Iraq, and Afghanistan attest. Here are some questions comparative politics might ask about the recent wave of revolution and democracy:

1. Where, historically, did democracy first appear? Why there? Is it connected with Protestantism?

2. Does democracy require certain philosophical and/or religious roots?

3. The American Revolution led to democracy, so why does this rarely happen elsewhere?

4. Why is democracy so difficult? Why does it often lead to chaos and dictatorial takeover?

5. Does democracy require a large middle class or certain levels of per capita wealth or education?

6. Which struggles are the most dangerous for the survival of democracy—class, religious, ethnic, or territorial?

international relations (IR)
Politics among countries.

followed up by many detailed questions. These five questions roughly follow the intellectual evolution of political science over a century: from history, to institutions, to political culture, to interactions, to policy.

1. *How has the past impacted current politics?* We pay little attention to the details of history—that's for historians—but ask, "What happened then that matters now?" How has the country's past set up its current problems? The rule of old monarchs and old regional conflicts may echo in present institutions, psychology, and quarrels.

2. *What are the main institutions?* Institutions are structures of power, sometimes spelled out in constitutions but often the slow buildup of usages evolved over time. Who really has power in this country? Is power divided or concentrated, democratic or dictatorial? How are the parliament and chief executive elected?

Comparison

Comparative Politics among Political Science Subfields

Comparative politics sees itself as the cornerstone of political inquiry (see box about Aristotle), but it is one subfield among several within political science. Comparative politics can and should inform the other subfields. Sometimes failure to do so weakens analyses.

International relations is often confused with comparative politics—because both deal with foreign events—but they are different. Comparative politics studies political interactions *within* countries, whereas international relations studies what happens *among* countries. **International relations (IR)** tends to look at countries like billiard balls colliding with each other on the world pool table; comparative politics looks inside each ball to see how it works. The two, of course, influence each other.

Policy makers who attempt to apply IR perspectives without analyzing what is going on *inside* the countries involved often err. Knowing little of Afghanistan's, Iraq's, and Libya's tribes, religions, ethnic hatreds, and tumultuous histories, Washington officials trained in IR plunged us into other countries' civil wars, conflicts that were difficult to end or withdraw from. Comparativists, on the other hand, need some IR to explain foreign influences on domestic politics.

U.S. politics, although focused on domestic institutions and processes, sometimes picks a comparative perspective in emphasizing either American exceptionalism or similarities with other countries. Comparisons among U.S. states or over time (such as the powers of the presidency in 1800, 1900, and 2000) can also use techniques of comparative politics.

Political theory, often focused on major thinkers, attempts to define the good polity. Aristotle understood that one of the best ways to do this is by comparing several systems.

Public administration, which studies how bureaucracies function, benefits greatly from a comparative perspective. Does administration depend more on institutions or political culture?

Constitutional law, focused entirely on the U.S. Constitution and legal system, can become myopic in supposing that words on paper alone determine the fate of the country. Some comparison could correct this.

Public policy studies the interaction of politics and economics in order to develop efficient programs. Comparative data on health care, energy policy, education, and much else can help eliminate wishful thinking and supposition in this crucial field.

3. *How does the political culture influence politics?* Much depends on the customs and psychology of the people, their political culture. Are they trusting or cynical? Does ideology play a major role—if so, which ideology—or are people mostly pragmatic? Is the country, or regions of it, religious or secular? Could democracy take root in this country?

demagogue
Manipulative politician who wins votes through impossible promises.

4. *What are the patterns of interaction?* Here we get to what is conventionally called "politics." Who does what to whom? How do parties win elections? Which are the most powerful interest groups, and how do they make their voices heard? Who tends to prevail? Are things stable or are reforms overdue?

Personalities

Aristotle

"You cannot be scientific if you are not comparing," UCLA's great James Coleman used to tell his students long ago. He was actually echoing the founder of political science, Aristotle, who recognized that comparison was the basis of this discipline, its cardinal method. Aristotle sent out his students to collect information on Greece's many city-states (*polis*), which he then compared in his *Politics*, the work that gave the study of governance its first empirical database. In contrast, Aristotle's predecessor, Plato, focused almost entirely on Athens and used reason with little data for his *Republic*. As Kant saw centuries ago, reason alone is highly fallible. Reasoning from a factual basis, on the other hand, can be powerful.

One of Aristotle's classifications of Greek city-states, a sixfold table, has endured for centuries and is still useful. Aristotle first counted the number of rulers: one, several, or many. Then he divided each into "rule in the interest of all" and "rule in the interest of self." The first Aristotle called the good, legitimate form of governance; the second he called the bad, corrupt form. Then he named them:

Number of Rulers	Legitimate Form *Rule in Interest of All*	Corrupt Form *Rule in Interest of Selves*
one	monarchy	tyranny
Several	aristocracy	oligarchy
many	polity	democracy

For Aristotle, the worst form of government was "democracy," which we would call mob rule. He had seen how **demagogues** swayed mobs to make themselves powerful and destroy ancient Athens. He had good things to say about aristocracy, rule of the best (Greek *aristos*), and the polity, a calm, moderate democracy. But any of the legitimate forms, warned Aristotle, can decay into its corrupt counterpart.

Aristotle also found that the best-governed city-states had large middle classes. A large lower class could be seduced by demagogues into plundering the property of the middle class. A too-powerful rich class, however, could ignore citizen needs and make themselves even richer and more powerful. Either way, the state soon comes to an end. But a large middle class, neither rich nor poor, seeks good, stable governance with limits on power. Notice how both these points help explain the difficulty of establishing democracy in several countries today.

5. *What do they quarrel about?* Here we get to ongoing issues, visible in the country's media or in talking with citizens. The chief issue is usually the **political economy**. Is the economy growing? Why or why not? What reforms are suggested? How did the government handle the 2008–2009 recession? Should income be redistributed from better- to worse-off citizens? Noneconomic issues sometimes loom: Do the country's regions seek more autonomy or even to break away? Should immigrants be excluded or assimilated? Should touchy parts of the nation's past be covered up or faced?

political economy
Mutual influence of politics and economy; what government should do in the economy.

Democracy

Defining Democracy

Democracy is not a simple thing or one that automatically grows after *authoritarian* or *totalitarian* regimes have fallen. We were naive about stable democracy soon coming to Russia and Iraq. Democracy is a complex balancing act, requiring a political culture with the right philosophical, moral, economic, and legal underpinnings. Most definitions of democracy include the following:

Accountability. Elected officials must face a real possibility of losing re-election. This induces them to adopt Friedrich's *rule of anticipated reactions*.

Equality. One person, one vote. No citizens can be excluded. All may run for office.

Competition. Several candidates and parties compete in free and fair elections. A one-party system cannot be democratic.

Alternation. Occasional turnovers in power must replace the "in" party with the "out" party.

Representation. "The room will not hold all," so a few fairly represent the many. The electoral system does this, either by single-member districts (as in the United States and Britain) or proportional representation (as in Germany and Sweden).

Free media. Only democracies permit the press—now including the new social media—to criticize the government. This is the quickest check for democracy.

Harvard's Samuel Huntington suggested a "two-turnover test" for stable democracy. Two alternations of government—elections where one party replaces another—indicate a firmly rooted democracy. Since the Polish Communist regime fell in 1989, Poland has had several electoral turnovers from left to right and back again, indicating a well-rooted democracy. Russia has never had a turnover and is not soon likely to. No turnovers, no democracy.

Freedom House (FH) in Washington uses a seven-point scale to annually rank countries on how much they accord citizens political rights and civil liberties. FH calls 1 to 2.5 "free," 3 to 5 "partly free," and 5.5 to 7 "not free." Russia slid lower during the Putin years, but Indonesia advanced with a new democracy. Some of FH's 2014 findings are shown in the table below.

United States	1.0	free
Canada	1.0	free
Britain	1.0	free
Japan	1.0	free
Brazil	2.0	free
India	2.5	free
Indonesia	2.5	free
Mexico	3.0	partly free
Turkey	3.5	partly free
Nigeria	4.0	partly free
Russia	5.5	not free
Iran	6.0	not free
China	6.5	not free
Cuba	6.5	not free
North Korea	7	not free

Nations and States

1.2   Contrast the terms *nation* and *state*.

The Latin root of **nation** means *birth*, but few nations now define themselves by race (Japan and Korea still try); rather, *nation* now means people with a common sense of identity who often share the same language, culture, or religion. Nation building is not quick, easy, or natural. To build modern France, kings united several regions first by the sword and then by language and culture. The United States is a bizarre mix of peoples, processed over time into holding a set of common values. India and Nigeria, both mixes of languages and religions, are still engaged in nation building.

State means governmental institutions and laws. Obviously, these are not states in the sense of the 50 U.S. states, which lack **sovereignty** because ultimately Washington's laws prevail. Historically, states preceded and often formed nations. Over the centuries, the French government, by decreeing use of a certain dialect and spelling and enforcing nationwide educational standards, molded a French consciousness. The French state invented the French nation. All nations are, to a certain degree, **constructed**, somewhat artificial.

We might settle on the term *country*, which originally meant a rural area where people shared the same dialect and traditions but broadened in meaning until it became synonymous with nation or state. Some used *nation-state* to combine the psychological and structural elements, but the term did not catch on. Nation-states were often defined as having territory, population, independence, government, and other attributes, but none of them are clear-cut.

Territory would seem to be a basic requirement, but what about those who have a strong sense of peoplehood but lack real estate? For example, the Jews turned their sense of nationhood into Israel, and the Palestinians now define themselves as a nation that is ready for statehood. And what happens when territorial claims overlap? History is a poor guide, as typically many tribes and invaders have washed over the land over the centuries. France's Alsatians, on the west bank of the Rhine River, speak German and have Germanic family names. But they also speak French and think of themselves as French. Should Alsace belong to France or Germany? Wars are fought over such questions.

Population is obviously essential. But many countries have populations divided by language or **ethnicity**. Sometimes the groups are angry and wish to break away. Like the ex-Soviet Union, ex-Yugoslavia was composed of several quarrelsome nationalities whose departure destroyed the country. All countries, to be sure, are more or less artificial, but over time, some, such as France, have psychologically inculcated a sense of common nationhood that overrides earlier regional or ethnic loyalties. Germany has done this more recently, and India and China are still working on it. In Nigeria, the process has barely begun.

Independence means that the state governs itself as a sovereign entity. Colonies, such as India under the British, become nation-states when the imperial power departs, as the British did in 1947. Diplomatic recognition by other countries, especially by the major powers, confirms a country's independence and helps its economy. China got a boost when

nation
Cultural element of country; people psychologically bound to one another.

state
Institutional or governmental element of country.

sovereignty
Last word in law in a given territory; being boss on your own turf.

constructed
Deliberately created but widely accepted as natural.

ethnicity
Cultural characteristics differentiating one group from another.

failed state
Collapse of sovereignty; essentially, no national governing power.

secularization
Diminishment of role of religion in government and society.

the United States recognized it in 1972. Some countries, however, are more sovereign and independent than others. East European lands during the Cold War were Soviet satellites; Moscow controlled their major decisions. Are Central American "banana republics," under U.S. influence, truly sovereign and independent? Sovereign independence may be a convenient legal fiction.

Government is the crux of being a state. No government means anarchy, with the high probability that the country will fall apart or be conquered. Some call countries such as Afghanistan and Somalia **failed states**. Sometimes government can precede states. The Continental Congress preceded and founded the United States. A government can be in exile, as was de Gaulle's Free French government during World War II. The mere existence of a government does not automatically mean that it effectively governs the whole country. In many of the developing lands, the government's writ falls off as one travels farther from the capital. In several Mexican states, drug lords fight virtual civil war against the Mexican government and army.

Geography

What Made the Modern State

Europe began to stir in the eleventh century (late Middle Ages), but the Renaissance—starting in the fourteenth century—accelerated growth in art, philosophy, science, commerce, and population across Europe. The political system changed from feudalism to absolutism as monarchs increased and centralized their power over the nobles. By the middle of the fifteenth century, Europe was set for a revolution:

- **1453** The Turks used cannons to crack open the walls of Constantinople. European monarchs quickly acquired the new weapon to subdue nobles and consolidate their kingdoms.

- **1454** Gutenberg printed with moveable type. Printing increased the spread of information, speeding up all other processes and displacing Latin with local tongues. Printed materials helped the national capital govern outlying provinces.

- **1488** The Portuguese rounded Africa in order to reach Asia, soon followed by …

- **1492** The New World opened. Countries with access to the sea (Spain, Portugal, England, France, and the Netherlands) rushed to Asia, Africa, and the Americas for trade and colonies.

- **1494** Italian monk Luca Pacioli codified double-entry accounting, making it possible to control large businesses, which encouraged growth.

- **1517** Luther nailed his 95 theses to the church door and founded Protestantism. Soon, Protestant kings split from Rome and set up national churches, as in England and Sweden.

- **1545** This led to the wars of religion, first the Schmalkaldic War of 1545–1555 and then the devastating Thirty Years War of 1618–1648. These conflicts increased state power and curtailed the church's temporal power, leading to **secularization**.

- **1602** The world's first stock exchange opened in Amsterdam to trade shares in the new Dutch East India Company.

- **1618–1648** The Thirty Years War forced state administration to greatly improve. Warring monarchs, desperate for money, needed reliable tax bases and tax collectors. France's Richelieu and Sweden's Oxenstierna founded modern, rational administration to control and tax an entire country. The state got its own budget, separate from the royal household budget.

In sum, nation-states are not as clearcut as supposed; their realities are messy but interesting. This is one reason for using the admittedly vague term "country": It avoids **reification**, a constant temptation in the social sciences but one we must guard against.

The Modern State

Whatever we call the modern state—country, state, or nation-state—we must recognize that its current form is relatively recent. To be sure, states appear at the dawn of written history. (Ancient kingdoms, in fact, invented writing in order to tax and control.) But the modern state is only about half a millennium old and traces back to the replacement of old European feudal monarchies with what were called "new monarchies" and subsequently the "strong state." There are many factors in this shift; it is impossible to pinpoint which were the causes and which the consequences. **Causality** is always difficult to demonstrate in the social sciences, but the box "What Made the Modern State" discusses changes that ushered in the modern state. Notice how they happened about the same time and how each reinforced the others in a package of incredible change.

By the end of the Thirty Years War in 1648, the feudal system had been displaced by the modern state. **Feudalism** had balanced power between monarch and nobles; it was loose and did not tolerate strong national government. It was not oriented to change or expansion. The new monarchies, on the other hand, were **absolutist**, concentrating all power in themselves, disdaining the old medieval constitution in which their powers balanced with nobles and using new economic, administrative, and military tools to increase their power. Royalist philosophers extolled the strong monarch and coined the term *sovereignty*. In consolidating their powers, monarchs had the concept of nation celebrated, giving rise to the notion of nationality, of belonging to a nation rather than merely being the subject of a hereditary ruler.

Nationalism

One can find a sort of nationalism far back in history—Israelites against Philistines, Romans against Carthaginians, Vietnamese against Chinese—but the French Revolution unleashed modern nationalism. As the armies of German princes closed in on the Revolution in 1792, the French people rallied *en masse* to repel the foe, believing they were defending both the Revolution and the *patrie* (fatherland), and the two concepts merged. France, the revolutionaries claimed, was destined to liberate and reform the rest of Europe. The concept of a nation embodying everything good was thus born, and it was spread throughout Europe by Napoleon's enthusiastic legions.

By its very nature, nationalism was contagious. The French soldiers turned into brutal and arrogant occupiers, and across Europe, local patriots rose up against them with the nationalism brought by the French. French nationalism thus triggered Spanish, German, and Russian nationalism. By the late nineteenth century, with German and Italian unification, most Europeans had either formed nationalistic states or desired to (for example, Poland). Thinkers

reification
Taking theory as reality; from Latin *res*, thing.

causality
Proving that one thing causes another.

feudalism
Political system of power dispersed and balanced between king and nobles.

absolutism
Royal dictatorship that bypasses nobles.

Comparing: Some Basic Figures

	Population		Per Capita GDP		Workforce	Infant Mortality
	in Millions 2014	Annual Growth Rate 2014	PPP* 2013	Growth 2013	in Agriculture	per 1,000 Live Births
Britain	64	0.54%	$37,300	1.4%	1.4%	4.4
France	66	0.45	35,700	0.2	3.8	3.3
Germany	81	−0.18	39,500	0.5	1.6	3.5
Japan	127	−0.13	37,100	2.0	3.9	2.1
Russia	142	−0.03	18,100	1.3	9.7	7
China	1,356	0.44	9,800	7.6	34.8	14.8
India	1,236	1.25	4,000	4.7	49.0	43.1
Mexico	120	1.21	15,600	1.2	13.4	12.6
Brazil	203	0.80	12,100	2.5	15.7	19.2
Nigeria	177	2.47	2,800	6.2	70.0	74
Iran	81	1.22	12,800	−1.5	16.9	39
United States	319	0.77	52,800	1.6	0.7	6.2

*Purchasing power parity, currencies corrected to take into account the local cost of living.

SOURCE: *CIA World Factbook*

Tables such as this are approximate and quickly out of date. Events change economic data wildly from one year to another. Figures from developing countries are not-too-accurate estimates. Population growth includes immigration, important for the U.S. figure. Averages conceal major inequalities between rich and poor and among regions within countries in income and infant mortality, especially in the developing lands. The last two items, percent of workforce in agriculture and infant mortality, indicate relative levels of development: the lower both are, the more developed the country is.

such as Germany's Hegel and Italy's Mazzini extolled the nation as the highest level of human (or possibly divine) development.

The modern state and its nationalism spread worldwide. Driven to expand, the Europeans conquered Latin America, Asia, and Africa. Only Japan and Turkey kept the Europeans out; Meiji Japan carried out a brilliant "defensive modernization." The European imperialists introduced nationalism to their subject peoples. By integrating and administering previously fragmented territories, the British in India, the French in Indochina, and the Dutch in Indonesia taught "the natives" to think of themselves as a nation that, of right, deserved to be independent. Now virtually the entire globe is populated by national states, each guarding its sovereign independence and many of them ablaze with nationalism.

Impact of the Past

1.3 Illustrate the impact a country's past has on its present politics.

Several leading political scientists argue that the way a political system began governs much of its subsequent development. Like a simple path that, over the centuries, turns into a road and then into a highway, political institutions and cultures gradually deepen the tracks laid down earlier until they are "time tested" and observed by most. This is called "path-dependent development." The fact that the United States was born in a revolt against concentrated power still makes Americans wary of giving Washington more power. China's millennia as a centralized bureaucratic empire, on the other hand, makes the concentration of power in Beijing seem natural.

Geography is an old and continuing influence on development. Physical geography concerns the natural features of the earth, whereas **political geography** studies what is largely human-made. There is, of course, a connection between the two, as physical limits set by nature influence the formation, consolidation, and governing mentality of political systems.

Also important is whether the country was unified early or late. For the most part, countries are artificial—not natural—created when one group or tribe conquered its neighbors and unified them by the sword. The founding of nations is usually a bloody business, and the longer ago it took place, the more stable a country is likely to be. We look at Sweden and say, "What a nice, peaceful country." We look at Afghanistan and say, "What a horror of warlords battling each other." Long ago, however, Sweden resembled Afghanistan.

The unification and consolidation of a country leave behind regional memories of incredible staying power. People whose ancestors were conquered centuries ago still act out their resentments in political ways, in the voting booth, or in civil violence. This is one way history has an impact on the present.

Becoming "modern" is a wrenching experience. Industrialization, urbanization, and the growth of education and communications uproot people from their traditional villages and lifestyles and send them to work in factories in cities. In the process, previously passive people become aware of their condition and want to change it. Mobilized by new parties, they start to participate in politics and demand economic improvement. This is a delicate time in the life of nations. If traditional **elites** do not devise some way to take account of newly awakened **mass** demands, the system may be heading toward revolution.

No country has industrialized in a nice way; it is always a process marked by low wages, bad working conditions, and, usually, political repression. The longer in the past this happened, the more peaceful and stable a country is likely to be. We must look for the stage of development a country is in. A country undergoing industrialization and modernization experiences domestic tensions that the already advanced countries have put behind them.

Religion is a crucial variable. Does the country have its church–state relationship settled? If not, it is a lingering political sore. Protestant countries had an easier time secularizing; their churches cut their ties to Rome, the state became stronger than the church early on, and the church stayed out of politics. In Roman Catholic countries, where the church had power in its own right, there was a long church–state struggle called the "clerical–anticlerical split," which is still alive in France and Mexico: Conservatives are more religious, and liberals and leftists are indifferent or hostile to religion. Iran now has the Muslim equivalent of a clerical–anticlerical split.

At a certain point in their development, countries become ready for democracy. Few poor countries can sustain democracy, which seems to require a large, educated middle class to work right. Attempts to implant democracy generally fail in countries with **per capita GDPs** below

political geography
How territory and politics influence each other.

elites
Those few persons with great influence.

mass
Most people; those without influence.

per capita
GDP divided by population, giving approximate level of well-being.

GDP
Gross domestic product; sum total of goods and services produced in a country in one year.

$6,000, but democracy usually takes root in countries that have per capita GDPs above $10,000. India is a large, fascinating exception. This is one way economics influences politics. Notice in the table in the previous section that several countries are in this borderline area.

As we learned in Iraq, democracy implanted by foreigners may not work. Countries have to be ready for it. Trying to start democracy too early often fails amid rigged elections, powerful warlords, and civil unrest. Democracy can also come too late. If the traditional elite waits too long, the masses may mobilize, turn radical, and fall into the hands of revolutionary demagogues. Democracy failed twice in Russia, in 1917 and 2000, and failed in Egypt in 2013. The gradual expansion of the **electoral franchise**, as in Britain, is probably best.

The widening of the franchise means the rise of political parties. On what was a party first based—the urban middle class, farmers, workers, or a religious denomination? When was it founded? What were its initial aims, and how has it changed over the years? Was the party strongly ideological? Left-wing parties argued that government should provide jobs, welfare, and education. Other parties, on the political center or right, either rejected the welfarist ideas, compromised with them, or stole them. Gradually, most developed countries become welfare states with heavy tax burdens.

Finally, history establishes political **symbols** that can awaken powerful feelings. Flags, monarchs, religion, and national holidays and anthems often help cement a country together, giving citizens the feeling that they are part of a common enterprise. To fully know a country, one must know its symbols, their historical origins, and their current connotation.

Key Institutions

1.4 **List the main institutional structures most modern countries have.**

For roughly the first half-century of modern political science, until World War II, most political scientists, including Woodrow Wilson, optimistically thought the formal structures of government—constitutions, parliaments, presidents—largely determined how systems functioned. The right setup on paper would create stable, effective governance. This is an overstatement, but it is clear that the wrong institutions can damage a political system, sometimes fatally. A political **institution** is a web of relationships lasting over time, an established structure of power. An institution may or may not be housed in an impressive building. With institutions, we look for durable sets of human relationships, not architecture.

electoral franchise
Right to vote.

symbol
Political artifact that stirs mass emotions.

institution
Established rules and relationships of power.

constitution
Written organization of a country's institutions.

We begin by asking who has power. When A commands, do B and C follow? Or do they ignore or counterbalance A? A nation's **constitution**—itself an institution—may give clues but does not always pinpoint real power centers. Britain's monarch and Germany's and India's presidents are more decorative than governing. The 1958 French constitution originally made the president strong, but that works only when the president commands a majority in the national parliament. Power in Iran is in the hands of the religious chief, not the elected president.

A major structural point is whether the system is presidential or parliamentary. Both systems have **parliaments**, but a presidential system has a powerful president who is elected and serves separately from the legislature; the legislature cannot vote out the president. The United States, Mexico, and Brazil are presidential systems. In parliamentary systems, action focuses on the prime minister, who is a member of parliament delegated by it to form a government (another word for cabinet). The prime minister and his or her **cabinet** can be ousted by a vote of no-confidence in parliament. Americans used to assume presidential systems were better and more stable than parliamentary systems, though recent problems might make Americans aware of the advantages of a parliamentary system, which can easily oust a chief executive. Besides, parliamentary systems, with the proper refinements such as Germany's, can be quite stable.

parliament
National assembly that considers and enacts laws.

cabinet
Top executives (ministers) of a government.

We ask how powerful the legislature is. In most cases, it is less powerful than the executive, and its power is generally declining. Parliaments still pass laws, but most of them originate with the civil servants and cabinet and are passed according to party wishes. In most legislatures (less so in the U.S. Congress), party discipline is so strong that a member of parliament simply votes the way party whips instruct. Parliaments can be important without originating many laws. They represent citizens, educate the public, structure interests, and, most important, oversee and criticize executive branch activities.

A parliament can have two chambers (bicameral) or one (unicameral). Two chambers are necessary in federal systems to represent the territorial divisions, but they are often extra baggage in unitary systems. Most of the countries studied in this book have bicameral legislatures.

How many parties are there? China is a one-party system, Russia is a dominant-party system, Britain and the United States are basically two-party systems, and France and Germany

Democracy

Waves of Democracy

The late Harvard political scientist Samuel P. Huntington saw democracy advancing in three waves. The first wave, from the American and French Revolutions through World War I, gradually and unevenly spread democracy through most of West Europe. But between the two world wars, a "reverse wave" of communist and fascist authoritarian regimes pushed back democracy in Russia, Italy, Germany, Spain, Portugal, and Japan.

The second wave, a short one, from the end of World War II until the mid-1960s, brought democracy to most of West Europe plus the many Asian and African colonies that got their independence. Most of Asia, Africa, and Latin America, however, quickly turned authoritarian.

Huntington's third wave began in the mid-1970s with the return of democracy to Portugal, Spain, and Greece and thence to Latin America and East Asia. In 1989, as Communist regimes collapsed, the third wave took over East Europe and, with the 1991 Soviet collapse, Russia. Even Mexico's long-dominant party relaxed its grip to let an opposition party win the 2000 presidential election. On paper, most of the world's countries are to some degree democratic (although a majority of humans still live in authoritarian systems). But, warned Huntington, get ready for another reverse wave as shaky democratic regimes revert to authoritarianism. Russia did precisely that.

political culture
Values and attitudes of citizens regarding politics and society.

cynical
Untrusting; holding belief that political system is wrong and corrupt.

legitimacy
Mass perception that regime's rule is rightful.

ideology
Belief system to improve society.

are multiparty systems. Party system is partly determined by a country's electoral system, of which there are two basic types, majoritarian and proportional. A majoritarian system, as in the United States and Britain, usually lets one party win a majority in parliament and encourages formation of two large parties. Proportional systems, where parliamentarians are elected according to the percentage of the vote their party won, as in Germany and Israel, rarely give one party control of parliament, so coalitions are necessary. Proportional representation encourages multiparty systems, which in turn may contribute to cabinet instability as coalition members quarrel.

Finally, we ask how powerful the country's permanent civil service, its bureaucracy, is. The bureaucracy today has eclipsed both cabinet and parliament in expertise, information, outside contacts, and sheer numbers. Some lobbyists no longer bother with the legislature; they go where the action is, to the important decision makers in the bureaucracy.

Political Culture

1.5   Identify the most common social cleavages and explain how they influence political culture.

After World War II, political scientists shifted emphasis from institutions to attitudes. The institutional approach was now seen as insufficient. On paper, after World War I, Germany's Weimar constitution was magnificent but did not work in practice because too few Germans supported democracy. By the 1950s, a new **political culture** approach to comparative politics sought to explain systems in terms of people's values. This is a two-way street, however, because attitudes determine government, and government determines attitudes. Americans became much more **cynical** in the wake of Vietnam and Watergate, for example, while Germans became more committed democrats as their country achieved economic success and political stability.

Legitimacy is basic to political culture. It originally meant that the rightful king was on the throne, not a usurper. Now it means that citizens think that the government's rule is valid and that it should generally be obeyed. Governments are not automatically legitimate; they have to earn respect. Legitimacy can be created over a long time as a government endures and governs well. Legitimacy can also erode as unstable and corrupt regimes come and go, never winning the people's respect. One quick test of legitimacy is how many police officers a country has. With high legitimacy, a country needs few police because people obey the law voluntarily. With low legitimacy, a country needs many police.

Regimes attempt to shore up their legitimacy by manipulating symbols. One symbol frequently manipulated is **ideology**. An ideology is a grand plan to save or improve the country (see box below). Typically, leaders don't believe their ideology in private as much as they say in public. But for mass consumption, the Soviets and Chinese cranked out reams of ideological propaganda (which, in fact, most of their people ignored). We ask how strong a country's ideologies are, and if they are hostile to each other.

Most of the other political systems explored in this book are ideologically moderate, but all espouse various ideologies to greater or lesser degrees: German Social Democrats are committed to the welfare state, British Conservatives to free-market economics, and Chinese Communists to "socialism with Chinese characteristics." Every system probably has some sort of ideology. A system run on purely **pragmatic** grounds— if it works, use it—would be nonideological, but such systems are rare. Even Americans, who pride themselves on being pragmatic, are usually convinced of the effectiveness of the free market (Republicans) or government intervention (Democrats).

Another contributor to political culture is a country's educational system. Nearly everywhere, education is the main path to elite status. Who gets educated and in what way helps structure who gets political power and what they do with it. No country has totally equal

pragmatic
Without ideological considerations; based on practicality.

Political Culture

What Is "Ideology"?

Political ideologies can be an important part of political culture. They are belief systems—usually ending in -ism—that claim to aim at improving society. Believers in an ideology say: "If we move in this direction, things will be much better. People will be happier, catastrophe will be avoided, and society will be perfected." Notice how ideology plays a considerable role even in the relatively pragmatic United States. An ideology usually contains four elements:

1. The *perception* that things are going wrong, that society is headed down the wrong path. Fanatic ideologies insist that catastrophe is just around the corner.

2. An *evaluation* or analysis of why things are going wrong. This means a criticism of all or part of the existing system.

3. A *prescription* or cure for the problem. Moderate ideologies advocate reforms; extremist ideologies urge revolution.

4. An effort to form a *movement* to carry out the cure. Without a party or movement, the above points are just talk without serious intent.

Marxism–Leninism is a perfect example of ideology. First, we have Marx's perception that capitalism is unjust and doomed. Second, we have Marx's theory that capitalism contains internal contradictions that bring about economic depressions. Third, we have a Marxist prescription: Abolish capitalism in favor of collective ownership of the means of production—i.e., socialism. And fourth, especially with Lenin, we have the determined movement to form a strong Communist party—the "organizational weapon"—to put the cure into effect by overthrowing the capitalist system. (How well does environmentalism fit this fourfold pattern?)

Ideologies are usually based on a serious thinker, often an important philosopher. Communism traces back to Hegel, classic liberalism to John Locke. But the philosopher's original ideas become popularized, vulgarized, and often distorted at the hands of ideologists who try to mass-market them. Deep thoughts are turned into cheap slogans.

Ideologies are always defective; they never deliver what they promise—perfect societies and happy humans. Be critical of all of them. Classic liberalism produced an underclass, Marxism–Leninism produced brutal dictatorships, and Iran's Islamic fundamentalism produced rule by rigid and corrupt clerics.

educational opportunity. Even where schooling is legally open to all, social, economic, and even political screening devices work against some sectors of the population. Most countries have elite universities that produce a big share of their political leadership, at times a near monopoly. The elite views formed in such schools determine much of a country's politics.

The Politics of Social Cleavages

Most societies split politically along one or more lines. These splits, or "cleavages," help establish the country's political culture and become its fault lines along which political interactions form. Here are some of the more politically relevant social cleavages.

SOCIAL CLASS Karl Marx thought social class determined everything. Whether one was bourgeois or proletarian determined political orientations. Marx held that middle- and upper-class people were conservative and working-class people were progressive or radical. This oversimplifies matters, as many poor people are conservative and many middle-class intellectuals are radical.

Still, social class does matter in structuring attitudes. The working class does tend toward the left, but never 100 percent, and it tends to the moderate left of social democracy rather than the radical left of communism. Such is the case with the German Social Democratic Party. Social class by itself seldom explains all political orientations. Other factors—such as religion and region—are usually present. The question, as political scientist Joseph LaPalombara put it, is, "Class plus what?"

GEOGRAPHIC REGION Most countries have regional differences that are politically important. Once a region gets set in its politics, it can stay that way for generations. Often the region remembers past conquests and injustices. Scotland still resents England, and likewise the south of France resents the north. The Muslim north and Christian south of Nigeria seriously dislike each other. Seacoast China is much richer than inland China. We must study the regions of a nation, what their politics are, and how they got to be that way.

RELIGION Religious struggles played major roles in most nations' histories and, in some countries, still do. You can predict with fair accuracy how French people will vote by knowing how often they attend Mass. You can partly predict how Germans will vote by knowing if they are Protestant or Catholic. In India, many Hindus and Muslims see each other in hostile terms. Christian–Muslim tension could rip Nigeria apart. Religion accounts for the formation of more political parties than does social class.

URBAN–RURAL Urban dwellers tend to be more aware of politics, more participatory, and more liberal or leftist. U.S. presidential elections graphically illustrate our urban–rural split.

There are other cleavages. In some countries, gender matters, as in the United States, where women vote more Democrat than men. In India, some jest, you do not cast your vote but vote your *caste*. Occupation, as distinct from social class, can also influence political attitudes. A miner and a farmer may have the same income, but the miner will likely be leftist and the farmer conservative. Age can be a political factor as well. Young people are usually more open to new ideas and more likely to embrace radical and even violent causes than older citizens. Germany's terrorists, China's Red Guards, and Iran's Pasdaran were all young.

Patterns of Interaction

1.6 **Describe how generalizations can lead to theory. Give examples.**

While all agree that history, institutions, and political culture contribute to politics, many modern political scientists see politics as intelligible games that are similar across countries and cultures. Typically, players everywhere try to maximize their advantage. India, Brazil, and Japan are historically and culturally very distinct, but politicians in all of them take money from special interests and strive to win elections by accusing opponents of perfidy. Why, mercy, even U.S. politicians do both. Competition creates what is conventionally called "politics"—who does what to whom—and forms the patterns of interactions of individuals, parties, interest groups, and bureaucracies.

fake state
Artificial country that splits apart or is absorbed.

Geography

Fake States

Over the years, I have studied five countries—four of them Communist, three of them federal systems—that no longer exist. These are not *failed states*, those without a functioning government. Instead, they are countries that could not stand the test of time and simply disappeared, either divided or absorbed. Because they were rather artificial, a better term might be "**fake states**."

No country comes with a warranty, and many states have folded over the centuries. A state may have officials, a flag, and a UN seat but lack the national political culture to sustain itself. You cannot impose legitimacy; it must grow from within, usually over centuries. Notice that federalism does not solve the problem of keeping fake states together but merely sets the stage for their breakup.

This Moscow elementary school principal, here photographed in 1973, thought he was taking his pupils on the path charted by Lenin, whose portrait was on the wall and whose bust was on the desk, to a radiant socialist future.

1. **The Soviet Union**, founded by Lenin in 1922, encompassed most of the old tsarist Russian Empire. The Communist Party and security police held together the Soviet federal structure, often brutally, of over 100 ethnic groups, which Soviets called "nationalities." Moscow thought it had solved the "nationalities question," but the 14 large nationalities, the ones that had their own republics, departed the economically declining Soviet Union in 1991. Three-quarters of Soviet territory continues as the Russian Federation, some of whose nationalities, especially in the North Caucasus, seek independence by violent means.

2. **Yugoslavia**, unlike Russia, had no existence prior to World War I but was patched together in 1918 from former Austro-Hungarian and Ottoman provinces. Its Serbian leadership and king alienated Croats, and local fascists set up a pro-Nazi Croatia after the swift German conquest of Yugoslavia in

1941. Tito's Partisans emerged victorious from the war and decreed a Communist federal system of six republics modeled on the Soviet Union. Tito outlawed separatism under the slogan "brotherhood and unity," but Yugoslavia did not jell, even though most citizens spoke Serbo-Croatian. After Tito died in 1980, its republic chiefs fought for power. Slovenia and Macedonia departed peacefully in 1991, but Serbia fought Croatia and Bosnia in the early 1990s. "Ethnic cleansing" killed thousands. I studied in Belgrade in 1963–1964 and was sad to see Yugoslavs murder each other. It did not have to happen. Tito's hyper-federal dictatorship was a structural mistake, but the right reforms, including democracy, might have kept Yugoslavia together.

3. **Czechoslovakia** was also assembled in 1918, from the former Austrian Bohemia and Moravia and the former Hungarian Slovakia and Ruthenia. Power and wealth was concentrated in the Czech lands, leading to Slovak resentment. Czech and Slovak are similar Slavic languages. At Munich in 1938, Britain and France gave Hitler the largely German Sudetenland; then he took the whole country in 1939 and made Slovakia a separate puppet state. Stalin put Czechoslovakia back together (but kept Ruthenia) and imposed a Communist regime in 1948. With democracy reborn in 1989, Slovaks began to demand independence, and in 1993, the federation split peacefully in the "velvet divorce." Democracy led to breakup. Both the Czech Republic and Slovakia are now members of the EU and NATO.

4. **East Germany**, founded as a child of the Cold War in 1949, was glad to be absorbed by West Germany in 1990. The Communist German Democratic Republic always lacked legitimacy, especially as its citizens could behold the prosperity and freedom of West Germany. Only the Berlin Wall, built in 1961, could keep them in. U.S. and Soviet tanks confronted each other at the Wall in 1961 and could have started World War III. The eastern parts of Germany, now heavily subsidized by the western parts, still have much cultural and economic catching up to do.

5. **South Vietnam** was the only one of the five invented by the United States. Vietnam was a French colony until Ho Chi Minh's Communists beat the French in 1954. Washington set up a separate South Vietnam in 1955 with a nationalist Catholic, Ngo Dinh Diem, as president to stem a takeover by Communist North Vietnam. But the corrupt and inept Diem regime never had much legitimacy; his own generals overthrew and killed him in 1963. The successor Saigon governments were unstable and unable, even with over half a million U.S. troops and billions of dollars, to beat back, first, Communist insurgency and, then, stealthy invasion by the North. Americans grew fed up with the war, and Nixon negotiated a face-saving U.S. exit in 1973. The larger and better-equipped South Vietnamese army melted away under a northern push in 1975. Now Hanoi governs a unified Communist Vietnam that seeks U.S. help to offset Chinese claims in the South China Sea. American firms now manufacture clothing and footwear in Vietnam.

South Korea was another U.S. invention but will likely last. North Korea, founded by a Stalin puppet, may not. The common weakness of fake states: little or no legitimacy. One can name other countries where this is currently a problem.

---

rational choice
Theory that people rationally pursue their advantage in voting and policies.

Some political scientists and economists argue that political moves are **rational choices**. Politicians and citizens aim for what they figure (sometimes mistakenly) is to their advantage. To win elections, politicians craft positions to please voters. Citizens pick candidates that most closely match their preferences. Accordingly, you can partly predict political behavior.

Elites play a major role. Even democratic politics is usually the work of a few. Most people, most of the time, do not participate in politics. But there are various kinds of elites, some more democratic than others. How much of these interactions is an elite game with little or no mass participation?

Interactions consider whether groups come together to compete or to strike deals. How do political parties persuade the public to support them? We look not for onetime events but for recurring things. Finding such patterns is the beginning of making **generalizations**, and generalizing is the beginning of **theory**. Once we have found a pattern, we ask why. The answer will be found partly in what we have learned about each country and partly in the nature of political life, where struggle and competition are normal and universal.

Some transactions are open and public; others are closed and secretive. The interactions of parties and citizenry are mostly open. Every party tries to convince the public that it is the one fit to govern. This holds equally true for democratic and authoritarian systems. Do they succeed? Whom do the parties aim for, and how do they win them over? By ideology? Promises? Common interests? Or by convincing people the other party is worse?

The parties interact with each other, sometimes cooperatively but more often competitively. How do they denounce and discredit each other? Under what circumstances do they make deals? Is their competition murderous or moderate? Parties also interact with the government. In China, the Communist Party basically *is* the government. In more politically open countries, parties try to capture and retain governmental power. How do parties form coalitions? Who gets the top cabinet jobs? Once in power, is the party able to act, or is it paralyzed by opposition forces?

Politics within the parties is important, as most parties have factions. In Japan, factions within the leading party battle each other as if they were separate parties. Does the party have left and right wings? How do its leaders hold it together? Do they pay off factions with ministerial positions? Do factional quarrels paralyze the party? Could it split?

Parties also interact with **interest groups**. Some groups enjoy "structured access" to likeminded parties. In Europe, labor unions are often linked formally to labor parties. Here we need to know: Does the party co-opt the interest group, or vice versa? How powerful are interest-group views in determining party policy?

Interest groups often decide it is not worth working on the electoral and legislative sides and instead focus their attention on bureaucracies. One of the key areas of politics is where bureaucracies and businesses interface. Are interest groups controlled by government, or vice versa? What kind of relationships do businesspeople and bureaucrats establish? Which groups are the most influential? These important interactions are generally out of the public sight and often corrupt. Corruption undermines legitimacy in China, India, Iran, Nigeria, and other developing lands. Political scientists are now starting to give corruption the attention it deserves.

generalization
Process of finding repeated examples and patterns.

theory
Firm generalization supported by evidence.

interest group
Association aimed at getting favorable policies.

China Lessons

Comparative Politics and China

Comparative politics is useful, especially on the looming question of whether China could turn democratic. A new box in each chapter suggests experiences of that country that may inform Chinese decisions. The Chinese Communist Party plans on ruling forever and rejects democracy, claiming it would lead to chaos. Comparativists can advise, "No, not necessarily, if you do it right." And in the not-too-distant future, the CCP might need to rethink its assumptions and reach out for models of the transition to more open governance. Comparativists can offer a few.

The first lesson comparative politics can offer is what can go wrong if the economic and social systems diverge from the political system. We take a leaf here from the Marxists' idea of **contradictions**. (You can amuse and embarrass Chinese students by quizzing them on Marxist terms. They all took mandatory Marxism classes, but few remember anything.)

Marx emphasized the "contradiction" between the economic basis of society and the political superstructure—specifically, the class struggle. The economy changes and brings new classes to the fore, but the political system stays rooted in the past. Eventually, the gap becomes so acute that revolution breaks out. Marx argued that the rapid industrialization of his day was creating contradictions that the bourgeois political structure could not handle. The industrial working class was paid too little to consume what it produced, leading to gluts and depressions. The "efficient" capitalist economy was too efficient and produced a contradiction that would kill it; it contained and even incubated the seeds of its own destruction. The faster the economy grew, the sharper the contradiction. Could the Chinese economy, which has set world growth records and created a large, educated middle class, avoid finding itself in a contradiction with the single-party government?

What They Quarrel About

1.7   Evaluate the importance of economics as a political quarrel.

Here we move to current policies, the political quarrels of the day. We start with economics, the universal and permanent policy quarrel over who gets what. Politics and economics are closely connected; one can make or break the other (which is why political scientists should have a grounding in economics).

First, is the economy of the country growing? Rapidly or slowly? Why? Are workers lazy or energetic? Are managers inept or clever? How much of the economy is supervised and planned by government? Does government help or hinder economic growth? If the economy is declining, could it lead to political collapse (as in the Soviet Union)? Why are some countries economic successes and others not? How big a role does politics play in economic growth?

Have unions and management reached durable understandings, or are strikes frequent? Have unions won laws on wages, benefits, and layoffs? Has this led to "labor-force rigidities" that slow growth? Does government influence wage increases? Beijing, afraid of worker discontent, ordered firms to deliver hefty pay hikes. Do workers have any say in running their companies? How much imported labor is there? How much unemployment?

contradiction

In Marxism, deep, opposing forces that can rip the system apart (modern term: *dysfunction*).

Once we have measured the economic pie, we inquire who gets what slice. How equal—or unequal—is the distribution of income and wealth? Does the government redistribute incomes to make people more equal, or does it let inequality grow? Does unequal distribution lead to social and political resentment? Heavy **redistribution** characterizes the welfare state, and all advanced democracies are to some extent welfare states. How high and how progressive are taxes? How many and how generous are welfare benefits? Do people want more welfare and higher taxes or less welfare and lower taxes? Which people? If stuck with an overgenerous welfare system, can the government trim it?

Most governments initially handled the 2008–2009 recession about the same way: massive spending to recover from the downturn and to cut unemployment. These "stimulus packages" varied from country to country—some emphasized exports, others domestic consumption; some developed infrastructure, others aided industries—but all pumped billions into their economies. Countries with very different systems adopted similar Keynesian approaches and went into deficit. Almost all bailed out banks with massive government funds. These bailouts were controversial, but fear of economic collapse gave countries little choice. After a couple of years, however, most European governments turned to *austerity* and cut government spending on the theory that it would restore business "confidence," but economies grew little.

There are, to be sure, noneconomic quarrels as well. Regionalism is persistent and growing. Britain, France, Russia, India, and Nigeria have breakaway regional movements. East and West Germany resent each other. Mexico's regions vote differently from one another. What are a country's regions? Which of them are discontented? Why are they discontented, and how do they show their discontent? Is there violence? Are there movements to decentralize or devolve power to the regions? One quarrel getting nastier throughout West Europe revolves around what to do with the millions of immigrants, mostly from the developing lands: Let in more, or keep them out? Integrate them, or send them home?

redistribution
Taxing the better off to help the worse off.

variable
Factor that changes and is related to other factors.

discontinuity
A break and new direction in the expected course of events.

analogy
Taking one example as the model for another.

dysanalogy
Showing that one example is a poor model for another.

Comparison

Country Experts Versus Comparativists

Should political scientists attempt to predict or at least anticipate what will happen in a given country? The profession is divided. Some argue that there are simply too many **variables**, most of which are hard to define, measure, and weigh. How could one untangle the complex interactions of economic growth, regional tensions, ideology, and personalities? Everything matters, but we do not know which matters most. Are one or a few variables the key? Which?

Prediction or anticipation concentrates the mind on the relevant variables. If one variable predicts moderately well, we focus on it and ignore variables that predict nothing. In doing this, we begin to theorize. If we stay only in the present, describing but refusing to predict, we admit that our findings are too flimsy to be used for much. Predicting, at least approximately, tests whether we really know our stuff.

Which is the best way to predict or at least anticipate? Specialists who immerse themselves in one country or region accumulate much data and details and write dissertations and articles about the area. They often know the language and, from interviewing local citizens, can delineate the varieties of opinions. Their books and articles are crammed with endnotes, some of them from original-language sources.

Their expertise is impressive, but they are often narrow and wrong. Few Soviet specialists foresaw the collapse of their subject matter. They were too optimistic that Gorbachev's reforms would work. And afterward, many Russia specialists confidently portrayed the establishment of democracy in Russia. They were again too optimistic in assuming that ending a dictatorship brings democracy. (Is there a built-in human tendency toward optimism? If so, we must be careful of optimistic analyses of China.) The Soviet/Russia area experts' mistaken predictions suggest they were following wrong variables.

Part of the problem is knowing too much about one country. Specialists suppose their details and data put them "inside" the system and enable them to anticipate its evolution. Kremlinologists and China watchers knew a lot about the rise and fall of Politburo personalities and evolution of state structures. But such studies assumed unilinear development and could not anticipate sudden breaks or **discontinuities**. Sovietologists got so specialized that they lacked comparative perspective. Are China specialists doing the same?

In contrast, comparativists have broader views but bring problems of their own. A comparativist might have less language or area expertise but be able to compare and contrast the country under consideration with similar cases across a continent or even the globe. They might find, for example, that democratization in Brazil spread to most Latin American countries at about the same time. It does not necessarily follow, however, that this pattern transfers to democratization in Central Europe or the Soviet Union. Scholars tried to make an **analogy** between Latin America and Central Europe and then between Central Europe and the Soviet Union. Many, however, failed to note the elements of **dysanalogy** between the cases. The Soviet Union, for example, had nothing resembling Poland's Solidarity, and neither does China today.

Comparing encourages seeking the relevant facts and variables; it forces one to theorize and then test the theories against reality. Single-country experts rarely do this. They assume that the accumulation of many facts will point to obvious conclusions without requiring that the facts be structured into a theoretical framework that makes sense and works in more than one country. This book contends that it is better to err on the side of being too broad (comparative politics) than being too narrow (country expertise). Just make sure you have the right analogies.

Review Questions

Learning Objective 1.1 Explain how comparative politics looks at the paralysis problem, p. 2.

1. What is the difference between comparative politics and international relations?
2. What was Aristotle's sixfold classification of political systems?
3. Define democracy.

Learning Objective 1.2 Contrast the terms *nation* and *state*, p. 7.

4. What is a *failed state*?
5. What made the modern state?
6. What unleashed modern nationalism?

and massacring inhabitants. The Celts were pushed back to Wales and Scotland, which became a "Celtic fringe." Some Celts fled to France and gave their name to Brittany. Preserving their distinct identity and languages (Cymric in Wales, Gaelic in Scotland), Britain's Celts never quite forgot what the newer arrivals did to them.

In the ninth century, Danish Vikings took much of eastern England but were eventually absorbed. A famous warning from this episode: Once you've paid the danegeld (protection money), you'll never be rid of the Dane. Other Vikings, Norsemen (Normans), had settled in France and gave their name to Normandy. In 1066, with the English throne in dispute, William of Normandy claimed it and invaded, defeating the English King Harold at Hastings. England changed dramatically. William replaced the Saxon ruling class with Norman nobles, who earned their **fiefdoms** by military service. The Normans brought thousands of French words that enriched English. Backed by military power, administration was better and tighter. William ordered an inventory of all his lands and population, which resulted in the Domesday Book. The **Exchequer** —the name derived from the French word for a checkered counting table—became the king's powerful treasury minister, who is still powerful. William and his descendants ruled both England and parts of France, so English forces fought several battles in France.

fiefdom
Land king grants to nobles in exchange for support.

Exchequer
Britain's treasury minister.

the Continent
British term for mainland Europe.

mixed monarchy
King balanced by nobles.

Magna Carta
1215 agreement to preserve rights of English nobles.

Magna Carta

The Normans also brought a political system that had first emerged on **the Continent**—feudalism, a contract in which lords granted vassals land and protection while the vassals supported the lord with military service. Feudalism appears when central authority breaks down and a money economy disappears, for then land and fighting ability are all that matter. The collapse of the Roman Empire meant kings could survive only if they had enough lords and knights to fight for them. The lords and knights in turn got land. Power here was a two-way street: The king needed the nobles and vice versa.

The **mixed monarchy** of the Middle Ages was a balance, which the nobles of Aragon expressed well in their oath to a new monarch: "We who are as good as you swear to you, who are no better than we, to accept you as our king and sovereign lord provided you observe all our statutes and laws; and if not, no." English history was a long struggle to keep the king within his feudal bounds and from turning into an absolute monarch, which happened in much of Europe. This English struggle laid the foundation for limited, representative government, democracy, and civil rights, even though the participants at the time had no such intent.

The Great Charter the barons forced on King John at Runnymede in 1215 never mentions liberty or democracy. The barons and top churchmen simply wanted to stop the king from encroaching on feudal customs, rights, and laws by which they held sway in their localities. In this sense, the **Magna Carta**, one of the great documents of democracy, was feudal and reactionary but did limit the monarch's powers—an important first step toward democracy. The Magna Carta kept the king in balance with the nobles, preventing either despotism or anarchy, the

United Kingdom of Great Britain and Northern Ireland

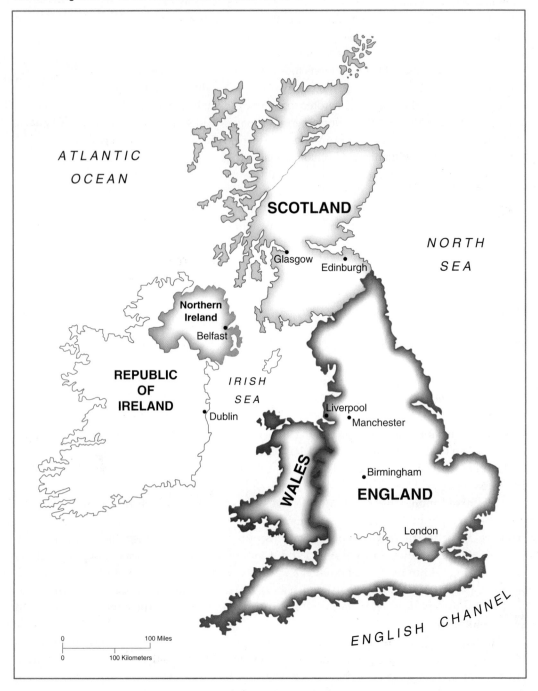

twin ills of the Continent, where countries either went to absolutism, as in France, or broke up into small principalities, as in Germany. British and, by extension, American democracy owes a lot to the stubborn English barons who stood up for their feudal rights.

The Rise of Parliament

English kings, often at war in France, needed taxes, so during the thirteenth century, they started calling to London two to four knights from each shire (roughly a county) and a similar number of burghers from towns to raise revenues. Local notables thus began participating in the affairs of state. Inadvertently, kings founded an institution in the thirteenth century that overshadowed the monarchy by the seventeenth century.

Parliament

When capitalized, Britain's legislature, now usually meaning the House of Commons.

Commons

Lower house of Parliament; the elected, important chamber.

Lords

Upper house of Parliament; now much less important than Commons.

anticlerical

Wants to get the Roman Catholic Church out of politics.

Parliament began as an extension of the king's court but, over the centuries, took on a life of its own. Knights and burghers formed a lower house, the House of **Commons**. Nobles and top churchmen formed an upper house, the House of **Lords**. Originally, Lords was more powerful, but, over time, Commons pushed Lords into a weaker role. A leading member of Commons became its Speaker, one who could speak to the king. Parliamentary privileges developed to prevent the arrest of members. Commons represented only a few locally wealthy or powerful males. Parliament, however, continued the blocking mechanism of the Magna Carta: It diffused power and prevented the king from getting too much.

Parliament got a major boost from Henry VIII (reigned 1509–1547), who needed Parliament in his struggle against Rome. Tensions grew between the Vatican and London because Henry needed the pope to grant him a divorce. His marriage to Catherine of Aragon had failed to produce the male heir Henry thought he needed to ensure stability after him. (Ironically, his daughter Elizabeth was possibly England's greatest monarch.)

The pope refused the divorce, so Henry summoned a parliament in 1529 and kept it busy for seven years, passing laws to break England away from Catholic influence. The head of the new Anglican Church, an Englishman, granted Henry his divorce in 1533. Henry had a total of six wives (and had two of them beheaded) in his quest for a male heir, which he never got.

Henry VIII's break with Rome changed English political culture. Countries that stayed Catholic—France, Spain, and Italy—split for centuries between pro-church and **anticlerical**

Geography

Invadability

Britain is hard to invade. The last successful invasion of England (by the Normans) was in 1066. The English Channel has served as a moat to keep Spaniards, French, and Germans from invading. Politically, this has meant that England was able to develop its own institutions without foreign interference, a luxury not enjoyed by most Continental lands. Militarily, it meant that England rarely had a large army, of great import in the seventeenth century when British kings were unable to tame Parliament because they had few soldiers.

Comparison

Common Law

One of England's lasting contributions is the **Common Law**, the legal system now also practiced in the United States (except in Louisiana), Canada, Australia, and many other countries once administered by Britain. Common Law grew out of the customary usage of the Germanic tribal laws of the Angles and Saxons, which stressed the rights of free men. It developed on the basis of **precedent** set by earlier decisions and thus has been called "judge-made law." After the Normans conquered England, they found the purely local nature of this law too fragmented, so they set up central courts to systematize the local laws and produce a "common" law for all parts of England—hence the name.

Common Law is based heavily on case law and differs from code law, which is used by most of the Continent (and Scotland) and of the world, and which emphasizes fixed legal codes rather than precedent and case study. Code law is essentially Roman Law that was kept alive in the Canon Law of the Catholic Church, revived by modernizing Continental monarchs and updated in 1804 into the *Code Napoléon*. Compared with code law, Common Law is flexible and adapts gradually with new cases.

Common Law
System of judge-made law developed in England.

precedent
Legal reasoning based on previous cases.

forces. England (and Sweden) avoided this problem because, early on, the state was stronger than the church and controlled it. In England, it was far easier to *secularize* society and politics than in Catholic countries, where the church stayed powerful. Henry unknowingly started an institutional shift of power from monarch to parliament. A century later, Parliament beheaded an English king.

Parliament versus King

In the late fifteenth century, several European monarchs expanded their powers and undermined the old feudal mixed monarchy. Kings proclaimed that they ruled by divine right— that is, that they received their authority directly from God without the pope as intermediary. Political theorists invented the idea of sovereignty and concluded it must lie in the monarch. All this gave rise to absolutism. By 1660, absolute monarchs governed most of Europe—but not England.

The seventeenth century brought uninterrupted turmoil to England: religious splits, civil war, a royal beheading, and a military dictatorship. The net winner, when the dust had settled, was Parliament. Trouble started when James I brought the Stuart dynasty from Scotland to take over the English throne after the death of Elizabeth I—the last Tudor—in 1603. James united the crowns of Scotland and England, but they remained separate countries until the 1707 Act of Union. James brought with him absolutist notions and thought existing institutions should simply support the king. This brought him into conflict with Parliament and with Puritanism, an extreme Protestant movement that aimed to reform the "popish" elements out of the Anglican Church. James preferred the church to stay just the way it was and promoted his version of the Bible. Harassed, some Puritans ran away to Massachusetts.

Geography

The United Kingdom

Britain's official name is the United Kingdom of Great Britain and Northern Ireland. "Great Britain" refers to the whole island, which includes Wales and Scotland as well as England. Standard usage is now simply "the UK." The British flag, the "Union Jack," symbolizes the three saints representing different parts of the United Kingdom. The larger red cross is the Cross of St. George of England, the diagonal white cross is that of St. Andrew of Scotland, and the thinner, diagonal red cross is that of St. Patrick of Ireland. (Note that this cross is off center.) Now some English nationalists display just the English flag (red cross on a white field). In Edinburgh, capital of Scotland, most of the flags are now Scottish (diagonal white cross on a blue field), an indication that the United Kingdom has grown less united. Symbols matter.

Several Scottish flags flank one Union Jack in Edinburgh, showing the strength of Scottish nationalism.

By now, Parliament felt equal with the king and even, in the area of raising revenues, superior. Hard up for cash, James tried to impose taxes without the consent of Parliament, which grew angry. James's son, Charles I (1625–1649), took England into wars with Spain and France, which increased the king's desperation for money. Charles tried to act like a Continental absolute monarch, but the English people and Parliament blocked him, leading to the English Civil War of 1642–1648, in which Royalists fought Parliamentarians, and the latter, aided by Puritans and the growing merchant class, won. The Parliamentarians created a "New Model Army," which trounced the Royalists. Charles was tried by Parliament and beheaded. He was not above the law.

From 1649 to 1660, England had no king. The only organized force was the army, led by Oliver Cromwell. Briefly, England became a **republic** called the **Commonwealth** under Cromwell, but discord

republic
Country not headed by a monarch.

Commonwealth
A republic; also organization of countries that were once British colonies.

Democracy

"One Man, One Vote"

Among the antiroyalists were **republicans**, called Levellers, who sought political equality. Soldiers in the New Model Army argued that people like themselves—tradesmen, artisans, and farmers—should have the vote. They were influenced by Puritanism, which taught that all men were equal before God and needed no spiritual or temporal superiors to guide them. (This Puritan notion helped found American democracy.)

One group of Levellers, meeting in Putney in 1647, even went so far as to advocate "one man, one vote." This radical idea was two centuries ahead of its time, and the more conservative forces of England, including Cromwell, rejected it out of hand. Still, the Putney meeting had introduced the idea of the universal franchise—that is, giving everybody the right to vote.

grew. To restore order, in 1653, Cromwell was designated Lord Protector, a sort of uncrowned king, and imposed a military dictatorship. When Cromwell died in 1658, most Englishmen had grown tired of turbulent republicanism. In 1660, Parliament invited Charles II, son of the beheaded king, to return from Dutch exile to the throne. The English monarchy was restored, but now Parliament was much stronger.

Charles II could not be an absolute monarch but tried to manipulate Parliament. Religion tripped him up. Charles was pro-Catholic and issued the 1673 Declaration of Indulgence, lifting laws against Catholics and non-Anglican Protestants. Parliament saw this as a return to Catholicism and blocked it. Anti-Catholic hysteria swept England with fabricated stories of popish plots to take over the country.

When Charles II died in 1685, his openly Catholic brother took the throne as James II. Parliament dumped James II (but let him escape) and invited his Protestant daughter Mary and her Dutch husband William to be England's queen and king. In this bloodless "Glorious Revolution" of 1688, England dumped the last Stuart. In 1690, William beat James in Ireland, an event still celebrated in Northern Ireland. A 1689 "Bill of Rights" (unlike its U.S. namesake) spelled out Parliament's relationship to the **Crown**: no laws or taxes without Parliament's assent. Most Englishmen approved. Parliament was now clearly supreme and could dismiss monarchs. In 1714, Parliament invited George I from Hanover in Germany to be king; the present royal family is descended from him. Since then, the British monarch has become increasingly a figurehead who "reigns but does not rule."

republican
In its original sense, supporter of movement to end monarchy.

Crown
The British government.

prime minister
Chief of government in parliamentary systems.

minister
Head of a major department (ministry) of government.

Prime Ministers and Democracy

George I spoke no English and preferred Hanover to London, so he gave executive power to a cabinet of ministers presided over by a first, or prime, minister. Headed by Sir Robert Walpole from 1721 to 1742, the cabinet developed nearly into its present form, but the **prime minister** could not pick his **ministers** (that was reserved for the king), and the cabinet was not responsible (literally, "answerable") to Parliament.

Absolutism had one last gasp. George III packed Commons with his supporters and governed with the obedient Lord North as his prime minister. One result was the U.S. Declaration of Independence, a revolution against the too-powerful king. Following the British defeat, William Pitt the Younger restored the cabinet and prime minister to power and made them responsible only to Commons, not to the king. This began the tradition—never written into law—that the "government" consists of the leader of the largest party in Commons along with other people he or she picks. As party chief, top parliamentarian, and head of government combined, the prime minister became the focus of political power in Britain.

Whigs
Faction of Parliament that became Liberal Party.

Tories
Faction of Parliament that became Conservative Party.

Reform Acts
Series of laws expanding the British electoral franchise.

Parliament was supreme by the late eighteenth century but not democratic or representative. By then, however, parties began to form. The labels **Whig** and **Tory** first appeared under Charles II, connoting his opposition and his supporters, respectively. Both names were at first used in jest: The original Whigs were Scottish bandits, and the original Tories were Irish bandits. At first these proto-parties were simply parliamentary caucuses, Tories representing the landed aristocracy, Whigs the merchants and manufacturers. Only in the next century did they take root in the electorate.

During the nineteenth century, a two-party system emerged. The Whigs grew into the Liberal Party and the Tories into the Conservative Party. Parliamentarians were not ordinary people. The House of Lords was limited to hereditary peers, and Commons, despite its name, belonged to landowners and better-off people, who often won by bribing the few voters. Whig democracy—democracy for the few—is standard in the opening decades of democratic development, as in the pre-Jackson United States. Mass participation usually comes later.

After the American and French Revolutions, however, Parliament had to expand the electorate. People talked about democracy and the right to vote. Under the impact of the Industrial Revolution and economic growth, two powerful new social classes arose—the middle class and the working class. Whigs and Tories, both elite, at first fought demands for the mass vote.

Gradually, though, the Whigs saw that political stability required bringing some ordinary Britons into politics to give them a stake in the system. They also realized that if they broadened the franchise, they would win many new voters. After much resistance by Tories, Parliament passed the **Reform Act** of 1832, which allowed more of the middle class to vote but still only expanded the electorate by half, to about 7 percent of adults. It established the principle, though,

Geography

Seacoast

A country with an outlet to the sea has a major economic advantage over landlocked countries. Sea transport is cheap and does not require crossing neighboring countries. Usable natural harbors also help. Peter the Great battled for years to obtain Russian outlets on the Baltic and Black seas. Atlantic Europe had an incredible advantage from the start. England's Atlantic orientation contributed to its empire, early industrialization, and prosperity.

Personalities

Hobbes, Locke, Burke

Thomas Hobbes lived through the upheavals of the English Civil War in the seventeenth century and opposed them for making people insecure and frightened. Hobbes imagined that life in "the **state of nature**," before "**civil society**" was founded, must have been terrible. Every man would have been the enemy of every other man, a "war of each against all." Humans would have lived in savage squalor with "no arts; no letters; no society; and which is worst of all, continual fear, and danger of violent death; and the life of man, solitary, poor, nasty, brutish, and short." To escape this horror, people would—out of self-interest—rationally join together to form civil society. Society thus arises naturally out of fear. People also would submit gladly to a king, even a bad one, to prevent anarchy. Hobbes's craving for stability and order marks him as a conservative.

John Locke saw the same upheavals but came to less harsh conclusions. Locke theorized that the original state of nature was not so bad; people lived in equality and tolerance with one another. But they could not secure their property: There was no money, title deeds, or courts of law, so their property was uncertain. To remedy this, they contractually formed civil society and thus secured "life, liberty, and property." Locke is to property rights as Hobbes is to fear of violent death. Americans are the children of Locke; notice the American emphasis on "the natural right to property." Many peg Locke as the originator of classic liberalism.

Edmund Burke, a Whig member of Parliament, was horrified at the French Revolution, warning it would end up as a military dictatorship (it did). The French revolutionists had broken the historical continuity, institutions, and symbols that restrain people from bestial behavior, argued Burke. Old institutions, such as the monarchy and church, must be pretty good because they have evolved over centuries. If you scrap them, society breaks down and leads to tyranny. Burke understood that **conservatism** means constant, but never radical, change. He wrote, "A state without the means of some change is without the means of its conservation." Progress comes not from chucking out the old but from gradually modifying the parts that need changing while preserving the overall structure, keeping the form but reforming the contents.

state of nature
Humans before civilization.

civil society
Humans after becoming civilized; modern usage: associations between family and government.

conservatism
Ideology of preserving existing institutions and usages.

that Commons ought to be representative of and responsive to citizens, not just notables. In 1867, the Conservatives under Prime Minister Benjamin Disraeli passed the Second Reform Act, which doubled the electorate, giving about 16 percent of adult Britons the vote. In 1884, the Third Reform Act added farmworkers and achieved nearly complete male suffrage. Women finally got the vote in 1918.

The British electorate grew incrementally. New elements—the middle and working classes—got the vote gradually, giving Parliament time to assimilate mass politics without an upheaval. It also meant citizens got the vote when they were sufficiently educated. Some other countries, such as Spain, instituted the universal franchise early, but the result was fake democracy, as crafty officials rigged votes among a poorly educated population. With the expanded voting franchise, political parties turned from parliamentary clubs into modern parties. They had to win over millions of voters by means of organization, programs, promises, and continuity. The growth of the electorate forced parties to become vehicles for democracy.

China Lessons

Forming Parties Inside Parliament

Britain's parties first developed inside the House of Commons; later they reached outside and organized their electoral bases. British parties began as informal parliamentary factions based on geography, religion, and interests. Some historians and political scientists believe this is what allowed the British party system to gradually evolve to democratic stability. Initially, local elections had no parties but were based on who had the best connections. The parliamentary factions—initially, who supported the Stuart kings (Tories) and who opposed them (Whigs) in the seventeenth century—faced and debated each other before the strife and anger of mass electoral politics began. Britain got used to Parliament as an institution before electing it democratically.

Countries where parties first organized outside the national legislature and had to fight their way into it in bitter elections developed radicalized and sometimes extremist parties. Germany and Russia are examples in the nineteenth century. Politics polarized before institutions could handle it. China could take a lesson by letting factions form in the National People's Congress (NPC) some years before allowing mass parties to form.

China has a head start here, as the Chinese Communist Party already has informal factions, simplified into pro-Mao leftists and free-market liberalizers. Actually, Chinese factions are partly based on geography and personal connections. A first step might be to let these factions establish themselves and debate in the NPC to get people used to the give and take of startup parties. Elections with mass parties should come later. If China started with free elections now, it could unleash demagoguery and chaos.

The Rise of the Welfare State

By the beginning of the twentieth century, with working men voting, British parties had to pay attention to demands for welfare measures—public education, housing, jobs, and medical care—that the Liberals and Conservatives had ignored. Expansion of the electoral franchise led to the **welfare state**. Pushing for this was the new Labour Party, founded in 1900. At first, Labour worked with the Liberals—the "Lib-Lab" coalition—but by the end of World War I, Labour pushed the Liberals into the weak third-party status they languish in to this day. Unlike most Continental socialists, few British Labourites were Marxists. Instead, they combined militant trade unionism with intellectual social democracy to produce a pragmatic, gradualist ideology that sought to level class differences in Britain. As one union leader put it, the British Labour Party "owes more to Methodism than to Marxism."

The early British labor movement was resentful and militant. In the 1926 General Strike, the trade unions attempted to halt the entire British economy to gain their wage demands. They failed. Labour was briefly and weakly in power under Ramsay MacDonald in the 1920s but then won big in 1945 to implement an ambitious welfare program plus state takeover of utilities, railroads, coal mines, and much heavy manufacturing. Since then, the chief quarrel in British politics has been between people who like the welfare state and state ownership and people who do not.

welfare state
Political system that redistributes income from rich to poor, standard in West Europe.

Democracy

"Power Corrupts"

Nineteenth-century British historian and philosopher Lord Acton distilled the lessons of centuries of English political development in his famous remark: "Power tends to corrupt, and absolute power corrupts absolutely." Acton feared the human tendency to abuse power. His insight is absolutely accurate—check today's news—and underlies democratic thinking.

The Key Institutions

2.2 Describe how Britain's electoral system—single-member districts with plurality win—influences their two-plus party system.

Britain's constitution does not consist of a single written document. Instead, it is a centuries-old collection of Common Law, historic charters, **statutes** passed by Parliament, and established custom. This eclectic quality gives the British constitution flexibility. Nothing can be declared "unconstitutional." Parliament—specifically the House of Commons—can pass any law it likes, letting the British political system change over time without a systemic crisis. Whereas the U.S. Supreme Court sometimes blocks changes as unconstitutional, this is rarely a problem in Britain.

The negative side to this was that Britain had little to guarantee human rights. In 1991, six men convicted as Irish Republican Army bombers in 1975 were freed with the shameful admission that confessions had been beaten out of them and the police had rigged evidence. The European Court of Human Rights ruled against British justice in several such cases. In 2000, Britain adopted the European Convention on Human Rights as domestic law, finally giving Britons the equivalent of a U.S. Bill of Rights. In 2009, Britain at last got a Supreme Court, although, under the doctrine of parliamentary supremacy, it lacks the crucial power of its U.S. counterpart to declare laws unconstitutional. It can rule on human rights, devolution, and officials who may have exceeded their authority. Its 12 members are appointed by the monarch on the advice of the prime minister and may serve until age 70.

The Monarch

"The Crown" originally meant the monarch but now means the British executive branch, including criminal prosecutors (e.g., *Crown v. Smith*). Britain has a separate "head of state" and "chief of government." The United States ignores this distinction because the two are combined in the presidency. In most of the world, however, a top figure without much power symbolizes the nation, receives foreign ambassadors, and gives patriotic speeches. This person—often a figurehead—can be either a hereditary monarch or an elected president, although not a U.S.-style president. Britain, Sweden, Norway, Denmark, the Netherlands, and Belgium are constitutional monarchies in which the head of state is largely symbolic with powers limited by a constitution (not the case

statute
Ordinary law, usually for a specific problem.

Comparison

The Origins of Two Welfare States

Both Britain and Sweden are welfare states, Sweden more so than Britain. How did this come to be? In comparing their histories, we get some clues.

- Swedish King Gustav Vasa broke with Rome in the 1520s, a few years earlier than Henry VIII. In setting up churches that were dependent on their respective states—Lutheran in Sweden, Anglican in England—the two countries eliminated religion as a source of opposition to government.

- Because of this, politics in both lands avoided getting stuck in a clerical–anticlerical dispute over the role of the church, as happened in France, Italy, and Spain. In Britain and Sweden, the main political split was along class lines: working class versus middle class.

- Britain and Sweden both developed efficient and uncorrupt civil services, which are an absolute essential for effective welfare programs.

- Workers in both countries organized strong, but not Marxist, labor unions: the TUC in Britain and the LO in Sweden.

These two labor movements gave rise to moderate, worker-oriented parties—Labour in Britain and the Social Democrats in Sweden—which over time got numerous welfare measures passed. One big difference is that the Swedish Social Democrats have been in power most of the time since 1932 and implemented a more thorough and more expensive welfare state. Another difference, a cultural one, is that Swedes are more pragmatic and flexible, and all Swedish parties joined without rancor in trimming their welfare state. Accordingly, although British parties show great interest in Sweden's reforms, they may not be able to copy them.

in Persian Gulf monarchies). This can be useful. Above politics, a monarch is psychological cement to hold a country together and has no important governing role. Historically, the above countries evolved into democracies, whereas France's and Germany's sudden loss of monarchs plunged them into chaos and dictatorship.

The great commentator on the British constitution, Sir Walter Bagehot, divided it into **dignified** and **efficient** parts. The monarch, as head of state, represents a dignified office with much symbolic but no real political power. The king or queen nominally appoints a cabinet of His or Her Majesty's servants, but the choice belongs to the prime minister, the "efficient" office in Britain. This chief of government is a working politician who fights elections, leads his or her party, and makes political deals. A prime minister does not have the "dignity" of the monarch, but there is an advantage in splitting the two positions. If chiefs of government do something foolish or illegal, they will catch the public's ire, but the blame will fall on the individual prime minister, while the head of state, the "dignified" office, is still respected. The system retains its legitimacy. Where the two offices are combined, as in the United States, if the president does something crooked, the public gets disgusted at both the working politician and the nation's symbolic leader. "The British do not need to love their prime minister," said one diplomat. "They love their queen."

dignified
In Bagehot's terms, symbolic or decorative offices.

efficient
In Bagehot's terms, working, political offices.

The 1997 death of Princess Diana, ex-wife of Prince Charles, jolted Britain, including the royal family. "Di" was the only royal with the common touch; her charity work and love life upstaged the cold and remote House of Windsor. Amid the outpouring of grief for Di came mutterings that the royal family did not care. Some even suggested dumping the monarchy. But old dynasties know how to survive, and the Queen and Prince Charles quickly became more public and outgoing. The 2011 royal wedding and 2013 birth of Prince George attracted worldwide attention.

Only a minority of Britons would end the monarchy for a republic; a thousand years of (mostly) continuity counts. Some (including Queen Elizabeth), however, suggest reforms that would cut government funds for the royal house and make female heirs to the throne the equal of males. Britain will experience major changes when Queen Elizabeth dies. Charles will likely accede to the throne, even with his 2005 remarriage to a commoner (herself divorced). The last time this happened, in 1936, King Edward VIII abdicated, but times have changed.

The Cabinet

The British cabinet differs from the U.S. cabinet. The former consists of members of Parliament (most in Commons, a few in Lords) who are high up in their parties and are important political figures. Most have lots of experience, first as ordinary members of Parliament (**MPs**), then as **junior ministers**, and finally as cabinet ministers. Prime ministers are powerful, but only with the solid support of their parties in Commons.

Originally, the British cabinet consisted of ministers to the king. Starting in the seventeenth century, the cabinet became more and more responsible to Parliament. A British minister is not necessarily an expert in his or her **portfolio** but is picked by the prime minister for political qualifications. Both major British parties contain several viewpoints and power centers, and prime ministers usually have representatives of these in the cabinet. When Prime Minister Margaret Thatcher (1925–2013, prime minister 1979–1990) ignored this principle by picking as ministers only Tories loyal to her and her philosophy, she was criticized as dictatorial and ultimately lost her job. Balancing party factions in the cabinet helps keep the party together in Parliament and in power. British cabinet government has been declining. Now the prime minister develops policy with a small personal staff and then informs the cabinet of it. British commentators fear the rise of a "command premiership" instead of cabinet government.

MP
Member of Parliament.

junior minister
MP with executive responsibilities below cabinet rank.

portfolio
Minister's assigned ministry.

fusion of powers
Connection of executive and legislative branches in parliamentary systems; opposite of U.S. *separation of powers.*

Notice that the British cabinet straddles the gap between "executive" and "legislative." The elaborate American separation of powers (adopted by the Founding Fathers from an earlier misperception of British government by Montesquieu) does not hold in Britain or in most of the world. The United Kingdom has a combining or **fusion of powers**.

The British cabinet practices "collective responsibility," meaning ministers all stick together and, in public at least, support the prime minister. Occasionally, ministers resign in protest over a major controversy (but keep their parliamentary seats). In recent years, the cabinet has consisted of some 20 ministers, although this number and portfolio titles change. Prime ministers design their cabinets; they add, drop, rename, or combine ministries, so each cabinet is different. Most

Democracy

The Queen Chooses a New Prime Minister

In 2010, an old ritual was repeated. Ostensibly, Queen Elizabeth II chose a new prime minister, but events unrolled according to the fiction that the prime minister is still chief advisor to the monarch.

Labour Prime Minister Gordon Brown, who had taken over from fellow Labourite Tony Blair in 2007, caught popular blame for Britain's economic reversals during the global financial meltdown. The Tories,

under the dynamic young David Cameron, won a plurality (but not a majority) of the 2010 elections and formed a coalition with the smaller Liberal Democrats. Immediately, Brown called on the Queen and formally resigned. A few hours later the Queen summoned Cameron, now the leader of the largest party in Commons, to Buckingham Palace and "asked" him to form a new government. He accepted.

countries function that way (not, of course, the United States). The Cameron cabinet consisted of the following "secretaries of state":

Chancellor of the Exchequer (treasury)	Transport
Lord Chancellor (heads judiciary)	Communities and Local Government
Foreign Affairs	Business, Enterprise, and Skills
Home Department (internal governance, including police)	Health
Environment, Food, and Rural Affairs	Northern Ireland
Energy and Climate Change	Wales
International Development	Scotland
Work and Pensions	Defense
Education	Trade and Industry
	Culture, Olympics, Media, and Sport

Generally, cabinet ministers are the top MPs of the Commons' largest party, although an occasional Lord may be named. In addition, several junior ministers and "parliamentary private secretaries" hold specialized offices in the cabinet. Below cabinet rank are more than 30 noncabinet departmental ministers and a similar number of junior ministers assigned to help cabinet and departmental ministers. All totalled, at any given time about 100 MPs also serve in the executive branch. The hope of being named to one of these positions helps keep most MPs obedient to the prime minister.

The 2010 British general elections produced a "hung parliament" in which no single party held a majority of Commons seats. Although common in the nineteenth century, there were no hung parliaments in the twentieth century. In 2010, Tories won only 307 of the 650 seats, so Cameron negotiated with Nick Clegg, head of the small (57 seats) Liberal Democratic Party, to produce Britain's first coalition since World War II. Most of the cabinet was Tory; the Lib Dems got some lesser portfolios. The two parties did not like each other.

For all intents and purposes, in Britain (and in most parliamentary systems), cabinet equals **government**; the two terms are used interchangeably. One speaks of the "government," what the United States

government

A particular cabinet, what Americans call "the administration."

calls the "administration," although the U.S. term has been spreading. When the "government falls," it simply means the cabinet has resigned. This happens rarely in Britain.

The Prime Minister

The prime minister, or PM for short (not to be confused with MP, which he or she also is), is the linchpin of the British system. Because the prime minister picks and controls the cabinet and heads the largest party in Parliament, he or she should be able to get nearly any measure passed. British parliamentarians are well disciplined; party **whips** make sure their MPs turn out for divisions and vote the party line. Yet prime ministers do not turn into dictators, chiefly because general elections are never more than five years away.

Prime ministers are usually cautious about introducing measures that might provoke public ire. When Labour PM Gordon Brown saw his popularity slipping, he knew he would lose if he "went to the country" with new elections; so he waited, hoping his party's fortunes would rise before the five years were up in 2010. They did not; the Tories won. Typically, prime ministers introduce moderate, piecemeal measures to avoid offending key blocks of voters. Fear of losing the next election keeps most prime ministers cautious.

A prime minister has to watch the major currents of opinion within party ranks. As in the United States, the two large British parties contain left, right, and center wings, as well as regional viewpoints, and a prime minister usually constructs the cabinet with top MPs representing several views. In cabinet meetings, the PM tries to fashion a consensus. Then the cabinet sells the policy to the MPs back in Commons. Party discipline is good but rarely total. The prime minister, through the chief whip, has a hold on the MPs, but never a perfect hold. Many leftist Labour MPs voted against Blair's centrist policies and the Iraq War. Those who do not "take the whip" (follow the party line on a vote), however, risk losing their nominations for reelection—in effect, getting

whip
Parliamentary party leader who makes sure members obey the party in voting.

Who Was When: Britain's Postwar Prime Ministers

Clement Attlee	Labour	1945–1951
Winston Churchill	Conservative	1951–1955
Anthony Eden	Conservative	1955–1957
Harold Macmillan	Conservative	1957–1963
Alec Douglas-Home	Conservative	1963–1964
Harold Wilson	Labour	1964–1970
Edward Heath	Conservative	1970–1974
Harold Wilson	Labour	1974–1976
James Callaghan	Labour	1976–1979
Margaret Thatcher	Conservative	1979–1990
John Major	Conservative	1990–1997
Tony Blair	Labour	1997–2007
Gordon Brown	Labour	2007–2010
David Cameron	Conservative	2010–

Personalities

David Cameron

David Cameron, leader of the Conservative Party, in 2010 became prime minister at age 44, like his Labour predecessor Tony Blair. Cameron, descended from nobility (as is his wife), was born in 1966 in London but raised in Oxfordshire. As befits his social class, he graduated Eton and Oxford, where he studied philosophy, politics, and economics, or PPE.

Born and educated to be a Conservative politician, after university he rose rapidly in Tory ranks, first in policy research, which included briefing Prime Minister John Major. Cameron lost his first attempt to win election to Parliament—as do most British politicians—in 1997 but won in 2001 and took over Tory leadership in 2005. Bright and selfconfident, he did not shy away from controversial policies.

Cameron's pleasant, outgoing personality and criticism of Labour policies initially put him and his party ahead. Cameron sees himself as a "modern compassionate conservative" and as an "heir to Blair," a centrist who minimized ideology in politics. Cameron's economic polity of *austerity*, however, produced no growth and hurt his chances for reelection. Some observers say he never got a grip on Britain's severe economic problems.

fired from Parliament, which happens in every election. If a party policy really bothers an MP, the member can "cross the aisle" to the other party in protest (as did the young Winston Churchill).

A prime minister can even be dumped by MPs. Labour and Conservative cabinets have had to withdraw or water down legislative proposals amid backbenchers' revolts, such as the one that ousted Thatcher in 1990. Labour **backbenchers** revolted against Blair's Iraq policy, in effect saying, "Blair, time for you to go." In 2007, he went. Commons can oust a PM on a **vote of no-confidence**, but that is rare; it indicates the ruling party has split so badly that its MPs are willing to give up power. Loss of a big measure, such as the budget, would require the PM to resign.

The PM does have a potent weapon: the power to call new elections whenever he or she wishes. By law, the Commons can go up to five years without a general election. **By-elections**, when an MP dies or retires, can come at any time and are closely watched as political barometers. Prime ministers call new general elections when they think the party will do best. A good economy and sunny weather can help. In 1974, Britain held two general elections because Prime Minister Harold Wilson thought he could boost Labour's seats (he did). In 2001 and 2005, Tony Blair called elections a year early to take advantage of good economic news and disarray in Conservative ranks; he won handily. Public opinion polls and by-elections help the prime minister decide when to ask the Queen to dissolve Parliament and hold new elections.

Since 1735, the British prime minister has resided in an ordinary brick row house, 10 Downing Street. This is deceptive, for Downing Street is the nerve center of **Whitehall**. Upstairs at "Number 10" is the prime minister's apartment. On the ground floor, in the back, the cabinet meets in a long white room. Number 10 connects to 12 Downing Street, the residence of the chief whip, the PM's parliamentary enforcer. The whip can visit without being seen from the street. Also connecting

backbencher
Ordinary MP with no executive responsibility.

vote of no-confidence
Parliamentary vote to oust prime minister.

by-election
Special election for a vacant seat in Parliament.

Whitehall
Main British government offices.

Democracy

Prime Ministers into Presidents

Political scientists have long noted that prime ministers are becoming more and more presidential. Postwar British prime ministers have increasingly concentrated and centralized power in their immediate office at the expense of the cabinet and Commons.

British prime ministers no longer pretend to be "first among equals" in the cabinet, which meets less often and decides issues less frequently. Like the U.S. cabinet secretaries, British ministers have become more like top administrators. Prime ministers preside over an enlarged staff at 10 Downing Street, headed with trusted advisors, and use them to make decisions, rather like the White House.

Prime ministers spend less time in Commons. Churchill voted in 55 percent of Commons divisions in 1951. Harold Wilson voted 43 percent of the time in 1974. Tony Blair voted just 5 percent of the time in Commons in 1997.

Some have called recent prime ministers "control freaks" who have broken with British tradition in order to amass personal power. Maybe, but personality alone does not explain the long-term trend for prime ministers everywhere to become presidential. One key factor is television, which centralizes election campaigns, emphasizes the top candidates, creates massive need for fundraising, bypasses parties and parliaments, and enables leaders to reach people directly. Other factors include the decline of legislatures, the growth of interest groups, and the tendency of voters to concentrate in the center of the political spectrum.

Parliamentary systems cannot operate as before. Systems as different as Britain, Germany, and Australia have tended to "presidentialize" themselves as prime ministers gain power and act as if they have been directly elected. In elections everywhere, parties showcase their leaders as if they were presidential candidates. Parliamentary systems will not turn completely into U.S.-type systems, but neither will any of them return to the pure parliamentary model, which was never completely realistic. Power long ago began shifting to prime ministers. A strong prime minister begins to resemble a U.S.-type president.

out of sight is 11 Downing Street, residence of the important Chancellor of the Exchequer, head of the powerful Treasury Ministry. Next door is the Foreign Office. At the corner of Downing Street, also connecting to Number 10, is the cabinet secretariat, responsible for communication and coordination among the departments.

Commons

In a parliamentary system like Britain's, voters choose only a parliament, which in turn chooses (and can oust) the executive branch, headed by a prime minister. The executive is a committee of the legislature. In a presidential system, such as the United States, voters choose both a legislature and a chief executive, and the two are expected to check and balance each other. In a parliamentary system, they do not check and balance but instead reinforce each other.

The cabinet is a committee of Commons sent from **Westminster** to nearby Whitehall to keep administration under parliamentary control. Commons is also an electoral college that stays in operation even after it has chosen the executive (the cabinet). In Lockean theory, legislative power has primacy, but in practice, Commons has rarely been free and independent and is becoming less so. Prime ministers lead and control Commons.

Westminster
Parliament building.

The two main parties in Commons—Conservative and Labour— face each other on long, parallel benches. The largest party is Her

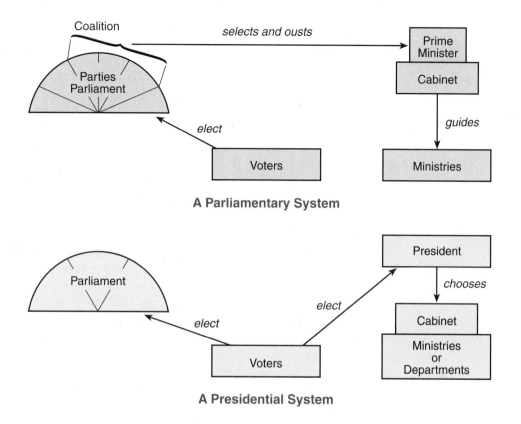

A Parliamentary System

A Presidential System

Majesty's Government; the other is Her Majesty's Loyal **Opposition**. Commons is very small—only 45 by 68 feet (14 by 21 meters)—and originally had only about 400 members. Its current membership of 650 makes it crowded. Unlike most modern legislators, Parliament members have no individual desks. For important votes, MPs pack in like sardines, sit in the aisles, and face each other in debate a few yards apart. The parallel benches go well with the two-party system; the half-circle floor plan of most Continental legislatures facilitates pie-like division into multiparty systems.

The chamber has always been small, ever since 1547, when Henry VIII first gave Commons the use of the St. Stephen's royal chapel. Each side has five rows of benches. Front row center on either side is reserved for the cabinet of the government party on one side and the **shadow cabinet** of the opposition on the other. Behind them sit the backbenchers, the MP rank and file. A neutral Speaker, elected for life from the MPs, sits in a throne-like chair at one end. The Speaker, who never votes or takes sides, manages the floor debate and preserves order; Conservative John Bercow has served as Speaker since 2009.

A table between the party benches is where legislation is placed (the origin of the verb "to table" a proposal). The Speaker calls the house to order at 11:30 A.M., and sessions can go on until 7:30 P.M. Unless "the

opposition
Parties in Parliament that are not in the cabinet.

shadow cabinet
Leaders of the *opposition* who aim to become the next cabinet.

whip is on"—meaning an MP must be there because an important vote is expected—many MPs are busy elsewhere.

Parliament opens each November with the Speech from the Throne by the Queen. The MPs file into the nearby House of Lords (neither monarchs nor lords may enter Commons) to hear Her Majesty read a statement outlining the policies "her government" will pursue. The speech has actually been written by the prime minister with no royal input.

Practically all legislation is introduced by the "government" (that is, the cabinet), and most passes nearly intact because of party discipline. What the PM wants, the PM usually gets. When a Tory government introduces bills, Tory MPs—unlike their American counterparts in Congress—rarely question them. The opposition, seated on the Speaker's left, challenges proposals. They question, denounce, and warn of dire consequences. There is no bipartisanship. The famous rhetorical ability of MPs often produces great debates.

Few MPs specialize. Traditionally, British parliamentary committees were also unspecialized; they simply went over the precise wording of bills. Eventually, MPs recognized the need for a more American type of committee system and, in 1979, 14 select committees were established to scrutinize the workings of the ministries, with the power to gather written and oral evidence. The select committees—with permanent, stable membership—resemble U.S. Congressional committees.

Commons is less important than it used to be. In most of the world, legislatures, the great avenues of democracy, are declining in power. Fewer people—especially young people—bother voting, and even fewer follow debates, which get less media attention. The debates matter little; thanks to Britain's (over)disciplined parties, prime ministers almost always get their way. To jump-start Commons back into life, MPs would have to ignore the whip and vote as they wish. A deliberate weakening of Britain's parties might make Commons exciting, unpredictable, and messy, like the U.S. Congress. But Capitol Hill has also been losing power to the White House. This may be an unstoppable world trend. Even so, legislatures are invaluable for scrutinizing executive power, holding it accountable, and occasionally ousting it. Thus they are still bulwarks of democracy.

Lords

Since 1958, distinguished Britons have been named Lords or Ladies of the Realm for their lifetimes only. In 1999, Parliament drastically reformed the House of Lords by kicking out most of its hereditary peers, thus turning it over to these life peers. This change has done nothing to enhance Lords' weak powers. Lords now has some 740 peers, most of them life peers, along with 92 hereditary peers and 26 top churchmen. Usually, fewer than 300 lords turn up; a quorum is three. A few lords are named to the cabinet or to other high political or diplomatic positions.

The British Parliament is nominally bicameral, but Commons limited Lords' powers over the centuries so that now "Parliament" really means Commons. Early on, Commons established supremacy in the key area of money—raising revenues and spending them. (This echoes in the U.S. provision that money bills originate in the House of Representatives.) Britain's seventeenth-century battles centered on the power of Commons, and it won. By 1867, Bagehot considered Lords a "dignified" part of the constitution. A unitary system like Britain really does not need an upper house; federal systems do, to represent the component parts. New Zealand realized this and dropped its upper chamber in 1951.

Since Britain's unwritten constitution does not specify or make permanent the powers of the two chambers, it was legally possible for Commons to weaken Lords. The 1911 Parliament Act allows Lords to delay legislation not more than 30 days on financial bills and two years (since 1949, one year) on other bills. Lords can amend legislation and send it back to Commons, which can (and usually does) delete the changes by a simple majority. Every few years, however, Lords jolts the government by forcing Commons to take another look at bills passed too quickly, sometimes serving as the "conscience of the nation." Lords is also able to debate questions too hot for elected officials—for example, abortion and homosexuality.

Most Britons agree that Lords is an anachronism ripe for reform but cannot agree on what to do with it. Blair's 1999 step depriving most hereditary peers of their seats made Lords meritocratic but not democratic. Occasionally, Commons considers making Lords fully or partially elected, like the U.S. Senate, but some fear that would dilute the legislative supremacy of Commons and turn Lords over to party politicians.

Supreme Court

In 2009, the Law Lords were split off from the House of Lords to form a new Supreme Court of the United Kingdom, located on Parliament Square in London. Some compared it to its U.S. counterpart, but there are big differences:

- The UK court has 12 "justices," few of whom are members of Lords, but they may use Lord as a courtesy title. They must retire at age 70 (75 for a dwindling number of oldsters), unlike the lifetime appointments of U.S. justices.

- Cases are mostly heard by a panel of five justices—sometimes by three, seven, or nine—rather than by the whole court.

- Vacancies are filled by the "president" of the court (equivalent to the U.S. chief justice) and deputy president in consultation with a Judicial Appointments Commission. This is an attempt to keep appoints professional, unlike the intensely political U.S. process.

- Because Britain has no written constitution and Parliament is supreme, the UK court cannot declare laws unconstitutional, but it may rule that usages are "incompatible" with UK or European Union rules on human rights. Accordingly, the UK court lacks the system-changing impact of U.S. Supreme Court decisions.

The Parties

Commons works as it does because of the strong British parties that formed in the late eighteenth century. A party that wins a majority of seats controls Commons and forms the government. British parties are more cohesive, centralized, and ideological than American parties. Earlier, British Labourites, who sometimes called themselves Socialists, favored **nationalization** of industry, welfare measures, and higher taxes. Conservatives, especially after Margaret Thatcher took them over, urged less government involvement and lower taxes.

nationalization
Government takeover of an industry.

The Liberal Party illustrates how smaller parties suffer under the British electoral system. In the nineteenth century, it was one of the two big parties, but by the 1920s, it had been pushed into a weak third place by Labour. Some former Labourites joined the Liberals in 1988 to become the Liberal Democrats. Although they have occasionally won 20 percent of the vote, they rarely get more than a few dozen Commons seats because their vote is territorially dispersed, so in only a few constituencies does it top Tories or Labourites.

As part of the 2010 coalition deal, the Lib Dems got a referendum in May 2011 on a modest electoral reform called "alternative vote" (AV), but voters rejected it. Instead of just one vote as under FPTP (see the following section, Britain's Two-Party System), AV lets voters rank candidates. If none get half of first preferences, second preferences from ballots for the *weakest* candidates are added until someone does get half. Also called "instant runoff," AV is used in several countries. Not as fair as PR, AV might have given the Lib Dems a few more seats, something the big parties did not want.

Scottish and Welsh nationalist parties have spurts of growth and decline. Their territorial concentration enables them to win a few seats in Westminster and many seats in the Scottish and Welsh assemblies instituted in 1999. (A parallel: the concentrated Québécois vote in Canada.)

Britain's Two-Party System

Britain is described as a two-party system, but some third parties are important. Britain, like many democracies, is actually a **"two-plus" party system**. In 1979, for example, the withdrawal of support by the 11 Scottish Nationalists in Commons brought down the Labour government in a rare vote of no-confidence. In general elections, the Liberal Democrats win enough votes to force Labourites and Conservatives to change some positions.

Britain's electoral system keeps two parties big and penalizes smaller parties. Britain, like the United States and Canada, uses **single-member districts** for elections. This old English system is simple: Each electoral district or constituency sends one person to the legislature, the candidate who gets the most votes, even if less than a majority, sometimes called "first past the post," FPTP. This system of single-member districts with **plurality** victors tends to produce two large political parties because there is a big premium to combine small parties into big ones to edge out competitors. If one of the two large parties splits, the other party, the one that hangs together, wins. **Proportional representation (PR)** systems do not put such a great premium on forming two large parties, contributing to multiparty systems.

Countries that inherited the British **majoritarian** system tend toward two large parties: one left, the other right, such as the U.S. Democrats and Republicans. India is an exception to this pattern, because its local parties are territorially concentrated so that India's parliament has dozens of parties. Canada has this to a lesser extent, permitting the separatist Bloc Québécois and socialistic New Democrats to win seats. New Zealand used to have the Anglo-American system, and it, too, yielded two large parties. It also left many New Zealanders discontent because other viewpoints got ignored, so its parliament in

"two-plus" party system
Two big parties and several small ones.

single-member district
Sends one representative to Parliament.

plurality
Largest quantity, even if less than a majority.

proportional representation (PR)
Electoral system of multimember districts with seats awarded by the percentage that parties win.

majoritarian
Electoral system that encourages dominance of one party in a parliament, as in Britain and the United States.

1993 adopted a new electoral law, modeled on Germany's hybrid system of half single-member districts and half proportional representation. New Zealand soon developed a more complex party system.

FPTP is simple but not fair or proportional. It advantages parties whose voters are distributed just right, neither overconcentrated nor too dispersed. The idea (as in U.S. gerrymandering) is to just edge out the second party in the most constituencies. There is no point in winning 100 percent of a constituency's vote. Once, a candidate won with just 26 percent of the vote in a four-party race in Scotland. In several postwar British elections, the party with the *second* most votes nationwide won the most seats. Reason: The bigger party got its votes overconcentrated in fewer constituencies. The opposite problem is when a party's votes are spread too thinly—the fate of the Lib Dems.

British Political Culture

2.3 **Illustrate the several ways that social class influences British politics.**

Britons are known (perhaps unfairly) for the large and often invidious distinctions made between and by social classes. Some of this may have already faded into the past. **Social class** can be analyzed two ways: objectively and subjectively. Objective analysis uses observable data such as income and neighborhood to place people into categories. Subjective analysis asks people to place themselves into categories. There are often discrepancies, as when, for example, a self-made businessman, thinking of his humble origins, describes himself as **working class**, or when a poorly paid schoolteacher, thinking of her university degrees, describes herself as **middle class**. In Britain and in most industrialized democracies, the main politically relevant distinction is between working class and middle class.

Objectively, class differences in Britain are no greater than in the rest of West Europe. Disraeli wrote that Britain was not one nation but two, the rich and the poor. Since then, the British working class has grown richer, the middle class bigger, and the small upper class poorer. But subjectively or psychologically, class differences remain. Working-class people live, dress, speak, and enjoy themselves differently than the middle class does. Class differences contribute to the way Britons vote, color the attitudes of unions and parties, and create Britain's elites through the education system.

social class
Layer or section of population of similar income and status.

working class
Those paid an hourly wage, typically less affluent and less educated.

middle class
Professionals or those paid salaries, typically more affluent and more educated.

meritocracy
Promotion by brains and ability rather than heredity.

public school
In Britain, a private boarding school, equivalent to a U.S. prep school.

"Public" Schools

Although many claim that Britain has become a **meritocracy** since World War II, having the right parents still helps. No society, including the United States, is purely merit based. One way the British upper and upper middle classes pass on their advantages is the **"public" school**—actually private and expensive—so called after its original purpose of training boys for public life in the military, civil service, or politics. Eton, Harrow, Rugby, St. Paul's, Winchester, and other famous academies have for generations molded the sons of better-off Britons into a ruling elite. British public schools are demanding and teach their 13- to 18-year-old pupils to be self-confident, self-disciplined, and bred to rule. Spy novelist John Le Carré recalled how his public schoolmates during World War II felt nothing but contempt for lower-class "oiks." Added Le Carré decades later, "nothing, but absolutely nothing, has changed."

Only 7 percent of young Britons attend private school—including day schools—but they make up more than 40 percent of students entering Oxford and Cambridge, because they are better prepared. (Note the parallel with U.S. "prep" schools.) The British public school system also generates an "old boy" network whose members help each other get positions in industry and government later in life. Most of Britain's elite have gone to public boarding schools, including more than half of Conservative MPs. Cameron was an Etonian, as were 18 other PMs. Fewer Labour MPs went to such schools. Most of Thatcher's and Cameron's ministers were educated at public schools, but only a minority of Blair's and Brown's.

Until the 1970s, most young Britons took a frightening exam at age 11 (the "11-plus") that selected the best for state-funded "grammar schools" but left most in "secondary modern" schools. In all but Northern Ireland, Labour governments phased out most of the selective grammar schools in favor of "comprehensive schools" for all, like U.S. high schools. This did not solve the twin problems of educational quality and equality. Now, better-off parents send their children to boarding schools, middle-class children go to private day schools, and working-class children go to mediocre state-funded comprehensive and technical schools, from which many drop out. Until after World War II, there was no free high school system in Britain. Only 65 percent of British 17-year-olds are still in school (including technical training), the lowest level of any industrial country (comparative figures: Germany, 97 percent; United States, 88 percent; Japan, 83 percent). British education is weak and still divided by class.

periphery
Nation's outlying regions.

vcenter–periphery tension
Resentment in outlying areas of rule by the nation's capital.

Geography

Centers and Peripheries

A country's capital is often called its "center," even though it may not be in the precise center of the land. Closer to the boundaries of the state is the **periphery**. Often these areas are more recent additions to the territory of the state. The inhabitants of some of them may still speak a different language and resent rule by the capital, such as the Russian-speaking eastern areas of Ukraine. This **center–periphery tension** is nearly universal among countries.

Over the centuries, England added Wales, Scotland, and Ireland. Resentment was so high in Ireland that Britain granted it independence in the twentieth century. Now Britain retains only Northern Ireland, long a source of resentment and violence.

Scotland and Wales also harbor grudges against rule by London and demand more home rule. Tony Blair's Labour government tried to calm these feelings by granting Scotland and Wales their own legislatures.

The U.S. Civil War was an effort by the southern periphery to cast off rule by Washington. In terms of culture and economics, the North and South really were two different countries, a gap that has been partly closed since then. The center of U.S. population, politics, economics, communications, education, and culture long remained in the northeast. This still fosters slight center–periphery tension; some western politicians express irritation at rule by Washington.

"Oxbridge"

Rhodes Scholarship
Founded by South African millionaire; sends top foreign students to Oxford.

class voting
Tendency of classes to vote for parties that represent them.

The elite universities of Oxford or Cambridge—"Oxbridge"—provide much of Britain's leadership. Nearly half of Conservative MPs are Oxford or Cambridge graduates (usually after attending a public school, such as Eton), while a quarter of Labour MPs are Oxbridge products. Thatcher, Blair, and Cameron were Oxonians. In Cameron's cabinet, 15 of 23 ministers were Oxbridge. In recent years, only Labour Prime Minister James Callaghan (1976–1979) and Conservative John Major (1990–1997) never went to college. In few other industrialized countries are political elites drawn so heavily from just two universities.

Since World War II, British education opened to the working and lower middle classes, by direct grant secondary schools and scholarships for deserving youths. Oxford and Cambridge became less class biased in their admissions, and many new institutions were founded or expanded. The percentage of British secondary school (high school) graduates continuing on to some type of higher education shot up from 14 percent in 1985 to nearly 40 percent today, approaching U.S. levels.

An Oxford or Cambridge degree—which takes three years to earn—commands respect and hones political skills. One popular major for aspiring politicians is "PPE"—philosophy, politics, and economics—in effect, how to run a country. Debating in the Oxford or Cambridge Unions trains students to think on their feet with rhetorical cleverness, the style of Commons. Many Oxbridge graduates carry a "sense of effortless superiority." One U.S. president (Clinton), two U.S. Supreme Court justices, and several U.S. cabinet secretaries attended Oxford on **Rhodes Scholarships**.

Class and Voting

Britain used to exemplify **class voting**. Most of the working class voted for the left party (in this case, Labour), while most of the middle class voted for the right (in this case, Conservative). Actually, class voting in Sweden was always higher than in Britain, but nowhere is it 100 percent, because some working-class people vote right and some middle-class people vote left.

Several factors dilute class voting. Some working-class people feel that Conservatives do a better job of governing. Some workers are sentimentally attached to the country's oldest party. The Tories win a chunk of the working class on economic growth, keeping taxes and deficits down, and keeping out immigrants. (Note the parallel with America's white working-class voting Republican.)

Going the other way, some middle-class people grew up in working-class families and vote like their parents. Many middle-class and educated Britons are intellectually convinced the Labour Party is the answer to an establishment-ruled, snobbish class system. Such intellectuals provide important leadership in the Labour Party. The leader of the Labour left for a long time was an aristocrat, Anthony Wedgewood Benn, or, as he liked to be known, Tony Benn.

The British generation that came of age during and after World War II, especially the working class, was quite loyal to the Labour Party, which swept to power in 1945. Since then, class voting has declined in Britain and other advanced, industrialized democracies, including

Geography

The 2010 Elections: Region trumps Class

A country's electoral geography—rooted in the history, resentments, and cultures of its regions—is long lasting. As illustrated in Britain, how a region voted in the past predicts how it will likely vote in the future. Labour lost overall in 2010 but scored above its national average in Scotland, Wales, and the industrial areas of London, Liverpool, Yorkshire, and the northeast—areas where it has long held sway. Geography now trumps social class: A better-off Scot is more likely to vote Labour than a working-class Englishman. The areas where the Conservatives fare above average (the blue-bordered portion) are mostly in England, especially in rural and suburban parts. In a nearly universal political pattern, large cities tend to vote left. Region strongly predicts the British vote, social class less so. Strong regional voting disparities make both Britain and the United States harder to govern: What pleases the north angers the south.

Blue: Where Tories Won above Average in 2010

the United States. Class is not as strong as it used to be in any country's voting patterns but is still a factor. In many countries, region now explains more than class.

civility
Good manners in politics.

British Civility

British **civility** is based on a sense of limits: Do not let anything go too far. Thus, while Labourites and Conservatives have serious arguments, they keep them verbal, which is not always the case in France, Germany, and Russia. British politicians are fairly decent toward one another.

But British civility does allow interrupting a speaker. In Parliament, a cabinet minister presenting a difficult case sometimes faces cries of "Shame!" or "Treason!" from the opposition benches. Margaret Thatcher faced Labourites chanting "Ditch the bitch." Insults and heckling are a normal part of British debates and are not viewed as out of bounds but rather as tests of a debater's poise and verbal skills. Amateur orators at the famous Speakers' Corner of Hyde Park in London can rant, but they too face heckling. British politics has turned uncivil on the question of race, and demonstrations and riots have led to deaths. Civility vanished in Northern Ireland amid a murderous civil war. British civility has been overstated; Swedes are more civil.

Pragmatism

Pragmatic has the same root as *practical* and means using what works regardless of theory or ideology. British political culture, like American or Swedish, is generally pragmatic. The Conservatives used to pride themselves on being the most pragmatic of all British parties. They were willing to adopt the policies of another party to win votes. In the nineteenth century, Disraeli crowed that he had "dished the Whigs" by stealing their drive to expand the voting franchise. In the 1950s, the returning Conservative government did not throw out Labour's welfare state; instead, it boasted that Tories ran it more efficiently. This changed with Thatcher's 1979 laissez-faire economic program. The fixity of her goals contributed to ideological debates within and between the two large and usually pragmatic parties. Pragmatism returned to the Tories after Thatcher. David Cameron proclaimed his centrist pragmatism as he trimmed overly generous welfare benefits, although not as much as Germany did under Social Democrat Schröder.

The British Labour Party historically offered little ideology beyond the welfare state. With the Callaghan government in the 1970s, however, ideological controversy engulfed Labour. Callaghan was a very moderate, pragmatic Labourite, hard to distinguish from moderate Conservatives. Militant Labourites, including some union heads, resented Callaghan's centrism and rammed through a socialist party platform despite him. The moderate wing of the Labour Party split off in 1981 to form a centrist party, the Social Democrats. A series of Labour Party chiefs pushed the party back to the nonideological center, leading to its 1997, 2001, and 2005 electoral victories.

There is and always has been a certain amount of ideology in British politics, but it has usually been balanced with a shrewd pragmatism to win elections and govern. The ideological flare-up of the 1980s in Britain made it perhaps the most polarized land of West Europe. Ironically, at this same time, French parties, long far more ideological than British parties,

Political Culture

The Shape of the British Electorate

Virtually all modern democracies show a strong clustering in the ideological center, with a tapering off toward the extremes: bell-shaped curves. Such a **center-peaked** distribution is probably necessary to sustain democracy, for it encourages **center-seeking** politics. A U-shaped distribution indicates extreme division, possibly heading toward civil war (for example, Spain in 1936). Pollsters and political consultants constantly remind their clients of the distribution of ideological opinion and warn them not to position themselves too far left or right. It took the Labour Party several electoral defeats to get the message. Tony Blair finally pushed Labour into about the 5 position (exact center) with vague but upbeat party positions. Cameron also pulled the Tories to the center.

Ideological Self-Placement of British Voters.

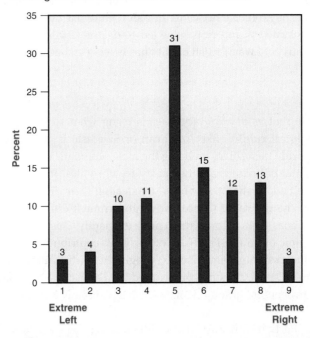

moved to the center. The British style is to "muddle through," improvising as they go. This may work with small problems, but not with a big problem such as Northern Ireland.

center-peaked
Distribution with most people in the middle, a bell-shaped curve.

center-seeking
Tendency of political parties toward moderate politics calculated to win the center.

Traditions and Legitimacy

British political usages still follow Burke's idea of keeping the forms but changing the contents. Most Britons like traditions and symbols. Some wince at the tabloid lifestyle of the younger generation of "royals," but few would abolish the monarchy in favor of a republic.

Parades with golden coaches and horsemen in red tunics are not just for tourists—although they help Britain's economy—they also deepen British feelings about the rightness of the system.

Traditions can also tame political radicals. Once they win seats in Commons, radicals find themselves playing according to established parliamentary usages. "Well, it simply isn't done, old boy," is the standard lesson taught to newcomers in Parliament. They may still have radical views, but they voice them within traditional bounds.

As used by political scientists, legitimacy means public perceptions that the government's rule is rightful. When a political system enjoys high legitimacy, people generally obey it. Legitimacy is closely related to **authority**, obeying duly constituted officials. British legitimacy and authority were famous, but they were exaggerated and oversold. Fewer than 5 percent of policemen carry guns in England and Wales (but most do in Northern Ireland).

During the 1970s, Britain turned violent. The Irish Republican Army (IRA) spread its murderous tactics from Ulster, planting bombs that killed dozens. In 1984, one bomb blew up near Prime Minister Thatcher. Criminals started using handguns. In Britain's cities, relations between police and youths, especially black youths, are hateful and contribute to urban riots, some of which turn deadly. After the 2005 London subway bombings, police shot and killed an innocent passenger on the mistaken suspicion that he was a terrorist. Some critics decried the gunplay as the Americanization of their police.

The Ulster Ulcer

Northern Ireland (sometimes called Ulster) illustrates how a system that works amid widespread legitimacy fails without it. Ulster is a split society, like Latin Europe—France, Spain, and Italy—where part of the population does not see the government as legitimate.

The Ulster problem is rooted in the eight centuries England ruled Ireland, at times treating the Irish as subhuman, seizing their land, deporting them, and even outlawing the Catholic faith. In the 1846–1854 potato famine, a million Irish starved to death while the English, with plentiful food stocks, watched (an example of what happens when you make too many babies, admonished English **Malthusians**). At that time, about a million and a half Irish emigrated, most to the United States. The Irish problem was the great issue of nineteenth-century British politics, "the damnable question" of whether to keep Ireland firmly under British control or grant it **home rule**.

In the spring of 1916, while the English were hard pressed in World War I, the "Irish Volunteers" (renamed the Irish Republican Army in 1919) attempted the Easter Rising to win freedom for Ireland. By 1922, after brutally crushing the rising, the British had had enough; Ireland became a "free state" within the British Commonwealth. In 1949, the bulk of Ireland ended this free-state status and became sovereign Eire, the Republic of Ireland.

But this did not solve the Northern Ireland problem; a majority of the 1.5 million people in its six counties are Protestant (descended from seventeenth-century Scottish immigrants) and are determined to remain part of Britain. Fiercely Protestant, for years these **Orangemen** treated Northern Irish Catholics as a different race and feared "popish" plots to bring Northern

authority
Political leaders' ability to be obeyed.

Malthusian
Malthus's theory that population growth outstrips food supply.

home rule
Giving a region some autonomy to govern itself.

Orangemen
After William of Orange (symbol of Netherlands royal house), Northern Irish Protestants.

Political Culture

Football Hooliganism

Underscoring the decline in British civility was the rise of football **hooliganism**, the violent rioting of some British soccer fanatics. Drunken fans sometimes charge onto the field in the middle of a game. In 1985, Liverpool fans killed 38 Italian spectators by causing their bleachers to collapse. All over Europe, the English fanatics are feared and sometimes barred from games.

What causes the violence? Some blame unemployment; the games offer the jobless one of their few diversions. But most hooligans are employed, and some earn good livings. Others see hooliganism as the erosion of civilization itself. "The truth is," said one self-confessed Manchester hooligan, "we just like scrappin'."

hooliganism
Violent and destructive behavior.

Ireland into the Catholic-dominated Irish Republic to the south. In control of Ulster's local government, the Protestants shortchanged the Catholic minority in jobs, housing, and even the right to vote for the Ulster legislature.

In 1968, Catholic protests started, modeled on U.S. civil rights marches. But Catholic nationalists, or "republicans," who sought to join the Republic of Ireland, soon battled with Protestant loyalists, or "unionists," who insisted that Northern Ireland stay part of Britain. The IRA enrolled Catholic gunmen, and Protestant counterparts reciprocated. Murder became nearly random. On "Bloody Sunday" in 1972, British paratroopers gunned down 13 peaceful Catholic marchers in Londonderry. Altogether, more than 3,600 were killed—including MPs, Earl Mountbatten, British soldiers, but mostly innocent civilians—and for some years the United Kingdom was the most violent nation in West Europe. Most Northern Irish welcomed a 1998 power-sharing agreement. Violence largely ended, but mistrust remains.

A Changing Political Culture

We are trying to put British political culture into perspective. Political scientists used to present Britain as a model of stability, moderation, calm, justice, and niceness. In contrast, France was often presented as a model of instability and immoderate political attitudes. The contrast was overdrawn; neither the British nor the French are as good or as bad as sometimes portrayed.

Observations of a country's political culture can err in two ways. First, if you are favorably disposed toward a country—and Americans are great Anglophiles (while many are Francophobes)—you may overlook some of the nasty things lurking under the surface or dismiss them as aberrations. For years, U.S. textbooks on British politics ignored or played down the violence in Northern Ireland. Such incivility seemed too un-British to mention. Riots in impoverished parts of British cities caught observers by surprise.

Second, studies of political culture are carried out during particular times, and things change. The data for Almond and Verba's famous book, *The Civic Culture*, were collected in 1959 and 1960. Their composite portrait of Britain as a "deferential civic culture" has not been valid for decades. British critics, mostly on the left, complain that Thatcher promoted individual greed and destroyed old communities and the sense of solidarity. Since World War II, Britain has undergone trying times, especially in the area of economics. This did not erase British culture wholesale; what had been latent simply became manifest.

Patterns of Interaction

2.4 **Explain why no country can be completely democratic.**

In Britain, as in most democratic countries, the relationship between people and political parties is complex, a two-way street in which each influences the other. The parties project something called **party image**, what people think of the party's policies, leaders, and ideology. Most voters, on the other hand, carry in their heads a **party identification**, a long-term tendency to think of themselves as "Tory" or "Democrat." Party strategy tries to project a party image that wins the loyalty of large numbers of voters and gets them to identify permanently with that party. If they can do this, the party prospers and wins many elections.

Both party image and party identification are reasonably clear in Britain: Most Britons recognize what the main parties stand for, and most identify with a party. The situation is never static, however, for the parties constantly change the images they project, and some voters lose their party identification and shift their votes.

In every country, parents contribute heavily to their children's party identification. In Britain (and the United States), if both parents are of the same party, most of their children first identify with that party, although this may later erode as young people develop their own perspectives. By the same token, party images are rather clear, and most Britons are able to see differences between their two largest parties: Labour aims to help people through social and educational reforms, and Conservatives aim at economic growth through hard work with little state intervention.

Until recently, most British voters were reliably Labour or Conservative. The *swing votes* are those who move their votes among parties, either because their party identification is not strong, or their perceptions of the parties' images shift, or both. A swing of a few percentage points can determine who will form the next government, for if each constituency shifts a little one way—say, toward the Conservatives—the Tory candidate will win in many constituencies. Single-member districts often exaggerate percentage trends and turn them into large majorities of **seats**.

The game of British electoral politics is in mobilizing all of a party's identifiers—that is, making sure their people bother to vote—plus winning over the uncommitted swing vote. In 1970, the Labour government of Harold Wilson suffered a surprise defeat by the Conservatives under Edward Heath. It was not because Labour identifiers suddenly switched parties; rather, some were unhappy with Wilson's policies and did not vote.

National and Local Party

Political scientists used to describe the British national party—Conservative or Labour—as nearly all-powerful, able to dictate to local party organizations whom to nominate for Parliament. Actually, there is a bargaining relationship between the parties' London headquarters and the local **constituency** party. The local party might have a bright local person it wants to run and ask the Labour or Conservative **central office** in London for approval. More often,

party image
Electorate's perception of a given party.

party identification
Psychological attachment of a voter to a political party.

seat
Membership in a legislature.

constituency
The district or population that elects a legislator.

central office
London headquarters of British political party.

Democracy

2010: A Hung Parliament

The May 2010 **general election** voted out Britain's Labour Party after 13 years in office but did not quite vote in the Conservatives. No party won a majority of seats—a rare thing with Britain's *majoritarian* system that had last happened in 1974—leading to a **hung parliament**. Typically, either Tories or Labour win a majority of Commons' seats (now increased back to 650 from the previous house's 646) with only a plurality of the vote, as Britain's electoral system overrepresents the winning party, just as in the United States. Since 1935, no British party has scored an actual majority. Turnout was a lackluster 65 percent (but up from 61 percent in 2005).

Labour had won three elections in a row (1997, 2001, and 2005) but was losing popularity after PM Tony Blair followed President Bush into the Iraq War in 2003. Critics called Blair "Bush's poodle." Only the Lib Dems opposed the Iraq War. In 2007, the successful Chancellor of the Exchequer Gordon Brown replaced Blair but quickly grew unpopular during the 2008–2009 recession. In ten years, Labour fell from 413 seats to 258.

The Conservatives under dynamic, young David Cameron gained in the popular vote and moved up from 30 percent of the seats to 47 percent, short of a majority. Initially, polls foresaw a Liberal Democratic surge under Nick Clegg—who "won" Britain's first televised election debates in 2010—but they gained only one percentage point in the popular vote and actually declined in seats because their voters were territorially dispersed. In 2010, the Tories needed 33,000 votes to win one seat and Labour needed 32,000, but the Lib Dems needed 112,000. Small parties, including the Scottish, Welsh, and Northern Irish parties, enjoyed an uptick, with 12 percent of the vote.

Labour suggested a coalition with the Lib Dems, but with only 315 seats, it would still have required support from small parties. Instead, after five days of negotiations, Tories and Lib Dems agreed to a coalition in which Clegg was deputy PM, the Lib Dems got some minor portfolios, and Cameron promised a referendum on reforming Britain's electoral system to more fairly represent small parties. Lib Dem voters, in some respects more radical than Labourites, were unhappy with the Lib Dems supporting Tory policies, and the Lib Dems declined sharply in the polls. Many called the coalition a mistake for the Lib Dems. When voter discontent with the two big parties boils up, the Lib Dems threaten to become Britain's second-largest party, ahead of Labour, but that would require a new electoral system and a coherent Liberal Democratic Party.

	% Votes		Seats	
	2010	**2005**	**2010**	**2005**
Conservative	36	32	306 (47%)	197 (30%)
Labour	29	35	258 (40%)	356 (55%)
Liberal Democrats	23	22	57 (9%)	62 (10%)

general election
Nationwide vote for all MPs.

hung parliament
One in which no party has a majority of seats; requires a *coalition.*

however, the central office suggests bright up-and-comers from elsewhere to the local party, which may or may not accept them. Britain has both national and local input into British candidate selection, with a veto on both sides. The U.S. system is purely local; essentially, candidates for Congress nominate themselves.

Some constituency organizations insist that a candidate actually live in the district. Americans expect all candidates to be from the district they represent; those who are not are called "carpetbaggers" and have an uphill battle. Most countries, however, including Britain,

safe seat
Constituency where voting has long favored a given party.

impose no such requirements, although being a local person can help. Some British constituencies like their people to establish a residence there once they have won, but many do not insist that their MP actually live there; after all, the MP's job is mainly in London, and periodic visits are sufficient for him or her to hear complaints and maintain ties with electors. In Britain, party is more important than personality. Usually, a minority of MPs are originally from the constituency they represent.

Parliamentary candidates hope to get **safe seats**. Party leaders are normally assigned very safe seats, for it is highly embarrassing if one of them loses his or her seat in the Commons. David Cameron, for example, represents Witney, a solid Tory constituency near Oxford. (Oxford itself goes Labour, a pattern also true of U.S. university cities, which go Democrat. Intellectuals tend to the left.) Some 450 (of 650) seats are usually considered safe.

What about the unsafe seats, those where the other party usually wins? These are the testing grounds for energetic newcomers to politics. The Conservative or Labour central offices in London may send a promising beginner to a constituency organization that knows it cannot win. Again, the local party must approve the candidate. Even if the candidate loses, his or her energy and ability are carefully watched—by measuring how much better the candidate did than the previous one—and promising comers are marked. For the next election, the London headquarters might offer the candidate a safer constituency, one where he or she stands a better chance. Finally, the candidate either wins an election in a contested constituency, is adopted by a safe constituency, or bows out of politics. Most of Britain's top politicians, including Thatcher, Blair, Brown, and Cameron, lost their first races and were transferred to other constituencies. There is no stigma attached; it is normal, part of the training and testing of a British politician.

Politics within the Parties

British political parties, like British cabinets, are balancing acts. In constructing their policies, party chiefs usually try to give various factions a say but keep matters under moderate control, with an eye to winning the next election. The Labour Party, portraying itself as more democratic, elects its leader at an annual party conference. Tories tried that for a time but, in 2005, reverted to their tradition of having only Conservative MPs, not a party conference, elect their chief.

Party leaders must balance between sometimes-extremist party militants and a generally moderate voting public. If a party takes too firm an ideological stand—too left in the case of Labour or too right in the Conservative case—it costs the party votes. Thus, party leaders tend to hedge and moderate their positions, trying to please both the true believers within their party and the general electorate. If they slip, they can lose party members or voters or both. When Labour veered left in the 1980s and the Conservatives followed their hard-right Thatcher course, the centrist Liberals won a quarter of the 1983 vote, a warning to both major parties.

Although long described as ideologically moderate, both Labour and Conservatives have ideological viewpoints within their ranks. The Labour Party has "left" and "right" wings. The

Marxist
Socialist theories of Karl Marx.

Trotskyist
Marxist but anti-Stalinist, follower of Leon Trotsky.

neoliberalism
Revival of free-market economics, exemplified by Thatcher.

left, springing from a tradition of militant trade unionism and intellectual radicalism, wants nationalization of industry, the dismantling of public schools, higher taxes on the rich, withdrawal from the European Union, and no nuclear weapons—British or American. Some **Marxists** and **Trotskyists** have won Labour offices. Labour moderates and centrists appreciate the welfarism of parties such as the Swedish Social Democrats but now want little government-owned industry or higher taxes. The Labour right is pro-NATO, pro-Europe, and pro-America in foreign policy. With Tony Blair, the Labour right won. For the 1997 election, Blair called his party New Labour. When young, leftish Ed Miliband narrowly won leadership of Labour in 2010, he dropped the New Labour label and tilted the party back to the left.

As an amorphous party proud of its pragmatism, Conservatives were long thought immune to ideology or faction. This is not completely true, for the Tories comprise two broad streams, which we might label as traditional and Thatcherite. The former is not U.S.-style conservative, advocating a totally free economy with no government intervention. Instead, the *traditional Tory* wants to take everybody's interests into account, plus traditional ways of doing things, under the guidance of people born and bred to lead. This has been called "one-nation Toryism" because it rejects notions of class divisions.

The Thatcherite wing (which traces back to nineteenth-century *liberalism* and is called **neoliberalism** in Europe and Latin America) is like American conservatism: They want to roll back government and free the economy. After World War II, this view crept into Conservative ranks and, with the 1975 elevation of Margaret Thatcher to party chief, moved to the forefront. Thatcher dubbed the traditional Tories "wets" and the militant Thatcherites "dries" (boarding school slang for frightened little boys who wet their pants and brave lads who do not).

The trouble here is that some traditional British Conservatives find total capitalism almost as threatening as socialism. As industries went bankrupt in record number, Thatcher faced a revolt of Tory "wets" against her "dry" policies. After John Major took over, Thatcherite MPs sought to dump him. Attitudes toward European unity still split the Tories. Thatcher favored the Common Market but opposed turning it into a European Union that infringed on British sovereignty. She and her followers were dubbed Euroskeptics. Major and his followers were enthusiastically pro-Europe—Euroenthusiasts—and supported the 1993 Maastricht Treaty, which created the present European Union. As Labour had done earlier, the Tories rebranded themselves as a centrist party by naming fresh, young David Cameron leader in 2005.

Parties and Interest Groups

Few politicians deliver what they promise. Americans are bothered by this, but it seems to be a universal rule of politics. Asked what guided his politics, Tory PM Harold Macmillan (1957–1963) responded: "Events, dear boy, events." Good intentions wither in the face of harsh realities.

In addition, politicians speak to different audiences. To party rank and file, they affirm party gospel, championing either the welfare state or free enterprise, as the case may be. To the electorate as a whole—which, as we saw, usually forms a bell-shaped curve—they tone down their ideological statements and offer vague slogans, such as "stability and prosperity" or "time for a change" to win the big vote in the center. But quietly, usually behind the scenes, politicians also strike important deals with influential interest groups representing industry, commerce, professions, and labor. A large fraction of the British electorate belongs to an interest group.

Around a quarter of the British workforce is unionized, down from half when Thatcher took office but still twice the level in the United States or France (but only half that of Sweden). Labor unions are constituent members of the Labour Party and, until 1993, controlled a majority of votes at Labour's annual conference. Unions still contribute most of the party's budgets and campaign funds and provide grassroots manpower and organization. Especially important are the views of the head of the **Trades Union Congress (TUC)**. No Labour Party leader can totally ignore Britain's union leaders.

This opened Labour to charges that it is run by and for the unions, which earned a reputation as too far left, too powerful, and too ready to strike. In selling his New Labour to the electorate, Blair partially broke the close association of labor federation to a social democratic party that had been the norm for Northern Europe. Dozens of union members sit as Labour MPs in Parliament; dozens more MPs are beholden to local unions for their election. This union bloc inside the Labour Party can force a Labour government to tone down measures that might harm unions. At times, however, Labour Party chiefs have made union leaders back down, warning that if the unions get too much, the Labour Party loses elections.

MPs known to directly represent special interests—**interested members**—are not limited to the Labour side. Numerous Tory MPs are interested members for various industries and do not hide it. When the connection is concealed or when money changes hands, an MP pushing for favors for a group becomes known as sleazy. The "sleaze factor" hurt the Tories under Major and Labour under Blair, some of whose aides sold peerages for cash. Politicians taking money on the side are found everywhere, in all parties, and even in modern, developed countries.

The Conservative counterpart of the TUC is the influential Confederation of British Industry (CBI), which speaks for most British employers but has no formal links to the Conservative Party, even though their views are often parallel. The CBI was delighted at Thatcher's antinationalization policies, although British industrialists gulped when they found this meant withdrawal of **subsidies** to their own industries. Thatcher could not totally ignore them, for CBI members and money support the Tories, and dozens of CBI-affiliated company directors occupy Conservative seats in Commons.

The Parties Face Each Other

There are two ways of looking at British elections. The first is to see them as one-month campaigns coming every few years, each a model of brevity and parsimony, especially compared with the long, expensive U.S. campaigns. Another way, however, is to see them as nearly permanent campaigns that begin the day a new Commons reconvenes after the latest balloting. The formal campaign may be only a few weeks, but, long in advance, the opposition party is planning how to oust the current government.

Trades Union Congress (TUC) British labor federation, equivalent to the U.S. AFL-CIO.

interested member MP known to represent an interest group.

subsidy Government economic aid to individual or business.

Question Hour
Time reserved in Commons for MPs to query ministers.

permanent secretary
Highest civil servant who runs a ministry, under a nominal minister.

knighthood
Lowest rank of nobility, carries the title "Sir."

The chief arena is Commons. British parliamentarians show no bipartisanship. The duty of the opposition is to oppose, and this they do by accusing the government of everything from incompetence and corruption to sexual scandal. The great weapon is embarrassment, making a cabinet minister look like a fool. The time is the **Question Hour**, held Monday through Thursday when Commons opens. By tradition, this hour is reserved for MPs to aim written questions at cabinet ministers, who are on the front bench on a rotating basis. Most Wednesdays at noon, for example, Prime Minister Cameron personally counters Tory criticism in Commons. Other cabinet ministers face questions on other days of the week. Each written question can be followed by supplementary oral questions. The opposition tries to push a minister into an awkward position where he or she lies, fluffs an answer, or becomes angry. The opposition means to show voters, "You see, they are not fit to govern."

The Cabinet and the Civil Servants

As we discussed earlier, British cabinet ministers are generalists, not specialists, and are chosen more for political reasons. The minister represents that ministry in cabinet discussions and defends it in Commons but does not really run the department; civil servants do.

Ministers come and go every few years; the highest civil servants, known as **permanent secretaries**, are there much longer. They often have an edge on their ministers in social and economic terms as well. Most permanent secretaries are knighted later in life, while few ministers are. Although **knighthood** is now purely honorific in Britain, it still conveys social superiority. Permanent secretaries earn more than ministers, in some cases nearly twice as much. Ministers find it nearly impossible to fire or transfer permanent secretaries, who have a say in determining who will replace them when they retire or leave for well-paid positions in private industry; they tend to be a self-selecting elite. Permanent secretaries always play the role of humble, obedient servants, but some ministers come to wonder just who the boss really is.

The permanent secretary is assisted by several deputy secretaries, who in turn are supported by undersecretaries and assistant secretaries. These positions look like those of an American department, but in Washington, all or most of those positions are filled by political appointees, serving at the pleasure of the president and resigning when a new president takes office. In Britain, only the ministers assisted by some junior ministers—about a hundred persons in all—change with a new government. What are temporary political appointees in the United States are permanent officials in Britain.

This gives them power. They are not amateurs but know their ministry—its personnel, problems, interests, and budget. Knowledge is power, and over time, top civil servants come to quietly exercise a lot of it. While permanent secretaries or their assistants never—well, hardly ever—go public with their viewpoints, they reveal them through the kinds of ideas, programs, bills, and budgets they submit to the minister, their nominal boss. The minister rarely knows enough about the workings of the ministry and must rely on civil servants. Accordingly, while most bills and budget proposals pass through the cabinet, they do not originate there. The permanent civil servants do the jobs that are the stuff of governance.

The real power among British ministries is **Treasury**, sometimes called the "department of departments." Treasury not only supervises the main lines of economic policy but has the last word on who gets what among the ministries. Anyone with a bright idea in British government—a new minister or an innovative civil servant—soon comes up against the stone wall of Treasury, "the ministry that says no." Britain's treasury minister goes by the old name of Chancellor of the Exchequer—originally the king's checker of taxes—and is now the second most powerful figure in the cabinet, the first being the prime minister. Some chancellors later become prime ministers, so the person in that office—currently George Osborne—is watched closely.

> **Treasury**
> British ministry that supervises economic policies and budgets of other ministries.
>
> **peerage**
> A lord or lady, higher than knighthood.

Treasury officials are smarter and more powerful than other bureaucrats. Operating on a team-spirit basis, Treasury chaps trust only other Treasury chaps, for only Treasury can see the whole picture of the British government and economy and how the many parts interrelate. Treasury has an image of cold, callous remoteness, "government by mandarins," but it is the pattern worldwide with any department, ministry, or bureau that controls the national budget. To budget is to govern, and he who controls the budget steers the government.

The Civil Service and Interest Groups

The relationship between interest groups and political parties is only one way for groups to make their voices heard and is often not the most important way. Much interest-group impact is in the quiet, behind-the-scenes contact with the bureaucracy. Indeed, with Parliament's role curtailed as a result of powerful prime ministers and party discipline, and cabinet ministers themselves dependent on permanent civil servants, many interest groups ask themselves, "Why bother with Parliament? Why not go straight to where the action is: the bureaucracy?"

Political Culture

The Utility of Dignity

The monarch's bestowal of an honor such as knighthood is a payoff system that serves a number of purposes. The granting of a knighthood (Sir) or a **peerage** (Lord) is a reward and an encouragement to retire, opening positions to new people. These honors also civilize recipients; even militant union leaders and rapacious businessmen start talking about the common good once they have titles in front of their names.

The Queen awards these and other distinctions only on the advice of the prime minister, who has a small staff that watches for meritorious civil servants, businesspeople, unionists, soldiers, politicians, scholars, artists, and writers and recommends who should get what. In addition to becoming knights and peers, distinguished Britons may be named to the Order of the British Empire, Order of the Garter, Order of Merit, Order of the Bath, the Royal Victorian Order, and many others. The granting of honors is a part of British political culture, a way of bolstering loyalty to and cooperation with the system.

This approach is especially common for business and industry; the major effort of the unions is still focused on the Labour Party. The reason for this is partly in the nature of what trade unions want as opposed to what business groups want. Unions want general policies on employment, wages, and welfare, which apply to tens of millions of people. Industry usually wants specific, narrow rulings on taxes, subsidies, and regulations that apply to a few firms. Thus unions tend to battle in the more open environment of party policy, while business groups prefer to quietly take an official to lunch.

In working closely with a branch of Britain's economic life, a given ministry comes to see itself not as an impartial administrator but as a concerned and attentive helper. After all, if that industry falters, it reflects badly on the government agency assigned to monitor it. In this manner, civil servants come to see leaders of economic interest groups as their "clients" and to reflect their clients' views. When this happens—and it happens worldwide, certainly in the United States—the industry is said to have "captured" or "colonized" the executive department.

Reinforcing this pattern is the interchange between civil service and private industry. A permanent secretary can make much more money in business than in Whitehall; every now and then, one of them leaves government service for greener pastures. (This pattern is especially strong in France and Japan.) By the same token, some business executives take high administrative positions on the dubious theory that if they can run a company, they can run government. Everywhere, cozy relationships develop between civil servants and private business.

How Democratic Is Britain?

The power of bureaucrats brings us to a fine irony. Britons marched toward democracy by first limiting the power of the monarch and then expanding participation, but now, many important decisions are only partly democratically controlled. Civil servants make much policy with no democratic input. Does this mean there is no real democracy in Britain? No, it means we must understand that no country really controls its bureaucracy and that parties and elections are only attempts to do so.

Indeed, most of the interactions we have talked about are not under any form of popular control. Ideological infighting, the influence of interest groups on parties and the bureaucracy, the relationship of top civil servants with ministers, and other interactions are removed from democratic control. The people do not even choose whom they get to vote for; that is a matter for party influentials. All the people get to do is vote every few years, and the choice is limited.

Some people have an exaggerated vision of democracy as a system in which everyone gets to decide on everything. Such a system never existed at the national level, nor could it. The most we can ask of a democracy is that the leading team—in Britain, the prime minister and cabinet—are held accountable periodically in elections. This makes them pay attention to the public good, holds down special favors and corruption, and makes sure the bureaucracy functions. It is in the fear of electoral punishment that Britain, or any other country, qualifies as a democracy. What Harvard's Carl J. Friedrich (1901–1984) called the **rule of anticipated reactions** keeps the governors on their toes. We will learn not to expect much more of political systems.

rule of anticipated reactions
Friedrich's theory that politicians plan their moves so as not to anger the public.

What Britons Quarrel About

2.5 **Compare recent political quarrels in Britain to those in the United States.**

The Political Economy of Britain

The 2008–2009 financial meltdown hurt Britain as much as it hurt the United States. British real estate and investment bubbles popped, producing a big recession, which both London and Washington initially combated by expanding credit and government stimulus packages (exactly what most major countries did). On both sides of the Atlantic, however, conservatives denounced the stimuli and prescribed austerity to restore business "confidence" as the only cure, which would come only when the budget was getting back into balance.

recession

A shrinking economy, indicated by falling GDP.

Liberal economists in both Britain and America argued this was exactly the wrong thing to do, a repeat of the policies that deepened and prolonged the Great Depression. They favored stimulus and urged deficit reduction only when economic recovery was well underway. To do it too soon would produce a "double dip" **recession**, they warned. In Britain and elsewhere, austerity policies did little to restore growth.

It was an old debate, one from the 1930s, when British economist John Maynard Keynes urged government deficit spending to push up "aggregate demand" and employment. Roosevelt applied such policies lightly by spending on public works and Social Security but then pulled back in 1937, producing another dip. Critics on the left say Roosevelt should have gone Keynesian stronger and longer. Critics on the right claim Keynesianism did nothing to get us out of the Depression and left a legacy of debt and inflation. Intellectually, nothing changed in the debate over Keynesian economics in 80 years.

Cameron's Austerity

Cameron's economic program featured drastic spending cuts, what is called "austerity." Tory Chancellor of the Exchequer George Osborne rolled back Labour's social spending with ultra-tight budgets aimed at eliminating deficits. The Obama administration—although mindful of Republican and Tea Party cries to do the same—held off drastic cuts. British unions protested peacefully, but some young Britons protested violently, especially over major university tuition hikes. Tory and Lib Dem standings in the polls drooped while Labour's rose. Who was right: U.S. Keynesians or British anti-Keynesians?

The U.S. economy recovered from the Great Recession slowly but faster than Britain's. It was hard to pinpoint blame, however, because other things were happening in the world economy that hampered Europe's recovery as a whole—high oil prices, currency parities, and droughts in many countries. Keynesians such as Princeton's Paul Krugman claimed that Britain (and much of the rest of Europe) was proof that austerity fails and that stimulus policies were clearly better. The U.S. economy was growing too slowly because Washington had applied only weak spending stimulus, he charged. Conservatives on both sides of the Atlantic adopted the old Scottish verdict of "not proven."

Britain had been in economic decline for decades. At first, it was only a relative decline, as the economies of West Europe and Japan grew more rapidly than the British economy. By the

Democracy

Pluralistic Stagnation

Harvard political scientist Samuel Beer decades ago advanced a provocative thesis on the cause of Britain's decline: too many interest groups making too many demands on parties who are too willing to promise everyone everything. (U.S. economist Mancur Olson made much the same point.) The result, said Beer, was **"pluralistic stagnation"** as British groups scrambled for welfare benefits, pay hikes, and subsidies for industry. The two main parties bid against each other with promises of more benefits to more groups.

Furthermore, in the 1960s, a strong British **counterculture** emerged that repudiated civility and deference in favor of stridency. With every group demanding and getting more, no one saw any reason for self-restraint that would leave them behind. Government benefits fed union wage demands, which fed inflation, which fed government benefits....

The interesting point about the Beer thesis is that it blamed precisely what political scientists long celebrated as the foundation of freedom and democracy: **pluralism**. Beer demonstrated, though, that it can run amok; groups block each other and government, leading to what Beer called the "paralysis of public choice." Many now see similar problems with the U.S. system.

---

pluralistic stagnation
Theory that out-of-control interest groups produce policy logjams.

counterculture
Rejects conventional values, as in the 1960s.

pluralism
Autonomous interaction of social groups with themselves and with government.

deindustrialization
Decline of heavy industry.

consumption
Buying things.

production
Making things.

productivity
Efficiency with which things are made.

inflation
Increase in most prices.

monetarism
Friedman's theory that the rate of growth of money supply governs much economic development.

1970s, however, Britain was in an absolute decline that left people with lower living standards as inflation outstripped wage increases. The first industrial nation saw Italy overtake it in per capita GDP in the 1980s. Even Britain's former colonies of Hong Kong and Singapore had higher per capita GDPs than Britain. In Britain, **deindustrialization** took place; in some years, the British GDP shrank. They called it the "British disease," and some Americans feared it was contagious. The 2008–2009 recession revived debate over Thatcher's cure for Britain's economic problems in the 1980s. Did it really work, or did it merely set up Britain for the downturn?

The "British Disease"

Thatcherites blamed the growth of the welfare state that Labour introduced in 1945, which let many **consume** without **producing** and subsidized inefficient industries. Unions, given most of what they demanded by previous governments, raised wages and lowered **productivity**. Welfare costs shortchanged investment, which meant insufficient production, which brought stagnating living standards. *Nationalized* and *subsidized* industries lost money. The result: **inflation** and falling productivity. The cure, in part, came from the **monetarist** theory of American economist (and Nobel Prize winner) Milton Friedman, which posits too-rapid growth of the money supply as the cause of inflation. Thatcher cut bureaucracy, the growth of welfare, and subsidies to industry in an effort to control Britain's money supply and restore economic health. The Cameron government basically accepted the Thatcherite views.

Comparison

The Cost of the Welfare State

The downside of the welfare state is its high cost. Government spending and total taxes as percentages of GDP are shown for 2009. This only approximates welfare spending, as not all of these expenditures are welfare; some go for defense, which is especially high for the United States, or for subsidies to industry or agriculture. Nowhere do taxes cover spending. The difference—usually more than ten percentage points—is passed along as deficits. Bear in mind that 2009 was a recession year, entailing higher spending and decreased tax revenues.

	Spending	Taxes
Sweden	56%	46%
France	55	42
Britain	52	34
Germany	48	37
Japan	42	28
United States	42	24

SOURCE: Organization for Economic Cooperation and Development

Labourites argued that the Thatcher policies were wrong and brutal. Unemployment at one point reached 14 percent of the workforce, thousands of firms went bankrupt, and Britain's GDP growth was still anemic. Even moderate Conservatives pleaded for her to relent, but Thatcher was not called the Iron Lady for nothing. She saw the economic difficulties as a purge Britain needed in order to get well. One of her economists said: "I don't shed tears when I see inefficient factories shut down. I rejoice." Thatcher and her supporters repeated, "You cannot consume until you produce." Gradually, the argument began to take hold, and in the 1980s, more working-class Britons voted Tory than voted Labour.

By the time the Tories left office in 1997, the picture was mixed but generally positive. Inflation was down, and economic growth was among the fastest in Europe. British industries that had been nationalized since the war to prevent unemployment were **privatized**. Competition increased with less regulation. Renters of public housing could buy their homes at low cost, a move that made some of them Conservatives. Unions eased their wage and other demands, and union membership dropped sharply. Many weak firms went under, but thousands of new small and midsized firms sprang up. Capital and labor were channeled away from losing industries and into winners, exactly what a good economic system should do.

Thatchernomics jolted workers out of their trade union complacency. When the government's National Coal Board closed hundreds of unprofitable pits and eliminated 20,000 jobs, miners staged a long and bitter strike in 1984, supported by some other unionists. Thatcher would not back down; after a year, the miners did. (At about the same time, President Reagan faced down striking air traffic controllers.) New legislation limited union chiefs' abilities to call strikes, and the number and length of strikes in Britain dropped drastically.

As in the United States in recent decades, income inequality grew in Britain. The number of Britons in families with less than half the average income increased under Thatcher and Major from 5 million in 1979 to 14 million in 1993. High youth unemployment led to urban riots (and still does). Regional disparities and resentments appeared between a rich, resurgent south of England,

privatization
Government sells off *nationalized* industries to private business.

Comparison

The Productivity Race

No production, no goods. Production is what gets turned out. Productivity is how efficiently it gets turned out. You can have a lot of production with low productivity, the Soviet problem that brought down the Communist regime. Productivity numbers, however, can deceive. During recessions, productivity goes up as workers are laid off, what is called the "productivity paradox."

The growth of productivity—the additional amount a worker cranks out per hour from one year to the next—is the measure of future prosperity. Rapid growth in productivity means quickly rising standards of living; low growth means stagnation or even decline. The percent growth of average annual "total factor productivity"—which measures the efficiency of both labor and capital—from 1990 to 2008 is shown in the table.

China's and India's rapid productivity growth was similar to Japan's in earlier decades. Newly industrializing countries, because they start from a low level, easily show big percentage gains. After a while, when all of the easy gains have been made, a country becomes more "normal," as Japan has. The major advanced economies all score the same slow gains.

Total Factor Productivity Growth, Annual Average, 1990–2008	
China	4.1
India	2.8
Japan	1.2
Britain	1.2
United States	1.1
Germany	1.1
France	1.0
Mexico	0.4
Brazil	0.3
Russia	0.2

SOURCE: OECD, UBS

with new high-tech industries, and a decaying, abandoned north, where unemployment hit hardest. Thatcher never did get a handle on government spending, much of which, like U.S. **entitlements**, must by law be paid. British welfare benefits actually climbed sharply during the Thatcher and Major years despite their best efforts to trim them. Cutting the welfare state is tempting but rarely successful; too many see their benefits as rights. Furthermore, in the late 1980s, a credit and spending boom kicked inflation back up to more than 10 percent, and the economy slumped into recession. Competitively, British productivity was low and its wages high, so Britain continued to lose manufacturing jobs to other countries.

Thatcher's main legacy is how she changed the terms of Britain's political debate. In 1945, Labour won on building a welfare state, and Tories had to compete with them on their own terms, never seriously challenging the premise that redistribution is good. Thatcher made the debate about productivity and economic growth; now Labour had to compete on *her* terms. It was a historic shift and one that influenced the political debate in other lands, including the United States. Labour Prime Ministers Blair and Brown did not repudiate Thatcher's free-market economic policies; they adopted them.

The flaw in the Thatcher (and Reagan) economic model was that it depended more and more on an overlarge financial sector amassing debts and risky loans, bubbles that had to pop on both sides of the Atlantic. When they did pop in 2008—triggered by the collapse of U.S.

entitlements

Spending programs citizens are automatically entitled to, such as Social Security.

subprime mortgages—both economies slid into major recession, which PM Brown fought with massive spending, leading to giant deficits and higher taxes on the rich. Brown looked inept and dishonest and became unpopular, leading to the 2010 Tory victory. Cameron's austerity policies, however, produced little growth, and the Tories started looking inept and out of touch, in poor shape for the next general election, which must be held by 2015. Electorates punish governments for not delivering prosperity.

The Trouble with National Health

The centerpiece of Britain's welfare state is the National Health Service (NHS), which went into operation in 1948 as part of Labour's longstanding commitment to helping working Britons. Before World War II, British medical care was spotty, and many Britons were too unhealthy and scrawny for military service during the war. Conservatives and the British Medical Association fought the NHS, but the tide was against them.

The British population is much healthier than it used to be. Infant mortality, one key measure of overall health standards, dropped from 64 out of 1,000 live births in 1931 to 5 now. The British working class especially benefited. Britons spend only 9 percent of their GDP on health care but are healthier than Americans, who spend 16 percent.

But NHS cannot keep up with skyrocketing costs, even though it eats nearly a fifth of the budget. As Britons have become more elderly, they consume much more medical care. Technical advances in medicine are terribly expensive, and the system requires many bureaucrats. With a staff of 1.5 million, the NHS is the third-largest employer in the world (behind the Chinese army and Wal-Mart), but personnel and facilities have not kept pace with demand. The money simply is not there. If surgery is not for an emergency, patients might wait a year or more. The debate in Britain is over whether to keep funding the NHS by general tax revenues, which Labour favors, or to adopt European funding models, which include mandatory employee and employer contributions and a bigger role for private health care.

Britain's Racial Problems

British society, like U.S. society, is split along racial and religious lines. Whites have little to do with nonwhites and Muslims, and there is animosity between them. Since 1958, racially based riots flare in Britain every few years. Nonwhites, most born in Britain, are now about 7 percent (4 percent South Asian and 2 percent black) of Britain's population, many ghettoized in the declining industrial cities in the north of England.

Every few years, arson, looting, and even murder hit English center cities, in some of the worst riots in Europe. Most of the participants are nonwhite. Labour chief Ed Miliband offers the standard leftist explanation that poverty, joblessness, and despair spark the riots. Tory policy shortchanges poor young people on education and jobs, he charges. PM Cameron offers the standard conservative explanation: Fatherless children, no discipline in home and school, and coddling of criminals lead to "slow-motion moral collapse." He vows tough anticrime responses. (Note the parallel with U.S. explanations: Democrats look to poverty, Republicans to laxity.)

The problem began as a legacy of empire. Britain in 1948 legally made the natives of its many colonies British **subjects**, entitled to live

subject
Originally, a subject of the Crown; now means British citizen.

and work in the United Kingdom. Although the colonies were granted independence from the late 1940s through the 1960s, as members of the British Commonwealth, their people were still entitled to enter Britain. In the 1950s, West Indians arrived from the Caribbean, then Indians and Pakistanis, taking lowly jobs that Britons did not want and then sending for relatives. For years, they labored in Britain's textile industry, but it closed, leaving many Muslims unemployed. Britain now has some 1.6 million Muslims, mostly Pakistanis. (France has far more Muslims.) Meanwhile, white resentment builds, especially among the working class in areas of industrial decline and high unemployment. Some Britons refer to "Londonistan" in a nonjoking way. In 1967, an openly racist National Front formed, advocating the expulsion of all "coloureds" back to their native lands. Skinheads, supporting the Front or its successor, the British National Party (BNP), enjoy "Paki bashing." With slogans such as "Rights for Whites," the anti-immigrant vote grew but never won a seat in Parliament. The BNP was much weaker than its Continental counterparts, such as the French National Front.

Two forces keep Muslims segregated: discrimination by whites and their own efforts to preserve their original faith and culture. A special irritant: Muslim women in full-face veils. Caught between two cultures, some unemployed and alienated Muslim youths fall under the sway of fanatic Islamist preachers. In 2005, four Muslim youths (three of Pakistani origin but born in England, one born in Jamaica) set off three bombs on London's Underground and one on a bus, which killed 56 and injured 700. Other bombings followed. A few bitter young Muslim Britons openly applaud terrorist bombings; some even celebrate 9/11.

Geography

Devolution for Scotland and Wales

Britain, a centralized unitary state, has become less centralized. Northern Ireland, Scotland, and Wales show the center–periphery tensions that afflict many countries. In general, the farther from the nation's capital, the more regional resentment. Wales has been a part of England since the Middle Ages; the thrones of England and Scotland were united in 1603, but only in 1707 did both countries agree to a single Parliament in London. The old resentments never died. Wales and Scotland were always poorer than England, leaving Welsh and Scots feeling economically ignored.

This aided the Labour Party. Voting Labour in Scotland and Wales became a form of regional nationalism, a way of repudiating rule by England, which goes Conservative. Center–periphery tensions reveal themselves in voting patterns. In the 1960s, the small Plaid Cymru (pronounced *plyde kum-REE*, meaning "Party of Wales") and the Scottish Nationalist Party grew, and both now win seats in Parliament.

Regional nationalism grew in many countries starting in the 1970s: Scottish and Welsh in Britain, Corsican and Breton in France, Quebecker in Canada, and Basque and Catalan in Spain. In the 1990s, the Soviet Union and Yugoslavia fell apart. There are several causes of local separatism. Local nationalists claim their regions are economically shortchanged by central governments. Some emphasize their distinct languages and cultures and demand that these be taught in schools. Many resent the bigness and remoteness of the modern state, the feeling that important decisions are out of local control and made by distant bureaucrats. Smoldering under the surface are historical resentments of a region that was conquered, occupied, and deprived of its own identity. Whatever the mixture, local nationalism can produce militants willing to use violence.

In Scotland, economic growth led to nationalism. When oil was discovered in the North Sea off Scotland in the 1960s, some Scots did not want to share it with the United Kingdom as a whole: "It's Scotland's oil!" Petroleum seemed to offer Scotland the possibility of economic independence and self-government, but now Scottish oil and natural-gas production is starting to decline. (Alberta also feels possessive about its oil.)

The leading issue for Welsh nationalists has been language, the ancient Celtic tongue of Cymric (pronounced *kem-raig*). Some 13 percent of Welsh speak Cymric, a number that has been growing as it is required in Welsh schools. Cymric is now officially coequal with English within Wales, which has a Cymric TV channel.

The Labour Party has been more open to home rule or autonomy for Scotland and Wales, what is called **devolution**, the center granting certain governing powers to the periphery. A 1977 devolution bill to set up Scottish and Welsh assemblies, however, failed in **referendums**. After the 1997 election, Tony Blair again offered Scotland and Wales their own parliaments, and this time the referendums passed. In 1999, at about the same time that Ulster got home rule, Scots and Welsh elected regional parliaments with a new voting system that could eventually be adopted for Britain as a whole. The German-style system gave each voter two votes, the first for FPTP single-member districts and the second for parties in multimember districts. The results of the second vote were used to "top off" the number of seats for each party until they were roughly proportional to its share of the votes.

The new assemblies have some powers in education, economic planning, and taxation. In 2011 elections to the 129-member Scottish Parliament, the Scottish National Party (SNP) trounced both Labourites and Tories to win an outright majority of seats. The SNP did a good job running Scotland, a point that encouraged other parts of the United Kingdom to think about devolution. For some Scots, devolution did not go far enough, but a 2014 referendum for full independence failed 44.7 percent "yes" to 55.3 percent "no", a parallel to Quebec's earlier failed referendums on sovereignty.

Britons do not use the word, but Britain now has **quasi-federalism**, and it could go further. Fewer citizens call themselves "British"; increasingly, they specify English, Scottish, or Welsh. Devolution may have started a logical sequence leading to federalism. Scottish and Welsh members of their respective assemblies get to vote on their own local affairs *plus*, in Westminster, Scottish and Welsh MPs get to vote on England's affairs. It is unfair, and two-thirds of the English now want their own *English* parliament. Logically, England—either as a whole or divided into regions—should have the right to govern its local affairs. (Or Scottish and Welsh MPs could refrain from voting on purely English matters.) England is divided into nine administrative regions, which could turn into federal units. A federal Britain, which is a long way off, could at last give the House of Lords a major function: representing the regions. Other unitary systems, such as in France and Spain, have loosened up into quasi-federal systems.

Tories have long wooed voters with calls for a "clear end to immigration" before it "swamps" British culture, but both major parties have, since 1962, tightened immigration to Britain so it is now very restrictive. Prime Ministers Blair, Brown, and Cameron all warned Muslim clerics who preached *jihad* to cease or face expulsion. Some worry about an erosion of civil rights in Britain, but many more applaud government vigilance.

devolution
Central government turns some powers over to regions.

referendum
Vote on an issue rather than for an office.

quasi-federal
Part-way federal.

Britain faces an old problem: How does a tolerant society handle militant intolerance? Britain, like all Western countries, debates where civil rights end and homeland security begins. No Western country tolerates *jihadis* on its soil. France and Germany face the identical problem, which is made worse by the fact that, historically, European lands have been countries of emigration, not countries of immigration. The United States handles

European Union (EU)
Quasi-federation of most European states; began in 1957 as the Common Market or European Community (EC).

euro (symbol: €)
Currency for most of Europe since 2002; worth around $1.25.

immigration better because it is populated by immigrants or their descendants. However, Americans, too, expect new arrivals to become patriotic Americans and get angry if they do not.

Britain and Europe

Historically, Britons did not see themselves as Europeans, and many still do not. Rather than joining the *Common Market*, forerunner of the EU (**European Union**), Britain emphasized its Commonwealth ties and "special relationship" with the United States. Britain stayed out of the 1957 Treaty of Rome, which set up the six-country European Community (EC; since 1993, EU), but in 1963, seeing the Continent's economic gains, London applied to join the EC. French President Charles de Gaulle vetoed British entry, charging that Britain was still too tied to the Commonwealth and the United States to be a good European member. By the time de Gaulle resigned in 1969, Britain was ready to join the EC, but not all Britons were. For traditional Tories, it meant giving up British sovereignty to the EC in Brussels. It meant higher food prices and British products competing with better and cheaper Continental imports. It opened Britain's fishing areas to all EC fishermen. Workers feared loss of jobs. Many Britons want to stay firmly British. The new UK Independence Party (UKIP), which aims to get Britain out of the EU and block influx of immigrants, scored increasingly well in elections.

The pro-EU argument held that Britain needs the competition that had invigorated European industries. Euroenthusiasts argue that geographically, strategically, economically, and even spiritually, Britain really is part of Europe and should start acting like it. The debate cuts across party lines, sometimes producing a strange coalition of right-wing Tories and left-wing Labourites, each opposing Europe for their own reasons. In 1971, under a Tory government, the Commons voted to join, but some Conservative MPs voted no and some Labourites voted yes. On January 1, 1973, Britain, along with Denmark and Ireland, made the Six the Nine.

When Labour returned to power, Prime Minister Harold Wilson offered the British public a first—a referendum, common in France but unknown in Britain, where Parliament is supreme. Most Britons voted in 1975 to stay in Europe, but one-third voted no. In 1975, a growing Europe was a good economic argument for Britain to join; a stagnant Europe no longer is. Many Britons, especially Tory MPs, want a "brexit" (British exit from the EU) or a loosening of ties to the EU. Both Tory and Labour chiefs cautiously favor the EU but take note of the rising UKIP vote. Lib Dems are the only openly pro-EU party. Some European leaders, tired of Britain always demanding special deals within the EU, would not mind a brexit. Cameron promised a referendum on leaving the EU, something many Britons wish. Others fear Britain would suffer economic isolation if it left.

Thatcher, a British nationalist and Euroskeptic, was tough on the EU. A common market was fine, she argued, but not a supranational entity that would infringe on Britain's sovereignty. Many Britons rejected joining the European Monetary Union (EMU) or adopting its new **euro** currency. Their slogan: "Europe yes, euro no." The EMU indeed ends an important part of sovereignty, the ability of each country to control its currency, and gives it to the European Central Bank in Frankfurt. Many Britons (and some other Europeans) feared that Europe's strongest economy—Germany—would dominate the EMU and set policy on money supply and interest rates. Britain (along with Denmark and Sweden) stood aside as the euro was introduced. Britain now has few Euroenthusiasts. When several euro countries' debts threatened to pull down the euro system, Britons were glad they had never adopted the euro. Britain seemed ready to prove that she never was a truly European country.

unilinear
Progressing evenly and always upward.

Britain's two centuries of rise and decline refute the idea that progress is **unilinear**. In the case of Britain, we see that what goes up can eventually come down. But this process is never static. Now that Britain is adjusting to its new reality—as one European country among many—regeneration has already begun. Other countries also show how societies and economies can change from static to dynamic. Never write off a country as hopeless.

Review Questions

Learning Objective 2.1 Contrast gradual historical change in Britain with tumultuous change in France, p. 26.

1. Why would a Pole be jealous of Britain's geography?
2. Contrast *mixed monarchy* with *absolutism*.
3. What is the *Common Law* and how did it originate?

Learning Objective 2.2 Describe how Britain's electoral system—single-member districts with plurality win—influences their two-plus party system, p. 36.

4. What is the difference between *head of state* and *chief of government*?
5. Contrast a British and U.S. cabinet and its members.
6. Can a British prime minister be more powerful than a U.S. president?

Learning Objective 2.3 Illustrate the several ways that social class influences British politics, p. 47.

7. Why is often hard to place individuals into social classes?
8. What is *center-periphery tension* and how does Britain illustrate it?
9. What is a *center-peaked distribution*?

Learning Objective 2.4 Explain why no country can be completely democratic, p. 55.

10. What is a *hung parliament*?
11. Must British parliamentary candidates be from their districts?
12. Why were Thatcher's economic policies called *neoliberalism*?

Learning Objective 2.5 Compare recent political quarrels in Britain to those in the United States, p. 63.

13. What was Cameron's austerity policy? Did it work?
14. What is *productivity* and why is it important?
15. Is *devolution* in Scotland and Wales really a type of federalism?

Key Terms

anticlerical, p. 29
authority, p. 53
backbencher, p. 41

by-election, p. 41
Celts, p. 26
center-peaked, p. 52

center–periphery tension, p. 48
center-seeking, p. 52
central office, p. 55

Further Reference

Allen, Robert C. *The British Industrial Revolution in Global Perspective.* New York: Cambridge University Press, 2009.

Barberis, Peter. *The Elite of the Elite: Permanent Secretaries in the British Higher Civil Service.* Brookfield, VT: Ashgate, 1996.

Bogdanor, Vernon. *The Coalition and the Constitution.* Oxford, UK: Hart, 2011.

Elliott, Larry, and Dan Atkinson. *Going South: Why Britain Will Have a Third World Economy by 2014.* London: Palgrave Macmillan, 2012.

Field, William H. *Regional Dynamics: The Basis of Electoral Support in Britain*. Portland, OR: F. Cass, 1997.

Foley, Michael. *The British Presidency: Tony Blair and the Politics of Public Leadership*. New York: St. Martin's, 2000.

Green, E. H. H. *Thatcher*. New York: Oxford University Press, 2006.

Hattersley, Roy. *Borrowed Time: The Story of Britain between the Wars*. Boston: Little Brown, 2007.

Hickson, Kevin, ed. *The Political Thought of the Conservative Party*. New York: Palgrave, 2005.

Jack, Ian. *The Country Formerly Known as Great Britain: Writings 1989–2009*. London: Jonathan Cape, 2009.

Kavanagh, Dennis, and Anthony Selden. *The Powers behind the Prime Minister: The Hidden Influence of Number Ten*. New York: HarperCollins, 2000.

King, Anthony, and Iain McLean, eds. *Rational Choice and British Politics: An Analysis of Rhetoric and Manipulation from Peel to Blair*. New York: Oxford, 2001.

McCormick, John. *Contemporary Britain*, 2nd ed. New York: Palgrave, 2007.

Moore, Charles. *Margaret Thatcher: The Authorized Biography: From Grantham to the Falklands*. New York: Knopf, 2013.

Norton, Bruce F. *Politics in Britain*. Washington, DC: CQ Press, 2007.

Overy, Richard. *The Morbid Age: Britain between the Wars*. London: Allen Lane, 2009.

Pincus, Steve. *1688: The First Modern Revolution*. New Haven, CT: Yale University Press, 2009.

Poguntke, Thomas, and Paul Webb, eds. *The Presidentialization of Politics: A Comparative Study of Modern Democracies*. New York: Oxford University Press, 2005.

Rawnsley, Andrew. *The End of the Party: The Rise and Fall of New Labour*. New York: Viking, 2010.

Rose, Richard, and Ian McAllister. *The Loyalties of Voters: A Lifetime Learning Model*. Newbury Park, CA: Sage, 1990.

Vinen, Richard. *Thatcher's Britain: The Politics of Social Upheaval in the Thatcher Era*. New York: Simon & Schuster, 2009.

Wall, Stephen. *A Stranger in Europe: Britain and the EU from Thatcher to Blair*. New York: Oxford University Press, 2008.

Chapter 3
France

Tourists flock to the Versailles Palace, built by Louis XIV, outside Paris.

 ## Learning Objectives

3.1 Explain the French pattern of revolution leading to tyranny.

3.2 Contrast the French semipresidential system with the U.S. presidential system.

3.3 Describe the split nature of French political culture.

3.4 Illustrate how referendums sound democratic but often are not.

3.5 Establish why French unemployment stays so high for so long.

WHY FRANCE MATTERS

Unlike Britain, France lurched suddenly into democracy—the French Revolution, which implanted the democratic ideals of "liberty, equality, fraternity." But instead of democracy, the Revolution "skidded out of control," leading to Napoleon. Radical and reactionary forces have battled each other ever since, producing an alternation between liberal regimes and conservative regimes. France introduces many key concepts in comparative politics, especially fragmentation and integration, and the problems they create. The old monarchy made France out of several tribes and regions, showing how nations are rather artificial or "constructed" entities. Tumultuous changes and regime instability left the French with negative views on government and produced, in de Gaulle's words, "a nation of complainers." Going back centuries, French modernizers set up a centralized state run by bureaucrats, which became a model for much of Europe and Japan. France also shows how a new constitution does not always solve underlying political paralysis. In France, as many say, nothing is simple.

Impact of the Past

3.1 **Explain the French pattern of revolution leading to tyranny.**

"France has everything," many French rightly boast, but it does not have England's moat and is vulnerable to land attack from the north and the east. France always had a large army, which helps explain the rise of French absolutism. France is divided into a north and a south, which culturally and temperamentally differ and, until relatively recently, even spoke different languages. Parallel with China, the northerners made their language standard nationwide, but southerners still have a distinct accent and resent rule by Paris.

The Roman Influence

Celts pushed into France and merged with the native Ligurians before the Romans conquered the area and called it *Gallia* (Gaul). Roman influence in France was longer and deeper than in England. The Angles and Saxons obliterated Roman culture in England, but the Germanic tribes that moved into Gaul became Romanized. Thus, English is a Germanic language and French a Romance language.

By the time Rome collapsed, one Germanic tribe, the Franks, had taken over most of present-day France. Their chief, Clovis—origin of the name Louis—was baptized in 496, and France has been mostly Catholic ever since, the "eldest daughter of the Church." The Franks under Charles Martel beat the Moors in 732, possibly saving Europe. His grandson, Charlemagne, in 800 founded a huge empire—the Holy Roman Empire—which encompassed what someday would be most of the six original EU countries. His empire soon disintegrated, but Charlemagne planted the idea of European unity.

The Rise of French Absolutism

After Charlemagne, France was split into several petty kingdoms and dukedoms, as was Germany. While Germany stayed divided until the nineteenth century, French kings unified and centralized as they pushed outward from the Paris area, the *Ile de France* (Island of France).

France

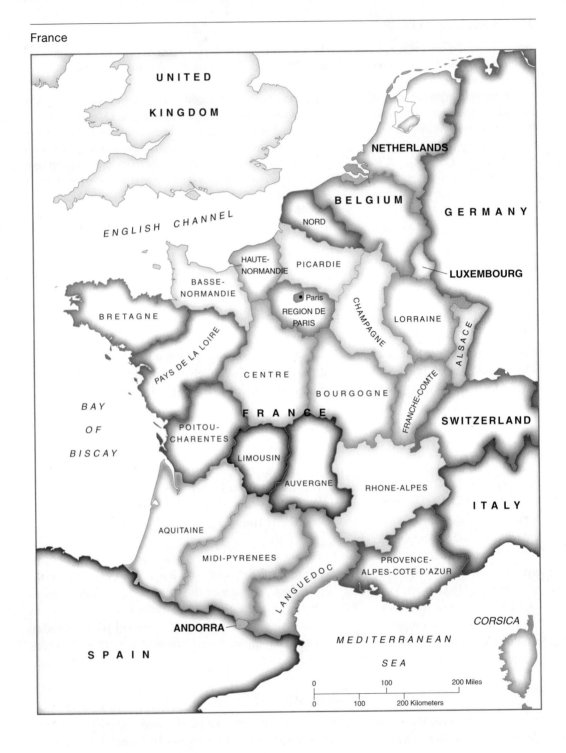

Feudalism in France began to give way to absolutism with the crafty Louis (pronounced *Lwie*) XI (ruled 1461–1483), who doubled the size of France until it neared its present shape. He also weakened the feudal nobles, ignored the **Estates-General**, and developed a royal bureaucracy to increase taxation. This pattern was strengthened for at least three centuries, leaving France still highly centralized. Louis XI also cultivated relations with Rome, and, unlike in England, the Catholic Church remained a pillar of the French monarchy. Protestant Huguenots were massacred and driven into exile. In 1589, however, the royal line of succession fell to a Protestant Huguenot, Henry of Navarre. The Catholic Church offered the throne to Henry only if he accepted Catholicism. Shrugged Henry famously: "Paris is well worth a Mass."

Under Louis XIII, Cardinal Richelieu became chief minister and virtual ruler from 1624 to 1642. Obsessed with French power and glory, Richelieu further weakened the nobles, recruited only middle-class bureaucrats, and sent out **intendants** to control the provinces for Paris. Richelieu was an organizational genius who put a permanent bureaucratic stamp on France. French nobles fought centralization but lost. In 1648 and again in 1650, some French **aristocrats** staged an uncoordinated revolt called the *Fronde*. Recall that, at this time, English nobles and their commoner allies beheaded a king who tried to act like an absolute monarch. In France, nobles lost the autonomy enjoyed by English lords.

"*L'état, c'est moi*" ("The state, that's me"), Louis XIV is often quoted as saying. Louis XIV (reigned 1643–1715) brought French absolutism to a high point. The Sun King increased centralization and bureaucratization, all aimed at his own and France's power. Louis XIV used his large army in almost continual warfare and handled much administration personally. He never convened the old parliament, the Estates-General. He constructed the **Versailles** Palace and made hundreds of nobles live there, reducing them to courtiers.

Louis XIV's policies of "war and magnificence" were financial drains. To make the French economy serve the state, his finance minister, Jean-Baptiste Colbert, practiced mercantilism, the theory that a nation was as wealthy as the amount of gold it possessed, to be accomplished by government supervision of the economy with plans, subsidies, monopolies, and tariffs. This set a

Estates-General
Old, unused French parliament.

intendants
French provincial administrators, answerable only to Paris; early version of *prefects*.

aristocrat
Person of inherited noble rank.

Versailles
Palaces and park on outskirts of Paris begun by Louis XIV.

Geography

Rivers

Navigable rivers are economic arteries, tying a country together and often boosting international trade. England's Thames also gives it an outlet to the sea. France's Seine, Rhine, Rhone, and Loire give it trade routes and outlets to the sea in all four points of the compass. French kings supplemented the rivers with canals, some of them still in use. The Rhine has for centuries been a West European highway from Switzerland to France, Germany, and the Netherlands. The Danube stitched together the Austro-Hungarian Empire, but for centuries, its outlet in the Black Sea was controlled by the hostile Turks. Russia's rivers flow the wrong way, either to the Arctic Ocean or to the Black Sea. China's economic and political life grew up around the Yellow and Yangzi rivers, the early Indian kingdoms along the Indus and Ganges.

core
Region where the state originated.

particularism
Region's sense of its difference.

Han
Original and main people of China.

pattern for most European countries and Japan—government-supervised economies. France instinctively turned to state economic supervision of the economy after the global meltdown of 2008, a continuation of Colbert's policies.

Louis XIV was an able monarch who impressed all of Europe; other kings tried to imitate him. French cuisine, architecture, dress, and language dominated the Continent. From the outside, the France

Geography

Core Areas

Most countries have an identifiable **core** area where, in most cases, the state originated. Some countries contain more than one core area, which can lead to tension. Typically, the country's capital is in its core area. Farther out are the peripheral areas, often more recent additions where people might speak a different language and resent rule by the core. This can turn deadly, as when Ukraine's Russian-speaking east, Turkey's Kurdish southeast, and Sri Lanka's Tamil north attempted to break away.

France is an almost perfect example of a core area, centered on Paris, spreading its rule, language, and culture to increase national integration. In the nineteenth century, wide areas of France still spoke a variety of dialects. French educational policy sent out school-teachers to turn "peasants into Frenchmen," in the words of historian Eugen Weber. Some peripheral areas still resent Paris. Brittany, Corsica, and Languedoc try to keep alive local dialects and regional culture. Extremists in Corsica practice occasional violence.

England is the core area of the United Kingdom. The Valley of Mexico is Mexico's, established and rein-forced by Toltecs, Aztecs, and Spaniards. The German core area is less clear because the many German ministates kept their sovereignty and dialects unusually long. Prussia led German unification in the nineteenth century and made Berlin the nation's capital. But the people of Catholic lands in the south and west disliked Prussia's authoritarianism and Protestantism. Germany remained riven by **particularism**, a factor that con-tributed to present-day federalism. Nazism was, in part, a contrived effort to bring all German regions under central control by means of lunatic nationalism.

Nigeria, assembled by British imperialists, has no core area, which is the root of its breakaway tribalism.

The Soviet Union had a huge gap between its Slavic core area and its non-Slavic peripheral areas. Russia's numerous nationalities are still distinct and discontent. The Slavic core of Russia, Belarus, and Ukraine gradually beat back Tatars, Turks, and Swedes until it straddled the vast belt where Europe meets Asia. Then the tsars sent expeditions eastward to claim Siberia to the Pacific. During the nineteenth century, Russia acquired the Caucasus and Turkic Muslim peoples of Central Asia, but not without a fight. Russification proved impossible, however, and fostered nationalist hatred against Moscow. The breakaway of republics from the Soviet Union is a type of decoloni-zation. The remaining Russian Federation still contains breakaway lands such as Chechnya.

China's core area was the Yellow River Valley, but before the time of Christ, it had consolidated a major empire. So numerous and united—despite occasional civil wars—were the **Han** Chinese that the addition to the kingdom of a few outer barbarians (Mongols, Tibetans, Turkic Muslims, and others) bothered the Han little. Recently, however, Central Asians have turned violent to protest rule by the Han and Beijing.

Japan, with Tokyo-Yokohama as its core area, has some center–periphery tension between East and West Japan and from agricultural and fishing prefectures. Iran has non-Persian-speaking peripheral areas that resent rule by Tehran. The U.S. core area began with the 13 colonies along the Atlantic sea-board, especially the northern ones, which are still somewhat resented by the rest of the union.

of Louis XIV looked more impressive than England. Without "checks and balances" to get in the way, the centralized French monarchy accomplished great things. But the English, by developing political participation, devised a more stable system.

Why the French Revolution?

Underneath its splendor, France in the eighteenth century was often near bankruptcy. Especially costly was French support for the Americans against Britain. The bureaucracy was corrupt and inefficient. Recognizing too late that mercantilism was bad economics, the regime tried to move to a free market, but by then, French industry and agriculture were used to state protection and wanted to keep it. New ideas on "liberty," "consent of the

Cartesian
After French philosopher René Descartes, philosophical analysis based on pure reason without empirical reference.

Enlightenment
Eighteenth-century philosophical movement advocating reason and tolerance.

general will
Rousseau's theory of what the whole community wants.

Personalities

Voltaire, Montesquieu, Rousseau

Three eighteenth-century French thinkers helped persuade many French, especially intellectuals, that the *ancien régime* was rotten and that a better system was possible. Their weapon was reason—abstract, **Cartesian**, logical—in contrast to English thinkers, who favored empirical reality. The French approach lends itself to radicalism.

Voltaire (1694–1778) was the epitome of the **Enlightenment**, doubting and ridiculing institutions such as the Catholic Church, which he saw as intolerant, irrational, and hypocritical. Voltaire's phrase *"Ecrasez l'infâme!"* ("Crush the infamous thing," meaning the Church) became the founding cry of *anticlericalism* and spread through most Catholic countries, including Mexico. France still retains some of the old clerical–anticlerical split.

The Baron de Montesquieu (1689–1755) traveled all over Europe to gather material for one of the first books of comparative politics, *The Spirit of the Laws.* Montesquieu was especially impressed with English liberties, which he thought resulted from the "checks and balances" of the different parts of their government. Actually, that English system had already passed into history, but the American Founding Fathers read Montesquieu literally. Montesquieu suggested that countries could rationally choose their

institutions, which the French have been doing ever since.

Jean-Jacques Rousseau (1712–1778), who was born in Geneva but lived in France, was the most complex and dangerous of these three thinkers. Rousseau hypothesized man in the state of nature as free, happy, and morally good. (Note the contrast to Hobbes's and Locke's states of nature.) He believed society corrupts humans, chiefly with private property, which leads to inequality and jealousy. Rousseau, in a famous phrase at the beginning of his book *The Social Contract,* wrote, "Man is born free but everywhere is in chains." How can humans be freed? Rousseau posited that beneath all the individual, petty viewpoints in society there is a **general will** for the common good, which could be discovered and implemented even though some people might object; they would be "forced to be free." Critics of Rousseau charge that he laid the intellectual basis for *totalitarianism* because his theory lets regimes crush dissent and claim that they "really know" what the people want and need.

The French political thinkers called for major, sweeping change; English thinkers called for slow, incremental change that preserved the overall system. The French thinkers fundamentally hated the existing state of affairs; the English did not.

ancien régime
French for old regime, the monarchy that preceded the Revolution.

constitutional monarchy
King with limited powers.

National Assembly
France's parliament.

Bastille
Old and nearly unused Paris jail, the storming of which heralded the French Revolution in 1789.

governed," and "the general will" undermined the legitimacy of the **ancien régime**.

Alexis de Tocqueville pointed out that revolutions tend to start when things are getting better. The French economy improved for most of the eighteenth century, but that increased expectations and awakened jealousies. As in Iran under the Shah, economic growth can destabilize. Then Louis XVI decided to reform the political system and provide for some representation. But, as in Russia and Iran, the reforming of an unjust and unpopular system often leads to revolution.

From Freedom to Tyranny

In 1791, the National Assembly constructed a **constitutional monarchy**, and if it had stopped there, the French Revolution might have resembled the English Revolution of a century earlier. But it was undermined from two sides: from the king and some aristocrats, who wanted to restore absolute power, and from a militant faction called the Jacobins, who wanted a radical revolution. Their cry: *"Liberté, Egalité, Fraternité!"* The king conspired with foreign princes to

China Lessons

Avoiding Revolution

Catastrophes frequently punctuate political development because ruling elites refuse to give way early enough and institute a series of gradual reforms that would admit wider sectors of the population into the political process. They refuse to budge because they fear (with some reason) losing power and opening the gate to chaos. Eventually, as tensions mount, the brighter among them recognize that things have got to change and suggest reforms. Typically, the regime postpones reforms until mass unrest breaks out and then gives way too suddenly, often leading to system collapse.

Louis XVI understood the growth of mass discontent and, in the spring of 1789, reconvened (for the first time since 1614) the unused parliament, the Estates-General, which was structured into three "estates"—one each for Catholic clergy, nobles, and commoners—that had to agree. The Third Estate was elected and was the largest. Because it represented the will of most, it demanded that all three estates meet together, allowing its greater numbers to override

the clerics and nobles of the First and Second Estates. Louis resisted the demand, which would indeed have transformed the still-feudal French political system. By the time he gave way, the radicalized Third Estate voted to turn the whole Estates-General into a new **National Assembly**.

A few weeks later, on July 14, an angry mob stormed the **Bastille**. Upon hearing of the incident, the king exclaimed, *"C'est une révolte,"* meaning something that could be put down. A duke corrected him: *"Non, Sire, c'est une révolution,"* the first modern usage of the word *revolution*.

Thus began the French Revolution. Louis XVI might have headed it off had he decided early to let the three estates meet together and enact major reforms, which might have taken the steam out of mass discontent. Instead, he waited until it was too late. He was guillotined in 1793 and replaced by the brief First French Republic. France had trouble finding stability and is now in its Fifth Republic. The moral: Don't wait until it is too late.

Geography

Bound France

An old but effective technique to learn geography requires the student to recite, from forced recall, the boundaries of a given country clockwise. By the time you can bound all our 11 countries (plus a few more for complex Africa), you will know where most of them are.

France is bounded on the north by Belgium and Luxembourg; on the east by Germany, Switzerland, and Italy; on the south by the Mediterranean Sea and Spain; and on the west by the Atlantic Ocean.

invade France and restore him to power. The 1792 German invasion helped the Jacobins take over. With a makeshift but enthusiastic citizen army—"the nation in arms"—they repelled the invaders at Valmy.

Power fell into the hands of the misnamed Committee of Public Safety under Maximilien Robespierre, a provincial lawyer and fanatic follower of Rousseau who was determined to "force men to be free." Instituting the **Reign of Terror**, Robespierre and his followers guillotined more than 20,000 people, starting with the king, queen, and nobles but soon also fellow revolutionaries such as Danton, who sadly noted before his execution: "The revolution devours its children." Finally, in 1794, during the revolutionary calendar's month of Thermidor, Robespierre's comrades, afraid they might be next, guillotined *him,* and the Terror ended.

The turmoil left the army as the only coherent institution, led by a young artillery officer, the Corsican Napoléon Bonaparte, who had led French armies in Italy and Egypt. A 1799 **coup d'état** overthrew the weak civilian Directory and set up the Consulate with Bonaparte as First Consul. Brilliant in both battle and civil reform, Napoleon crowned himself emperor in 1804.

Napoleon loved conquest. As Henry Kissinger pointed out, a revolutionary power, like France in the midst of hostile conservative monarchies, can feel secure only by conquering all potential threats. Napoleon, with bold tactics and a large, enthusiastic army, mastered all Europe. But faced with a British-led coalition, harassed by Spanish guerrillas, and frozen in the Russian winter, Napoleon was defeated and exiled to the Mediterranean island of Elba in 1814. He tried a comeback the next year, and thousands of his old soldiers rallied to fight at Waterloo and lost.

Napoleon claimed to be consolidating the Revolution but set up a police state. Trying to embody Rousseau's *general will*, Napoleon held several **plebiscites**, which he always won. He unleashed **chauvinism** by proclaiming France Europe's liberator. Napoleon was not just a historic accident, though, for we shall see similar figures emerge in French politics. When a society is badly split, as France was over the Revolution, power tends to gravitate into the hands of a strongman, and democracy does not have a chance.

The Bourbon Restoration

Europe was relieved once Napoleon was exiled to a remote island in the South Atlantic and the brother of Louis XVI was restored to the

Reign of Terror
Robespierre's 1793–1794 rule by guillotine.

coup d'état
Military takeover of a government.

plebiscite
Referendum; mass vote for issue rather than for candidates.

chauvinism
After Napoleonic soldier named Chauvin; fervent, prideful nationalism.

Comparison

Brinton's Theory of Revolution

Harvard historian Crane Brinton, in his 1938 *The Anatomy of Revolution*, argued that all revolutions pass through similar stages. He compared several revolutions, but his main model was the French. Brinton saw the following stages:

- The old regime loses its governing effectiveness and legitimacy. It becomes inept and indecisive. Intellectuals, especially, become **alienated** from it. An improving economy provokes discontent and jealousy.

- Antiregime groups grow. A political problem—such as whether the three estates should meet separately or together—that the old regime cannot solve triggers the revolution. Rioting breaks out, and troops sent to crush it desert to the rioters. The antiregime people easily take power amid popular rejoicing.

- Moderates initially seize power. They oppose the old regime, but as critics rather than as revolutionaries. They want major reform rather than total revolution. Extremists call them weak and cowardly, and indeed they are not ruthless enough to crush the extremists.

- Extremists take power because they are more ruthless, purposeful, and organized than the moderates. In what Brinton likened to a high fever during an illness, the extremists whip up a revolutionary frenzy, throwing out everything old, forcing people to be good, and punishing real or imagined enemies in a reign of terror. In France, this stage came with Robespierre; in Iran, with Khomeini.

- A **Thermidor**, or calming-down period, ends the reign of terror. Brinton likened this to a convalescence after a fever, because human nature cannot take the extremists and their revolutionary purity for too long. Power may then fall into the hands of a dictator who restores order but not liberty—a Napoleon or a Stalin.

Brinton's theory became a classic and has largely stood the test of time. Revolutions do seem to pass through stages, although their timing varies. Mexico, Russia, China, and Iran followed the Brinton pattern.

French throne as Louis XVIII. In the **Bourbon** Restoration, exiles returned to France to claim their old rights. Many French disliked them and sighed, "They learned nothing and they forgot nothing."

France was badly split. Most aristocrats hated the Revolution, while most commoners supported at least a version of it. The Catholic Church was reactionary, for the Revolution had confiscated church lands and ended its tax privileges. French Catholics for generations opposed the anticlericalist republicans, who in turn mistrusted the church. Residuals of the clerical–anticlerical split persist in France. But France had also changed in the quarter century after the Revolution. Parliaments now mattered; kings could no longer rule without them. Napoleon's civil reforms were preserved. People insisted on equality before the law.

At first, the French, tired from upheaval and warfare, accepted the Bourbons. But by 1830, rioting broke out and, in a semilegal switch, the liberal Duc d'Orleans, Louis-Phillipe, replaced the last Bourbon, Charles X. He, too, proved inept, and a small uprising in that revolutionary year of 1848 brought the brief Second Republic.

alienated
Psychologically distant and hostile.

Thermidor
Revolutionary month when Robespierre fell; a calming down after a revolutionary high.

Bourbon
French dynasty before the Revolution.

Democracy

Left, Right, and Center

The way delegates were seated in the National Assembly during and after the French Revolution gives us our terms for radical, conservative, and moderate. In a half-circle chamber, the most radical delegates, those representing the common people, were seated to the left of the speaker's rostrum, and the most conservative, those representing the aristocracy, were seated to the right. This allowed like-minded legislators to caucus and avoided fist fights.

The precise meanings of left, right, and center have varied, but the left favors greater equality of incomes, welfare measures, and government intervention in the economy. The right, now that it has shed its aristocratic origins, favors individual achievement and private industry. The center tries to synthesize the moderate elements in both viewpoints. Those just a little to one side or the other are called center-left or center-right.

The French have historically turned from tumultuous democracy to authoritarian rule. In 1848, they overwhelmingly elected Napoleon's self-proclaimed nephew, Louis Napoleon, as president. Using plebiscites, in 1852, he turned the Second Republic into the Second Empire with himself as Emperor Napoleon III. This brought two decades of peace and progress until Bismarck in 1870 goaded France into war with Prussia. The Germans quickly trounced the over-confident French, surrounded Paris, and shelled it daily, but there was no French government left to surrender. Common citizens took over Paris and ruled through the **Paris Commune**, which conservative French troops crushed, killing some 20,000 Parisians.

The Third Republic

Amidst near anarchy, the Third Republic, France's first stable democracy, was born. A humiliating peace with Germany cost France Alsace (which has many German-speaking people) plus a billion dollars in gold. The French ached for revenge and transferred their traditional enmity of Britain to Germany.

The accidental Third Republic, although chronically unstable, lasted until World War II. It was basically conservative and **bourgeois**. France was not healed during the Third Republic's long tenure, and social tensions mounted. A **reactionary** Catholic right dreamed of authoritarian rule, while the left organized Socialist and, later, Communist parties. Economic and population growth was slow, and France slipped further behind rapidly growing Germany. Still, the Third Republic staggered through the ordeal of World War I, which cost France a million and a half lives. France turned bitter and defeatist even though it was on the winning side. France regained Alsace but had no stomach to fight again.

French defeatism aided Nazi Germany, which swept easily through France in May–June 1940. Only one French unit fought well, a tank column commanded by an obscure colonel named de Gaulle, who had long warned of the need to develop armored forces. The French thought they could prevent a repetition of World War I by building

Paris Commune
Citizen takeover of Paris government during 1870–1871 German siege.

bourgeois
Middle class.

reactionary
Seeking to go back to old ways; extremely conservative.

Geography

A Tale of Two Flags

The Bourbon flag was blue and white with a fleur-de-lis (iris). (Today's Quebec flag is blue and white with four irises.) The Revolution introduced the tricolor of red, white, and blue. The Bourbon restoration brought back the old flag, for the tricolor symbolized everything the aristocrats hated. In 1830, the Orleanist monarchy, to mollify revolutionary sentiment, brought back the tricolor, France's flag ever since.

 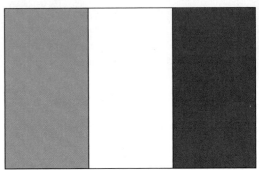

the **Maginot Line**, but fixed defenses cannot move; in 1940, the Germans simply went around them on the north.

Vichy: France Splits Again

The Germans largely let the French run occupied France. Named after the town of Vichy in central France where it was set up, the **Vichy** government was staffed by authoritarian reactionaries. The aged Marshal Pétain, hero of World War I, became chief of state, and an opportunistic politician, Pierre Laval, became premier without elections. Some French thought Vichy was an improvement over the Third Republic, which had voted the **Popular Front** into power in 1936. "Better the Nazis than the Communists," muttered Vichy supporters. French SS units fought in Russia. French police rounded up Jews for deportation to death camps. French workers went to Germany. Most French prefer to forget that many collaborated with the Germans and even liked them.

Again, France split as other French, many of them leftists, joined the **Résistance**, an underground network that sabotaged and spied on the Germans, rescued British and American airmen, and occasionally killed collaborators. French Communists, who refused to attack Germans until the 1941 invasion of Russia, became the most effective underground fighters and emerged from the war with prestige and a good organization.

Charles de Gaulle (promoted to general in the last days of the Third Republic) rallied the French with a broadcast from London: "France has lost a battle, but France has not lost the war!" Organizing

Maginot Line
Supposedly unbreachable French defenses facing Germany before World War II.

Vichy
Nazi puppet regime that ran France during World War II.

Popular Front
Coalition government of all leftist and liberal parties in France and Spain in the 1930s.

Résistance
World War II French underground anti-German movement.

Political Culture

The Dreyfus Affair

The split nature of French society leaped out with the trial of Captain Alfred Dreyfus, a Jewish officer on the French general staff. In 1894, Dreyfus was accused of selling secrets to the Germans; a biased military court used fake evidence to send him to Devil's Island for life. It soon became clear that Dreyfus was not the culprit and had been convicted by bigoted officers.

Those defending Dreyfus—the *Dreyfusards*, generally liberals and leftists—supported the republican traditions of equality. Novelist Emile Zola penned his *J'accuse!* (I accuse!), charging the government with covering up for the military. The *Anti-Dreyfusards*—reactionary aristocrats, army officers, fanatic Catholics, and anti-Semites—were equally passionate in defense of prerevolutionary values. Most French took one side or the other; there was even street fighting.

The French Supreme Court finally exonerated Dreyfus in 1906, but the affair revealed that France's civilized veneer concealed reaction and anti-Semitism. A Viennese journalist at the trial, Theodore Herzl, was so shocked that he organized a world **Zionist** movement to save Jews from what he (correctly) feared would be worse outbursts.

French-speaking people around the world—France's sizable colonies and thousands who fled from France—de Gaulle declared a provisional government composed of **Free French** expatriates. In North Africa, the Normandy landings, and the liberation of Paris in 1944, the Free French Army helped the **Allies** win. During the war, de Gaulle came to think of himself as the savior of France, a modern Joan of Arc.

The Fourth Republic

From 1944 to early 1946, de Gaulle headed a provisional government. A newly elected constituent assembly, dominated by parties of the left, drafted a constitution for the Fourth Republic that gave great power to the legislature. De Gaulle warned that the Fourth Republic would have the same institutional weaknesses as the Third and resigned. He retired to a small town until the people called him back to save France again 12 years later.

De Gaulle was right about the Fourth Republic, which was plagued by a weak executive, a National Assembly paralyzed by small, squabbling parties, and frequent changes of cabinet. The result was, as before, **immobilisme**. Politicians played power games; they were good at wrecking but not at building. The Fourth Republic might have endured if not for the terrible problems of **decolonization**, which the fractious parliamentarians could not solve. First was Indochina, a French colony since the 1880s, occupied by the Japanese in World War II and then reclaimed by France. War between France and the Communist Vietminh broke out in 1946 and dragged on until the fall of the French fortress of Dienbienphu in 1954. (The United States came close to jumping into the conflict that year but backed off.)

Algeria was worse. The French had been there since 1830, at first to suppress piracy but later to settle. Close to a million Europeans

Zionism
Jewish nationalist movement that founded Israel.

Free French
De Gaulle's World War II government in exile.

Allies
World War II anti-Axis military coalition.

immobilisme
Government inability to solve big problems.

decolonization
Granting of independence to colonies.

Political Culture

France's Political Eras

The political history of France is rich and complex and reinforces France's split political culture. Notice how conservative and radical eras roughly alternate as if in perpetual conflict.

Name	Years	Remembered for
Old Regime	–1789	Absolutist monarchy; centralized administration; supervised economy
Revolution	1789–1799	Tumult; repels invaders; Reign of Terror; Thermidor
Napoleon	1799–1814	Redoes civil code; conquers most of Europe; crowns self emperor
Bourbon Restoration	1815–1830	Restores monarchy in badly split France
Orleanist	1830–1848	Liberal monarchy
Second Republic	1848–1852	Attempted liberal republic
Second Empire	1852–1870	Louis Napoleon's conservative stability
Third Republic	1871–1940	Bourgeois liberal democracy
Vichy	1940–1944	German puppet government
Provisional Government	1944–1946	De Gaulle-led coalition
Fourth Republic	1946–1958	Unstable, fractious, immobilized; Indochina and Algeria
Fifth Republic	1958–	De Gaulle's strong presidency; state-led modernization

dominated Algerian economic, social, and political life; Algeria was declared part of France. Algerian nationalists revolted in 1954 with urban terrorism. The French army hunted down nationalists and tortured them. When politicians in Paris opposed the Algerian War, the French army in Algeria began a *coup d'état* in 1958. Paratroopers were ready to drop on their own country; France tottered on the brink of civil war. At the last minute, both sides agreed to call back General de Gaulle, who demanded as his price a totally new constitution, one that would cure the ills of the Fourth Republic.

The Key Institutions

3.2   Contrast the French semipresidential system with the U.S. presidential system.

Unlike the British constitution, French constitutions—15 of them since the Revolution—are written but often altered over time. Americans regard their Constitution as sacred, but the French and most other Europeans have seen constitutions come and go and are willing to rewrite them.

premier
French for prime minister.

president
Elected head of state, not necessarily powerful.

By 1958, many French agreed that the Fourth Republic was flawed and unable to settle the Algerian War. The chief problem was the weak executive, the **premier**. The **president** was simply a figurehead, typical of European republics. The premier depended on unstable **coalitions**. Faced with difficult issues, one or more coalition parties could drop out, vote no-confidence against the government, and bring it down. In all, there were 20 cabinets ("governments") in less than 12 years. The Fourth Republic embodied all the weaknesses of a multiparty parliamentary system that still plague Israel. Such a system can work well and with stability, as in Sweden, but it depends on the party system and the national political style. Given French parties and political culture, a pure parliamentary system may never work well.

coalition
Multiparty alliance to form government.

deadlock
U.S. tendency for executive and legislature, especially when of opposing parties, to block each other; current term: *gridlock*.

Who Was When: The Fifth Republic's Presidents

Charles de Gaulle		1959–1969—re-elected in 1965, resigned in 1969
Georges Pompidou	Gaullist	1969–1974—died in office
Valéry Giscard d'Estaing	UDF	1974–1981—served one term
François Mitterrand	Socialist	1981–1995—re-elected in 1988
Jacques Chirac	neo-Gaullist	1995–2007—re-elected in 2002
Nicolas Sarkozy	neo-Gaullist	2007–2012—served one term
François Hollande	Socialist	2012–2017—likely to lose reelection

A Semipresidential System

Most European governments are parliamentary, like Britain, and depend on votes in parliament to form a government. In a presidential system, such as the United States, Mexico, and Brazil, the executive does not depend on parliamentary support, but the president and the legislature may **deadlock**, producing something similar to the *immobilisme* that stalls parliamentary systems.

The French Semipresidential System

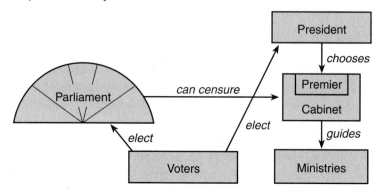

The French Semipresidential System

semipresidential

System with features of both presidential and parliamentary systems.

Elysée

Presidential palace in Paris, equivalent to U.S. White House.

De Gaulle hated the Fourth Republic's executive weakness, but neither did he like the U.S. system with its checks and balances, so he devised a **semipresidential** system, a hybrid with both an executive president and a premier (see graphic). De Gaulle ruled by commanding the largest party in the National Assembly, so, for its first 28 years, the Fifth Republic functioned as a presidential, or even "superpresidential," system. Only with the parliamentary elections of 1986—which produced a conservative National Assembly while a Socialist president was still in office—did we finally see real semipresidentialism.

The Fifth Republic's constitution continues, but since de Gaulle (1958–1969), the president's powers have weakened. Originally, the president was elected for seven years and could be reelected without limit. Amid complaints, terms were shortened in 2000 to five years, and in 2008, presidents were limited to two consecutive terms. Originally, the president was selected by an electoral college of parliamentarians and local office holders. De Gaulle decided he wanted no politicians to stand between him and the people, so a 1962 referendum made the president directly elected.

The constitution divides powers between president and premier but was unclear. Presidents appoint premiers and have a say in naming cabinet ministers. No parliamentary approval is required. Until 1986, the president was assured of an obedient National Assembly and handpicked ministers as helpers to carry out the president's program. The president presided at cabinet meetings. Virtually all foreign and defense affairs were in his hands (still mostly the case). The **Elysée** originated most legislation, often with the advice of ministers, and could even force the National Assembly to vote simply yes or no on executive proposals. The president, however, does not have the power to veto legislation. De Gaulle saw the role of president in almost mystical terms, as a "guide" and "arbiter" of the nation.

One important—and overused—power de Gaulle liked is the calling of *referendums*. Such mass votes on issues are recent and rare in Britain but long a part of French usage, especially by leaders who believe they embody the general will and communicate directly with the people, bypassing the politicians. De Gaulle called five such plebiscites and won each except the last. Feeling repudiated, he resigned, perhaps establishing another constitutional tradition.

Another power of French presidents is the ability to invoke emergency powers in time of danger. While many democracies have such an emergency provision, it can be abused, as Hitler used Article 48 of the Weimar constitution to snuff out freedom. Article 16 of the French constitution seems to place no limits on what a president can do during an emergency, a situation that is up to the president to define. (U.S. President Bush 43 took a leaf from de Gaulle in claiming similar powers following 9/11, what was called the "unitary executive theory," but it is disputed.) During such an emergency, the National Assembly must meet, but it has no power to block presidential decisions. The emergency clause has been invoked only once—in 1961, when the same generals who put de Gaulle into power tried to overthrow him for pulling out of Algeria—and it was a genuine emergency.

Presidential dominance came to an end with the National Assembly elections of 1986, which produced a legislature controlled by conservative parties while President François Mitterrand, a Socialist, had two years remaining in his seven-year term. For the first time, the president did not control the National Assembly. No one knew how to handle it; the constitution was unclear. Some feared a hostile deadlock and paralysis of government. Others thought that Mitterrand would have to resign to allow election of a conservative president. Instead, Mitterrand played a waiting game that kept him president but reduced the powers of the presidency. Mitterrand thus clarified the French constitution and set a precedent for when the same situation occurred in 1993 and 1997.

neo-Gaullist
Chirac's revival of Gaullist party, now called Union for a Popular Movement (UMP).

cohabitation
French president forced to name premier of opposing party.

In 1986, Mitterrand called on the leader of the largest conservative party (sometimes called **neo-Gaullist**), Jacques Chirac, to become premier and then went along with most of Chirac's cabinet choices and legislation, which rolled back many of Mitterrand's socialist experiments in the economy. The two struck an informal bargain—called **cohabitation**, living together but not married—in which Chirac concentrated on domestic affairs and Mitterrand on foreign and defense policy plus the symbolic functions of the presidency. In 1993, faced with another conservative victory in parliamentary elections, Mitterrand named another neo-Gaullist, Edouard Balladur, as his premier. In 1997, after a Socialist victory in the early parliamentary elections he had called, President Chirac named Socialist chief Lionel Jospin as premier.

Cohabitation—apart from the president's love life—is now unlikely. Two reforms deliberately make (almost) sure that the president and premier will be of the same party: (1) since 2000, the presidential term has been cut to five years; and (2) since 2002, parliamentary elections come one month after presidential elections. This eliminates the two-year overhang to a presidential term. France does not have U.S.-style "midterm" elections, but the split could recur if the opposition wins parliamentary elections a president calls early, a mistake Chirac made in 1997. If a president, in a crisis, say, calls legislative elections early and loses, Paris knows how to handle it: cohabitation again. During cohabitation, French presidents were not as strong as de Gaulle was, and premiers were stronger than he intended. Now, without cohabitation, presidents are back in full power. Institutions change according to circumstances.

If the French want to permanently avoid cohabitation, they could cut the last link between legislative and executive branches (the "can-censure" arrow) and become a straight presidential system, U.S. style. True, the U.S. system often deadlocks between the White House and Capitol Hill, but the president still has plenty of power to govern without permission from Congress.

Premier and Cabinet

Until cohabitation, French ministers, including the prime minister, were mostly the president's messengers; the premier pushed presidential measures through parliament. Under cohabitation, however, Premiers Chirac, Balladur, and Jospin brought much power to that office by pursuing their own legislative agendas. Even with no cohabitation since 2002, the premiership did not return to de Gaulle's subservient model. French presidents like to appear above ordinary politics, so they let their premiers do the heavy work, especially on the economy. The precise balance of powers between president and premier in France has not been settled and is likely to change with new personalities and situations. Hollande's first premier resigned in 2014 amid a weak economy and Socialist unpopularity. His second, Spanish-born Manuel Valls (he became a French citizen at age 20), backed away from socialism in favor of very moderate welfarism.

Democracy

France's Presidential Election of 2012

Neo-Gaullist President Nicolas Sarkozy came into office in 2007 pledging to free up the economy. When the global financial meltdown hit in 2008, however, he kept with French tradition and used state supervision, which yielded little. Having lost the neoliberal vision he campaigned on, Sarkozy's popularity plunged—typical for French presidents—leaving him exteremly vulnerable in 2012. Sarkozy, the son of an immigrant Hungarian aristocrat (who abandoned the family), was a brash, energetic outsider, not the staid product of a *grande école*.

His Socialist challenger, François Hollande, was more typical of the French elite: a brilliant graduate of three elite schools who climbed to the top of the Socialist Party under President Mitterrand. Hollande was something of an accidental candidate. The leading contender for the Socialists, Dominique Strauss-Kahn, head of the International Monetary Fund, was arrested for sexual assault in New York City, taking him out of the running. The Socialists emphasized Hollande's calm, attractive personality and help-the-poor policies in contrast to Sarkozy's impetuous temper and unsuccessful economic policies.

Hollande's big themes echoed those of Mitterrand decades earlier: equality, regulation of finance (as a high civil servant, he specialized in auditing finances),

turnout
Percentage of those eligible who vote in a given election.

subsidized jobs, and tax increases on corporations, banks, and the wealthy. Like many European politicians on the left, he denounced austerity policies that seemed to prolong the recession. He also pledged to legalize same-sex marriage, one of the few promises he delivered on.

French elections are held in two rounds. The first round on Sunday (most European elections are on Sundays), April 22, had ten candidates. The results are shown in the table. Only the two top vote winners then went on to the decisive second round two weeks later, which Hollande won 52 to 48 percent with strong support from young voters, the less well off, and public sector workers. Both rounds drew 80 percent **turnouts**.

Eight minor candidates took 44 percent of the first-round vote. Many French protest against the system by voting for no-chance parties in the first round, figuring that only the second round counts, and everyone knew it would be between Sarkozy and Hollande. In 2002, such frivolous voting for several left parties dropped Socialist Premier Lionel Jospin into third place on the first round and out of the contest. The French left was more careful in 2007 and 2012, concentrating on the Socialist candidates to make sure they would be in the second round. Marine Le Pen of the anti-immigrant National Front did better in the first round in 2012 than her father did in 2007.

First Round		
François Hollande	Socialist	28.6%
Nicolas Sarkozy	Union for a Popular Movement	27.2
Marine Le Pen	National Front	17.9
Jean-Luc Mélenchon	Left Front	11.1
François Bayrou	Democratic Movement	9.1
Eva Joly	Europe Ecology-Greens	2.3
Nicolas Dupont-Aignan	Arise the Republic	1.8
Philippe Poutou	New Anticapitalist Party	1.2
Nathalie Arthaud	Workers' Struggle	0.6
Jacques Cheminade	Solidarity and Progress	0.3
Second Round		
Hollande		51.6%
Sarkozy		48.4

Premiers pick ministers, who do not have to be approved by the National Assembly but usually are. A cabinet not to the liking of parliament could be censured and ousted. Accordingly, Socialist Mitterrand felt he had to name neo-Gaullists Chirac and Balladur as premiers because they had majority support in parliament. This is the general basis for selecting prime ministers throughout Europe.

The president cannot directly fire a premier, but, if they are of the same party, the president may persuade the premier to resign. Chirac got Premier Jean-Pierre Raffarin to resign in 2005 after French voters rejected the EU constitution. Socialist President Mitterrand had earlier named and dropped several Socialist premiers; two of them served less than a year. Hollande dropped his first premier, a Socialist, in 2014. Cohabitation may actually favor a premier's tenure in office, because the president cannot use party pressure to get premiers to resign. During the first two cohabitation periods, Mitterrand had no party leverage over his neo-Gaullist

Personalities

François Hollande

François Hollande's name indicates the origin of a sixteenth-century ancestor. Hollande was born in 1954 in Rouen in the north of France, son of a conservative doctor, but the family moved to a Paris suburb when he was 13. Very bright, Hollande jumped through elite French educational hoops: the Higher Commerce School, Sciences-Po, and National Administration School (ENA, see below for the Great Schools). He was raised Catholic but has not practiced any religion for years.

After ENA, Hollande joined the prestigious Court of Audiors (*Cour des Comptes*) that monitors the finances of France's government and many state-owned firms. During the 1970s, he climbed the ranks of the Socialist Party and became first secretary in 1997. In 1981, he lost his first parliamentary election in the south-central Corrèze department against Jacques Chirac, later president. He won there in 1988, lost in 1993, and won again in 1997. As in much of Europe, legislators do not have to be from the district they represent, although French politicians often become mayors to show they have local roots. More than 60 percent of National Assembly deputies also hold local elected offices, often as mayors. Hollande and his premier Valls were mayors while also in parliament. Jacques Chirac was mayor of Paris even as he was prime minister. Holding both local and national office simultaneously is unheard of in the United States but common elsewhere.

At ENA, Hollande took up with classmate Ségolène Royal, the unsuccessful Socialist candidate for presidcnt in 2007. They cohabited (literally) from 1978 to 2007 as unmarried "civil union partners" and had four children, but he left her for magazine writer Valérie Trierweiler, whom he left in 2014 for actress Julie Gayet. At the same time, Hollande named Royal minister for ecology, a post she had held 22 years earlier under Mitterrand. Socialist President Mitterrand had a "parallel family." Most French voters shrug off such private matters. (But they bother American and British voters. Why the difference?)

With President Sarkozy deeply unpopular, Hollande won the Socialists' first U.S.-style primary in 2011 (also held in two rounds) and then beat Sarkozy in 2012. He pledged to reverse Sarkozy's austerity program with major stimulus spending but was under severe pressure from Germany not to. He quarrelled openly with German Chancellor Angela Merkel over austerity. His vow to raise taxes on those making €1 million ($1.3 million) a year to 75 percent drove a few into exile and was ruled unconstitutional. Like Mitterrand 30 years earlier, Hollande's economic policies produced a shambles. He named a new premier to reverse socialist policies and woo business with investment-friendly proposals. Many thought Hollande simply did not know what to do, and his paralyzed Socialist government become the most unpopular in modern French history. He seemed certain to be a one-term president.

deputy
Member of French and many other parliaments.

technocrat
Official, usually unelected, who governs by virtue of economic skills.

interior ministry
In Europe, department in charge of homeland security and national police.

premiers, Chirac and Balladur, who lasted two years until new elections. Curiously, Socialist Lionel Jospin, in cohabitation with Gaullist Chirac, was one of France's longest-serving premiers (1997–2002). Divided government may be good for France.

Another difference from parliamentary systems is that a French **deputy** chosen to be a minister must resign his or her National Assembly seat. (A replacement is elected along with each deputy, so there is no need for by-elections, as in Britain.) In parliamentary systems such as Britain, ministers keep their seats in parliament, but de Gaulle wanted to make sure ministers could not run back to parliament to protest his policies. Also unlike Britain, French ministers do not have to be members of parliament; many are experienced administrators and nonparty **technocrats** who have never been elected to anything. De Gaulle picked as one of his premiers Georges Pompidou, who had never run in an election (but who went on to become an effective president in his own right).

Like other European cabinets, the French cabinet can be easily remade to suit the premier. Ministries are not quite the same as U.S. departments, which are firmly fixed by statute and change only after great deliberation. Paris ministries, often renamed, are almost ad hoc combinations of existing French agencies and bureaus and change according to the policy goals of the executive. Premier Valls's cabinet had 16 ministries:

Foreign Affairs	Agriculture
Defense	Ecology
Economy	Culture and Communication
Interior	Social Affairs
Justice	Decentralization and State Reform
Finance	Housing
Education	Women's Rights, Youth, and Sports
Labor	Overseas France

The U.S. Department of the Interior runs parks and forests; a European **interior ministry** guards the internal security of the country and includes police. America got a vague equivalent with the Department of Homeland Security in 2002, except the FBI is not part of it. Having repeated changes in ministries sounds chaotic to Americans, but the same career civil servants still run the various bureaus; the changes are only at the top, at the ministerial level. In France, we see bureaucrats actually running the country, a pattern developed even more fully in Japan.

The National Assembly

France's main legislative body, the 577-member National Assembly, is elected every five years (or sooner if the president wishes it) but has lost much of its power. During the Third and Fourth Republics, the National Assembly made and unmade cabinets and controlled the executive. Some say this sort of parliamentary system has a weak executive and strong legislature, but the legislature was not strong either. Divided into several quarrelsome parties that were unable to form stable coalitions, the French National Assembly was no more able to govern than were the cabinets. The government "fell" every few months on average.

The "fall" of a parliamentary government does not mean the entire system collapses; indeed, little changes. It just means there is a quarrel among the parties so that the cabinet coalition no longer commands a majority in parliament. The cabinet then resigns, is ousted in a vote of no-confidence, or limps along as a minority government. After several days or weeks of negotiations, another cabinet that wins majority approval is put together with the same ministers in the same jobs. Instead of too much change, parliamentary systems often suffer from too little. As the French have said for decades, "*Plus ça change, plus c'est la même chose*" ("The more it changes, the more it stays the same"). Some French premiers of the Fourth Republic were so intent on keeping the coalition together that they were unwilling to risk new policies. The result was *immobilisme*.

Meeting in the windowless **Palais Bourbon**, deputies prior to 1958 played politics with each other and ignored France's problems. They concentrated on either getting into the cabinet or bringing it down. Things changed with the Fifth Republic, ending the legislators' paradise.

The National Assembly no longer makes cabinets; the premier does, in consultation with the president. Indeed, the relationship between the cabinet and the legislature has been deliberately weakened, but one link remains: The National Assembly can **censure** a cabinet, indicating its extreme displeasure. The president, on the other hand, can dissolve the National Assembly for new elections before the end of its normal five-year term, which is what Chirac did in 1997. The president is limited to one dissolution per year.

The premier and president, not the legislature, now set the agenda and originate most bills. This is also true in Washington, but in Paris, if the government specifies, its proposals must be considered without amendments on a take-it-or-leave-it basis called a *blocked vote*, which prevents parliamentary dilution of legislation. The National Assembly has little time to consider legislation: It meets no more than five and a half months a year, it has only six committees, and a bill cannot be bottled up in committee but must be reported out.

The government is able to pass many laws by simple decree, provided the premier and the president agree. The 1958 constitution specifies the types of laws that must go through parliament; presumably, no other laws need to. While most decrees concern details, the power of government decree also extends to the budget. Here, the legislature has lost its original purpose—the power of the purse. Any parliamentary motions to either decrease revenues (a tax cut) or increase spending (a new program) are automatically out of order. And if the parliament cannot settle on the budget within 70 days, the government may make it law by simple decree.

The French upper house, the *Sénat*, is less important. Only federal systems really need upper chambers, and France is a unitary system. The French Senate has 326 members elected for nine years each—with elections for about a third every three years—by a gigantic electoral college made up of National Assembly deputies plus more than 100,000 regional and municipal councilors that overrepresent rural France. The Sénat looks after farms and is sometimes called the "agricultural chamber." It may also criticize and amend government bills, but the National Assembly can override its objections by a simple majority.

Palais Bourbon
Paris house of French National Assembly.

censure
Legislative condemnation of executive.

National Front
French anti-immigrant and
anti-EU party.

The French Multiparty System

Party system can be crucial to stable governance. Some prefer two-party systems, but multiparty systems can be stable and effective, as in Sweden, Switzerland, Holland, and Belgium. France has, at present, two large parties and three small ones, plus a sprinkling of minor parties. The largest and currently ruling party is the center-left Socialist Party (PS). The Union for a Popular Movement (*Union pour un Mouvement Populaire*, UMP), commonly referred to as "neo-Gaullists," occupies the center-right. On the far right, the anti-Muslim and anti-EU **National Front** gets a protest vote for president but few parliamentary seats. The once-mighty French Communist Party, running in 2012 as part of the Left Front, has drastically shrunk.

The electoral system, as French political scientist Maurice Duverger argued long ago, has a powerful influence on party system. The traditional electoral system of the Fifth Republic—single-member districts with runoff—is actually taken from the Third Republic. Like Britain and the United States, France uses single-member districts but, instead of a simple plurality to win (FPTP), requires a majority (more than 50 percent). If the candidate does not get it on the first ballot—usually the case—the contest goes to a runoff a week later, this time with either the top two candidates or those with at least 12.5 percent of the eligible voters of that district. Now

Democracy

France's Parliamentary Elections of 2012

France's parliamentary elections followed the presidential victory of François Hollande and gave 280 of the National Assembly's 577 seats to his center-left Socialist Party, up 94 seats from 2007 but still less than a majority and thus requiring parliamentary support from some small leftist parties. The UMP fell 119 seats from 2007 to win only 194 seats. Several smaller parties and some independents won a handful of seats.

A few candidates won actual majorities in their districts, and they were declared winners immediately.

In most districts, however, voters went to a runoff a week later. Candidates who had polled fewer than one eligible voter in eight in the first round were dropped. In most districts, weaker candidates also withdrew and endorsed the candidate who most matched their preferences. For example, a New Center candidate who scored lower would withdraw and urge his supporters to vote for the UMP candidate in the second round. As with the presidential contest, the second round is the decisive one.

	1st Round	2nd Round	Total Seats
Socialists	29%	41%	280 seats
Union for a Popular Movement (UMP)	27	38	194
Left Front (incl. Communists)	7	1	10
Europe Ecology-Greens	5	4	17
National Front	14	4	2
New Center	2	2	12
Radical Party of the Left	2	2	12
small leftist parties	3	3	22
small rightist parties	4	2	15

only a simple plurality is needed to win. The second round, then, is the decisive one; the first round is a bit like U.S. primaries. Like the U.S. and British single-member systems, seats are not closely proportionate to votes.

Presidential elections run under similar rules. All but the top two candidates for president are eliminated in the first round; a second round two weeks later decides between the top two. In the first round of 2002, leftists scattered their votes and let the National Front's Jean-Marie Le Pen come in second, humiliating France. To prevent a recurrence, France could drop the two-round system and go to a simple plurality win (FPTP) in one round. That would force small parties to coalesce into larger parties *before* the election.

The French system permits several parties to exist but not necessarily to win; the Anglo-American systems discourage third parties. Proportional representation systems, on the other hand, permit small parties to exist and even win. In Germany, for example, a Green vote

unitary
System that centralizes power in the capital with little autonomy for component areas.

first-order civil divisions
Main territorial units within countries, such as departments in France.

prefect
French *préfet*; top administrator of department.

Midi
French for "noon"; the South of France.

Geography

Decentralizing Unitary Systems

A state's territorial organization—its "civil divisions" and their relationship to the capital—can heighten or dampen center–periphery tensions, although no sure-fire formula has been found. There are two approaches, **unitary** and federal. More than Britain, France is a unitary system, a carryover from monarchical times, whereby the **first-order civil divisions**—counties in Britain, departments in France, prefectures in Japan—have little autonomy and serve mostly as administrative conveniences for the national capital.

These units can be changed and their boundaries redrawn with little ado. The leading executives in these civil divisions are appointed and supervised by the national government. France's **prefects** are perhaps the best examples of how the unitary state rules. There are, to be sure, elected county, departmental, and municipal councils, but their powers to tax and spend are limited. Any major project must be cleared with, and usually funded by, the national authorities. Most countries in the world are unitary systems. (U.S. states, although they look like federal systems, are actually unitary.)

The advantage of a unitary system is that it gives greater control to the center for rational administration and modernization. Standards can be enforced nationally. Central administration can knead disparate groups into a single nationality, as France has done over the centuries. The unitary system best suits a country like Japan that is not too large or does not contain different cultures and languages.

There are several difficulties with unitary systems. One is that they may ignore the wishes of local people, especially those at the periphery. Crushing the **Midi** caused centuries of resentment. Many of today's *méridionaux* (southerners) see themselves as a race separate from the northerners. Thus, a unitary system may foster center–periphery tensions. Corsican and Breton violence are illustrations of France's incomplete integration of regional subcultures.

Further, a unitary system, because it is so uniform, can be too rigid and make big, nationwide mistakes that in a federal system would be implemented and corrected piecemeal, as the components try various policies. Often, there is too much national control over purely local issues. Even trivial matters such as a new traffic light might have to be approved by Paris or Tokyo.

Britain, France, and Spain, in recent years, loosened their unitary systems by instituting regional autonomy. Britain devolved some home rule to Scotland, Wales, and Northern Ireland. France's 22 regions and Spain's 17 *autonomías* now have elected councils with considerable decision-making powers on economic growth, education, housing, and other regional concerns. Although not nearly federalism, these unitary systems have moved in a quasi-federal direction.

The change in France under Mitterrand is particularly striking, for it rolled back a tradition that started with Louis XI. French monarchs tried to erase regional differences but sometimes only worsened local resentments. Napoleon perfected this centralizing and homogenizing pattern. He abolished the historic provinces and replaced them with smaller, artificial units called **départements** named after rivers. The departments were administrative conveniences to facilitate control by Paris. Each department—there are now 96 (plus four for overseas territories)—is administered by a prefect, a lineal descendant of Richelieu's old intendant, now an official of the Interior Ministry. Prefects, very bright and highly trained (often at the ENA) monitored laws, funds, and mayors with Olympian detachment.

In 1982, Mitterrand passed a law that reduced the domain of prefects and increased local autonomy. Elected councils in the departments and regions got policy-setting and taxation powers in education, urban and regional planning and development, job training, and housing. Soon, French local and regional government became more important, and elections to their councils were hotly contested. Competition set in as cities, departments, and regions sought to attract new industries. Local taxes increased, but the ways of assessing them became widely divergent and innovative.

The subnational units of French government started acting somewhat like American states, developing their own strategies for prosperity. France in no sense became a federal system—indeed, its decentralization did not go as far as Spain's during this same period—but decentralization was Mitterrand's most important and lasting contribution to the French political system.

département
Department; French first-order civil division, equivalent to British county.

of more than 5 percent wins dozens of seats for that party. But the French party system is rooted in French society, and this is a more complex and fragmented society than the British or American. In any case, the French party system seems to be coalescing into two large blocs, one left and one right. Over the decades, there have been fewer and fewer relevant parties in France.

The Constitutional Council

In the 1980s, a little-noticed branch of the French government started drawing attention: the Constitutional Council. Although it was part of the 1958 constitution, it came into its own as a buffer between Mitterrand and the conservative-dominated parliament during his two cohabitation periods. Some started comparing it to the U.S. Supreme Court, but it is quite different.

- Both have nine members, but the French serve for nine years, not for life. Three members of the French court are appointed each by the president, the speaker of the National Assembly, and the speaker of the Senate.

- The French Council members are rarely lawyers and see their role as political rather than legal. The U.S. Supreme Court sees its role the other way around.

- The scope of the French Council is limited. It can review the constitutionality of laws only after they are passed by parliament but before they have been signed by the president. It considers cases not from lower courts but on demand by the executive or any 60 members of either chamber of parliament.

- Rather than establishing legal precedents as the U.S. Supreme Court does, the French Constitutional Council has acted as a brake against hasty and ill-considered legislation. As such, the ruling parties in France tend to dislike its decisions, while the opposition parties often like them.

Geography

Sailing the Mediterranean

On your luxury yacht, you are sailing in a great, clockwise circle around the Mediterranean Sea, always keeping the shore a few kilometers to port (left, for you landlubbers). You enter through the Strait of Gibraltar. Which countries do you pass, one after another, on your left?

Spain, France, Italy, Slovenia, Croatia, Bosnia (minute shoreline), Croatia again, Montenegro, Albania, Greece, Turkey, Syria, Lebanon, Israel, Egypt, Libya, Tunisia, Algeria, and Morocco.

The role and powers of the U.S. Supreme Court are unique. Some French thinkers would like to see their council become more like the U.S. Supreme Court. The German Federal Constitutional Court is one of the few that approach the Supreme Court in importance.

French Political Culture

3.3   Describe the split nature of French political culture.

Catholic countries have a nasty split absent in Protestant (and Eastern Orthodox) countries. The role of the church has long been one of the defining characteristics of Catholic countries. When Britain and Sweden broke with Rome, the new Anglican and Lutheran churches subordinated churchmen to the state; they could not turn to Rome or play an independent political role.

In Latin European countries—France, Italy, and Spain—the Roman Catholic faith retained its political power, supporting conservative regimes and retaining special privileges, such as control of education, tax exemption for church lands, and a considerable say in government policy. Because of this temporal power, many people in Latin Europe followed Voltaire's anticlericalism (see box earlier in this chapter). After the French Revolution and Italian unification (in the mid-nineteenth century), many people wanted a purely secular state—that is, one with no church influence in government. That was easy to do in America, where there was no single established church, but it was hard in France, Italy, and Spain, where church and state were intertwined. To separate them required drastic surgery: sale of church lands, banning of some Catholic orders (such as the Jesuits), and state rather than church control of schools. In reaction to this anticlericalism, the church turned from conservative to reactionary, even seeking monarchical restoration, because that would restore church privileges.

The battle raged for more than a century (even in Mexico). At one point, the Vatican instructed faithful Catholics to avoid involvement with the "Jacobin" Republic. During the Dreyfus affair, French clericalists and anticlericalists opposed each other, sometimes violently. Finally, in 1905, the National Assembly completed separation of church and state. Until the twentieth century, to be for the Republic meant to be anticlerical. The great World

Political Culture

How to Celebrate a 200-Year-Old Revolution

The French Revolution still divided France in 1989. Even choosing the official historian for the bicentennial was a political problem. Conservative historians called the Revolution a horrible mistake, the root of France's subsequent troubles. Radical or leftist historians, on the other hand, read into the Revolution the harbinger of all things good and of the Bolshevik Revolution in Russia.

In François Furet, the Mitterrand government found its historian: a former Marxist who had abandoned radicalism to produce a moderate and sober synthesis. Furet admired the revolutionary ideals but argued that the collapse of the monarchy and takeover of the revolution by extremists made it "skid out of control" (*dérapage*), part of the logic of revolutions. Furet's thinking parallels Crane Brinton's (see earlier box).

A change in the political context enabled Furet and other French intellectuals to accept this troubling analysis of the French Revolution. For decades, many naively celebrated the 1917 Russian Revolution as a continuation of the French Revolution. With the erosion of French leftism and decay of Soviet communism, French intellectuals saw that the Bolshevik Revolution had been a mistake. But if it was, then the French Revolution itself must have been badly flawed. The new attitude about communism forced the French to reevaluate their own revolution.

War I premier, Georges Clemenceau—*le tigre*—was a passionate republican and supporter of Dreyfus. He recalled how his father used to tell him that the only thing worse than a bad priest is a good one.

The French left—including the Socialists—still draws most of its supporters from the anticlerical tradition. The right—chiefly the Gaullists—attracts mostly people from the pro-Church tradition. Indeed, in most Catholic countries—including Mexico and Brazil—how often people go to Mass partially predicts their votes; strongly Catholic means politically conservative. (A parallel: religious Americans tend to conservatism.)

Most French are baptized Catholic, but only 13 percent of French Catholics attend Mass weekly. (Europeans in general are much less religious than Americans.) Although the great battles between clericalists and anticlericalists have subsided, issues such as abortion and state control of Church schools can still bring protesters to the streets of Paris. Once established, social and political cleavages have tremendous staying power. France now practices *laïcité*, the keeping of religion out of public life, something stronger than the "separation of church and state" in the United States, where public figures are expected to appear religious.

French Patriotism

France has a mystique, a drawing power that can equally attract conservatives such as de Gaulle and Socialists such as Mitterrand. The conservatives are drawn to French civilization, its Catholic roots, and its *grandeur* (greatness). Liberals and leftists, on the other hand, are drawn to the liberty, equality, and fraternity espoused by the French Revolution and see France as guarding these ideals. Some French envision their land as a person, a princess, or even a Madonna. The dramatic and stirring **"La Marseillaise"** shows the passion of French patriotism.

French patriotism in the abstract, however, does not carry over into the real, grubby, daily life of French politics. The French are more cynical about politics than are Britons or Americans. The French may be the world's greatest complainers: Nothing works right; reforms fail; all governments are crooked; presidents quickly lose popularity. France in the abstract is glorious; France in the here and now is shabby. De Gaulle said France needs national greatness, for only with such a vision can the French rise above the sordid reality and pursue the mythical ideal.

Sarkozy was elected in 2007, in part, because of his ability to project an idealistic vision of a reinvigorated France with a neoliberal twist. The French initially liked the notion, but once Sarkozy was in power, they quickly grew disillusioned with him, as they do with all presidents. His ratings fell, and *anti-Sarkozysme* dominated media and political talk. One book described Sarkozy's rule as "egocracy." Then Hollande won with the leftist take on French ideals, but he was soon seen as weak and ineffective and became deeply unpopular. The French oppose—just about anyone and anything—brilliantly. In the end, though, they knuckle under to authority.

Where did this political schizophrenia come from? Part of the problem is historical, traceable to the centralization of French kings, who implanted a centralized state that tried to plan and build rationally but in practice often failed. The French, educated to expect a powerful government to help them (the ideal), are always disappointed when it does not (the real). Every new French government, for example, promises to cut France's high unemployment rate. It fails, leaving French citizens bitter. The solution: Either stop promising or dismantle the impediments to a free economy that would hire more people. Few French politicians are willing to do either.

French **statism** also stunted the development of a voluntary, do-it-ourselves attitude, one common in the United States. France has no tradition of voluntary groups undertaking local governance. When locals take responsibility and something goes wrong, they can only blame themselves. In France, with all responsibility, until recently, in the hands of the central government, people blame Paris.

Centuries of **bureaucratized** administration also left the French used to living by lots of uniform, impersonal rules. This creates the resentment of the little citizen on one side of the counter facing the cold, indifferent bureaucrat on the other. Centralization and bureaucratization are the products of the "order and reason" approach to governance that has been practiced in France for centuries. Order and reason, unfortunately, are always deficient in practice, and the French become unhappy with a reality that always falls short of ideals.

"La Marseillaise"
French national anthem.

statism
Idea that a strong government should run things, especially major industries.

bureaucratized
Heavily controlled by civil servants.

A Climate of Mistrust

In personal relations, many French are distant to and mistrustful of people outside their family. Indeed, attitudes of mistrust are widespread throughout Latin Europe, although with modernization, mistrust has receded. (Trustful attitudes prevail in North Europe and Japan.) Harvard's Laurence Wylie in 1950–1951 found villagers in the Vaucluse, in the south of France, constantly

privatism
Concerned only with one's personal life; unsocial.

suspicious of *les autres*, "the others," who talk behind your back, blacken your name, and meddle in your affairs. The best way to live, people there agreed, was not to get involved with other people and to maintain only correct but distant relations with neighbors. French philosopher Jean-Paul Sartre voiced a very French feeling about interpersonal relationships when he wrote, "*L'enfer, c'est les autres*" (Hell is other people). He meant, in his 1944 play *No Exit*, that having to get along with others is hell.

Although it has receded in recent decades, the French still tend to **privatism**. French houses often have high walls topped by broken glass set in concrete. Traditionally, French people rarely entertained at home—they would go to a restaurant instead; inviting outsiders to your table was an invasion of family privacy. (This has changed, however; I have been invited into several French homes for superb meals.) Special mistrust is reserved for the government. Wylie's villagers understood that all government is bad, a necessary evil at best. The duties of a good citizen, which schoolchildren memorize in their civics course, are mere ideals, but in the real world, government is corrupt, intrusive, and ineffective. French children learn to love *la patrie* (the fatherland) in the abstract but to disdain politics in the here and now. Politics is best kept private and personal; discussing politics with others only leads to arguments. Besides, it is none of their business.

Geography

The Persistence of Region

In 1936, the leftist Popular Front won in the shaded *départements* (map, left). In 1981, Socialist François Mitterrand won the presidency with a very similar pattern (map, right). Maps of recent elections look much the same. Region, as well as social class and religion, often produces distinct and durable voting patterns.

1936: Popular Front Vote

1981: Mitterand Vote

School for Grinds

As everywhere, schooling contributes to political culture. The French curriculum, like Japan's, is heavy on memorization and tends to produce diligent grinds rather than lively intellects. Children put in long school and homework hours and are graded harshly. Until recently, all French children learned the same thing, established by the Ministry of Education in Paris, with no local input. Starting in the late nineteenth century, Paris used uniform education to replace local dialects and subcultures with a nationwide Frenchness. Back in the day, an education minister could tell by his watch what Latin verb was being conjugated all over France. Since then, French school curricula have become less centralized and less classical.

lycée
French academic high school.

baccalauréat
French high school exam and diploma.

The curious thing about the standardized, memorized French education, however, is its deeply humanistic and individualistic content that exposes students to ideas that would be banned in U.S. high schools (such as those in the novel *The Immoralist*). The flunk rate is high, and many must repeat a year. The stress and anxiety contribute to privatistic individualism and periodic rebellion.

The French claim equality of educational opportunity. France has few English-style boarding schools for the rich, but, as everywhere, opportunities are still skewed. The lofty content of French education is tilted toward middle- and upper-class children. Working-class and peasant children, not exposed to correct speech—and the French are maniacs about their language—or to abstract, intellectual thoughts, begin school at a disadvantage and have lesser chances at higher education. (Is educational stratification in the United States similar?)

The academic high school in France is the **lycée**, developed by Napoleon to train army officers. Most lycées are state run and in cities; few are in rural France. Admission is competitive, and the curriculum is demanding. Students complete the lycée with an examination at age 18 and get a **baccalauréat** (invented by Napoleon), which entitles them to university admission. Now, as the result of government policy to upgrade French educational levels, more than 70 percent of French young people earn the "*bac.*" Two-thirds of a million took exams in 2013, now in 91 specialized subjects, many of them technical and vocational. But public *lycées* suffer from dilapidated buildings, crowded classrooms, and crime. (Sound familiar?) Middle-class French parents, afraid of school decay, prefer private *lycées.* French student

Geography

"Every Country Has a South"

This old saw contains much truth. Except for very small countries, the south of most lands in the Northern Hemisphere is poorer and less developed than the north. Industry historically started in the north of France, Germany, Italy, Spain, and the United States. People in the south of these countries are often described as fun loving but slow and lazy, northern people as efficient and hard working. The south votes differently from the north. People of France's *Midi* describe themselves as a different, Mediterranean race that does not like the cold, Germanic northern French. Centuries ago, Montesquieu proposed that climate produces culture. Does it?

grande école

French for "great school"; an elite, specialized college.

Ecole Nationale d'Administration (ENA)

France's school for top bureaucrats.

protests over school conditions periodically shake the government, reminders of the 1968 Events of May.

The "Great Schools"

The **grandes écoles** are the elite of French higher education. French universities, which stress the "impractical" liberal arts, are nearly free, unselective, and mediocre. Anyone with a bac can get into one—now 1.5 million students crowd France's 82 universities—but many drop out. Altogether, some 45 percent of French 20- to 24-year-olds are in full-time education, the highest percentage in Europe and comparable to the United States. Reforms to let universities select students competitively and charge tuition are shouted down. The result: No French university makes the global top 40.

In contrast, the "Great Schools" skim off the brightest and most motivated 4 percent through rigorous entrance exams, train (rather than "educate") them in the practical matters of running a country, and then place them in top civil service and managerial positions. The Great Schools form the people who run France. No other country has anything quite like them. It would be as if West Point produced not army officers but leading administrators. Some denounce the *grandes écoles* as elitist and undemocratic, as they admit few working-class or Muslim students.

There are over 200 Great Schools, but three are truly elite. The *Ecole Polytechnique* was used by Napoleon to train military engineers. Called X for short, *xiens* have their pick of technology and management jobs when they graduate. The *Ecole Normale Supérieure*, founded by Napoleon to create loyal lycée instructors, still produces many of France's leading intellectuals—including Jean-Paul Sartre, Raymond Aron, and President Georges Pompidou. The newest Great School, founded by de Gaulle in 1945, the **Ecole Nationale d'Administration (ENA)**, quickly became the most important. Many of the country's top civil servants are "enarchs," as they call themselves.

Many ENA students are already graduates of the *Institut d'Etudes Politiques* in Paris, itself a *grande école* (and still known as "Sciences-Po," a birthplace of modern political science). Getting into the ENA is even harder; typically, fewer than one in ten pass the legendary written and oral exams to join the entering class of 80 or so. ENA students get monthly stipends and spend half

Political Culture

How Would You Do on the "Bac"?

In about 12 hours of nationwide essay exams spread over a week, France's 17- or 18-year-old lycéens face questions such as the following, taken from the philosophy section of a recent baccalauréat exam. How would you do? Choose one. Spend no more than two hours.

- Why defend the weak?
- What is it to judge?
- Is it reasonable to love?

French students now get their choice of bac exams. Some are scientific or technical; the most prestigious is math (because you cannot bluff). The French government is trying to move students from the humanities to technology.

of their 27 months interning in government ministries. Most ENA graduates get high positions in the civil service. About one-third of France's prefects and ambassadors are ENA graduates. Cabinets typically illustrate "enarchy." President Chirac (class of 1959) and former Premier de Villepin ('80, along with his sister, Véronique) graduated ENA, as did 2007 Socialist presidential candidate Ségolène Royal ('80) and Socialist President François Hollande (also '80).

In 2007, Royal lost to Sarkozy, a law graduate of an ordinary university, who was proud that only two ministers in his first cabinet were ENA graduates, but his last cabinet had six. French governments seem unable to do without enarchs, although some think ENA has passed its peak of influence. Extensive privatization has shrunk the number of positions running state-owned industries, and many bright young people now prefer MBAs and private industry. France's most prestigious MBA is from the HEC (*Ecole des Hautes Etudes Commerciales*), another Great School (and one of Hollande's).

The Great Schools epitomize the best and worst of French education. Students have to be very smart and hard working. But they also have to be cold, logical, and removed from ordinary people. Products of the *grandes écoles* may be brilliant, but they often lack common sense and humanity. Some critics call them, pejoratively, *technocrats*—people who rule by technical criteria. Trained by the state, they tend to propose statist solutions.

Whether lycée, university, or Great School, the teaching style is cold, distant, and uninvolved. Class discussion is rare, and questions are from the instructor, not the students. Long ago at the University of Toulouse, I tried to break this pattern and urged student participation. I was met with silence; they were uncomfortable with class discussion. (More recently, I had the same experience with Chinese students.)

Political Culture

The French–U.S. Love–Hate Relationship

The French have contradictory attitudes toward America. Some are deeply anti-American. Many French intellectuals dislike the United States, its compassionless capitalism, its lack of culture, and its global hegemony, all symbolized by McDonald's. French critics call the United States a "*hyperpuissance*" (hyperpower) that tries to remake the world in its own image. But France, they say, will go its own way, based on its own traditions and culture. Millions of French people (including President Sarkozy), however, like America and President Obama. The French flock to U.S.-made movies and eat "McDos."

French elites try to hold back American cultural penetration. They outlaw English words ("*franglais*") and limit the number of U.S. movies and TV shows. They reject a totally free market and cling to state ownership and supervision. What bothers French elites? First, they look back to the time when French power, language, and culture (and cuisine) dominated Europe. They resent being replaced by U.S. power and the English language. De Gaulle, miffed at not being treated as an equal by Roosevelt and Churchill during the war, led France on nationalistic and anti-U.S. paths. France, not the United States, was to lead Europe. Many French, especially in the Foreign Ministry, still follow this design.

Little by little, however, French ways resemble American ways—"*le business à l'américaine*" (an example of franglais). The international economy requires it; much business is now global and conducted in English. French firms buy American firms and vice versa. Some French Great Schools now offer English-language MBAs.

compartmentalization
Mentally separating and isolating problems.

ideal–typical
Distilling social characteristics into one example.

Sociologist Michel Crozier wrote in 1964 that the French have *"l'horreur du face-à-face."* Outside of family, French people feel uncomfortable with face-to-face relationships. Some tourists find the French unfriendly, but they are reserved and formal to everyone. The French style is opposite to that of the American, which values informality and friendliness. To avoid face-to-face relationships, the French prefer structure and formality with clear but limited impersonal rules that keep out of one's private domain.

Freedom or Authority?

Lack of trust, fear of face-to-face relationships, and rigid and rote education contribute to a French inability to choose between freedom and authority. The French tend to want both the abstract *liberté* and the controlled bureaucracies. The solution is **compartmentalization**: The private French person loves freedom, while the public French person wants reason, order, and formal, impersonal rules. A typical French person has been described as an anarchist who secretly admires the police but could equally be a policeman who secretly admires the anarchists.

This mental split produces a longing for freedom and a perfect society but an equal tendency to surrender to authority and an imperfect society. The balance is unstable; from time to time, the quest for liberty bursts out, as in 1789, 1830, 1848, the Paris Commune of 1871, the Events of May 1968, and the 2005 youth riots, most of which ended with a surrender to authority. French political culture has been described as limited authoritarianism accompanied by potential insurrection.

Legitimacy in France is much weaker than in Britain. Most French distrust the regime, think democracy is not working in France, and think France is in decline. Some even argue that the Fifth Republic has not worked right since de Gaulle and that it is time for a Sixth Republic. France may be due for another bout of tumultuous change.

Social Class

France, like Britain, is a class society. The gap between the French working and middle class is big, and, until recently, social mobility has been dampened. In France, as in Britain, few who are born working class or Muslim climb the income ladder. Distribution of income in France is more unequal than in Spain. The rich live superbly in France; the poor scrape by.

Class differences tend to reinforce other cleavages in French society—clerical–anticlerical, urban–rural, radical–conservative, even, to a certain extent, North–South. That is, these factors tend to line up on one side—never perfectly, of course, but enough to produce a left–right split in French voting. Very broadly, here are the **ideal–typical** French voters of the left and the right.

Left Voter	Right Voter
Working class	Middle class
Anticlerical	Pro-church
Urban	Rural or small town

The Great Calming Down

French intellectuals were, for much of the postwar period, attracted to Marxism. Observing the huge gap between the ideal of equality and the reality of inequality, many educated French turned to Marxism and sometimes to membership in the Communist Party. Philosopher Jean-Paul Sartre backed leftist causes and urged other intellectuals to become *engagé*. His conservative adversary Raymond Aron, another *normalien*, disparaged Marxism as "the opium of the intellectuals," a play on Marx's statement that "religion is the opium of the masses."

Under Mitterrand, if not before, this changed. French intellectuals grew disillusioned with Marxism, communism, and traditional leftist positions. The French Communist Party declined to irrelevance. In the 1970s, a new generation of French intellectuals criticized the Soviet Union and communism. The Soviet-approved 1981 coup in Poland by a Polish general reminded many French of Marshal Pétain in the service of Germany during World War II.

Democracy

The Centrist French

The real winner of recent French elections has been neither the left nor the right but the center. Observers saw the "normalization" of French political life and a healing of the great split in French society. Politicians of the left and right tended to move to the center. A poll that asked the French to place themselves on a nine-point ideological scale, from extreme left to extreme right, resembled the centrist results in Britain and Germany. Such a "center-peaked" unimodal distribution of ideological values is basic to stable democracy.

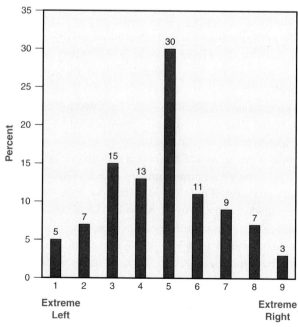

Self-Placement of French Voters on a Left/Right Ideological Scale

volatile
Rises and falls quickly.

The election of a Socialist government in 1981 brought the left to power, but they soon found it was easy to criticize a conservative government but hard to run a government yourself, to fix the economy, assume a role in world affairs, and transform French society. As a result, many French intellectuals became moderates, and some even urged free-market capitalism. The Mitterrand presidency helped free French society from the allure of leftist ideology and guide it to a pragmatism that still endures. French politics became centrist, like politics in most of Europe. (Curiously, at this same time, U.S. politics polarized, and the middle ground shrank. Any idea why?) With the bicentennial, much of the passion that earlier surrounded the French Revolution was passé. French politics entered into what might be termed "the great calming down" of moderation. As François Furet put it, "The Revolution is over."

Patterns of Interaction

3.4   Illustrate how referendums sound democratic but often are not.

Party image and voter identification with parties are less developed in France than in Britain. Many French voters do not have long-term party preferences, and French parties tend to come and go and change their names, blurring their images. One result is that many voters are not attached to one party and scatter their votes as a form of protest. In 2002, this led to a top contender, Socialist Premier Jospin, getting knocked out of the presidential race by a right-wing extremist. In most of West Europe, elections show only small swings of a few points from the previous contest, but not in France, where new parties can rise and fall within a few years. French parties may gain or lose 10 to 20 percentage points from their previous showing. French voting can be **volatile**.

Most French parties have changed their names, especially the Gaullists. From 1947 to 1952, it was the Rally of the French People (RPF). When de Gaulle came to power in 1958, they became the Union for the New Republic (UNR); then, in 1967, the Democratic Union for the Fifth Republic (UD-V^e); in 1968, the Union for the Defense of the Republic (UDR); in 1971, the Union of Democrats for the Republic (with the same initials, UDR); in 1976, the Rally for the Republic (RPR); and in 2002, the Union for a Presidential Majority (UMP), quickly renamed the Union for a Popular Movement (still UMP).

A U.S. political scientist would argue that French parties cannot build party identification with so many name changes. But the Gaullists—since 1976 known as the "neo-Gaullists"—saw themselves less as a structured political party than as a patriotic rally and felt the name changes showed they were always starting fresh. Neo-Gaullist Nicolas Sarkozy was elected president in 2007. What makes sense in one political culture does not in another.

The Socialists, founded in 1905, originally called themselves the French Section of the Workers International, or SFIO. In 1969, merging with some smaller left groups, they changed the name to the *Parti Socialiste* (PS). In 1981, the PS under Mitterrand won both the presidency and the National Assembly. It again became the largest party in parliament in 1997 but shrank to second largest in the 2002 and 2007 elections. It rebounded in 2012 with the victory of François Hollande. French Socialist leaders talk left but, once in power, govern from the center.

The French center is unusually messy; many centrist figures strive for prominence and do not like to merge into one party. The Union for French Democracy (*Union pour la Démocratie Française*, UDF) began as a parliamentary grouping in 1962 and first ran in elections in 1966 as the Republicans. In 1974, its leader, Valéry Giscard d'Estaing, was elected president and later merged several small centrist parties with the Republicans to form the UDF, a loose federation of five center-right parties. For the 2007 parliamentary elections, the UDF split into the New Center (NC) and Democratic Movement *(MoDem)*. The French center, where small parties continually combine, split, and change names, has been aptly called "the eternal swamp."

The Communists (PCF) plunged from a quarter of the parliamentary vote to a few percent running as the Left Front. On the right, the National Front emerged in 1986 as the anti-immigrant party and has grown. Even more complicating, left parties often run jointly as the United Left or Common Program (Socialist and Communist), and right parties as the Presidential Majority or Alliance (Gaullists and New Center).

The French party system is not as complex as it used to be; it is down from ten parties in 1958 to perhaps four relevant ones today. France's parties have been consolidating and forming into two blocs—one left and one right—possibly headed for a "two-plus" party system. Much depends on whether the Union for a Popular Movement (UMP) can unite the French right. Schematically, it looks like below figure.

The two blocs are divided internally. The Communists and other far-left parties are always feuding with the Socialists, and the small centrist parties are constantly trying to eat into the neo-Gaullists. None of the other parties wants anything to do with the National Front, now resurgent and led by Marine Le Pen, the founder's daughter, who emphasizes anti-globalization. In terms of voter appeal, however, the two blocs fit into two great French tendencies of which we spoke earlier. The left favors ways to make people more equal by taxing the rich, controlling the economy, and providing more welfare benefits. The right favors change based on economic growth and modest reforms. Both look to a strong state, but the left dislikes free-market solutions, while Sarkozy claimed to favor some of them. Sarkozy in office did not implement a competitive economy, which the UMP never supported, but reflexively turned to statist solutions. The National Front wants to end immigration and dismantle the EU.

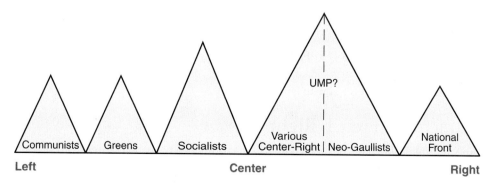

Eurocommunism
1970s move by Italian
Communists away from
Stalinism and toward
democracy.

Stalinist
Brutal central control over
Communist parties.

The Fractured French Left

In most countries, Socialist and Communist parties have been natural enemies ever since the Communists followed Lenin's command and broke from the Socialists shortly after World War I. Typically, where one was strong, the other was weak. Britain, Sweden, Germany, and Spain all had large socialist-type parties and small Communist parties. In Italy, on the other hand, a large Communist Party—now renamed the Democratic Party of the Left—overshadowed the Socialists. In France, it used to be that way, but, during the 1970s and 1980s, the Socialists grew and the Communists shrank, so that now the PS is by far the largest left party in France.

The two parties have common roots. The PCF, in 1920, broke away from the Socialists. In a battle that raged over the twentieth century, the Communists claimed that the Socialists were not militant enough, that they abandoned revolutionary Marxism for gradual, pragmatic reformism. The PCF echoed the Soviet line. The Communists did not join the Resistance until Germany attacked the Soviet Union in 1941. After Stalin's death, however, the PCF gradually became more moderate. It denounced the 1968 Soviet invasion of Czechoslovakia and claimed to favor **Eurocommunism**, but many feared it was still **Stalinist**.

Socialists and Communists formed an unstable alliance. The two parties hated each other but knew they needed each other. The second round, or runoff, of a French election places a great premium on combining parties, for, in the French runoff, a simple plurality wins. If the Communists and Socialists ran separately on the second ballot, they would always lose to the combined Gaullists and other center-right parties. Accordingly, the left parties—the PS, PCF, and now many small leftist parties—generally support the strongest left candidate, regardless of party, on the *second* ballot. It is the French electoral system that drives rivals on the French left together.

When François Mitterrand took over the Socialist Party in 1971, it was overshadowed on the French left by the Communists, who regularly won a fifth or more of the vote. Given France's peculiar electoral system—single-member districts with runoff—Mitterrand knew the PS could not grow on its own. He also knew that much of the Communist vote was not from committed Communists; it was a protest vote that could be won over by an attractive Socialist Party. He cleverly embraced the Communists, used them, won away their lukewarm supporters, and then discarded the PCF. In 1984, a shrunken PCF left the cabinet and kept shrinking.

The decline of the French Communists, however, left the French left still fragmented, as it spawned several far-left parties trying to grab the PCF's militant tradition and worker and intellectual electorate. In the 2012 presidential election, four far-leftist candidates fragmented the left vote on the first ballot. In France, as in most of Europe, at least a third of the electorate vote for one leftist party or another—ranging from the Socialists at center-left to the Communists at medium-left to far-left Trotskyists.

The Fractured French Right

The French right is likewise fragmented. France has one large party on the right, but two smaller ones speak to other parts of the electorate. Some trace the division of the French right back to the Revolution, which produced (1) an ultraconservative monarchist right, (2) a moderate

Orleanist right, and (3) a populist Napoleonic right. Today, these three strands are represented by the (1) National Front (FN), (2) Democratic Movement (*MoDem*, descended from the old UDF), and (3) neo-Gaullists. Farther right, the National Front and other small groups spit venom at immigrants and the European Union.

For the right, ideology and doctrine are less important than personality. Gaullists traditionally have been skeptical of European unity and the free market, while most small centrist parties have been for them. But in speaking to the same middle-class electorate, some of these small parties and the Gaullists often cooperate and agree on a single parliamentary candidate on the first ballot. The neo-Gaullists often attempt a grand merger of smaller parties into their Union for a Popular Movement (UMP), but that is difficult because on the right—and this is true of many countries—personality becomes the dominant issue.

Here, the shadow of de Gaulle still looms, tearing the French right between those who want to keep his image alive and those who favor more-traditional center-right politics. De Gaulle was a Napoleonic figure above parties. Like Franco, Mussolini, and Latin American military dictators, de Gaulle hated parties, blaming their incessant squabbles for all the troubles of the Third and Fourth Republics. De Gaulle did not even much care for the Gaullist party; he never formally headed or endorsed it. The Gaullist party was simply his tool to control the National Assembly. In the legislative elections of 1968, the Gaullists won 46 percent of the popular vote and an outright majority of National Assembly seats.

A single charismatic figure leading a national movement is a tough act to follow. Such a leader does not tolerate other important personalities around him; he prefers obedient servants. As a result, when de Gaulle departed in 1969, he left a vacuum that no one since has filled. His former premier, Georges Pompidou, won the presidency that year, but by the time he died in 1974, the Republican candidate, Valéry Giscard d'Estaing (who later formed the UDF), was more attractive than the Gaullist candidate. De Gaulle had never institutionalized his movement into a durable party. The real genius in politics is one who builds lastingly; de Gaulle did not.

Trying to fill the vacuum, Jacques Chirac in 1976 reorganized the moribund Gaullists into the Rally for the Republic, commonly called "neo-Gaullist." Intelligent but slick, he alienated many French by his high-handedness. Chirac alternately quarreled and made up with the UDF. Pushed into a less-active role when he was forced to cohabit with a Socialist cabinet after the 1997 election, Chirac gave up party leadership. Chirac and his party won in 2002 by default because Socialist Jospin was knocked out in the first round by frivolous left voting. The problem for the Gaullists parallels that of the Socialists: What do we stand for now? Most French now consider Gaullism *passé*, a conservative mood rather than a party.

The neo-Gaullists show that there are several types of conservatism. When Nicolas Sarkozy was interior minister under President Chirac, he fought with Premier Dominique de Villepin. Both were UMP and conservatives, but Sarkozy was pro-market and pro-United States, while de Villepin wanted to preserve the French welfare state and oppose U.S. power. Sarkozy was a more modern, market-oriented conservative, de Villepin a traditional French big-government conservative. Conservatism means different things in different countries.

As on the left, the French electoral system makes rightist parties compete with each other on the first round but ally on the second round. The difference on the right is that it is a struggle between ambitious party leaders who want to be president. If two parties merge, the leader of the smaller party becomes a second fiddle, something most politicians do not accept.

charisma
Pronounced "kar-isma"; Greek for gift; political drawing power.

Events of May
Euphemism for riots and upheaval of May 1968.

In France, everything fragments. One way to cure electoral fragmentation: Drop the first round of elections and go to straight FPTP, U.S. and British style, which would force like-minded parties together. The first round, a kind of primary, may not be necessary. Already, the large UMP and Socialists practice a kind of primary election by having online votes for nominees.

The Stalemate Cycle

French politics runs in a roughly cyclical pattern. "Normal" politics in France leads to a stalemate in which political groups, constantly feuding among themselves, block major change. This paralysis in turn leads to an explosion every generation or two. To get out of the paralysis, the French have repeatedly turned to a hero, a charismatic figure above politics. French politics requires a Napoleon from time to time. France's current stagnant economy with all serious reforms blocked suggests the buildup to another breaking point and another hero. Do not count on a stable France.

After a dozen years of revolutionary turmoil, France welcomed the first Napoleon as a hero to end the chaos. Half a century later, it turned to Louis Napoleon for the same reason. In 1940, the French parliament actually voted dictatorial powers for the aged Marshal Pétain. As the chaotic Fourth Republic faltered, de Gaulle returned in 1958 to save France from civil war over Algeria. None of de Gaulle's successors have had a fraction of his **charisma**.

Political Culture

The Events of May 1968

The right calls it the **Events of May**, the left "the Movement": A month of student and worker strikes and street battles with police revealed that under the law-and-order surface of Gaullist France throbbed the old revolutionary tradition—almost like a scene from *Les Mis*. France's old conservative–radical split had not completely healed; it still ran through French society like a California fault line ready for another earthquake.

Trouble began at the University of Nanterre in a suburb of Paris (later, Sarkozy's university). Students, fed up with bad facilities and curricula, staged a strike that quickly spread to most universities and many factories. France split again, this time largely along age lines; the young were tired of obeying the old. One slogan: "It is forbidden to forbid." The CRS (*Compagnies Républicains de Sécurité*, riot police) waded into groups of protesters with tear gas and truncheons. De Gaulle placed troops and tanks around Paris.

But then the riots burned out, like many previous uprisings in French history. De Gaulle promised more participation and held parliamentary elections in which Gaullists won an actual majority of the National Assembly. "When the French are fearful," noted one French political scientist, "they swing to the right," the tendency in many countries.

Some see recent protests as resurgences of French revolutionary feeling. But 2005 rioting was confined to young Muslim males, alienated from French society, without goals or purposes; some called it simple vandalism. In 2006, students protested against a new employment law. After the 2007 election of Sarkozy, young people rioted and shouted, "Sarko fascist!" In 2009, many French students closed their universities in opposition to Sarkozy's plans to make them competitive and autonomous. The commonality of all these: angry young people marginalized by the system.

De Gaulle believed he had ended France's recurrent stalemates by constructing a Fifth Republic with a strong president. At first it appeared to work. France withdrew from Algeria, streamlined its party system, and surged economically. In 1968, however, all hell broke loose (see box on the "Events of May"), and people began to wonder if the Fifth Republic still had some of the ills that had plagued predecessors.

Mitterrand also discovered that the transformation of French politics was not as complete as de Gaulle believed. De Gaulle's personal popularity ensured not only his election as president but a large Gaullist party in the National Assembly. This made it easy to govern; the Palais Bourbon rubber-stamped any law or budget de Gaulle wanted. The Fifth Republic did not depend on the unstable coalitions of the Third and Fourth. But how much did it depend on the same party maintaining control of both the executive and legislative branches?

France found out in 1986. With the election of a National Assembly dominated by the Republicans and Gaullists, Mitterrand named a conservative as premier but stayed on as president. *Cohabitation* kept the government functioning, but only because Mitterrand let Premier Chirac name ministers and pursue conservative policies. Mitterrand played a waiting game, letting Chirac take the blame for unpopular policies. After some time, when Mitterrand's popularity eclipsed Chirac's, Mitterrand began to oppose some of Chirac's policies. A U.S.-style deadlock emerged as neither the president nor the premier could get his way. Chirac controlled parliament, but Mitterrand could denounce his legislative program and criticize him personally. The second cohabitation period was somewhat more relaxed as Mitterrand, probably aware he was dying, attempted little. In the third cohabitation period, 1997–2002, Chirac named Jospin premier. It worked fairly well, but underneath was a smoldering discontent that gave Le Pen the edge on Jospin in the first round of the 2002 presidential election.

Sarkozy ran and won on a platform of breakthrough, of economic and educational modernization that used more free-market solutions. The 2008–2009 global recession, however, made Sarkozy pull back into the traditional statist mold. Hollande promised a welfarist breakthrough but produced only stagnation and discontent. France, like Japan, always seems ready to change but rarely does, and not by much. Political patterns, once planted, endure.

Referendum Madness

French presidents like plebiscites, or referendums, to pose major questions directly to the people without going through elected representatives in parliament. The referendum, recent and rare in Britain, has been used 20 times since 1793 in France, where it fits Rousseau's idea of the general will. On the surface, it sounds very democratic—the people directly express their wishes.

In reality, plebiscites can be tricky—a manipulative, authoritarian gimmick. The key power in a referendum belongs to the one who writes the question, which can be posed in such a simplified way that almost rigs the vote. Furthermore, a referendum usually comes after the decision has already been made and the leader just wants popular endorsement.

De Gaulle held several plebiscites, not merely to gain mass approval for a given policy but to reinforce his personal rule. After every referendum, he could turn to his old enemies, the traditional politicians, and say, "You see, the people support me. Who needs you?" In French political theory, derived from Rousseau, a nation run by a leader communicating directly with the people—without parties, parliaments, politicians, or interest groups getting in the way—is the ideal democracy. Some, however, see in this model the seeds of dictatorship.

De Gaulle attached his personal prestige to each referendum. "If the nation rejects the measure," he in effect told France, "it also rejects me, and I shall resign." This worked every time until the last. In 1958, people were glad to get a new constitution. In 1961 and 1962, they were delighted to see Algeria become independent and French troops come home. But de Gaulle's second referendum of 1962 raised questions. De Gaulle had made a mistake in the 1958 constitution in having the president chosen by a gigantic electoral college composed of local officeholders, whom he assumed would be conservative and pro-de Gaulle; they were not. So in October 1962, bypassing the National Assembly, he asked the voters to amend the constitution to directly elect the president. The referendum passed with a 62 percent yes vote, but this represented only 46 percent of the total electorate, far less than de Gaulle expected.

The hint was clear—the French were happy to get out of Algeria but not so happy about tinkering with the constitution—but de Gaulle ignored it. In 1969, de Gaulle again sought to demonstrate mass support. He picked a narrow issue that did not require a plebiscite: the reform (that is, weakening) of the Senate and the setting up of regional subunits. The French people said no, and, true to his word, de Gaulle resigned. He went back to the village of Colombey-les-Deux-Eglises, where he died the following year.

Since then, there have been five referendums. In 1972, Pompidou held one on enlarging the Common Market to include Britain, Ireland, and Denmark. Mitterrand's 1988 referendum on granting the Pacific territory of New Caledonia greater independence passed, but with only a 37 percent turnout. In 1992, Mitterrand brought the Europe-unifying Maastricht Treaty before the French electorate, which narrowly endorsed it. A 2000 referendum to cut the presidential term to five years had only a 31 percent turnout. The 2005 French referendum to ratify a new EU constitution failed, humiliating Chirac. In none of these cases were referendums needed to solve a constitutional problem. Rather, presidents tried to use a referendum to bolster mass support and deflect attention away from more serious matters. Voter apathy and negativity suggest that the French have tired of referendums. (Have Californians?)

Fragmented Labor Unions

In Britain, we saw how interest groups were well organized and powerful, especially big labor and big business. This pattern is true of North Europe in general. In France and in Latin Europe, generally, there are plenty of interest groups, but they are usually splintered along party lines.

In Britain (and Germany and Sweden), there is one big labor federation. In France (and Italy and Spain), there are several labor unions—Communist, Socialist, Catholic, and independent unions—competing against each other. The Communist-led CGT (*Confédération Générale du Travail*) is considered powerful in France, but, on a comparative basis, it is weak. Indeed, only 8 percent of the French workforce, mostly in the public sector, is organized into unions; even U.S. unions are proportionally bigger (12 percent of the workforce).

French unions also quarrel among themselves. The CGT has collided angrily with the smaller, Socialist-oriented CFDT (*Confédération Française Démocratique du Travail*) and nonparty *Force Ouvrière*. Labor's voice in France is weak and divided. Accordingly, French unions are strong neither in bargaining with management nor in making an impact on government. There are many strikes in France, but they are short because unions lack strike funds. Transportation workers disrupt rail and subway service every few years.

French unions engage in political strikes, actions aimed at policy rather than bread-and-butter demands. The largest union, the CGT, is led by Communists, so the government ignores their demands. French unions often protest closures or layoffs at state-owned industries, much as in Thatcher's Britain. In 2010, French workers took to the streets to block a government proposal to raise retirement age from 60 to 62. Few French unions take the American view that a union is a device to negotiate better terms with management, not a political tool.

The weakness of French unions makes them more, rather than less, militant and ideological. Feeling that the government ignores them, French workers are more bitter than German or Swedish workers, where strong unions have a voice in government. In those two countries, large and well-organized unions have become moderate and pragmatic.

Medef
French business association.

structured access
Permanent openness of bureaucracy to interest-group demands.

dirigiste
Bureaucrats directing industry; closely connected to French statism.

Business and the Bureaucracy

French business is little more influential than labor. The French Enterprise Movement (*Mouvement des Entreprises de France*, **Medef**) seeks reforms to cut taxes, privatize pensions, and free up labor laws. Only business creates jobs, it argues, a Thatcherite view that is just catching on in France, but Medef does not have much political access. Unlike Americans, most French people see business as callous, exploitive, and inhumane. Few French politicians are openly pro-business the way American politicians are. It would be bad politics in France.

Mitterrand ignored business interests to pursue a leftist economic program, so French businesses cut investment in France and increased it in the United States. Mitterrand backed off. Premier and later President Chirac privatized large sections of France's nationalized industries, including a state-owned television network, but never endorsed a free-market society. Socialist Jospin continued privatization but talked about worker rights. Sarkozy talked about "economic patriotism" rather than a free economy. Hollande sought the old socialist remedies of a bigger state and massive taxes on the rich, but. like Mitterrand 30 years earlier, had to back off.

Medef is not as influential as the CBI in Britain because of French individualism. A French firm prefers to work alone with discreet contacts with the bureaucracy. One business advantage: Many French executives and high civil servants are graduates of the same *grande école* and move back and forth between top jobs in government and industry. This gives France's major firms **structured access** to the machinery of administration, something small-business people, farmers, and labor unionists do not enjoy. It also builds up bitterness and frustration in the latter groups that explode from time to time in angry parties such as the National Front, in produce dumping by farmers, and in wildcat strikes. The political-bureaucratic systems of North Europe, by providing access for all major groups, generally avoid such outbursts.

French business has little influence on policy. Unlike Anglo-American pluralism, French political theory still follows Rousseau's notion that interest groups are immoral—because they represent partial wills rather than the general will—and views such groups as illegitimate. The French tradition is **dirigiste**, from the top down, ignoring interest-group demands

Comparison

The Rise of Europe's Angry Right

For some years, most European lands have had angry rightist parties led by charismatic speakers, such as France's National Front, Austria's Freedom Party, Germany's National Democrats, Netherlands' Party for Freedom, and Italy's Northern League. While they differ on some issues, all are anti-immigrant, anti-crime, and anti-EU and draw 15 to 20 percent of the vote.

Some call them fascist, but they deny it and are probably not. Rather, they voice voter concerns that conventional politicians ignored for years. Many Europeans really do not like Muslim immigrants and "multiculturalism." Mainstream politicians have been too politically correct to talk about this. Likewise, European elites have almost reflexively favored the EU even though many ordinary citizens fear the loss

of their countries' sovereignty, culture, and jobs in a united Europe. Anti-immigrant politicians simply filled the gap left by the conventional politicians. This is also happening inside the U.S. Republican Party.

Is this a threat to European democracy, or is it democracy in action? If one party does not give voters what they want, another party will. In any country, a certain percentage of disgruntled citizens is receptive to the simplified arguments of populist demagogues. America has its share but has some advantages: (1) Americans are used to immigrants from all continents, and (2) many of the alienated Americans do not vote. (Perhaps we should be grateful for our low electoral turnout.)

and doing what civil servants deem best for French power and prestige. This gives great power to bureaucrats.

Government by Bureaucracy

France has been developing its bureaucracy for five centuries. Almost every change of regime has led to growth in the number (now five million) and functions of French bureaucrats. During the revolving-door cabinets of the Fourth Republic, people used to say that the fall of governments did not really matter because the bureaucracy ran the country. Tocqueville recognized the problem in 1856, when he complained that France's administration regulates too much, as if it is in charge of everything. The same charge holds true today.

Civil servants oversee most of the French economy, leading to lack of competition. Japanese bureaucrats are a close comparison. France has several nationalized industries—aircraft, automobiles, coal mines, banks, steel, gas, and electricity—in addition to the areas that are state run throughout Europe, such as the PTT (post, telephone, and telegraph) and the railroads. Workers in these industries are not civil servants, but top management people are. Every French teacher, from kindergarten to university, is a civil servant.

The top civil servants are the several thousand who staff the Paris ministries, the **Grands Corps**, most of whom are graduates of one of the Great Schools. Even more powerful than their British counterparts, French civil servants of the administrative class (about the top 20 percent) run France. If anything, bureaucratic power grew with the Fifth Republic, for de Gaulle hamstrung the National Assembly so it provided no policy counterweight to, or check on, the

Grands Corps
Top bureaucrats of France.

administrative class. By long French tradition, many politicians were themselves civil servants, often graduates of the ENA or of another

Comparison

"Putting on the Slippers"

The movement of top French civil servants to the executive suites of industries is called *pantouflage*, or "putting on the slippers." Japan has the exact same pattern, called "descent from heaven." In France, a graduate of the *Ecole Polytechnique* or the ENA, after a few years in a Paris ministry, can slip into a cushy, high-paying management job, often in a firm he or she used to deal with as an official. Half the chief executives of France's 40 largest firms are graduates of the ENA or X, and most have been civil servants. *Pantouflage* is an important connecting link between French business and bureaucracy. It also invites corruption, which seems endemic in France. Several top French administrators have been caught using business connections to supplement their income.

grande école. Many ministers and National Assembly deputies are civil servants, leading to government of the bureaucrats, by the bureaucrats, and for the bureaucrats.

French bureaucrats often do their jobs well, but their bureaucratic attitude alienates their countrymen: aloof, arrogant, cold, logical, and rigid. They do interact with representatives of business, labor, and farming citizens on thousands of committees and councils. The highest of these is the national Social and Economic Council, but many of its members are named by the government, and its advice is usually ignored as "unobjective." The French bureaucratic approach is called **tutelle**, for they act more as tutors than as servants of the public.

The real elite running France is the *Inspection Générale des Finances* (IGF). Selected from among the top ten ENA graduates each year, the superbright *inspecteurs des finances* snoop all around France to see how public funds are spent. The rest of the government fears them. Few countries have the precise equivalent of the **Inspection**. It would be as if the U.S. Government Accountability Office (GAO), a branch of Congress, had the enforcement powers of the FBI. *Inspecteurs* of all ranks and ages agree to always see each other. Inspectors who "put on the slippers" (see box) still have clout, as they offer each other the best public and private jobs. And if they tire of these, they can return to the IGF at a top salary.

The civil service in France is powerful and uncontrolled by elected officials, who sometimes denounce the bureaucracy as an "administrative labyrinth" or even as "administrative totalitarianism." But they can do little about it. We should not think France is unique in this regard, for no country has devised a way to fully control its bureaucracy. France, with more and longer bureaucratization, merely reveals the pattern more fully. In Japan, it reaches a high point. Almost every effort to reform, trim, or democratize bureaucracy entails adding *more* bureaucrats. In France, Mitterrand introduced a ministry for the reform of administration—another layer of bureaucracy.

We can see here why the French people, faced with an unresponsive, undemocratic bureaucratic maze, turn frustrated and bitter. Where bureaucracy thrives, democracy shrivels. In trying to fix this, France's top politicians step into a contradiction. Modern states need lots of bureaucracy—to run welfare programs, supervise industry, and plan the economy. Privatization means loosening bureaucratic controls

tutelle
French for tutelage; bureaucratic guidance.

Inspection
Short for General Finance Inspection; very top of French bureaucracy, with powers to investigate all branches.

and letting market forces guide society. Most mainstream French politicians oppose this, for it would mean turning away from what they regard as the humane French model of the welfare state and toward a savage "Anglo-Saxon" market system. Again, France is stuck.

What the French Quarrel About

3.5   Establish why French unemployment stays so high for so long.

The Political Economy of France

The French economy, which had grown only slowly in the nineteenth and early twentieth centuries, awoke as if from a slumber after World War II with growth rates reaching 6 percent a year. The French still remember the period of 1945–1975 as *les trentes glorieuses* (the 30 glorious years), something true of several countries, including the United States, Germany, and Japan. After that, however, French growth slowed and unemployment climbed. Much of France's industry is uncompetitive, saddled with high *unit labor costs*. Most French know their country is in economic decline, but few are willing to suffer the temporary pain of reforms, and no French leaders are willing to carry them out. France has no equivalent to Britain's Margaret Thatcher or Germany's Gerhard Schröder, who cut the welfare state and made the workforce more flexible, painful reforms that worked. Hollande's minor reform for labor flexibility in 2013 split his Socialist Party. Without serious reforms, many now foresee a grim future for the French economy.

What invigorated France after World War II? The typical French business was a small family affair that emphasized keeping it in the family and earning a good living, not growth. This meant lots of little firms. Rather than compete, the French **petit bourgeois** sought state protection to set prices and keep out foreign competition by high tariffs. This cozy arrangement held back France's economy.

The French elite, smarting from German conquest and eager to restore France to world leadership, planned for growth. A Planning Commission provided economic research and incentives for **indicative planning** to encourage—but not force, Communist style—French businesses to expand in certain sectors and regions. (Japan's MITI did this even more.) Foreign competition also motivated the French economy, first the European Coal and Steel Community (ECSC) in 1952, then the Common Market in 1957, which dismantled France's protective tariffs. At first, French businesses feared more-efficient German industry, but French firms learned to compete and gained major sales in the Common Market. French business firms changed, becoming bigger, more modern, and expansion-oriented. But success brought its own problems.

Big Guys versus Little Guys

petit bourgeois
Small shopkeeper.

indicative planning
Government suggestions to industry to expand in certain areas.

France's myriad neighborhood shops, during the 1950s, faced brutal competition from supermarkets and department stores that forced out many small shops. Some call this capitalism run amok or the Americanization of France, but it is just the modernization of an old-fashioned economy. France also had too many small farms; it remained a nation of peasants unusually long. A third of the French workforce was still in agriculture at the end of World War II. Since 1950, over three-fourths of France's farms, mostly small, have disappeared. Now French agriculture, efficient and mechanized, overproduces, and French farmers often dump produce on highways to protest prices below production costs. France is the world's second-largest food exporter (first place: the United States) and the EU's largest food producer. One French idea: Instead of subsidizing farmers to produce more than is needed, pay them to look after the environment.

flash party
One that quickly rises and falls.

protectionism
Keeping out imports via tariffs and regulations in order to help domestic producers.

The small shopkeepers and farmers who get squeezed out are angry and contribute to France's electoral volatility. They shift allegiances rapidly to whoever promises their survival. The Gaullists have been a major beneficiary, but some votes go to extremist parties. There is no nice solution to the problem of too many small shops and farms. Attempts to retain them are hopeless and reactionary, the stuff of demagoguery. (How do U.S. communities react to a proposed Wal-Mart?)

In 1953, Pierre Poujade founded the Union for the Defense of Shopkeepers and Artisans (UDCA) to protect small-business people. Tinged with reaction and anti-Semitism, Poujadism caught fire and, in the parliamentary elections of 1956, won 12 percent of the popular vote; some thought it was the coming party. It turned out to be a **flash party**, however; Poujadism disappeared in 1958 when de Gaulle took over the French right. Le Pen was a Poujadist and, some say, continued its views in his National Front.

Comparison

European and U.S. Attitudes on the State

France, like most of Europe, approves of a more powerful and expensive welfare state than Americans do. The French constitution promises a "decent means of existence." French welfare recipients get about 50 percent more than their U.S. counterparts. Few French like capitalism, and most do not mind state ownership of industry.

Starting far back in the Old Regime, *étatisme* (statism) became part of French political culture. Also early, some French thinkers recognized that it was bad economics. France coined the term *laissez-faire* ("leave us be"). The French Physiocrats in the eighteenth century invented the free-market argument and profoundly influenced Adam Smith. In the mid-nineteenth century, French economist Frédéric Bastiat ridiculed trade **protectionism** by suggesting Paris protect French candlemakers from "the ruinous competition of a foreign rival"—the sun.

There is a major U.S.–EU cultural difference on welfare and state ownership. Many European politicians, especially leftists, attack capitalism. "We will not become like the cruel U.S. economy," they say (not noticing France's large Muslim underclass). Few French share the American view that capitalism is basically a good thing, flexible and competitive with opportunities for all, where achievement is up to individuals. Seymour Martin Lipset defined the American ethos as "competitive individualism." Europeans value solidarity: Society as a whole should look out for its weakest members. This is especially strong in French political culture and resists change.

conservatism
Desire to preserve or return to old ways.

The Privatization Question

For much of the postwar period, one-fourth of French business and industry was state-owned, more than any other West European country. Now, after major privatization programs, 22 percent of the French workforce is still in the public sector, among the highest in Europe. In addition, the French government has majority ownership of some 1,500 private-sector businesses. Some industries, such as telecoms and railways, were always state-owned in Europe. Some, such as cars and steel, were taken over to keep them from closing and creating unemployment. High-tech areas, such as aircraft, nuclear power, and computers, are state-owned prestige industries that boost France's world standing.

Traditionally, the French left demanded more nationalization, including all big banks and industries. They argued that under state control, big industries would pay workers fairly, hire more people, and produce what French people really need rather than capitalist luxuries. Traditionally, much of the French right also liked state-owned industries, believing that they contributed to national greatness and were best run by brilliant *xiens* and *énarques*. De Gaulle supported a major state sector in heavy and high-tech industry. Remember, **conservatism** in Europe is not the same as conservatism in America. In recent elections, no party has run as free marketeers.

Waves of privatization and deregulation by both left and right governments roll in about every two decades but then roll back, leaving France still with too much state ownership, too many controls, and too many rules. French leaders flinch at privatization in fear of making unemployment, already high, any worse. French public-sector unions demonstrate against

Comparison

European and U.S. Conservatism

Conservatism in Europe is not the same as in the United States. For Europeans, U.S.-style conservatism is not conservatism at all; it is the classic *liberalism* of Adam Smith: little government and a free market. European conservatism likes strong states to supervise the economy for the sake of national power. They like strong leaders and see nothing wrong with statism and the welfare state. Prime examples: de Gaulle and the Gaullists.

Gradually, however, U.S.-style conservatism took hold in European conservative parties, spurred by intellectuals who saw that defending old class privileges and uncompetitive, state-owned industries retards growth and job creation. They called the movement "neo-liberalism," a revival and updating of Adam Smith. Prime examples: Margaret Thatcher and the Tory "dries." The movement appeared in France with Premier Raymond Barre's efforts in the late 1970s to liberalize the French economy. Even the Socialists realized in the early 1980s that state ownership of industry was a problem. Sarkozy mentioned neoliberal economics but did not deliver. France has privatized much industry but rejects a U.S.-style free market because the French have a cultural block against what they call "savage liberalism." A 2010 poll found that 65 percent of Chinese said capitalism works well and should be kept, compared with 55 percent of Americans, 45 percent of Britons and Germans, and only 15 percent of French.

privatization, which would end their high pay and early retirements. One plus of still having plenty of government regulation: France (and Germany) is careful about loans to home buyers and so did not suffer the property boom and bust the United States did.

Giscard d'Estaing's center-right government in the 1970s had the strongest commitment to privatization, but the pain of change led to the Socialist victory of 1981. Good economics is sometimes bad politics. But, as Mitterrand discovered, good politics is sometimes bad economics. Generous policies on welfare, wages, and benefits brought inflation, stagnation, and higher unemployment. The Socialists nationalized several large firms and banks but discovered that they lost money. In 1983, Mitterrand reversed course in favor of private business and a market economy. "You do not want more state?" asked Mitterrand. "Me neither." (Compare with Clinton: "The era of big government is over.") Hollande duplicated Mitterrand's turnaround.

Believers in socialism retreated in the 1980s; some abandoned leftism. Chirac reoriented the Gaullists toward privatization of state-owned industry. Much was sold, but unemployment was so huge that it led to the Socialists' 1997 parliamentary election victory. Jospin promised to slow or reverse privatization, but in practice, he sold more French state-owned enterprises than all five of his immediate predecessors put together, never using the word "privatization," for that is an Anglo-Saxon policy. President Sarkozy, who initially favored a vigorous market economy, in the face of the 2008 financial meltdown, backed away from free-market reforms, proclaiming, "The state must absolutely intervene, impose rules, and invest." (Note how U.S. Presidents Bush and Obama did the same but phrased it in reluctant terms to fit America's anti-statism.)

Unemployment: The Giant Problem

Unemployment in France (and West Europe generally) has long been high and seemingly incurable, at times twice the U.S. level. French unemployment topped 11 percent in 2013, a postwar high. And Europe's high unemployment has occurred when, for the most part, its economies were growing. Many believe the key problem is European **labor-force rigidities**, related to West Europe's generous welfare and unemployment benefits, which discourage the unemployed from seeking new jobs. Wages and **social costs** are so high that European firms are reluctant to hire new workers. A French employer pays almost half as much in taxes as in wages. Some 40 deductions must be enumerated on French pay stubs. Laws in most of Europe prevent easy layoffs by requiring hefty severance pay.

Hence, the reluctance of French firms to hire: It is too expensive, involves much red tape, and they may not be able to let workers go in a downturn. The solution for business-people: Either (1) do not hire anyone, (2) hire on the **informal economy**, or (3) set up shop in another country. French businesses do all three. Europe's high off-the-books workforce indicates an economy choked with taxes and controls. In France, as in all of Europe, the working class generally votes left to protect jobs and wages—even when protection creates inefficiencies and unemployment—while managers press to roll back restrictions and free up the labor market. The U.S. labor force is much more flexible; wages and social costs are

labor-force rigidities
Unwillingness of workers to take or change jobs.

social costs
Taxes for medical, unemployment, and pension benefits.

informal economy
Off-the-books transactions to avoid taxes and regulations.

low, and hiring and layoffs are easy. Result: The U.S. economy creates more jobs, something Europeans envy.

High French unemployment also puts a brake on further privatization. One-fifth of French workers are in the public sector, compared with one-seventh in the United States and Britain and one-sixth in Germany. (Those figures are not just "bureaucrats" but anyone who works for any form or level of government, including military personnel, police, and schoolteachers.) French public-sector workers enjoy job security plus good pay, benefits, and retirement plans. Their unions stage strikes over any efforts to trim these bounties, and Paris usually backs down, a pattern shared by other statist systems. Paris faces strikes by public-sector unions over their lush retirement benefits that permit them to retire young on full pensions. (Is this a problem in U.S. states?)

Another contributor to high unemployment: the euro. To join Europe's single-currency club, France was supposed to bring its budget deficit down to 3 percent of GDP and maintain a *franc fort* (strong franc). Britain said to hell with the euro and dropped out of the European Monetary Union (EMU), but Chirac was determined, partly for reasons of prestige, to stay in, whatever the domestic economic costs. Many consider *austerity* foolishly rigid and the chief cause of high unemployment that costs incumbents reelection. Many European countries exceed the 3 percent deficit limit to hold down unemployment and do not apologize. The EMU does not get them reelected; their voters do.

Comparison

Nuclear Power à la Française

The French complain and quarrel about many things, but nuclear energy is not one of them. Most French accept nuclear energy, and none of the major parties is against it. The French, short of other energy sources, have gone all out for nuclear power. France has 59 nuclear power stations that produce 75 percent of its electricity, compared with 29 percent in Japan, 26 percent in Germany, 18 percent in Britain, 20 percent in the United States, 3 percent in India, and 2 percent in China. French nuclear-generated electricity costs less than half of America's, and France builds reactors for a fraction of U.S. costs. Responding to environmentalists, in 2012, Hollande said he would cut French dependence on nuclear power to 50 percent; he didn't.

Here we see some of the occasional advantages of centralized, technocratic rule. Electricité de France, the state-owned utility, developed a single type of reactor and stuck with it. Competing U.S. manufacturers proffered a variety of designs, some not well tested. When Paris gives the word to build a reactor, the political, financial, regulatory, and managerial sectors mesh under central direction, and the project gets done on time. In the United States, those sectors quarrel and have no central guidance, and the project takes years longer than it should. Environmentalist groups in France—not very big or powerful—have no legal power to block or delay projects. Nuclear power plants are an important part of France's export trade. The very strengths of the American system—decentralization, competition, light regulation, and pluralist interplay—have tripped up the U.S. nuclear industry.

How to cure unemployment? All incoming French governments swear it is their top priority, but most are voted out, in part, because they fail to dent the problem. The Jospin government's bright idea originated in Germany: France cut its work week from 39 to 35 hours without cuts in pay on the theory that firms would hire more workers. It did not help; the law simply forced firms to become more efficient and raise labor productivity. France thus stumbled into the paradox that higher productivity means fewer workers.

Youth unemployment in France is especially high, the result of a too-high minimum wage and education that leaves many unskilled. France tried to end laws that keep firms from easily hiring and firing with a 2006 proposal that would have allowed workers under age 26 to be let go within their first two years on a job. Most French opposed the move, and young people protested in the streets, so the government dropped the plan. The French, like many Europeans, have difficulty understanding that making it hard to let workers go means firms hire few new workers even in good times; they fear getting stuck with them in slack times. America's easy-hire, easy-fire policy contributes to labor-force flexibility and U.S. job growth.

President Sarkozy got new laws that bypassed the 35-hour work week by taxing overtime pay more lightly—"Work more to earn more"—and letting firms negotiate hours with employees. Unemployment benefits can now end if recipients reject job offers. The Socialists and trade unions opposed the changes, and Hollande pledged to reverse them. Little came of these minor reforms. As the global economic downturn increased French unemployment, both Sarkozy and Hollande reacted with the usual French statist remedies, and no major political party offered any alternatives. No one has come up with a legislative cure for unemployment.

Geography

The Geography of Migration

The Third World is trying to get into the First. The reason: economic opportunities. Pakistanis in Britain, Algerians in France, Turks in Germany, and Mexicans in the United States indicate the same problem: not enough jobs in the home country. Japan tries to block foreign job seekers, but even there, one finds Filipino, Thai, Sri Lankan, and other workers. There is one place where you can walk from the Third World into the First: the Mexico-U.S. border. In a kind of osmosis, migrants are drawn through a membrane (border) by the pressure of unemployment.

But is this a problem? From a purely economic standpoint, no. The immigrants take jobs local people shun in favor of welfare. And the rich countries have few babies and many retirees. Without immigrants, there would be too few workers to pay for the oldsters' pensions. Part of the problem is that immigrants preserve their old cultures in the new country. In France, discrimination and limited schooling mean immigrants and their children do not master French, gain few job skills, and become ghettoized. This, in turn, fuels resentment against immigrants and has led to the British and French National Fronts and the German National Democrats. Close parallel: some western U.S. Republicans who rail against illegal immigrants.

Muslim
Follower of Islam; also adjective
of *Islam*.

France's Racial Problems

France has more **Muslim** immigrants than Britain and Germany. Now numbering between five and six million, perhaps 9 percent of France's population, most are from former French colonies in West and North Africa. They flee misery and unemployment to take the hardest, dirtiest, lowest-paid work in France, but many are still unemployed, especially young people. Most are now French citizens and live in shabby high-rise public housing.

Most French say there are too many Muslims in France, and some want them sent home, which the National Front advocates. All of France's main parties are against any more newcomers, so that now (legal), immigration is as tight as in Britain, and France turns away hundreds of thousands of desperate refugees each year. Said Sarkozy (whose father fled Hungary): "France needs immigrants, but France cannot and should not welcome *all* immigrants."

The French republican ideal posits a single French identity without subgroups. France has no affirmative action and does not even collect official data on racial, religious, and ethnic groups the way the U.S. Census does. France now has millions of citizens of color who are treated as permanent foreigners.

France now has angry Muslim youths who look a lot like the black underclass of U.S. ghettoes. Often from broken homes, they slide into unemployment, gangs, drugs, and petty crime, a few into Islamic extremism. The police harass them, and they hate the police. In 2005, young males, mostly Muslim, rioted for three weeks across France and burned more than 8,000 cars. Tough police methods and a curfew finally quelled the riots. Then-Interior Minister Sarkozy, in charge of France's police, called the rioters "scum" and vowed to "clean out" their neighborhoods. Most French agreed, but few said so openly. Riots break out every few years, and Hollande did not touch the problem.

A running issue was Muslim female attire. Many Muslim girls wore the traditional *hijab* (headscarf), required by their religion, in school. France, intent on keeping religion out of schools, outlawed it in 2004. Fearing an influx of Muslim extremism, in 2011, France outlawed the *niqab* or *burqa*, the head-to-toe garment worn by devout Muslim women, and most French agreed, although some Muslims protested. Thundered one *imam* (Muslim cleric): "Allah's law takes precedence over French law." The French deported him, as they do any Muslin preacher who advocates *jihad.* A 1996 French law lets judges detain people for "association with wrongdoers involved in a terrorist enterprise." Faced with terrorism, the French pay less heed to human rights than do the British or Germans. After 9/11 and the London bombings, the United States and Britain moved closer to the French zero tolerance position.

Most French politicians agree that the immigrants should integrate into French economic and cultural life, but they disagree on how. Improving immigrant housing, schooling, and jobs all cost money. The tax burden falls most heavily on the municipalities where there are the most immigrants, one reason the National Front vote is the strongest where there are more Muslims. The Socialist and other left parties are willing to spend more. Trying to

Comparison

Is There a VAT in Our Future?

European governments raise some 30 percent of their revenues through hefty (10 to 20 percent) **value-added taxes (VAT)**. In contrast, U.S. sales taxes at the state level average around 6 percent and altogether make up only 15 percent of all U.S. taxes. But European VATs are invisible; they are calculated at every stage where value is added to a product (as when pieces of cloth are sewn together to make a shirt), not added to the purchase price at the cash register, as in America. Accordingly, European governments reason that it is less painful. Washington, faced with budget deficits, sometimes talks about a "consumption tax" or "national sales tax," in effect a VAT, because they are reluctant to raise income taxes on average citizens.

curb radical tendencies and encourage dialogue, Paris, in 2003, created the French Council of the Muslim Faith. The racial gap heals briefly when Muslim players win soccer games for France.

France and Europe

Unlike Britain, France took the lead to build a united Europe. Indeed, the idea originated with two French officials, Jean Monnet and Robert Schuman, after World War II. France was one of the original six of the ECSC and then of the Common Market. Members cut tariffs with each other and let in workers from member countries. The Market's invigorating effects boosted French economic growth. The EU's **Common Agricultural Program (CAP)** eats 40 percent of the EU budget, and French farmers are the biggest beneficiaries. French farmers like this; German and Dutch taxpayers do not.

French voters rejected a new EU constitution 55 to 45 percent in 2005, showing their displeasure with the elites who run France and the EU. A 2013 Pew poll found only 41 percent of French favored the EU (compared to 60 percent of Germans and 43 percent of Britons). Most French leaders favor European unification, partly because they see France leading a united Europe, but they disagree on what kind of a Europe they want. Not all want a full federation, for that would blot out French sovereignty. Charles de Gaulle voiced this in the 1960s when he spoke of a *Europe des patries* ("Europe of fatherlands," later the view of Britain's Margaret Thatcher). This is especially true as unified Germany becomes Europe's leader, not France. And how big should the EU be? Should it include Turkey? The farther eastward the EU expands, the more it makes Germany its natural hub, something many French oppose. Since German unification in 1871—after it beat France—France has worried about its large, powerful neighbor to the east that now hectors France to stick with austerity. France and Germany are the twin pillars of the EU, but unless France gets its financial house in order, some warn, the entire eurozone could collapse.

value-added taxes (VAT)
Large, hidden national sales taxes used throughout Europe.

Common Agricultural Program (CAP)
EU farm subsidies, the biggest part of the EU budget.

Comparison

Medical Care and Costs

France delivers some of the world's best medical care at moderate cost, the World Health Organization concluded in a 2000 study—the first to compare medical delivery worldwide, and one so controversial it has not been updated. The Japanese are the healthiest people in the world (probably related to diet) and spend less, but those are indications of health, not of medical care.

Worldwide, medical costs increased from 3 percent of gross world product in 1948 to 9.7 in 2007. Americans spend by far the most on medical care but are less healthy than many who spend less (again, diet). The United States does little to hold down costs, so insurance struggles to keep up with high-tech care and new, costlier drugs. Most of Europe has nationwide insurance (usually a mix of public and private) that covers everyone and caps costs. But Europeans pay in other ways, through long waits and not-so-high-tech treatment: de facto rationing. Will the new U.S. health care reform hold down soaring medical costs?

	WHO Ranking 2000	Health Expenditures per Person 2009	Percentage of GDP 2010
France	1	$4,840	11.9
Japan	10	3,754	9.5
Britain	18	3,440	9.6
Germany	25	4,723	11.6
United States	37	7,960	17.9
Mexico	61	525	6.3
Iran	93	287	5.6
India	112	44	4.1
Brazil	125	734	9.0
Russia	130	476	5.1
China	144	191	5.1
Nigeria	187	67	5.1

SOURCE: World Health Organization, CIA World Factbook

Review Questions

Learning Objective 3.1 Explain the French pattern of revolution leading to tyranny, p. 75.

1. How does French history illustrate *absolutism*?
2. What is a *core* area? Give examples.
3. What could the French Revolution teach China about democracy?

Learning Objective 3.2 Contrast the French semipresidential system with the U.S. presidential system, p. 86.

4. What is France's *semipresidential* system?
5. What are France's main political parties?
6. Explain France's *unitary* system. How has it decentralized?

Learning Objective 3.3 Describe the split nature of French political culture, p. 97.

7. In what countries has *anticlericalism* developed? Why?

8. What is "enarchy" and why does it persist in France?

9. What do the French think of America? Which French?

Learning Objective 3.4 Illustrate how referendums sound democratic but often are not, p. 106.

10. Could France experience upheaval again? Why?

11. Why are *referendums* part of French tradition but not of British?

12. Explain Europe's angry right. What are they angry about?

Learning Objective 3.5 Establish why French unemployment stays so high for so long, p. 116.

13. Contrast U.S. with French attitudes toward capitalism.

14. How would you cure high French unemployment?

15. Compare U.S. and French attitudes toward immigrants.

Key Terms

alienated, p. 82
Allies, p. 85
ancien régime, p. 80
aristocrat, p. 77
baccalauréat, p. 101
Bastille, p. 80
Bourbon, p. 82
bourgeois, p. 83
bureaucratized, p. 99
Cartesian, p. 79
censure, p. 93
chauvinism, p. 81
coalition, p. 87
cohabitation, p. 89
Common Agricultural Program (CAP), p. 123
compartmentalization, p. 104
conservatism, p. 118
constitutional monarchy, p. 80
core, p. 78
coup d'état, p. 81
deadlock, p. 87
decolonization, p. 85
département, p. 96
deputy, p. 92
dirigiste, p. 113
Ecole Nationale d'Administration (ENA), p. 102

Elysée, p. 88
Enlightenment, p. 79
Estates-General, p. 77
Eurocommunism, p. 108
Events of May, p. 110
first-order civil division, p. 95
flash party, p. 117
Free French, p. 85
general will, p. 79
grande école, p. 102
Grands Corps, p. 114
Han, p. 78
ideal–typical, p. 104
immobilisme, p. 85
indicative planning, p. 116
informal economy, p. 119
Inspection, p. 115
intendants, p. 77
interior ministry, p. 92
labor-force rigidities, p. 119
"La Marseillaise", p. 99
lycée, p. 101
Maginot Line, p. 84
Medef, p. 113
Midi, p. 95
Muslim, p. 122
National Assembly, p. 80
National Front, p. 94
neo-Gaullist, p. 89

Palais Bourbon, p. 93
Paris Commune, p. 83
particularism, p. 78
petit bourgeois, p. 116
plebiscite, p. 81
Popular Front, p. 84
prefect, p. 95
premier, p. 86
president, p. 86
privatism, p. 100
protectionism, p. 117
reactionary, p. 83
Reign of Terror, p. 81
Résistance, p. 84
semipresidential, p. 88
social costs, p. 119
Stalinist, p. 108
statism, p. 99
structured access, p. 113
technocrat, p. 92
Thermidor, p. 82
turnout, p. 90
tutelle, p. 115
unitary, p. 95
value-added taxes (VAT), p. 123
Versailles, p. 77
Vichy, p. 84
volatile, p. 106
Zionism, p. 85

Further Reference

Begley, Louis. *Why the Dreyfus Affair Matters.* New Haven, CT: Yale University Press, 2010.

Berenson, Edward, Vincent Duclert, and Christopher Prochasson, eds. *The French Republic: History, Values, Debates.* Ithaca, NY: Cornell University Press, 2011.

Bowen, John. *Can Islam Be French? Pluralism and Pragmatism in a Secularist Society.* Princeton, NJ: Princeton University Press, 2009.

Cobb, Matthew. *The Resistance: The French Fight against the Nazis.* New York: Simon & Schuster, 2010.

Evans, Martin. *Algeria: France's Undeclared War.* New York: Oxford University Press, 2011.

Hazareesingh, Sudhir. *In the Shadow of the General: Modern France and the Myth of de Gaulle.* New York: Oxford University Press, 2012.

Judt, Tony. *Past Imperfect: French Intellectuals, 1944–1956.* Berkeley, CA: University of California Press, 1993.

Levy, Jonah D. *Tocqueville's Revenge: State, Society, and Economy in Contemporary France.* Cambridge, MA: Harvard University Press, 1999.

Miller, Mary Ashburn. *A Natural History of Revolution: Violence and Nature in the French Revolutionary Imagination, 1789–1794.* Ithaca, NY: Cornell University Press, 2011.

Robb, Graham. *The Discovery of France: A Historical Geography from the Revolution to the First World War.* New York: Norton, 2007.

Roger, Philippe. *The American Enemy: The History of French Anti-Americanism.* Chicago: University of Chicago Press, 2005.

Sa'adah, Anne. *Contemporary France: A Democratic Education.* Lanham, MD: Rowman & Littlefield, 2003.

Schama, Simon. *Citizens: A Chronicle of the French Revolution.* New York: Knopf, 1989.

Shields, James. *The Extreme Right in France: From Pétain to Le Pen.* New York: Routledge, 2007.

Short, Philip. *A Taste for Intrigue: The Multiple Lives of François Mitterrand.* New York: Holt, 2014.

Smith, Timothy B. *France in Crisis: Welfare, Inequality, and Globalization since 1980.* New York: Cambridge University Press, 2005.

Stone, Alec. *The Birth of Judicial Review in France: The Constitutional Council in Comparative Perspective.* New York: Oxford University Press, 1992.

Weil, Patrick. *How to Be French: Nationality in the Making since 1789.* Durham, NC: Duke University Press, 2008.

Chapter 4
Germany

Berlin's Kaiser Wilhelm Memorial Church is left ruined as a reminder of World War II.

Learning Objectives

4.1 Contrast Germany's political development with those of Britain and France.

4.2 Characterize the German voting system.

4.3 Explain how Germany's past lingers in current politics.

4.4 Explain why a center-peaked unimodal distribution of political values is necessary to sustain democracy.

4.5 Compare Germany's and Japan's postwar economic recoveries.

WHY GERMANY MATTERS

Germany is probably the European country that offers the most lessons for political scientists. We learn how, depending on circumstances, democracy can fail or work. We see that borders can be artificial. Germany's late unification and subsequent plunge into lunatic nationalism teach us what can go wrong in the construction and stabilization of a new country. West Germany's postwar recovery teaches us what sound economic policy can do. Bonn's postwar constitution shows that with a few deft reforms—a hybrid voting system, constructive no-confidence, and a two-plus party system—an unstable country can become a stable democracy. Germany's electoral system—where voters pick one party plus one individual—is especially instructive in exploring the advantages and disadvantages of single-member districts and proportional representation, and how it is possible to combine the two. And Germany's recent reunification shows how expensive it is to combine two very different systems. (Koreans, take note.)

Impact of the Past

4.1 **Contrast Germany's political development with those of Britain and France.**

Germany has natural borders only on its north and south (the Baltic Sea and Alps), a fact that contributed to its tumultuous history. Germany has expanded and contracted over the centuries, at times stretching from Alsace (now French) to East Prussia (now Polish and Russian). After World War II, its eastern wing was chopped off, and the country was divided into eastern and western occupation zones, which, in 1949, became East and West Germany. The two reunified in 1990, but Germany is smaller than the Second Reich before World War I.

Germany's location in the center of Europe and the flat, defenseless North European Plain imposed two unhappy options. When Germany was divided and militarily weak—its condition for most of its history—it was Europe's battleground. But when Germany united, it dominated Europe; it was big, populous, and strategically located. Some Europeans still fear a united Germany. As in most of Europe, Celts, several Germanic tribes, Huns, Romans, Slavs, and Jews made Germans a highly mixed people, contrary to Nazi race theory.

Germany

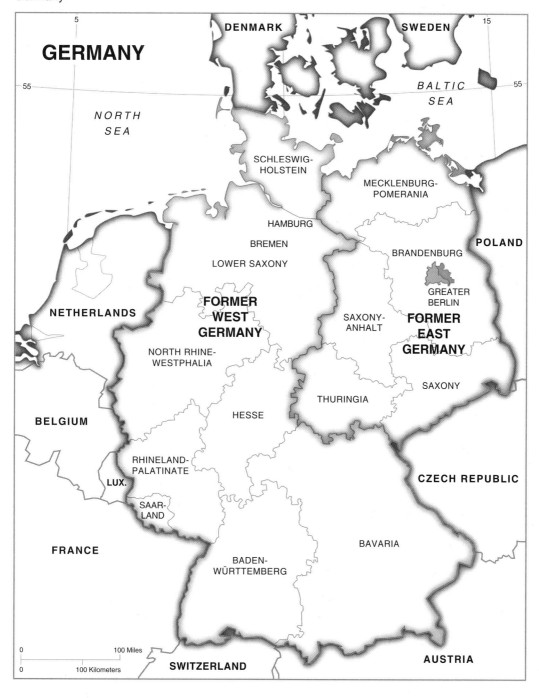

GERMANY

DENMARK

SWEDEN

BALTIC SEA

NORTH SEA

SCHLESWIG-HOLSTEIN

MECKLENBURG-POMERANIA

HAMBURG

BREMEN

BRANDENBURG

POLAND

LOWER SAXONY

GREATER BERLIN

NETHERLANDS

FORMER WEST GERMANY

NORTH RHINE-WESTPHALIA

SAXONY-ANHALT

FORMER EAST GERMANY

BELGIUM

HESSE

THURINGIA

SAXONY

RHINELAND-PALATINATE

LUX.

SAAR-LAND

CZECH REPUBLIC

FRANCE

BAVARIA

BADEN-WÜRTTEMBERG

0   100 Miles

0   100 Kilometers

SWITZERLAND

AUSTRIA

Fragmented Germany

Germanic tribes helped destroy the overextended Roman Empire, but, in 800, the Frankish king Charlemagne (German: Karl der Grosse) was crowned in Rome and called his huge realm the Holy Roman Empire (which, Voltaire later quipped, was "neither holy, nor Roman, nor an empire"). It soon fell apart, but the German part continued calling itself that until Napoleon ended the pretense in 1806. Unlike England, where king and nobles balanced, or France, where absolutism upset the balance, in Germany, nobles gained power until, by the thirteenth century, the emperor was a mere figurehead while princes and churchmen ran hundreds of principalities.

Geography

Boundaries: Lines on a Map

Maps make boundaries look real, natural, and permanent, but most are artificial and changeable. To be legal and stable, a border must be agreed upon in a boundary treaty and demarcated with physical markers. Few borders in the world are like that. Germany's boundaries, for example, consolidated, expanded, and contracted with great fluidity (see maps).

Germany's boundaries were widest under Bismarck in 1871 and under Hitler before and during World War II. The Second Reich (1871–1918) included much of present-day Poland and Prussia. With defeat in World War I, Germany lost part of Prussia and Pomerania to make a "Polish corridor" to the Baltic. Alsace returned to France. Hitler's Third Reich (1933–1945) expanded the map of Germany by adding Austria, Bohemia (now the Czech Republic), Alsace, and parts of Poland. These lands were stripped away with Germany's defeat in World War II. Germany was two countries from 1949 to 1990.

Which are the "correct" boundaries for Germany? Historical, moral, and even demographic claims are hotly disputed. Hitler attempted to draw Germany's borders to include all Germans, but people are not neatly arrayed in demographic ranks with, say, Germans on one side of a river and Poles on the other. Instead, they are often "interdigitized," with some German villages in Polish territory and Poles living in some German cities. Whatever border you draw will leave some Germans in Poland and some Poles in Germany.

Poland's boundaries are also perplexing. As the empires that had partitioned Poland since the 1790s (Germany, Austria, and Russia) collapsed in World War I, Polish patriots under Pilsudski reestablished Poland, but it included many Lithuanians, Belorussians, and Ukrainians. Stalin never liked that boundary and, during World War II, pushed Soviet borders westward. In compensation, Poland got former German territories so that now, its western border is formed by the Oder and Neisse rivers. Millions of Germans were expelled. In effect, Poland was picked up and moved more than 100 miles westward!

Control of borders is a chief attribute of sovereignty, and nations go to great lengths to demonstrate that they alone are in charge of who and what goes in and out across their borders. Some of the first points of violence in Lithuania and Slovenia were their passport and customs houses. In forcibly taking over these border checkpoints, Soviet and Yugoslav federal forces, in 1991, respectively attempted to show that they, rather than the breakaway republics, were in charge of the entire national territory. They did not succeed, and their countries fragmented.

Boundary questions abound, such as India's border with Pakistan (especially over Kashmir), China's borders with India and with Russia, Venezuela with Guyana, Argentina with Chile (over Tierra del Fuego) and with Britain (over the Falklands), Syria with Lebanon (over the Bekaa Valley), Morocco with Algeria (over the former Spanish Sahara), and Iraq with Iran (over the Shatt al-Arab waterway). Such questions cause wars.

The Catholic-Protestant struggle accentuated Germany's fragmentation. Martin Luther in the early sixteenth century reflected the feeling of much of northern Germany that the Roman church was corrupt and ungodly. The North German princes did not like paying taxes to Rome and found Lutheranism a good excuse to stop. South Germany and the Rhineland stayed mostly Catholic, and the north and east turned predominantly Protestant, a pattern that endures.

Religion caused two wars in Germany. In the first, the Schmalkaldic War (named after the town of Schmalkalden where Protestant princes formed a coalition) of 1545–1555, the **Habsburg** Emperor Charles V nearly succeeded in crushing Lutheranism. The Protestants, however, allied with Catholic France to beat Charles. Deciding which parts of Germany should be Catholic and which Protestant, the Religious Peace of Augsburg in 1555 devised the formula *cuius regio, eius religio*—"whoever reigns, his religion." Thus, the religion of the local prince decided an area's religion, which deepened the disunity of Germany and princely power.

The **Thirty Years War** (1618–1648) was much worse. Again, at first the Catholic Habsburgs won, but Cardinal Richelieu feared Habsburg power would encircle France, so he aided the Protestants. In international relations, power and national interests often trump religious or ideological affinity. A Swedish army under King Gustavus Adolphus fought brilliantly in Germany for the Protestants; he was killed in battle there. Until World War I, the Thirty Years War was the worst in human history. Germany lost perhaps 30 percent of its population, most by starvation. The Treaty of **Westphalia** in 1648 confirmed *cuius regio* and left Germany atomized into 360 small states.

England broke with Rome; the return of Catholic kings to London merely confirmed the power of Parliament. In France, the Catholic Church and *ancien régime* stayed loyal to one another while many French turned anticlerical, dividing French society into conservative Catholics and anticlerical radicals. Germany split into Catholic and Protestant, leading to a long and ruinous war, fragmentation, and centuries of mistrust between Germans of different denominations.

Habsburg
Catholic dynasty that once ruled Austria-Hungary, Spain, Latin America, and the Netherlands.

Thirty Years War
1618–1648 Habsburg attempt to conquer and catholicize Europe.

Westphalia
Treaty ending the Thirty Years War.

Prussia
Powerful North German state; capital Berlin.

Junker
(Pronounced YOON care) From *junge Herren*, young gentlemen; Prussian nobility.

The Rise of Prussia

Brandenburg, later known as **Prussia**, in the eighteenth century took over much of the eastern Baltic coast, Silesia, and parts of the Rhineland. In the eastern Baltic regions, a type of nobility had developed, descended from the old Teutonic knights: the **Junkers**, who owned great estates worked by obedient serfs. Unlike the English lords, they were not independent but a state nobility, dependent on Berlin and controlling the civil service and military. The Junkers bequeathed their obedience, discipline, and attention to detail to modern Germany. Prussian kings, with potential enemies on all sides, became obsessed with military power, leading to Voltaire's wisecrack that Prussia is not a country with an army but an army with a country.

Frederick the Great (reigned 1740–1786) kept the strong Prussian army in such high readiness that it frightened larger states. Administering his kingdom personally, Frederick

The Changing Shape of Germany

Charlemagne's Holy Roman Empire

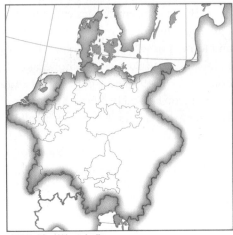

1648: After Westphalia

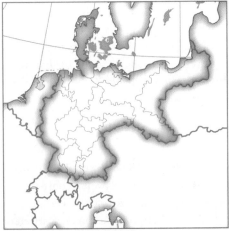

1815: The German Confederation

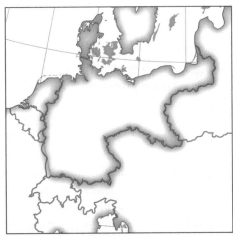

1871: The Second Reich

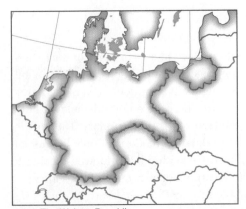

1919: The Weimar Republic

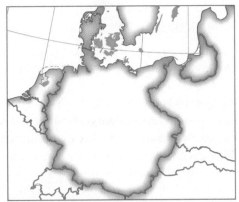

1939: Hitler's Third Reich

1945: Occupied Germany (Four Zones)

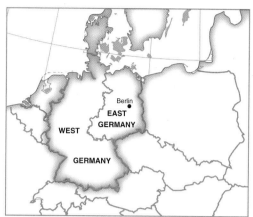

1949: Two Germanies

1990: Reunited Germany

became known as the "enlightened despot" who brought art and culture (Voltaire stayed at his court for a while), as well as military triumphs and territorial expansion, to Prussia. A brilliant commander and daring strategist, Frederick was a model for later German nationalists, including Hitler.

German Nationalism

At the time of the French Revolution, there were still more than 300 German states. Prussia and Austria were the strongest, but they too fell to Napoleon. German liberals, fed up with the backwardness and fragmentation of their country, at first welcomed the French as liberators and modernizers. Napoleon consolidated the many German ministates—but not Prussia or Austria—into about 30, calling them the Confederation of the Rhine, and introduced laws to liberalize the economy and society. The French also infected all of Europe with the new idea of **nationalism**. German nationalism led to three German invasions of France—1870, 1914, and

nationalism
Belief in greatness and unity of one's country and hatred of rule by foreigners.

Geography

Mountains

Mountains can serve as defensive barriers, making a country hard to invade. The Alps guard Germany's southern flank; the Pyrenees do the same for France. Russia, with no mountains until the Urals rise up to form Europe's border with Asia, had nothing to block the Mongols (who passed south of the Urals), Swedes, and Germans. Mountains can also slow political and economic development. Mountainous countries, such as Spain and Mexico, may be harder to unify, as the nation's capital cannot easily penetrate regions shielded by mountains. As the West Virginia motto says, *Montani Semper Liberi* (Mountaineers Are Always Free). Because much of Japan is too mountainous for farms or factories, most Japanese live in the narrow coastal strips.

1940. German nationalism became romantic, angry, and racist and celebrated a *Volksgeist*, a combination of *Volk* (people) and *Geist* (spirit), implying a superior Germanic racial spirit. German geographers coined the term **Lebensraum** to argue that Germany was entitled to more territory. (Japanese militarists argued precisely the same.) Long before Hitler, many Germans favored expansionist nationalism.

After Napoleon's defeat, German thinkers wanted a unified and modernized nation, but the reactionary Austrian Prince Metternich helped create a German Confederation of 39 states to rebuild European stability. In 1848, revolutions broke out all over Europe as discontented **liberals** and nationalists sought to overthrow the **Metternichian system**. German liberals met in Frankfurt to set up a unified, democratic Germany. They offered the king of Prussia leadership of a German constitutional monarchy, but he refused it with the remark that he "would not accept a crown from the gutter." The army cleared out the National Assembly in Frankfurt, and German liberals either converted to pure nationalism or immigrated to the United States.

The Second Reich

German unification was imposed from above, by Prussia, and was the work of a staunch conservative, Otto von Bismarck, who had seen the liberals in action in 1848 and thought they were fools. Bismarck, who became Prussia's prime minister in 1862, was not a German nationalist but a Junker monarchist who sought German unification to preserve Prussia. In 1862, when the Prussian parliament deadlocked over the military budget, Bismarck simply decreed new taxes and spent the money, declaring, "Not by speeches and majority decisions will the great questions of the time be decided—that was the fault of 1848 and 1849—but by iron and blood."

Bismarck used war to solve the great question of who was to lead a unified Germany, Prussia, or Austria. In a series of three limited wars— in 1864 against Denmark, in 1866 against Austria, and in 1870 against France—Bismarck first consolidated the many German states behind Prussia, then got rid of Austria, then firmed up German unity. The new Second **Reich** (Charlemagne's was the first) was actually proclaimed

Lebensraum
German for "living space" for an entire nation. (Note: All German nouns are capitalized.)

liberal
European and Latin American for free society and free economy. (Note very different U.S. meaning.)

Metternichian system
Contrived conservative system that tried to restore pre-Napoleon European monarchy and stability.

Reich
German for empire.

Personalities

Bismarck's Dubious Legacy

Otto von Bismarck, Germany's chancellor from 1871 to 1890, was a Prussian Junker to the bone, and the stamp he put on unified Germany retarded its democratic development for decades. Many compared Bismarck and Disraeli as dynamic conservatives, but English and German conservatism were very different. Disraeli's Tories widened the electorate and welcomed a fight in Parliament. Bismarck hated parties, parliaments, and anyone who opposed him. Bismarck left Germany an authoritarian and one-man style of governance that was overcome only after World War II.

Bismarck's **Kulturkampf** with the Catholic Church sharpened Catholic resentment against the Protestant north, a feeling that lingers. Bismarck's most dangerous legacy was in his foreign policy, which combined **Machtpolitik** and **Realpolitik** to unify Germany.

Germany's real problem was that Bismarck used power politics for a limited end, the unification of Germany. His successors picked up his amoral *Machtpolitik* but discarded the restraints, the *Realpolitik*. Bismarck, for example, could have easily conquered all of Denmark, Austria, and France but did not because he knew it would destabilize Europe. Bismarck used war in a controlled way, to unify Germany rather than to conquer Europe. Once he got his Second Reich, Bismarck kept potential enemies from forming coalitions against it.

Bismarck cautioned that supporting Austrian ambitions in the Balkans could lead to war. "The entire Balkans," he said, were "not worth the bones of one Pomeranian grenadier." That was precisely the way World War I began. Bismarck's successors, men of far less ability and great ambition, let Austria pull them into war over the Balkans. The tragedy of Bismarck is that he constructed a delicate balance of European power that could not be maintained without himself as the master juggler.

---

in France, at Versailles Palace, in 1871. After that, Bismarck aimed for stability, not expansion.

The Second Reich, lasting from 1871 to 1918, was not a democracy. The legislature, the **Reichstag**, had only limited power, namely, to approve or reject the budget. The chancellor (prime minister) was not "responsible" to the parliament—he could not be voted out—and handpicked his own ministers. The German **Kaiser** was not a figurehead but actually set policy. The many German states retained much autonomy, a forerunner of the present federal system.

German industry grew, especially iron and steel, and with it came a militant and well-organized German labor movement. In 1863, Ferdinand Lassalle formed the General German Workers' Association, partly a union and partly a party. In 1875, the group became the *Sozialdemokratische Partei Deutschlands* (**SPD**), now the oldest and one of the most successful social democratic parties. Bismarck suppressed the SPD in 1878 but offered welfare measures himself. In the 1880s, Germany became the first country with medical and accident insurance, a pension plan, and state employment offices. Germany has been a welfare state ever since.

Kulturkampf
Culture struggle, specifically Bismarck's with the Catholic Church.

Machtpolitik
Power politics (cognate to "might").

Realpolitik
Politics of realism.

Reichstag
Pre-Hitler German parliament; its building now houses the *Bundestag*.

Kaiser
German for Caesar; emperor.

SPD
German Social Democratic Party.

revisionism
Rethinking an ideology or reinterpreting history.

Dolchstoss
German for "stab in the back."

Versailles Treaty
1919 treaty ending World War I.

Weimar Republic
1919–1933 democratic German republic.

The Catastrophe: World War I

The Second Reich might have evolved into a democracy. Political parties and parliament grew in importance. After Bismarck was retired in 1890, the SPD became Germany's largest party, with almost one-third of the Reichstag's seats, and grew moderate, abandoning Marxism for **revisionism**, the idea that socialism can grow gradually through democratic elections. After Bismarck, Germany's foreign policy turned expansionist. Kaiser Wilhelm II saw Germany as a great imperial power, dominating Europe and competing with Britain overseas. German naval armament began in 1889, touching off a race with Britain to build more battleships. Wilhelm supported the Boers against the British in South Africa and the Austrians who competed with the Russians to grab the Balkans. By Sarajevo in 1914, Germany had surrounded itself with enemies, exactly what Bismarck had tried to prevent.

The Germans, with their quick victory of 1870 in mind, marched joyously off to war. In early August of 1914, the Kaiser told his troops: "You will be home before the leaves have fallen from the trees." All of Europe thought the war would be short, but it took four years and over 10 million lives until Germany surrendered. Many Germans could not believe they had lost. Right-wing Germans promoted the **Dolchstoss** myth that Germany had been betrayed by democrats, socialists, Bolsheviks, and Jews. Fed nothing but war propaganda, Germans did not understand that the army and the economy could give no more. The **Versailles Treaty** blamed the war on Germany and demanded 132 billion in gold marks ($442 billion in today's dollars) in reparations. Germany was stripped of its few colonies (in Africa and the Pacific) and lost Alsace and the Polish Corridor. Many Germans wanted revenge. Versailles led to Hitler and World War II.

Republic without Democrats

The **Weimar Republic**—which got its name from the town of Weimar, where its federal constitution was drawn up—started with three strikes against it. First, Germans had no experience with a republic or a democracy. Second, for many Germans, the Weimar Republic lacked legitimacy; it had been forced upon Germany by the victors and "backstabbers." Third, the punitive Versailles Treaty humiliated and economically hobbled Germany.

Geography

Bound Germany

Germany is bounded on the north by the Atlantic, Denmark, and the Baltic Sea;

on the east by Poland and the Czech Republic;

on the south by Austria and Switzerland;

and on the west by France, Luxembourg, Belgium, and the Netherlands.

To reinforce your knowledge, sketch out and label Germany and its neighbors. Note also the old border between East and West Germany that disappeared with unification in 1990.

Geography

Bound Poland

Poland is bounded on the north by the Baltic Sea, Russia (Kaliningrad Oblast), and Lithuania; on the east by Belarus and Ukraine; on the south by Slovakia and the Czech Republic; and on the west by Germany.

Poland

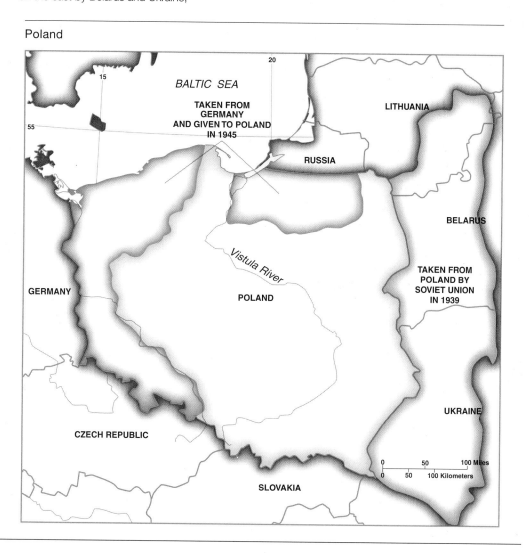

Only an estimated one German in four was a wholehearted democrat. Another quarter hated democracy. The rest went along with the new republic until the economy collapsed and then aligned with authoritarian movements of the left or right. Weimar Germany, it has been said, was a republic without republicans and a democracy without democrats.

hyperinflation
Very rapid inflation, more than 50 percent a month.

opportunist
Unprincipled person out for himself or herself.

Berlin, in a crisis with France over reparations, printed money without limit, bringing a **hyperinflation** so insane that by 1923, it took a wheelbarrowful of marks to buy a loaf of bread. Families whose businesses and savings were wiped out were receptive to the Nazis. The period left an indelible mark, and to this day, the German government, more than any other in Europe, emphasizes preventing inflation. For fear of triggering inflation, Chancellor Angela Merkel kept a balanced budget that did not stimulate the economy and berated France and the United States for deficit spending. Even the SPD agreed with her.

By the mid-1920s, the economy stabilized, but cabinets changed frequently: 26 in 14 years. The Social Democrat, Catholic Center, and Conservative parties were the largest; the Nazis were tiny. When the world Depression started in 1929, moderate parties declined, and extremist parties—Nazis and Communists—grew (see box below). The more people out of work, the higher the Nazi vote. In late 1932, the Nazis won 35 percent of the German vote, and the aged President Hindenburg, a conservative general, named Hitler as chancellor in January 1933. In March 1933, the Nazis won 44 percent of the vote as Hitler consolidated his power. The Weimar Republic, Germany's first democracy, died after an unstable life of 14 years.

The Third Reich

Nazi was short for the National Socialist German Workers Party. Nazism, like other forms of fascism, had a fake socialist component that promised jobs and welfare. The Nazis did not put industries under state ownership like the Soviet Communists; instead, they practiced *Gleichschaltung* (coordination) of the economy under party supervision. Many Germans got work on government projects, such as the new *Autobahn* (express highways). The Nazis never won a fair election, but by the late 1930s, a majority of Germans supported Hitler, whom they saw as restoring prosperity and national pride.

Most Germans had not been enthusiastic about democracy, and few protested the growth of tyranny. Some Communists and Socialists went underground, to prison, or into exile, and some old-style conservatives loathed Hitler, who, in their eyes, was an Austrian guttersnipe. But most Germans got along by going along. For some, membership in the Nazi party offered better jobs and snappy uniforms. Many ex-Nazis claimed they joined only to keep their jobs or further their careers, and most were probably telling the truth. You do not need true believers to staff a tyranny; **opportunists** will do just as well. The frightening thing about the Nazi regime was how it could turn normal humans into cold-blooded mass murderers.

Geography

Bound Hungary

Hungary is bounded on the north by Slovakia; on the east by Ukraine and Romania; on the south by Serbia and Croatia; and on the west by Slovenia and Austria.

Democracy

Polarized Pluralism

Columbia University political scientist Giovanni Sartori used the term **polarized pluralism** to describe what happens when a multiparty democracy such as Weimar's or Spain's in the 1930s turns extremist. Centrist parties face opposition on both their right and left. Competing for votes in a highly ideological atmosphere, parties engage in a "politics of outbidding" by offering more-radical solutions. Voters flee from center to extremes, to parties dedicated to overthrowing democracy.

Compare the percentage of votes German parties got in 1928 with what they got in 1933 and the "center-fleeing" tendency is clear.

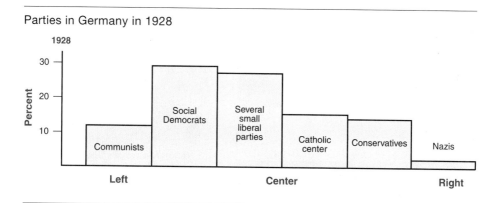

Parties in Germany in 1928

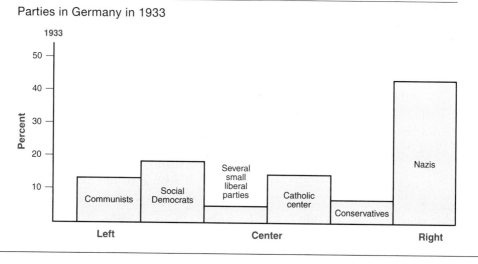

Parties in Germany in 1933

Hitler aimed for war. At first, he just consolidated Germany's boundaries, absorbing the Saar in 1935, Austria and the Sudetenland in 1938, and Czech lands in 1939. Germany's former World War I enemies, still war weary, did nothing to stop him. German generals were ready to overthrow Hitler if the British said no to his demands at Munich

polarized pluralism

A multiparty system of two extremist blocs with little in the center.

Geography

Another Tale of Two Flags

Like France, Germany's divided loyalties have been symbolized by its flags' colors. The German nationalist movement's flag was black, red, and gold, colors of a Prussian regiment that fought Napoleon. By 1848, it symbolized a democratic, united Germany. Bismarck rejected it and, for the Second Reich's flag, chose Prussia's black and white, plus the white and red of the medieval Hansa commercial league.

The Reich's collapse in 1918 and the founding of the Weimar Republic brought back the democratic black, red, and gold German flag. Hitler, a fanatic for symbols, insisted on authoritarian black, red, and white colors. The Bonn Republic adopted the present German flag with the original democratic colors.

Two German Flags

in 1938. But Hitler's victories without fighting persuaded the generals to follow him. Finally, when Hitler invaded Poland in September 1939, Britain and France declared war. France was overrun, Britain contained beyond the Channel. By the summer of 1940, Germany or its allies ruled most of Europe.

Jews, less than 1 percent of the German population, were portrayed as a poisonous, foreign element and were deprived, one step at a time, of their civil rights, jobs, property, citizenship, and finally lives. In 1941, Hitler ordered his **Final Solution**. Death camps, mostly in Poland, killed some 6 million Jews and a similar number of inconvenient Christians (Poles, gypsies, and others). A new word was coined to describe it: **genocide**.

Hitler—just a week before he attacked Poland in 1939—completed a **nonaggression pact** with Stalin. In the summer of 1941, however, Hitler assembled the biggest army in history and gave the order for "Barbarossa," the conquest and enslavement of the Soviet Union, but

Final Solution
Nazi program to exterminate Jews.

genocide
Murder of an entire people.

nonaggression pact
Treaty to not attack each other, specifically the 1939 treaty between Hitler and Stalin.

the Russian winter and Red Army devoured entire German divisions. From late 1942, the war went downhill for Germany.

The Occupation

This time, there could be no Dolchstoss myth; Germans watched Russians, Americans, British, and French fight through Germany. At Yalta in February 1945, the Allied leaders agreed to divide Germany into four zones for temporary occupation; Berlin, deep inside the Soviet zone, was similarly divided. German government vanished, and the country was run by foreign occupiers.

Initially, the Allies, shocked by the Nazi concentration camps, treated Germans harshly, but that reversed with the onset of the *Cold War*, which grew in large part out of the way the Soviets handled Germany. The Soviets, having lost some 27 million in the war, looted Germany by shipping whole factories to the Soviet Union and flooded the country with inflated military currency. The British and Americans, distressed at the brutal Soviet takeover of East Europe, revived German economic and political life in their zones. The U.S. **Marshall Plan** pumped billions of dollars into German recovery. In 1948, the British and Americans introduced a currency reform with a new **deutsche Mark** (DM), which ended Soviet looting in the western zones. In retaliation, the Russians blockaded Berlin, which was supplied for nearly a year by the American-British **Berlin airlift**. The Cold War was on, centered in Germany.

In 1949, the Western allies returned sovereignty to West Germany in order to ensure its cooperation against Soviet power. A few months later, the Soviets set up East Germany. Both German regimes were children of the Cold War, and when it ended—often dated to the fall of the Berlin Wall in late 1989—prosperous and democratic West Germany swallowed weak and dependent East Germany.

Marshall Plan
Massive U.S. financial aid for European recovery.

deutsche Mark
German currency from 1948 to 2002.

Berlin airlift
U.S.–British supply of West Berlin by air in 1948–1949.

Political Culture

Germany's Political Eras

Name	Years	Remembered for
Holy Roman Empire	800–1806	Charlemagne, fragmentation, religious wars
Nineteenth Century	1806–1871	Consolidation, modernization stir
Second Reich	1871–1918	Bismarck unites Germany; industry and war
Weimar Republic	1919–1933	Weak democracy; culture flourishes
Nazis	1933–1945	Brutal dictatorship; war; mass murder
Occupation	1945–1949	Allies divide and run Germany
Federal Republic	1949–	Democracy; economic miracle; unification; from Bonn to Berlin

Federal Republic of Germany
Previously West Germany, now all of Germany.

Grundgesetz
Basic Law; Germany's constitution.

federalism
System in which component areas have considerable autonomy.

Land
Germany's first-order civil division, equivalent to U.S. state; plural *Länder*.

Mitteleuropa
Central Europe.

The Key Institutions

4.2   Characterize the German voting system.

In 1949, the founders of the **Federal Republic of Germany** (FRG) took some elements from the 1848–1849 Frankfurt and 1919 Weimar constitutions in drafting the new **Grundgesetz** (Basic Law). They designated Bonn as West Germany's temporary capital and revived German **federalism**, in part to repudiate Nazi centralization. Germany's *Länder* have more autonomy than U.S. states. Communist East Germany continued the Nazi pattern of centralized rule with 14 administrative districts without autonomy, each named after its leading city. Unification in 1990 recreated five East German Länder, so now the Federal Republic has 16 Länder: 10 from West Germany, 5 from East Germany, and Greater Berlin.

Berlin, 110 miles (180 kilometers) inside East Germany, was supposed to be under four-party occupation. The Soviets, however, in 1949, turned East Berlin into the capital of East Germany (which they called the German Democratic Republic, GDR), and the American, British, and French sectors effectively became part of West Germany. Bonn counted West Berlin as its eleventh **Land**, although the city sent only nonvoting representatives to Bonn. Berlin became the official capital of united Germany in 1991.

The President

Germany's federal president (*Bundespräsident*) is a figurehead with few political but many symbolic duties. Like the monarchs of Britain and Scandinavia, the German president is, in Bagehot's terms, a "dignified" rather than an "efficient" position. The French president of the Third and Fourth Republics and today's Israeli president are other examples of weak presidencies. The U.S., Mexican, Brazilian, and current French presidents are examples of strong presidents.

Geography

From Bonn to Berlin

The 1991 debate that restored Berlin as the capital of united Germany was a conflict over core areas. Bonn, a small town in the Catholic Rhineland well to the west, had been West Germany's capital since 1949. It shifted Germans' attention westward in values, economics, and alliances.

Berlin, near the eastern border of Germany, was the capital of Protestant Prussia and then Germany's capital from 1871 to 1945. Moving back to Berlin shifted Germans' attention to the problems of poorer, former-Communist East Germany. Some feared that it could turn Germany from the West and back to the old concept of a German-dominated **Mitteleuropa**.

As "head of state" rather than "chief of government," the German president receives new foreign ambassadors, proclaims laws (after they have been passed by parliament), dissolves the **Bundestag** (upon the chancellor's request), and appoints new chancellors (after the leading party has named one). The president, elected by a special Federal Assembly composed of all Bundestag members plus an equal number from the state legislatures, serves five years and may be reelected once. A semiretirement job, it usually goes to distinguished public figures.

Bundestag
Lower house of German parliament.

chancellor
German prime minister.

constructive no-confidence
Parliament must vote in a new cabinet when it ousts the current one.

The German presidency in recent years has lost stability and prestige. In 2010, former International Monetary Fund head Horst Köhler of the CDU resigned, during his second term as president, over media criticism. His successor, former CDU Lower Saxony governor Christian Wulff, resigned amid corruption charges in 2012. Former East German Lutheran pastor Joachim Gauck, active in exposing Stasi (secret police) abuses, had been the SPD candidate for president in 2010 and was elected with the support of all parties in 2012.

The Chancellor

Germany has a weak president but a strong **chancellor**. In contrast to the Weimar Republic, the FRG chancellorship has been stable and durable. Part of the reason is that the Basic Law requires the Bundestag to simultaneously vote *in* a new chancellor if it wants to vote *out* the present one. This reform, **constructive no-confidence**, makes ousting a chancellor between elections rare (used only once, in 1982) and ended a problem of parliamentary (as opposed to presidential) governments—namely, their dependence on an often-fickle legislative majority.

The strong chancellorship is a legacy of Konrad Adenauer, a tough, shrewd politician who helped found the Federal Republic and served as chancellor during its first 14 years. First occupants, such as Washington, can define an office's powers and style for generations. Adenauer, named chancellor at age 73, led firmly and made decisions that stretched the new constitution to the limits. A Catholic Rhinelander, he formed the CDU, consolidated a "two-plus" party system, pointed Germany westward into NATO and the EU, and established a special relationship with France. Adenauer made the German chancellor as powerful as the British prime minister. Chancellors pick their own cabinet (like the British PM) and must defend government policies in the Bundestag and to the public.

Who Was When: Germany's Chancellors		
Konrad Adenauer	CDU	1949–1963
Ludwig Erhard	CDU	1963–1966
Kurt Georg Kiesinger	CDU	1966–1969
Willy Brandt	SPD	1969–1974
Helmut Schmidt	SPD	1974–1982
Helmut Kohl	CDU	1982–1998
Gerhard Schröder	SPD	1998–2005
Angela Merkel	CDU	2005–

The Cabinet

The typical German cabinet is usually smaller than the British and is now even smaller than the 15-department U.S. cabinet. As is usual in Europe, ministries are added, deleted, and reshuffled from one cabinet to another. Chancellor Merkel, after extensive negotiations between the two coalition parties, named a cabinet with 14 ministries, 10 headed by Christian Democrats and 4 by Free Democrats:

Foreign Affairs	Health
Interior	Families
Justice	Labor
Finance	Education
Economy and Technology	Development (foreign aid)
Defense	Environment
Agriculture	Transport

Personalities

Angela Merkel

Angela Merkel is unusual in several ways. She is Germany's first woman chancellor and the first from East Germany. Her English and Russian are nearly perfect. A Protestant, she heads a heavily Catholic party. She wants more free-market economics than much of her own CDU/CSU wishes. She is now in her second marriage and has no children.

Merkel was born in West Germany but went as a baby to East Germany, where her pastor father was assigned a church. She grew up entirely in East Germany but kept her critical views of the Communist regime to herself. Extremely bright, she earned a doctorate in physics at Leipzig University and did research in quantum chemistry. (Thatcher graduated Oxford in chemistry.)

When the Berlin Wall fell in late 1989, Merkel helped organize a conservative party that merged with the CDU. Elected to the Bundestag, she still represents a constituency in Mecklenburg-Pomerania. Chancellor Helmut Kohl appointed Merkel to his cabinet, first as minister of women and youth and then environment. After Kohl's defeat in 1998, Merkel became CDU chair in 2000.

By the early 2000s, SPD Chancellor Gerhard Schröder was politically stalled and losing popularity. He reformed Germany's slow-growth and high-unemployment economy but got little support from his own SPD, which fights any cuts in welfare benefits. Unable to govern, a frustrated Schröder arranged a Bundestag defeat to call elections in 2005, a year early. Schröder, an outgoing personality and good speaker, was more popular than his party. "Angie," as Merkel's supporters call her, was a bland speaker, less popular than her party (a situation that reversed in 2009). Personality matters in German politics, and the CDU saw its early 20-point lead over the SPD narrow to a maddening tie.

After two months of negotiations, the CDU and SPD agreed to a **grand coalition** with Merkel as chancellor. Merkel wanted to go further with reforms to free the economy and trim the welfare state, but the SPD half of her cabinet limited her to what she called "small steps." Merkel, in 2009, denounced the money-pumping policies of central banks—including the U.S. Fed—as inflationary. This struck a chord with German voters and turned Merkel into Germany's most popular politician for the September 2009 elections, which returned her to the chancellorship as head of a CDU-FDP coalition.

Most Germans liked her calm and steady if uncharismatic personality, but in her second term, criticism mounted that she followed rather than led, trying to please everybody and changing policies almost as if frightened. Merkel pledged liberalizing reforms but backed down in the face of public opinion. She found nuclear power acceptable until the Fukushima nuclear accident but then pledged to close all 17 of Germany's reactors by 2022. She had Germany abstain on a UN Security Council resolution against Libya, isolating Germany from its Western allies. She urged other European countries to follow her austerity policy (she calls it "budget consolidation") but supports the euro while not taxing Germans to bail out weaker economies—policies that conflict with one another. Although offering little vision or European leadership, Merkel's calm and steady approach propelled her to a third electoral victory in 2013.

The chief job of the interior ministry is protection of the constitution (*Verfassungsschutz*), including monitoring extremist parties and movements. The protection office's chief resigned in 2012, accused of ignoring the murder of Turks by neo-Nazis and of shredding documents to cover up the case. The federal interior ministry, however, controls only the small Federal Criminal Police and Border Police; all other police are at the *Land* or municipal levels.

As in Britain (but not in France), German cabinet ministers are also working politicians with Bundestag seats. Like their British counterparts, they are rarely specialists in their assigned portfolio. Most are trained as lawyers and have served in party and legislative positions. Below cabinet rank, a parliamentary state secretary is assigned to each minister to assist in relations with the Bundestag, as in Britain.

The Bundestag

Germany never had a strong parliamentary tradition, so Konrad Adenauer placed little faith in the Bundestag. The Reichstag (whose building the Bundestag now occupies) was weak under both Bismarck and Weimar. Since 1949, the Bundestag has established itself as a pillar of democracy and an important branch of government. Success has been gradual and incomplete, and some Germans still do not respect the Bundestag (which still gets higher ratings than Americans give their Congress).

The Bundestag has at least 598 members (but usually more) and now totals 631. Deputies are elected for four years, but elections can be called early. In a parliamentary system, the legislature cannot so harshly criticize the administration as does the U.S. Congress. After all, the Bundestag's majority parties form the government. The Bundestag is neither the tumultuous National Assembly of the French Third and Fourth Republics nor the docile rubber stamp that de Gaulle created. It is not the colorful debating chamber of Britain's Commons. On balance, the Bundestag has less independent power than the U.S. Congress but more than the French National Assembly and possibly even the British Commons.

One interesting point about the Bundestag is that a third of its members are women, typical of North European systems that use proportional representation (PR), which allows parties to place women candidates high on party lists. Single-member electoral districts are less fair to women than those that use PR. By law, at least 40 percent of Sweden's Riksdag must be women. The number of women in most parliaments has grown fast in recent years—now 45 percent of Swedish, 26 percent of Mexican, 22 percent of British, 19 percent of French, and 17 percent of U.S. national legislators are women. Japan lags with 11 percent, still an improvement.

Geography

Federations

The prefix **Bundes-** proudly announces that Germany is a federal system, one that gives major autonomy to its components, such as U.S., Indian, Mexican, Brazilian, or Nigerian states; German Länder; or Canadian provinces. The components cannot be legally erased or split or have their boundaries easily changed; such matters are grave constitutional questions. Certain powers are reserved for the federal government (defense, money supply, interstate commerce, and so on) while other powers are reserved for the components (education, police, highways, and so on). Large countries or those with particularistic languages or traditions lend themselves to federalism.

The advantages of a federal system are its flexibility and accommodation to particularism. Texans feel Texas is different and special; Bavarians feel Bavaria is different and special; Québécois feel Quebec is different and special; and so on. If one state or province wishes to try a new formula to, say, fund health care, it may do so without upsetting the state–federal balance. If the new way works, it may be gradually copied. If it fails, little harm is done before it is phased out. U.S. states, in this regard, have been called "laboratories of democracy." Governments at the Land or state level also train politicians before they try the national level. Examples: Texas Governor George Bush, Lower Saxony Premier Gerhard Schröder, and Mexico State Governor Enrique Peña Nieto.

A federal system may achieve a stable balance between local and national loyalties, leading gradually to a psychologically integrated country, such as the United States, Germany, and Switzerland. But this does not always work. Soviet, Yugoslav, and Czechoslovak federalism actually fostered resentments of the component "republics" against the center. When their Communist parties weakened, local nationalists took over and declared independence.

The disadvantage of federal systems can be inconsistent and incoherent administration among components. Many federal systems lack nationwide standards in education, environment, welfare, or health care. To correct such problems, federal systems, over time, tend to grant more power to the **center** at the expense of the states. Prime example: the United States.

Unitary systems, such as Britain and France, tug in the direction of federalism, whereas federal systems tug in the direction of central administration. This does not necessarily mean that the two will eventually meet in some middle ground; it merely means that neither unitary nor federal systems are finished products and that both are still evolving.

The Bundestag's strong point is its committee work, most of it behind closed doors, where deputies, especially opposition members, can criticize. German legislative committees are more important and more specialized than their British counterparts. German party discipline is not as tight as the British so that deputies from the ruling party can criticize a government bill while opposition deputies can agree with it. In the give and take of committee work, the opposition is often able to get changes in legislation. Once back on the Bundestag floor—and all bills must be reported out; they cannot be killed in committee—voting is mostly on party lines with occasional defections on matters of conscience. Each ministry has a relevant Bundestag committee to deal with, and ministers, themselves Bundestag members, sometimes attend committee sessions.

In a parallel with French deputies, Bundestag membership is heavy with civil servants. German law permits bureaucrats to take leaves of absence to serve in the Bundestag. Many members are from interest

Bundes-
German prefix for "federal."

center
In federal systems, the powers of the nation's capital.

groups—business associations and labor unions. Together, these two groups usually form a majority of the Bundestag, contributing to the feeling that parliament is dominated by powerful interests. Scandals have revealed that many Bundestag members get "secret money" from private firms for no work, a parallel with British MPs' "sleaze factor."

Federal Constitutional Court
Germany's top court, equivalent to U.S. Supreme Court.

extreme multipartism
Too many parties in parliament.

The Constitutional Court

Few countries have a judiciary equal in power to the legislative or executive branches. The United States and Germany are two; both allow their highest courts to review the constitutionality of laws. The **Federal Constitutional Court** (*Bundesverfassungsgericht*, BVerfG), located in Karlsruhe, was set up in 1951 partly on the U.S. model, to prevent misuse of power, and was a new concept for Europe. It is composed of 16 judges, 8 elected by each house of parliament, who serve for nonrenewable 12-year terms. The BVerfG operates as two courts, or "senates," of 8 judges each to speed up the work. Independent of other branches, the court decides cases between Länder, protects civil liberties, outlaws dangerous political parties, and makes sure that statutes conform to the Basic Law.

The Constitutional Court's decisions have been important. It has declared illegal some right and left extremist parties on the grounds that they sought to overthrow the constitution. In 1979, it ruled that "worker codetermination" in running companies was constitutional. In 1983 and 2005, it found that chancellors had acted within the constitution when they arranged to lose a Bundestag vote of confidence in order to hold elections early. In 1994, it ruled that Germany can send troops overseas for peacekeeping operations. In 1995, it overrode a Bavarian law requiring a crucifix in every classroom. More recently, it has developed a "duty to protect" individuals from both public and private mistreatment and "proportionality" between conflicting rights, as between a free press and individual privacy, including computer privacy. In 2009, it warned that the EU constitution could not override German democracy and sovereignty. The BVerfG, because it operates within the more rigid code law system, does not have the impact of the U.S. Supreme Court, whose decisions are precedents throughout the U.S. common-law system.

From "Two-Plus" to Multiparty System

Much of the reason the FRG government worked well is the party system that evolved after 1949–one that may have ended in 2005. The Weimar Reichstag suffered from **extreme multipartism**; a dozen parties, some of them extremist, made it impossible to form stable coalitions. The Federal Republic seemed to have fixed that, and Germany turned into a "two-plus" party system. German governments consisted of one of the two large parties in coalition with one small party. Britain, with its majoritarian system, usually gives one party a majority in parliament. Germany's proportional system, on the other hand, seldom produces single-party governments. A two-plus party system is somewhere between a two-party system and a multiparty system.

Recent elections, however, turned Germany back into a multiparty system that makes coalition formation harder. Indeed, in much of Europe, discontented citizens, fed up with the two big, stodgy parties, vote less for them and more for Greens, anti-immigrant, anti-EU, leftist, and other small parties. (Some Americans wish for a third party, but the electoral system works

Greens
Environmentalist party.

against it.) The two-plus system is splintering. Germany now has five relevant parties.

The Christian Democratic Union (*Christlich Demokratische Union*, CDU) is now chaired by Angela Merkel, who became chancellor in 2005. Its Bavarian affiliate is the Christian Social Union (CSU). Together, the two are designated CDU/CSU. The original core of the CDU was the old Catholic Center Party, one of the few parties that held its own against the growth of Nazism. After World War II, Center politicians like Adenauer opted for a broad center-right party, one that welcomed Protestants. Like France's Gaullists, the CDU never embraced a totally free market (and still does not); instead, it promoted a "social market" economy. The CDU/CSU has been the largest party in every election except 1972 and 1998, when the SPD pulled ahead. In 2013, the CDU/CSU was the largest party, with 42 percent of the PR vote, not enough to govern alone.

The Social Democratic Party (*Sozialdemokratische Partei Deutschlands*, SPD) is the mother party of European democratic socialism—it turned 150 in 2013—and the only German party that antedates the Federal Republic. Starting out Marxist, the SPD gradually revised its positions until, in 1959, it discarded all Marxism. Its electoral fortunes grew, and it expanded beyond its working-class base into the middle class, especially intellectuals. Now a center-left party, the SPD's socialism is basically support for the welfare state. Its leadership is generally centrist, but it still contains leftists who try to gain control. From 1998 to 2005, the SPD governed in coalition with the Greens. In 2005 and 2013, it polled under the CDU, with which it formed a grand coalition. In the 2009 election, the SPD won just 23 percent of the vote and became the main opposition party. In 2013, it won 26 percent of the PR vote and returned to a grand coalition with the CDU.

The small Free Democratic Party (*Freie Demokratische Partei*, FDP) is a classic liberal party—that sometimes calls itself "the Liberals"—that seeks to cut government, welfare, and taxes in favor of individual free enterprise. (Liberalism in Europe means about the opposite of U.S. liberalism.) From 2009 to 2013, the FDP served as junior partner in coalition with the CDU. The FDP used to be placed in the center of the political spectrum between the CDU and SPD but now is often to the right of the CDU on free-market questions. The FDP climbed to 14.6 percent in 2009, a measure of how Germans disliked the CDU-SPD grand coalition but slumped below the threshold to 4.8 percent in 2013 and was out of the Bundestag for the first time in the party's history. It desperately struggles to revive.

In 1983, a new ecology-pacifist party, the **Greens**, first made it into the Bundestag. From 1998 to 2005, they governed in coalition with the Social Democrats. In 2013, the Greens won 8 percent. Pulled between militant environmentalists and pragmatic realists, Greens want to phase out Germany's nuclear power plants and put hefty "eco-taxes" on gasoline. Their electoral fortunes grew with Japan's nuclear disaster, and in 2011, a Green became a state governor for the first time. Another SPD-Green coalition is possible.

As soon as the Wall came down in 1989, the CDU and SPD, with money and organization, elbowed aside the small, new East German parties that had spearheaded the ouster of the Communists. One regional East German party survived, the Party of Democratic Socialism (PDS), composed of ex-Communists and those who felt ignored by the new system. In 2005, it joined disgruntled SPD leftists to form a new Left party (*Die Linke*). In 2013, buoyed by the recession and joblessness, it pulled 9 percent of the national vote but was second largest in the east. Some small rightist parties, including neo-Nazis, win seats in local and Land elections but not in the Bundestag.

The Bundesrat

Neither Britain nor France really needs an upper house because they are unitary systems. The German federal system, however, needs an upper house, the **Bundesrat**. Not as powerful as the U.S. Senate—a coequal upper house is a world rarity—the Bundesrat represents the 16 Länder and has equal power with the Bundestag on taxes, finances, and laws that affect the federal-state balance. The Bundesrat can veto bills, but the Bundestag can override the veto. On more-serious bills, the matter goes to a mediation committee with 16 members from each house, but compromise often eludes them. When the Bundesrat is in the hands of the opposition party, Germany has the divided legislature often found in the United States when one party controls the House and another the Senate.

The Bundesrat has 68 members. Small German Länder get three seats each, more populous four, and the most populous six. Each Land appoints its delegates and usually sends to Berlin the top officials from the **Landtag**, who are also cabinet members in the Land government. They may be from different parties (if the Land government is a coalition), but each Bundesrat delegation votes as a bloc, not as individuals or as parties, because they represent the whole state.

A Split Electoral System

Britain and the United States use single-member districts with plurality win ("first past the post," FPTP), a system that anchors a deputy to a district but does not accurately reflect votes for parties nationwide; seats are not proportional to votes. (It also overfocuses U.S. representatives on voters back home rather than on the country as a whole.)

Bundesrat
Literally, federal council; upper chamber of German parliament, represents states.

Landtag
German state legislature.

mixed-member (MM)
Electoral system combining single-member districts with proportional representation.

China lessons

Representation at Three Levels

Germany's hybrid **mixed-member (MM)** electoral system—sometimes called a parallel system—is impressive for combining the simplicity of single-member districts with the fairness of PR. It also represents Germans at two levels, one district and one state. Italy, Japan, New Zealand, Mexico, and the Scottish and Welsh parliaments adopted variations of it. Russia tried it from 1993 to 2003, but Putin did not want critics winning single-member seats in the Duma, so he returned to straight PR.

China could do Germany one better by representation in the National Peoples Congress (NPC) at three levels. China could have (1) single-member districts for about half of NPC seats, (2) PR at the province level for about a third, and (3) PR at the national level for the remaining sixth. (The fractions could be adjusted.) A separate ballot for the third level would not be necessary; just add up the PR votes in all the provinces and use that to apportion the national seats. The idea here is to give Chinese a local representative who knows the district, plus those who represent the province, plus some who look out for China as a whole. Such a system might also help the United States override the localism deadlock of congressional elections.

Democracy

2013: A Split Electoral System in Action

The 2013 Bundestag elections were lackluster. Germans simply did not know what to do about the looming euro crisis. They wanted to hold Europe together but were reluctant to lead Europe and bail out other countries. Turnout was only 72 percent.

Like the British Labour Party, the SPD was torn between veering left and staying centrist. Some deserted it for the Left. The CDU held together better, but both campaigns were boring. Chancellor Merkel came across as calm and intelligent. SPD chancellor candidate Peer Steinbrück, who had earlier served as finance minister in the grand coalition, made many gaffes. Germans did not want to further bail out weaker eurozone members, an issue that benefitted the CDU. Election posters featured portraits of Merkel and Steinbrück, almost as if it were a presidential election.

The CDU/CSU was again the largest party in the Bundestag, with 311 seats to the SPD's 193, still less than a majority. The FDP for the first time did not make it into the Bundestage, so the CDU/CSU, after five weeks of negotiations, reformed its grand coalition with the Social Democrats. With 504 seats, the CDU-SPD coalition has a huge majority, but the two are far apart on several policies, paralyzing bold moves and leaving only two small parties to oppose—not healthy for democracy.

Germany's MM electoral system (see box) is based on PR, but about half the seats are filled from single-member districts with plurality win (as in Britain). First, notice that the percentage of vote (on the right-hand, PR ballot) is close to the percentage of Bundestag seats except that the parties got more seats than their percentage of the votes. This is partly because some small parties (the neo-Nazi National Democrats, for example) won less than 5 percent and got no seats. Further, ticket-splitting—voting, as many did in 2013, for the individual CDU candidate on the left-hand half of the ballot but for the FDP on the PR right-hand side—won the CDU more seats than did the percentage of their party votes. The Greens and Left won seats almost entirely on the second ballot, the party list. More than 15 percent of the 2013 vote went to parties that did not reach the 5 percent threshold and thus got no seats.

Those who win a single-member constituency (the left half of the ballot) keep the seat even if it exceeds the percentage that their party is entitled to from the PR (right half of the ballot) vote. These "bonus seats" (in 2013, most of them went to the CDU) make the Bundestag larger than its nominal size of 598 seats; it now has 631 members. Is the German electoral system now clear to you? Not to worry. Many Germans do not fully understand it. Basically, just remember that it is a split system: roughly half single-member districts and half PR, but PR sets the overall share of seats. It is not perfectly proportional, because the parties that get below 5 percent get no seats; they are apportioned among the parties that met the threshold.

	% of PR Vote	Seats
CDU/CSU	41.5	311 (49.4%)
Social Democrats	25.7	193 (30.5%)
Left	8.6	64 (10.2%)
Greens	8.4	63 (10.0%)

"You Have Two Votes": A German Ballot

Stimmzettel

für die Wahl zum Deutschen Bunderstag im Wahlkreis 63 Bonn
am 27. September 1998

Sie haben 2 Stimmen

⊗ ↓　　　⊗ ↓

hier 1 Stimme
für die Wahl
eines/einer Wahlkreis-
abgeordneten

hier 1 Stimme
für die Wahl
einer Landesliste (Partei)
- maßgebende Stimme für die Verteilung der Sitze
insgesamt auf die einzelnen Parteien -

Erststimme　　　**Zweitstimme**

Erststimme		Zweitstimme	
1 **Kelber**, Ulrich — **SPD** — Sozialdemokratische Partei Deutschlands — Dipl. Informatiker, Bonn-Beuel, Neustraße 37	◯	◯ **SPD** — Sozialdemokratische Partei Deutschlands — Franz Müntefering, Anke Fuchs, Rudolf Dreßler, Wolf-Michael Catenhusen, Ingrid Matthäus-Maier	1
2 **Hauser**, Norbert — **CDU** — Christlich Demokratische Union Deutschlands — Rechtsanwalt, Bonn-Bad Godesberg, Elfstraße 26	◯	◯ **CDU** — Christlich Demokratische Union Deutschlands — Dr. Norbert Blüm, Peter Hintze, Irmgard Karwatzki, Dr. Norbert Lammert, Dr. Jürgen Rüttgers	2
3 **Dr. Westerwelle**, Guido — **F.D.P.** — Free Demokratische Partei — Rechtsanwalt, Bonn, Heerstraße 85	◯	◯ **F.D.P.** — Freie Demokratische Partei — Dr. Guido Westerwelle, Jürgen W. Möllemann, Ulrike Flach, Paul Friedhoff, Dr. Werner H. Hoyer	3
4 **Manemann**, Coletta — **GRÜNE** — BÜNDNIS 90/ DIE GRÜNEN — Dipl. Pädagogin, Bonn, Humboldtstraße 2	◯	◯ **GRÜNE** — BÜNDNIS 90/DIE GRÜNEN — Kerstin Müller, Ludger Volmer, Christa Nickels, Dr. Reinhard Loske, Simone Probst	4
		◯ **PDS** — Partei des Demokratischen Sozialismus — Ulla Jelpke, Ursula Lötzer, Knud Vöcking, Ernst Dmytrowski, Astrid Keller	5
		◯ **Deutschland** — Ab jetzt ... Bündnis für Deutschland — Horst Zaborowski, Dr. -Ing. Helmut Fleck, Dietmar-Lothar Dander, Ricardo Pielsticker, Uwe Karg	6
		◯ **APPD** — Anarchistische Pogo-Partei Deutschlands — Rainer Kaufmann, Matthias Bender, Daniel-Lars Kroll, Markus Bittmann, Markus Rykalski	7
8 **Müchler**, Frank — **BüSo** — Bürgerrechts-bewegung Solidarität — Buchhändler, Düsseldorf, Ohligserstraße 45	◯	◯ **BüSo** — Bürgerrechtsbewegung Solidarität — Helga Zepp-LaRouche, Karl-Michael Vitt, Andreas Schumacher, Hildegard Reynen-Kaiser, Walter vom Stein	8

Proportional representation (PR) makes the party's percentage of seats nearly proportional to its votes. Weimar Germany had a PR system, part of its undoing. PR systems are fairer but often put too many small parties into parliament, including antidemocratic ones, and make coalitions hard to form and unstable because several parties must agree. Israel, with over a dozen parties in parliament, suffers these consequences of pure proportional representation.

The German system combines both systems. The voter has two votes, one for a single representative in one of 299 districts, the other for a party. The party vote is the crucial one because it

party list

In PR elections, party's ranking of its candidates; voters pick one list as their ballot.

threshold clause

In PR systems, minimum percentage party must win to get any seats.

determines the total number of seats a party gets in a given Land. Some of these seats are occupied by the party's district winners; additional seats are taken from a **party list** (the right-hand column on the sample ballot) to reach the percentage won on the second ballot. The party list of persons the party proposes as deputies is the standard technique for a PR system. Leading party figures are assigned high positions on the list to ensure that they get elected.

The German system works like proportional representation—percentage of votes (nearly) equals percentage of Bundestag seats—but with the advantage of single-member districts. It is known as mixed-member proportional (MMP), as it preserves overall proportionality. (The systems discussed in the box below are just mixed-member, as they do not have overall proportionality.) As in Britain and the United States, German voters get a district representative, so personality counts in German elections. It is a matter of pride among FRG politicians to be elected from a single-member district with a higher percentage than their party won on the second ballot. It shows voters like the candidate better than his or her party.

For most of the postwar years, the German system cut down the number of parties from the Weimar days until it was a two-plus system (a big CDU and SPD, plus a small FDP). One reason: A party must win at least 5 percent nationwide to get its PR share of Bundestag seats, a **threshold clause** designed to keep out splinter and extremist parties. More recently, however, new small parties have made it into parliament: the Greens and the Left. Even if below 5 percent, a party gets whatever single-member constituency seats it wins.

German parties get government campaign funds, but after the election. A party that makes it into the Bundestag gets several euros for each vote, and parties' contributions and membership fees are matched 50 percent by federal funds. A German national election costs taxpayers $150 million or more (cheap by U.S. standards).

German Political Culture

4.3   Explain how Germany's past lingers in current politics.

A German woman once told me how the Americans, in the last days of World War II, had bombed her hometown, a place of no military value. The town was a mess: Bodies lay unburied, water and electricity were out, and food supplies were unmoved. What did the townspeople do? She shrugged, "We waited for the Americans to come and tell us what to do."

Such were the beginnings of democracy in West Germany: a foreign implant grafted onto a people who were used to being told what to do. Can democracy be transplanted? (Even in Iraq?) Has it taken root in Germany? Germany's institutions are fine; the FRG's Basic Law is a model constitution. But, as we saw with Weimar, good institutions fail if people do not support them. Are German democratic values sufficiently strong and deep to withstand economic and political hard times?

Historically, Germany has a long liberal tradition—but a losing one. It grew out of the Enlightenment, as in France. In Britain, democracy gradually triumphed. In France, democracy and reaction seesawed back and forth, finally reaching an uneasy balance. In Germany, on the other hand, democracy was overwhelmed by authoritarian forces. In 1849, the German liberals were driven out of the Frankfurt cathedral. In Bismarck's Second Reich, they were treated with contempt. In the Weimar Republic, they were a minority, a pushover for authoritarians.

liberal democracy
Combines tolerance and freedoms (liberalism) with mass participation (democracy).
denazification
Purging Nazi officials from public life.

East Germany attempted to develop "people's democracy" (communism) rather than **liberal democracy** in the Western sense. Although communism and fascism are supposed to be opposites, both made individuals obedient and powerless. Many East Germans were confused and skeptical at the onrush of democracy from West Germany in 1990; they had known nothing but authoritarian rule since 1933. Now education in the East German *Länder* does not scrutinize the Communist past, and many youngsters do not understand that it was a dictatorship where the Stasi imprisoned and tortured dissidents.

Communist East Germany illustrates how legitimacy, authority, and sovereignty connect. The GDR had weak legitimacy, especially as East Germans compared their lot with free and prosperous West Germans. The regime needed a massive police apparatus and the Berlin Wall, which undermined the authority of GDR rulers. As soon as they could disobey them, East Germans did, in November 1989 when the Wall fell. Then, without a leg to stand on, East German sovereignty evaporated, and the GDR fell into the FRG's hands. Like falling dominoes, weak legitimacy toppled into authority that then collapsed sovereignty.

The Moral Vacuum

A liberal democracy requires certain moral foundations. If you are entrusting ultimate authority to the people through their representatives, you have to believe that they are generally moral, even a bit idealistic. Without this belief, a democracy lacks legitimacy. People may go along with it, but with doubts. Such was the Weimar period. Next, the Nazis left a moral vacuum in Germany, and filling it was a long, slow process, one hampered by the persistence of ex-Nazis in high places. Every time one was discovered, it undermined the moral authority of the regime. People, especially young people, thought, "Why should we respect democracy if the same old Nazis are running it?"

Immediately after the war, the Allied occupiers tried to "denazify" their occupation zones. Party members, especially officials and the Gestapo (secret police), lost their jobs and sometimes went to prison. Henry Kissinger, then a U.S. Army sergeant, rounded up Gestapo agents in the town he was running by advertising in the newspaper for experienced policemen; when they showed up, he jailed them. Still, aside from the 177 war criminals tried at Nuremberg (25 sentenced to death), **denazification** was spotty, and many Nazis got away, to Latin America or to new lives in Germany. Many made themselves useful to occupation authorities and held high positions in business, politics, and the civil service.

The new FRG's judicial system, staffed with Nazi holdovers, kept mass murderers from trial until the 1960s, when younger prosecutors were willing to pursue cases their elders let pass. A few Nazi war criminals were still being tried after 2000. The Cold War also delayed examining the Nazi past. By 1947, the Western Allies decided they needed Germany to block Soviet power, so they stopped looking for war criminals (as did U.S. occupiers in Japan).

Bonn authorities did not wish to "open old wounds." West German (and U.S.) intelligence and diplomatic services for years had known Nazi mass murderer Adolph Eichmann was in

Holocaust
Nazi genocide of Europe's Jews during World War II.

multiculturalism
Preservation of diverse languages and traditions within one country; in German, *Multikulti*.

reparations
Payment for war damages.

Argentina, but did nothing. When the Israelis caught him in 1960 (tried in 1961, hanged in 1962), Bonn feared that the trial would incriminate current officials, specifically Chancellor Adenauer's top assistant Hans Globke, who had worked on Nazi racial laws in the same office as Eichmann. A German trade deal persuaded Jerusalem to not mention any current Bonn officials in the trial.

Two presidents of the Federal Republic, Walter Scheel of the FDP and Karl Carstens of the CDU, and one chancellor, Kurt Kiesinger of the CDU, had been Nazi party members. All asserted they were nominal members, just opportunists out to further their careers when the Nazis controlled all promotions. While none was accused of any crime, what kind of moral authority did "just an opportunist" lend to the highest offices of a country trying to become a democracy?

The Remembrance of Things Past

Can a society experience collective guilt? Was it realistic to expect Germans as a whole to feel remorse for Nazi crimes? German fathers said little, and history textbooks in some Länder skipped the Nazi period, leaving young Germans in the 1950s and 1960s ignorant about the Nazis and the **Holocaust**. West Germans tried to blot out the past by throwing themselves into work, making money, and spending it conspicuously. The results were spectacular; the economy soared, and many Germans became *Wunderkinder* (wonder children), businessmen who rose from rubble to riches. But material prosperity could not fill the moral and historical void. Many young Germans in the 1960s were dissatisfied with the materialism that covered up a lack of deeper values. Some turned to far-left and, later, "green" politics.

This factor contributed to radical and sometimes violent politics in the 1970s and 1980s. The radicals were not poor; some were from wealthy families. Prosperity and materialism, in fact, rubbed them the wrong way. Said one rich girl: "I'm sick of all this caviar gobbling." She joined the terrorists and helped murder an old family friend, a banker. (She and other gang members were arrested in 1990 in East Germany, where the secret police, the Stasi, had protected them.) The Baader-Meinhof gang committed murder and bank robbery in the name of revolution, and some young Germans agreed that German society had developed a moral void with nothing to believe in but "caviar gobbling." As William Faulkner wrote: "The past isn't dead; it isn't even past."

German Catholic writer Heinrich Böll coined the term *Vergangenheitsbewältigung* ("coping with the past") in the 1950s to urge Germans to face the past squarely and admit some collective guilt. Many German intellectuals take this as necessary to found real German democracy. If Germans cannot come to grips with their own past, if they try to cover it up, Germany could again be taken over by mindless nationalists, cautioned former President Richard von Weizsäcker and leftist writer Günter Grass.

The 1979 American-made TV miniseries "Holocaust" riveted Germans' attention and triggered books, films, and school curricular changes. Many Germans, however, tired of hearing about the Holocaust and accused leftists of using guilt to promote **multiculturalism** and political correctness. Germany has paid some $60 billion in **reparations** for the Holocaust, and many Germans felt this was enough. Some felt Germany was being picked upon.

Communist East Germany avoided coming to grips with the past by denying it was their past. "We were not Nazis," taught the Communist regime, "We fought the Nazis. So we have nothing to be ashamed of or to regret. The Nazis are over there in West Germany." East Germany avoided moral responsibility by trying to portray the Nazis as a foreign power, like Austria has done. This is one way East German attitudes lagged behind West German attitudes.

political generation
Theory that age groups are marked by the great events of their young adulthood.

postmaterialism
Theory that modern culture has moved beyond getting and spending.

The Generation Gap

Long ago, I saw how a German family reacted when one of the daughters found an old poem, *"Die Hitlerblume"* (the Hitler flower), comparing the *Führer* to a blossom. The three college-age children howled with laughter and derision: "Daddy, how could you go along with this garbage?" The father, an old-fashioned authoritarian type, turned red and stammered, "You don't know what it was like. They had everybody whipped up. The times were different." He was embarrassed.

German political attitudes have undergone rapid generational changes. Younger Germans are more open, free-spirited, democratic, and European. Most give allegiance to democracy and European unity. Only a few personality problems hanker for an authoritarian system. Feeling distant from the Nazis, they are also little inclined to ponder Germany's past.

No longer are German women confined to *Kinder, Küche, Kirche* (children, kitchen, and church); most now work outside the home and participate in politics. German youngsters are

Political Culture

Political Generations in Germany

Hungarian-born sociologist Karl Mannheim coined the term **political generations** to describe how great events put a lasting stamp on young people. We can see this in Germany. Today's young Germans were formed by the fall of the Berlin Wall in 1989. Sometimes called "89ers," they stand in marked contrast with previous German generations: the 45ers, who climbed out of the rubble and rebuilt a new Germany, and the 68ers, who rebelled against complacent materialism.

Many 68ers changed over time. Chancellor Schröder had been a Marxist Juso (Young Socialist) who turned quite centrist. Green leader Joschka Fischer dropped out of high school and fought police in the streets but became a popular and effective foreign minister. Otto Schily had been a far-left lawyer who defended terrorists but joined the SPD and became interior minister, which includes internal security. Most Germans were unbothered by their pasts.

The 89ers are relatively few (because of Germany's one-child couples) and worry about unemployment and destruction of the environment. They exemplify the **postmaterialism** found throughout the advanced industrialized world. Raised in prosperity with no depression or war, young Britons, French, Germans, Japanese, and Americans tend to ignore their parents' values and embrace few causes. They are tolerant, introspective, fun-loving, and not drawn to conventional political parties (although some like the Greens) or religions or marriage and family.

Now some younger Germans repudiate the rebellion of the 68ers and playfulness of the 89ers by returning to the *bourgeois* values of earlier times (*die neue Bürgerlichkeit*). Relying on the welfare state is less fashionable; self-reliance and volunteering is back in. Hippie clothing is out; nicely dressed is in. Such people helped boost CDU electoral fortunes.

output affect
Attachment to a system based on its providing material abundance.

system affect
Attachment to a system for its own sake.

not so obedient, and German fathers no longer beat them as in the old days. If democracy starts in the home, German democracy now has a much better foundation. With millions of immigrants from all corners of the globe, Germany is also more diverse, colorful, and relaxed.

The typical German of today is far more democratic than in 1949, when the Federal Republic was founded. Those inclined to dictatorship and racism dwindle—but never to zero—while those who favor democracy and human and civil rights are a solid majority.

Is the change permanent? Political scientist Sidney Verba, in the 1960s, drew a distinction between **output affect** and **system affect** in his discussion of German political culture. The former means liking the system for what it produces (jobs, security, and material goods), the latter, liking the system because it is perceived as good. Verba thought Germans showed more of the first than the second; that is, they liked the system while the going was good— they were "fair-weather democrats"—but had not yet become "rain-or-shine democrats" like Britons or Americans. West Germans now embrace democracy, but some East Germans still judge democracy by the cars and jobs it provides.

Many Germans now argue that Germany has become a "normal" country with no special guilt about the past. Most Germans were born after the Nazis, and German democracy is as solid as any. As good Europeans, Germans should help prevent massacres in Bosnia and Kosovo, a majority of Germans felt, thus breaking the FRG taboo against using German forces outside of Germany. Until recently, most Germans hid their patriotism, but now, many politicians say they are patriotic and proud to be German.

The younger generation of Germans has new concerns about jobs and the environment that did not bother the older generation. A distance has developed between many young Germans and the mainstream political parties. In the German party system, newcomers must slowly work their way up the ranks of the major parties, starting at the local and state levels, before they can have a say at the national level. By the time they can, few are young. In the meantime, they are expected to obey party dictates and not have much input. Some youth organizations of both the Social Democrats and Free Democrats became so rambunctious that they had to be disowned by their parent parties. For many young Germans, both the Christian Democrats and Social Democrats, who alternated in power, looked staid and elderly, and neither was responsive to young people.

Belatedly, some German politicians recognized the problem. Former President Richard von Weizsäcker worried about "the failure of my generation to bring younger people into politics." Young Germans, he noted, "do not admire the moral substance of the older generation. Our economic achievement went along with a very materialistic and very selfish view of all problems."

Young Germans also turned away from the United States, which, in the 1950s and 1960s, had been their model in politics, lifestyles, and values. The assassination of President Kennedy—who had recently proclaimed *"Ich bin ein Berliner"* at the Berlin Wall—horrified Germans and made them wonder about the United States. Then some young Germans compared the Vietnam War to Hitler's aggression. Rising tensions between East and West and the warlike posture of President Reagan convinced many that the United States was willing to incinerate Germany.

Personalities

Willy Brandt as Turning Point

One sign of democracy taking root in Germany was the 1969 election that made Willy Brandt chancellor. It would have been impossible even a few years earlier, for Brandt represented a cultural change. First, Brandt was an illegitimate child, a black mark that Adenauer used in election campaigns. Second, Brandt was a Socialist, and, in his youth in the North German seaport of Lübeck, had been pretty far left. No Socialist had been in power in Germany for decades, and the CDU kept smearing the SPD as a dangerous party. Third, Brandt had fled to Norway in 1933, become a Norwegian citizen, and not reclaimed his German nationality until 1947. He was even falsely accused of fighting Germans as a Norwegian soldier.

But many Germans, especially younger ones, admired Brandt as a German who had battled the Nazis—literally, in Lübeck street fights—not "just an opportunist" like other politicians. Brandt represented a newer, better Germany as opposed to the conservative, traditional values of Adenauer and the CDU.

As mayor of West Berlin from 1957 to 1966, Brandt showed that he was tough and anti-Communist in standing up to Soviet and East German efforts at encroachment. A leading figure in the SPD, Brandt supported its 1959 dropping of Marxism. In 1964, he became the SPD's chairman, and this boosted the party's electoral fortunes.

In 1966, the SPD joined the cabinet in a grand coalition with the CDU, and he became foreign minister. Here, Brandt showed himself to be a forceful and innovative statesman with his **Ostpolitik**. In 1969, the SPD won enough Bundestag seats to form a small coalition with the FDP, and Brandt became the FRG's first Socialist chancellor. Germany looked more democratic under an anti-Nazi than an ex-Nazi (his predecessor, Kiesinger).

In 1974, a top Brandt assistant was unmasked as an East German spy. (West Germany was riddled with them.) Brandt, regretting his security slip, resigned to become the grand old man of not only German but West European social democracy. By the time he died in 1992, he could see the fruits of his Ostpolitik.

Such attitudes fed the Green and later the Left parties, which do best among young voters. A new German nationalism no longer follows in America's footsteps. Instead of automatically looking west, some young Germans look to a reunified Germany taking its rightful place as the natural leader of Central Europe. Some turned anti-U.S. and anti-NATO. The entirely new situation created by German unification, the end of the Cold War, and fighting in Bosnia, Kosovo, Iraq, and Libya made many Germans reject involvement in foreign troubles. It was ironic that the United States—which had tutored Germans to repudiate war—became the object of German antiwar feeling.

Ostpolitik
Literally "east policy"; Brandt's building of relations with East Europe, including East Germany.

Schooling for Elites

Germans respect the academic title "Herr Doktor." Eleven of Chancellor Merkel's 15 cabinet members (including herself) have academic doctorates. The thirst for doctorates brought down Defense Minister Karl-Theodor zu Guttenberg of the CSU in 2011 when much of his 2006 law dissertation was found to be plagiarized. The aristocratic Guttenberg resigned from both the cabinet and the Bundestag. Many Germans thought it was a pity because Guttenberg

Political Culture

The Ossi-Wessi Split

When the Wall came down in late 1989, there was much celebration and good will. **Wessis** were generous to the **Ossis**, but soon they soured on each other. The Ossis kept demanding the bounties of the prosperous West as a right; after all, they were all Germans, and the Wessis had so much. The Wessis did not see things that way. "We've worked hard for more than 40 years for this," they argued, "Now you Ossis must do the same." With newly acquired D-Marks from West German taxpayers, Ossis snatched up modern products while their own economy collapsed. Many West Germans quickly developed negative stereotypes of East Germans living well at Wessi expense.

The costs of bringing East Germany up to West German levels sharpened resentments. The East German economy was in far worse shape than foreseen and needed huge bailouts. Much industry had to be closed, and unemployment shot up. West German business executives talk down to their East German counterparts. Wessis think the Communists trained the Ossis into inefficiency. Ossis feel belittled by and alienated from the West German system that was quickly imposed on them. This has led to an increase in East German consciousness, which is now greater than before unification.

Some Ossis feel alienated in modern German culture and develop nostalgia (*Ostalgie*) for what they imagine were the good days in old East Germany. They recall not being obsessed with money and material possessions but enjoying a slower lifestyle and group solidarity. Modern society is too hectic and competitive, some Ossis feel. They forget about the security police and punishment for dissenters. Many Ossis who left for West Germany keep quiet about their origins. Few Ossis and Wessis marry one another, feeling that a cultural gap separates them.

Ossis shift their votes from one election to the next—first to the CDU, then to the SPD, and recently to the Left, the party of ex-Communists, people worried about their pensions, and Ossis who feel the other parties ignore them. The collapse of East Germany left citizens disoriented and lacking something to believe in. "Freedom" is not clear enough; some are still ideologically socialist and crave order and a system that guarantees their livelihood. One of the lessons of Germany's unification: You have to pay as much attention to psychological and social transitions as to economic ones. South Korean delegations have studied German unification. Gradually, however, the time is healing the values gap between young Ossis and Wessis.

Wessi
Informal name for West German.

Ossi
Informal name for East German.

was popular and effective, a prospective chancellor. He was replaced as defense minister by another aristocrat with a doctorate, Thomas de Maizière, of French Huguenot descent.

German schooling parallels that of Britain and France: Skim off the best and neglect the rest. In all three lands, changing to less-stratified systems is difficult and controversial. Germany has a three-tier system. At age 10, exams select the brightest half to go to a *Gymnasium* to earn an *Abitur* (like the French *bac*) for university admission. These are mostly children of middle-class and educated people. Other young Germans go to a *Realschule* (for white-collar jobs), and weaker performers to a *Hauptschule* (for blue-collar jobs). The system marks Germans for life: Where you start is where you stay. Trying for greater equality, in the 1960s, some *Gesamtschulen* (comprehensive schools), resembling U.S. high schools, opened but did not catch on. Most German politicians have attended *Gymnasien* and universities. Proposed reforms to make the system less class-biased are rejected by better-off parents.

There is no German equivalent of Britain's Oxbridge or France's Great Schools. As in America, the typical German politician has studied law, although, in Germany, this is done at the undergraduate rather than the postgraduate level. German (and other European) legal systems produce different attitudes than the Anglo-American common-law system does. Continental law developed from Roman law—usually in the updated form of the Napoleonic Code—and emphasizes fixed rules. The common law, on the other hand, is judge-made law that focuses on precedent and persuasion; it is flexible. The former system produces lawyers who go by the book, the latter lawyers who negotiate and make deals. Consequently, German politicians are heavily law oriented rather than people oriented.

romanticism
Hearkening to an ideal world or mythical past.

Much of the work of the Bundestag, for example, is in the precise wording of bills, making that house a rather dull, inward-looking chamber that wins little admiration from the public. Likewise, cabinet ministers see their role heavily in terms of carrying out laws. Every cabinet has many lawyers; often the chancellor is one.

Economists also play a bigger role in German politics than in most other countries. One German chancellor had a PhD in economics: Ludwig Erhard. Under Adenauer, rotund, jolly Economics Minister Erhard charted Germany's rise to prosperity; later, he became chancellor. Helmut Schmidt, an economics graduate, succeeded Brandt as SPD chancellor and managed to keep both inflation and unemployment low in Germany while much of the world went through a major recession. In Germany, economists are not just advisers but often important policy makers.

The German Split Personality

The French often seem split between demanding impersonal authority and rebelling against it. The Germans have a sort of split personality, too, but it is between **romanticism** and realism.

Most of the time, Germans are pragmatic realists—hard working, thrifty, clean, orderly, cooperative, family oriented. But a romantic streak runs through German history. Nineteenth-century intellectuals (such as composer Richard Wagner) reveled in the *Volksgeist*. Nazi youth really believed they were building a "thousand-year Reich." In the 1970s, far-left terrorists sought utopia by assassination. The latest German romantics are the Greens, who long for a pastoral idyll free of industry and pollution. German romanticism also manifests itself in the striving for perfection, which may lead Germans to undertake absurd projects. Hitler's plan to conquer all of Europe, including Russia, is an infamous example.

Germans set high store by achievement. To work harder, produce more, and proudly let others know it seems to be part of German culture (although fading among young Germans). This helps explain Germany's rise after the war to Europe's number-one economic power. Both East Germany's leader Walter Ulbricht and West Germany's Helmut Schmidt toured their respective camps giving unsolicited advice on how other countries should copy the German economic miracle. East Germany's economy, although not as spectacular as the Federal Republic's, nonetheless made it the envy of the East bloc. Back when the Wall stood, I told an anti-Communist West Berliner that East Berlin also looked prosperous. He nodded and said, "Of course. They're Germans, too."

center-seeking

Parties trying to win a big centrist vote with moderate programs.

Perhaps the archetypal German figure is Goethe's Faust, the driven, ambitious person who can never be content. This quality can produce both great good and evil. Former Chancellor Helmut Schmidt, an archetypical German realist, once said, "Germans have an enormous capacity for idealism and the perversion of it."

Patterns of Interaction

4.4 Explain why a center-peaked unimodal distribution of political values is necessary to sustain democracy.

With unification—and even a little before—German politics became less stable and more complex. The party system is no longer "two-plus"; the Greens and Left make it a multiparty system. The two large parties lost some of their votes to smaller parties. This made coalition formation more difficult, for now a German coalition may require three partners instead of the previous two. With nine possible coalition combinations, German cabinet formation is now less stable and predictable.

Weimar collapsed with the shrinking of moderate parties and growth of extremist parties—"polarized pluralism." Could this happen in the Federal Republic? The large parties, for good political reasons, stick close to the center of the political spectrum, making political competition **center-seeking**. Before reunification, West German voters chose among three moderate parties (there were several tiny parties on the ballot) that could combine in only three

The Shape of the German Electorate: The Self-Placement of German Voters on a Left/Right Ideological Scale

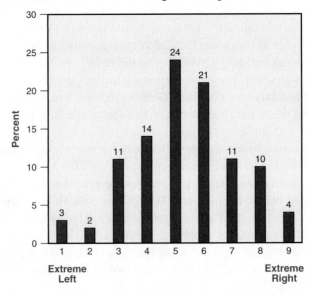

Geography

Sailing the Baltic

Back on your luxury yacht, you are sailing in a great, clockwise circle around the Baltic Sea, always staying with land a few kilometers to port (left). Upon entering the Skagerrak, which countries do you pass on your left?

Norway, Sweden, Finland, Russia, Estonia, Latvia, Lithuania, Russia again (Kaliningrad Oblast), Poland, Germany, and Denmark.

different coalitions (CDU and FDP, CDU and SPD, SPD and FDP). This made West German politics stable compared with more tumultuous multiparty systems, but now Germany is also a multiparty system.

Parties and the Electorate

Social scientists repeatedly find that political opinion in most modern democracies resembles a bell-shaped curve: Most citizens are in the center, with fewer and fewer as one moves to the left or right: a **unimodal** distribution of opinion. (A **bimodal** distribution indicates extreme division, what happened during Weimar.) Routinely, Europeans are asked to place themselves on a one-to-nine ideological scale, one for the most left and nine for the most right. Germany comes out, like most West European countries, as a bell-shaped curve (see graph).

When party leaders understand the bell shape of the electorate, either through polling or by election results, they usually tailor their *party image* to appeal to the middle of the opinion spectrum. If the Social Democrats are too far left—say, at two on the nine-point scale—by advocating nationalizing industry and leaving NATO, they please left-wing ideologues but do poorly in elections, because few Germans are at the two position. So the SPD tones down its socialism and emphasizes democracy plus welfare measures, moving to the four and then five position. Now it gains enough centrist votes to become Germany's governing party. To be sure, some on the SPD left move to the Greens or Left. But which is better—staying ideologically pure or winning elections?

That is a thumbnail history of the SPD. A century ago, the Social Democrats started to shed their Marxism, in practice if not yet in theory. In the 1950s, seeing the CDU triumphantly win the center, they decided to break out of their left-wing stronghold. Meeting in Bad Godesberg (just outside Bonn) in 1959, they drew up a Basic Program so moderate one can hardly find any socialism in it. Marxism was *kaputt*; the SPD proclaimed itself "rooted in Christian ethics, humanism and classical philosophy."

While the Social Democrats moved rightward, the Christian Democrats had already taken a broad swath of the ideological spectrum, claiming to stand for everything—a party of all Germans—just as the British Conservatives claim to represent all Britons. The CDU downplayed its conservatism, for it, too, understood that if the party image were too rightist, it would lose the big prize in the center. The result is two large parties that have generally tried to

unimodal
Single-peaked distribution.

bimodal
Two-peaked distribution.

Weltanschauung
Literally "world view"; parties offering firm, narrow ideologies.

catchall
Nonideological parties that welcome all.

be centrist but in so doing have rubbed their respective left and right wings the wrong way. They also make politics boring.

As they turned into a center-left party, the SPD allowed the area on their left to be taken over by newer, more radical parties, the Greens and Left. (In one study, Green voters placed themselves at 3.4 on the scale.) Partly to try to win over these leftist voters, partly in response to Juso (see box above) influence within the SPD, and partly out of irritation at the hawkishness of the Reagan administration, the SPD moved leftward in the late 1980s, much like the British Labour Party had done earlier. The SPD came out against U.S. nuclear missiles in Germany and nuclear power plants, two key Green demands. But the shift hurt the SPD in elections.

The SPD is still pulled in two directions. Tugging leftward is the traditional socialist wing, based heavily on workers and older people, that wants to help those in need and preserve the welfare state. Tugging rightward is the centrist majority of the SPD, which understands the need to trim pensions, subsidies, bureaucracy, unemployment, and regulations that slow economic growth. The left–right tug within the SPD resembles that of the British Labour Party and U.S. Democrats.

The Chancellor and the Electorate

Two factors especially hurt the SPD in the 1990s. The CDU's embrace of rapid unification made the SPD look narrow and carping in its warnings about the expense and economic impact of quick merger. "Go slow and think it through" was the SPD message, not a popular one in 1990, although their "I told you so" won them some votes in 1994. SPD chancellor candidates in 1990 and 1994 were too clever and radical for most German voters. In 1998, the SPD took a leaf from Tony Blair's 1997 success in Britain: Assume vague, centrist positions; emphasize that the conservatives have been in office too long; and offer a younger, outgoing personality for prime minister. The SPD, in effect, learned the unimodal shape of the German electorate in the 1950s and 1960s, forgot it in the 1980s, and relearned it in the late 1990s, but, with their shopworn defense of welfare benefits in elections since, may need to learn it again.

In Germany, as in most advanced countries, personality has become more important than ideology. With the decline of **Weltanschauung** parties (see box below) and the shift of large parties to the center of the political spectrum, the personality of candidates is often what persuades voters. Some call it the Americanization of European politics, but it is less a matter of copying than it is of reflecting the rise of **catchall** parties. Throughout Europe, election posters now feature the face of the top party leader who would become prime minister. Although voting may be by party list, citizens know that in choosing a party they are actually electing a prime minister. In 2013, Merkel was more popular than her party as a whole and far ahead of the SPD's unimpressive Steinbrück.

German (and British) campaigns are conducted almost as if they were for the direct election of a president—as in the United States and France. Officially, there is no "candidate for chancellor," but in practice, the leaders of the two big parties are clearly identified as such—in the media, on billboards, and in the public mind—so that much of the campaign revolves around the personalities of the two leading candidates.

Democracy

The "Catchall" Party

In prewar Europe, many political parties used to imbue their supporters with a "view of the world" (*Weltanschauung*) corresponding to the party's ideology and philosophy. This was especially true of parties on the left, and it came to a high point in Weimar Germany. After World War II, most Weltanschauung parties disappeared as they broadened their appeal or merged into bigger parties.

Noting their demise, German political scientist Otto Kirchheimer coined the term "catchall party" to describe what was taking their place: big, loose, pluralist parties that have diluted their ideologies so they can accommodate many diverse groups of supporters. His model of a catchall party was the CDU, a political vacuum cleaner that draws in all groups:

farmers, businesspeople, labor, women, Catholics, Protestants, white-collar workers, blue collar, you name it.

For a while, under crusty Kurt Schumacher, the SPD tried to stay a Weltanschauung party, defining itself in rigid and ideological terms that turned away many middle-of-the-road voters. Since 1959, the SPD, too, has become a catchall party, appealing to Germans of all classes and backgrounds. Indeed, by now the catchall party is the norm in modern democracies. Almost axiomatically, any large party is bound to be a catchall party—for example, the French neo-Gaullists, Canadian Liberals, British Conservatives, Japanese Liberal Democrats, and, of course, both major U.S. parties.

A German candidate for chancellor must project strength and levelheadedness. In a country that still fears inflation, the candidate's economic background plays a big role. Two of Germany's postwar chancellors have been economists. The candidate's adherence to democratic rules also matters, and Franz Josef Strauss's authoritarian streak contributed to his 1980 defeat.

Personality counts in German elections. The CDU/CSU had the steady, optimistic Helmut Kohl (1982–1998) and now the calm, cautious pragmatism of Angela Merkel, dubbed *"Mutti"* (mom). Much of postwar German politics can be described as parties groping for the right leader to bring them to power in the Bundestag and chancellor's office. When they find the right ones—such as Adenauer, Kohl, and Merkel of the CDU—they stick with them. Were it not for his security slipup, Brandt could have played a similar role for the SPD.

German Dealignment?

For many years, political scientists have worried that American voters have shown an increasing **dealignment** with the main parties. Some decades ago, U.S. parties used to present a fairly clear party image, and most voters carried around in their heads a fairly clear party ID. Where the two connected (for example, U.S. Democrats and blue-collar workers) grew reliable party–voter "alignments." These could change every few decades in what were called "realignments," new matches of voters to parties. But some think U.S. voters are dealigning: Their preferences, often unfocused, connect with no party on a long-term basis. Their votes easily shift in response to candidate personality and clever advertising.

Britain, France, and Germany also show evidence of electoral dealignment. Many Germans dislike both major parties and doubt that

dealignment
Voters losing identification with any party.

Political Culture

Bavaria's Own Party: The CSU

Bavaria is the Texas of Germany, a land with its own distinctive politics. On principle, the Christian Social Union (CSU) never let itself be absorbed into the CDU. Instead, it calls itself an allied party and boasts of having turned once-pastoral Bavaria—where it has at times won a majority of the vote—into the most prosperous Land of Germany and a model for the others. The CSU is more Catholic and to the right of the CDU on immigrants, radicals, and welfare. The four CSU ministers in Merkel's third cabinet preach a tough line against government bailouts and debt.

one does better in office than the other. German electoral turnout, as in most of Europe, is falling, from a high of 91 percent in 1972 to 72 percent in 2013. More Germans now scatter their votes among small parties across the political spectrum. The whimsical Pirate Party enjoyed a brief surge by mixing left and right themes with internet piracy.

Dealignment is the normal and natural maturation process that most advanced democracies go through. One step in this process is the formation of the catchall party (see earlier Democracy box). If two catchall parties face each other, their positions can become so moderate and similar that they risk becoming boring. Exciting new choices, programs, or personalities are few. Green leader Joschka Fischer was popular because he was not boring. (After his fourth divorce, he got a young girlfriend. Imagine that in U.S. politics.)

Meanwhile, society is hit by problems few could imagine a generation ago: immigration, environmental degradation, the movement of jobs to low-wage countries, and crushing tax and debt burdens. None of the catchall parties has any convincing solution; all waffle in some middle ground. Also, suddenly gone is the cement that helped hold the system together: the Soviet threat. It is a disorienting time, and none of the great catchall parties provides much in the way of guidance. The public response is lower voter turnouts and small and less-stable shares of the vote for the catchall parties—in a word, dealignment.

The Bundestag and the Citizen

One reason German elections have become almost presidential elections for chancellor is the murky status of the Bundestag in the minds of many voters. They know what the chancellor does but are not too clear on what the Bundestag does. Part of the blame for this rests on the concept Bundestag deputies have of their role. The **Rechtsstaat** tradition is focused on laws. The Bundestag, now housed in the old Reichstag building in Berlin, is staffed heavily by lawyers and civil servants and has become a law factory.

But is it not a legislature's purpose to legislate? Not entirely. By confining their activities to law books and committee meetings, the Bundestag deputies have failed to grasp the less obvious functions of a legislature. Equally important is the role of a legislature in overseeing the activities of the national government, catching corruption and inefficiency, uncovering scandals, threatening budget cuts, and keeping the bureaucrats on their toes.

Rechtsstaat
Literally, state of laws; government based on written rules and rights.

Publicity cures much governmental wrongdoing. Too-cozy relationships between ministers and businesses thrive in the dark. It is in this area that the Bundestag has been weak. Although there are commissions of inquiry and a question hour, the former are not pursued as thoroughly as on Washington's Capitol Hill—where televised committee hearings are a major preoccupation—and the latter is not carried out with as much verve as in Commons. (Bundestag deputies can be quite insulting, but they often sound crude rather than clever.) In functioning as little but lawmakers, German legislators have contributed to the boredom problem.

One function the Bundestag neglects is education. The way legislators operate, argue, and conduct themselves is a great teacher of democracy. The Bundestag does not generate good press because it is a dull story. U.S. senators and representatives get more attention because they do interesting and unpredictable things, like disobeying their own party, something that rarely happens in Germany.

Another legislative function is to represent people. Voters must feel that someone is speaking for them and understands their needs. The Bundestag suffers from a problem common to all elected legislatures: It is not representative of voters. The average Bundestag deputy is close to 50 years old, male, trained as a lawyer, and employed as a civil servant, party leader, or interest-group official.

Germany's well-organized parties generally require members to slowly work their way up the ranks before they are put on a ballot. Accordingly, candidates tend to be older, seasoned party loyalists rather than fresh, new faces. Unlike in the American system, few German candidates "come from out of nowhere" to win on their own. Candidates tend to be a piece of the party machine. The result is unrepresentative representatives. Many Germans do not feel represented, finding instead that the Bundestag is where the powerful interests of society work out deals with little reference to the common citizen. Such feelings contribute to the Green and Left vote.

The Union-Party Linkup

Unions in Germany are still strong but not what they used to be, another sign of the fraying of Germany's "consensus model" (discussed below). One historical characteristic of North Europe—and here we include Britain and Sweden along with Germany—has been the close relationship between labor unions and social democratic parties. Unions are large and cohesive; blue-collar workers are heavily organized, and their unions form a single, large labor federation. Such federations support the social democratic parties with money, manpower, and votes. Often, union leaders run for office on the party ticket. In Latin Europe, labor is weakly organized and fragmented. U.S. labor, now in decline, no longer has the political input of North European labor, where unions founded the welfare state.

In Britain, unions are actual constituent members of the Labour Party. In Sweden, the gigantic LO is so close to the Social Democrats that some of their top personnel are the same. The German Basic Law forbids a formal union-party tie, but here, too, everyone knows that labor support is an important pillar of the SPD.

In the United States, 11 percent of the labor force is unionized; in Germany, 20 percent is (in Sweden, some 50 percent). Eleven German industrial unions—the largest is the metalworkers, *IG Metall*, with 2.4 million members—are federated into an umbrella organization, the

Democracy

Germany's Coalitions

Two-party coalitions have been the norm for Germany—usually one large party and one small party. When either of the two large parties (CDU or SPD) gets around 40 percent of the vote (and of Bundestag seats), it forms a coalition with a small party that won around 10 percent and thus controls a (bare) majority of the Bundestag. This gives rise to coalition possibilities 1 through 4, which have governed the FRG thus far:

1. Christian-Liberal Coalition: The CDU/CSU wins the most Bundestag seats but less than half and so needs the FDP's seats to form the coalition that governed for much of the FRG's history. Called the "bourgeois coalition," it returned to power from 2009 to 2013 but not since, as the FDP was out of the Bundestag.

2. Social-Liberal Coalition: The SPD edges out the CDU in Bundestag seats, but still less than half, and so turns to the FDP to build the coalition that supported Brandt and Schmidt in the 1970s.

3. Grand Coalition: If the two big parties, the CDU and SPD, shrink to around one-third of the vote, and the small parties get about 10 percent each, then coalitions 1 and 2 become impossible. The two big parties may then have to make a coalition with each other, as they did in the late 1960s, in 2005–2009, and after the 2013 election.

4. Red-Green Coalition: If the SPD (red) gets, say, 40 percent and the Greens get 10 percent, they build a social-ecological coalition, which ruled from 1998 to 2005 and could happen again.

Five other coalitions are possible but unlikely:

5. "Traffic Light" (*Ampel*) Coalition: Red, green, and yellow (for the FDP). If the SPD won under 40 percent, it might need two small coalition partners, each with 6 to 10 percent of Bundestag seats, in order to build a majority. The Liberals, if they ever revive, and Greens, however, are ideologically incompatible and oppose each other.

6. "Jamaica" Coalition (named after the colors of the Jamaican flag): This coalition would be the right-wing counterpart of the *Ampel*—black (CDU), yellow (FDP), and green. The FDP and Greens, however, dislike each other.

7. An SPD-Left Coalition: The new Left is too far left for most other parties, but in a pinch, the SPD could turn to it.

8. An all-left coalition: If the SPD gets about a third and the Greens and Left both get around 10 percent, all three could form a leftist coalition.

9. A "government of national unity" of all parties: These can be useful for emergency situations such as war, but not for much else. According to the theory of coalitions, you stop adding partners once you have topped 50 percent; there is no point to adding more. And an all-party coalition would not stay together for long.

Deutscher Gewerkschaftsbund (DGB) with 7 million members, down from 11.8 million in 1990. (U.S., British, French, and German unions have all declined. Is this permanent or reversible?)

The DGB is still heeded by the Social Democrats, but not as much as before. Union leaders are regularly consulted by SPD chiefs and get some of what they want: an elaborate welfare system, a short work week, and even directors' seats on the boards of large companies (more on this below). Many SPD Bundestag deputies have union ties. In 2001, five service unions formed the 2.2-million-member Verdi (*Vereinte Dienstleistungsgewerkschaft*) to organize everything from clerks to nurses to civil servants. Service unions such as Verdi have different demands than do the industrial unions in the DGB. As the industrial sector shrinks in favor of services, unions shift, too. In modern societies, unions grow heavily among government employees and teachers.

The catchall nature of the SPD prevents any one group from dominating it. The more the SPD seeks votes in the political center, the more it turns away from close cooperation with unions. (The British Labourites faced the same problem; when they let the unions dominate, they lost.) Starting in the 1970s, the SPD and unions diverged. Chancellor Helmut Schmidt (1974–1982), representing the SPD right, was a better democrat and economist than socialist. Union relations with the SPD cooled. The Schröder government told unions that raising wages and benefits worked against adding new jobs and that cutting benefits and flexible work rules boost the economy. The unions did not want to hear it and grew angry at Schröder. Some unionists went to the Left party, and in 2009, IG Metall endorsed no party. Schröder's controversial reforms, however, laid the groundwork for Germany's subsequent prosperity.

The management side shows a similar pattern. The powerful *Bundesverband der Deutschen Industrie* (Federation of German Industries, BDI) has warm connections with the CDU but not as close as those of unions with the SPD. The BDI wants flexible labor contracts and tax cuts, points the CDU also likes. One point of conflict: German business wants select immigration (such as computer specialists) to fill high-tech vacancies, but the CDU/CSU says no to all immigration. When the Social Democrats are in power, the BDI finds it can get along with them, too. As in most democracies, big business is happy to work with all parties. The major focus of business is the bureaucracy, not the parties. Providing information to the relevant ministry, explaining to civil servants why regulations should be modified, going along with government economic plans—in these and other ways, business quietly cements ties with government.

The Länder and Berlin

Britain and France are unitary systems that have moved, respectively, to devolution and decentralization. Germany is a federal system that some would like to make a little more centralized. Both unitary and federal systems are under pressure to move toward a middle ground. Centralization in France was rigid and inefficient, and it ignored local wishes and regional pride. Federalism in Germany is often uncoordinated, powerless, and deadlocked and encourages federal-state squabbles. The distinctions between unitary and federal systems are overdrawn; some see the emergence of a new "regional" pattern midway between unitary and federal.

Germany is probably more federal than the United States; that is, its Länder run more of their own affairs and get a bigger portion of taxes than do American states. For example, individual and corporate income taxes are split between Berlin and the Länder with equal 42.5 percent shares; local governments get 15 percent. The Länder also get 45.9 percent of the value-added tax, the large but hidden sales tax used throughout Europe. The poorer Länder— the new eastern ones—get additional funds. German Länder are directly plugged into the federal tax system, an idea Americans might consider.

Germany's federalism has some drawbacks. With no nationwide police force, law enforcement is a Land affair. Terrorists who commit their crimes in one Land can flee to another, counting on communication and coordination foul-ups to delay police. Cleaning the polluted Rhine River took decades because such matters are controlled by the states, and each sees its

Geography

Elections and Maps

Virtually all elections show geographical voting patterns and regional variations in party strength. A map of Britain showing where parties score best, for example, seldom needs to be changed; major parties tend to preserve their regional strength. Once rooted, regional voting patterns can persist for decades. Here are some of the patterns.

1. *Cities vote left (liberal in U.S. terms).* Urban areas are usually to the left of rural areas. Cities are places of education, intellectuals, and critics calling for change and reform. Workers tend to be urban and discontent over wages and benefits. The countryside tends to be calmer, more accepting of the status quo, and often still controlled by political bosses or old traditions. Rural and farming people often resent urban intellectuals for having more experimental notions than common sense.

    England outside of the big cities votes Conservative; central London votes Labour. Catholic Bavaria votes Christian Social, but Munich votes Social Democrat. Paris needs some qualification, for, in Paris, the better-off people live in the city while the working class lives in the suburbs. This gives Paris a conservative core but a "red belt" around the city, now eroding as the old working-class suburbs gentrify. In Russian elections, the big cities, led by Moscow and St. Petersburg, more strongly support relatively liberal parties than does the countryside, which likes Putin and fears economic disruption. Iranian city dwellers are more moderate or liberal, rural people more religious and traditional. U.S. elections show strong urban–rural splits.

2. *Every country has regional voting.* Regions vote their resentments. Typically, the periphery votes against the core area. If the core votes for party X, the periphery votes for party Y. If the periphery was conquered long ago, it remembers this eternally, as has the U.S. South. Scotland and Wales show their resentments toward England by voting Labour, but England stays Tory. France south of the Loire River and Spain south of the Tagus River tend to go Socialist, acting out their resentments toward, respectively, Paris and Madrid. The south of Brazil, on the other hand, now tends to oppose the Labor Party. As the Soviet Union's republics held free and fair elections, many strongly nationalistic republic governments took office and proclaimed their independence. Lithuanians' and Georgians' hatred of Moscow led them to nationalistic parties.

3. *Voting follows religion.* Religious attitudes tend to be regional. Indeed, the religion factor is one explanation for points 1 and 2. Big cities tend to be less religious than small towns, inclining the cities to vote liberal or left. Some regions have different religions than the core area. Scottish Presbyterians show their difference from the Anglicans by not voting Tory. Some German Protestants still see the Christian Democratic Union as a Catholic party and therefore vote against it, a tendency muddied by other factors. Immediately after unification, largely Protestant East Germany went CDU, but it has since swung to leftist parties—the SPD and Left. Religion helped to pull the Soviet Union apart, as Muslim republics installed Islamic regimes that were implicitly anti-Christian. In the Caucasus, persons of Christian origin, even if irreligious, feel threatened. Surrounded by hostile Islamic peoples, they elect implicitly anti-Muslim Christian governments, as in Armenia and Georgia.

Compare Percentage of Catholics per Land (left) to Percentage of CDU/CSU Vote per Land (right)

With the exception of North Rhine-Westphalia and Saarland, a high percentage of Catholics accompanies heavy CDU/CSU voting. Former East Germany has few Catholics.

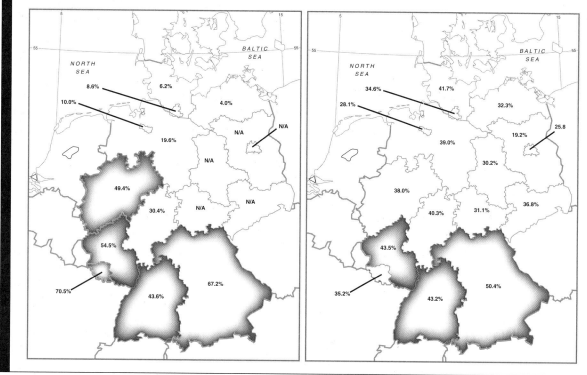

environmental responsibilities differently. In 1986, the Bundestag set up a federal environment ministry, but it could not override Land environment ministries. And decentralized education made it impossible for federal authorities to insist that schools cover the Nazis and their crimes.

The German Länder, like American states, resist moves that would erode the powers of Land officials, and they have the perfect means to do so: the Bundesrat, which is often in the hands of the opposition party. Bundesrat delegations are composed of the state's political chiefs. The Bundesrat must concur on any move that would alter the balance between federation and state, and they usually reject such moves. The Bundesrat, like the U.S. Senate, acts as a check on both the cabinet and the lower house. A 2006 reform trimmed the Bundesrat's blocking powers in exchange for allowing the Länder to have control of education, civil service pay, and other areas, which made Germany more federal.

German Voting Patterns

In Britain, the vote follows region and social class. Labour usually wins Scotland, Wales, and large industrial cities plus much of the working class. French voting is similar, with the added factor of clerical or anticlerical. West German voting also tended to follow region, class, and religion, but the addition of East Germany in 1990 muddied this. Dealignment muddied it further.

In Germany, religion means Catholic or Protestant. German Catholics are more likely to vote CDU; therefore, heavily Catholic Länder such as Baden-Wurttemberg generally go with the CDU. The CSU long had Catholic Bavaria sewn up. Farther north, in the largely Protestant Länder, the SPD tends to do better, as they do in large cities. In a parallel with the U.S. vote, in Germany, the rural and small-town vote tends strongly to the CDU. German workers, especially those who belong to a union, are generally more loyal to the SPD than British workers are to the Labour Party. Thus, an *ideal-typical* SPD voter in Germany is a Protestant worker in a large northern city. His or her CDU counterpart is a middle-class Catholic in a small southern town. The Free Democrats appeal to some of the Protestant middle class, the Greens to young people, and the Left to East Germans and those left out of prosperity.

East Germany—although it is almost completely Protestant and, pre-1933, voted mostly SPD—went heavily Christian Democrat in 1990. As the costs and disappointments of unification became clear, some East Germans moved to the SPD, confirming the SPD as a party that is more attractive to Protestants and urban workers. But a good number of Ossis lent their votes to the Greens, then to the ex-Communist Party of Democratic Socialism, and then, in 2005, 2009, and 2013, to the Left. German voting, like the German party system, has become more complex and less predictable.

What Germans Quarrel About

4.5   Compare Germany's and Japan's postwar economic recoveries.

The Political Economy of Germany

European countries are welfare states, but now they are asking how much welfare they can afford. One-third of Germany's GDP goes for social spending, a heavy tax burden on Germany's manufacturing competitiveness. Germany's welfare system is Europe's oldest and has grown and is accepted by just about everyone. Even some Social Democrats, however, now worry that their generous welfare provisions could price them out of the market. Both CDU and SPD governments cut unemployment and welfare benefits. German pensions are generous, but to pay for them, German workers must contribute 20 percent of their wages, and this will soon rise to 30 percent if present trends continue. Without further drastic reforms, the German welfare system will impose an impossible burden on the younger generation.

Nothing produces economic miracles, it has been said, like losing a war—surely the case in West Germany and Japan following World War II. There was simply nothing to do but work. Some German factories were destroyed by Allied bombing. The Red Army ripped out machine tools and shipped them back to the Soviet Union. The British and Americans patched up their old industries, but the Germans were forced to rebuild theirs with new and more-efficient equipment.

Basically, rapid economic growth comes from wages that lag behind productivity, as in Germany and Japan. After the war, German workers' skills were still high, and much of

Germany's infrastructure was intact. At first, labor unions practiced **wage restraint** to let capital grow until it provided jobs and good wages for all. This period—from the 1950s through the 1970s—was the time of Germany's rapid growth (as well as France's and Japan's). In contrast, British and U.S. productivity lagged behind wage increases.

wage restraint
Unions holding back on compensation demands.

Wirtschaftswunder
German for "economic miracle."

unit labor costs
What it costs to manufacture the same item in different countries.

The aftermath of war had some psychological benefits. Almost everybody was poor; food and fuel were barely sufficient for survival. This produced greater material equality among Germans; income distribution was more equitable in Germany (and Japan) than in the victorious countries. Consequently, the bitter class antagonisms found in Britain and France did not develop in Germany. Everyone started from a similar low level, and most West Germans felt that everyone got a share of economic growth. Furthermore, defeat in the war and empty stomachs left Germans with more modest expectations than was the case for Britons or Americans, who expected a bountiful economy. For West Germans, hard work and economic recovery were their only outlets for national pride.

Under the leadership of the CDU and Economics Minister (later Chancellor) Ludwig Erhard, West Germany produced growth so rapid it was called the **Wirtschaftswunder**. While Britain turned to Labour's welfare state and France to *planification* after World War II, West Germany relied mainly on market forces. Bonn, like Tokyo, supervised the macroeconomy but left the microeconomy private—no government takeovers—and both Germany

Comparison

Who Wins the Manufacturing Race?

It is not necessarily those with the lowest wages who win the global manufacturing race. What you need is lower wages combined with good productivity. The table below shows how the situation looks among five industrialized democracies.

Hourly labor costs, here for 2005, include bonuses, benefits, and social security and other taxes (such as health insurance), which, in Germany, add 80 percent to regular wages. These "social taxes" are low in the United States and Japan. **Unit labor costs** combine total labor costs with productivity. The clear winner: the United States, which benefits from a cheaper dollar. Productivity figures change constantly and are closely monitored as signs of a nation's economic vitality. China beats them all by several miles, but standardized, accurate Chinese data are hard to come by.

	Average Hourly Labor Costs	Unit Labor Costs
Britain	$26	165
France	25	145
Germany	33	140
Japan	22	125
United States	22	100

SOURCE: U.S. Department of Labor, Swedish Employers Federation

soziale Marktwirtschaft
"Social market economy";
Germany's postwar capitalism
aimed at reconstruction and
welfare.

Modell Deutschland
German economic model.

consensus
Agreement among all
constituent groups.

Mitbestimmung
"Codetermination"; unions
participating in company
decisions.

and Japan recovered quickly. Erhard's **soziale Marktwirtschaft** was basically a free market with bank loans for social goals, such as rebuilding Germany's bombed-out cities. It continued and expanded the welfare state begun by Bismarck. Some called it "capitalism with a conscience."

During the 1970s, the **Modell Deutschland** that stressed **consensus** among all social groups was successful and admired. In it, no one's views were ignored. Workers, for example, have **Mitbestimmung**, which gives unions a role in overall company policy. Each large firm has a supervisory board with half its directors chosen by labor and half by top management and big shareholders. For example, in 1999, BMW's ten worker representatives on the board vetoed a proposed executive they did not like and got one they did. Codetermination is one reason Germany has few strikes; workers feel they are part of the system.

Like most countries, Germany suffered during the 2008–2009 recession, but less than other industrialized lands, and, for a while, enjoyed an export upsurge. The German economy in 2010 grew 3.6 percent, the highest of the advanced industrialized countries (but fell to 0.5 percent in 2013). During the 1970s and 1980s, Germany's postwar miracle tapered off as wages and welfare benefits climbed until German wages surpassed U.S. wages, social taxes were much higher, and productivity was no longer growing quickly. America got more competitive; wages had been essentially stagnant since the early 1970s, but productivity grew. The U.S. welfare floor, always much lower than the German, is less of a tax burden. U.S. labor costs, when benefits and social taxes are reckoned in, are much lower than German labor costs. Until recently, individual and corporate taxes and regulations were heavier in Germany than in America. Under such pressures, German capital fled abroad. German investment in the United States created some two-thirds of a million American jobs. Your BMW was made in Georgia, your Volkswagen in Tennessee.

By the 1990s, Germans enjoyed short work weeks (35 hours), long vacations (six to eight weeks), the world's highest pay, lush unemployment benefits, male retirement at 63 (women at 60) with good pensions, and almost no strikes. With these *labor-force rigidities*, however, firms hired few new workers. The result: Formerly labor-short Germany has been hit by recurring bouts of unemployment, at times over 10 percent (twice as high in the east as in the west). GDP growth does not guarantee low unemployment, which can persist even when the economy is growing.

In a 1996 austerity package, the Bundestag cut Germans' health, unemployment, and welfare benefits and gradually raised the retirement age to 65 for men and 63 for women (now being slowly raised to 67, already the U.S. norm). Kohl's CDU government defended the cuts as moderate, necessary, and supported by most Germans, who were fed up with high taxes. Opponents of the cuts, including the SPD, called them "socially obscene" and the "destruction of the welfare state." The cuts helped the SPD win the 1998 elections, but Schröder had to deliver similar austerity budgets, tightening of welfare benefits, and greater work and wage flexibility. The left wing of his SPD howled—some deserted to the new Left—but the economy allowed him no choice. And it worked. The German economy, thanks to strong exports, suffered little from the 2008–2009 recession.

Comparison

The German and U.S. Economies

Germany weathered the 2008–2009 recession much better than did the United States. There was no German debt bubble to burst. German mortgages were always hard to get—often requiring 50 percent down—and few Germans use credit cards, much less max them out. Like Japanese, Germans are thrifty.

The famous *Mittelstand*—small and medium-sized firms, many in metalworking—spearheaded German growth. Some 20 percent of Germany's economy is in manufacturing; in the United States, only about 11 percent is. Manufacturing is a more stable basis for an economy than are financial services, which grew massively in the United States (and Britain). Germany's Mittelstand gets loans from local savings banks (*Sparkassen*) that know the

firm, whereas much U.S. credit flows through distant giant banks that gamble with complex and risky investments.

As a result, Germany, already a major exporter, was ready to supply booming countries such as China, India, and Brazil with the cars, power generators, and machine tools they need. Germany runs a major trade surplus, the United States a major trade deficit. Worldwide, Germany has gained the most from globalization. America does not make as much as Germany for export. U.S. exports, however, have begun to turn around. U.S. productivity is up, a weaker dollar makes American goods more competitive, and natural gas provides cheap energy. Americans are learning how to export again.

Merging Two Economies

The sudden merging of two very different systems was and still is a difficult economic hurdle. Over 45 years, the free-market West German economy had become a world giant. The centrally controlled and planned East German economy, although it was the envy of the East bloc, had a per capita GDP one-third that of West Germany. West German products were desired throughout the world; East German products were sold mostly to the Soviet bloc plus some Third World lands too poor to afford better. Two very different German economies existed side by side but with little trade between them, so they did not directly compete.

In 1990, the physical and political barriers between the two Germanys suddenly disappeared. West German currency and products flooded into East Germany, and the East German economy collapsed with a speed and thoroughness no one had foreseen. East Germans ceased buying East German products as soon as they could buy nicer West German goods. As gigantic state subsidies ended, East German factory and farm production plummeted, and unemployment shot from essentially zero into the millions. Few East German enterprises survived the transition to a market economy.

Saving the East German economy required tons of money, far more than anticipated—€1.6 trillion ($2.3 trillion) so far—from the federal government. Ultimately, of course, it comes from West German taxpayers. Some €80 billion (3 percent of Germany's GDP) flows to the east every year in subsidies. Thus, the first great quarrel of united Germany grew out of how to merge the two economies and who was going to pay for it. Chancellor Kohl said the bailout of the East German economy could be done without higher taxes, but the next year, he put a 7.5 percent "solidarity surcharge" on income taxes. It was unpopular but necessary.

Geography

How Germany Unified

The collapse of Communist East Europe in 1989 surprised most observers, who did not comprehend how inefficient and slow-growing its economies were. The Soviet Union, falling behind the West, had to call off the Cold War and cut loose its dependent East European satellites. As soon as their citizens realized Moscow would no longer send in the Soviet army, they threw out their Communist governments. In East Germany (the GDR), events unrolled rapidly.

1. The hardline Honecker regime in East Berlin rejects reforms for most of 1989, but East Germans, seeing reforms elsewhere in the Soviet bloc, become restless.

2. Hungary lets East Germans exit into Austria. The Communist regime in Budapest had pledged not to let East German tourists flee to the West, but in the summer of 1989, they stop enforcing this pledge. Debt-burdened Hungary, by then under reform-minded Communists, gets some nice financing from Bonn. Economic carrots had long been part of West German policy in East Europe. Hearing about the open border, thousands of East Germans "vacation" in Hungary but proceed to West Germany. East Berlin protests, but Budapest shrugs. By September, more than 18,000 East Germans flee via Hungary, another 17,000 via Czechoslovakia. East Germany closes its border with Czechoslovakia to stanch the flow.

3. Demonstrations break out in GDR in September, centered in Leipzig. In October, Soviet party chief Mikhail Gorbachev visits to urge reform and warn his East German counterpart Erich Honecker, "Life punishes those who delay." Gorbachev wishes to be rid of the problems and expenses of maintaining a Soviet empire in East Europe. Some 100,000 protesters march in Leipzig chanting, "Gorby! Gorby!"

In 1961, the Berlin Wall went up, here guarded by East German police and soldiers.

4. Honecker orders a "Chinese solution" like the massacre at Tiananmen Square that June, but security chief Egon Krenz fears catastrophe and countermands the order. On October 18, Honecker is out and Krenz becomes party chief and president. By now, a million East Germans, led by intellectuals in the New Forum movement, protest for democracy.

5. On November 9, 1989, East German officials order the Berlin Wall opened to gain some good will and time for reform. Locked in since 1961, tens of thousands of East Germans pour into the West. Liberal, reform-minded Communists take over and pledge free elections.

6. Too many East Germans pour into the West, seeking the good life of West Germany. Some half a million come across in the four months after the Wall opens, overburdening West Germany's job and apartment market, financial resources, and patience. Stay home, Chancellor Kohl urges; we will merge and lift your living standards soon enough.

7. Free East German elections in March 1990 put Christian Democrats in power. They see things Kohl's way and want speedy unification; this is why East Germans voted CDU.

8. Bonn gives East Germans a generous exchange rate. East German marks are not worth much, but East Germans argue that they have worked for and saved *Ostmarks* for decades. They demand a one-to-one exchange. Bonn gives them one to one for each Ossi's first 2,000 marks (about $1,000) and one *Westmark* for two *Ostmarks* above 2,000. The rate is a bribe to get Ossis to stay put. On July 2, 1990, the Westmark becomes the official currency in both Germanys.

9. East Germans buy everything Western, nothing Eastern, turning their backs on their own products, now seen as junk. Suddenly, competing in a free market with the West, the East German economy collapses; it never had a chance to adjust.

10. East and West German governments quickly negotiate a treaty in which the FRG absorbs the GDR as five new Länder, putting all of Germany under the Basic Law and into the EU and NATO. It is a takeover, not a merger of equals, and sets up Ossi resentment. On October 3, 1990, there is again one Germany.

To prevent or slow this sequence would have meant going back to step one and getting the Honecker regime committed to liberalizing the economy, but Honecker was a devoted Communist to whom marketization meant abandoning communism. And once East Germans started pouring across, Bonn could not rebuild the wall to make East Germans wait at home. Gradual unification might have been better, but events took charge.

Can an economic miracle work in East Germany? The desperate postwar situation that made West Germans work so hard is not found in post-Wall East Germany. Under communism, East Germans did not develop attitudes of hard work and entrepreneurial risk taking. They got used to a welfare system that offered security but few incentives for individual exertion. Ossis say, "It's not our fault that the Communists saddled us with an inferior economic system. Besides, you Wessis got billions of dollars in U.S. Marshall Plan aid; we got ripped off by the Soviets. So it's only fair that you boost us up to your standard of living, and quickly."

West Germans reject such attitudes, which seem like excuses to avoid work. On average, an Ossi's output is 70 percent that of a Wessi. Why set up factories in East Germany when you can get good productivity out of Poles and Czechs, whose labor costs are a fraction of German levels? Resentment flared in each half of Germany against the other half.

Bailing Out the Euro

Germans were among the most enthusiastic supporters of European unity, but, recently, many have grown critical. First, they did not like giving up their rock-solid DM for the new euro in

eurozone
The 19 (out of 28) EU countries that use the euro currency.

European Central Bank
Supervises interest rates, money supply, and inflation in the euro area, like the U.S. Fed.

bailout
Emergency loan to prevent a collapse.

Gastarbeiter
"Guest workers"; temporary labor allowed into Germany.

2002. But worse, they hated bailing out spendthrift weaker members of the **eurozone**. The Bundesbank, remembering the worthless Weimar and Nazi currencies, had been tough on inflation. At German insistence, euro members had to limit their budget deficits to 3 percent to block inflation. The **European Central Bank** (ECB), located in Frankfurt, was supposed to supervise and fine any government that went over, but soon, nearly everyone cheated to fund generous welfare benefits. Particularly egregious were Portugal, Ireland, Greece, and Spain (conveniently dubbed the PIGS), whose deficits all topped 10 percent.

When this was revealed in 2010, both the euro and the whole European Union were threatened by the prospective default of several members. To stave off collapse, the eurozone's financial ministers assembled a **bailout** package of nearly $1 trillion. The richer countries, chiefly Germany, furnished the most money. Germans exploded; many were willing to kick Greece out of the eurozone or drop out themselves. Germans charged that the EU was a "transfer union," a device to transfer taxes from hard-working countries to profligate cheats. Most Germans think the FRG gives too much money to the EU, and many want to return to their old reliable marks.

Merkel had to strike a fine balance on bailing out the euro. She knew it had to be done but also knew that Germans hated it. "The euro is our common fate, and Europe is our common future," Merkel said, but demanded a German veto over future bailouts. Economists had warned that monetary union without *fiscal* union could bring such crises, but few Europeans want a powerful EU to supervise their national budgets. German politicians feared that new far-right parties would use anger at the EU to win votes in 2013, as such parties do elsewhere in Europe. Whether Germany is stingy or generous in bailing out other countries, the euro crisis demonstrated that Germany leads Europe.

The Flood of Foreigners

Like Britain and France, Germany gets immigrants from poor countries seeking jobs while citizen resentment of them builds. There are 7 million foreigners in Germany (8.5 percent of Germany's population), mostly from Mediterranean nations (Turkey, ex-Yugoslavia, Greece, Italy, and Spain). More than 2 million are workers; the rest are spouses and children.

The trend started in 1955 when the economic miracle had absorbed all working Germans and was still short of labor. Italian and later Spanish **Gastarbeiter** were invited to West Germany, and they came, eager for the plentiful jobs. Soon, Germans began abandoning dirty, dangerous, and unskilled work for better positions, leaving their old jobs to foreigners. At first, the impact seemed temporary: The migrant workers were supposed to stay three years and rotate back home. But the "guest workers," faced with unemployment at home, often remained and sent for their families. Large numbers began arriving from Turkey, where unemployment is especially high. There are now some 4 million Muslims in Germany, two-thirds of them Turks. Whole neighborhoods have turned Turkish, and the Turkish *döner kebab* (lamb slices and salad in a pita) has become Germany's fast food (highly recommended). The "guests" had come to stay.

By the 1980s, poor people worldwide had discovered Germany's very liberal asylum law. Upon arriving, foreigners had only to claim they were politically persecuted back home,

Geography

Citizenship: Blood or Soil?

Europe traditionally used **jus sanguinis** to determine citizenship: If your parents were German, you are German. The United States, from its beginning, used **jus soli**: If you were born here, you are American. Other countries of immigration, such as Australia and Brazil, also use *jus soli*. Slowly and grudgingly, Germany is introducing *jus soli*. Under SPD sponsorship, a 2000 law allows German citizenship for those who have resided 8 years (down from 15) in the FRG and makes citizenship automatic for children born in Germany, provided one parent lived there 8 years. This is a major switch in Germany's definition of who is a German, and it provoked conservative opposition. Elections went against the SPD over the citizenship issue.

although motivation was usually economic. Legal tangles let asylum seekers stay in Germany for years, all the while on welfare. The FRG, along with Austria, strengthened border controls and expelled many undocumented visitors. Amid great political controversy (with the SPD fighting it), the asylum law was tightened to exclude most claimants. Britain, which also had a liberal asylum policy, had to do the same.

jus sanguinis
Latin for "right of blood"; citizenship based on descent.

jus soli
Latin for "right of soil"; citizenship given to those born in the country.

Unskilled and poorly educated, many Muslims are unemployed, poor, and at odds with the host-country culture. They are accused of living off welfare and supporting Islamic radicalism. Some Muslims want Islamic family law to govern such traditional practices as wife beating, instant divorce, and "honor killings" of unchaste women. The 9/11 plot was hatched by Arab students in Hamburg. Most Germans demand that Muslims accept German culture and law or leave. As in the United States, multiculturalism came under criticism. "Multiculturalism has utterly failed," said CDU Chancellor Merkel. A former finance official claimed, in a popular 2010 book, *Germany Abolishes Itself*, that high-birthrate Muslims refuse to integrate and will swamp low-birthrate Germans. One-third of Germans agreed with him, and two-thirds opposed any more immigration, as does the CDU/CSU.

Americans are used to immigrants, but Germany, long a nation of emigration, is not. Immigration, as in all of Europe, has been tightened. Germany issues limited numbers of "green cards" (they borrow the U.S. term) to skilled immigrants, such as 20,000 computer specialists from India. Conservative politicians huffed: *"Kinder statt Inder"* (Children instead of Indians), but the German fertility rate would have to shoot up to an impossible 3.8 (from the current 1.4) to fill the need for workers. As more Germans retire, Germany will need some quarter of a million new workers a year. Many come from Spain, where youth unemployment tops 50 percent. Spain is also in the EU, so Spaniards are free to work in Germany, and many stay.

FRG law allows a person of German descent from Russia or Romania, whose ancestors had left Germany centuries ago, to get instant FRG citizenship. A Turk, on the other hand, born and raised in Germany could not, until recently, become a German citizen. The law was reformed in 2000, and now, 45 percent of Muslims residing in Germany are citizens and are integrating into German society, much like the U.S. melting pot. There are SPD and Green Bundestag members of Turkish origin.

xenophobia

Fear and hatred of foreigners.

Warsaw Pact

Soviet-led alliance of Communist countries, now defunct.

Comecon

Trading organization of Communist countries, now defunct.

Bonn Republic

West Germany, 1949–1990, with the capital in Bonn.

Berlin Republic

Reunified Germany, since 1990, with the capital in Berlin.

Throughout West Europe, **xenophobia** grows, and most countries have anti-immigrant parties that win 15 percent or more of the vote. Interestingly, such parties are weak and divided in Germany, where the anti-immigrant stance has been preempted by the CDU/CSU. If all xenophobic Germans supported one party, however, it could win seats in the Bundestag. More than 100 Turks and Africans have been killed, but police and courts paid little attention until the 2011 arrest of a neo-Nazi Ossi trio that had murdered ten over seven years to get Turks to leave Germany. The police admitted they had been blind to racist terrorism and had explained away the deaths as Turkish gang killings. Thousands of Germans rallied to protest against xenophobia and violence. (Notice how U.S. Republicans resemble the CDU on the immigration issue, Democrats the SPD.)

Is Berlin Weimar?

By most measures, the Federal Republic of Germany is an unqualified success story. Its constitution, leading parties, and economy deserve to be studied by other countries. But some observers have wondered if, under the glittering surface, democracy has taken firm root. How will German institutions function with a multiparty system instead of a two-plus party system? What if the German economy tanks? Could the present democracy go the way of Weimar's?

All survey data have said no. Germans have grown more democratic in their values. By now, they are at least as committed to a pluralist, free, democratic society as the British and French. They weathered terrorism and economic downturns as well as any of their democratic neighbors. Gradually, with much pain and complaint, East Germans are turning into free-market democrats.

Things have changed in both the domestic and international contexts of German democracy, however. Germany's consensus and welfare state has become rigid and costly. Like most of West Europe, Germany's wages, taxes, welfare benefits, and overregulation have led to chronic high unemployment. Competition from low-wage, low-tax countries is fierce, and many German firms have moved production to Poland, the Czech Republic, or Slovakia. Berlin hotels send their laundry to Poland.

Both Germanys were products of the Cold War. At times, a third of a million U.S. soldiers were stationed in West Germany and more than half a million Soviet soldiers in East Germany. This situation was tense but stable. The FRG was firmly anchored to NATO and the European Union, the GDR to the **Warsaw Pact** and **Comecon**. Suddenly, the international context changed. The Cold War is over, and Germany is unified. The Soviet troops left, and very few U.S. troops remain. The **Bonn Republic** was anchored to the West. Will the new **Berlin Republic** stay cemented to Western ideals and institutions, or could it someday go off on its own, with a nationalistic and expansionist foreign policy?

Unlikely. German democracy is solid. Most Germans have become good Europeans, and most major politicians are committed to Europe. The German army ended conscription and

Geography

Demography as Politics

Demography has become a major political issue in Germany and many other countries. Most industrialized countries produce too few babies. Chancellor Merkel made Germany's birth dearth one of her chief projects, although she herself did not set a good example. Despite hefty children's allowances, an average German woman bears only 1.4 children, one of the world's lowest **fertility rates** (which is not the same as the "birthrate," a different measure). Some 2014 estimated fertility rates are listed below.

Notice that China and Iran are at European levels. Replacement fertility rate is 2.1—one for each parent and a little to spare—the level at which a population will hold steady, and it is found in few advanced industrialized countries. Large families are not prized, and women now have increased educational and career options. These rates take no account of immigration and are one reason why some countries need immigrants to support an aging and retired population.

By 2025, an estimated 24 percent of Germans and Japanese will be 65 or older; some 20 percent of Britons, French, and Americans will be in that age bracket. By 2050, Germany's population is projected to shrink from 81 to 70 million. Former East Germany is already depopulating. All of West Europe faces the problem of soon having too few people in the workforce supporting too many people in retirement. Germany already has the heaviest burden, with two working persons supporting one retiree, one reason German taxes are high.

Merkel's government introduced "parents' pay": 14 months of stipends after birth for each child, based on parents' salaries, to encourage middle-class women to have more babies. They also expanded daycare facilities to aid working mothers. Historically, such supports have not reversed low birthrates. Germany still needs more immigrants and later retirements, both of which are already happening.

Japan	1.4	United States	2.0
Germany	1.4	France	2.1
Russia	1.6	Mexico	2.3
China	1.6	World	2.5
Brazil	1.8	India	2.5
Britain	1.9	Nigeria	5.3
Iran	1.9		

shrank to 180,000. It has no ABC (atomic, biological, or chemical) weapons. Three of Germany's European neighbors (Britain, France, and Russia) have nuclear weapons, which by itself means that Germany will never go on the warpath. Germans have no taste for militarism, for they have seen what it leads to. Germany sent nearly 9,000 troops for peacekeeping in Afghanistan, Kosovo, Lebanon, and Bosnia but is not eager for more assignments. Germany has accomplished so much more by peaceful economic means than it could ever obtain by warlike means. The Weimar analogy is misplaced on present-day Germany.

demography
Study of population growth.

fertility rate
How many children an average woman bears.

Review Questions

Learning Objective 4.1 Contrast Germany's political development with those of Britain and France, p. 128.

1. When did Germany first unify? Why so late?
2. Why did the *Weimar Republic* fail?
3. What and when were the three German *Reichs*?

Learning Objective 4.2 Characterize the German voting system, p. 142.

4. Contrast Germany's president with its chancellor.
5. In how many ways is Angela Merkel interesting and different?
6. What could China learn from Germany's electoral system?

Learning Objective 4.3 Explain how Germany's past lingers in current politics, p. 152.

7. Should countries study the dark parts of their past? Why?
8. What are political generations and where do they come from?

9. Contrast East and West German political culture.

Learning Objective 4.4 Explain why a center-peaked unimodal distribution of political values is necessary to sustain democracy, p. 160.

10. Explain how the German party system has become more complex.
11. What is a *catchall* party and why is it now standard worldwide?
12. Explain the North European union-party linkup.

Learning Objective 4.5 Compare Germany's and Japan's postwar economic recoveries, p. 170.

13. Could German reunification have gone much differently, that is, slower?
14. Does Germany have a duty—moral and/or political—to bail out the euro?
15. Contrast *jus solis* with *jus sanguinis*. Who uses which?

Key Terms

bailout, p. 176
Berlin airlift, p. 141
Berlin Republic, p. 178
bimodal, p. 161
Bonn Republic, p. 178
Bundes-, p. 146
Bundesrat, p. 149
Bundestag, p. 143
catchall, p. 162
center, p. 146
center-seeking, p. 160
chancellor, p. 143
Comecon, p. 178
consensus, p. 172
constructive no-confidence, p. 143
dealignment, p. 163
demography, p. 179

denazification, p. 153
deutsche Mark, p. 141
Dolchstoss, p. 136
European Central Bank, p. 176
eurozone, p. 176
extreme multipartism, p. 147
Federal Constitutional Court, p. 147
federalism, p. 142
Federal Republic of Germany, p. 142
fertility rate, p. 179
Final Solution, p. 140
Gastarbeiter, p. 176
genocide, p. 140
grand coalition, p. 144
Greens, p. 148
Grundgesetz, p. 142

Habsburg, p. 131
Holocaust, p. 154
hyperinflation, p. 138
Junker, p. 131
jus sanguinis, p. 177
jus soli, p. 177
Kaiser, p. 135
Kulturkampf, p. 135
Land, p. 142
Landtag, p. 149
Lebensraum, p. 134
liberal, p. 134
liberal democracy, p. 153
Machtpolitik, p. 135
Marshall Plan, p. 141
Metternichian system, p. 134
Mitbestimmung, p. 172
Mitteleuropa, p. 142

Further Reference

Bessel, Richard. *Germany 1945: From War to Peace.* New York: HarperCollins, 2009.

Cramme, Olaf, and Patrick Diamond, eds. *After the Third Way: The Future of Social Democracy in Europe.* London: I. B. Tauris, 2012.

Crawford, Alan, and Tony Czuczka. *Angela Merkel: A Chancellorship Forged in Crisis.* New York: Bloomberg, 2013.

Darmstaedter, Friedrich. *Bismarck and the Creation of the Second Reich.* Piscataway, NJ: Transaction, 2008.

Frei, Norbert. *Adenauer's Germany and the Nazi Past.* New York: Columbia University Press, 2002.

Fritzsche, Peter. *Life and Death in the Third Reich.* Cambridge, MA: Harvard University Press, 2008.

Glaessner, Gert-Joachim. *German Democracy: From Post World War II to the Present Day.* New York: Berg, 2005.

Hancock, M. Donald, and Henry Krisch. *Politics in Germany.* Washington, DC: CQ Press, 2007.

Karapin, Roger. *Protest Politics in Germany: Movements on the Left and Right since the 1960s.* State College, PA: Pennsylvania State University Press, 2007.

Kornelius, Stefan. *Angela Merkel: The Chancellor and Her World.* London: Alma, 2013.

Kramer, Jane. *The Politics of Memory: Looking for Germany in the New Germany.* New York: Random House, 1996.

Meyer, Michael. *The Year That Changed the World: The Untold Story behind the Fall of the Berlin Wall.* New York: Scribner, 2009.

Nooteboom, Cees. *Roads to Berlin: Detours and Riddles in the Lands and History of Germany.* London: MacLehose, 2012.

Ozment, Steven. *A Mighty Fortress: A New History of the German People.* New York: Harper, 2005.

Posen, Adam S. *Reform in a Rich Country: Germany.* Washington, DC: Institute for International Economics, 2006.

Simms, Brendan. *Europe: The Struggle for Supremacy, from 1453 to the Present.* New York: Basic Books, 2013.

Sinn, Hans-Werner. *Can Germany Be Saved? The Malaise of the World's First Welfare State.* Cambridge, MA: MIT Press, 2007.

Steinberg, Jonathan. *Bismarck: A Life.* New York: Oxford University Press, 2011.

Stern, Fritz. *Five Germanys I Have Known.* New York: Farrar, Straus & Giroux, 2006.

Taylor, Frederick. *Exorcising Hitler: The Occupation and Denazification of Germany.* New York: Bloomsbury, 2011.

___*The Downfall of Money: Germany's Hyperinflation and the Destruction of the Middle Class.* New York: Bloomsbury, 2013.

Weitz, Eric D. *Weimar Germany: Promise and Tragedy.* Princeton, NJ: Princeton University Press, 2007.

Chapter 5
Japan

"Floating Torii" of Miyajima (near Hiroshima) is a Shinto shrine.

 ## Learning Objectives

5.1 Describe the effects of Japan's long and strong feudalism.

5.2 Explain the brief tenures of Japanese prime ministers.

5.3 Contrast Japanese and U.S. political cultures.

5.4 Describe the theory of "no one in charge" in Japan.

5.5 Explain how Japan's booming economy could go flat.

WHY JAPAN MATTERS

Can democracy be imported? Japan illustrates two attempts at importing democracy, the first by Japanese liberals copying foreign models a century ago and the second by American occupation forces after World War II. The first clearly failed in the 1930s; the second worked, but not quite the way it works in the West. Japanese political culture is just too different. Japan can no longer be taken for granted as a country of rapid economic growth and political stability. Both have frayed, leaving Japanese insecure and worried in what some call a "national malaise." Japan's postwar boom has been over since 1990; China eclipsed it to become the world's second-largest economy in 2010. Japan, like Mexico, was a *dominant-party system* for decades. Alternation was rare and brief. In terms of attention and prestige in Asia, Japan has become marginal to China. Where will this lead? To Japan's reform and renewal, to slow decline, or to a new, angry nationalism? Japan can serve as a warning to other lands—including the United States—that bubbles burst and the rich and powerful do not stay that way forever.

Impact of the Past

5.1   **Describe the effects of Japan's long and strong feudalism.**

Japanese see themselves as a pure-blooded single tribe, but their ancestors came from several parts of the Pacific Rim, especially from Korea. The Japanese and Korean languages are related, and some scholars suggest that the imperial family is of Korean origin—a controversial point, as older Japanese tend to look down on Koreans. Japan and Korea both owe much to Chinese culture.

Japan has four main islands, making it hard to unify. Mountainous Japan has little arable land, much devoted to rice, a crop so important that it became part of the religion. Early Japanese pushed back the original inhabitants, the *Ainu*, developing a warrior ethos. Japanese were undisturbed on their islands for many centuries, adopting Chinese culture but avoiding Chinese takeover. *Confucianism* and *Buddhism* arrived in the sixth century from China but took on Japanese characteristics. Many Japanese words are from Chinese.

Japanese called their land *Nihon* ("sun origin," also pronounced *Nippon*), from the national myth that all Japanese are descended from the Sun Goddess. Marco Polo recorded the Mongol name *Zipangu*, which, among Westerners, turned into "Japan." In 1274 and 1281, Mongol Emperor Kublai Khan invaded Japan. Japan trembled, but Japanese samurai fought off the Mongols, and both times a "divine wind" (*kamikaze*) wrecked the invasion fleets. The Japanese nobility celebrated themselves as a superior warrior race until 1945.

Japanese Feudalism

Japan was long dominated by clans and their leaders. According to tradition (still practiced in the **Shinto** faith), Jimmu, a descendant of the Sun Goddess, founded the Land of the Rising Sun in 660 BC. Myth aside, by the seventh century AD, central Japan had largely unified on the Chinese imperial model, bolstered by Confucianism and ruled by a *tenno* (emperor). Under the forms of Chinese centralized rule, however, the clans exercised control and kept figurehead emperors in the palace.

Shinto
Japan's original religion; the worship of nature, of one's ancestors, and of Japan.

Japan

Feudalism grows as central authority breaks down, which occurred in Japan from the ninth to the twelfth centuries and led to seven centuries of feudalism, ending only in the nineteenth century. China overcame feudalism early to become a bureaucratic empire. England overcame feudalism slowly in favor of limited, constitutional government. France overcame feudalism through absolutism. Japan, it has been argued, was feudal so long and deeply that feudal characteristics remain in bowing, politics, and education.

shogun
Feudal Japanese military ruler.

The essence of feudalism is power diffused and quarreled over among autonomous lords, each supported by warrior-helpers, whose knightly code—in Japan, *bushido*, the way of the *bushi* or *samurai* (warriors)—stresses obedience, honor, and selfless commitment to duty. The sure sign of feudalism is castles—the lords needed secure home bases—and Japan has many. Medieval Europe—with its trinity of king, lords, and knights—corresponds to medieval Japan, where they were respectively the *tenno* (starting about 1600 eclipsed by the **shogun**), *daimyo* (regional lords), and *samurai* ("those who serve"). Europe started growing out of feudalism before the fifteenth century, as modernizing monarchs crushed their aristocratic competitors and founded the "strong state" of centralized power and sovereignty. Japan lagged centuries behind.

The European Jolt

The first Europeans to reach Japan were, as usual, Portuguese, in 1543, followed by Spaniards in 1587 and Dutch in 1609. The Japanese could not keep them out, and soon European traders and Catholic missionaries made inroads. St. Francis Xavier turned the Jesuits to converting Asia by learned argumentation and better knowledge of astronomy (to impress imperial courts). As many as 150,000 (2 percent of Japan's population) converted by 1582. Japan's rulers feared Christianity was the opening wedge of foreign takeover (which it was in much of the world) and banned it in 1597. Over a few decades, missionaries were excluded and Japanese Catholics slaughtered. In 1635, Japanese were forbidden to travel abroad under the shogunate's policy

Geography

Japan and Britain

Japan and Britain are similar: Both are islands that derived much of their culture from the nearby continent. Why then are they so different? England early became a great industrial seapower, exploring, trading with, and colonizing much of the world. Japan stayed home and did not develop industry beyond the craft level. There were no Japanese fleets or explorations.

They faced different nearby powers. Europe was fragmented into many competing states and rarely a threat to England. Indeed, England played power balancer on the Continent by injecting its armies into Europe's wars to make sure a unified Europe could never invade England.

Japan faced a unified China that was a threat, as demonstrated by the two Mongol invasion attempts of the thirteenth century. Early on, Japan decided isolation was safest and, in the ninth century, cut most of its contacts with and borrowings from China and turned inward. Unlike European monarchs, Asian monarchs did not engage in competitive expansion, so Japan had no incentive to discover new lands.

Tokugawa
Dynasty of *shoguns* who ruled
Japan from 1603 to 1868; also
known as the Edo Period.

gaijin
Literally, "outside person";
foreigner. (Japanese suffix "jin"
means person, thus Nihon-jin
and America-jin.)

Meiji
Period of Japan's rapid
modernization, starting in 1868.

of seclusion known as *sakoku* ("chaining of the archipelago"), which lasted until the mid-nineteenth century.

The **Tokugawa** clan won a major battle in 1600 and established a powerful shogunate, combining feudalism, military rule, and police state. Spies were everywhere, especially watching the *daimyo*, who had to spend much time or leave their family at the palace (as in the France of Louis XIV). The Tokugawa founded the Japanese police state and brought Japan two centuries of peace, prosperity, and isolation. The Tokugawa moved the capital from Kyoto (now a Buddhist cultural site) to Edo (modern Tokyo). Aside from one Dutch trading post on an island in Nagasaki harbor, Japan shut the door to foreigners. The Tokugawa shoguns feared that **gaijin** ways and wares were threats to Japanese stability, but they kept informed of the outside world through Chinese couriers.

The Forced Entry

By mid-nineteenth century, Japan was distinctive, prosperous, and highly developed, with little Western influence. A wealthy merchant middle class supported an artistic highpoint. Most Japanese would have preferred to be left alone.

The United States did business on the China coast. Western sailors were shipwrecked on Japanese islands and could be gotten back only with difficulty, through the Dutch trading post. Furthermore, Japan looked ripe for commercial expansion. In 1846, two U.S. warships called at Yokohama (Tokyo's port) to request diplomatic relations but were rebuffed. Then U.S. President Millard Fillmore ordered Commodore Matthew Perry to open Japan. Perry arrived in 1853 with four ships that combined steam power with sails. The Japanese were frightened by these fire-belching sea monsters, which they called *kurofune* ("the black ships") and begged Perry to return next year. The shogun and his helpers feared Western penetration. They saw how China was "being molested by foreign devils" and feared the foreigners would undermine their rule (they did), but, after much discussion, Edo decided it could keep the world out no longer. When Perry returned in 1854, a large Japanese imperial delegation met him and acceded to his demands for diplomatic and trade relations. Soon, Europeans followed in Perry's wake, and Japan quickly opened.

The 1868 Meiji Restoration

The long and peaceful Tokugawa period had made the samurai superfluous, but, in 1868, some found a new calling: to save Japan by modernizing it quickly, before the West could take it over. With the accession of the new Emperor Mutsuhito, whose era took the name **Meiji**, these samurai had the emperor declare a "restoration" of his power (it really was not) and issue a series of "imperial rescripts" in 1868 that ordered the modernization of everything from education and the military to industry and commerce. The Tokugawa were out, but the emperor remained as a nationalistic symbol for rule by samurai clans.

The Meiji modernizers—using a two-millennia-old Chinese phrase, "Rich nation, strong army!"—changed everything, and, in a generation, Japan went from the Middle Ages to the

Geography

Cruising the Sea of Japan

Your aircraft carrier enters the Sea of Japan (called the East Sea in Korea) from the south, through the Korea Strait. Cruising in a clockwise direction, which countries do you pass to port (left)?

South Korea, North Korea, Russia, and Japan. (It looks like China has a tiny seacoast here, but it does not.)

modern age. The *daimyo* lost their big hereditary estates (but got good deals in the new industries). Feudalism ended, and all Japanese were legally equal. No longer could a samurai legally kill someone who disrespected him. (Even today, those of samurai origin are proud of it, but it confers no special advantages.) It was a controlled revolution from above, the only kind Japan has known.

Daimyo and samurai clans were given monopolies on branches of industry and ordered to develop them. These formed the basis of industrial conglomerates, the *zaibatsu*. Japanese were sent to copy the best of the West: British shipbuilding and naval warfare, French commercial law and civil organization, and German medical care, steelmaking, and army organization. For funds, the peasants were squeezed for taxes.

Some educated Japanese liked democracy, but the Meiji modernizers preferred Bismarck's authoritarianism and copied the political system of newly unified Germany. The 1889 Japanese constitution included a monarch, an elected parliament, and political parties, but underneath, patterns of governance were Japanese and brokered by traditional power holders. It only looked democratic and modern.

Japan's economy grew rapidly. From 1885 to 1919, Japan doubled its per capita GDP, a 2 percent annual growth rate unheard of at the time. (Now, 2 percent is slow growth.) Japanese products, starting with textiles, charged onto the world market using cheap labor to undercut Western producers. (More recently, China did the same.) The purpose of Japanese economic growth, however, was less to make Japanese prosperous than to make Japan powerful. Some argue that this impulse still influences Japanese (and Chinese) economic policy.

The Path to War

With its new Western arms, Japan picked a fight with and beat China in 1895, seizing Taiwan as its prize (and keeping it until 1945). Then it gradually took over Korea—which was even more of a hermit kingdom than Japan had been—and made it a Japanese colony in 1910. If these moves sound wicked, note that the West had earlier taken Asia by force, so why should Japan not do the same?

In 1904, amid growing tensions, Japan, without warning, attacked the Russian Far Eastern Fleet on the Manchurian coast. With discipline, enthusiasm, bold officers, and British naval and German army advisors, the Japanese beat the incompetent Russians on land and sea. U.S. opinion favored the Japanese—Teddy Roosevelt called them "plucky little Nips"—because repressive tsarist Russia had a poor reputation in the United States. President Roosevelt

Comparison

A Japanese Model of Industrialization?

Japan's rapid modernization is sometimes offered as a model for the developing areas. But it was not free-market capitalism; it was state-led modernization with much government guidance and funding. And it was not nice or painless; some samurai families got rich while peasants were turned into a downtrodden proletariat. Worse, its centralization set up Japan for takeover by militarists and later, after World War II, by bureaucrats intent on economic growth regardless of foreign or domestic costs. Now Japan must reform a government-led industrializing machine that has become a hindrance. And Japanese-style modernization would not work in countries with completely different cultures.

personally mediated an end to the war (in Portsmouth, New Hampshire) and won a Nobel Peace Prize.

Several *zaibatsu* conglomerates grew into economic giants that bought control of political parties. Japanese politicians, like some today, took money from private industry. In 1927, even before the Great Depression, the Japanese economy collapsed. The rich *zaibatsu* got richer as the middle class got poorer and peasants starved. Japanese army officers, whose families and soldiers were often just off the farm, resented the economic concentration and crooked politicians. The officer corps, a hotbed of right-wing nationalism and emperor worship, turned against the democracy and capitalism that bloomed in the 1920s and subverted them.

With no civilian control, the Japanese military ran itself without even informing the cabinet or diplomats. The war minister was a general, and the navy minister was an admiral; they got whatever budget they demanded. Japanese armed forces were split by rival cliques—feudalism again—who sometimes fought each other. Emperor Hirohito, although largely a figurehead, approved and supported plans to expand his empire. No one was in charge.

The Japanese army conquered Manchuria in 1931 and there built a state within a state, aimed at conquest. Soon the army controlled the Tokyo government, and civilian politicians obeyed the military or were assassinated. Japanese learned to say nothing critical, as the dread *Kempeitai*, called the "thought police," kept tabs on everyone. The ideology of the militarists— who supposed that the "Japanese spirit" was invincible—was similar to that of the Nazis: a combination of racism, extreme nationalism, militarism, and a bit of socialism. Both defined their peoples as a biologically superior, warrior race, destined to conquer their regions and dominate inferior peoples. Both were convinced they needed new lands for their growing populations. Both built societies on military lines into tight, obedient hierarchies. Both offered the working class and farmers some economic help. The difference is that the Nazis did it through a party, the Japanese through the army; parties in Japan were unimportant. It was no great surprise when Imperial Japan linked up with Nazi Germany in the 1936 Anti-Comintern Pact and, in 1940, joined the Axis. The two had little contact during the war and, fortunately for both Russians and Americans, did not coordinate their military campaigns.

The Japanese propaganda line was "Asia for the Asians." The evil American and European colonialists were to be kicked out and the region enrolled in what Tokyo called the Greater

Geography

Another Tale of Two Flags

Related to their sun goddess myth, some Japanese clans used a sun flag at least six centuries ago. With the Meiji modernization, Japan needed a national flag. The head of the powerful Satsuma clan in southern Japan suggested the present flag—*Hinomaru*, or rising sun—that was first used in 1860 (by the first diplomatic delegation to the United States). One sinister Japanese flag, with beams radiating out, became a symbol of militaristic expansion. The army version had thicker red rays, the navy version thinner. U.S. occupiers abolished the sun-ray flag, but the Naval Self-Defense Force resumed using it in 1954.

The national anthem *Kimigayo* ("His Majesty's Reign") was also used by the militarists until 1945. Like the *Hinomaru*, it was never written into postwar law or required at ceremonies. Nationalistic politicians wanted to require both, but leftist teachers, fearing a recrudescence of militarism, opposed it and still do. The Diet finally made both official and legal in 1999. Japanese students and teachers are now required to face the flag and sing the anthem.

Two flags

East Asia Coprosperity Sphere, led, of course, by Japan. Some anticolonial Asians went over to the Japanese (Ne Win of Burma, Sukarno of Indonesia, and Subhas Chandra Bose of India), although the Japanese turned out to be worse colonialists and racists than the Westerners. The Japanese governed with a bloody hand, mostly through the *Kempeitai*.

The Great Pacific War

In 1931, the Japanese army in Manchuria blew up a railway track at Mukden (the Manchu name, now Shenyang) and claimed the Chinese Nationalist army did it. Based on this lie, the Japanese army quickly conquered all of Manchuria and set up a puppet state they named **Manchukuo**. Tokyo's civilian prime minister protested and was assassinated. The Tokyo government was not in charge; the army operated on its own. The League of Nations condemned Japan, so Japan walked out of the League. Britain and France, with extensive Asian colonies, did not want to antagonize Japan, so they kept silent. The United States, as an avowed "big brother" to China,

Manchukuo
Japanese puppet state in Manchuria.

protested with words but not with military power, which convinced the Japanese militarists that the Americans were bluffing.

In 1937, the Japanese army began the conquest of all of China. The United States supported China, but, wishing to avoid war, took only cautious steps—in 1940, it embargoed oil and scrap steel to Japan, and, in 1941, froze Japanese assets in American banks and organized the Flying Tigers. The Japanese military saw these steps as an undeclared war and planned Pearl Harbor. They hoped that by knocking out the U.S. Pacific Fleet, they would persuade Washington to leave the Western Pacific to them. This ignored American rage, something the militarists could not comprehend across the cultural gap. The Japanese people were informed of and consulted on nothing.

The war was unusually cruel, what one American historian called "war without mercy." Both Japanese and Americans killed war prisoners and inflicted vast civilian damage. Japanese soldiers fought to the death, because the emperor forbade surrender, which meant shame. The nuclear bombing of Hiroshima and Nagasaki in August 1945 tilted Emperor Hirohito to peace, even though some generals wanted to keep fighting. The Japanese language is subtle and avoids blunt statements, so Hirohito went on radio (for the first time ever) to explain to his ruined country why Japan would have to "endure the unendurable" and surrender: "Developments in the war have not necessarily gone as well as Japan might have wished." It was a classic Japanese understatement.

Up from the Ashes

Japanese cities were gray rubble by 1945. Starvation loomed. With no resistance, General Douglas MacArthur and his staff moved into one of the few Tokyo buildings still standing, Dai-Ichi Life Insurance (later, one of the world's largest banks). Emperor Hirohito soon called on MacArthur to express his willingness to take blame. MacArthur, speaking as one emperor to another, told him he could keep his throne, but as an ordinary mortal, not as a "living god," something most Japanese already understood. To get Japan on the U.S. side in the Cold War, in 1947, the U.S. occupation began covering up Hirohito's support for the war and blaming General Hideki Tojo, the wartime prime minister, and a few dozen helpers, who were tried by an international military tribunal and hanged. Critics claim that MacArthur's "reverse course" of 1947 let Japan avoid coming to grips with its wartime horrors.

In 1946, MacArthur's staff wrote a new constitution in ten days to block a Japanese attempt to just lightly revise their prewar constitution. Resembling British institutions, it guaranteed freedom, parliamentary democracy, and peace. Japanese elites did not like the MacArthur Constitution—among other points, it made the emperor merely the symbol of Japan—but grudgingly accepted it when the emperor endorsed it.

The 1947 constitution has not functioned precisely as written, as Japanese power does not flow in neat, Western-type channels. Industry revived, much of it under the supervision of those who had run the war machine. The *zaibatsu* were broken up, but as the Cold War started, MacArthur let banks reassemble them under the new name of *keiretsu*, giant industrial-financial combinations with the same names as the *zaibatsu*. MacArthur also let many of the old elites return to political power. Japanese patterns keep reasserting themselves.

Political Culture

Japan's Political Eras

Since the Tokugawa shogunate, Japan's political eras are named for the reigns of each emperor. Indeed, for domestic use only, lunar years in Japan are those of the emperor's reign. Thus 2012 is given as year 24 of the reign of Akihito. Wherever they can, the Japanese do it their way.

Name	Years	Remembered for
Edo Period	1603–1868	Tokugawa shogunate; military feudalism; isolated Japan
Meiji	1868–1912	Rapid modernization under "restored" emperor; military expansionism begins
Taisho	1912–1926	Normal but corrupt democracy
Showa	1926–1989	Militarists take over, lead country to war; postwar economic boom
Heisei	1989–	Economic slowdown; efforts at reform

The Key Institutions

5.2   **Explain the brief tenures of Japanese prime ministers.**

Japanese institutions resemble British ones, but they do not function in the same way. The Japanese monarchy, which was constitutionally divine until 1945, for most of history was a figurehead. Some older and more conservative Japanese still see the monarch as divine and will not criticize him. Many younger Japanese, like Britons, admire the monarchy as a symbol of tradition and stability. The three postwar royal marriages were all to commoners, which helped popularize the Imperial Household.

The constitution specifies that the emperor has no "powers related to government." He does ritual and ceremony. Let off the hook by MacArthur, Hirohito for the first time met his subjects face to face and became a symbol of the poor, little Japanese bravely making do under U.S. occupation. In speeches, Emperor Akihito, son of Hirohito (reigned 1926–1989), is vague and idealistic. For a while, the Imperial House had no male heirs, the only kind Japanese law permits. Changing the law to allow for an empress stalled in the Diet. Conservatives protested, but most Japanese approved. It was the modern, liberal thing to do, and Japan long ago had eight empresses. The problem was temporarily solved when a younger brother produced a son in 2006.

Weak Prime Ministers

Japan's prime ministers have been mostly weak and rarely the real power. Their stay in office is often comically short. A few, including Junichiro Koizumi (2001–2006), were strong, but their powers hinged on mastery of the fractious Liberal Democratic Party (LDP) and did not carry on to their successors. Following Koizumi, Japan had six prime ministers in five years. Voters, less deferential and fed up with a weak and incompetent LDP, finally voted in the opposition

Personalities

Shinzo Abe

After a long line of brief prime ministers—some lasting less than a year—Shinzo Abe (pronounced *ah-bay*) tried to invigorate Japan's stagnant economy. As is typical in Japan, his position is quasi-inherited. His maternal grandfather Nobusuke Kishi was LDP prime minister from 1957 to 1960. For his service in Manchuria and in the Tojo cabinet during the war, Kishi was accused of war crimes but let out of prison in 1948 as part of MacArthur's "reverse course" to fight leftism. Abe's father, Shintaro Abe, was Japan's longest-serving foreign minister.

Born in 1954, Abe graduated in political science and worked his way up in the LDP's Mori faction. In 1993, Abe won election to his father's seat in the House of Representatives from Yamaguchi prefecture and has held it ever since. Japanese voters judge candidates partly by their bloodlines. In 2006, Abe became prime minster, but, amid economic stagnation and scandal—his agriculture minister committed suicide—Abe resigned just a year later. He looked like another short-term prime minister.

Abe reconsolidated his and the LDP's position and, after three years of ineffectual DPJ governance, came roaring back with a landslide win in late 2012. Abe paraded his right-wing nationalist credentials. He has visited the controversial Yasukuni shrine many times, even as prime minister, despite American warnings. He has denied there were any Korean sex slaves during the war but now keeps quiet about it. He wants to redo Japanese schoolbooks to eliminate blame for the war. All this plays well with many Japanese voters but enrages China and Korea.

But it is economics that will make or break Abe's tenure. His initial policies produced growth,and his popularity soared. He named a new central bank chief, who loosened the money supply, thereby lowering the overvalued yen. He pumped out stimulus packages and removed restrictions that Japanese commerce sheltered behind. Japanese began spending again. Soon, however, "Abenomics" faltered; growth was anemic, and support for Abe declined.

Democratic Party of Japan (DPJ) in August 2009, but its prime ministers were also weak and short-lived, so they voted back in the LDP in 2012.

In keeping with Japan's feudal traditions, political office is partly inherited. Five of Japan's recent prime ministers have been sons or grandsons of prime ministers. The United States has its political dynasties—the Kennedys and Bushes—but nothing like Japan, where some 40 percent of LDP legislators (and 20 percent of the DPJ) are descendants of legislators. Voters note the names of political heirs and the pork their fathers delivered.

Americans often mistake Japanese prime ministers for their British or German counterparts. In trade talks, for example, the Japanese prime minister visits Washington and makes some concessions to the U.S. side, but then nothing changes. The prime minister does not have the power, in the face of major interest groups and in government ministries, to follow through.

There have been 15 Japanese prime ministers in two decades, most lackluster but one of them effective: Koizumi. Tokyo cabinets last an average of a year and a half, but not from losing votes of confidence or the splintering of coalitions in the manner of the French Fourth Republic. Until 1993, the **Liberal Democrats (LDP)** had a comfortable Diet majority and could brush off no-confidence motions.

The problem has been the fragmented nature of the two big parties. The leaders of the LDP's several factions made and unmade prime

Liberal Democrats (LDP)
Japan's long-dominant party, a *catchall*.

ministers and ministers in behind-the-scenes deals. Many ministers were simply frontmen for their factions. Some claim that LDP faction leaders were more powerful than prime ministers. LDP politicians have passed up chances to become prime minister because faction chief was more powerful. Typically, the leader of the dominant LDP faction, called half in jest the "shadow shogun," arranged backroom deals with bosses of the LDP's nine factions to support a new prime minister. Reformers hope to overcome this feudal arrangement, but it persists. Except for a brief coalition (of LDP splinter parties) in 1993–1994, the LDP was in power until 2009 and returned to power in 2012. The DPJ also had a shadow shogun, its former chief Ichiro Ozawa, who was disgraced in a fund-raising scandal, went on trial, and lost influence.

Diet
Name of some parliaments, such as Japan's and Finland's.

The Japanese Diet

The Japanese diet is optimal: light on fat, cholesterol, and calories. The Japanese Diet is marginal: heavy on payoffs, pork, and political squabbling. The 1947 constitution specifies the bicameral **Diet** (legislature) as the "highest organ" of Japanese government. Not strictly true in Europe, it is even less true in Japan. By law, the president of the ruling party automatically becomes prime minister but can be ousted if the cabinet resigns or the Diet is dissolved for new elections. Much of Japan's real decision-making power lies elsewhere, in the powerful ministries.

Japan's lower house, the House of Representatives, has 480 members, 300 elected from single-member districts and 180 on the basis of proportional representation by party lists in 11 regions, a *mixed-member* system. The house's term is a maximum of four years. The new Japanese system, which began only with the elections of 1996, resembles the German hybrid system but does not use PR to set the overall number of seats per party (the German system, which does, is *mixed-member proportional*).

As in all parliamentary systems, the lower house can be dissolved early for new elections, which Prime Minister Koizumi did in 2005 (and won a resounding victory). The non-LDP coalition of 1993 rewrote some of the rules that had been widely blamed for Japan's endemic political corruption. (See box on reforming Japan's electoral system.)

Japan's lower house is more powerful than the upper, the House of Councilors, always the case. The upper chamber may reject a bill from the lower, but the latter may override with a two-thirds majority. The upper house has no say in selecting prime ministers. The House of Councilors has 247 members elected for six-year terms; half are elected every three years. It cannot be dissolved early. The elections of 2012 and 2013 gave the LDP a majority of both the lower and upper houses, respectively. Whatever legislation the LDP wants, it can get.

Behind the show of parties, elections, and debates, the larger question of any parliament is whether it actually controls government policy. The career professionals who staff the Tokyo ministries regard most Diet members as clowns who pass around the **pork barrel** to get reelected but have little interest in running government. The Diet, like Britain's Commons, has a Question Time, but top bureaucrats answer most of the questions, not ministers. The anti-bureaucrat DPJ stopped that practice during their brief tenure. The bureaucrats disliked the DPJ for interfering with their running of Japan.

pork barrel
Government projects that narrowly benefit legislators' constituencies.

The Parties

Japan, India, and Mexico were, until recently, examples of dominant-party systems, ones with several parties but one party much stronger than the others. The big party could theoretically be voted out, but it stayed in power for decades. Over time, all three nations grew out of this pattern as voters became fed up with the dominant party. Russia is now our best example of a dominant-party system. For most of Japan's postwar era, one party, the pro-American LDP, was so strong that some jested Japan was a "one-and-a-half party system." (The much weaker Socialists were the "half" party.)

The Liberal Democrats were a 1955 amalgamation of several centrist and conservative parties that had been ruling Japan since 1947. With the Cold War, the United States worried that radical Japanese parties, the Communists and Socialists, might turn Japan neutral or pro-Soviet, so the Americans encouraged the mergers that created the LDP.

The Liberal Democrats, although described as center-right, barely cohered as a party; only the winning of elections and gaining of spoils kept it together. Some saw the LDP as less of a party than an electoral alignment of factions grouped around powerful chiefs, like old samurai clans that used money instead of swords. Asked his political views, one local LDP activist proudly proclaimed, "I am a soldier in the Tanaka faction." This feudal arrangement meant that no single faction or chief dominated for long, and no one was interested in or responsible for policy. The LDP is "conservative" not out of ideological convictions but merely because it fundamentally opposes change. There are no important ideological divisions within the party either, only loyalties to chiefs, some of whom had been unsavory holdovers from the World War II militarist government.

In the early 1990s, the LDP fell into disarray. Dozens of leading LDP politicians stalked out to form centrist-reformist parties—Japan Renewal, Japan New Party, and New Party Harbinger—that constantly reshuffled and renamed themselves. In 1998, many of them, plus some Socialists, coalesced into the Democratic Party of Japan (DPJ), which, in 2009, trounced the LDP. The center-left DPJ, like leftist European parties, boosted welfare spending—child allowances, guaranteed pensions, and farm subsidies. It rejected U.S.-type "market fundamentalism" and showed an anti-U.S. nationalism. The uneasy mixture of former Liberal Democrats and Socialists makes the DPJ as incoherent and faction ridden as the LDP. Fed up with economic stagnation, voters threw out the DPJ and brought back the LDP in late 2012.

The old "half party," the Japan Socialist Party (JSP), was formed with the approval of MacArthur's occupation government because it repudiated the militarist regime. The JSP hit an electoral high in 1958 with nearly one-third of the vote but declined because it was doctrinaire and rigid. The JSP, for example, urged neutralism for Japan and gave the Soviet Union and North Korea the benefit of the doubt while criticizing the United States. Renamed the Social Democrat Party of Japan, it joined and ditched the shaky 1993–1994 coalition, then bizarrely joined with its LDP archenemies in a 1994–1996 coalition with a Social Democratic leader as a figurehead prime minister. With the Social Democrats standing for nothing very clear, voters abandoned it, and the SDPJ now has only 2 (two!) of the 136 seats that it had in 1990.

A fifth of voters, fed up with Japan's paralysis, went, in 2012, to the new Restoration Party, whose nationalistic chief, Osaka mayor Toru Hashimoto, advocates strong leadership, shrinking the bureaucracy, and an end to apologizing for "comfort women"—mostly Koreans forced to become army sex slaves during the war, an explosive issue in South Korea. Less-privileged Japanese tend to support the strange New Komeito, or Clean Government Party, a 1960s offshoot of the Buddhist Soka Gakkai movement that many think is warped and fanatic. Komeito formed a coalition with the LDP from 1999 to 2009 and again in 2012.

alternation in power
The electoral overturn of one party by another.

The puny score of Social Democrats and Communists in 2012 shows a Japan with almost no left, an odd situation matched only by Ireland. In most other advanced industrialized countries, a combined left (including center-left) gets some 40 percent of the vote. Japan, dominated by centrist and rightist parties, is an outlier. (Any ideas why?) Surveying Japan's messy and changing party system, we can say that no party is really strong. Almost half of Japanese say they support no party because all are ineffective.

Japan's Electoral System

Japan's former electoral system was blamed for its weak parties and lack of **alternation in power**. Elections for the lower chamber were by 130 multimember districts. Instead of European-style proportional representation, Japanese voted for one candidate rather than for one party, and the winners were simply those with the most votes. If there were seven candidates in a four-person district, the four highest vote getters were elected. Candidates of the same party competed against each other, a system that begged for factionalism and corruption within the LDP. The need for campaign money became desperate, and with that came the influence of private donors.

The short-lived coalition elected in 1993 brought in some German-style electoral reforms. First, they divided Japan into 300 single-member districts, but their numbers were not equal; rural districts were still overrepresented. In 1976, one rural vote was worth five times an urban vote to elect a Diet member; in 1980, four times; in 1990, three times; and in 2011, still 2.43 times. Japan's Supreme Court ruled in 2011 that the difference could be no greater than two times, but this was not implemented in time for the 2012 election. The discrepancy magnifies the voice of Japan's farmers and lets the LDP win most rural prefectures. The LDP-dominated Diet long kept out imported food and subsidized inefficient Japanese farmers, giving Japanese consumers the world's highest food prices and angering foreign food exporters, such as the United States. Abe cut farm subsidies and told farmers to get more efficient.

Now, after the 1993 reforms, 300 districts elect only one member each by simple plurality (not necessarily a majority) of the votes. This was supposed to cut the number of parties in the Diet, since such systems penalize small parties. Still, every Japanese election sees several small parties, either old or startups. Next, now that candidates from the same party no longer compete against each other, the reform was supposed to overcome factionalism within parties. It did not.

The remaining 180 members of the lower house are now elected by proportional representation in 11 regions. This, too, aimed at healing party factionalism because candidates run on party lists rather than as competitors. This was supposed to give Japan's parties greater ideological coherence. The reformers' goal was a responsible two-party system with alternation in power, finally achieved 16 years later with the DPJ's ouster of the LDP in 2009. The trouble is

METI
Japan's powerful Ministry of Economy, Trade, and Industry (formerly MITI).

that the DPJ, in terms of factions and taking money, looked a lot like the LDP and lasted in power only three years.

Elections for the upper chamber are similar. Each prefecture has from two to eight councilors, based on population, and voters have two ballots; one is for a single-member district with plurality winning, which fills 149 seats. Proportional representation at the national level fills another 98 seats. Rural prefectures and their elderly farmers are overrepresented, allowing them to block needed reforms. A unitary system such as Japan really does not need an upper house.

The Ministries

Who, then, holds power in Japan? First, there is no single power center; it is diffused among several centers. Many argue that the 19,000 career bureaucrats at the ministries' executive levels, particularly the Finance Ministry and Ministry of Economy, Trade, and Industry (**METI**)—formerly the famous MITI, the Ministry of International Trade and Industry—are the real powers in Japan. The Ministry of Land, Infrastructure, and Transport (formerly Ministry of Construction) has great clout, too, as it distributes big public works contracts to please the "road tribe," politicians representing Japan's overlarge construction industry. The three most important ministries—trade, finance, foreign affairs, plus the national police, which is not a ministry but a powerful agency—usually assign top civil servants as secretaries to the prime minister, a further bureaucratic hold on power.

The Japanese cabinet, like most European cabinets, can be easily changed from year to year, with ministries combined, renamed, or instituted. Recent cabinets had the following ministries:

Foreign Affairs	Health, Labor, and Welfare
Justice	Agriculture, Forestry, and Fisheries
Finance	Economy, Trade, and Industry (METI)
Defense	Land, Infrastructure, and Transport
Internal Affairs and Communications	Environment
Education, Culture, Sports, Science, and Technology	

In addition, the cabinet included several "ministers of state" for lesser-ranked specialized functions, such as disaster management. A minister may get more than one portfolio (as in France), and the ministries can be easily renamed and reshuffled. Japan's chief cabinet secretary is second in command after the prime minister and official cabinet spokesperson, a position that can lead to the top. Only in 2007 was Defense made a full cabinet ministry. At least five ministries or agencies deal with economic development. One minister, such as for finance or foreign affairs, typically also serves as deputy prime minister.

At least half of the ministers, including the prime minister, must be members of the Diet, of either house, but most are members of the lower house. Occasionally, specialists or academics not in the Diet are brought in. The ministers are not necessarily experts in their portfolios (ministerial assignments), which are based more on political criteria than on subject matter competence. Bureaucrats run the ministries, not ministers.

Democracy

The 2012 Elections: A Hybrid System in Action

In 2012, after three years of three fumbling DPJ prime ministers, a revived LDP booted out the DPJ in elections for the House of Representatives. The LDP once again has a big majority, while the DPJ, which had won in 2009 in a landslide but did nothing to end Japan's two decades of economic stagnation, is busted low. Shinzo Abe, who did poorly in his year as LDP prime minister in 2006-2007, resumed office in late 2012 with plans to invigorate the economy.

The election provided both good news and bad news. It reaffirmed Japan's ability to alternate parties in power, one of the measures of democracy. But it also showed extreme electoral volatility, which could undermine governing stablity. We cannot be sure that the 1993 electoral reforms produced this dual result, as many other things also changed in Japan: a more critical younger generation, LDP and DPJ paralysis decades of economic stagnation, and the rise of politics based on personalities rather than on payoffs. Turnout in 2012 was 59 percent, down 10 percentage points from 2009. The Diet's lower chamber looked like this:

If the LDP had won 320 seats (two-thirds), it would have had the power in the lower chamber to pass bills without the assent of the upper chamber. Japanese voters had stuck with the LDP for more than half a century, but the LDP's corruption and payoffs to interest groups finally made them fed up. Even rural voters abandoned the LDP in 2009; most returned in 2012. The DPJ had promised to fix everything but fixed nothing. Some take the ousters of the LDP in 2009 and DPJ in 2012 as democratic signs: Japanese voters no longer cling to the status quo but are at last punishing incompents. Their message to the parties: Fix the mess or you're out.

	Single-Member Seats	PR Percent Votes	PR Seats	Total Seats	Change from 2009
Liberal Democratic Party (LDP)	237	28%	57	294	+175 seats
Democratic Party of Japan (DPJ)	27	15	30	57	−251 seats
Restoration Party	14	21	40	54	+54 seats
New Komeito	9	12	22	31	+10 seats
Your Party	4	9	14	18	+10 seats
Tomorrow Party	2	6	7	9	+9 seats
Communists	0	6	8	8	−1 seat
Social Democrats	1	2	1	2	−5 seats
Other parties and independents	6	1	1	7	
Total	**300**		**180**	**480**	

As in Europe, every party in a coalition has at least one top leader appointed as a minister. The eight-party coalition of 1993, for example, had ministers from eight different parties. Even the small parties got a portfolio, but the parties with the most seats got several. Such distributions of ministries are payoffs used to form and hold a cabinet together. Below the minister, a civil-service vice minister really runs the ministry. The Japanese vice ministers, who

Political Culture

Why Is Wa?

Wa, social harmony, may be the key to Japanese culture. Japanese learn to seek *wa* with each other. Japanese love *beisu-boru* but seldom argue with an umpire. *Wa* gives Japan its cooperative group-mindedness. (Notice how the only way to play Pokémon is by cooperation.) Critics charge that *wa* is a device for social control, conformity, and obedience. Anyone questioning or criticizing disturbs the domestic peace and harmony. *Wa* can also induce corporate and government bureaucrats to cover up financial problems rather than face them.

correspond to British *permanent secretaries*, are more powerful than their nominal bosses, also the case in most of Europe. Reportedly, the vice ministers used to meet twice weekly to draw up the agenda the cabinet followed the next day, something that may still be happening. The ministries' top appointed officials—appointed internally on the basis of merit, as defined by the individual ministry, not on the basis of political connections—have years of experience and knowledge; the minister may last only a few months in office. This gives the top civil servants much power and the feeling that they run Japan. The DPJ declared that politicians—not bureaucrats—would henceforth call the shots, but the bureaucratic rule largely continued.

Japanese Territorial Organization

Japan is a unitary system that looks a bit like a federal system. It has 47 administrative divisions, 43 of them **prefectures**, after the French *prefect*, the head of a *département*. The other four are special situations: Tokyo, Osaka, and Kyoto are run as large metropolitan districts, and the thinly populated northernmost island of Hokkaido is one big district.

The Japanese situation resembles the modern French territorial structure: unitary but with certain local-democracy features. The Ministry of Internal Affairs in Tokyo still oversees prefectural matters and can override local officials, which raises local ire. Each prefecture has an elected governor and unicameral assembly to decide local matters and raise local taxes that cover only about 30 percent of spending, what Japanese call "30 percent autonomy." Unfortunately, an estimated 80 percent of prefectural spending is ordered by Tokyo—what Americans call "unfunded mandates." Fuming at Tokyo's interference, several prefectures have launched "tea party" type parties to repudiate both the LDP and DPJ.

Japanese Political Culture

5.3   Contrast Japanese and U.S. political cultures.

prefecture
First-order Japanese civil division; like French department.

Japan is one of the few non-European countries that modernized while retaining its own culture. Facilitating Japan's modernization was the *absence* of deep religious values. Japanese religion, light and flexible, never blocked change. Japan took on some appearances of

Political Culture

The Roots of Nihonjin-Ron

Japanese political culture is so distinctive that some Japanese claim their brains are physically different. During the war, the militarists touted this racist explanation, and some politicians still claim that the Japanese culture and work ethic are superior to the West's. There are several theories of *nihonjin-ron*, and it is probably a combination of all.

- *Shintoism* taught that Japan and the Japanese are a wonderful, perfect society superior to others.
- *Buddhism* still teaches the renunciation of desire, enduring pain and difficulties, and being careful and mindful of all persons and things.
- *Confucianism* taught that one is born into a strict hierarchy and must obey authority and defer to superiors with great politeness.
- *Feudalism*, deep and prolonged in Japan, taught all to obey, honor, and respect superiors and keep their place, and it diffused power among several centers. Bowing, a remnant of feudalism that has largely died out elsewhere in Asia, is still strong in Japan.
- *Dependency* was until recently inculcated into young Japanese by their parents and teachers. Unlike young Americans, Japanese were not trained for independence but to remain dutiful and submissive to the authority of both the job and the government.
- *Rice farming* required sharing water and working in teams. Some argue that this made Japanese cooperative but conformist.
- *Crowded* into a small land, Japanese had to develop nice manners and cooperation to make daily life possible. (This would not explain New Yorkers.)

Western culture but kept its inner core of Japaneseness (*nihonjin-ron*, literally, "discourse on the Japanese"). For this reason, many observers see Japan as a unique civilization.

Germany and Japan were defeated in World War II, but missing from the U.S. occupation of Japan was the denazification practiced, however imperfectly, in Germany. Japan had no Nazi-type party to blame or put on trial (just army officers), and MacArthur retained the emperor and Japanese political structures. Japanese bureaucrats and politicians carried over from wartime assignments and quietly resolved not to change Japan too much. For decades, Japanese media and textbooks did not mention their army's massacres of civilians, "comfort women," or Unit 731's germ and gas experiments on prisoners, some of them Americans. Whereas some Germans showed guilt about the Nazi past, until recently, few Japanese openly expressed guilt over wartime brutality.

Only recently have some Japanese officials admitted war guilt—or is it shame?—for World War II. In 1991, Emperor Akihito apologized to Koreans for Japan's colonial occupation (1910–1945). In Beijing in 1992, he told Chinese officials that he "deeply deplored" Japan's long (1937–1945) war in China, which killed, by Beijing's estimate, 35 million Chinese. His father, Hirohito, had stayed silent about World War II. Several prime ministers have apologized, but Japan's signals are mixed. Some right-wingers still do not admit the truth or show remorse, claiming that Japan was never aggressive or brutal and had fought only "for self-defense and the independence of Asian countries." A 1995 Diet proposal for a resolution of apology was dropped in the face of a petition signed by 5 million Japanese and supported by most of the LDP.

Political Culture

Guilt Versus Shame

Some argue that Japanese, unlike Westerners, are not driven by **guilt** but by the more superficial feeling of **shame**, of not upholding group standards. Guilt is woven into the Judeo-Christian ethos. The idea that God gives you moral choices and judges you is an important component of Western civilization and, according to some, the basis of Western individualism.

Japanese religion—and the Japanese are largely irreligious—has no such basis. In Shintoism, a form of animism that includes one's ancestors, there is no God or code of morality besides serving and obeying. State Shinto was refined into an organized religion by the Meiji modernizers to ensure loyalty and was turned into a pillar of nationalism. Buddhism, which exists side by side with Shintoism, is vague on the existence of God; Lord Buddha was merely enlightened, not divine. Either way, from Shinto or Buddha, few Japanese are on guilt trips.

Instead of guilt, according to this theory, Japanese are motivated by shame. To let down the group is a terrible thing. In World War II, many Japanese preferred death to surrender, which meant shame. (Americans who surrendered were shameless cowards worthy only of harsh treatment.) One Japanese soldier who hid on Guam until 1972 said, upon his heroic return, "I have a gun from the emperor and I have brought it back." He added: "I am ashamed that I have come home alive." Bringing shame to the family deters most crime in Japan. Police use shaming in interrogation, and prosecutors bring only sure cases to court, leading to a 99 percent conviction rate, one rivaling China's. The shame theory helps explain Japanese anti-individualism and the suicides of prominent Japanese, including the crooked agriculture minister in 2007.

guilt
Deeply internalized feeling of personal responsibility and moral failure.

shame
Feeling of having behaved incorrectly and of having violated group norms.

Japanese politicians visit Tokyo's controversial Yasukuni Shrine. They claim they just want to pay respect to Japan's 2.5 million war dead, but the Shinto shrine also honors Japan's militarist past and 14 Class A war criminals—including wartime chief Tojo—hanged by the Americans. Prime Minister Koizumi visited in 2001, but prime ministers since have stayed away so as not to anger China and South Korea. Its attached museum portrays the war as Japan's liberation of Asia from Western imperialists. Fascistic youths in World War II uniforms parade at Yasukuni. LDP chiefs cultivate the important Bereaved Families Association as well as right wingers and militarists. Beijing claims such gestures show continuing Japanese militarism.

Japan's Education Ministry screens textbooks to promote unity and patriotism. Doubts and war crimes get screened out in favor of mild wording, such as "Japan caused inconvenience to neighboring Asian countries." Many Japanese are genuinely sorry for what Japan did to its Asian neighbors, but such bland gestures give the outside world the impression that Japan only halfheartedly admits war guilt. Germany apologized better, earlier, and more publicly.

The view of themselves as permanent underdogs colors Japanese life. We are, they used to say, confined to a small country with few natural resources and devastated by war. But by 1970, Japan was a rich society with no need for protection for any of its sectors. Psychologically, though, many Japanese, especially older people, act as if they are trapped in wartime and postwar poverty and scarcity. Thus, they "make do" with high tariffs (777.7 percent on rice)

Political Culture

Japan's Critical Christians

Religion strongly influences political culture, and one clear difference is Japan's lack of Christianity. Christians (mostly mainstream Protestant) form less than 1 percent of Japan's population and are not growing much. (The Jesuits in the sixteenth century did better, converting 2 percent.) Although Christian-related schools and colleges (many with U.S. ties) are numerous and popular, few students are drawn to Christianity. Western-style weddings, complete with marriage chapels and white gowns, are popular but just for show.

Japan's Christians see themselves as an embattled, prophetic minority. They no longer face discrimination, just indifference. They deplore the lack of higher values among Japanese, whom they see caught up in "secular materialism"—the godless getting of money and things. They see Shintoism and Buddhism as empty ritual, providing relaxation therapy but no moral grounding. Japanese Christians are willing to face Japan's responsibility and guilt for World War II and to warn that Japan's new emphasis on "patriotism" could be misused.

Christianity always had an uphill struggle in Japan, where it was regarded as a foreign subversion of Japaneseness. Christianity brings with it individualism, guilt, and equality, but Japanese are content in their irreligiosity. In contrast, more than a quarter of South Koreans are Christians. Koreans, under the long Japanese oppression, saw churches (many U.S.-sponsored) as a comfort and support for their Koreanness.

and prices, cramped living quarters, and obedience and loyalty to company and bureaucratic authority. Young Japanese, educated and exposed to foreign norms, are rapidly breaking out of this pattern.

The Cult of the Group

Americans pride themselves on individualism, Japanese on groupness. We are trained from childhood to "be ourselves" and to attract attention: "Hey, look at me!" Older Japanese were taught to fit into the group and not attract attention: "It is the nail that sticks up that gets pounded down," goes a Japanese folk adage. Many Japanese feel they communicate with and understand only other Japanese. More plausibly, Japanese groupness grew from centuries of isolation and feudalism, which made Japanese obedient. The crime rate is very low. (There are practically no private handguns in Japan.) Students obediently hit the books, although younger Japanese less so. Japanese bureaucrats instruct businesspersons on correct strategies, something no American businessperson would tolerate.

Compared with American individualists, Japanese try not to attract attention or make a fuss, an attitude called *enryo*. One should always be polite and smile and not sue but should settle disputes quietly. (Japan has fewer lawyers than U.S. law schools produce each year.) Japanese medical costs are half America's, and Japanese have lower infant mortality and live longer (much of it due to diet). Wow, maybe we should try a little *enryo*.

But Japanese are shortchanged in civil and legal rights. Until recently, they rarely sued but settled obediently for the sake of social harmony, usually in favor of the stronger party, even if their own claim was valid. Under police interrogation (some lasting for days, with no

Comparison

How Would You Do on a Japanese Exam?

This solid geometry problem is from an entrance examination to Japan's elite Tokyo University. It is aimed at young Japanese in their last year of high school.

A regular pyramid with a height of V and a square base of width a rests on a sphere. The base of the pyramid passes through the center of the sphere, and all eight edges of the pyramid touch the surface of the sphere, as is shown in the illustration.

How do you calculate (1) the height of V and (2) the volume that the pyramid and sphere share in common?

Well, you say, I'm not a math major and should not be expected to know such advanced stuff. But this question is from the exam for *humanities* applicants.

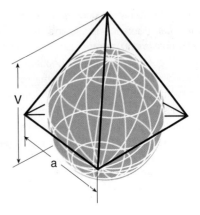

lawyer present), most arrested Japanese confessed, even the innocent. Recognizing the inequities of the justice system, Japanese universities are expanding their law programs, and Japanese courts added juries in 2009. Japanese are now less obedient and more aware of their rights.

Education for Grinds

The Japanese are strong on education, one of the keys to their success. The Japanese workforce is better educated than the American, especially in mathematics, the basis of all high-tech operations. On average, Japanese high school graduates know more math than do American college graduates. Children do their homework—often supervised by "education mamas"—with a determination that leaves French grinds far behind.

Japanese youngsters compete to get into the right schools and universities. As an almost perfect **meritocracy**, all admissions are based on tests; athletic ability or family connections help little. Many Japanese youngsters take cram courses after school. Young Japanese endure "examination hell" to get into the right high school or university. Not long ago, some of those who did poorly on exams committed suicide out of shame. Once into college, however, many Japanese students relax and do little work until their junior year, when they take exams that lead to jobs. Few Japanese students do graduate study, so few seek a high grade point average. Where you studied—Tokyo University (*Todai*) is the best—matters more than grades for getting a job.

Few Japanese students care or know about politics, often the case in advanced industrial countries, what is called *postmaterialism*. Leftist professors influence a few students to criticize the system. Upon graduation, though, many Japanese students get a haircut and a new suit and become obedient *sararimen* ("salary men"). Entrepreneurialism is rare; young Japanese seek jobs with big companies . Only recently have some young Japanese started their own companies.

meritocracy
Advancement based only on intellectual ability.

Comparison

Destined to Misunderstand?

Viscount Eiichi Shibusawa (1840–1931), one of the founders of modern Japanese business and an advocate of strong U.S.–Japanese ties, grew exasperated with the difficulties he encountered. Wrote Shibusawa: "No other countries exist which are as different from each other as the United States and Japan. These two countries seem to have been destined to misunderstand one another."

This shows up in the distinct U.S. and Japanese business cultures. For example, two business seminars are held in New York City, one for 25 Japanese executives in America, the other for 25 American executives working for Japanese firms in the United States. The Japanese, all men, arrive in dark suits and keep their coats on even though the room is hot. They take exactly the allotted ten minutes for a coffee break. They ask no questions until they get to know each other over lunch. They politely defer to the speakers.

The American group includes eight women. Many of the men immediately take off their coats in the hot room. Chatting during the coffee break lasts more than 20 minutes. The Americans ask many questions, and some dispute the speakers.

These are just a few of the cultural differences between Japanese and American managers. Americans view conflict within the firm as normal; Japanese practice *ne-mawashi*, patient discussion leading to consensus that all then follow. American managers want quick profits; Japanese want bigger market share and greater efficiency, building for the long run. American firms hire people for specific skills and then downsize them when they are no longer needed. Japanese firms hire for what the person can learn and contribute and try not to let the employee go. American managers respond to questions quickly and directly, for that indicates frankness. Japanese managers pause before answering and give discreet replies, for that indicates thoughtfulness. It does seem we are destined to misunderstand each other.

Japanese education is heavily based on rote learning and multiple choice exams. Traditionally, creativity and innovation were not prized, a style that is being rapidly and deliberately changed to let Japan compete globally. Debate, for example, used to be taught only as part of English-language instruction, implying that only with foreigners does one have disagreements. Today, many Japanese classes include debate to help Japanese communicate better among themselves as well as with the world. Fast learners in Japanese classrooms are assigned to help the slow, which is good both for education and groupness.

Death of a Sarariman

Traditionally, Japanese *sararimen* liked to stay with one company, and the company tried to offer lifetime employment, something the economy no longer permits. Most Japanese employees felt duty-bound to stay with their firm; American-style job hopping was frowned upon as opportunistic and disloyal. Corporate downsizing has made Japanese more job mobile. Japanese work hard; 12-hour days are common. Some Japanese die of overwork, an illness called *karoshi*. Families have sued the companies that worked the fathers to death.

Japanese work hard and produce much but ask for little. *Sararimen* live in small apartments and commute for an hour in crowded railcars. The cost of living is among the world's highest, especially for housing. Japan has only a meager social safety net or social security system, so

Japanese save for hard times and retirement. They are bigger savers than Germans, and the capital this made available for investment explains much of Japan's postwar economic growth. (Chinese savers are now doing the same for the Chinese economy.)

Much of this has changed. Now many companies hire *haken* (temporary workers from job agencies) to save money. Some 20 million Japanese do not have full-time, permanent jobs. Unemployment appeared in the 1990s as lifetime jobs, always part mythical, ended.

The "New Human Race"

The generation gap is wide in Japan. Older Japanese are amazed at how younger Japanese have changed and call them the *shin jinrui*, the new human race. Young Japanese are several inches taller than their grandparents, the result of more protein and not kneeling. McDonald's and KFC are among Japan's most popular fast food restaurants. Change in the postwar Japanese diet (higher fat) has produced obesity, previously unknown among Japanese youngsters.

Young Japanese have different attitudes. With jobs scarce and apartments expensive, many young Japanese work as *freeters* (temporaries) and live with their parents, never marrying. They see they will get only low-paid temporary jobs their whole life, so they are not oriented to economic growth or personal ambition. Might as well just have fun. Some are frustrated that the older generation, with secure jobs and benefits, refuses to make way for the younger. "Japan has the worst generational inequality in the world," noted one professor. A Japan that ignores a generation of potential innovators and entrepreneurs will not found new Kyoceras and Hondas.

Since Perry, Japanese political culture has been a rearguard action to preserve the core of *nihonjin-ron*. Gradually and grudgingly, Japan accepted *gaijin* ways, but superficially and altered. The Meiji modernizers in effect said: "We have to modernize to prevent the West from taking us over. But we will do it our way." After World War II, Japan essentially said: "We have to become a capitalist democracy. But we will do it our way."

Comparison

Changing Political Cultures in Germany and Japan

Both Germany and Japan long had feudal hierarchies and stressed obedience. Both marched to war under dictators who manipulated traditional-looking symbols. Neither country took to democracy until it was imposed on them after World War II. The devastation of war and lean postwar years taught both to work hard and ask for little. Reliable conservative parties— respectively, the CDU and LDP—delivered prosperity, and voters stayed with them. The difference is that Germany shed its postwar stability in about a generation; the Japanese are taking two or more generations.

Why is Japan slower? First, Japan's feudalism lasted longer and its obedience patterns were deeper than Germany's. Second, Japan was more isolated even after World War II, and it had no Common Market to make it more open. Third, Japan did not go through the reeducation that West Germany did after the war. Fourth, Japan was a poor country, poorer than most of West Europe, until the 1960s. As Japan got richer and more open to the world, its political culture grew less distinctive.

Patterns of Interaction

5.4   **Describe the theory of "no one in charge" in Japan.**

Japanese politics is an **iron triangle** consisting of leading politicians, economic interest groups, and the ministries. New prime ministers often vow to break the triangle but have only dented it. The triangle works like this: Politicians promise most economic interest groups—especially agriculture and the construction industry—to look out for

iron triangle
Interlocking of politicians, bureaucrats, and businesspeople to promote the flow of funds among them.

them. The ministries deliver money and guidance. In return, the interest groups deliver campaign funds, enabling the politicians to outspend rivals. (Some politicians also put funds in their own pockets.)

The ministries and agencies adjudicate the various demands by contracts, loans, regulations, subsidies, and trade protection. The ministries, the commanding corner of the triangle, focus narrowly on their industries and sectors and protect them by controlled markets in which competition is limited or excluded, making the Japanese economy—which looks like a free-market economy—one of the world's most regulated. Although recently reformed a little, thousands of regulations govern every aspect of the Japanese economy. The ministries build regulated markets under the control of bureaucrats, a setup reminiscent of the mercantilist system of the French kings. Japanese consumers pay for it in some of the world's highest prices.

Democracy

Japan's Major Interest Groups

Japanese interest groups resemble the French model; that is, they are usually subordinate to bureaucrats and, until recently, did not dispute the ministry that supervises them. Japanese pluralism is not the same as American pluralism, where interests strive to capture the relevant agency or, failing that, fight it. Here are some top Japanese interest confederations:

- **Keidanren**, Federation of Economic Organizations, the most important business group, speaks for most large corporations and used to work closely with METI to promote exports. Now it is working around ministerial control in favor of deregulation and competition.
- **Shin Rengo**, Japanese Trade Union Confederation, was formed from the 1989 merger of smaller union federations and speaks for 8 million members in a moderate and nonideological voice,

even though it still has some ties to the Social Democrats.

- **Nissho**, Japan Chamber of Commerce and Industry, with good ties to the LDP, seeks to curb competition, large stores, discounting, and foreign imports.
- **Nokyo**, Central Union of Agricultural Cooperatives (Japan Agriculture, JA), with nearly 10 million members, argues for self-sufficiency in food. The state-sponsored JA warns the LDP that it will lose farm votes if Japan opens to agricultural imports.
- **Nikkyoso**, Japan Teachers Union, is left wing, pacifist, and critical of government. It is tied to the Social Democrats.
- **Jichiro**, the Prefectural and Local Public Employees Union, is Japan's largest single union and is quite influential. It is also leftist and tied to the Social Democrats.

Bureaucrats in Command

Japan's ministries came from the militaristic system of the 1930s and 1940s. Munitions, heavy industry, the development of Manchuria, transportation and communications, and many other sectors were under state control and supervision. Indeed, the very founding of the modern Japanese economy during the Meiji Restoration was planned and controlled by the state. Japan has not really known a free-market economy.

After the war, the same bureaucrats who ran Japan's war economy planned its recovery. They did it well, with the argument that nothing but Japan's economic growth mattered, and they were the only people who knew how to do it. This is not a "socialist" system, for it kept ownership private and did not redistribute income from rich to poor. It was not directly aimed at living standards but at the growth of the Japanese economy as a whole. Neither is Japan a "statist" system (as in France and Mexico), where the state is the number one capitalist and owns major industries. Perhaps we should call Japan "guided capitalism."

The Japanese bureaucratic method is to leave industry in private hands but to persuade—often over dinner and drinks—the industry to go a certain way. The targets are the areas where Japan can undercut foreign producers and gain a big world-market share. Industries certified as growth leaders get long-term, low-interest loans from banks connected to the important ministries. Those industries not moving down desired paths do not get loans. This is a far more subtle way of steering an economy than Soviet-type socialism. (It also meant, by the 1990s, that many loans were mistakes that ruined Japanese banks. There is a downside to everything.) The Japanese approach is similar to the French "indicative planning," but stronger and more effective because it makes the cash flow and utilizes the cooperative Japanese setting where business generally obeys government.

The new Ministry of Economy, Trade, and Industry (METI), which took over the role of the Finance and the Ministry of International Trade and Industry (MITI) in 2001, mostly does a

Comparison

Bureaucratic Elites in France and Japan

The concept of a strong bureaucracy ignoring elected officials is nothing new. France has had such a system for decades. The Japanese bureaucratic elite resembles the French *grand corps*. Both groups are very bright and highly educated and placed into the top executive positions with mandates to modernize and upgrade their economies. Both think that they alone can save their countries and that elected politicians are a nuisance.

The French are trained in a Great School, such as the National Administration School, whereas the brainiest young Japanese get into Tokyo University, *Todai*, which is publicly funded. Upon graduation, both enter fast tracks to the executive level, and both may retire early into better-paying jobs in private industry. The French bureaucratic elite disdains the views of interest groups, whereas the Japanese listen to the groups but then persuade them to follow the ministry.

A big difference is that French bureaucratic elites cooperate across ministries. The Japanese are soon immersed in their ministries' closed environments and ignore other ministries or elected officials. Many criticize the ministries for having no grand plan to lift Japan out of economic stagnation; they just want to throw more money at the sectors they supervise.

good job. The brightest graduates are promoted rapidly and given major responsibilities while still young. Their modest salaries lead some to move into private industry in midcareer (what the Japanese call "descent from heaven" and the French call "putting on the slippers"), and the ministry does not mind, as this broadens its ties with industry (and, with it, occasional corruption). Japan recovered quickly after World War II and went on to set economic growth records. But bureaucratic guidance may have distorted the Japanese economy and plunged it into difficulties later.

Foreigners criticized Japan's bureaucracy as too powerful, but Tokyo dismissed that as "Japan bashing." By the 1990s, however, many Japanese agreed that the ministries and regulations had to be reformed. Yesterday's Japan bashing became today's conventional wisdom. One of the DPJ's main campaign promises was to put the bureaucrats under cabinet control.

It was not easy; the bureaucrats are used to their power. Fumed one high official of the powerful and conservative Finance Ministry, "We won't accommodate them, I assure you. They will accommodate us." In 2002, the popular and outspoken woman foreign minister was

Democracy

The Politics of Natural Disasters

Japan had been counting on nuclear as a main electricity source, but the 2011 earthquake, tsunami, and radiation leaks on its northeast coast quickly ended that dream and turned into a political issue. What is officially called the East Japan Great Earthquake, at magnitude 9.0 the biggest ever recorded in Japan, moved the main island of Honshu 8 feet to the east. More than 23,000 died, most from the tsunami. Especially young Japanese have little confidence in nuclear power, and, for a time, all of Japan's 54 nuclear reactors were shut down; some have since restarted. Abe claims Japan cannot do without nuclear power and wants most back on line.

Nothing could have stopped plate tectonics in 2011, but many claimed that government failures made things worse: The sea wall should have been higher, the nuclear power stations stronger, emergency services better, and information faster and more honest. Tokyo Electric Power, owner of the nuclear stations, had insufficient government supervision and downplayed the danger. The DPJ prime minister was charged with lack of leadership and resigned. The accusation "no one in charge" appeared, and trust in government and the economy took a hit.

Natural disasters often become political. The media, the opposition, and grieving citizens all look for someone to blame, which is sometimes justified. The 1995 Kobe earthquake, which killed nearly 6,500, brought charges of inadequate concrete standards. Likewise, China's 2008 Sichuan earthquake—which killed 90,000, including 19,000 schoolchildren—raised claims of shoddy and corrupt school construction, which Beijing promptly silenced. Hurricane Katrina, which flooded New Orleans in 2005, unleashed charges of incompetence at the federal, state, and local levels.

The interesting question about the 2011 earthquake and tsunami is what it will do to the Japanese psyche. Previous calamities have accelerated change. The 1923 Tokyo earthquake, which killed 140,000, aided the rise of militarism. Two nuclear bombs turned Japan to peaceful growth. The weak response to Kobe sped the LDP's ouster. Some say that the Japanese attitude of *gaman* (endurance, part of Zen doctrine) and voluntarism of 2011 will contribute to Japanese self-confidence and recovery.

scandal
Corrupt practice publicized by news media.

walking-around money
Politicians' relatively small payments to buy votes.

slush fund
Secret, unbudgeted, and unaccountable money used by politicians.

money politics
Lavish use of funds to win elections.

¥
Symbol for yen (and Chinese yuan); Japan's currency; worth about ¥100 to $1.

fired when the ministry's civil servants mutinied over her attempt to impose accountability. Japanese bureaucrats do not like politicians telling them what to do.

Japan's economic downturn showed that bureaucrats were unable to reverse the slump; the old formulas no longer worked. Impatient, the powerful private advisory body to the prime minister, the Federation of Economic Organizations (Keidanren), organized its own Competitiveness Committee in 2008 and made tough recommendations to the government, bypassing METI. Keidanren's message: Fix this creaky economic machine or we move our factories overseas. By 2010, Japanese companies were already doing 30 percent of their production in other countries. The bureaucracy lost prestige. Todai law students, Japan's best, who used to enter the civil service, turned to private industry.

Corruption Scandals

Another leg of the iron triangle, connecting the government to interest groups, contributes to corruption. **Scandals**, accompanied by officials' resignations and sometimes arrests, are not rare in Japan. Even prime ministers have been brought down. It used to be widely accepted, among both foreign and Japanese observers, that a little corruption was normal in Japan and that most Japanese did not mind it. **Walking-around money** is part of many political systems, and voters expect favors from politicians. In 2010, it was revealed that prime ministers have long had a **slush fund** they use to win support. Japanese now criticize corrupt politicians when the amounts are too big, the conflicts of interest too obvious, the methods of donation secretive, or the sources too dirty.

Everyone knows that many public works such as dams, highways, and bridges are unneeded—Japan uses more concrete a year than the United States—but they reward contractors, who kick back a percentage into party or personal coffers. Japan has been called a "construction state," implying payoffs. Komeito was founded in the 1950s as the "clean government party" to fight corruption.

Corruption is rooted in Japan's **money politics**, as many candidates do not stress party platform or personality but the nontrivial cash gifts they hand out to constituents, the funds for which they must raise themselves. A typical incumbent spends an estimated ¥120 million (some $1.2 million) a year but gets an allowance of only ¥20 million. The rest has to be raised somewhere, by the donations of friends, supporters, businesses, and even gangsters. By the early 1990s, the entire LDP was looking dirty, too conservative, and incapable of rehabilitating Japan's ailing economy. Some LDP politicians, generally younger and with an eye to the future, began bailing out of the party before it also tarnished them and began forming new parties. In 1993, voters, many now openly fed up, deserted not only the LDP but also the perennial second party, the Social Democrats, who were also tarred with scandal.

The increasing clamor over corruption amid Japan's slow-growth economy shows that the Japanese voting public is growing more mature, democratic, and frustrated. What an older generation accepted as normal, a younger generation brands as dirty, dishonorable, and undemocratic. Notice how, at this same time, Italian and Brazilian politicians were also brought down by the sort of corruption that had been going on for decades. These scandals were good signs, for they showed that people worldwide understand that they are ill served by corrupt governments.

No Leadership

One explanation of contemporary Japan is that behind a facade of orderly government, there is no real leadership, no one in charge. Some see it as a legacy of Japan's long and deep feudalism, which diffused power. Japanese political culture discourages bold or charismatic leadership. Few prime ministers lead; they briefly occupy the office until their unpopularity persuades faction chiefs to replace them. The faction chiefs do not really lead either; instead, they amass feudal power with which to battle one another. And parliamentarians do little but collect money in order to ensure their reelection. And even the mighty bureaucracies lead only in their narrow subject areas. Japanese government rumbles on, looking efficient, but no one steers it.

The "no one in charge" theory helps explain the uncoordinated drift of Japan into World War II: The government in Tokyo wanted peace, but the army pushed into China. The theory explains the difficulty in getting trade commitments from Tokyo: The prime minister promises to open the Japanese market to American products, but Japanese bureaucrats quietly ignore policy changes that come from outside their ministry, which has been likened to a feudal fiefdom, without common purpose or leadership.

The "no one in charge" theory also suggests that Japan is institutionally underdeveloped, unable to handle the economic problems of the twenty-first century, including economic distortions that produced a long slump and trade imbalances. The big question for Japan now is whether any party is coherent enough to carry out necessary reforms. Previous reform efforts budged Japan only a little.

No Losers

Related to the "no one in charge" theory is the understanding that no one gets injured by economic change. Although whale meat is now a trivial part of the Japanese diet, Tokyo defends the right of Japanese whalers to slay the endangered animals. Why? To give into international pressures would put whalers out of business, and, in this country, no one gets hurt. A single farmer on three acres of eggplants blocks the badly needed expansion of Tokyo's overburdened Narita airport. Why? To expand the airport would put the farmer out of business, and in this country, they do not do that.

The "no losers" impact on Japanese politics is to stifle change. Interest groups such as small retailers have been able to block and delay construction of big department stores and supermarkets. It took years to open Toys"R"Us in Japan; small shopkeepers objected. (It is now Japan's biggest toy retailer.) Japan is slowly modernizing its retail sector, and most Japanese are now happy to shop in large stores.

Democracy

Who Bribes Whom?

There are two important flows of money in modern politics. The first is from interest group to political party, an effort to get favorable policies that is found everywhere—in Europe, the United States, and Japan. It attracts the most media attention.

A much bigger money flow, however, is from government to voting bloc, designed to win votes. It, too, is found everywhere and has grown, as all modern governments pay off various groups with spending programs, construction projects, subsidies, and trade protection. This form of bribery is probably a bigger motivator of politicians' choices. Fear of alienating a voter bloc makes cowards out of most politicians.

Mostly governments bribe groups rather than the other way around.

Typically, politicians strive for their immediate advantage (namely, getting reelected) and pay little attention to outcomes (such as war, budget deficits, or inflation). Politicians have to play short-term games and ignore long-term consequences. Those who do not can be voted out. Campaign-law reforms, either in Japan or in the United States, pay no attention to the more important type of bribery, the "earmarks" (polite term for *pork*) so beloved of both Japanese and U.S. politicians.

Informally, Japan has a **unit veto** system, one in which any component, no matter how small, can veto an innovation desired by most. Farmers have especially benefited. Even within the Tokyo area—at 35 million people the world's largest metropolitan area—there are small patches of farmland that the owners will not sell to make way for badly needed apartment houses, and they are supported by laws and lavish subsidies. Japanese consumers lose through the high prices and cramped life they must endure.

Reform without Change

France and Italy have been described as "blocked societies" for the way entrenched interests paralyze needed reforms. Typically, such systems rumble on until pressures for change crack apart the old setup. De Gaulle's 1958 arrival in power exemplified how a blocked society dramatically unblocks. Japan has a similar but perhaps worse problem, for there is no one in charge and no single center of power that can bring about major changes. Some observers see Japan as stuck in an institutional paralysis that caused its economy to slow and its status as regional leader to lapse.

For years, Japanese prime ministers have pledged to deregulate the Japanese economy—now they call it *risutora*, "restructuring"—but most prime ministers offer minor, almost cosmetic reforms that change little. Many Japanese favor major reforms—Keidanren strongly backs them—hoping to kill as many as four birds with one stone. Namely, deregulating the strongly regulated Japanese economy, including its barriers to foreign imports, could reinvigorate the economy, raise living standards, reduce trade surpluses, and curb the bureaucracy. In Japan, reform is always coming but never arrives.

unit veto
Ability of one component to block laws or changes.

Democracy

Can "Money Politics" Be Broken?

Did Japan's electoral and campaign-funding reforms of 1993 work, or is money politics so deeply rooted in Japanese political culture that legal tinkering cannot end it? It is an old question: Which is more important, **structure** or psychology?

Japan's money politics, alas, continued. Reforms do not necessarily work as planned. The United States has gone through several reforms of campaign financing only to find that both candidates and contributors come up with new ways to beat the system. (Now it is **soft money**.) The underlying problem is the need for campaign funds and the need to please blocs of voters.

Japan, the United States, Britain, France, and Germany all have different electoral systems, but each has recurring scandals related to fund-raising. Why? Because in each system, parties and candidates figure out ways to skirt the law. And in each system, some candidates use campaign contributions for personal expenses, which often leads to additional scandals. Notice the underlying similarity: Politicians of all nationalities are addicted to money. In the words of California political boss Jesse Unruh, "Money is the mother's milk of politics."

What Japanese Quarrel About

5.5   Explain how Japan's booming economy could go flat.

The Political Economy of Japan

Like Germany, the Japanese economy soared after World War II but then leveled off, until rapidly expanding China surpassed it in 2010 as the world's second-largest economy. Over time, Germany's and Japan's postwar economic advantages faded. From 1990 to 2010, Japan's GDP grew little. Japan illustrates well how economic growth tends to form an "S-curve"—first a slow traditional economy, then something triggers a few decades of rapid growth, and finally growth levels off. From 1955 to 1970, Japan's growth averaged a marvellous 9.5 percent a year, but from 1971 to 1990, only 3.8 percent, and from 1991 to 2010, a measly 0.8 percent. Now Singapore, Hong Kong, and Taiwan all have higher per capita incomes (corrected for *PPP*) than Japan.

After the war, "made in Japan" suggested a product was junk, but Japan climbed out of the junk stage in the 1950s. In 1960, Japan was the richest country in Asia but still had a per capita GDP of only $380 (around $2,600 in today's dollars), one-eighth the American per capita GDP. By 1990, Japan's per capita was nominally higher than America's. The Korean War of 1950–1953 brought U.S. military contracts for clothing, footwear, and other items to low-bid Japanese producers. (The Vietnam War was the catalyst for South Korea's industrial takeoff in the late 1960s.) Soon, U.S. manufacturers of civilian goods gave contracts to Japanese firms. Quality improved, and costs were a fraction of U.S. costs. In the 1960s, Japanese cars were looked down on, but by the 1970s, they were respected for fuel economy and workmanship.

structure
Institutions of government such as constitution, laws, and branches.

soft money
In U.S. politics, funds given to parties and other groups rather than to candidates in order to skirt restrictions.

Four Tigers
South Korea, Taiwan, Hong
Kong, and Singapore.

Now, Toyota is the world's largest car company. A continual pattern has been to underestimate the Japanese product—until it puts you out of business.

As in postwar West Germany, Japanese did not ask for much: a job that put food on the table. In politics, most were cautious and voted for moderate conservatives. In 1990, however, Japan's extraordinary economic growth ended with a major recession and unemployment. The collapse of Japan's stock market and real estate bubbles left corporations and banks looking poorer and foolish. The LDP started looking incompetent. Younger Japanese, educated and traveled, saw how people in other countries did not live in rabbit hutches and pay exorbitant prices. Many were no longer willing to support the status quo.

Not long ago, the Japanese economy was the marvel of the world. A popular 1979 book was titled *Japan as No. 1*. Many saw the "Japanese model" as a new, different, and better system; no one imagined it could nosedive. Many now suspect there was never a Japanese success formula, but for years, business writers sold books by simplifying factors such as these:

CONFUCIANISM Several East Asian countries show similar patterns of rapid growth. China and the **Four Tigers** have also grown fast. Culturally, all share a Confucian culture, which stresses education, hard work, stability, and obedience. It frowns on high personal consumption; people should save, not spend. Some argue that a Confucian work ethic gave East Asia the functional equivalent of a Protestant work ethic.

PRODUCTIVITY High productivity and low wages make for rapid growth. For some decades, Japanese productivity stayed ahead of wages, giving Japan an opening to produce much of the world's advanced consumer electronics. Japanese factories could simply put more high-quality labor into a product—no longer the case.

EDUCATION Japan (and the Four Tigers) pays a lot of attention to education, especially K–12. Education is supervised at the national level and compulsory. This gives Japan a highly skilled labor force, one that can read, follow instructions, and do math. (Much of the U.S. labor force cannot.) Interestingly, Japan and its high-growth neighbors pay less attention to college education, finding that much of it contributes little to economic growth.

SAVINGS Japanese save a lot and consider debt shameful; Americans save little and accumulate big debts. Japanese use credit cards far less than Americans do and pay off balances monthly. In Japan, thrift is an old tradition, and pension plans, welfare, and social security are weak, so Japanese put aside money. Many economists think that savings alone explains Japan's past phenomenal economic growth. Savings made Japanese banks the world's biggest in the 1980s. The vast capital available for investment encouraged businesses to expand until they overexpanded; then banks loaned even more to these "zombie" companies, piling up bad loans. Japan's banks finally *wrote off* about half of the dud loans and put the banking system on the road to recovery. Many argue that Japanese save too much; their frugality keeps Japan's economy flat. Japanese households sit on a staggering $18 trillion in savings.

STATE SUPERVISION This is controversial both in Japan and abroad. Is state supervision, going back to the Meiji modernizers and continuing with MITI and the Finance Ministry, a key factor in Japan's rapid growth? Most other fast-growth East Asian economies have state supervision as well. (Hong Kong, however, has none.)

The value of state planning has not been proved. Some economists say Japan simply got its **macroeconomy** or "fundamentals" right and might have done as well or better without state supervision of the **microeconomy**. Some Japanese firms prospered with no help from a ministry, and some with much help did poorly. (Sony founder Akio Morita publicly disdained government help.) The only way to demonstrate that Japanese economic intervention worked is to have two very similar countries operate under different policies, one with state supervision and the other without, and see which grows faster.

macroeconomy
Big picture of a nation's economy, including GDP size and growth, productivity, interest rates, and inflation.

microeconomy
Close-up picture of individual markets, including product design and pricing, efficiency, and costs.

From Bubble to Burst

Japan's economic bubble burst first and worst, nearly two decades earlier than the U.S. meltdown. The 1990s were the "lost decade" of Japan's economy, and the following decade was not much better. Poverty and inequality increased. From 1955 to 1973, Japan's economy grew rapidly, but then the S-curve took hold. In some years, Japan's economy actually declined, for three main reasons: (1) competition from lower-wage Asian lands, (2) an aging workforce, and (3) a yen that is much too high. Investment mistakes were made. MITI prodded and financed Japanese electronics firms to lose vast sums developing the "fifth generation" of computers and high-definition television. MITI encouraged Japan's 11 (eleven!) car makers to expand until they overexpanded.

Government and banks pushed the export sectors (cars, electronics) into high levels of automation, productivity, and efficiency. (Profitability, alas, was rather poor.) Other sectors got left behind. Distribution was predominantly by expensive and inefficient neighborhood mom-and-pop stores. U.S.-style discounting was denounced for ruining family shops. Gradually, though, as Japanese found they could buy Sonys and Canons cheaper in the United States, foreign retail chains were allowed to open in Japan.

China Lessons

Beware the S-Curve

Japan's recovery from the devastation of World War II followed the classic *S-curve* of economic growth. Japanese growth accelerated during the 1950s and 1960s, setting records for the time (since eclipsed by China), but slowed in the 1970s and 1980s, flattened in 1990, and has been weak and fitful since. Many causes are named: decline in births (and hence an aging workforce), high labor costs, offshoring of production to lower-cost countries, capital from bank loans rather than from stocks, focus on market share rather than on profits, and stock market and property bubbles that burst. China is now developing many of these same problems.

The underlying problem is that no economy grows rapidly forever. Most form an S-curve that slows after 30 or so years, from several percent a year to a few percent. No cure has been found for this tendency, neither governmental austerity nor deficit spending. The lesson for China: Plan ahead for a moderation of your growth tempo—which is already underway—and explain to citizens that it is a sign of economic maturity. China will continue to grow, just not at its record-shattering pace.

Geography

Living Without Lebensraum

German thinkers of the nineteenth century came up with overly deterministic theories of *geopolitics* such as *Lebensraum* (living space), eagerly embraced by the Nazis and Japanese militarists as justification for their imperial expansion. After their defeat, Germans and Japanese learned that they have never lived so well as when confined to their present crowded countries. If you have the economy, you do not need much land. Prosperity depends not so much on territory as on smart, energetic people and sound economic policy.

Agriculture got left behind. The typical Japanese farm of a few acres was inefficient, but the Agricultural Ministry protected Japanese farmers from cheaper imports. This cost Japanese consumers dearly and angered Japan's trading partners. Nearly three-quarters of Japanese farmers are part-time anyway, a pattern typical of industrializing countries. The average Japanese farmer is 66 and farms less than five acres. In purely economic terms, farmers should sell their small holdings, either to more-efficient farmers or for building apartments. There is protected and tax-exempt farmland in and near major cities that should be subject to market forces.

During the 1990s, Japanese grew dissatisfied with their economy as the shortcomings of the supervised system became clear. Under bureaucratic guidance, the Japanese economy produced **excess liquidity**, which fueled stock market and real estate bubbles, which both burst in 1989. The Tokyo stock exchange lost most of its peak value and recovered only slowly. Japan went into **deflation**, the great plague of the 1930s, and got stuck in it. The Bank of Japan refused to do anything about it. Many economists reckon that deflation is worse than inflation, as it shrinks the value of homes and businesses. Some Japanese who bought apartments around 1990 saw them lose half their worth but still have to pay off huge mortgages, also a U.S. problem.

excess liquidity
Too much money floating around.

deflation
Decrease in prices; opposite of inflation.

deficit
Government spends more in a given year than it takes in.

debt
Sum total of government *deficits* over many years.

insolvent
Owes more than it owns.

To fight the slowdown, Tokyo threw trillions of dollars into public works spending, giving Japan the world's biggest **deficits** and national **debt** but producing little economic growth. Tokyo did what it had always done—bail out any troubled economic sector—but no government can bail out everything forever.

Bailing out firms merely disguises their illnesses and blocks the market's signals that these companies must change or fold. Tokyo tried to keep Japan's large banks from collapsing, although, based on their assets, several were **insolvent**. Japanese and foreign analysts worry that foolish investments help weak banks and businesses mask problems but do not solve them. Abe cut back Japan's huge farm subsidies but had to face Japan's highly organized JA. In 2005, LDP Prime Minister Junichiro Koizumi vowed to privatize Japan

Post's massive savings bank and insurance functions and release their billions into investments, but subsequent chiefs retreated from the project. Politicians like to do pork with postal savings, postal bureaucrats form a powerful lobby, and many villages' social life centers on the post office. In Japan, as in many lands, reforms are thwarted and paralysis thrives.

Japan is now undercut by low-cost competitors. Other lands have taken over several sectors that used to be Japanese: steelmaking, shipbuilding, and consumer electronics. China now does much of the world's manufacturing. Japanese camera firms have moved much of their production to Southeast Asia. Japanese should not despair; it just means Japan has become a mature economy with modest growth rates. And Japan has an excellent foundation for long-term prosperity: a well-educated population, a magnificent high-tech sector, and vast investment capital.

Holding down domestic consumption while accumulating capital resources boosted economic growth. But pursued too long, it overshot the mark and produced serious imbalances. The yen, held too low for too long, suddenly shot from 330 to the dollar to 80 to the dollar. (The value of the yen is expressed in how many yen per dollar, so when the yen goes "up," it is getting cheaper in relation to the dollar; when the yen goes "down," it is getting more expensive. With the euro, conversely, up means up.) The strong yen hurt Japanese export products but enabled Japanese to live better from cheap imports.

Abe's Three Arrows

How to revive a stagnant economy is Japan's big political question. Prime Minister Shinzo Abe offered "three arrows" for this: (1) fiscal stimulus, (2) monetary easing, and (3) structural reforms. For the first, Abe pumped ¥10.3 trillion into public works spending. For the second, Abe named the new head of Japan's central bank and told him to print more currency to deliberately weaken the yen from 77 to the dollar to more than 100. For the third, Abe's longer-term structural reforms to free up Japan's market, including lifting import restrictions, were resisted and came to little, making Abe look weak.

Initially, Japanese consumers were spending again, and the economy perked up, but many doubted that it would continue. Japan already carries massive government debt—245 percent of GDP in 2014 (U.S.: 100 percent)—which Abe attempted to reduce. Japan's workforce was still rapidly aging, with too few workers to replace them. Critics charged that none of Abe's arrows hit Japan's underlying problems.

To an extent, Abe was trying to correct Japan's long-term trade imbalances, specifically its mammoth **trade surpluses**, especially with the United States, which MITI was obsessed by, a sort of latter-day mercantilism. If the Japanese had simply consumed more—including more imported goods—at an earlier date, they might have avoided the excess liquidity that fueled the stock market and real estate bubbles. Too many yen chased investments to the sky; then the bubbles burst. (Note how China is duplicating this pattern of export mania while shortchanging domestic consumption.) Abe pledged to join the U.S.-backed Trans-Pacific Partnership (TPP) talks to cut trade barriers and correct trade imbalances, but the powerful JA farm lobby is adamant against letting in foreign foodstuffs, and farmers are an important LDP constituency.

write off
Lender admits that a *nonperforming loan* will never be repaid.

nonperforming loan
One that is not being repaid.

Should Japan Rearm?

Since World War II, Japan has preached and practiced peace. MacArthur's staff put a "no-war clause" (Article 9) into Japan's new constitution, stating that military forces "will never be maintained." The Korean War in 1950 made some wonder if Japan should stay defenseless and depend on U.S. protection. A 1954 law allowed Japan to build "Self-Defense Forces," but Tokyo informally limited defense spending to 1 percent of GDP. Japan has only some 238,000 in its armed forces, but they are well trained and equipped. As China staked out territorial claims far into the South and East China seas and North Korea lobbed rockets over Japan as "tests" and built nuclear weapons, the United States and Japan dusted off their defense alliance.

Japanese leftists argue that even their Self-Defense Forces are at odds with both the letter and spirit of the constitution. Radical nationalists, some of them in the Abe cabinet, on

Comparison

Japanese and U.S. Economic Problems

Many Americans worry that the U.S. national debt—now equal to its GDP—predicts economic collapse and must therefore be urgently fought by cutting our annual budget deficits. If we don't, our trading partners will dump dollars and impoverish us. Others argue that we are in a still-fragile recovery and drastic cuts in federal spending would push us back into recession. Some tried to use Japan to prove their respective cases, but the lessons were murky.

After 1990, to fight underconsumption and deflation, Tokyo pumped money into public works, and the economy began to rebound. In 1997, believing the recession was over, and short on revenue, Tokyo raised Japan's national consumption tax (a sort of sales tax) from 3 to 5 percent. Japan plunged into a double-dip recession that lingers still. "Aha!" exclaim U.S. Republicans, "you see what happens when you raise taxes?" Counter U.S. Democrats: "Aha! You see what happens when you snip off fiscal stimulus too soon?" Desperate for revenues, Abe raised the tax to 8 percent in 2013.

Even though Japan has the world's highest national debt, the yen, far from collapsing, stayed strong. Global investors still liked safe private Japanese firms even though government debt weakened its credit ratings. Likewise, the U.S. dollar declined only a little because there are few other economies where investors can safely park large sums. In neither country did big national debt sink their currencies. Actually, both Tokyo and Washington try to weaken their currencies to promote exports.

Much attention focused on both countries' banks, which had shoveled out loans that went bad. The banks pretended they would be repaid until that became unbelievable and they crashed. Finally, in 2002, the Tokyo Finance Ministry's tough new audits declared the full amount of bad debts and forced Japan's "zombie banks" to **write off** their **nonperforming loans**. Likewise the U.S. Congress, under intense lobbying, let banks overstate the value of their bad loans after the 2008 financial meltdown.

Some economists warned that without major reforms, Japan could be America's future. But the U.S. economy avoided deflation and began to recover. Deficits and debt predict neither economic turnaround nor collapse. Each country has its own deep-seated problems that cannot be cured by monetary policy alone. Demographics and political culture may explain more. Japan's population is aging and shrinking, America's is young and growing. Especially, older Japanese, raised in frugality and making do, prefer saving to buying. Americans have no such problem.

the other hand, demand a restoration of the samurai spirit and would end the constitution's pacifist clauses and even acquire a few nuclear weapons to counter Chinese and North Korean threats. Abe, a rightwing nationalist, seeks to revise Article 9, something most Japanese favor but a few intellectuals fear. An assertive, rearmed Japan would sharpen Sino-Japanese conflict.

support ratio
Number working compared to number retired.

Public and newspaper opinion turned anti-Abe in 2013 when he quickly passed a tough new secrecy law, boosting jail terms from one year to ten for leaking secrets. Four-fifths of Japanese opposed the law, and Abe's popularity dropped 10 percentage points, to below 50 percent. A group of academics called the law the biggest threat to democracy since World War II. Abe may not be able to accomplish his rearmament agenda.

The United States wants Japan to be able to defend itself and lead regional security—as Japan did splendidly in Cambodian peacekeeping—and encourages Japan to do more, but not go nuclear. Japan sent 550 noncombat troops to Iraq, something Japanese disliked. Okinawans want to close the big U.S. base there, but Tokyo wants to keep it. LDP governments seek U.S. protection; the DPJ had pledged to "reexamine" the U.S.–Japan alliance but decided to keep Japan under the U.S. umbrella, something most Japanese want.

Should Japan expand its Self-Defense Forces? Japan's neighbors used to fear Japanese military power, but now, facing China and North Korea, other Asian countries see Japan as a strategic partner and counterweight to China. Many Japanese and their neighbors now think that Japan should become a normal country with a credible but unthreatening defense capability. A showdown looms in the East China Sea: At the same time, in late 2012, nationalistic new leaders took power in Beijing and Tokyo, both pledging to never back down over ownership of the tiny but contested Diaoyu (in Chinese) or Senkaku (in Japanese) Islands in the East China Sea. Are Americans willing to fight to keep the Senkakus in Japanese hands?

Geography

Running out of Japanese

In 1975, the number of births in Japan started to drop. In 2005, Japan's population began to shrink and, with its very low fertility rate, will drop below 100 million by midcentury. Japan's colleges worry that the number of 18-year-olds, which declined by half since 1974, will not be enough to fill classrooms. Industry lacks sufficient workers. By 2030, a third of Japanese will be over 64. Some politicians promise families a monthly allowance for every child, but such subsidies rarely reverse declining fertility rates.

The biggest worry is how to support Japanese in retirement—and Japanese are the longest-lived and fastest aging in the world—with so few workers. Japan's pension system will soon be in the red. The **support ratio** is projected at 1.2 working Japanese to 1 retiree by 2050. In Germany, it will be 1.6, and in the United States, 2.6, but they admit foreign workers; Japan admits very few. Only 1.7 percent of Japan's population is "foreign," and that includes Chinese and Koreans whose families have lived in Japan for generations. Japanese discriminate against immigrants—even against Japanese born in Brazil and Peru. Japan, a semiclosed society, must open up.

Review Questions

Learning Objective 5.1 Describe the effects of Japan's long and strong feudalism, p. 183.

1. How does Japanese feudalism resemble European feudalism?
2. What and when was the Meiji Restoration?
3. Was Japan's march to war inevitable?

Learning Objective 5.2 Explain the brief tenures of Japanese prime ministers, p. 191.

4. Why have Japan's prime ministers tended to be weak and brief?
5. Which has been Japan's dominant party and why?
6. How is Japan organized territorially?

Learning Objective 5.3 Contrast Japanese and U.S. political cultures, p. 198.

7. What is the difference between guilt and shame? Which characterizes Japan?
8. Why has postwar Japan had such difficulty in coming to grips with its past?

9. What are the cultural problems of Japanese firms operating in America?

Learning Objective 5.4 Describe the theory of "no one in charge" in Japan, p. 205.

10. Describe the Japanese *iron triangle*.
11. Is Japan run by its bureaucrats? Then what role does Japanese democracy have?
12. Do interest groups bribe government, or does government bribe interest groups?
13. Why is the Japanese system so hard to change?

Learning Objective 5.5 Explain how Japan's booming economy could go flat, p. 211.

14. What is the *S-curve* in economic growth? Is it inevitable?
15. Did Prime Minister Abe's "three arrows" economic program work?
16. Should Japan rearm in order to stand up to China?

Key Terms

alternation in power, p. 195
debt, p. 214
deficit, p. 214
deflation, p. 214
Diet, p. 193, p. 193
excess liquidity, p. 214
Four Tigers, p. 212
gaijin, p. 186
guilt, p. 200
insolvent, p. 214
iron triangle, p. 205
Liberal Democrats, p. 192

macroeconomy, p. 213
Manchukuo, p. 189
Meiji, p. 186
meritocracy, p. 202
METI, p. 196
microeconomy, p. 213
money politics, p. 208
nonperforming loan, p. 216
pork barrel, p. 193
prefecture, p. 198
scandal, p. 208
shame, p. 200

Shinto, p. 183
shogun, p. 185
slush fund, p. 208
soft money, p. 211
structure, p. 211
support ratio, p. 217
Tokugawa, p. 186
trade surplus, p. 215
unit veto, p. 210
walking-around money, p. 208
write off, p. 216
¥, p. 208

Further Reference

Buruma, Ian. *Inventing Japan, 1853–1964.* New York: Modern Library, 2003.

Calichman, Richard, ed. *Contemporary Japanese Thought.* New York: Columbia University Press, 2005.

Carlson, Matthew. *Money Politics in Japan: New Rules, Old Practices.* Boulder, CO: Lynne Rienner, 2007.

Curtis, Gerald L. *The Logic of Japanese Politics: Leaders, Institutions, and the Limits of Change.* New York: Columbia University Press, 2000.

Dower, John W. *Ways of Forgetting, Ways of Remembering: Japan in the Modern World.* New York: New Press, 2012.

Estévez-Abe, Margarita. *Welfare and Capitalism in Postwar Japan: Party, Bureaucracy, and Business.* New York: Cambridge University Press, 2008.

Feifer, George. *Breaking Open Japan: Commodore Perry, Lord Abe, and American Imperialism in 1853.* New York: HarperCollins, 2006.

Gordon, Andrew. *A Modern History of Japan: From Tokugawa Times to the Present.* New York: Oxford University Press, 2003.

Hayes, Louis D. *Introduction to Japanese Politics,* 5th ed. Armonk, NY: M. E. Sharpe, 2008.

Hrebenar, Ronald J., and Akira Nakamura, eds. *Parties and Politics in Contemporary Japan: The Post-Koizumi Era.* Boulder, CO: Lynne Rienner, 2009.

Kingston, Jeff. *Contemporary Japan: History, Politics and Social Change since the 1980s.* Hoboken, NJ: Wiley-Blackwell, 2010.

Koo, Richard C. *The Holy Grail of Macroeconomics: Lessons from Japan's Great Recession.* Hoboken, NJ: Wiley, 2010.

Martin, Sherry L., and Gill Steel, eds. *Democratic Reform in Japan: Assessing the Impact.* Boulder, CO: Lynne Rienner, 2008.

McNeill, David, and Lucy Birmingham. *Strong in the Rain: Surviving Japan's Earthquake, Tsunami, and Fukushima Nuclear Disaster.* New York: Palgrave Macmillan, 2012.

Mulgan, Aurelia George. *Power and Pork: A Japanese Political Life.* Canberra: Australian National University Press, 2006.

Nathan, John. *Japan Unbound: A Volatile Nation's Quest for Pride and Purpose.* Boston: Houghton Mifflin, 2004.

Packard, George R. *Edwin O. Reischauer and the American Discovery of Japan.* New York: Columbia University Press, 2010.

Pilling, David. *Bending Adversity: Japan and the Art of Survival.* New York: Penguin, 2014.

Pyle, Kenneth. *Japan Rising: The Resurgence of Japanese Power and Purpose.* New York: Public Affairs, 2007.

Ruoff, Kenneth J. *Imperial Japan at Its Zenith: The Wartime Celebration of the Empire's 2,600th Anniversary.* Ithaca, NY: Cornell University Press, 2010.

Sugimoto, Yoshio. *The Cambridge Companion to Modern Japanese Culture.* New York: Cambridge University Press, 2009.

Chapter 6
Russia

Kremlin walls face domes of St. Basil's cathedral in Moscow.

Learning Objectives

6.1 Explain how Russia's geographical location governed its political development.

6.2 Compare and contrast the Soviet system with the new Russian system.

6.3 Illustrate how "civil society" underpins democracy.

6.4 Explain why reforming Russia is a recurrent problem.

6.5 Contrast the Russian and Chinese economies.

WHY RUSSIA MATTERS

Russia's actions in Ukraine showed dangerous nationalism and pointed toward a new cold war in which Russia again allies with China. Russia and China took two paths out of communism, neither of which led to democracy. Russia attempted reforms that led to collapse, whereas China made economic but not political reforms. So far, Beijing seems far cleverer than Moscow, but China's transition is also risky. Russia shows how the march to democracy can reverse. The end of the Soviet Union in late 1991 and the apparent founding of a democracy did not produce rule of law and alternation in power. Instead, Russia stalled in an authoritarianism with democratic trappings. Many Russians resent losing the Cold War and believe they are threatened by U.S. power. Only a minority were ever democrats, and most supported the strong president who brought stability and prosperity, although discontent over crime and corruption grows. Because Russia's economy is based on oil and natural gas exports, its prosperity and stability are shaky.

Impact of the Past

6.1   **Explain how Russia's geographical location governed its political development.**

Russia is immense, stretching nine time zones across the northern half of Asia. Actually, only a small part of Russia is in Europe—that is, west of the Urals, the nominal dividing line between Europe and Asia—although that is where most Russians live. A country as big and ethnically diverse as Russia may require strong central control backed by force to hold it together, a point that inclines Russia to **tyranny**.

Without natural boundaries, Russia is easy to invade from east or west, although its size and harsh winters doomed the invasions of Charles XII of Sweden, Napoleon, and Hitler. Winters give Russia a short growing season, making agriculture chancy, with crops failing an average of one year in three. Vast **Siberia** and its weather are hostile to settlement, and its mineral and forest wealth is hard to extract. Plans to develop Siberia go back to tsarist days, but Siberia is now depopulating.

Russia long had difficulty reaching the open sea. The first Russian states were landlocked; only under Peter the Great at the beginning of the eighteenth century did Russians overcome the Swedes to reach the Baltic and the Turks to reach the Black Sea. The North Russian ports ice over in winter, and the Black Sea is controlled by the Turkish Straits, still leaving European Russia without year-round, secure ports. One of the great dreams of tsarists and Communists alike was for warm-water ports under exclusive Russian control.

The Slavic People

Occupying most of East Europe, the Slavic peoples are the most numerous in Europe, with languages that are similar but written differently. The Western Slavs (Poles, Czechs, Croats, Slovenes, and Slovaks) were Christianized from Rome; hence, their alphabet is Latin. The Eastern Slavs (Russians, Ukrainians, Serbs, Bulgarians, and Macedonians) were converted by Eastern Orthodox monks from **Constantinople**, and their languages are written in a variation of the Greek alphabet called **Cyrillic**, after St. Cyril, one of the monks who first converted Slavs.

tyranny
Coercive rule, usually by one person.

Siberia
That part of Russia east of the Ural Mountains.

Constantinople
Capital of Byzantium, conquered by Turks in 1453.

Cyrillic
Greek-based alphabet of Eastern Slavic languages.

Tatar
Mongol-origin tribes who ruled Russia for centuries. (*Not Tartar.*)

Ukraine
From Slavic for "borderland"; country south of Russia.

Their Orthodox Christianity and Cyrillic writing contributed to Russians' cultural isolation from the rest of Europe. The ideas that modernized Catholic and Protestant Europe penetrated Russia much later. Rome sparked new thoughts in West Europe, but the headquarters of the Orthodox faith, Constantinople, under the Turks, ceased to provide intellectual guidance. At the same time West Europe experienced the Renaissance, which rippled outward from Catholic Italy, Russia stayed isolated and asleep. It missed most of the Enlightenment.

A bigger factor in Russia's isolation was its thirteenth-century conquest by the Mongols, later known as **Tatars**. The Mongols crushed the first Russian state, centered at Kiev in present-day **Ukraine**, and dominated for two centuries. While West Europe moved ahead, Russian culture under the barbaric Mongols declined. It took five centuries for Russia to catch up with the West.

Russia

Geography

Bound Russia

Russia is bounded on the north by the Arctic Ocean;

on the east by the Bering Sea and Sea of Okhotsk;

on the south by North Korea (tiny), China, Mongolia, Kazakhstan, Azerbaijan, Georgia, and the Black Sea;

and on the west by Ukraine, Belarus, Latvia, Estonia, Finland, and Norway.

The Russian **exclave** of Kaliningrad Oblast (region), formerly Königsberg of old East Prussia, is wedged between Poland and Lithuania on the Baltic.

Russian Autocracy

Under the Tatars, the duchy of Moscow became the most powerful Russian state and eventually beat the Tatars. Moscovy's Ivan the Terrible (1530–1584), the **tsar**, expanded Russian territory down the Volga to the Caspian Sea and into Siberia. Ivan's brutal use of force set a standard for later rulers, and many Russians still like strong and ruthless leaders. When the Russian nobles (*boyars*) came into conflict with Ivan, his secret police, the *Oprichnina*, exiled or executed them. The Russian nobility never again played an autonomous role in political life. The result was **autocracy** under the tsar. Unlike West Europe, Russia never experienced the mixed monarchy of nobles, church, commoners, and king. Accordingly, Russians had no experience with limited government, checks and balances, or pluralism. As Ivan grew older, he became madder. Able to trust no one, he murdered those around him—even his own son—at the least suspicion. By the time he died, he had carved out the modern Russian state.

Russians accepted autocracy because they felt that, without a firm hand at the top, the system would degenerate into anarchy, which happened in the early seventeenth century, the "Time of Troubles." Russia suffered unrest, banditry, civil war, and a Polish invasion. Russians willingly served a powerful state. The Russian Orthodox Church, which the tsar also headed, became a pillar of autocracy, teaching the faithful to worship the tsar as the "little father" who protected all Russians. The tsar was both head of state and head of church, a pattern called **caesaropapism**. Russia became a "service state" in which all walks of life, from nobles to peasants to priests, served the autocrat. Western concepts such as liberty and individual rights were absent.

During the fifteenth and sixteenth centuries, Russia actually moved backward as previously free peasants became serfs, tied to the land to labor for aristocrats. While West Europe ended serfdom centuries earlier, in Russia, the vast majority were poor and ignorant farm laborers who occasionally revolted.

exclave
Part of country separated from main territory.

tsar
From "caesar"; Russia's emperor; sometimes spelled old Polish style, *czar*.

autocracy
Absolute rule of one person in a centralized state.

caesaropapism
Combining the top civil ruler (caesar) with the top spiritual ruler (pope), as in Russia's tsars.

Westernizers
Nineteenth-century Russians
who wished to copy the West.

Slavophiles
Nineteenth-century Russians
who wished to develop Russia
along native, non-Western lines;
also known as "Russophiles."

zemstvo
Local parliament in old Russia.

Forced Modernization

By the time Peter I became tsar in 1682, Russia lagged behind West Europe. Peter, who stood 6 feet 9 inches (206 cm), forced Russia to modernize and become a major power. He personally handled Russia's legislation, diplomacy, war, and technical innovation and was the first tsar to travel in West Europe. Admiring its industries, he ordered them duplicated in Russia. Nearly continually at war, Peter pushed the Swedes back to give Russia an outlet on the Baltic, where he ordered a magnificent new capital built, St. Petersburg (later Leningrad), modeled after Amsterdam, to serve as Russia's window to the West.

Copying the tight Swedish administrative system, Peter divided Russia into provinces, counties, and districts, each supervised by bureaucrats drawn from the nobility. All male nobles had to serve the tsar from age 15 until death, either as bureaucrats or military officers. Even the bureaucrats were organized on military lines, with ranks and uniforms. The Russian government penetrated deep into society. A census counted the males available for military conscription, and each community had a quota. Draftees served for life. Taxation squeezed everybody as Peter ordered his officials to "collect money, as much as possible, for money is the artery of war."

When Peter died in 1725, Russia was more modern and Westernized but still behind West Europe. Peter the Great founded a pattern of forced modernization from the top, pushing a poor, giant country forward despite itself. Russia paid dearly. The peasants, heavily taxed, were worse off than ever. The Westernized nobility—forced, for instance, to shave for the first time—was cut off from the hopes and feelings of the peasantry. The pattern continued for a long time.

Westernizers and Slavophiles

Napoleon's invasion of Russia and capture of Moscow in 1812 made Russian intellectuals painfully aware of Russia's backwardness. Many sought to adopt Western politics and institutions, including a constitutional monarchy to limit the autocratic powers of the tsar. These were called **Westernizers**. Others disliked the West, which they saw as spiritually shallow and materialistic. Russia must cultivate its Slavic roots and develop institutions and styles different from and superior to the West's. "Russia will teach the world" was their view. These **Slavophiles** (literally, "lovers of the Slavs"), who stressed the spiritual depth and warm humanity of Russian peasants, were romantic nationalists. This pattern appears in cultures that reject Western materialism in favor of traditional spiritual values. In Russia, the old debate still echoes: Liberal reformers are still pro-West while conservative authoritarians are anti-West nationalists.

Marxism Comes to Russia

Calls for reform during the nineteenth century made little progress. All tsars rejected becoming a constitutional monarchy. Even Alexander II, the "tsar-liberator," carried out only limited reforms. In 1861, he issued his famous Edict of Emancipation, freeing serfs from legal bondage. Most of them remained in economic bondage, however. He set up district and provincial assemblies called **zemstvos** but gave them only marginal local power. Reforms often make revolution

Personalities

Lenin, the Great Revolutionary

Some claim that Lenin sought revenge against the tsarist system that hanged his older brother in 1887 for his part in a bomb plot against the tsar. That cannot be proved, but it is clear that Lenin was dominated by a cold, contained rage for revolutionary socialism in Russia.

Born Vladimir Ilyich Ulyanov in 1870 to a provincial education official, Lenin was from the intellectual middle class rather than the proletariat—a pattern common among revolutionary socialists. Lenin was quickly expelled from university for subversive activity and sent into rural exile. The self-disciplined Lenin taught himself and breezed through law exams with top marks.

In the early 1890s, Lenin, like many Russian intellectuals, discovered Marx and wrote Marxist analyses of the rapidly growing Russian economy. Recognized as a leading Marxist thinker, Lenin quickly rose in underground revolutionary circles.

In December 1895, while editing an illegal socialist newspaper, Lenin was arrested and sent to prison for a year, followed by three years' exile on the Lena River in Siberia. There he took the name Lenin, the man from the Lena. The solitary hours gave him time to read, learn foreign languages, and write. Released in 1900, Lenin fled to Zurich, Switzerland, where he spent most of the next 17 years. Until taking power in Russia in 1917, Lenin never held a job.

In Swiss exile, Lenin at times worried there would never be a revolution in Russia. The working class was concentrating on higher wages rather than revolution. The Russian Social Democratic Labor Party was small, with only a few thousand members in Russia and in exile. Lenin transformed this small party into an effective underground force. Size was not important; organization was everything. His 1902 pamphlet *What Is to Be Done?* demanded a tightly disciplined party of professional revolutionaries, not a conventional social democratic party open to everybody. Under Lenin, the early Communists forged the "organizational weapon": the Party.

In answering the question of how proletarian revolution could come to preindustrial Russia, Lenin greatly changed Marxism. Marx theorized that revolution would come in the most advanced countries, where the proletariat was biggest. Lenin said, not necessarily: Revolution could come where capitalism is weakest, where it is just starting. **Imperialism** had changed capitalism, Lenin argued, giving it a new lease on life. By exploiting weaker countries, the big imperialist powers were able to bribe their own working class with higher wages and keep them quiet. Where capitalism was beginning—as in Russia, with heavy foreign investment—was where it could be overthrown. The newly developing countries, such as Russia and Spain, were "capitalism's weakest link," said Lenin.

Lenin also disagreed with Marx's insistence that peasants could never be revolutionary. Lenin believed that, under certain conditions and leadership, peasants could turn revolutionary and, throwing their weight in with the small working class, provide a massive revolutionary army. (Three decades later, Mao Zedong elaborated on these themes to argue that China, a victim of imperialism, could have a socialist revolution based entirely on the peasantry. Mao completed the train of thought that Lenin started.)

Lenin was not a great theoretician but a brilliant opportunist, switching doctrine to take advantage of situations, like all successful revolutionaries. He was less concerned with pure Marxism than with using it to overthrow the system he hated. Once in power, he practiced the same bloody ruthlessness later associated with Stalin. It is not clear that, had Lenin lived, he would have been any better than Stalin.

more likely. Alexander's reforms were regarded by an increasingly critical *intelligentsia* (the educated class) as not nearly enough, and many became bitter and frustrated.

Some intellectuals tried agitating the masses. In the 1870s, thousands of idealistic students put on peasant clothes and tried "going to the people" in the villages to incite radical

imperialism
Powerful countries turning other lands into colonies.

Narodniki
From Russian for "people," *narod*; radical populist agitators of late nineteenth-century Russia.

anarchism
Radical ideology seeking to overthrow all conventional forms of government.

proletariat
According to Marx, class of industrial workers.

communism
Economic theories of Marx combined with organization of Lenin.

Bolshevik
"Majority" in Russian; early name for Soviet Communist Party.

action. These **Narodniki** made no progress; the peasants ignored them or turned them over to the police. Other intellectuals turned to **anarchism** and violence, believing that killing the right official constituted "propaganda of the deed," a way to arouse the inert Russian masses. One group of revolutionaries, *Narodnaya Volya* (People's Will), after seven attempts, killed the tsar with a bomb thrown into his carriage in 1881.

According to Marx's theory, Russia was far from ready for proletarian revolution. There was not much of a **proletariat** in agricultural Russia, where industrialization was just beginning in the late nineteenth century. Marx believed revolution would come first in the most industrially advanced countries, such as Britain and Germany. Marxism, though, caught on more strongly in Russia than anywhere else. Marx's works were eagerly seized upon by frustrated Russian intellectuals who wanted change but did not have a theoretical framework for it. Here at last, they believed, they had found a reason and a means to carry out a revolution.

There were several schools of Marxism in Russia. "Legal Marxists," noting Russia's underdevelopment, thought the country must first go through capitalism before it could start on socialism. Marx's deterministic view of history saw it developing in economic stages—first capitalism, then socialism—so the Legal Marxists believed they must first promote capitalism. (China's rulers may hold similar notions.) Another school of Russian Marxism, "economism," sought better wages and working conditions through labor unions. They resembled West European social democrats, whose Marxism mellowed into welfarism.

Opposing these two gradualist schools were militants who demanded revolution. They argued they could "give history a shove" by starting a revolution with only a small proletariat, gain power, and then use the state to move directly into socialism. Lenin made some theoretical changes in Marxism so it fit Russian conditions (see Lenin box). Since then, the doctrine of Russian **communism** has been known as Marxism-Leninism. In 1898, several small Marxist groups formed the Russian Social Democratic Labor Party. Immediately penetrated by the *Okhrana*, the tsarist secret police, many of the party's leaders went into exile in West Europe. Its newspaper, *Iskra* (The Spark), was published in Zurich and smuggled into Russia. One of its editors was Lenin.

In 1903, the small party split over a crucial question: organization. Some wanted a normal party like the German Social Democrats, with open membership to enroll the Russian working class. Lenin scoffed at this, arguing that tsarist secret police would crush an open party. Instead, he urged a small, tightly knit underground party of professional revolutionaries, more a conspiracy than a conventional party. Lenin got his way. At the 1903 party congress in Brussels, Belgium (it could not be held in Russia), he controlled 33 of the 51 votes. Although probably unrepresentative of total party membership, Lenin proclaimed his faction **Bolshevik** (majority), and the name stuck. The *Menshevik* (minority) faction at the congress continued to exist, advocating a more moderate line.

Curtain-Raiser: The 1905 Revolution

At the beginning of the twentieth century, two expanding powers, Russia and Japan, collided. The Russians were pushing eastward to the Pacific by building the immense Trans-Siberian Railway, the last leg of which ran through Manchuria. Japan was pushing up from Korea into Manchuria, nominally part of China. The tsar's cabinet, certain they could beat any Asian army and hoping to deflect domestic unrest, thought war with Japan was a good idea. Said the interior minister: "We need a little victorious war to stem the tide of revolution." Instead, the Japanese fleet launched a surprise attack against the Russians at Port Arthur and then beat the Russians on land and sea. The 1904–1905 Russo-Japanese War revealed the tsarist military was unprepared, inept, and stupid.

Duma
Russia's national parliament.

In Russia, rioting and then revolution broke out. Some naval units mutinied (fictionalized in Eisenstein's film classic *Battleship Potemkin*). Workers briefly seized factories in St. Petersburg. Tsar Nicholas II decreed reforms: freedoms of speech, press, and assembly and the democratic election of a **Duma**. Briefly, his 1905 October Manifesto looked as if it would turn autocracy into constitutional monarchy; however, the tsar and his reactionary advisors backed down on their promises. Nicholas, none too bright, refused to yield any of his autocratic powers. Four Dumas were subsequently elected, but each was dissolved when it grew too critical. Finally, the Duma was turned into an undemocratic debating society without power.

The Duma was Russia's last hope for a peaceful transition to democracy. People in modern times need to feel that they participate at least in a small way in the affairs of government. Parties, elections, and parliaments may be imperfect means of participation, but they are better than violent revolution. Since the failed Decembrist revolt of 1825, Russian intellectuals had been trying to tell this to the tsar, but he refused to listen.

World War I and Collapse

Communists spoke of the Russian Revolution as a Marxist inevitability, but it was a consequence of World War I. Lenin himself, in early 1917, doubted he would live to see a revolution in Russia. Things were not so terrible in Russia before the war. The Duma struggled to erode tsarist autocracy and, in time, might have succeeded. Industry grew rapidly and culture flourished. Peasants, now free to own land, turned into prosperous small farmers. The war changed everything. Repeating their overconfidence of 1904, the Russian army was quickly ground up by the Germans. Troops deserted, the economy fell apart, and peasants seized their landlords' estates. The government was paralyzed, but the tsar refused to change anything.

By 1917, the situation was desperate. In March, a group of democratic moderates seized power and deposed the tsar. Resembling Western liberals, the people of the Provisional Government hoped to modernize and democratize Russia. The Western powers, including the United States, welcomed them, thinking they would rally Russians to continue the war. The Kerensky government tried to stay in the war, by then impossible. If Kerensky had betrayed the Western Allies and made a separate peace with Germany, he might have retained power.

Personalities

Kerensky: Nice Guys Lose

In the late 1950s at UCLA, I saw and heard Alexander Kerensky speak. The past lives. Still fit and articulate in his 70s, Kerensky recalled his brief stint (July to November 1917) as head of Russia's Provisional Government. One man in the audience, a Russian emigré, asked angrily why Kerensky did not use his power to have Lenin killed. Kerensky reflected a moment and said, "Sometimes, when you have power, it's hard to use it."

A decent man, Kerensky would not have a political opponent murdered. The Western Allies begged him to keep Russia in the war, and he could not betray them. Living in New York City, he spent his years justifying his short tenure and denouncing both the Bolsheviks and Russian rightists who tried to bring him down. He died in 1970 at age 89.

Meanwhile, the German General Staff, looking for a way to knock Russia out of the war, sent the agitator Lenin into Russia to create havoc. In April 1917, Lenin and his colleagues traveled in a famous "sealed train" across Germany, Sweden, and Finland to Petrograd, the World War I name for St. Petersburg. Lenin, at that point, served German purposes.

At Petrograd's Finland Station, Lenin issued his stirring slogan, "Bread, Land, Peace," speaking respectively to workers, peasants, and soldiers. He saw that a "dual authority" was trying to rule Russia. The Provisional Government controlled the army and foreign policy, but a council (*soviet* in Russian) of workers, soldiers, sailors, and revolutionaries ran Petrograd. Soon these councils appeared in many Russian cities. The soviets' composition was mixed, with the Bolsheviks a small minority. Lenin pursued a double strategy: Make the soviets the only effective governing power, and make the Bolsheviks the dominant power in the soviets. Lenin's slogan for this: "All Power to the Soviets." The Bolsheviks' tight organization and discipline paid off. In a situation of chaos, the best organized—not necessarily the biggest—win.

The Revolution and Civil War

The initial seizure of power in October 1917 was easy. Soldiers and sailors loyal to the Petrograd soviet took over the Winter Palace to oust the Provisional Government. Control of all Russia was difficult and bloody. Lenin headed the new government and immediately took Russia out of the war, accepting a punitive peace treaty from the Germans at Brest-Litovsk in March 1918. It was a dictated treaty (*Diktat* in German) that enabled the Germans to seize large areas of Russia and redeploy nearly a million troops to the western front.

Feeling betrayed and concerned that allied military supplies would fall into German hands, the Western Allies sent small expeditionary forces into Russia. American troops actually fought the Bolsheviks in North Russia and Siberia in 1918–1919. This started the Soviet propaganda line that the capitalist powers tried to strangle the infant Bolshevik regime in its cradle.

From 1918 to 1920, civil war raged. The White Army, led by tsarist Russian officers and supplied by Western Allies, tried to crush the Communists' Red Army. Both sides were ruthless in a life-or-death struggle. Millions perished from starvation. The Red Army invaded Poland in 1920, hoping to trigger a Europe-wide socialist revolution. Instead, the Poles threw back

Personalities

Stalin: "One Death Is a Tragedy; A Million Is a Statistic"

The Soviet system was more Stalin's than Lenin's. Lenin died in 1924, at age 54, before he could fully form the system. Exactly who is to blame for the horrors that developed—Lenin or Stalin—is controversial. Some argue that if Lenin had lived, he would have set Russia on the path to "true socialism." Others say that the structure Lenin created—concentrating power first in the Party, then in the Central Committee, and finally in himself—made abuse of power inevitable.

Stalin aptly illustrates Acton's dictum, "power corrupts." Stalin lived to amass political power. Born Yosif Vissarionovich Djugashvili in 1879, son of a poor shoemaker, Stalin lacked Lenin's intellectual background and education. Some of Stalin's behavior comes from his Georgia homeland in the Caucasus, where fiery people are given to personal hatred and blood feuds. In Georgia, "Soso" (his Georgian nickname) is still praised as a local boy who made good.

The young Djugashvili started to study for the Orthodox priesthood but soon joined the Georgian Marxist underground as an agitator and strike organizer. Repeatedly arrested, jailed, and exiled to Siberia, he always managed to escape. (There is some evidence that he was a double agent for the tsarist police.) He took the underground name Stalin, Russian for "man of steel."

Never a great theoretician, Stalin attracted Lenin's attention as a non-Russian who could write the Bolsheviks' nationalities policy. Stalin played only a moderate role in the 1917 revolution but was named commissar for nationalities in 1918 and then was chosen as the party's first general secretary in 1922, Lenin's worst mistake. Lenin thought the new office would be a clerical job with little power. Lenin and Stalin were never close—although Stalin's historians tried to make it look that way—and toward the end of his life, Lenin urged the party to reject Stalin as "too rude."

It was too late. Using his position as **gensek**, Stalin organized the **CPSU** to his advantage by promoting to key posts only those personally loyal to him, giving him the edge over his rival, Leon Trotsky, organizer of the Red Army. Stalin beat Trotsky in party infighting and had him expelled from Russia in 1929 and murdered in Mexico in 1940. Reviled as a deviationist traitor, Trotsky did try to organize an anti-Stalin opposition within the CPSU, a point that fed Stalin's natural **paranoia** and led him to shoot officials on the slightest suspicion of disloyalty.

Stalin played one faction against another until, by the late 1920s, he was the Kremlin's master. Stalin was determined to modernize regardless of human cost and began the Soviet Union's forced industrialization. Farmers were herded into collectives and forced to produce for the state, sometimes at gunpoint. Better-off farmers, the so-called *kulaks*, were "liquidated as a class," a euphemism for killed. Economic development was defined as heavy industry, and steel production became the chief goal of the man of steel.

In 1934, during the second Five-Year Plan, Stalin, obsessed with "Trotskyite" disloyalty, began his **purges**: up to one million party comrades killed, some after they confessed to being British spies or Trotskyite "wreckers." Stalin ordered all managers to train two replacements. Stalin even had most of his generals and colonels shot, a blunder that hurt the Soviet Union in the 1941 German attack. Hundreds of thousands arrested on fake charges also perished, many in Siberian forced-labor camps. In total, Stalin's orders led to the death of six to nine million people—estimates are still disputed—during collectivization and the purges.

Was Stalin mad? There was some Trotskyite opposition to him, but he exaggerated it. It was Plato who first observed that any tyrant, even one who starts sane, must lose his mind because he can trust no one. More than a question of personality, Stalin shows what happens when one person assumes total power. The Communists did not like to admit it, but it was their *system* that was at fault more than any particular individual.

During his lifetime, Stalin was deified as history's greatest linguist, art critic, Marxist theoretician, engineer, agronomist, and so forth. His communization of East Europe led to the **Cold War**. By the time he died in 1953—while preparing yet another purge—Stalin had turned the Soviet Union into *his* system, and, in basic outlines, it never changed much. When Mikhail Gorbachev attempted to seriously reform it, the system collapsed. Today, Stalin's crimes are unmentioned, and he is again praised as a symbol of Russian power.

---

gensek
Russian abbreviation for "general secretary"; powerful CPSU chief.

CPSU
Communist Party of the Soviet Union.

paranoia
Unreasonable suspicion of others.

purge
Stalin's "cleansing" of suspicious elements by firing squad.

Cold War
Period of armed tension and competition between the United States and the Soviet Union, approximately 1947–1989.

war communism
Temporary strict socialism in Russia, 1918–1921.

New Economic Policy (NEP)
Lenin's economic policy that allowed private activity, 1921–1928.

Five-Year Plans
Stalin's forced industrialization of the Soviet Union, starting in 1928.

capital goods
Implements used to make other things.

consumer goods
Things people use, such as food, clothing, and housing.

the Red Army and seized parts of Ukraine and Belarus. Lenin and his colleagues saw there would be no world revolution and settled for building the world's first socialist country.

War Communism and NEP

The Bolsheviks tried to plunge directly into their utopian system with a ruined economy. This **war communism** led immediately to starvation, and only the charity of American grain shipments (supervised by Herbert Hoover) held deaths to a few million. To motivate workers, Lenin ordered: "He who does not work, neither shall he eat" (from 2 Thessalonians 3:10).

Lenin realized that Russia was far from ready for pure socialism, so he pulled state control back to the "commanding heights" of heavy industry and let most of the rest of the economy revert to private hands. This period of Lenin's **New Economic Policy (NEP)** brought relative prosperity to Russia; farmers worked their own land, "nepmen" ran small businesses, and life relaxed. But the NEP did not move the Soviet Union, as it was now called, toward socialism. It is likely that Lenin intended the NEP to be only a temporary rest before socialist construction.

Stalin took full power in the late 1920s and, in 1928, began the first **Five-Year Plan** to accelerate collectivization and industrialization (see Stalin box). Peasants resisted giving up their fields, farm production dropped, and millions (especially Ukrainians) were deliberately starved to death. In new factories, workers toiled with primitive tools to produce **capital goods**. Setting a pattern for all Communist countries, **consumer goods** were neglected, and the standard of living declined. The forced industrialization of the 1930s was brutal, but some argue that it gave the Soviet Union the industrial base to repel the 1941 German invasion.

The war caused 27 million Soviet deaths. The Nazis cared nothing for Slavic lives and starved to death Russian prisoners of war. Faced with extinction, the Soviet Union pulled together. Stalin, like Lenin, understood the Russian nationalism beneath the Communist surface. Reviewing troops marching from Moscow to the nearby front, Stalin mused that they were not fighting for communism or for Stalin but for Mother Russia. In Russia today, World

Geography

Another Tale of Two Flags

At the end of 1991, the Communist red flag (with the gold hammer and sickle) came down as the Soviet Union dissolved. Red had been the color of socialist movements (taken from the red shirts of Italian unifier Garibaldi) since the nineteenth century, and the Bolsheviks used it in 1917. The old tsarist flag was developed by Peter the Great, who brought the Netherlands tricolor back with him from his stay in Dutch shipyards in 1699 but changed the stripes from the original Dutch (from the top: red, white, and blue) to white, blue, and red, sometimes with an imperial double-headed eagle (from Byzantium) in the center. The Provisional Government removed the eagle in 1917; this is what the Russian Federation revived as its flag in 1991.

War II is called the Great Patriotic War. By the time he died in 1953, Stalin had transformed a backward country into a giant empire and major industrial power. He also founded a system that, in the long run, proved to be inefficient and unreformable and finally collapsed in 1991.

The Key Institutions

6.2 Compare and contrast the Soviet system with the new Russian system.

Russia resembles the **weak state** common in Latin America, where crime and government interpenetrate. As in Mexico, the police engage in criminal activities. Corruption, lawlessness, and insecurity are now the Russian norm. In a climate of fear, Russians flock to a strong leader. Putin, by arbitrarily shifting top power to himself when be became prime minister in 2008 and then back to the presidency when he resumed it in 2012, showed that Russia's institutions are still flimsy, dominated by strong personalities.

Russia has slid partway back to authoritarianism, and democracy has an uphill struggle. Accordingly, we must consider two models: the old Soviet system formed under Stalin and a post-Communist system that tried to break with the past but did not succeed. The end of the Soviet Union in late 1991, we now realize, was less than system change. The new Russian government was not a new broom and did not sweep clean. Virtually all of the current leadership was trained by the old Soviet system; many are former (or current) security police. Russia's constitution overconcentrates power in the presidency, and President Putin concentrated it more. Much of the old Communist system underlies today's Russia.

The Stalin System

The Soviet system started by Lenin and perfected by Stalin lasted into Gorbachev's tenure. The system changed over time, but not much. Its main structural features were as follows.

THE COMMUNIST PARTY IN COMMAND Said Lenin: "The Communist Party is not a party like other parties." Lenin meant that the CPSU would not compete democratically but was constitutionally defined as

weak state
One unable to govern effectively; corrupt and crime ridden.

Central Committee
Large, next-to-top governing body of most Communist parties.

apparatchik
"Man of the apparatus"; full-time CPSU functionary.

Politburo
"Political bureau"; small, top governing body of most Communist parties.

republic
First-order civil division of Communist federal systems, equivalent to U.S. states.

"the leading and guiding force of Soviet society." No other parties were permitted, and no factions were allowed inside the CPSU. The Party did not run things directly but was a central brain and nervous system that transmitted policy lines, oversaw the economy, reported discontent, and selected, promoted, and supervised the system's personnel. There was much overlap between Party and state systems so that, at the top, most government ministers were also on the Party's **Central Committee**.

Party membership was tightly controlled. Less than 7 percent of the Soviet population were Party members, selected on the basis of good records as workers, students, or youth leaders. The Party was organized like a pyramid: primary party organizations at the bottom; district, province, and republic party conferences in between; and an all-union party conference at the top. A committee presided over each. Each level "elected" delegates to the next-highest level (actually, they were handpicked from above) in what was called "democratic centralism." Party administrators, **apparatchiki**, held the *apparat* together.

The All-Union Party Congress of some 5,000 delegates would meet for a few days every few years, ostensibly to elect the Central Committee of about 300 full members and 150 candidate members. The Central Committee would meet twice a year, usually just before the meeting of its government counterpart, the Supreme Soviet, because the membership of the two bodies overlapped.

Above the Central Committee and really in charge was the **Politburo**, a full-time decision-making body with about a dozen full members and six candidate members. Politburo decisions were automatically approved by the Central Committee, whose decisions were approved by the Party Congress, and so on down the line. A general secretary (*gensek*), called in the West the "party chief," ran the Politburo, and he became supreme boss of both Party and state. In most Communist systems, the party chief is the most powerful figure because he controls the *apparat* and selects *apparatchiki* who are personally loyal to him.

A LESS IMPORTANT STATE STRUCTURE The Supreme Soviet, with 1,500 members, was not a real parliament. It met only a few days a year to rubber-stamp laws drafted by the top echelons of the Party. Nominally bicameral, the Supreme Soviet "elected" a governing Presidium of 20 members that overlapped with the Politburo. The Presidium simply decreed laws and served as a collective presidency, with its chairman called the "president" of the Soviet Union. Since Brezhnev, the Party general secretary was also named president to make clear that he headed both state and Party.

The Supreme Soviet also chose a cabinet, the Council of Ministers, with some 85 highly specialized ministries, mostly concentrated on branches of the economy. The Council of Ministers rarely met for collective deliberation. Only Politburo members served as prime minister, or minister of state security (KGB), interior, defense, and foreign affairs—the "power ministries."

A CENTRALIZED FEDERAL SYSTEM The Soviet Union was a federation dominated by Moscow through the Party. The Soviet Union had some two dozen major nationalities and many more minor ones—104 in all. The 15 largest each got their own Soviet Socialist **Republic** (for example, the Uzbek SSR), which together made the USSR (Union of Soviet Socialist Republics).

Who Was When: Soviet Party Chiefs		
Party Chief	**Ruled**	**Main Accomplishments**
Vladimir I. Lenin	1917–1924	Led Revolution; instituted War Communism, then NEP
Josef Stalin	1927–1953	Five-Year Plans of forced collectivization and industrialization; purges; waged World War II; self-deification
Nikita Khrushchev	1955–1964	Destalinized; experimented with economic and cultural reform; promised utopia soon; ousted
Leonid Brezhnev	1964–1982	Partially restalinized; refrained from shaking up system; let corruption grow and economy slow
Yuri Andropov	1982–1984	Cracked down on corruption and alcoholism; suggested major reforms but soon died
Konstantin Chernenko	1984–1985	*Nichevo*
Mikhail Gorbachev	1985–1991	Initiated sweeping change; unwittingly collapsed Soviet system

The Russian Federative Republic was by far the biggest and is still a federation of autonomous regions for its many ethnic groups. The chief purpose of Soviet federalism was preservation of language rights. Stalin, who developed Soviet nationality policy, recognized that language and culture are powerful and let each nationality feel culturally autonomous while in fact they were politically subordinate. Stalin's formula: "National in form, socialist in content." This deception was unstable. All three of the world's Communist federal systems failed—messy in the Soviet Union, bloody in Yugoslavia, but peaceful in Czechoslovakia—and the huge Russian Federation still has problems with unity.

The tsarist system imposed a unitary pattern on the empire that was so hated that old Russia was called "the prison of nations." With the Bolshevik Revolution, Finland and the Baltic states of Lithuania, Latvia, and Estonia happily escaped to independence. (In 1940, Stalin swallowed the Baltics and treated their citizens cruelly.) With Gorbachev's *glasnost* (openness) policy of relative freedom of speech and press, the nationalities question erupted, and, in 1991, all 15 republics departed from the union and legally dissolved it.

Many ex-Soviet nationalities resent other nationalities. Attitudes border on racism. Particularly delicate is the question of the 25 million Russians who now live outside of Russia. The Russian army has made clear that it will use force to protect them and has already done so in Moldova, where several hundred Romanian speakers were gunned down. The newly independent republics fear antagonizing Russia.

Soviet federalism failed for several reasons. First, there are too many national groups to give each their own territories. Second, the nationalities are dispersed; in Uzbekistan, for example, there are Tajiks, Russians, Jews, Tatars, Koreans, and many others in addition to Uzbeks. No clean line could separate Soviet nationalities. Third, Stalin devised the system with borders deliberately drawn to create ethnic tensions, letting Stalin arbitrate disputes so the republics would depend on him. Fourth, the center held too much power, so the federalism was not genuine. The Soviet Union paid the price for Stalin's fake federal system. Some fear that the current Russian Federation of 89 components will not stay together.

A GIGANTIC BUREAUCRACY Karl Marx argued that, after socialism eliminated class differences, the state would "wither away." German sociologist Max Weber countered that socialism required much more state power and a larger bureaucracy. Weber was right. The

nomenklatura
List of sensitive positions and people eligible to fill them, the Soviet elite.

Gulag
The Soviet central prisons administration.

siloviki
"Strong men"; security officials who now control Russia (singular *silovik*).

Gosplan
Soviet central economic planning agency.

Soviet bureaucracy had some 18 million persons administering every facet of Soviet life. Bureaucrats—slow, inflexible, inefficient, and corrupt—helped ruin the Soviet Union.

The CPSU interpenetrated and guided the bureaucracy, the Party's *kontrol* function, appointing and supervising all important officials. Incompetent or crooked ones could get demoted or transferred to a remote area. Officials were cautious and went by the book. If they were effective, the Party could promote them into the **nomenklatura**, a list of some 600,000 important positions and another list of reliable people eligible to fill them.

SECURITY POLICE Security police—sometimes called "secret police," after the Nazi Gestapo—are what make dictatorships work and last. Unlike regular police, security police are highly political and focus on preventing any criticism, dissent, or movements that might harm the regime. They often use terror, "the linchpin of the Soviet system," the key element that held it together.

Lenin instituted the *Cheka* (short for Extraordinary Commission) immediately after the Revolution to annihilate opponents. Stalin turned it into the NKVD (People's Commissariat for Internal Affairs), which set up the **Gulag**. After Stalin, it became the KGB (Committee on State Security), with more refined and subtle methods. Russians still use "Chekist" for a member of the security police.

Some three-quarters of a million KGB agents were everywhere: guarding borders and in factories, hotels, and universities, watching anyone who contacted foreigners or dissented against the system. Millions of citizens had KGB dossiers, from which the KGB was able to recite even trivial incidents from years earlier. Part-time informers, *stukachi* (squealers), fed material to the KGB.

While the KGB could not actually try most cases—which went to a regular court—they rigged evidence. As the KGB used to say, "Give us the man and we will find you the crime." Dissidents could lose jobs, get sent to psychiatric hospitals, be denied university entrance, have their rooms bugged, and lose the right to live in a city by the KGB.

Although the KGB was formally dissolved along with the Soviet Union, its chief component reappeared as the Federal Security Service (FSB in Russian), which is staffed by old KGB hands and does the same tasks: supporting the authorities and eliminating any threats to their power. President Putin handpicked top FSB officials from a network of old comrades. The FSB has strong powers to investigate and arrest, even from anonymous accusations. Murder and corruption run rampant, but the FSB arrests few, suggesting they are in on the crooked deals. Three of Yeltsin's prime ministers in a row were high up in the old KGB and then in the FSB. Putin was a KGB officer and then head of the FSB, and most of his top appointees—known as **siloviki**, the strong ones or tough guys—are drawn from the security organizations. As Putin says, "There is no such thing as a former Chekist."

CENTRAL ECONOMIC PLANNING The State Planning Committee, **Gosplan**, was the nerve center of the Soviet economic system, setting how much of what was produced each year and setting longer term targets for some 350,000 enterprises. Under Stalin, central planning industrialized the Soviet Union quickly, albeit at terrible human cost. But it also meant inefficiencies

Democracy

1991: The Coup That Failed

In August 1991, as Gorbachev was on vacation in Crimea, most of his cabinet tried to overthrow him. An eight-man *junta* (Russians used the Spanish loan word) of conservatives, calling themselves the "Emergency Committee," said Gorbachev had taken ill and declared his vice president the acting president.

Some Western experts had been predicting a coup for three years. Gorbachev's reforms, cautious as they were, threatened the Soviet system and the jobs and comforts of the Soviet ruling elite. Gorbachev had been warned repeatedly of their anger. In December 1990, Foreign Minister Eduard Shevardnadze resigned in public protest at what he said was a coming dictatorship.

Gorbachev zigzagged between promising major reforms and reassuring Party conservatives that he would not reform too much. In 1991, Gorbachev again favored reform and, with the leaders of nine of the Soviet republics, drafted a new union treaty that would give the republics great autonomy within a market economy. This was the last straw for the conservatives. The day before the treaty was to be signed, they staged their coup.

For three days, the world held its breath. Would the coup by not-very-bright Kremlin apparatchiks succeed? They seemed to hold the upper hand. Among them were the head of the military, the KGB, and the interior ministry. The following are some of the reasons the coup failed:

- Few supported the coup. Tens of thousands of citizens favoring democracy publicly opposed the coup. Gorbachev was not very popular, but the junta was much worse.

- Boris Yeltsin stood firm. About a mile and a half from the Kremlin is the parliament of the Russian Republic, then presided over by reformist Yeltsin. Yeltsin and his helpers holed up in the building and declared the junta's decrees illegal. A tank column sent to take the building instead sided with Yeltsin and defended it. Thousands of Muscovites came to stand guard and to protest the coup. Yeltsin's toughness galvanized opposition.

- The Soviet armed forces started to split. Many commanders either stood on the sidelines or opposed the junta. Facing a bloody civil war, the junta lost its nerve.

- International pressure opposed the coup. Major countries made it clear that the Soviet economy, desperate for foreign help, would get none. Foreign broadcasts (heard by Gorbachev himself) heartened the antijunta forces.

A haggard Gorbachev returned to Moscow vowing further reform. The junta was arrested (one committed suicide). The coup attempt hastened the end of the Soviet Union, revealing Gorbachev as indecisive and weak. Yeltsin bumped him out of power and proclaimed an independent Russia. Democracy got a brief chance.

---

and shortages of items the Gosplan ignored. One year, no toothbrushes were produced in the entire Soviet Union, a Gosplan oversight. The planned, centrally directed Soviet economy slowly ran down and fell behind the dynamic economies of the West and Asia. Gorbachev had to dismantle it.

The New System

In the months after the failed coup of August 1991, the old Soviet system collapsed, and from the remains emerged a new Russian system that looks democratic on paper but is not.

NO MORE SOVIET UNION All of the 15 Soviet republics declared their independence. The Baltic republics especially—Lithuania, Latvia, and Estonia—led the way. They expelled Soviet police, issued their own passports and visas, and took control of their borders. The other republics soon followed, and now all are independent, some more than others. Ukraine had been part of tsarist Russia for centuries and was the breadbasket of the Soviet Union, but many Ukrainians resented Moscow's rule, especially after they finally learned what Stalin's farm collectivization had done to them—deliberately starved three million to death. Eastern Ukrainians, on the other hand, mostly Russian-speaking, fought to break away from Kiev in 2014.

Belarus (formerly Belarussia, the area between Russia and Poland), which had never been an independent country or harbored much separatist feeling, voted for independence, too. But Belarus still uses the Russian ruble as currency and gets sweetheart trade deals with Russia. Its army is closely linked to the Russian army. Belarus in reality never cut its Russian ties and is now ridiculed as Europe's last dictatorship.

The scariest problem was the ethnic tension that came out in the republics. Minorities who had lived in peace for generations (because the KGB was watching) became the target of nationalist resentment. In the Caucasus, blood flowed. Many republic politicians played the nationalist card, which easily turned into violence. Their messages were simple and effective: Georgia for the Georgians, Uzbekistan for the Uzbeks, Armenia for the Armenians, even Russia for the Russians.

All of the Central Asian republics plus Azerbaijan have a Muslim majority and speak a Turkic language, except the Tajiks, who speak a type of Persian (like Iran). There has been Muslim–Christian violence between Azeris and Armenians and in Georgia. Inside the Russian Federation, the North Caucasus produces murderous terrorists. All together, however, far more were killed in ex-Yugoslavia. A big question: In which direction will the authoritarian ex-Soviet Muslim republics go—toward the modern example of Turkey, to Islamic fundamentalism, back to a militarily dominant Russia, or tied by trade to an economically dominant China?

A COMMONWEALTH OF INDEPENDENT STATES Most of the Soviet Union's 15 component republics agreed to form the Commonwealth of Independent States (CIS), with headquarters in Minsk, Belarus. Conspicuously missing were the three Baltic republics and Georgia. Georgia was later forced, in the middle of a civil war abetted by Moscow, to sign the CIS treaty. No one quite knows what the powers of the CIS are, but most agree that it is part of Moscow's plan to regain control over the ex-Soviet republics—in effect, to rebuild the Russia of Peter the Great. Some republics need ties with Russia. First, 8 of the 12 CIS member republics are landlocked and need Russia for access to the outside world. Industrially, all are tied to the Russian economy for manufactured goods and energy, although now the Central Asian states—the five "stans"—do more business with China.

A NEW CONSTITUTION Along with voting for a new parliament, in late 1993, Russians approved a new and completely different constitution, one somewhat modeled on de Gaulle's 1958 French constitution.

Semipresidentialism Russia follows the French (and Chinese) pattern of a strong president, but from 2008 to 2012, Putin played with the constitution by making the president weak and the prime minister strong so that Putin could continue as the real power after his two terms. Institutions that can be easily remade are weak and fake. French semipresidentialism has both an executive president and a prime minister but gives top power to the president. The Russian president is elected for two six-year terms (it was four years, but Putin "suggested" making it six, starting in 2012) but can repeat after an interval, which Putin did in 2012. The president sets basic policy and names the prime minister and other top officials, and he can veto bills and dissolve parliament. In many areas, the president can simply rule by decree and give himself strong emergency powers. There is no vice president; if the president dies or is incapacitated, the prime minister serves as acting president until elections are held within three months. This happened when Yeltsin suddenly resigned at the end of 1999 and Putin took over.

By prearrangement, after completing his two terms as president in 2008, Putin became prime minister and made clear that power had shifted to that office. The new president, Putin protégé Dmitri Medvedev, smiled and obeyed Putin. In 2012, he obeyed Putin again and stood aside so Putin could run for a third term as president. The president names and fires prime ministers, but they must be confirmed by the Duma. Because Putin still dominates the Duma, this is no problem. If the Duma should reject the president's nominee for prime minister three times, the president can dissolve the Duma and hold new parliamentary elections.

A Federal System   The federal system carries over from the old Soviet structure. The country's official name is the Russian Federation; it consists of 83 regions—most of them *republics*—21 of which are predominantly non-Russian. Each region is supposed to be bound by treaty to the Federation, but not all have signed, and they do not all like Moscow's rule. One Caucasian Muslim republic, Chechnya, which had resisted Russian rule since its original tsarist conquest, won temporary autonomy but was shelled into ruin.

During the 1990s, local strongmen—"elected," but not democratically—turned republics into corrupt personal fiefdoms. Putin ended that by giving himself the power to appoint republic governors. He also created seven new large regions and personally appointed their

Geography

The Ex-Soviet Republics

Learn the names and approximate location of each of the 15 former Soviet republics; they are now independent countries, but many are under Russian influence. (See the map at the beginning of the chapter.) To help you remember the republics, note that there are three groups of three, plus a Central Asia group of five (the five "stans"), plus a Romanian area.

Slavic	Baltic	Caucasian	Central Asian	Romanian-Speaking
Russia	Lithuania[†]	Georgia	Turkmenistan*	Moldova (formerly Moldavia)
Ukraine	Latvia[†]	Armenia	Kazakhstan*	
Belarus	Estonia[†]	Azerbaijan*	Kyrgyzstan*	
			Uzbekistan*	
			Tajikistan*	

[†]*Not in CIS*

Predominantly Muslim

Democracy

1993: The Second Coup That Failed

The 1991 coup was attempted by members of Gorbachev's own executive branch and stopped by members of the Russian (not Soviet) parliament in its White House some distance from the Kremlin. The October 1993 coup attempt was by a paralyzed parliament that occupied the White House and was crushed by armed forces under President Yeltsin, who was now in the Kremlin.

The trigger of the 1993 attempt was Yeltsin's order to dissolve the Russian parliament and hold new elections. (The old Supreme Soviet disappeared with the USSR at the end of 1991.) The Russian parliament was elected in 1989 under the old regime; accordingly, it was incoherent and incapable of passing a new constitution. Yeltsin could no longer govern with this parliament, and, indeed, it was high time for free and fair parliamentary elections.

But the old parliament did not like being put out of business and called Yeltsin dictatorial. A majority of deputies declared the dissolution unconstitutional and holed up in the White House, hoping that the country and especially the army would side with it. They did not; instead, tanks shelled the White House until it caught fire.

Yeltsin won, but he lost. New elections were held in December 1993, but by then, so many Russians were disillusioned with reforms that brought crime, inflation, and unemployment that they voted in a parliament, now called the State Duma, that was heavily antireformist and anti-Yeltsin. Yeltsin had to dump many reformist ministers.

governors from FSB ranks. Mayors and governors can be fired. Like old Soviet federalism, the new gives most power to the center. To be sure, unruly Russia needs considerable centralized power to hold together. Under Yeltsin, Russia was falling apart, so Putin did what he had to do.

A Bicameral Parliament Russia's bicameral parliament resembles the U.S. Congress but no longer has any power to contradict the Russian presidency. The lower house, the **State Duma**, has 450 deputies elected for up to five years. The Duma passes bills, approves the budget, and confirms the president's nominees for top jobs. It can vote no confidence in a cabinet and, along with the upper house, can theoretically override a presidential veto with a two-thirds majority. That is unlikely, as Putin's United Russia has a narrow majority of Duma seats.

The upper house, the Federation Council, consists of 166 members, 2 named by each of the 83 regional governments of the Russian Federation. Because Putin named the regional governors, he indirectly picked the regions' deputies for the Federation Council. The Council's duties differ somewhat from the Duma's. Only the Federation Council can change internal boundaries and ratify use of armed forces abroad. It appoints top judges and prosecutors and can remove them. The president controls both houses of parliament, and they pass any law he wants, including laws that give him more power.

A Proportional Electoral System In 2005, Putin had the Duma institute straight *proportional representation* with voting by party list and not for individuals. This replaced the system Yeltsin instituted, a *mixed-member* system inspired by Germany, with half of the Duma's 450 seats elected by proportional representation, and half by single-member districts with plurality win. Under the PR system, there are no longer any independent candidates because there are no more single-member districts, and the threshold is now 7 percent (up from 5).

State Duma
Lower house of Russia's parliament.

Democracy

Russia's Surprising 2011 Parliamentary Elections

Although Russia's December 2011 Duma elections were rigged by ballot-box stuffing, voters still delivered a surprise rebuke to Putin's United Russia Party, showing that Putin faced growing opposition and suggesting that civil society was emerging, aided by the new social media.

To protest corruption, stagnant living standards, and Putin's announcement that he would soon resume the presidency, many Russian voters turned to other parties, including the Communists, which scored major gains. Fair elections would have given United Russia much less. Thousands of urban Russians, mobilized by the new electronic media, risked police beatings to protest the electoral fraud in the streets.

Election monitors and opposition groups were severely restricted, and some were arrested. State-controlled television showcased United Russia and ignored other parties. Putin had earlier eliminated the single-member constituencies and made the system straight PR with a 7 percent threshold that knocked out some small, democratic parties. The dramatic difference of two elections:

	2011		2007	
	Percentage Votes	Seats	Percentage Votes	Seats
United Russia	49.5	238	64.3	315
Communists	19.2	92	11.5	57
A Just Russia	13.2	64	7.7	38
Liberal Democrats	11.7	56	8.1	40

A Constitutional Court The constitutional court is borrowed chiefly from the United States but with some French and German features. The Russian Constitutional Court has 19 judges appointed by the president and confirmed by the upper house. These judges are supposed to be independent and cannot be fired. They may act both on citizens' complaints and on cases submitted by government agencies. The court is supposed to make sure all laws and decrees conform to the constitution. Putin, however, put it back under political control so that it does little to promote the rule of law in Russia.

A Dominant-Party System

From a one-party Soviet system, Russia fragmented into a system of many weak parties to become now a dominant-party system. Several Russian political parties sprang up quickly but were divided and personalistic, like Latin American parties. Russia's top parties aimed chiefly at getting their leaders elected. In the 1999 Duma elections, five parties had present or former prime ministers as leaders. Putin invented the United Russia (*Yedinaya Rossiya*) Party, his vehicle to win the presidency and dominate the Duma. United Russia is like a diluted and personalized CPSU, informally called "the party of bureaucrats." It has no ideology.

Party system is one foundation of political stability. Britain is a "two-plus" party system, France is a multiparty system, and Germany has turned from a "two-plus" to a multiparty system. Putin marginalized competing parties to make Russia a dominant-party system with

Personalities

Putin: The KGB President

Russian President Vladimir Putin (pronounced POOH-tin) came from the KGB bureaucracy but governs with tsarist values and techniques. Putin is a cold, secretive, and nationalistic authoritarian, the builder of a "sovereign democracy"—a thinly disguised authoritarianism—that attempts to regain Russia's old borders. He is also a control freak, worried about another Soviet-type collapse and intent on crushing any protest. He is convinced that only his firm rule can save Russia, something the tsars also believed.

In late 1999, Putin rose from obscurity to powerful president of the Russian Federation, first as acting president and then elected in 2000. In August 1999, Yeltsin named Putin, then 46 years old, as his fifth prime minister in 17 months. Many thought that Putin was another temp, but Yeltsin soon designated him as successor. Yeltsin—ill, drunk, and unpopular—resigned at the end of 1999, and Putin constitutionally became acting president.

Putin's rapid rise was not accidental but was a quiet KGB coup, one planned years in advance. Putin graduated from law school in 1975 and went into the KGB, where he became a lieutenant colonel in spy operations in East Germany. As the Soviet Union collapsed—and the KGB knew precisely how bad the system was—the KGB placed many officers into state positions in order to later reconstitute authoritarian power. Putin went into St. Petersburg's municipal administration and became vice mayor in 1994. In 1996, Yeltsin brought him to the Kremlin to supervise relations among Russia's regions and, in 1998, made him head of the FSB. In 1999, Putin was named secretary of the powerful Security Council and then premier, his first substantial public exposure. His election to president in 2000 (on the first round) was his first run for any office.

Putin is bright, but his great strength is his background and comrades in the KGB (now FSB), who have *kompromat* on Russia's most powerful people. They know who is corrupt and stashes money overseas, including politicians and oligarchs. Putin and dozens of other KGB, military, and other *siloviki* set up an invisible system inside the official Russian state. *Siloviki* were placed in charge of state-controlled industries and got rich.

Most Russians detested the danger and decay of the Yeltsin years and initially accepted Putin's authoritarianism. By new laws, threats, demotions, or criminal trials, Putin's people control the bureaucracy, courts, media, Duma, regional governors, oligarchs, and private groups. Occasional assassinations, rarely solved, silence persistent critics. Putin basks in heroic media exposure and high approval ratings, both of which he engineers. Russians always liked strong, one-man rule.

Putin created mass support by renewing the war in Chechnya. Alleged Chechen bombs in several Russian cities killed hundreds. Russians wanted revenge. Putin's orders to crush Chechen rebels drew nearly complete support to easily win the presidency in 2000 and reelection in 2004. His popularity soared again when he took over parts of Ukraine in 2014, "protecting" their Russian-speakers from "fascist" Ukrainians. The controlled mass media fawn on Putin.

Economic stability and growth, largely from oil and gas exports, made most Russians content. Putin's popularity plunged, however, after he rigged parliamentary elections in 2011 and announced that he would resume the presidency in 2012. Some Russians, fed up with corruption and manipulation, want Putin out.

Putin turned bitterly hostile to Washington over U.S. help for Russian and Ukrainian democracy, which he portrays as attempts at subversion. He allows private industry in some sectors but has Russia's oil and gas—which provide most of its export earnings—back under Kremlin control. Putin's goals are those of a good KGB officer: restore Russia's power and old borders. His chief technique: Russian nationalism.

Democracy

Russia's 2012 Presidential Elections

Russian presidential elections are modeled on the French two-round system, minus the democracy. Russia's March 2012 presidential elections unrolled as Putin wished, giving Putin a resounding first-round victory. As in the parliamentary elections a few months earlier, critics say rigging undercounted the amount of opposition to Putin.

After the 2011 parliamentary elections, won by Putin's United Russia, Putin announced that he was taking back the presidency after the one term of Dmitri Medvedev, a close Putin protégé who followed him from St. Petersburg's municipal administration to the Kremlin in 1999. Putin served as his prime minister but was the real power. Medvedev politely stood aside for Putin's third term, and Putin made Medvedev his prime minister. Putin noted that Franklin Delano Roosevelt's four terms did not harm U.S. democracy.

Serious opposition candidates were effectively eliminated, and the candidates that ran against Putin did not even campaign. Many Russians, to be sure, liked the stability and economic growth Putin had brought. Turnout was an unenthusiastic 65 percent, as voters knew the fix was in. If no one had won a majority, a runoff two weeks later would have decided between the top two. Russian television, owned by corporations tied to the Kremlin, supported only Putin. The 2012 election was not democratic, as there was essentially no competition, and competition is the crux of democracy. The 2012 results, none too reliable, are shown in the table below.

Candidate	Party	Percentage
Vladimir Putin	United Russia	64
Gennady Zyuganov	Communist	17
Vladimir Zhirinovsky	Liberal Democrat	6
Sergei Mironov	A Just Russia	4

no checks or balances on an all-powerful executive. Politics in such systems revolves around struggles, mostly unseen, within the big party for power and spoils, such as control of industries. Russians could theoretically elect a Duma to offset the president, but with the Russian preference for a strong hand at the top and the main media in government hands, United Russia will likely continue to dominate for some years.

Russian Political Culture

6.3   Illustrate how "civil society" underpins democracy.

As the Soviet regime declined and collapsed in the late 1980s and early 1990s, the word "democracy" had a positive ring among Russians. The leading political party was *Demrossiya*, Democratic Russia. Now, after having lived through several years of economic decline, lawlessness, and national weakness, few Russians care about democracy. They want food on the table, order, and stability, and most believe that the authoritarian Putin gives it to them. Polls find that only a minority of Russians think democracy is always best, and half think Stalin

oligarchy
Rule by a few.

kleptocracy
Rule by thieves.

was a wise leader. Schools never educated Russians on the crimes of Stalin, who is once again praised. Germans imperfectly faced their past, Japanese less so, but Russians (and Chinese) hardly at all.

Ignoring the crucial factor of political culture, we naively assumed that the collapse of the Communist regime would unleash liberal democracy and free-market prosperity. Instead, it brought monumental lawlessness and poverty. A handful of **oligarchs** got very rich buying state business (especially oil) at giveaway prices. Mafia gangs were into everything, including the government. Some called the system, half in jest, a **kleptocracy**. The breakdown demonstrated what some scholars long suspected, that under the law-and-order surface of Soviet rule, Russian society was very weak—indeed, it had been made deliberately weak—and could not sustain a free democracy, at least not for some time.

The Russian Difference

Central Europe discarded its Communist regimes in 1989, and within five years, Poland, the Czech Republic, and Hungary were democracies with growing market economies. Starting in 1992, the Soviet Union tried to make the same transition but collapsed economically and politically.

Catholic Central Europe faces west; Eastern Orthodox Russia does not (see Huntington box). The CPSU captured Russian *nationalism* and Russian pride. For Central Europeans, communism was imposed and at odds with indigenous nationalism. Central Europe became Communist much later (after World War II) than the Soviet Union (during World War I). Russians had most of a century of Communist rule (1917–1991), so three generations knew only one system. The tsarist system had not been democratic either and was just in the early stages of economic development.

Russians were used to jobs (constitutionally guaranteed) and a low but predictable standard of living. Apartments were scarce and tacky but cost little. Few Russians worked hard; there was no point to it. Now, suddenly, Russians were told their jobs were not guaranteed and that reward comes from hard work. The result was psychological disorientation and fear. The economy declined sharply, and the old legitimacy of Party and leaders collapsed. Gorbachev and Yeltsin lost their early credibility; they zigged and zagged too long on the economy.

In the vacuum of belief, cynicism and despair reigned. Some Russians rediscovered their Orthodox church, which grew after the Communist collapse but has not kept growing. Few attend Orthodox services. Many Russians believed in nothing and said everything was going wrong. Most are still politically numb and care nothing for democracy. But people have to believe in something; cynicism cannot sustain a society. Western values of a free society, of morality rooted in religion, of civil rights, and of individual achievement in a market economy are talked about by some intellectuals but not widely held. Seven decades of Communist rule stomped them out.

The Mask of Legitimacy

For decades, the CPSU pounded into Soviet skulls that the regime was legitimate—that is, its rule was rightful—and was leading the country through the difficulties of "building socialism" to the working utopia of communism. No one can say how many believed it. Foreigners were

Geography

Huntington's "Civilizational" Divide in Europe

In an influential but controversial 1993 article in *Foreign Affairs*, Harvard political scientist Samuel P. Huntington argued that, with the Cold War over, profound differences of culture were dividing the world into several "civilizations" that have trouble understanding each other. These civilizations mostly follow religious lines: West European (with a North American branch), Slavic/Orthodox, Muslim, Hindu, Confucian, Japanese, and Latin American.

In Europe, said Huntington, the key geographic line is still where Eastern Orthodoxy meets the two branches of Western Christianity—Catholicism and Protestantism—a line running south from Finland and the Baltic republics (Lithuania is mostly Catholic, Latvia and Estonia mostly Lutheran) and along the eastern borders of Poland, Slovakia, Hungary, and Croatia. West European civilization, initially in Protestant countries, led the way to democracy and capitalism. Catholic Europe followed more recently. Poland, the Czech Republic, and Hungary all turned quickly to market systems and democracy after ousting their Communist regimes in 1989. (Hungary, alas, has recently turned partway back to authoritarianism.)

But notice that Slavic/Orthodox countries such as Russia, Ukraine, Serbia, Bulgaria, and Romania have difficulty in making this transition. Basic assumptions about individual freedom and choice, private property, personal rights, and the rule of law that are widespread in West Europe have not developed in the same way in Slavic/Orthodox Europe. One key point: Orthodox culture is less individualistic, and this helps account for economic behavior.

Economic *shock therapy* (the sudden introduction of a free market) soon brought rapid growth to Poland. Applied in Russia, it simply collapsed the economy—"shock without therapy." Many observers suggest the differences between Poland and Russia are cultural, that Poland has always faced west and Russia has not. Huntington's theory does not mean that other civilizations cannot become free-market democracies, just that it may take some time.

treated to performances of marchers, youth delegations, and seemingly frank conversations with officials that showed the system worked. In private, one could meet dissident intellectuals, bitter workers, and even Party members who had come to doubt the system.

rump state
Leftover portions of a country after dismemberment.

Geography

Bound Serbia

Serbia is bounded on the north by Hungary;

on the east by Romania and Bulgaria;

on the south by Macedonia, Kosovo, and Montenegro;

and on the west by Bosnia and Croatia.

In 2003 Yugoslavia, a **rump state**, changed its name to Serbia and Montenegro. The old Yugoslavia of 1918–1941 and 1945–1991 (areas with color) included Slovenia, Croatia, Bosnia, and Macedonia, all of which are now independent. In 2006, Montenegro (Black Mountain) voted in a referendum to depart from the federation. Serbia lost its outlet to the sea and returned to what it was called before World War I. In 1999, Serbia lost control of Kosovo and its largely Albanian population, who, in 2008, proclaimed Kosovo independent, which Serbia and Russia did not recognize. With the bounding exercises you have now done, you should be able to locate most countries of Europe. Which European lands have not been named in our bounding exercises?

Serbia

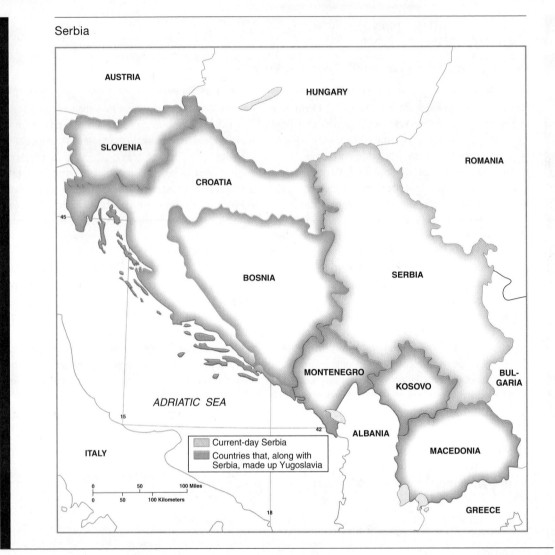

When Gorbachev permitted increased freedom of expression in the late 1980s, **glasnost**, criticism poured out. Freed from fear of the police, the media criticized the bureaucracy, the Party, and the corruption of both. The mask of Soviet legitimacy slipped away to reveal a system that satisfied few, but there was no consensus on what should replace it. The broad masses (Russian: *narod*) generally wanted a cleaned-up socialism that guaranteed everyone a good standard of living. They showed little understanding of democracy or a market system. Many better educated understood that socialism was defective and should be scrapped in favor of free politics and free economics. Those whose jobs depended on the old system saw change as a threat. And many Russians simply did not know what to think. They had never before been asked for their opinions.

glasnost
Gorbachev's policy of media openness.

Many Russians turned to Russian nationalism, a powerful impulse long manipulated by the Communists, and to newly freed Russian

Orthodox Christianity. Russian nationalism and the Russian Orthodox faith, however, cannot cement Russia together: Twenty-one ethnic republics are non-Russian, mostly Tatar and Muslim (more than 10 percent of Russia's population), and harbor their own nationalism and separatism. No symbols unite all Russians. Some like the new tricolor flag (based on a tsarist design); others want to bring back the red flag with hammer and sickle. National day is no longer November 11 to celebrate the revolution (although thousands, out of nostalgia, still parade) but June 12 to celebrate "Russia Day," when it proclaimed sovereignty in 1990 (for which few parade). Most Russians deplore the breakup of the Soviet Union.

The Illusion of Ideology

Some studies of the Soviet Union paid great attention to Marxist-Leninist ideology. In truth, for many years, ideology had counted for little in the Soviet Union; with *glasnost*, it disappeared. Much Soviet "ideology" was Russian national pride masking feelings of inferiority. Marxism, by predicting the collapse of the capitalist West, told Russians that they would soon emerge superior. They were "building socialism," which at a certain point would surpass the United States and turn into a Communist utopia with no social or economic problems. In earlier decades, some Soviets believed it, but American academics exaggerated the role of ideology as the basis of the Soviet system. The true basis was opportunism. Young people joined the Party to get into universities, to win job promotions, or to become military or

Political Culture

The Philosophical Gap

One key difference between us and the Russians is philosophical; namely, we are the children of John Locke, and they are not. Few Americans study the philosopher who is at the root of much of our thinking, but most have assimilated what the seventeenth-century English thinker had to say: People are rational and reasonable; they have a natural right to life, liberty, and property. Government is good if it preserves these rights and bad if it infringes on them. If this sounds like the Declaration of Independence, it is; Jefferson was an ardent Lockean, as were most of the Founding Fathers. Ever since, Americans have taken to Locke like a duck takes to water; we love his commonsense emphasis on small government and individuals working for the good of themselves and their families. To Russians, this is not common sense.

Russian thought comes out almost the opposite of Locke and traces back to the geographical dilemma of living on a defenseless plain: Either build a strong state or perish. Plugging into the Russian tradition of a strong state is Jean-Jacques Rousseau, the radical eighteenth-century French thinker whose theory of the general will rejected Lockean individualism in favor of using state power to "force men to be free." With Locke, people form society, and then society sets up a state, all with an eye to preserving property.

With Rousseau, the flow goes the other way: The state, guided by the general will, molds society and then redoes individuals. Marxists added a class-struggle gloss to this; Lenin bought the package and then sold it to the Russian people. Without a new philosophical outlook, one taken mostly from the West, the Russians will likely stay trapped in their *statist* frame of mind, one that it took India, Brazil, and Mexico decades to get out of.

civil society
Associations larger than the family but not part of government, and the pluralistic values that come with them.

socialize
To teach political culture, often informally.

civilian officials. Most were cynical and cared nothing for Marxism-Leninism. They were motivated by careers, not ideology.

Marxism is basically a method of analysis, one that stresses social classes and their conflicts. As such, it stayed far livelier in the West, where it faced constant argument and challenge. In the Soviet Union, it atrophied. Applying Marxist analyses to Soviet society was the last thing the *apparat* wanted, as it would have revealed a pampered Party elite lording it over a wretched proletariat. Soviet Marxists focused on the West and cranked out clichés, such as the "sharpening of contradictions" and "increasing tempo and magnitude of crises." The West was supposed to collapse soon. After some decades, few took it seriously. Soviet students took required classes on Marxism-Leninism with the enthusiasm of American students going to compulsory chapel.

The constant mouthing of a dead doctrine created a climate of cynicism, hypocrisy, and opportunism. With the collapse of the Soviet system, Marxism-Leninism collapsed like the house of cards it always was. Marxist ideology was always a defective foundation, but nothing has replaced it, and cynical and hopeless attitudes are still widespread.

The Rediscovery of Civil Society

Political scientists since Tocqueville (in his brilliant *Democracy in America* in the 1830s) have held that the crux of democracy is the autonomy of **civil society**. Independent enterprises, churches, associations, and the media interact with each other and with government to produce democracy. No pluralism, no democracy. The crux of the Soviet system, however, was the stomping out of civil society by the state. Nothing was to be autonomous; everything was to be under state supervision, in turn supervised by the Party. The CPSU had deliberately crushed civil society, and the Soviet collapse left a vacuum in its place. Some anticipated that civil society would emerge in post-Communist Russia as it had in Central Europe.

Initially, civil society did emerge in Russia, and within a few years, some 450,000 private groups and charities were voicing citizen concerns. In 2005, however, an obedient Duma passed two Putin measures to bring civil society under government control. One law requires all associations to register with the state, effectively banning nongovernmental organizations (NGOs), especially foreign-funded foundations that promote democracy and civil rights. Another law set up a "Public Chamber" of 126 distinguished citizens, supposedly representatives of civil-society organizations, to monitor government and strengthen democracy. Few were fooled, and many called it a smokescreen to strengthen Putin's power. The crux of civil society is the autonomy of its many groups; place them under state control and they are no longer civil society.

The concept of civil society starts with the understanding that state and society are two different things, although they clearly influence each other. Society over time evolves informal usages and customs that make living together possible. The "civil" (as in civilized) indicates a reasonable level of trust, politeness, public spirit, and willingness to compromise. A civil society, through parents, churches, and schools, **socializes** its members to right behavior and "rules of the game" that continue even when the state, through its police and bureaucrats, is not watching.

The state, the formal institutions that wield power, cannot substitute for civil society, although the Communists tried. Attempting such a substitution creates a system where people lack basic civility and see no need to play by informal rules of the game. Businessmen cheat, and mafia gangs muscle into all sectors of the economy. Politicians attack each other hysterically, immoderately, with no possibility of compromise; they have never learned restraint. Citizens feel little need to obey the l aw if they can get away with breaking it. Legitimacy is terribly weak.

contradiction
In Marxism, a big, incurable problem that rips the system apart (current equivalent: dysfunction).

The West had centuries to build up its civil societies. Churches, often with threats of eternal damnation, inculcated right behavior. Philosophers such as Hobbes and Locke explained rationally why civil society is necessary. The market system generated usages to keep dealings fair and predictable, enforced by contracts, laws, and courts. All of this has been missing in Russia since the 1917 Revolution. Americans tended to take their civil society for granted until corporate misdeeds reminded them that businesses without ethics undermine the whole system. When communism fell, we thought democratic institutions and a market economy in Russia would quickly bring civil society. We now see that, without the philosophical, moral, economic, and legal understandings of civil society, Russia turns back to authoritarianism.

Natural Egalitarians?

Marxism-Leninism may have vanished in Russia, but Russians tend toward extreme equality, a natural socialism. Russians resent differences of wealth and enviously try to bring the better off down to their level. Most Russians hated the new-rich oligarchs and were delighted to see

Political Culture

The Economics Gap

Another basic point that was overlooked is that people have to learn capitalism. A market economy may occur naturally (whenever buyers and sellers meet), but it is not understood naturally. You have to take courses in market economics and read books and articles about it. Soviet courses covered "bourgeois economics" in the history of economic thought but gave it short shrift as a doomed system riven with **contradictions**, unfairness, and depressions. When their system collapsed, only a few Russian economists grasped market economies.

Especially missing was how money plays an autonomous role. Marxist economics has no theory of money. I have tried the following mental experiment in a seminar (at the U.S. Army War College) of U.S., Central European, and Russian colonels, all bright and well

educated. Imagine, I tell them, a miniature country with ten citizens, each of whom works in one hamburger shop. They make a total of ten hamburgers a day, and each is paid $1 a day. Then, each buys one hamburger a day with their $1. The government decides to raise the pay of each to $2 a day (by printing an extra ten $1 bills). The workers' output is still ten hamburgers a day. Within a day or two, what is the price of a hamburger?

The Americans responded instinctively: $2! The East Europeans and Russians did not get it. "You haven't given us enough data," they said. Well, how would you explain it? It is not so simple. Phrases like "supply and demand" by themselves do not explain much. What we accept as basic and self-evident, Russians do not. (By the way, once you can explain the parable, you have a rudimentary theory of money.)

Putin break and jail them. Some observers argue that the Russian peasantry, who for centuries tilled the soil in common and shared the harvest, developed highly egalitarian values, which the Communists nourished. Perhaps so, but values are not genetic; they are learned and can be unlearned, given the right conditions. Until new values are learned, however, the old ones can trip up the best-laid plans of reformers.

Americans also favor equality, but it is "equality of opportunity": Everyone has a chance; the results are up to you. Most Russians do not understand this kind of equality; they expect "equality of result," with each person collecting the same rewards. Those who get ahead are presumed to have cheated, exploited, or bribed (actually, many have). "The rich are living on

Political Culture

The Moral Gap

America has corporate crooks and cheats, but what would America be like if one could go back over three generations and strip out most moral teachings? What if no one could trust anyone else? The result would be rather like Russia today.

Russians had ethical training, but it was relativistic, superficial, and based on Marxist theories of social class. That which helps the working class is good, went the litany. The Soviet state helps the working class, so it must be good. The Communist Party is devoted to the working class, so it must be very good. The state and the Party must therefore be obeyed, respected, and defended. Anyone who goes against them is insane, a wrecker, or a spy. Crime is something that happens only in capitalist countries, where the poor are forced to steal. Private property is inherently wicked, because it has been stolen from the workers who produced it.

Under communism, there were no moral absolutes. The Russian Orthodox Church, tightly controlled by the government, confined itself to religious ritual. By contrast, the Polish Catholic Church, for centuries the pillar of Polish civil society, stayed free of state control and critical of communism, always trying to face Poland westward. Religion matters.

Soviet citizens soon learned to treat the system with cynicism. With the KGB and its informants everywhere, no one could trust anyone else, and they still do not. With no individual responsibility, stealing, especially from the state, was okay. After all, it really belonged to no one. Under communism, rip-offs and bribery were the norm.

The Soviet collapse made things worse, unleashing a spirit of "anything goes." Nothing happens without bribes. People who were smart, ruthless, or well connected grabbed whole industries. Russia was robbed from within by its own bureaucrats. Because Soviets had always been taught that capitalists and *biznesmeny* (long a term of derision, now adopted as a loan word) were crooks and their gains were ill gotten, many Russians went into business with that image as their norm. The crime rate shot up; only Colombians are more likely to be murdered than Russians. Massive protection rackets, enforced by professional *keelers* (another loan word), were all right because they were just stealing from capitalist thieves.

A modern capitalist culture needs a moral basis; people have to be able to trust each other. Such a system draws from religious and ethical teachings, legal enforcement, and the knowledge that cheating businesses get few repeat customers. It may take a long time to build up this moral consensus. We made the mistake of thinking it would automatically arrive with the free market, which we supposed to be self-policing. We too recently discovered that U.S. financial institutions are not self-policing but need regulation. For Russians, a free market means legal cheating. For capitalism to work properly, both in Russia and America, the moral gap must be filled.

our poverty," said one elderly Russian lady. In polls, most Russians say that the free market and small state are wrong for Russia; only a few favor them. American values of individual work and achievement lend themselves to capitalism; Russian values, until recently, have not.

Caucasus
Mountainous region between Black and Caspian seas.

Central Asia
Region between Caspian Sea and China.

Russian Racism

With *glasnost*, hate-filled racist attitudes latent among the Soviet nationalities came into the open. Under Soviet law, nationality was stamped in internal passports, and, contrary to U.S. usage, nationality throughout East Europe and the ex-Soviet Union does not equal citizenship. For example, one can be a Russian citizen of the Komi nationality. This approach is asking for trouble, because it encourages minority groups to demand independent states. Educated Russians admire the U.S. approach, which prohibits the official identification of citizens by race or national origin.

And Russians pigeonhole by nationality. Some are acceptable, others despised. Russians respect the Baltic peoples as European, civilized, and "cultured." But Russians speak scathingly of the Muslim peoples of the **Caucasus** and **Central Asia** as lawless and corrupt mafiosi

Political Culture

The Legal Gap

Much of Russia is lawless, one characteristic of the weak state. Russian police and courts are chaotic and easily bribed. As in India and Mexico, motorists are used to paying off traffic cops. Law is used selectively: Regime opponents get arrested and convicted, but major assassinations go unsolved, and corrupt officials are untouched. Said one Russian law expert ruefully, "The only lawyer around here is a Kalashnikov," a favorite weapon of *keelers*. A nosy lawyer, Sergei Magnitsky, died in prison. Female punk rockers were sent to a penal colony for insulting Putin.

The Soviet legal structure broke down, and it was deficient to begin with. Soviet law paid minimal attention to property. Any big property (land, factories) automatically belonged to the state, and stealing state property could be harshly punished as a form of treason. The Lockean notion that property is a natural right and basis for human freedom was rejected out of hand. Russians, having been inculcated with the Marxist notion that "all property is theft," have trouble grasping the democratic and capitalist notion that "private property means personal freedom."

Weak or absent in the old Soviet socialist legal code, which Russia inherited, are such basics as ownership, contracts, torts, and bankruptcy. If you set up a business in the United States or West Europe, you are reasonably confident your property and earnings will not be taken from you. In Russia, you have no confidence. Not only are business and property laws new, there is no legal culture built up over the years that regards these areas as important. One result is that foreigners and Russians alike are reluctant to invest in Russia; many have lost everything.

By way of contrast, Poland adopted its excellent Commercial Code in 1935, borrowed heavily from the Italian. The Polish Communist regime never repealed this code, and after the Communists' ouster in 1989, Polish jurists put it into practice. Both Poles and foreigners enjoy legal protections and made the Polish economy grow fast. Russia finally passed commercial and criminal codes in 2002, based, in part, on Western legal concepts.

who make too many babies. The theme of the differential birthrate comes up often. Most Russian families nowadays have one child (also the norm in West Europe). Muslim families have many children. Some Russians fear that their stagnant numbers will be swamped by a tide of inferior peoples. When bombs blew up apartment houses in 1999, killing close to 300 people, the Russian government and people eagerly blamed alleged Chechen terrorists and supported a new war to crush them. Caucasians and Central Asians who had long run market stalls were expelled. Putin said it was to protect "native Russians" from the Asian "semi-gangs."

The non-Russian nationalities feel little affection for Russians. In Central Asia, several republics have made their local language the only official language. Educated Uzbeks, for example, know Russian perfectly but now speak only Uzbek to make local Russians feel unwelcome. Many Russians got the message and left Central Asia. Virtually none have fled from the Baltic republics, however, and some Russians there even support independence. They feel that they are treated fairly by the cultured Balts. They fear the Muslims of the Caucasus and Central Asia. (After 9/11 and the 2013 Boston bombings, so do Americans.)

Anti-Semitism, deliberately cultivated in tsarist Russia, is back but unofficial and played down in public statements. Russian nationalists and Communists point to the handful of oligarchs of Jewish or partly Jewish origin and see a sinister international conspiracy called "Zionism." Small nationalist parties of skinheads urge violence against Jews, and nearly one million Jews emigrated from the former Soviet Union to Israel. Most Russians, however, condemn anti-Semitism, and, in 2002, President Putin got the Duma to pass a law against ethnic extremism.

A Culture of Insecurity

Average Russians are terribly insecure. In the 1990s, crime, corruption, and economic decay dominated their lives. Some used the phrase "Weimar Russia" to suggest a coming fascism. Before Putin took power, most Russians described the situation as "tense," "critical," or "explosive" and expected anarchy. Most feel Putin made life more secure; they like his power and overlook his undemocratic methods. The 2008–2009 global downturn again made Russians insecure, and Putin's approval ratings, although higher than any Western leader's, began to slump. The 2014 Ukraine crisis boosted Putin's popularity.

One thing angers Russians (and Chinese) and keeps legitimacy from growing: corruption. Russians know their system is hugely corrupt—Transparency International rates it worse than China—and nothing is done to fix it. Many Russians say corruption got worse under Putin, although he claimed to be fighting it. No one trusts civil servants or police. Only the trickle down of oil and natural gas revenues keep Russians quiet. A regime that depends on the fickle global price of oil is not on solid ground.

"We could have been contenders," Russians seem to be saying. "We once had a great empire that challenged the Americans; suddenly it vanished." Although support of client states around the globe was a net drain on the Soviet economy, many Russians were proud of their power. The feeling of belonging to a mighty empire served to quiet discontent over shortages and poor living conditions. Every time a new client signed up—Cuba, Vietnam, Ethiopia, Angola—Russians could say, "See, we really are the wave of the future." The loss of empire was a psychological letdown for Russians.

Democracy

Free Media

One of the basic components of democracy—in addition to competitive elections—is a free press. The easiest way to tell if a country is democratic is to see whether its mass media are controlled or muzzled. If television, radio, newspapers, and magazines routinely criticize the regime and remain in business, you probably have a democracy. The government closing these entities down or taking them over signals authoritarianism. Freedom of information is indispensable to democracies but undermines dictatorships.

Russia sharply but quietly restricts the media. Most of the national media, especially television, has been taken over by government-linked corporations and the rest cowed into "self-censorship," afraid that they will be next. The Kremlin, never stating its intentions, forced the oligarchs to relinquish their television networks and newspapers—which had supported first Yeltsin and then Putin in elections. Moscow also prosecutes Russian writers and journalists for critical views. Several have been maimed or killed, the perpetrators never caught. Although not as bad as in Communist times, all of Russia's national media praise Putin.

Russians used to feel that they were the equals—maybe the superiors—of the Americans; now the arrogant Americans sneer at Russia. Indeed, Russians believe, it was Americans who craftily engineered the fall of the Soviet Empire and the collapse of the Soviet Union. Now they are moving in for the kill—the destruction of Russia. What else could the extension of NATO eastward—by adding Central Europe and the Baltic states—mean? See what they did to our little Slavic brother Serbia? And now with Ukraine? The Americans gave Russia little money and a lot of bad economic advice, making sure our economy collapsed.

Observers were distressed at Russia's signs of *paranoia* and *xenophobia*. The Soviet and, later, Russian systems collapsed from their own chiefly economic weaknesses; it was not a U.S. plot. Moscow rejected most Western economic urgings and then got angry when Western banks refrained from investing. Foreign support for building democracy in Russia was not an attempt to take over Russia. Such a victim mentality contributes to the growth of nationalist authoritarianism of the sort that leaped out in 2014 over Ukraine.

One leading study of Nazi Germany blamed its rise on "the politics of cultural despair," a situation where everything seems to have failed, where civil society has dissolved and nothing has taken its place. Many Russians now despair at the crime, corruption, and high living costs and say they would like to emigrate. (Few, however, complain about lack of democracy.) The better off stash getaway money and buy properties in West Europe.

How far can despair go before something snaps? Under Yeltsin, Russia was headed for the abyss; Putin pulled it back just in time. The economy grew—based heavily on oil and natural gas exports—and few Russians worried about the choking off of pluralism and democracy. When oil and natural gas prices fell, so did Putin's generous budgets and popularity, illustrating the danger of trying to buy legitimacy with cash. To last, "performance-based legitimacy" must be firmed up into "institution-based legitimacy," something absent in Russia.

Personalities

Failed Reformers: Nikita Khrushchev

The Soviet Union had petrified under Stalin. Nikita Khrushchev attempted to revitalize the system and move it toward communism again. He was only partly and briefly successful, for much of the Soviet party and bureaucracy resisted. We now realize Khrushchev was not the undisputed master of the Kremlin that Stalin was and had to overcome opposition. Like Gorbachev, he failed.

Born in 1894 of an ethnic Russian family in Ukraine, Khrushchev joined the Bolsheviks shortly after the revolution and worked his way up through Party jobs. A protégé of Stalin, Khrushchev did some of the dictator's dirty work in the 1930s, which earned him a full Politburo membership in 1939. During the war, he was a political general on the Ukrainian front. After the war, he organized Party work in Ukraine and then the Moscow region and carefully packed the leadership with his supporters, the key to success in Soviet politics.

Stalin's death in 1953 unleashed a power struggle. All the Politburo had feared Stalin and longed for stability and personal security. Accordingly, they immediately had the head of the secret police, Lavrenti Beria (like Stalin, a Georgian) shot, putting the security police under Party control. The first post-Stalin premier, Georgi Malenkov, advocated relaxing the system and producing more consumer goods. But Khrushchev was made CPSU first secretary, a post that was always more powerful, and built a coalition against Malenkov, who, in 1955, was demoted to minister for power stations. The Soviet leadership abandoned violent death as a way to run a political system.

To consolidate his power and trump his enemies within the Party, Khrushchev took a dramatic step: He denounced Stalin to a Party congress. A CPSU that was still Stalinist was immobile, incapable of reform or innovation, and blocked the productive potential of the Soviet Union under a blanket of fear and routine. At the Twentieth Party Congress in February 1956, Khrushchev delivered a stinging, hours-long tirade against the "crimes of Stalin," who, he said, had murdered thousands of Party comrades and top military officers. Stalin had built a **cult of personality** that must never be allowed again.

Communist parties the world over were based on Stalin worship, and when the speech leaked (with help from the CIA), all hell broke loose. Soviet tanks crushed a Hungarian uprising; Poland nearly revolted. In the West, longtime Communists resigned from the party. In China, Mao Zedong was horrified at Khrushchev for undermining the Communist camp by denouncing its symbol. Thus began the Sino–Soviet split.

To revitalize the Soviet economy, Khrushchev proposed decentralization. Outvoted in the Politburo, he called a 1957 Central Committee meeting packed with his supporters and backed by the army, which forced his opponents, the "antiparty group," to resign. But CPSU leaders grew irritated at his "harebrained schemes" to boost production (especially of consumer goods), eliminate class differences (everyone would have to work before college, even the elites' children), and outfox Americans by placing missiles in Cuba. They considered him a reckless experimenter and liberalizer, and, in October 1964, the Politburo *voted* him out of office, a rare thing in Communist systems. He retired and died in 1971.

The Khrushchev era brought major changes in domestic and foreign policy. A generation of young Party members, including Gorbachev, came of age wanting economic reform. These people, "Khrushchev's children," later staffed the Gorbachev reform effort. Khrushchev was a flamboyant, can-do character, who promised major change. He stressed consumer goods over heavy industry, and this infuriated managers and the military. He permitted publication of anti-Stalin works, then backed off when things got out of hand. Khrushchev tried to reform against the interests of the Party *apparatchiki*, the same people who brought down Gorbachev.

Ultimately, Russia can become as democratic as Germany or Spain, but not under conditions of chaos. Putin restores order and is better than Communists, extreme nationalists, and gangsters, but he does not aim for full-fledged democracy. Thrust onto an unprepared population in the midst of economic decline, democracy and capitalism have not yet taken root in Russia. Spain under Franco was a police state, but strong economic growth made a majority of Spaniards middle class, and, in the late 1970s, Spain moved easily to democracy. If Putin can do something similar for Russia, he may be remembered favorably.

cult of personality
Personal glorification of a dictator.

shock therapy
Sudden replacement of socialist economy by market economy.

Patterns of Interaction

6.4   Explain why reforming Russia is a recurrent problem.

Going back two centuries, Russian politics has been a tug-of-war between reformist and conservative forces. Post-Communist Russian politics reflects, and to some extent continues, Soviet and even earlier Russian patterns. Since tsarist times, Russia has needed major reform, but conservative forces block reform. A hundred years ago, educated Russians could recognize the problem: How to reform a system that keeps reverting back to old patterns?

Reformers versus Conservatives

Russia has few rules or institutions to regulate and moderate political clashes. Without experience in multiparty competition, a free press, voluntary associations, tolerance, and simple politeness, the new forces freed by the ending of Party control began a new game without rules. The clashes were chaotic and made worse by insiders who grabbed state enterprises cheap.

Earlier editions of this book argued that under the uniform surface of Soviet political life existed a permanent struggle between liberals and conservatives, the former for major change toward Western models, the latter for standing pat with the essentially Stalinist system. This conflict continues in the post-Soviet era. Reformers who rallied to Gorbachev and then to Yeltsin hearkened back to the Russian Westernizers of the nineteenth century who wanted to import Western ways nearly wholesale: a market economy, free democracy, and individualistic philosophy. This led the new reformists to attempt the economic **shock therapy** recommended by Columbia economist Jeffrey Sachs, which earlier worked in Bolivia and Poland. In Russia, such therapy was never fully and correctly applied, and the economy plunged downward. The reformers resigned or were dismissed.

The term "conservatives" covers a broad swath, from moderates to extremists who oppose the thorough restructuring of the Russian economy. Russia may need reforms, some concede, but they must be our reforms tailored to our conditions. Some old-line Party types would go back to a centralized command economy. Like the old Russophiles of the nineteenth century, they reject Western models and would turn inward, to Russia's roots; accordingly, they are nationalistic.

Russian "centrists" sought a middle ground of moderate reforms cushioned by continued state subsidies and ownership. Unfortunately, under Yeltsin, this approach led to incredible corruption. Thoroughgoing reformers and democrats, such as the small Yabloko party (which is no longer in the Duma), are weak because few Russians share their Western-type thinking.

President versus Parliament

Russia's executive and legislative bodies were at serious odds in the 1990s, and their competing claims led to anger and violence. Then Putin tamed the Duma. The initial problem, as noted earlier, was the carryover from Soviet times of a Russian parliament elected under the Communists in 1989. Most members of this parliament stood firm with Yeltsin during the abortive coup of 1991. But then Yeltsin gathered more power into the office of the presidency, and parliament claimed that Yeltsin was becoming dictatorial. His dissolution of parliament to hold new elections prompted the coup attempt of 1993 (see previous boxes). Then parliamentary elections turned into slaps at Yeltsin. Yeltsin backed down and made a string of cautious reformers his prime ministers but fired each after a few months.

But is this not just democracy in action? An executive starts showing dictatorial tendencies and implements policies that go further and faster than citizens want, so the citizens, through their elected representatives in parliament, put on the brakes. That is the way the State Duma liked to see itself, but the problem in Russia is trickier. Without major economic reforms, democracy in Russia does not stand a chance. But such reforms are seldom initiated by purely democratic means because they inflict too much pain, at least temporarily. Major reforms need strong executive leadership; a fragmented parliament cannot do it. If the executive is blocked, the result will likely not be democracy but chaos, and out of chaos grows dictatorship.

The Taming of the Oligarchs

Moscow privatized ("piratized" might be more accurate) the Russian economy in a way that made a few people incredibly wealthy. Clever wheeler-dealers, some of them already in management (who understood the value of state-owned firms, chiefly in the oil and natural gas industries), bought the companies ultracheap with borrowed money. Most of what they did was legal because there were few laws governing the sales. Russia privatized badly.

These oligarchs, as they were soon called, either had or quickly developed ties to leading politicians. One top oligarch was Boris Berezovsky, a math professor turned used car king and then media and oil magnate. His money, newspapers, and TV network helped first Yeltsin and then Putin win election. Putin then had Berezovsky prosecuted and took his properties. Berezovsky fled to Britain and was the target of assassination attempts. He hanged himself in 2013. Several other oligarchs, fearing prosecution, also fled abroad.

Russia's oligarchs did not act like the old U.S. "robber barons," who invested and then reinvested to make the economy and jobs grow. Russian oligarchs simply stripped assets from their companies—for example, selling oil abroad—and did not reinvest the money but stashed it in foreign (Swiss, Cayman Islands, Cyprus) banks. They did not like paying taxes or competing in a free market. As they got rich, the Russian economy got poor.

Russians, with their penchant for equality, hated the oligarchs and liked how President Putin cracked down on them. Most are in jail or in exile. Putin's *siloviki* targeted some for tax

Comparison

Totalitarian versus Authoritarian

Since the 1930s, political science has debated the nature of modern dictatorships. Some developed theories and models of **totalitarianism** to explain Mussolini's Italy, Hitler's Germany, and Stalin's Soviet Union, whose total control aimed at remaking society. Carl J. Friedrich and Zbigniew Brzezinski argued that totalitarian dictatorships have these six points in common:

1. An official ideology
2. A single, disciplined party
3. Terroristic police control
4. Party monopoly of the mass media
5. Party control of the armed forces
6. Central direction of the economy

Widely accepted for years, the totalitarian model came under criticism as unrealistic and oversimplified. Far from total, the systems of Mussolini, Hitler, and Stalin were quite messy. Many citizens knew the regimes were frauds; plans were often improvised. The dictators like their systems to *look* total. Totalitarianism was an attempt at total control that always fell short.

"Totalitarianism" fell into disfavor and was replaced by **authoritarianism**, which can be quite brutal but does not aim for total control. A dictator—such as Spain's Franco, Chile's Pinochet, or Brazil's generals—monopolizes politics, but much of the economy, religion, and culture are semifree. Most or all of the six points listed earlier are missing.

Political scientist Jeane J. Kirkpatrick, in 1980, argued that there is still a distinction between the two terms. Authoritarian regimes, more loose and open, can change and reform themselves into democracies. This happened throughout Latin America in the 1980s. Totalitarian systems, especially Communist ones, she argued, cannot reform; they are too rigid. The Communist regimes of East Europe and the Soviet Union never did reform; they collapsed.

---

evasion (in a system where everyone cheats on taxes) and forced them to turn over their companies—including oil and gas industries, television networks, and newspapers—to government fronts. Under Putin, most of the big Russian media came under state control, and few dared criticize him.

Mikhail Khodorkovsky, once Russia's richest man, lost his huge (and well-run) Yukos oil firm, allegedly for fraud but more likely for trying to bring in U.S. partners. He got two rigged trials and 10 years in prison. Putin got Yukos by having Kremlin-controlled Rosneft buy it cheap. Like many Russians, he felt that something as important as energy should never have been privatized. Putin also wanted to stop Khodorkovsky from becoming a political rival. At the end of 2013, Putin freed Khodorkovsky, who now lives in Switzerland.

Russia still has oligarchs, but they are tame, either government officials or those beholden to Putin, who have taken over major industries and the media. They kick back money to the Kremlin, making top Russian politicians extremely wealthy. Some claim Putin's power lies in his tsar-like ability to settle disputes among oligarchs. Transparency International calls Russia one of the most corrupt countries in the world. The original oligarchs were egregious, greedy, and sometimes criminal, but their television stations and newspapers briefly gave Russia freedom of information.

totalitarianism
Attempts to totally control society, as under Stalin and Hitler.

authoritarianism
Dictatorial rejection of democracy, but milder than *totalitarianism*.

Personalities

Failed Reformers: Mikhail Gorbachev

"Life punishes those who delay," said Soviet President Gorbachev, in 1989, as he urged the East German Communist regime to reform before it was too late. The East Berlin regime ignored Gorbachev and collapsed. But Mikhail Sergeyevich Gorbachev did not grasp that he, too, was engaging in delayed and halfway reforms that would collapse the Soviet regime and his own tenure in power.

Amid great hopes, Gorbachev assumed the top Soviet political position—CPSU general secretary—in 1985. The Soviet Union had gradually run down during Brezhnev's 18-year reign; growth slumped while cynicism, alcoholism, and corruption grew. Two elderly temporaries, Andropov and Chernenko, followed as the Soviet system atrophied. Gorbachev—age 54, a mere kid in Politburo terms—announced wide-ranging reforms to shake up the Soviet system.

Born into a peasant family in the North Caucasus in 1931, Gorbachev graduated in law from Moscow University in 1955 and returned to his home area for Party work. As CPSU chief of Stavropol province in 1970, he impressed Brezhnev, who summoned him to Moscow in 1978. Gorbachev, by now, was under the wing of Andropov, head of the KGB, and Mikhail Suslov, a Politburo kingmaker from Stavropol. Gorbachev was elected to the Central Committee in 1971, to candidate member of the Politburo in 1979, and to full member in 1980. When Andropov took over in 1982, Gorbachev assisted him and his tough anticorruption policies.

In 1985, Gorbachev began reforms to turn the Soviet Union into a modern, possibly democratic, system. He announced "new thinking" in foreign policy that led to arms control agreements with the United States and to the freeing of East Europe from the Communist regimes imposed by Stalin after World War II. With these steps, the Cold War ended.

Gorbachev ordered *glasnost* in the Soviet media, which became more pluralist, honest, and critical.

Corrupt big shots were fired. Gorbachev also urged *demokratizatzia*; competitive elections were introduced, and a partially elected parliament convened.

Gorbachev first tried to fix the economic system with old remedies: verbal exhortations, antialcohol campaigns, "acceleration," and importing foreign technology. After hesitating too long, he ordered **perestroika**, which slowly began to decentralize and liberalize the Soviet economy. Farms and factories made more of their own decisions and kept more of their own profits. Private cooperatives were permitted. But it was too little, too late. By 1989, economic disaster loomed. Soviet living and dietary standards fell and angered everyone.

With a freer press, the many nationalities (including Russians) demanded greater autonomy or even independence. Violence between ethnic groups flared. The *apparat* and *nomenklatura* sabotaged economic reforms by hoarding food and raw materials. Some generals and the KGB indicated that they would not stand for the chaos, which was leading to the dismemberment of the Soviet Union, so Gorbachev pulled back from reforms and tightened up in late 1990.

In early 1991, Gorbachev favored reform again. In opposition, conservative hardliners in his own cabinet—handpicked by Gorbachev—attempted a coup against him in August 1991. The coup failed due to splits in the Soviet armed forces and the stubbornness of Russian President Boris Yeltsin, who then pushed a weakened Gorbachev from office and broke up the Soviet Union by pulling the vast Russian federation out of it.

In part, Gorbachev had himself to blame for the Soviet collapse. He dawdled too long and changed course too many times. He sought to preserve the Party and "socialism" and never did adopt an economic reform plan. Life indeed punished him who delayed.

Democracy

Runaway Systems

Yale political scientist Robert Dahl noted that powerful people tend to use their resources (legal, political, economic) to gain more resources. If there are no counterbalancing institutions or strong laws to check them, some amass power without limit: Stalin. Engineers call this a **runaway system**, which keeps concentrating power until it breaks. (Example: The New York Yankees used their resources to buy more top ballplayers, who won more games, which netted the Yankees even more resources, which enabled them to buy. . . .)

Putin illustrates the runaway-system theory. Gradually and skillfully—never revealing his ultimate intentions—he amassed power, never reaching the point where he had "enough." One indicator: Putin did not leave power in 2008 after his two four-year terms; he made himself prime minister, with power still in his hands. Putin named and supervised a puppet president. Then, after one term, Putin became president again and postponed democracy several more years.

The Two Mafias

Criminal conspiracies (Russians use the loan word *mafiya*) are important interest groups in Russia and have two levels. On the street, strongarm rackets make all businesses pay protection money and make fake deals, enforced by *keelers* and contract hits. At a higher level, *siloviki* connected to and serving the Kremlin run major industries. Anyone in their way or who annoys the regime gets murdered—bankers, reformers, defectors (Alexander Litvinenko, poisoned in London), journalists (including top muckraker Anna Politkovskaya), old people (for their apartments), American businessmen, and Duma members. Most "banks" simply launder money.

perestroika
Russian for "restructuring"; Gorbachev's proposals to reform the Soviet economy.

runaway system
Influential people use their resources to amass more resources.

And no one is brought to justice, indicating that the regime either hires the contract killers or orders the police not to interfere. The FSB could solve such cases but does not. Putin controls the FSB. The hallmark of the developing areas is the penetration of crime into politics. In this respect, Russia has regressed to Third World status.

Russian mafiosi flaunt their new wealth, flashy cars (any make you can name, often stolen), clothes, lady friends, and parties. The average Russian hates those who rapidly enrich themselves as they degrade Russia, and this hatred feeds support for politicians who vow to crack down on them. Thus, lawlessness helped President Putin consolidate his power. Russians have long argued that without strict supervision and draconian controls, they are the most lawless of peoples. Americans, they say, have internal controls that Russians lack. Historically, freedom in Russia meant chaos and bloody anarchy, so Russians welcome a "good tsar" to restore order.

Why Did We Miss It?

The most stupendous change of the late twentieth century took academics, journalists, and intelligence analysts by surprise. Why did we fail to anticipate—notice that I use the word "anticipate" rather than "predict"—the collapse of the Soviet Union? Only a handful of

Personalities

Failed Reformers: Boris Yeltsin

Gorbachev was the first *prezident* (Russians use the loan word) of the Soviet Union. Boris Yeltsin was the first *prezident* of the Russian Federation. As with Gorbachev, both Russians and the world initially hailed Yeltsin as a great reformer who would make a prosperous and peaceful Russia. Both Gorbachev and Yeltsin disappointed with halfway, half-hearted reforms that ruined the economy and their approval ratings. Neither was a convinced democrat; by background and training, both acted like Party big shots. Yeltsin, who resigned the presidency at the end of 1999 and died in 2007, was a gutsy risk taker who put his career and even his life on the line.

Born in 1931 (as was Gorbachev) near Yekaterinburg in the southern Urals to a poor peasant family, Yeltsin studied engineering and worked in the housing industry in his hometown. Joining the Party in 1961 at age 30, Yeltsin was promoted to the Central Committee in 1976. He was noticed as an energetic manager and reformer, and Gorbachev elevated him to head the Moscow Party organization in 1985 and made him a candidate member of the Politburo. A natural populist, Yeltsin, unlike other Soviet leaders, mingled with the people and denounced the privileges of the *nomenklatura*. The common people rallied to him.

In a 1987 speech to the Central Committee, as the Soviet system weakened, Yeltsin attacked Party conservatives by name for dragging their feet on reform. For that, he was relieved of his Party posts and demoted, but he bounced back. In the first partly competitive election in 1989, he ran on his populist credentials and easily won election to parliament, where he criticized Gorbachev for dawdling on reforms. Shifting his attention to the Russian (as opposed to the Soviet) government, Yeltsin won election to the Russian parliament in 1990.

Yeltsin sensed that the Soviet Union was doomed, but Russia would survive. In July 1990, Yeltsin resigned from the CPSU and won fair elections to become president of the Russian Federation in 1991. This gave him another edge on Gorbachev, who had never been popularly elected to anything.

In the attempted coup of 1991, Yeltsin became a hero, standing firm on a tank in front of the Russian parliament. Mocking Gorbachev as an indecisive weakling, Yeltsin pulled the Russian Federation out of the Soviet Union in late 1991, thus collapsing the entire structure. Conservatives think it was a terrible mistake to break up the Soviet Union.

As president, Yeltsin went from bad to worse. Frequently drunk or ill, Yeltsin and his ministers bungled privatization, the economy tanked, corruption soared, and Russians turned bitterly against him. Consulting no one, Yeltsin ordered the crushing of breakaway Chechnya. Although reelected in 1996 as the lesser of two evils, during his last years in office, Yeltsin's public approval rating was under 5 percent. The Duma tried to impeach him but was too divided. One of Yeltsin's favorite stunts was, every few months, to blame his prime ministers for economic failures and replace them. He resigned in shame at the end of 1999 and died in 2007. Some claim that a first president other than Yeltsin might have set up a stable Russia.

historians and economists sounded warnings. A demographer made the most accurate prediction: Years in advance, Nicholas Eberstadt saw overall system decay in the statistical decline of Soviet health. Most political scientists saw more of the same, with some reforms. Beware of making similar mistakes with China.

Why did political scientists miss the signs pointing to collapse? There were several mental blocks that we built for ourselves, mostly by reading each others' books and articles, what intelligence officers call "incestuous amplification."

Comparison

The Timing of Reforms

In addition to cultural factors, the timing or *sequencing* of reforms can make a crucial difference to the successful founding of democracy. The differences in timing between what happened in Central Europe and what happened in Russia are instructive.

First, in Central Europe (Poland, Czechoslovakia, and Hungary), a broad anti-Communist movement formed while the Communists were still in power. By the time liberal Communists held free elections in 1989 or 1990, an aware electorate completely voted the Communists out. It was a new broom sweeping clean. The initial winner was the broad catchall of anti-Communist forces, the leader of which became either the president (Walesa of Poland and Havel of Czechoslovakia) or the prime minister (Antall of Hungary). Later, these catchalls fell apart, but they had done their job: Communism was out, and democracy and market economies were established. In a few years, these countries joined NATO and the EU.

Russia had no nationwide anti-Communist catchall movement like Solidarity or Civic Forum. The Communists never allowed that. Instead, they held semifree elections but did not allow themselves to be voted out of power. Gorbachev, who was never elected to anything, stayed in office believing he was supervising important reforms.

But Gorbachev still faced major conservative (that is, Party) forces and continually changed course in the face of them. Sensing his weakness, Party conservatives attempted to overthrow him. After their defeat, the Party was finally ousted from office (late 1991) but was still influential in parliament, industry, and the countryside. Yeltsin, with no mass movement behind him, attempted serious reform but was still blocked by conservative forces, some of them remnants of the Party.

If Russia had done it like Central Europe, there would have been multiparty elections in late 1991 instead of late 1993. At the earlier date, there might have been sufficient enthusiasm to elect a proreform majority; by the latter date, the declining economy had produced despair and a backlash. This happened in Central Europe as well; in both Poland and Hungary, economic hardship gave electoral wins to their Socialist parties (ex-Communists). But, by then, democracy and a market economy were established. The Socialists accepted the market system and merely made minor adjustments in the "social safety net" of Poland and Hungary.

The desirable sequence, as illustrated by Central Europe: First, form a broad mass movement; second, thoroughly oust the Communists in elections; third, institute political and economic reforms. The Russians tried to do it backward.

1. *Lousy Empirical Data.* Much of the Soviet system was secret; we had to piece together flimsy indicators and infer how the system worked. We filled the informational vacuum with theory, much of it misleading. In Yugoslavia, by way of contrast, scholars could get accurate data and candid interviews. As early as the 1960s, some saw cracks in the Yugoslav federation. Little theory came out of studies of Yugoslavia, as researchers did not need to theorize; they had facts. Lacking facts, Soviet specialists theorized. The moral: We are only as good as our data.

2. *Systems Theory.* Since the 1960s, political scientists had been trained to see all countries as *political systems* that have varying structures but perform the same functions. Whenever the system is thrown off balance, it always corrects itself, by new leaders, parties, or reforms. Systems were presumed to be resilient and durable, possibly immortal. Systems theorists could not imagine system collapse.

3. *Anti-Anticommunism.* The anticommunist hysteria of the early Cold War years, especially McCarthyism, was so primitive that some thinkers gave Communist systems the benefit of the doubt. Specialists tended to accept Communist systems as givens (as did systems theorists) and to conduct detailed studies of how they worked. Anyone who suggested Communist systems were inherently flawed and doomed was read out of the profession as speculative, right wing, and unscholarly.

4. *Undervaluing Economics.* Many Soviet specialists paid little attention to economics; they assumed that politics dominated economics. (Economists assume the opposite.) Few appreciated that a deteriorating economy eventually drags the entire country down with it. Some economists called attention to Soviet economic decline for years.

5. *System Reformability.* Political scientists supposed that Soviet problems could be fixed with reforms. (This, too, derives from systems theory.) If the system has an economic or structural problem, it will correct it, was the bland assumption. Eventually, some thought, the Soviet system would turn into a social democratic welfare state. The brittleness of the Soviet system occurred to few. It was not reformable.

6. *Fixation on Personalities.* Because reforms are necessary, they will be carried out; they just need the right personality. Ah! Here comes Gorbachev, the man both the United States and the Russian liberals have been waiting for. His reforms will produce a democratic Soviet Union. In this way, we read into Gorbachev heroic and reformist qualities he never had.

Transition to What?

Starting in the mid-1970s, democracy replaced dictatorships in Portugal, Spain, and Greece, and then in Latin America, East Asia, and (in late 1989) East Europe, until most of the globe was, to some extent, democratic. Soon, academics developed theories of "transitions to democracy."

But not all transitions led to democracy. Some countries enjoyed only brief democratic interludes—such as Russia and Venezuela—but became unstable or authoritarian with democratic trappings. Samuel Huntington noted that, after every wave of democracy washes in, a reverse wave washes out, as in the rise of the totalitarian dictatorships between the two world

China Lessons

Petrification or Pluralism

Duke University political scientist Jerry Hough argued, in 1972, that the Soviet Union faced a choice between "petrification or pluralism." The Soviet economy and politics were becoming increasingly rigid, he wrote, and could be saved only by loosening up and allowing some pluralist inputs. Hough was right in the short term but wrong in the longer term. The Soviet system had indeed become rigid, but liberalizing it, as Gorbachev attempted in the late 1980s, simply collapsed the system.

The Soviet system was more fragile than most outsiders realized and could not handle Gorbachev's several major reforms at once. Economic reforms should have come decades earlier to produce a large, educated middle class. China, by doing this first, has been ten times more intelligent than the Soviet Union. Although the Chinese Communist Party (CCP) now lets a variety of people join—even capitalists!—it provides for no pluralist input from civil society, such as churches and labor unions. China would be well advised to start allowing civil-society inputs early.

wars. The United States could not get Iraq and Afghanistan to transition to democracy.

The collapsed Soviet system did not transition to democracy. Much of the old system carried over into the new, killing democratic hopes. Culturally, only a minority understood or wanted genuine democracy. Economically, Russia collapsed under Yeltsin; people feared chaos and the breakup of the federation. Putin was the necessary if authoritarian corrective to this slide. If it had not been Putin, it would have been someone worse.

input-output table
Spreadsheet for economy of entire nation.

What Russians Quarrel About

6.5 **Contrast the Russian and Chinese economies.**

The Political Economy of Russia

The Soviet collapse is not merely a historical question. Observers fear that the present Russian system has fallen into similar economic and political stagnation and that what happened then can happen again. Political scientists need to become more aware of the potential for system collapse.

Many Russians refuse to believe that the Soviet Union collapsed largely because of the inherent economic inefficiency of socialism. They blame sinister forces, especially the Americans, the functional equivalent of the "stab in the back" myth that so harmed Weimar Germany. The real explanation is that socialist economies—meaning state-owned and centrally planned, "Communist" if you prefer—work poorly. They do not collapse overnight but slowly run down. Centrally planned economies can grow fast, as did the Soviet Union under the Five-Year Plans. A largely preindustrial country borrowed capitalist technology and threw all its resources, including labor, into giant projects. From the 1930s and into the 1960s, it seemed possible that the Soviet economy could reach U.S. levels.

But as the Soviet Union tried to catch up, its economy became more complex and harder to control. Gosplan's **input-output tables** required hundreds of mathematicians to make the thousands of calculations to set economic targets on a centralized basis. Product quality was poor, as only quantity was calculated and required. Designs, often copied from old Western products, were out of date. Efficiency counted for nothing; there was not even a Russian word for efficiency (the closest was "effective"). Many factories produced things nobody wanted.

The consumer sector, deliberately shortchanged, offered too few products to motivate Soviet workers, who had to wait years for an apartment or a car. Accordingly, workers did not exert themselves but chuckled: "They pretend to pay us, and we pretend to work." Many took afternoons off to shop for scarce goods; standing in lines took hours each week. These and other factors made Soviets angry with the system. During the 1960s, the Soviet economy began to slow, especially in comparison to the surging economies of West Europe and the Pacific Rim. By the 1970s, decay was obvious.

The system, however, could have lumbered on in shabby backwardness. The real killer was technological lag, especially in the Soviet military. Computers were transforming Western businesses, research labs, and military systems. The Soviets fell behind in computerization, and the Soviet military faced obsolescence. U.S. President Ronald Reagan promoted a "Star Wars"

infant mortality rate
Number of live newborns who die in their first year, per thousand; standard measure of nation's health.

shield in space that would make America invulnerable. An important sector of the Soviet military thus turned to economic and technological reform out of the fear of falling behind. Many thinking Soviet Party people, especially younger ones, knew, by the 1980s, that economic reforms were urgent and were eager for someone like Gorbachev. But by themselves, they could not prevail against the conservative forces of managers and *apparatchiki*, many of whose jobs were at stake. It took the high-tech sections of the armed forces to ally themselves with Gorbachev and give the green light to economic reforms to lead to military technology to equal the American threat.

At no time did Mikhail Gorbachev adopt a thoroughgoing plan for economic reform. His advisors presented him with several plans, each bolder than the previous, but he never implemented any. He never wanted capitalism; instead, he sought a middle path or "third way" between capitalism and socialism. Gorbachev hesitated and changed his mind more or less annually, one year for economic reform, the next year against. Later, he admitted several mistakes. First, he later said, he should have liberalized agriculture, as the Chinese did under Deng. Instead, Gorbachev tried a couple of timid steps that he inherited from his mentor, the late Andropov: "intensification" and an antialcohol campaign. Both failed.

When it came to real reforms, Gorbachev choked, both out of fear of the consequences and in the face of massive resistance by conservative Soviet forces. Gorbachev finally freed most prices but did not privatize industry, resulting in too many rubles chasing too few goods: inflation. Everyone wanted dollars as the ruble dwindled in value. Worried citizens feared bottomless economic decline. Against this background, Gorbachev's own cabinet plotted a coup in 1991. Before the year ended, the Soviet Union was dissolved, Gorbachev was a private citizen, and Yeltsin was president of a new Russian Federation. At last, reform started looking serious, but Yeltsin, too, faced opposition from conservative forces.

Geography

Running Out of Russians

Almost all industrialized countries produce few babies, but Russia is in serious demographic decline. In 1989, before the Soviet collapse, an average Soviet woman (many non-Russian) bore 2.17 children. Now, an average Russian woman bears only 1.6 children (up from 1.2 a few years before), still a low fertility rate, which is not the same as the birthrate, a different measure (number of births per 1,000 population). Putin tried to remedy this with financial incentives for more babies, but Russian families still tend to have only one child.

In Russia, declining health standards raised the **infant mortality rate**, but, lately, it has improved to 7 per 1,000 live births, still worse than West Europe. During the 1990s, expectant mothers were poorly nourished and so were their babies. The Russian death rate climbed; life expectancy of adult men dropped to 60 years, lower than in many developing countries. Result: Russia's population shrinks by several hundred thousand a year. In 2006, Putin called demography "Russia's most acute problem today."

HIV/AIDS is strong in Russia. Alcohol consumption (some of it poisonous home brew) is prodigious, killing tens of thousands of Russians a year. Russian environmental poisoning, both chemical and nuclear, is among the world's worst, and environmentally caused diseases are common. (Russia's closest rival: China.) Many factories just dump toxic and nuclear wastes into shallow landfills. The air in Russia's industrial cities is dangerous. "To live longer," said one official, "we should breathe less."

Geography

Yugoslavia: A Miniature Soviet Union?

The former multiethnic Balkan federal system of Yugoslavia resembled the ex-Soviet Union. Both countries had a Slavic core nationality: Russian in the Soviet Union and Serb in Yugoslavia. Serbs and Russians are both Eastern Orthodox Christians and use the Cyrillic alphabet. Both defined themselves as the founders and guarantors of their respective nations and regarded breakaway republics as traitors.

The other nationalities resented this overbearing attitude. In each country, an advanced northwest (the Baltic republics in the Soviet Union and Slovenia in Yugoslavia) grew tired of being held back by the less-developed core nationality, which economically drained the advanced area. Interestingly, the Baltics and Slovenia declared their independence first.

The second-largest nationality in each country was also Slavic, but with a distinctive culture and resentments against being bossed by the center; thus, Ukraine and Croatia quickly broke away. In the south, feisty Muslim nationalities demanded greater autonomy

and fought neighboring Christian nationalities (the Azeris against the Armenians and the Bosnian Muslims and Kosovar Albanians against the Serbs). In most of the newly independent republics in both the ex-Soviet Union and ex-Yugoslavia, the "new" leaders had been local Communist bosses prior to independence.

A final touch: Russians and Serbs, respectively, formed the bulk of the officer corps of the old Soviet and Yugoslav armies. They were conservative, dedicated to keeping their countries intact, and not adverse to using force to do so. In 1991, both armies started intervening directly in politics. The key difference is that conservative Communists took over in Belgrade and, with the army's generals in agreement, attempted to hold Yugoslavia together by force. When that quickly failed, they turned to building a Greater Serbia by military conquest, coupled with "ethnic cleansing." In the ex-Soviet Union, the death toll was not as large, but it, too, experienced wars in the Caucasus region, which could return.

The Rubble of the Ruble

The Russian economy, unlike China's, is unimpressive. Russia's dangerous dependency on oil and natural gas exports puts it on a roller coaster: down in the 1990s, up at the turn of the century, down sharply in the 2008–2009 recession, booming in the mid-2000s, then slow in the 2010s. When oil is high, Russia acts rich, but its income goes mostly to Kremlin cronies who control state-related industries. In the good years, Moscow has budget surpluses and cash reserves, and money trickles down to make most Russians content with the economy and the government. In the bad years, budgets shrink and Russians get angry. Aside from energy and mineral exports, Russia produces little else. Government subsidies prop up inefficient Soviet-era industries that cannot compete with other lands' manufactured goods. Productivity and investment are weak because entrepreneurs fear seizure of their property and imprisonment for "tax evasion." Better to take your capital and go abroad.

Russia is another example of the "oil curse" seen in Mexico and Nigeria. Russia could have had stable, diversified growth if Gorbachev and Yeltsin had seriously restructured the Soviet/ Russian economy, but they stayed on the path of energy and mineral exports. Poland initiated a *shock therapy* at the beginning of 1991 and, in two years, had overcome inflation and industrial decline to enjoy rapid growth.

Yeltsin's first prime minister (until late 1992) and later finance minister, the dynamic reformer Yegor Gaidar, tried shock therapy when he privatized the large, obsolete Communist

asset stripping
Selling off firm's property and raw materials for short-term profit.

public finances
What a government takes in, what it spends, and how it makes up the difference.

flight capital
Money that the owner sends out of the country for fear of losing it.

hard currency
Noninflating, recognized currencies used in international dealings, such as dollars and euros.

default
Country announces that it cannot pay back a loan.

industrial enterprises. Inefficient and overstaffed and with no concern for consumers, many Soviet plants actually *subtracted* value from the raw materials they processed. But these industries were the wealth and power of the bureaucrats who ran them and gave employment to those who listlessly worked in them. Accordingly, the industries pressured Moscow to keep the subsidies flowing. In any rational system, they would have been declared bankrupt. But you cannot throw millions of people out of work all at once, protested many Russians.

A handful of clever operators bought up factories and raw materials cheap and turned themselves into a new class of capitalists. Many of these industries still got government subsidies (such as cheap energy), which gave the new owners enormous profits for exported oil and minerals. Much of the profit did not return to Russia but went into foreign banks, a pattern typical of South America. Because this capital was not recycled back into the Russian economy, the rest of the economy declined, making poor people poorer. Capitalism in Russia began as **asset stripping**, which is no basis for long-term growth.

In August 1998, the dysfunctional economy crashed. **Public finances** lagged. Russia was collecting less than half the taxes it was supposed to—everyone cheated on taxes—and the budget went dangerously into deficit, so the Yeltsin government simply printed more money. Banks—and anyone in Russia could open a bank—were unregulated and made unsecured loans to friends. The chief monetary instrument of Russian banks was U.S. $100 bills, some of them counterfeit. Knowing the perils of keeping money in Russia, many stash billions in **flight capital** offshore (possibly $200 billion in 2014). When the system crashed in 1998, the ruble lost three-quarters of its value in relation to **hard currencies**. Many banks closed, leaving depositors with nothing. Russia's fledgling stock markets dived. Some industries collapsed. Russia **defaulted** on its loans (biggest losers: German banks, who lent more than $30 billion to Russia) and had to beg for new credit. Badly burned, foreign investors fled Russia.

Russians felt angry and betrayed. The Americans had told them that the free market is the path to prosperity, but it brought only misery. A third of Russians fell below the official (very low) poverty line. Actually, Russia had never fully implemented a market system. Much Western advice was ignored. Most of the $66 billion in Western aid disappeared. There were too many government subsidies and tax breaks, and too few rules and regulations that keep a market economy steady. Money, always a weak point with Russians, was just something you printed. In the words of one Russian reformer, it was "the most expensive economic education in history."

Before the 1998 collapse, some people got rich fast while many went hungry. Having long been taught by the Communists that material equality is good and just, Russians witnessed the explosive growth of inequality. Some *biznesmeny* and mafiosi (the two words are linked in the Russian mind) enjoyed new wealth while most Russians lived worse than ever.

Initially, some good emerged from the rubble of the ruble. Fake businesses collapsed, and entrepreneurs started investing their profits in Russia. In the years of high oil prices, Russia's economy grew by several percent a year. Russia's trade balance was very positive, the federal budget enjoyed surpluses, and inflation eased from 80 percent in 1998 to a few percent. Putin's

Geography

Putin and Geopolitics

Russians are unhappy and fearful because their former Central European satellites (Poland, the Czech Republic, Hungary) joined NATO in 1999 and the former Soviet republics of Lithuania, Latvia, and Estonia joined NATO in 2004, along with Bulgaria, Romania, Slovakia, and Slovenia. NATO, the Cold War enemy, has taken over Russia's former security belt. No Russian likes this, and Putin tries to counter it.

Putin, in many respects a tsarist figure, practices the Kremlin's traditional **geopolitics**. Territory, in this nineteenth-century view, equals security (not necessarily true). Starting under the tsars but reemphasized by Stalin, it became an article of Kremlin faith that Russia needed a defensive belt against invasions by Teutonic Knights, Swedes, Napoleon, Imperial Germany, and Nazi Germany. After World War II, Moscow organized East Europe as the *Warsaw Pact*, a shield against NATO. To keep the shield, Khrushchev crushed the 1956 Hungarian uprising, and Brezhnev crushed the 1968 Prague Spring. Both nearly invaded Poland.

But East Europe was an economic and military drain on the Soviet Union and blocked improved relations with the West. By 1989, Gorbachev had decided to no longer support the Communist regimes of East Europe; they fell. In a few years, all these lands joined NATO. Some critics say NATO's eastward expansion caused Russian hostility, for the Kremlin was bound to take it as a threat. When Georgia and Ukraine moved to join NATO, Putin stopped them, and most Russians, in fear of invasion from the West, cheered. We must ask whether Putin's policy was a reasonable defensive move or an exaggerated aggressive move.

---

reforms of taxes, banks, and land sales promoted growth. Hourly wages grew twelvefold—from less than half a dollar to more than $12—from 1999 to 2012. Said Putin in 2002: "Our economy must grow much faster" (Stalin said the same in 1931), and Putin largely delivered.

geopolitics
Influence of geography on politics and use of geography for strategic ends.

But some of Putin's policies worked against rational, long-term economic growth. He seized the properties of oligarchs he disliked, such as Khodorkovsky, and of foreign investors, giving the entire Russian oil and gas industry to *siloviki*, who both serve the Kremlin and get rich. Seeing Kremlin friends take over major firms persuaded capitalists, both foreign and domestic, to not invest, stunting Russian growth. Why develop a business if it will be taken from you?

Recover the Lost Republics?

Putin described the breakup of the Soviet Union as "the greatest geopolitical catastrophe of the century" and worried that the "epidemic of collapse has spilled over into Russia itself." Most Russians agreed. Russians call the non-Russian republics that departed from the Soviet Union in 1991 the "near abroad." Most of them had been part of the tsarist empire, and many Russians still think of them as belonging to Russia. Some want to restore the Russian empire, especially the Russian army, which still has troops in most of the ex-Soviet republics.

In many ex-Soviet republics, the "new" leaders are old Party big shots whose corrupt and authoritarian rule continues. One crucial factor in Russian thinking concerns the 25 million ethnic Russians who live in the near abroad. (The term does not refer to the former East European satellites such as Poland and Hungary.) Some Russians in these newly independent countries feel threatened. Moscow claims the right and duty to rescue them by military means. Putin

Geography

Trouble in the North Caucasus

Violence is ongoing in Russia's **North Caucasus** despite—or maybe because of—Moscow's bloody efforts to tame it. The poor, angry region is a long-term Russian problem. Like all mountainous regions, it is hard to control and enables small ethnic and religious groups to keep distinct cultures and resist outside rule. The rugged region—home to more than six million people divided into 40 ethnic groups—is mostly Muslim. Stalin consolidated the largest of them into their current borders. From west to east, they are Karachayevo-Cherkessia, Kabardino-Balkaria, North Ossetia, Ingushetia, Chechnya, and Dagestan.

The tsarist army subdued the region in the early nineteenth century. Tolstoy wrote that the conquest created something "stronger than hatred, for [the Chechens] did not regard those Russian dogs as human beings." Emblematic was the tsarist fortress built in 1784: Vladikavkaz (Master of the Caucasus), now the capital of North Ossetia. The locals despised Russian rule, and Russians despised them as bandits. In 1944, Stalin accused several Caucasian nationalities of collaborating with the German invaders and brutally exiled entire ethnic groups to Central Asia.

Decades later, a Chechen, Jokar Dudayev, became a general in the Soviet air force. Assigned to an Estonian airbase in the 1980s, Dudayev sympathized with the Estonians, who, like Chechens, hated Russian rule. Dudayev blocked the landing of Soviet troops in early 1991, helping Estonia win independence. He then retired, won an election in Chechnya, and proclaimed its independence as the Soviet Union broke up in late 1991. But Chechnya, unlike Estonia, had never been a "union republic"; it was part of the Russian Federation, and Moscow feared unrest spreading to all the North Caucasus.

Yeltsin, in late 1994, gave the order to quickly crush Chechen independence, but the Russian army was pathetic, and Chechens fought boldly and tenaciously. Some 80,000, mostly civilians, were killed, and the capital, Grozny, was shelled into ruin. Most Russians, even military officers, hated the war; partly because of it, Yeltsin's popularity plummeted. After a shaky peace in 1996, war reignited in 1999. Russians bloodily occupied Chechnya and installed an ex-rebel as puppet chief. News coverage is blocked out; those bold enough to report the horrors are assassinated.

The problem is bigger than Chechnya. Heavy-handed repression by Russian security forces throughout the North Caucasus deepens ethnic hatreds, turning many into Islamist extremists, some of whom talk of a North Caucasus *caliphate*. Suicide bombings are common, and security forces retaliate brutally. "We showed weakness, and the weak are trampled upon," said Putin, echoing Stalin. After the 2013 Boston bombing by ethnic Chechens, Putin could in effect say, "Now do you see what we face?" Some fear the unravelling not only of the North Caucasus but of the whole Russian Federation.

North Caucasus
Mountainous region north of Georgia and Azerbaijan, including Chechnya.

now looks like he is using this as an excuse to seize all or part of the near abroad.

Recovery of the lost republics could come about by more-subtle means: economics. As the economies of other republics plunged downward, some turned desperately to Moscow for help. Under the banner of the Commonwealth of Independent States, Moscow delivers some aid (for example, a good deal on oil and natural gas) but, in return, gets trade concessions and general obedience. Moscow successfully used this approach on Belarus—which now uses the Russian ruble as its currency—and sometimes interrupts the flow of natural gas to Ukraine.

In Georgia and Ukraine, Putin used military power. The Muslim Abkhazians of western Georgia broke away by force of arms, many supplied quietly by the Russian army. Georgia had originally refused to join the CIS in 1991 but, faced with military defeat, did so in 1994. In 2008,

Georgian forces attempted to reassert control over breakaway South Ossetia, but Russian forces smashed them back. Moscow claimed it was protecting human rights and local desires for independence from Georgia, but it was actually warning Georgia to not join NATO.

middle way
Supposed blend of capitalism and socialism; also called "third way."

In 2014, the corrupt Ukrainian regime was overthrown by street protesters demanding to realign with the EU and NATO. Putin was enraged; for him, Ukraine is still a Russian province and should bow to Moscow. Khrushchev had transferred Crimea to Ukraine in 1954, but it is still home to the Russian Black Sea fleet. Putin infiltrated soldiers and annexed Crimea. He then aided Russian-speaking separatists to break away from Ukraine. Basically, Putin won; Ukraine was too weak, and the West had no practical way to counter Putin, who threatened to "protect" other Russian-speakers in the ex-Soviet republics. A new cold war threatened.

Should the West oppose him? Military confrontation could result if Putin targets NATO members Lithuania, Latvia, and Estonia. Moscow used economic bribes, threats, and armed infiltrators to recoup the near abroad. Gazprom, 51 percent owned and totally controlled by the government,

Comparison

A Middle Way for Socialism?

Confusion surrounds the term *socialism*. Many Russians and East Europeans now tell you that they no longer know what the word means. Some call the welfare states of Scandinavia "socialist" because freely elected social democratic governments have gradually introduced elaborate medical, unemployment, educational, housing, and other programs to lift up the lower rungs of society: cradle-to-grave welfare. These social democratic or labor parties started out Marxist, but all of them shed it. They are all based on large labor union federations and aim to wipe out poverty without coercion or state ownership.

And here is where Scandinavian *welfarism* differs sharply from communist-style socialism. The Scandinavian lands have little nationalized industry. The bulk of the economy is private and capitalist. Swedish managers especially developed a ferocious reputation for efficient, money-making plant operation. Taxes, to be sure, are high, but the economy is otherwise free. Scandinavia's welfarism was developed after and on top of a capitalist industrial base. First came capitalism; then came welfare. It is doubtful if the order can be reversed or if they can be built simultaneously.

No one has yet found a way to combine capitalism and socialism on a long-term, stable basis. For a while, such a combination seems to work, but soon the private sector bumps into the restricted, slow-moving state sector. The private sector needs raw materials, labor, infrastructure, and transportation on a flexible, ever-changing basis. The state sector, still run by a central plan, cannot possibly deliver and has no incentive to. If you have state enterprises join the private-sector market, you gradually desocialize the economy. It gets more efficient but less socialist. Eventually, you must either bury the socialist sector as a bad experiment or recontrol the private sector. The mix will not hold steady; you must go one way or the other. China faces this choice.

Putin's ultimate problem—inherited from his predecessors—was that he thought there was a **middle way** between a centrally planned socialist economy and a free-market economy. Reforms, some argue, can blend a market economy with a socialist economy. Some Russians still think that the state can keep the "commanding heights" of heavy industry while permitting small enterprises to operate in a free market. This is what Lenin did with the NEP in the early 1920s, a model mentioned by Gorbachevites. But the NEP was inherently flawed and was running down in the late 1920s when Stalin dropped it in favor of forced industrialization. Many Russians, including Putin, still suppose they can find a middle way that is uniquely Russian. Experience suggests that middle ways lead to unstable, inflationary systems.

current account balance
A country's exports minus its imports.

sold natural gas cheap to those ex-Soviet states that stayed loyal. Those who turned westward saw prices double. The move into Ukraine underscored Putin's Soviet-era mentality—some say tsarist-era—and alarmed Europe, which gets much of its natural gas from Russia.

Which Way Russia?

Many observers of the Russian economy see a botched job. Free-market capitalism has not taken root. Oligarchs looted state enterprises and stashed the money abroad; then Putin stole it back. The oil and gas industries have returned to state control. After an initial flurry of foreign investment in the 1990s, investors learned that *siloviki* tied to the Kremlin run most large enterprises and block competition. Most foreign investors pulled out, and few now try to enter the Russian market. Corruption and lawlessness link authorities (including the police) and mafias. There are, to be sure, some good signs. Part of Russia's economy is private and, after the collapse of 1998, grew. Inflation dropped, and **current account balances** are positive, thanks to oil exports. Health and economic indicators have improved.

Which way will Russia face, east or west? Moscow is frosty toward Washington—Putin compared U.S. policies to the Third Reich—while it builds ties to Beijing. Unfortunately, in some ways, Russia and China are natural allies, both nurturing grudges against the West and with complementary economies, Russian raw materials traded for Chinese manufactured goods. In the long run, to be sure, Russia may not want to serve as junior partner and raw materials supplier to China. The last thing the United States needs is another Sino-Russian bloc and a new cold war. Russia is a problem, a huge angry country that feels it has been humiliated. Moscow's message: "Treat us with respect and keep out of our affairs!" A country that alters borders by military force, however, is bound to create a hostile environment.

Clearly, Russia is no democracy. Freedom House demoted Russia from "partly free" to "not free," closer to dictatorship than to democracy. Can Russians eventually govern themselves in a moderate, democratic fashion? I think they can, but it will take many years. There is nothing genetically authoritarian about Russians. In the twentieth century, Germans and Spaniards were deemed unfit for responsible self-government, but now they are practicing democracy as well as any Europeans. Which path Russia takes—toward peace and democracy or toward expansion and autocracy—will form much of this century's political developments.

Review Questions

Learning Objective 6.1 Explain how Russia's geographical location governed its political development, p. 221.

1. How has religion contributed to Russia's isolation?
2. Explain Russian *autocracy*. Is it still practiced today?
3. Explain how Marxism came to Russia.

Learning Objective 6.2 Compare and contrast the Soviet system with the new Russian system, p. 231.

4. How much of the old Stalin system lingers in Russia today?
5. Will Putin be in power essentially as long as he wants?
6. What points indicate that Russia is not a democracy?

Learning Objective 6.3 **Illustrate how "civil society" underpins democracy, p. 241.**

7. How could the ex-Communist regimes of Central Europe quickly become democratic, but not Russia?

8. Argue that Russia was psychologically unprepared for democracy.

9. How did the 2014 Ukraine crisis strengthen Putin?

Learning Objective 6.4 **Explain why reforming Russia is a recurrent problem, p. 253.**

10. What is the difference between *totalitarian* and *authoritarian*?

11. Contrast Russia's *oligarchs* with America's big capitalists.

12. Why did Western observers not see the Soviet collapse coming?

Learning Objective 6.5 **Contrast the Russian and Chinese economies, p. 261.**

13. Could the right reforms have saved the Soviet economy? Why weren't they made?

14. What could China learn from the Soviet collapse? Or have they learned it?

15. Argue that Putin is attempting to reassemble the old Soviet Union.

Key Terms

anarchism, p. 226
apparatchik, p. 232
asset stripping, p. 264
authoritarianism, p. 255
autocracy, p. 223
Bolshevik, p. 226
caesaropapism, p. 223
capital goods, p. 230
Caucasus, p. 249
Central Asia, p. 249
Central Committee, p. 232
civil society, p. 246
Cold War, p. 230
communism, p. 226
Constantinople, p. 221
consumer goods, p. 230
contradiction, p. 247
CPSU, p. 229
cult of personality, p. 252
current account balance, p. 268
Cyrillic, p. 221
default, p. 264
Duma, p. 227

exclave, p. 223
Five-Year Plans, p. 230
flight capital, p. 264
gensek, p. 229
geopolitics, p. 265
glasnost, p. 244
Gosplan, p. 234
Gulag, p. 234
hard currency, p. 264
imperialism, p. 225
infant mortality rate, p. 262
input-output table, p. 261
kleptocracy, p. 242
middle way, p. 267
Narodniki, p. 226
New Economic Policy (NEP),
   p. 230
nomenklatura, p. 234
North Caucasus, p. 266
oligarchy, p. 242
paranoia, p. 229
perestroika, p. 256
Politburo, p. 232

proletariat, p. 226
public finances, p. 264
purge, p. 229
republic, p. 232
rump state, p. 243
runaway system, p. 257
shock therapy, p. 253
socialize, p. 246
Siberia, p. 221
siloviki, p. 234
Slavophiles, p. 224
State Duma, p. 238
Tatar, p. 222
totalitarianism, p. 255
tsar, p. 223
tyranny, p. 221
Ukraine, p. 222
war communism, p. 230
weak state, p. 231
Westernizers, p. 224
zemstvo, p. 224

Further Reference

Aron, Leon. *Russia's Revolution: Essays, 1989–2006.* Washington, DC: AEI Press, 2007.

Åslund, Anders, and Andrew Kuchins. *Russia: The Balance Sheet.* Washington, DC: Peterson Institute, 2009.

Brent, Jonathan. *Inside the Stalin Archives: Discovering the New Russia.* New York: Atlas, 2008.

Brown, Archie. *The Rise and Fall of Communism.* New York: HarperCollins, 2009.

Cohen, Stephen F. *Soviet Fates and Lost Alternatives: From Stalinism to the New Cold War.* New York: Columbia University Press, 2009.

Colton, Timothy J. *Yeltsin: A Life.* New York: Basic Books, 2011.

de Waal, Thomas. *The Caucasus: An Introduction.* New York: Oxford University Press, 2010.

Feifer, Gregory. *Russians: The People behind the Power.* New York: Hachette, 2014.

Figes, Orlando. *Revolutionary Russia, 1891–1991: A History.* New York: Metropolitan, 2014.

Gaidar, Yegor. *Russia: A Long View.* Cambridge, MA: MIT Press, 2012.

Gessen, Masha. *The Man without a Face: The Unlikely Rise of Vladimir Putin.* New York: Penguin, 2013.

Goldman, Marshall I. *Petrostate: Putin, Power, and the New Russia.* New York: Oxford University Press, 2008.

Hill, Fiona, and Clifford G. Gaddy. *Mr. Putin: Operative in the Kremlin.* Washington, DC: Brookings, 2013.

Hughes, James. *Chechnya: From Nationalism to Jihad.* Philadelphia: University of Pennsylvania Press, 2007.

Judah, Ben. *Fragile Empire: How Russia Fell In and Out of Love with Vladimir Putin.* New Haven, CT: Yale University Press, 2013.

Ledeneva, Alena V. *Can Russia Modernise? Sistema, Power Networks and Informal Governance.* New York: Cambridge University Press, 2013.

Naimark, Norman M. *Stalin's Genocides.* Princeton, NJ: Princeton University Press, 2010.

Panyushkin, Valery. *12 Who Don't Agree: The Battle for Freedom in Putin's Russia.* New York: Europa, 2011.

Plokhy, Serhii. *The Last Empire: The Final Days of the Soviet Union.* New York: Basic, 2014.

Politkovskaya, Anna. *A Russian Diary: A Journalist's Final Account of Life, Corruption, and Death in Putin's Russia.* New York: Random House, 2007.

Pomper, Philip. *Lenin's Brother: The Origins of the October Revolution.* New York: Norton, 2010.

Remington, Thomas F. *Politics in Russia,* 7th ed. New York: Longman, 2012.

Richards, Susan. *Lost and Found in Russia.* New York: Other Press, 2010.

Roxburgh, Angus. *The Strongman: Vladimir Putin and the Struggle for Russia.* London: I. B. Tauris, 2014.

Shevtsova, Lilia, and Andrew Wood. *Change or Decay: Russia's Dilemma and the West's Response.* Washington, DC: Carnegie Endowment, 2011.

Soldatov, Andrei, and Irina Borogan. *The New Nobility: Russia's Security State and the Enduring Legacy of the KGB.* New York: PublicAffairs, 2010.

Solzhenitsyn, Aleksandr, ed. *Voices from the Gulag.* Evanston, IL: Northwestern University Press, 2010.

Zubok, Vladislav. *Zhivago's Children: The Last Russian Intelligentsia.* Cambridge, MA: Harvard University Press, 2009.

Zimmerman, William. *Ruling Russia: Authoritarianism From the Revolution to Putin.* Princeton, NJ: Princeton University Press, 2014.

Chapter 7
China

Dramatic karsts draw tourists to South China's Guangxi province.

 Learning Objectives

7.1 Describe China's "bureaucratic empire" and how it compares with Europe's political development.

7.2 Outline the main points of China's current political model.

7.3 Identify the main sources of discontent in today's China.

7.4 Compare and contrast China's Great Leap Forward and its Cultural Revolution.

7.5 Explain why Beijing wants to "rebalance" China's economy.

WHY CHINA MATTERS

The Soviet lurch to democracy is a model for doing everything wrong. Can China do it better? Its economic growth has been amazing, but no one can be sure how China will end up. For some three decades, the assumption has been that its market economy will eventually pull China into democracy. The Beijing regime says that will not happen and is vigilant to suppress any movement it does not control. Beijing has built a distinctive "Chinese model" that combines one-party political control with a semifree economy that makes most urban Chinese content with their new material possessions. Can this system last over the long term? Even more worrisome is the strong Chinese nationalism—in part deep and genuine, in part hyped by the regime—that claims most of the East and South China Seas. If China's economic growth slows, will the regime deflect domestic discontent with nationalism? There are risks in any transition to democracy, but China could, if the regime were not so frightened, become democratic sooner than Russia. More likely, however, is that Beijing will not budge until it is too late.

Impact of the Past

7.1   Describe China's "bureaucratic empire" and how it compares with Europe's political development.

China is big, but only one-third of it is arable, growing rice in the well-watered south and wheat in the drier north. China now has less than a quarter acre of farmland (and currently shrinking) for each Chinese, and this has long imposed limits on politics, economics, and social thought.

Rice cultivation, for example, uses much water and labor to get major crops (two and even three times a year in South China) from small plots. This labor-intensive farming, until recently, meant that most Chinese stayed peasants and encouraged strong family organization and obedient, cooperative behavior. It also meant that a central authority controlled water canals and determined who got how much water. Irrigation helps explain why Mesopotamia, Egypt, and China produced history's first kingdoms and empires.

The Bureaucratic Empire

China, in sharp contrast to Europe, unified and ended feudalism very early, becoming a bureaucratic empire. During the Bronze Age, small but rather advanced kingdoms (about at the level of ancient Greece) appeared along the Yellow River—the Xia around 2000 BC, the Shang around 1600 BC, and the Zhou around 1045 BC. (Confucius was a public official and philosopher of the late Zhou kingdom.) After the Spring and Autumn Period and Warring States, times of many kingdoms and warfare from 771 BC to 221 BC, the short-lived Qin dynasty (earlier spelled Ch'in, origin of the Western name for China) unified the first Chinese empire, the **Middle Kingdom** (*Zhōngguó*).

Middle Kingdom
China's traditional and current name for itself, "in the middle of the heavens" (translation of *Zhōngguó*).

Han
Early dynasty, 206 BC to 220 AD, that solidified China's unity and culture. Ethnic meaning: main people of China.

Mandarin
High civil servant of imperial China; now main language of China.

The next dynasty, the **Han** (206 BC to 220 AD), developed Confucianism into a bureaucratic empire that replaced the old aristocratic families with a **Mandarin** class impartially selected by examination in classic texts, which stressed obedience, authority, and hierarchy.

Geography

Bound China

China is bounded on the north by Kazakhstan, Russia, and Mongolia;

on the east by Korea and the Yellow, East China, and South China Seas;

on the south by Vietnam, Laos, Myanmar (formerly Burma), India, Bhutan, and Nepal;

and on the west by Pakistan, Afghanistan (minutely), Tajikistan, and Kyrgyzstan.

By knowing China's boundaries, you can label most of mainland Asia. Only Cambodia, Thailand, and Bangladesh do not border China.

China

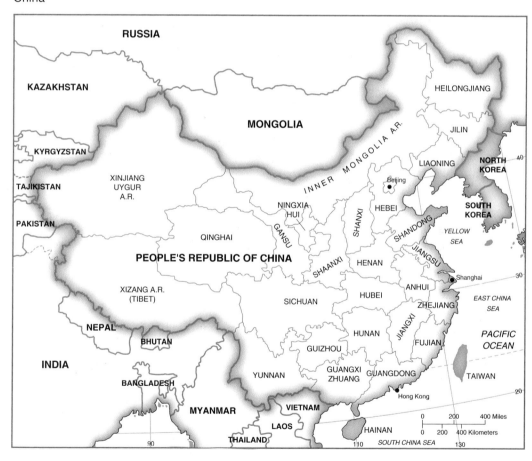

A gentry class of better-off people were literate intermediaries between the Mandarins and the 90 percent of the population that were peasants.

China and Rome invite comparison. Both arose and achieved their greatest glory at about the same time. At their peaks, they were about the same size. The two empires knew of each

dynastic cycle
Rise, maturity, and fall of an imperial family.

Mandate of Heaven
Old Chinese expression for legitimacy.

Mongol
Central Asian tribes combined by Genghis Khan; ruled China as the Yuan dynasty in the thirteenth and fourteenth centuries.

Manchu
Last imperial dynasty of China, 1644–1912; also known as *Qing*.

steady-state
A system that preserves itself with little change.

other and traded a little via the Silk Road and by sea. Both achieved high civilizations in terms of art, architecture, administration, commerce, and writing. But there are many contrasts. In the first century AD, Buddhism arrived in China from India but never established itself as a state religion before it faded. Rome eventually accepted Christianity, which became Europe's unifying culture. Rome kept expanding until it overexpanded and fell to barbarians. China was not keen on expansion but tried to keep out barbarians with a Great Wall. (Only the last dynasty, the non-Chinese Manchus, annexed Taiwan, Tibet, Mongolia, and Xinjiang in the late seventeenth and eighteenth centuries—before the Dutch, British, or Russians could grab them.) The Roman economy was based on slaves, and China's on peasants, giving China more stability. The Han developed paper, silk, the compass, and the rudder, putting them ahead of Rome in technology.

The chief difference is what the two empires left behind. When the Western part of the Roman Empire fell to barbarians in 476 AD, it fragmented into separate states and stayed that way. After the Han, China, too, suffered periods of fragmentation and chaos, but during their four centuries, the Han implanted a culture so deep that later dynasties used it to put China back together. Chinese intellectuals always insisted that China was one entity; China broken into separate kingdoms always seemed wrong. China, it has been said, is not a country but a civilization with 4,000 years of cultural continuity.

Dynasties rose and fell every few hundred years in a **dynastic cycle**. As the old dynasty became increasingly incompetent, water systems were not repaired; famine, wars, and banditry appeared; and corruption and palace conspiracies grew. As more influential families got their lands exempted from taxation, peasants had to pay heavier taxes, until they revolted. The emperor seemed to lose the **Mandate of Heaven**—that is, his legitimate right to rule. A conqueror, either Chinese or foreign (**Mongol** or **Manchu**), then took over a delegitimized empire and exercised a new Mandate of Heaven, restoring administration and taxation. After some generations, though, the new dynasty fell prey to the old ills, and Chinese, especially the literate, began think the emperor had lost his heavenly mandate, and the cycle started over.

Two millennia of bureaucratic empire still mark China. Not a feudal system like Japan, China unified and centralized early. An emperor at the top set the direction and tone, Mandarins carried out the emperor's writ, and gentry ran local affairs. For centuries, China was the world's greatest civilization and biggest economy, far ahead of Europe. By around 1500, however, Europe began surging ahead, eventually surpassing China. One factor: China was one state when Europe was many states. Europe's monarchs competed for wealth, power, and new territories, whereas huge, unified China faced no competition. Soon, expansionist European empires controlled much of the world. Chinese today know that China was a great civilization, one humiliated by the West.

With little new territory to expand into, Chinese society evolved **steady-state** structures aimed at stability. Labor-saving devices would render peasants jobless and were not encouraged. China's achievements in science and technology did not contribute to an industrial revolution. Commercial expansion was discouraged. Instead of a Western mentality of reinvestment, growth, and risk taking, Chinese merchants sought a steady-state relationship with peasants and officials; they depended heavily on government permits, monopolies, and set prices.

Except for Buddhism from India, China took little interest in anything foreign. The Middle Kingdom was surrounded by barbarians who were walled out or awed. Chinese culture could uplift the near barbarians (Koreans and Vietnamese), who could then **kow-tow** and pay tribute to the emperor. This *tributary system* was quite different from the diplomacy developed in Europe, where other lands were sovereign and treated diplomatically as equals. For China, other lands should simply pay tribute.

kow-tow
Literally, "head to the ground"; to kneel and bow deeply.

Confucianism
Chinese philosophy of social and political stability based on family, hierarchy, and manners.

Political Culture

Confucianism: Government by Right Thinking

Confucianism is not a religion but a philosophy of governance. The scholar Confucius (551–479 BC) advised rulers that good, stable government resulted from correct, moral behavior in ruled and rulers alike. People can be improved, but they must understand their roles and perform them obediently. Sons must be subservient to fathers, wives to husbands, younger brothers to elder brothers, and subjects to rulers. The ruler sets a moral example. Pure spirit and careful manners create a conservative political culture more effective and durable than mere laws.

Confucianism emphasized that good government—the very idea of which was a Confucian invention—starts with thinking correct thoughts in utter sincerity. If things go wrong, it indicates rulers have been insincere. The system did not depend on Confucianism alone; it also had strong police controls that permitted no dissent. Mao Zedong disdained old China, but he adapted Confucianism's stress on right thinking with a Marxist twist that one was a proletarian not because of working-class origin but because one had revolutionary, pure thoughts.

Curiously, Confucianism survives more in Japan than in China, often the case of ideologies transplanted from their country of origin. Japanese are still inculcated with politeness and decorum, bowing and obedience. Such behaviors have largely disappeared in China, the result of more than a century of revolution

Confucius is buried in his home town, Qufu, Shandong Province, now a pilgrimage site.

and war. Mao Zedong tried to finish off Confucianism with his "destroy the four olds" campaign, part of the Cultural Revolution of the late 1960s. Now Beijing is refurbishing Confucianism as a tool of social control. Some propose making it China's official religion.

Ming
Chinese dynasty between
Mongols and Manchus,
1368–1644.

pinyin
Literally, "spell sound"; current
system of transliterating
Chinese.

China's superiority complex poorly equipped it to handle European penetration.

China was centuries ahead of Europe in naval technology, including the compass and watertight compartments. From 1405 to 1433, the **Mings** sent huge naval expeditions under Admiral Zheng He, a Muslim eunuch (common among court officials), all around the Indian Ocean. If the Chinese fleets had rounded Africa or crossed the Pacific, China would have discovered Europe and the Americas. But Ming officials decided that the expeditions were too costly and China had everything it needed. For centuries, China mostly stayed home.

Political Culture

Chinese Words in Roman Letters

In contrast to Western alphabetic writing systems, China, starting nearly 4,000 years ago, developed an ideographic system based on symbolic word pictures, a system copied and modified by Korea, Vietnam, and Japan. Literacy involves memorizing thousands of characters, much harder than Western phonetic systems. The characters are politically useful, however, precisely because they do not represent specific sounds. People speaking very different languages—the Wu and Cantonese of South China or even Japanese—can read the same newspaper. This was a great help in unifying China, which is still a country of many different languages. An official did not need to speak the emperor's language in order to understand his written edicts. In the 1950s and 1960s, Beijing simplified the characters, making them easier to learn and transmit electronically.

Chinese is also tonal, like singing. Mandarin Chinese has four tones (in addition to no tone). Speak a syllable with the wrong tone and you have said a completely different word, sometimes to comic effect. Chinese sounds are very different and cannot be precisely transliterated into English. One system, the Wade-Giles, devised in the 1860s by two Cambridge dons, was used for more than a century but poorly matched spoken Chinese.

In 1958, Peking—sorry, Beijing—introduced a new phonetic system, **pinyin**, to help Chinese

schoolchildren learn to pronounce their own language. Pinyin indicates tones with accent marks, but it is still an imperfect guide to spoken Chinese sounds. In 1979, China made pinyin the official standard for transliteration. There are no books or newspapers in pinyin, which is used only to learn Chinese and for street signs. Computer programs now let you type in a pinyin word, and instantly a matching Chinese character pops up. You may still see Wade-Giles spellings in older books. Here are some examples:

Wade-Giles	Pinyin
Mao Tse-tung	Mao Zedong
Chou En-lai	Zhou Enlai
Kuomintang	Guomindang
Peking	Beijing
Nanking	Nanjing
Chungking	Chongqing
Shanghai	Shanghai (the same!)
Szechwan	Sichuan
Sinkiang	Xinjiang (X sounds "hs")
Canton	Guangdong
Hong Kong	Xiang Gang
Ch'in	Qin (Q sounds "ch")
Tsingtao	Qingdao

The Long Collapse

For some 2,000 years, China absorbed invasions, famines, and new dynasties. The old pattern always reasserted itself; it was the most rational way to rule the Middle Kingdom. But as the modern epoch impinged on China, the system could not handle two new factors: population growth and Western penetration. In 1741, China's population was 143 million; just a century later, in 1851, it had become an amazing 432 million, the result of new crops (corn, potatoes, and sweet potatoes from the Americas) and internal peace under the Manchus. Taxation and administration lagged behind population growth, which hit in the nineteenth century as the Manchus were going into the typical decline phase of their dynastic cycle.

Opium Wars
Nineteenth-century British (and French) campaigns to keep China open to opium imports.

treaty ports
Areas of China coast run by European powers.

extraterritoriality
Privilege of Europeans in colonial situations to have their own laws and courts.

sphere of influence
Semicolonial area under control of major power.

At about the same time, the West penetrated and disoriented China. In a clash of two cultures—Western dynamism and greed versus Chinese stability—China was no match. Over roughly a century, old China went into convulsions and breakdowns, which, some fear, still lurk under the surface. Portuguese navigators reached China in 1514. Gradually, they and other Europeans gained permission to set up trading ports on the coast. For three centuries, the Imperial government disdained the foreigners and their products and tried to keep both to a minimum. In 1793, for example, in response to a British mission to Beijing, the emperor commended King George III for his "respectful spirit of submission" but pointed out that there could be little trade because "our celestial empire possesses all things in prolific abundance." But the West, especially the British, pushed on, smelling enormous profits in the China trade.

Matters came to a head with the First **Opium War** of 1839 to 1842. The British imported opium from India, flouting Chinese law, and popularized opium smoking. When a zealous Imperial official tried to stop opium imports, Britain went to war, invoking the principle of "free trade." Britain easily won, but the Chinese still refused to admit that the foreigners were superior. Moaned one Cantonese: "Except for your ships being solid, your gunfire fierce, and your rockets powerful, what good qualities do you have?" For the Chinese, war technology was not as important as moral quality, a view later adopted by Mao Zedong.

The 1842 Treaty of Nanjing (Nanking in Wade-Giles) wrested five **treaty ports** from China. Britain got Hong Kong Island as an outright colony. In the treaty ports, foreigners held sway, dominating the commerce and governance of the area, and enjoying **extraterritoriality**, meaning they were not subject to Chinese law but had their own courts, a point deeply resented by both Chinese and Japanese. In the Second Opium War of 1856–1860, an Anglo-French expedition occupied Beijing, burned down the Summer Palace, and forced China to add nine more treaty ports. China called the imperialist land grabs "unequal treaties."

Around the treaty ports grew **spheres of influence**, understandings among the foreign powers as to who exercised control. The British, French, Germans, Russians, and Japanese carved up the China coast. Foreign powers turned the treaty port of Shanghai into a major and modern trading center. Shanghai quickly became China's leading city both in size and commercial importance and still is. China was reduced to semicolonial status.

Japan also took advantage of China's weakness. Every Japanese incursion generated passionate nationalism in China. In 1894, Japan started a war with China, took Taiwan, and

Taiping
Religion-based rebellion in nineteenth-century China.

Boxer
Chinese antiforeigner rebellion in 1900.

warlord
General who ran province after collapse of empire in 1911.

Nationalist
Chiang Kai-shek's party that unified China in the late 1920s, abbreviated KMT.

made it Japanese from 1895 to 1945. In 1915, Japan issued its Twenty-One Demands on China that would have turned it into a Japanese protectorate. Chinese were furious. On May 4, 1919, the Versailles peace conference decided to allow Japan to keep the former German concession in Shandong Province, the seizure of which had been Japan's contribution to the Allied side in World War I. Beijing students protested and rioted, and anti-Japanese demonstrations broke out. The May Fourth Movement that followed was the training ground for young Chinese Nationalists and Communists. In a parallel to the German invasion of Russia in World War I, Japanese incursions into China led to the Communist takeover in 1949. Foreign invasion rather than mass uprising brought communism to both Russia and China.

From Empire to Republic

Internally, too, the Empire weakened. Rebellions broke out. From 1851 to 1864, the **Taipings**—espousing a mixture of Christianity and Confucianism—baptized millions in South China and nearly overthrew the Manchus in a rebellion that cost more than 20 million lives. In 1900, with the backing of some reactionary officials and the empress dowager, the antiforeign **Boxer** movement, based on traditional temple-boxing exercises, killed missionaries and their converts and besieged Beijing's Legation Quarter for 55 days. What the Chinese call the "Eight Powers Expedition" of British, French, German, Russian, American, Japanese, Austrian, and Italian troops broke through and lifted the siege. The foreigners then demanded indemnities and concessions from the tottering Imperial government.

Could China have adapted itself to the new Western pressures? Japan had; with the 1868 *Meiji Restoration*, it preserved the form of empire but shifted to modernization and industrialization. Many young Chinese demanded reforms to strengthen China, especially after their humiliating defeat by Japan in 1895. In 1898, the young Emperor Guangxu gathered reformers around him and, in the famous Hundred Days, issued more than 40 edicts, modernizing everything from education to the military. Conservative officials and the old empress dowager would have none of it; they carried out a coup, rescinded the changes, and put the emperor under house arrest for the rest of his short life. Old China could not reform itself.

Younger people, however, especially army officers, grew fed up with China's weakness and became militant nationalists. Many Chinese studied in the West and were eager to modernize China. Socialist and Marxist ideas from Europe intrigued Chinese intellectuals. Under an idealistic, Western-trained doctor, Sun Yixian (Sun Yat-sen in Wade-Giles), disgruntled provincial officials and military commanders overthrew the Manchus in 1911. In the absence of central authority, so-called **warlords** fragmented China from 1916 to 1927.

The **Nationalist** Party, or Guomindang (in Wade-Giles, Kuomintang, KMT), gradually overcame China's chaos. Formed by Sun shortly after the Manchu's overthrow, the Nationalists were guided by intellectuals (many of them educated in the United States), army officers, and businesspeople. Their greatest strength was in the South, especially in the coastal cities where there was the most contact with the West. They restored the ancient capital of Nanjing ("Southern Capital") as their capital.

Political Culture

U.S. Involvement in China

The United States has had long and deep ties to China. Some of Boston's leading families profited early from the China trade (including the sale of Turkish opium). While the British carved up China's coast, we prided ourselves on being above that sort of imperialism (but we did use the treaty ports). In 1900, Secretary of State Hay issued the **Open Door** notes to stop the dismemberment of China. We saw ourselves as China's "big brother" and "favorite people," who were only there to help and seized no territory. (Chinese historians now call the Americans imperialists who just used the Open Door to get a share of the China trade.)

American churches sent hundreds of missionaries to China in the nineteenth and early twentieth centuries to make the Chinese Protestant and prosperous. Henry Luce, born in China in 1898, the son of a Presbyterian missionary, arrived at Yale speaking Chinese. All his life, Luce carried the missionary view that we can and must uplift China by supporting the Chinese Nationalists. Luce founded *Time* magazine in 1923 and put Nationalist chief Chiang ten times on its cover. Opinionated and influential, Luce used *Time* to rail against Chinese Communists and U.S. Democrats (he conflated the two).

U.S. support for China had to bring us into war with Japan. When Japan conquered Manchuria in 1931, Secretary of State Stimson issued his *nonrecognition doctrine*. When Japan began its conquest of all of China in 1937, we increasingly embargoed trade with Japan, leading to Pearl Harbor. China could not be more than a minor theater of operations for the U.S. war effort. The Japanese occupied the entire China coast, so only a trickle of U.S. supplies could reach China by air and by the Burma Road from India. During the war, U.S. officials attempted to get Chinese Nationalists and Communists to work together against the Japanese, but they remained bitter enemies.

When the Communists took over China in late 1949, U.S. Republicans such as Luce intoned, "Who lost China?" and blamed the Democrats. The "Old China Hands" among U.S. diplomats were purged from the State Department for letting the Communists take over China—they could not have done anything about it—leaving Washington, for decades, without experts who knew China firsthand. Washington broke all ties with mainland China in 1949 and did not resume them until Nixon's visit in 1972. We fought China in Korea. The 23 years of U.S.-Chinese hostility, however, was an aberration in a history of two centuries of good ties.

After Sun died in 1925, General (later Generalissimo) Chiang Kai-shek (Jiang Jieshi in pinyin) took over the Nationalists and launched a series of military expeditions to control portions of China. While many Americans hailed Jiang as the founder and savior of the new China, Nationalist rule was weak and corrupt. The Western-oriented city people who staffed the Nationalists did not reform or develop the rural areas where most Chinese lived, often under the thumb of rapacious landlords. Administration became terribly corrupt. And the Nationalists offered no unifying ideology to rally the big majority of Chinese, the peasants.

The Nationalists might have succeeded were it not for the Japanese invasion. In 1931, the Japanese army seized Manchuria and, in 1937, began the conquest of all of China. By 1941, they had taken the entire coast, forcing the Nationalists to move their capital far up the Yangzi River from Nanjing to Chongqing. Jiang's forces did not put up heavy resistance to the Japanese advance (neither did the Communists); instead, they conserved their forces until a U.S. victory returned them to power.

Open Door
U.S. policy of protecting China.

Geography

Sailing the East China Sea

Your aircraft carrier enters the East China Sea from the south, the Taiwan Strait. Sailing clockwise in a great circle that includes the Yellow Sea to the north, which countries do you pass?

On your left you pass China, North Korea (steer well away), South Korea, Japan (including its Ryukyu Islands), and Taiwan.

The Communist Triumph

One branch of Chinese nationalism, influenced by Marx and the Bolshevik Revolution, decided that communism was the only effective basis for a nationalist revolution. The Chinese Communists have always been first and foremost nationalists, and, from its founding in 1921, the Chinese Communist Party (CCP) worked with the Nationalists until Jiang, in 1927, decided to exterminate them as a threat. The fight between the KMT and CCP was a struggle between two versions of Chinese nationalism.

Stalin, who knew little of China, mistakenly advised the Chinese Communists to base themselves on the small proletariat of the coastal cities, but Mao Zedong rose to leadership of the Party by developing a rural strategy he called the **mass line**. Mao concluded that the real revolutionary potential in China was the poorest peasants, a major revision of Marx. Mao, considered a maverick in the CCP, organized peasants in 1931 in Jiangxi Province into a small Chinese Soviet Republic. In 1934, with KMT forces surrounding their "Jiangxi redoubt," some 80,000 began their incredible Long March of 5,000 miles (8,000 km) to the relative safety of Yan'an far to the north in Shaanxi Province. The march took more than a year and led across mountain ranges and rivers amid hostile forces. Only 6,000 survived. The Long March became the epic of Chinese Communist history. Self-reliant and isolated from the Soviets, Mao developed his mass line of working with the peasants and guerrilla warfare.

China's war against Japan weakened the Nationalists, giving the advantage to the Communists. Besides stocks of captured Japanese weapons from the Soviet takeover of Manchuria in 1945, the Chinese Communists got little but bad advice from the Soviets and felt they never owed them much in return. In 1947, full-scale civil war resumed between the KMT and CCP, which the Communists won in late 1949. Mao and the CCP came to power largely on their own, a point that contributed to the later Sino–Soviet split.

After World War II, the Nationalist forces were much larger than the Communists' and had many U.S. arms. Nationalist strength, however, melted away as hyperinflation destroyed the economy, corrupt officers sold their troops' weapons, and war weariness paralyzed the population. The Nationalists had always neglected the rice roots of political strength: the common peasant. The Communists, by cultivating the peasantry (Mao himself was of peasant origin), won a new Mandate of Heaven. In 1949, the disintegrating Nationalists retreated to the island of Taiwan as the Communists restored Beijing ("Northern Capital") as the country's capital and proceeded to

mass line
Mao's theory of peasant-based revolution for China.

China Lessons

Brinton's Stages of Revolution

Harvard historian Crane Brinton (see our France chapter), in his 1938 classic *The Anatomy of Revolution*, compared four revolutions: the English, American, French, and Russian. (Any historian who compares becomes an honorary political scientist.) He found that revolutions pass through similar stages. One commonality during the first stage is the "alienation of the intellectuals." Educated people increasingly find the old regime ridiculous and ineffective, not worthy of their psychological support. Instead, they transfer their allegiance to proposed new and better possible forms of governance, and the regime loses its legitimacy.

Brinton did not include the Chinese revolution; he wrote before the Communists' 1949 victory. The Chinese revolution, however, could fit Brinton's outline, including the alienation of intellectuals. Chinese intellectuals indeed became alienated from the Qing dynasty, whose court factions blocked modernization, leaving China powerless and unable to repel European and Japanese incursions.

The initial seizure of power is easy, often over a small problem the regime mishandles. Indeed, China's Double Ten (October 10, 1911; pity it did not come a year earlier), the day celebrated as the start of the revolution, began as a local squabble over railway ownership. At first, relative moderates take over and hold power for a while, but in competition with more radical forces. Two governments, each proclaiming itself the true bearers of revolution, exist side by side in conflict. In China, the Nationalists were relative moderates, and

by 1927, they were in a civil war with the Communists. Then, wrote Brinton, the extremists oust the moderates. The extremists are better organized, more ruthless, and know exactly what they want. Once in power, they plunge the country into a revolutionary frenzy and punish all who block their march to utopia. Mao's 1949 victory, execution of landlords, Great Leap Forward in the late 1950s, and Cultural Revolution in the late 1960s would fit Brinton's extremist phase except that it was stretched out in several iterations.

The final phase, Thermidor, marks the end of the frenzy and a calming down. It was named after the month in which Robespierre and his colleagues were deposed and guillotined. After all the upheaval, people are tired of revolution and want to get on with their lives with some security and comfort. Deng Xiaoping's market-oriented reforms starting in 1979 could be the Chinese equivalent of a Thermidor.

Brinton added that there may be aftershocks. Just as a series of minor tremors may follow a major earthquake, so may smaller upheavals follow a big revolution, starting again with regime decay and alienation of the intellectuals. Could China be showing some of these signs? China's class structure, thanks to economic growth, is now far more complex than it used to be. Are all of these classes equally content? It may pay to think a bit like Marxists in examining China's classes, unless you believe that the Chinese Revolution ended the class struggle.

implement the world's most sweeping revolution. On that occasion, Mao voiced his nationalistic sentiments: "Our nation will never again be an insulted nation. We have stood up." Even today, in its race for respect and prestige, China is still putting Mao's words into action.

The Key Institutions

7.2 **Outline the main points of China's current political model.**

Of the three greatest twentieth-century dictators, Mao was the bloodiest. Yale's Timothy Snyder made the grisly calculation that under Stalin's orders, 6 to 9 million civilians died, and under Hitler, 11 million. And these do not include military personnel. Mao's orders killed perhaps

40 million of his countrymen, most by starvation. The few Chinese who publicly discuss Mao's horrors are threatened or jailed. Since Mao, however, China has moved away from a *totalitarian* model and developed a distinctive system of political control with a partial market economy.

The New Chinese Model

Although never officially promulgated, several commentators, both Chinese and foreign, argue that China has devised a new and effective political and economic model, one much better suited to China than either Soviet-style communism or Western liberal democracy. They claim the Chinese model yields spectacular growth and stability. Departing from it—say, by introducing democracy—invites division and chaos, some warn. Therefore, they suggest, China will be governed along these lines:

1. China is ruled by one party, the Communist Party (CCP), with no competition or (open) factions.
2. The elite of the CCP—the Standing Committee—makes all important decisions.
3. No autonomous civil society outside of state control is permitted.
4. Since 2002, the CCP's elite serves for fixed terms and selects bright and educated successors in advance.
5. The Party renews itself by admitting young technocrats and businesspeople.
6. Corruption is to be kept in check by a Party commission.
7. Administration is decentralized to provincial and local levels.
8. Smaller parts of the economy are in private hands, but the big parts, including banking, are still state owned or controlled.
9. Foreign economic ties—investments and exports—are encouraged.
10. Chinese are to be kept content through rising material consumption and national pride.
11. The regime crushes small organized discontent but bends to really big spontaneous discontent.

Other observers, both Chinese and foreign, doubt that the model will work in the long run. The Chinese model is not quite unique or a first. Brazil was also governed by very bright *technocrats* with a similar "authoritarian developmentalism" from 1964 to 1985, with three big differences: Brazil was only mildly authoritarian, it had no ruling party, and its generals deliberately and gradually "decompressed" their rule into democracy.

The first three of the above model's points fit the standard totalitarian model, but others diverge from it. The fourth point resembles Mexico's method of selecting new leaders under the long reign of PRI. Mexico's president picked his successor from loyal, proven PRI officials. Doing this, China solves the problem of succession crises that accompanied changes of Soviet leadership. It also makes sure top leaders are bright and well educated. Top Chinese leaders no longer die in office but retire after two terms, having selected their replacements. China's new leaders are known years in advance. In 2007, Xi Jinping was tipped for president in 2013.

The fifth point is also more flexible and clever than the Soviet model. It resembles the *co-optation* practiced by PRI in Mexico and generals in Brazil. Bright young talent—academics, technocrats, and businesspeople—must not stay outside of the Party, where they may form a dissenting class, but are invited into the Party, provided they are patriotic. The only ideology

they need is China's progress; Mao Thought is unimportant. Young
Party members are rewarded and kept loyal by career advancement. In
this way, the Party stays vital and current and avoids becoming isolated
from society. But it also means opportunists join the Party for self-gain,
fostering corruption.

Zhongnanhai
Walled compound for China's
top leaders next to Forbidden
City in Beijing.

The sixth point, control of corruption, is the weakest part of the Chinese model and could
bring it down. Like Russians, average Chinese hate the corruption that is widespread and
rooted among the very officials the regime depends on. The Party's Central Commission for
Discipline Inspection, supposed to be powerful, makes only superficial and spotty inroads.

The seventh point, administrative decentralization, is also problematic. China is a unitary,
not a federal system, but Beijing promotes economic growth by permitting much provincial
and local interpretation of laws: Do whatever gives you the fastest growth. But this has led
to wildly different laws and usages among provinces, and corruption. What is allowed in one
province is prohibited in the next. Construction permits—fertile soil for bribery everywhere—
are quick and easy in one city, slow and expensive in another.

The last point also departs from the Soviet model. The Kremlin paid little attention to discontent, but the **Zhongnanhai** backs down in the face of mass discontent before it can threaten
the regime. Critical individuals or groups are jailed, but if millions of Chinese complain loudly
or ignore the law, the regime bends. Mass starvation in 1958–1961 made Beijing end the brutal
communal farms and let peasants return to individual farming. The illegal migration of rural
millions to the cities forced Beijing to allow it. Under mass pressure, unenforced laws can suddenly get enforced and new ones passed. Unsafe milk, crooked officials, and rural poverty
bring new programs and policies. In this way, Beijing practices a kind of *regime accountability*,
like a democracy but without the divisions and tumult. Any attempt to challenge the regime, of
course, such as happened in Tiananmen Square and Xinjiang, is crushed.

The China model is a fascinating experiment that tries to blend control at the top with
growing freedom at the bottom. Several authoritarian regimes admired the Chinese model. But
can it work over many years? Or will the contradictions built into it force changes in the model
or even its abandonment?

The Importance of the Party

China is still a party-state. Supposedly "the party of workers and peasants," the CCP is actually
the party of officials. China's 1982 constitution repeatedly specifies that everything runs "under
the leadership of the Communist Party of China." As in all Communist countries, neither competing parties nor factions within the CCP are permitted. Eight fake tiny puppet parties exist
for show but are under the CCP. Behind the scenes, CCP factions exist, often based on geography, such as the "Shanghai Clique," that sometimes go on to occupy top positions in Beijing.
Some analysts claim China is run by "weak leaders but strong factions" based on nepotism and
cronyism. Factional disputes occasionally burst out into public view.

China is no longer a one-man dictatorship but the dictatorship of a small Party elite riven by
factions. After Mao and Deng died, China's top rulers have adhered to fixed term limits—two
5-year terms—and do not stay in power forever. China has evolved a method for the orderly
and regular renewal of top personnel, something the Soviet Union never did. Most Soviet chiefs

Geography

Heavenly Government: Concentrated and Isolated

The Mongols who founded the Yuan dynasty first made Beijing China's capital in 1267, and it mostly stayed that way. The first two Ming emperors in the fourteenth century set up their capital in Nanjing, but the third Ming emperor returned it to Beijing. The southern-facing Nationalists restored Nanjing as their capital in 1928, but to escape the Japanese, they had to flee far up the Yangzi River to make Chongqing their wartime capital.

The Mings also founded the **Forbidden City** as the divine center of Beijing in the early fifteenth century on a strict north–south axis; the main entrance is the Meridian Gate, supposedly aligned with heaven. **Geomancy** was always important in traditional China. Only the emperor, his family, and a relatively few officials and servants were allowed to enter the walled, 178-acre City, which contains numerous halls and temples. The Forbidden City aimed to impress Chinese (and later foreigners) by awe and magnificence. Unfortunately, it was also a huge, costly, extravagant tax drain, which isolated the emperor and overconcentrated power too far north to be in China's original core area, which is to the south, in the Yellow and Yangzi river valleys.

The Communist regime, starting in 1961, at great expense restored the Forbidden City to make it the Imperial Palace Museum, the country's number-one tourist attraction. It shows that the Communists have returned China to its deserved status at the center of heaven. Mao gave his 1949 "China has stood up" speech from the Gate of Heavenly Peace overlooking the wide-open **Tiananmen** Square, at the south of which sits Mao's mausoleum (officially a "memorial hall").

Forbidden City
Emperor's walled palace complex in Beijing.

geomancy
Divinely correct positioning of structures.

Tiananmen
Gate of Heavenly Peace, Beijing's main square.

simply died in office, as did Mao. The lack of a succession mechanism produced at least two problems: (1) rule by the elderly (gerontocracy) and (2) messy succession battles (for example, Stalin and Trotsky after Lenin's death). In this and other ways, China has been cleverer than the Soviet Union.

The Soviet Parallel

We must specify "before and after" in describing Chinese political institutions. The break in China was not as sharp as the 1991 Soviet collapse, but Russia has turned partway back to authoritarianism. China had no interlude comparable to Russia's attempt at democracy in the 1990s; it merely shifted into a lighter authoritarianism. The original Communist institutions Mao set up after taking power in 1949 were closely modeled after Stalin's Soviet system, but now the system is looser and freer. Indeed, tourists enjoying the sights, shopping, and cuisine might not notice they are in a Communist country.

The institutions of China's government are similar to what the Soviet Union had: interlocking state and Party hierarchies. For example, the National Party Congress has many of the same members as China's legislature, the National People's Congress. (The two are easy to confuse. Just remember, one is Party, the other state.) Typically, a Chinese leader first climbs into the upper ranks of the Party and then assumes high government jobs as well. In Communist systems generally, position in the Party determines who also gets governing power within the state structure. China's Party general secretary, for example, soon becomes its president.

Comparison

Indirect Analysis of Authoritarian Systems

Democracies are easier to study than authoritarian systems. In democracies, we can get a variety of data, much of it quantified, on public opinion, party positions, election results, legislative votes, and policy shifts. With authoritarian systems, we can get only the policy shifts, and they are veiled by obscure wording. It may take a while to figure out what has changed.

During the Cold War, academics and journalists developed indirect techniques to study Soviet politics. Dubbed **Kremlinology**, they focused on who in the Kremlin got promoted, demoted, or executed. By associating these personnel shifts with their positions and statements, observers inferred the direction of Kremlin politics. Stalin's replacement of Foreign Minister Maxim Litvinov in 1939 by Vyacheslav Molotov, for example, signaled a major shift in Soviet foreign policy, from trying to gain Western allies to making a deal with Hitler.

Even who stood next to whom atop Lenin's tomb could be significant. In 1953, after Stalin's death, Kremlinologists noted that security police chief Lavrenti Beria was missing from the lineup. "Maybe he had a cold," scoffed one American editor. Actually, Beria had already been shot as a threat to other Politburo members. In Kremlinology, little things mean a lot.

The equivalent, dubbed "China watching" (much of it from Hong Kong) during the Cold War, applied similar techniques to China. Who is under whose protection? Did Premier Zhou Enlai quietly protect Deng Xiaoping from the ravages of the Cultural Revolution? (Yes, in order to ensure a pragmatic successor.) Did Deng fire Party General Secretary Zhao Ziyang in 1989? (Clearly, because of Zhao's soft line on the Tiananmen demonstrators.)

A newer example: In 2012, the Politburo's Standing Committee shrank from nine members to seven. The only two candidates for the nine-man committee with known reformist views did not make it onto the smaller committee. China watchers suggest that the committee was trimmed to bar political reformists—associated with outgoing Premier Wen Jiabao— and retain tight political control to implement urgent economic liberalization. One can separate economic reforms from political reforms, but not forever.

China watching, like all indirect political analysis, has to be based on fragmentary evidence, speculation, and anecdotes, which can lead to mistakes. Some China specialists took at face value an unverified (and probably bogus) report that Mao on his deathbed in 1976 handed Premier Hua Guofeng a note saying, "With you in charge, I am at ease." Hua seemed secure as Mao's successor, but behind the scenes, Deng Xiaoping sidelined Hua and kicked him out of the Politburo in 1981, surprising some China watchers. Don't bet the farm on indirect analysis. Unfortunately, until the politics of the Zhongnanhai opens up, indirect analysis is all we have.

China, however, adds a Third World twist to Communist governance: The army has also been quite important, at times intervening directly in politics, as happens in other developing countries. Typically, armies intervene not merely to grab power but to save the country from disorder and breakdown. Until China is no longer vulnerable to upheaval, we cannot be sure the army will not intervene again.

Kremlinology
Noting personnel changes to analyze Communist regimes.

As in the old Soviet model, each state and Party level ostensibly elects the one above it. In practice, the Party handpicks delegates to be elected from the lower to the higher congresses. In China, townships elect congresses every two years, which then elect some 2,800 county congresses every three years, which in turn choose provincial and big-city People's Congresses every five years. In the old days of Mao, factories were the main base units of political organization; now it is townships. The provincial People's Congresses then elect the unicameral National People's Congress (NPC) of nearly 3,000 delegates—some 70 percent of them government officials—for a five-year term.

As in the old Soviet Union, this parliament is too big to do much at its nine- or ten-day annual sessions. At times, NPC sessions allow motions from the floor, debate, contested committee elections, and negative votes. Some hope that the NPC can turn into a real parliament with checks on the executive, a major step to democracy. But that would require letting NPC delegates form links with outside groups and other members, whom they could mobilize and represent—in a word, parties. An individual NPC delegate introducing a minor bill is no substitute for pluralism. Standing alone, the delegate is nothing; with groups behind them, they are the building blocks of democracy. A faint beginning could be seen in NPC joint motions and bills, each of which requires the signatures of at least 30 delegates. If this were to expand and solidify, the NPC would have the making of parliamentary parties (but not yet mass parties). Centuries ago, such groupings in Britain's House of Commons marked the beginning of parties.

The NPC Standing Committee (not to be confused with the Politburo's seven-member standing committee) of about 155 is theoretically supreme, but it, too, does not have much power to oversee the executive branch. The chairman of the Standing Committee is considered China's head of state or president. The top of the executive branch is the State Council, a cabinet of approximately 40 ministers (specialized in economic branches) and a dozen vice premiers led by a premier, China's head of government. China, therefore, has both a president and a premier and resembles the semipresidential system de Gaulle devised in France, in which the president (since Deng's death) is more powerful than the premier. Most of China's current top leaders graduated in engineering or science and worked in those fields. China's governing elite is now among the world's most educated and technocratic.

The Party

Like the old Soviet Communist Party (CPSU), the Chinese Communist Party (CCP) is constitutionally and in practice the leading political element of the country. With 85 million members (and growing roughly 1 percent a year), the CCP is large but, at 6.3 percent of China's population, is proportionately smaller than the CPSU was in the Soviet Union. To fight complacency and corruption, the Party retires millions of old-timers and recruits well-educated young academics, technocrats, and businesspeople, who see Party membership as a way to get jobs. In this way, the Party *co-opts* them, but many are nominal members, and some privately criticize the system. CCP leaders no longer wear military-style Mao suits. Instead, in coat and tie (usually red), they look like modern executives. Party members must attend a three-week course every year to learn the latest line, which they immediately shrug off.

Beida
Short name for Beijing University, long China's best (equivalent to Japan's *Todai*).

Comintern
Short for Communist International; the world's Communist parties under Moscow's control.

With the economic changes since the late 1970s, the CCP has lost authority and a sense of mission. In place of Maoism, its only ideal is a strong, stable China. In today's China, lust for money trumps all else. Some Communist officials now use their positions for personal gain; massive corruption is pervasive. If not revitalized, the CCP could implode, leaving China without a backbone. Such revitalization would have to include, at a minimum, (1) a new, realistic statement of mission

Personalities

Tandem Power: Mao and Zhou

For more than a quarter of a century, until both died in 1976, power in Beijing was divided between Party Chairman Mao Zedong and Premier Zhou Enlai. This set a Chinese pattern of tandem power that still operates and may now be sufficiently *institutionalized* to continue.

Both were of rural backgrounds, but Mao was born in 1893 into a peasant family in inland Hunan Province, while Zhou was born in 1898 into a gentry family in coastal Jiangsu Province. Mao's father had worked his way up from poverty to property and was counted as a "rich peasant," exactly the kind Mao ordered tried and executed by the millions in the early 1950s. Mao said his background let him understand China's peasants, but his cold-blooded policies showed no sympathy for them.

Mao went away to school but, in late 1911, briefly became a soldier in the revolution against the dying Manchu dynasty. Mao never attended a university but graduated in 1918 from Hunan's teacher-training school. Already a radical nationalist, while there, he organized the New People's Study Society, a precursor of the CCP. Arriving in Beijing during the anti-Japanese May Fourth Movement of 1919, Mao got a job as a library assistant at the famous **Beida**. In 1921, when Chinese Marxists with **Comintern** help founded the Chinese Communist Party (CCP) in Shanghai, Mao was one of the founders.

Zhou went to a top high school and then to Japan in 1917 to study. Japan, having beaten Russia in 1904–1905, was then an example and magnet for nationalists throughout Asia, including Chinese and Vietnamese. The 1919 May Fourth movement brought an exodus of Chinese students from Japan, and Zhou returned to China. Already a student radical, Zhou was jailed briefly in 1920. Upon release, Zhou went to France in 1920 to study, but, with the founding of the CCP, he worked at recruiting Chinese students in Europe to join the Communists. Zhou returned to China in 1924 to participate in Sun's Nationalist revolution. Mao had no experience outside of China.

As with most young Chinese early in the twentieth century, Mao and Zhou were passionate Chinese nationalists before they turned to Marxism. Neither of them had much higher education, although both studied, debated, and published in Chinese leftist circles. Under Moscow's orders, the young CCP worked in alliance with the Nationalists. Zhou was in charge of political education at the Nationalist military academy at Whampoa in Guangzhou, where Nationalist Jiang Jieshi was commandant. In 1927, Zhou became CCP military director. As KMT forces approached Shanghai that year, Zhou organized workers to take over the city. But Jiang, who was suspicious that the Communists planned to ultimately seize power, massacred them by the thousands, and both Mao and Zhou barely escaped with their lives.

The next decade set the Mao-Zhou relationship. Mao concluded from his work with peasants that they were the means to China's revolution. Zhou and many other CCP members initially rejected Mao in favor of Stalin's "proletarian line," which argued for a series of worker uprisings in China's coastal cities. Stalin knew little about the world and nothing about China. By 1931, after all uprisings had failed, Zhou changed his mind and joined Mao in his Jiangxi redoubt. From there, the two led the arduous Long March to the north. By the time they arrived in Yan'an, Mao was clearly the leader of the CCP, and his "mass line" of basing the revolution on the peasantry prevailed.

Mao dominated mainly by force of intellect. Other CCP leaders respected his ability to theorize in clear, blunt language. Mao became the Party chief and theoretician but did not supervise the day-to-day tasks of survival, warfare, and diplomacy. These became Zhou's jobs; he was the administrator of the revolution. Never bothering to theorize, Zhou was a master at shaping and controlling bureaucracies, clever compromise, and political survival amid changing lines. Asked for his views on the French Revolution, the cagey Zhou declined to comment on what he referred to as such a recent event.

Zhou always supported Mao, although at times, in the shambles of the Great Leap Forward (1958–1961) and the Cultural Revolution (1966–1976), he tried to stabilize things and limit damage. Mao was the abstract thinker and more radical, Zhou the pragmatic doer and more conservative. Mao could spin out his utopian dreams, but Zhou made the bureaucracy, military, and economy function. Zhou's pragmatic views won out; all China's top leaders since 1977 have been Zhou's ideological descendants. Mao's radicalism, however, lingers among some.

of where the Party wants China to go and (2) open disagreements among Party factions that media and citizens could discuss publicly, a step toward democracy.

In organization, the CCP parallels the defunct CPSU. Hierarchies of Party congresses at the local, county, provincial, and national levels feed into corresponding Party committees. At the top is the National Party Congress; composed of some 2,200 delegates and supposed to meet at least once in five years, this congress nominally chooses a Central Committee of about 370 members. Because both bodies are too big to run things, real power is in the hands of a Politburo of, currently, 25 top Party leaders and generals. But this, too, is not the highest level. Within the Politburo is a Standing Committee, now with seven members, who decide everything important. The CCP general secretary, who also serves as China's president, and the premier are Standing Committee members.

China's nervous system is its 30 million Party **cadres**, who resemble the old Soviet *apparatchiks*. Whoever controls the cadres controls China. In 1979, Deng Xiaoping began easing out both incompetent old-timers and extreme leftists from the Cultural Revolution. Quietly, Deng brought in younger, better-educated cadres dedicated to his moderate, pragmatic line. The CCP's secretive Central Organization Department names all senior officials, much like the old Soviet *nomenklatura*. The CCP's Central Commission for Discipline Inspection tries to root out graft and corruption, of which there is plenty in China.

The Army

Most top figures in the Chinese elite hold both high state and high Party offices, as in the old Soviet Union. In China, though, they also hold high positions atop the military structure through the important Central Military Commission, which interlocks with the CCP's Politburo. Mao, Deng, and Jiang were all chairmen of the Military Commission, as is China's current president. Part of his power is his relation to the military.

From the beginning, the People's Liberation Army (PLA) has been so intertwined with the CCP that it is hard to separate them; this is what political scientist Robert Tucker called "military communism." Mao wrote, "Political power grows out of the barrel of a gun," but "the Party commands the gun, and the gun must never be allowed to command the Party." As the Communists took over China in the 1940s, it was the PLA that first set up their power structures. Until recently, China's executive decision makers all had extensive military experience, often as political commissars in PLA units. Said Zhou Enlai, who had been involved in military affairs since the 1920s: "We are all connected with the army."

cadre
Communist member serving as an official; Chinese: *gànbù*.

Personalities

The Invisible Puppeteer: Deng Xiaoping

Deng Xiaoping had been purged from Chinese politics twice before becoming "senior vice premier" in 1977, a deceptive title for China's undisputed boss. And Deng sought no fame or glory; unlike Mao, he built no personality cult. Deng seldom appeared in public or in the media but governed in the Confucian tradition: quietly, behind the scenes, chiefly by picking top officials. The late MIT political scientist Lucian Pye called him the "invisible puppeteer." This former protégé of Zhou Enlai—who, like Zhou, was a pragmatic administrator rather than a theorizer—set China on its present course and gave China its current problems.

Deng was born in 1904 into a rural landlord family. Sent to study in France, Deng was recruited there by Zhou Enlai and soon joined the Chinese Communists. As one of the political commissars and organizers of the People's Liberation Army, Deng forged strong military connections. Rising through major posts after 1949, Deng was named to the top of the Party—the Politburo's Standing Committee—in 1956.

Deng was not as adroit as Zhou and kept getting into political trouble. An outspoken pragmatist, Deng said after the Great Leap: "Private farming is all right as long as it raises production, just as it does not matter whether a cat is black or white as long as it catches mice." During the Cultural Revolution, this utterance was used against Deng to show that he was a "capitalist roader." Deng dropped out of sight and lost his official position. A mob crippled his son during the Cultural Revolution.

But the little man—Deng was well under 5 feet tall—bounced back in 1973 when moderates regained control. In 1975, he seemed to be ready to take over; he spoke with visiting U.S. President Ford as one head of state to another. But just a month later, Deng was again in disgrace, denounced by the radicals of the **Gang of Four** as anti-Mao. Again, he was stripped of his posts,

but old army buddies gave him sanctuary in an elite military resort. The adaptable Deng bounced back. With the arrest of the Gang of Four in 1976, moderates returned, among them Deng, and, in July 1977, he was reappointed to all his old posts. Many Chinese leaders, badly shaken by the Cultural Revolution, looked to old comrade Deng to restore stability.

In 1978, Deng, then already 74, proclaimed his famous "Four Modernizations" of agriculture, industry, science, and defense. In the veiled language of authoritarian regimes, Deng mentioned permitting "side occupations," which turned out to mean individuals could work growing, making, and selling things for profit. A few words triggered a massive shift, and now streets are lined with shops and restaurants run by entrepreneurs. Deng also urged "adaptation to local conditions," meaning the provinces and localities were freed from lock-step central direction, the starting signal for the rapid industrialization of the southern coastal regions.

Deng started China on its present course by splitting economics from politics. He offered the Chinese a new deal: Work and get rich in a partly market economy but leave politics to the Party. China's economic growth amazed, but will massive economic changes eventually influence politics? How much inequality can China take without unrest? Is this growth sustainable? Apparently, Deng never gave much thought to the contradictions he was creating, and they are now China's chief problems.

Deng was no "liberal." He encouraged economic reform but blocked any moves toward democracy, as have his successors. In 1989, Deng brutally crushed the prodemocracy movement in Beijing's Tiananmen Square. Although weak and reclusive in the 1990s, Deng still quietly controlled Beijing's top personnel and main policy lines until he died in 1997 at age 92.

When the Cultural Revolution broke out in 1966, the army first facilitated, then dampened, and finally stopped the Red Guards' rampages. By the time the Cultural Revolution sputtered out, the PLA was in de facto control of most provincial governments and most of the

Gang of Four
Mao's ultraradical helpers, arrested in 1976.

paramilitary
National police force organized
and equipped like a light army,
such as the French CRS.

Politburo. Several Politburo members are still active military men (but none of the Standing Committee are). At various times during mobilization campaigns, the army is cited as a model for the rest of the country to follow, and heroic individual soldiers are celebrated in the media.

Armies, as guardians of their countries' security, define whatever is good for them as good for the country. Anyone who undermines their power earns their opposition. During the Cultural Revolution, Defense Minister Lin Biao fanatically supported Mao's program to shake up the Party and state bureaucracy. (The army was scarcely touched.) As the chaos spread, however, military commanders worried that it was sapping China's strength and military preparedness. Lin became increasingly isolated within the military. In 1971, Lin attempted a coup, tried to assassinate Mao, and fled to the Soviet Union in a plane that crashed. Mao's bodyguard, the secretive Unit 8341, foiled the Lin plot, and Lin's supporters were purged from the military. The PLA thus helped tame Maoist radicalism. Lin's attempted coup revealed a latent praetorianism that marks it as a Third World country.

China's leaders realize that the army is a poor way to control domestic unrest. The PLA disliked mowing down students in Tiananmen in 1989. To deal with such situations, Beijing built up the People's Armed Police (PAP), now 700,000 strong, a **paramilitary** police force like the French CRS. The PAP, under PLA control, are sometimes called "internal security forces" or "riot police." The PAP quelled the 2009 riots in Xinjiang with PLA backup.

China's leaders pay special attention to the PLA and increase its budget, but the PLA, with 2.3 million members, is still poor and underequipped. To supplement its budget, the PLA went massively into private industry and ran some 15,000 businesses. Worried about PLA corruption, smuggling, and loss of mission, President Jiang ordered the army to get out of business and get back to soldiering. They complied, indicating that the Party still commands the gun. The PLA is a conservative, nationalist force in Chinese politics, for, almost axiomatically, an army stands for order and sees disorder as a security problem. When chaos threatens, the army moves. The PLA's naval branch (PLAN) is eager to show its growing strength and stand up to the United States and Japan in the China Seas.

A Decentralized Unitary System

China, like most countries, is organized on a unitary rather than federal basis, but its provinces and municipalities operate almost like units of a federal system, with what critics claim is too much local autonomy. The problem is an ancient one in China: how to govern a huge country from one capital city. Imperial China did it imperfectly through the Mandarin system. Mao did it through the Communist Party's cadres, but he damaged the coherence and morale of the Party through his periodic upheavals. Now, with China dedicated to making money, local Party bosses simply boost the local economy and line their own pockets. They say, in effect, "Heck, Beijing wants fast economic growth, and that's what I'm doing." China's unitary system has too little central control to overcome massive problems of a poisoned environment, health and safety, and corruption. Beijing has laws for all these problems, but they are not enforced locally.

China has 23 provinces and 4 huge cities—Beijing, Chongqing, Shanghai, and Tianjin—which count as provinces. In China, a "small" city like Jinan, capital of Shandong Province, has 6 million people (the same as Tennessee). China has 200 cities with populations of over 1 million. China lists Taiwan as a province, something many Taiwanese do not wish for. Hong Kong and Macau—handed back from, respectively, Britain in 1997 and Portugal in 1999—are "special administrative regions," allowed to keep their laws (including driving on the left) and market economies for 50 years. Beijing, however, quietly supervises them.

Personalities

China's Third to Fifth Generations of Rulers

In 1989, when Deng Xiaoping at age 85 gave up his last formal post—chairman of the powerful Central Military Commission—he made sure two protégés took over: Party General Secretary Jiang Zemin (who also took on the title of president) and Premier Li Peng. They were, respectively, 63 and 61, the "third generation" of Beijing's Communist rulers. In 1998, when Li's two 5-year terms were up, he was replaced as premier by Zhu Rongji, then 70.

All three of these leaders kept firm central control of politics while encouraging the growth of a market economy. All silenced troublesome intellectuals. All were graduate engineers—still largely the case today—giving their rule a technocratic bent. None was popular, nor did they seek popularity. None returned to the visions of Mao, but all were cautious about major change. None suggested democracy in China's future. In late 2002, Jiang gave up his Party position, and in 2003, Premier Zhu retired.

China got its "fourth generation" of Communist leaders at the Sixteenth Communist Party conference in late 2002. Succeeding Jiang was Vice President Hu Jintao, then 59. An engineer, Hu was formally elected China's president by the National People's Congress in March 2003. Jiang tried to stay influential, as chair of the Central Military Commission, but in 2004, at age 78, he reluctantly stepped down, and President Hu became China's military chief, thus completing the triple transfer of power—head of party, of executive, and of military. Succeeding Premier Zhu in 2003 was Deputy Premier Wen Jiabao, then 60. Wen trained as a geologist but worked in finance and agriculture and was extremely bright.

The fifth generation arrived in 2012–2013. Party chief and President Xi Jinping is considered a "princeling," the child of a revolutionary leader. His father was a guerrilla chief in Shaanxi Province and later vice chairman of the National People's Congress but was purged by Mao and later rehabilitated by Deng. Xi, born in 1953, was "sent down" in 1969 but became village party secretary before he was allowed home in 1975 to study chemical engineering at Tsinghua. Bright, pragmatic, and with the right connections, he rose quickly in the administration of booming Fujian and Zhejiang provinces. Premier Li Keqiang, born in 1955, the son of a local official, was also sent down but returned to get a law degree at Beida and later a doctorate in economics, making him one of three economists on the Standing Committee, a new thing.

Generations of Chinese Communist Rulers			Accomplishments
First	Mao and Zhou	1949–1976	Won revolution, brutally communized, destructive upheavals
Second	Deng	1977–1989	Calmed China, allowed private enterprise, crushed Tiananmen
Third	Jiang, Li, Zhu	1989–2002	Foreign investment, rapid growth
Fourth	Hu and Wen	2002–2012	Technocratic rule to promote China's power and prestige
Fifth	Xi and Li	2012–2022 (presumed)	Stabilize economy and shift it toward mass consumption

autonomous region
Soviet-style home area for ethnic minority.

Uighur
Muslim, Turkic-speaking ethnic group, bordering ex-Soviet Central Asia.

Xinjiang
China's northwesternmost region, home of *Uighurs*.

Tibet
Himalayan region of China with distinct language and culture.

China also has five **autonomous regions**, a concept borrowed from Stalin's organization of the Soviet Union, where large nationalities got their own Soviet republics and smaller ones got autonomous regions within the republics. China's purpose here is the same as Stalin's: to give ethnic groups use of their language. The most troublesome are the 8 million Turkic-speaking Muslim **Uighurs** of Central Asia in **Xinjiang** (literally "new frontier," named by the Manchu Qing dynasty). The regime arrests Uighurs of the East Turkestan Islamic Movement as dangerous terrorists with links to al Qaeda.

Tibet has a distinctive Buddhist culture and long ago was independent. First acquired by the Mongols in the thirteenth century as part of their Yuan dynasty, Tibet (Xizang) has been claimed by China ever since. The PLA crushed a major Tibetan independence uprising in the 1950s and a smaller one in 2008. Inner Mongolia (*Nei Mongol*), home of nomadic Buddhist herders, covers a huge swath along China's northern border. Stalin set up Outer Mongolia as independent Mongolia, a buffer on Russia's underbelly. China's autonomous regions have been gradually brought under Beijing's control by settling millions of *Han* Chinese in them.

Chinese Political Culture

7.3   Identify the main sources of discontent in today's China.

There is growing ferment in China, but it is not on the brink of democracy. Aside from intellectuals, few Chinese have clear notions of democracy, and few thirst for it. Perhaps, in a generation, a majority will, but at present, most just want jobs, rising living standards, and national pride, which the regime delivers. The question now is whether China is developing sufficient social, economic, and cultural bases to eventually sustain a democracy. There are grounds for hope.

Many Third World countries lack a consistent political culture that has grown slowly over time. Instead—as in Mexico and Iran—they have imported and distorted waves of outside ideas that rarely blend into a coherent whole. And each wave of ideas is overthrown, often violently, by the next. We can see, for example, at least three layers in Chinese political culture. They sometimes reinforce and sometimes contradict one another.

Traditional Culture

Many values ingrained over three millennia of Chinese civilization have carried over into the People's Republic. No one, not even Mao, could wipe them clean. When the Communists restored Beijing as the capital in 1949, they were restoring an old symbol. Jiang's Nationalists had moved the capital to Nanjing, but many felt that Beijing was the legitimate one. Top government offices are in the Zhongnanhai, a compound next to the Forbidden City of the emperors. Tiananmen (Gate of Heavenly Peace) Square is still Beijing's parade and demonstration area, much like Red Square is in Moscow.

Another value from China's history is the conviction that China is one country and must never be divided, first articulated by Confucian intellectuals in reaction to the time of Warring

States. The Qing (Manchu) dynasty annexed Taiwan only in 1683 (to stop Taiwanese pirates and a Dutch takeover), but Chinese still feel strongly that it is an eternal part of China and must soon reunify with the motherland, even if that requires force.

The Communists' bureaucrats and cadres perform much the same function as the old Mandarins and gentry. Reciting a developmentalist line instead of Confucius, the new elites strive to control and guide China, now aiming at growth and modernization. Mao himself recognized the similarity of old and new when he denounced the bureaucrats as the "new Mandarins" during the Cultural Revolution. Deng Xiaoping governed in the old Confucian style.

Another carryover from Old China: Age confers special qualities of wisdom and leadership. Mao died at 82 and Zhou at 78, both in office. When he returned to power in 1977, Deng Xiaoping was 73. In his early 90s, he was still politically influential although weak and deaf. Former President Jiang and Prime Minister Zhu still governed in their 70s. Trying to break the tendency to gerontocracy, the Party now does not appoint anyone over 70 to a new position.

Nationalist China

Overpowering traditional Chinese values is the more recent nationalism that has dominated China's intellectual life for a century. Chinese nationalism, like Asian and Middle East nationalism generally, is the result of a proud and ancient civilization suffering penetration, disorientation, and humiliation at the hands of the West and Japan. This can induce rage and the feeling that the native culture, although temporarily beaten by foreigners, is morally superior and more enduring. Mao and Zhou began as young patriots urging their countrymen to revitalize China and stand up to the West and to Japan. In our day, Chinese, Russians, and Iranians still act out their resentment of the West, especially of America. Most of what China does today—from space launches to claiming the China Seas—is out of nationalism. For the sake of Chinese power, Beijing accepts some capitalism. Chinese communism is, at heart, Chinese nationalism.

In Asia, Chinese and Japanese nationalists vowed to beat the West at its own game, building industry and weaponry but making them serve the traditional culture. The Japanese modernizers, starting with the 1868 Meiji Restoration, succeeded; the Chinese have not yet completed this process. As in the old Soviet Union, the prevailing Chinese attitude is the nationalist drive to catch up with the West. During their good economic growth years—the mid-1950s and since 1980—Chinese leaders were proud of their rapid progress. The Great Leap Forward and the Cultural Revolution set the economy back decades. A pragmatic moderate such as Zhou or Deng always had a powerful argument against such disruptions: They harm growth and weaken China. Basically, this is a nationalist argument and one used by pragmatists today.

Chinese are deeply patriotic, increasingly in an angry way. Part is genuine, part is hyped by the regime. Anti-U.S. Chinese nationalism is growing, in part over Taiwan and Tibet and American complaints on human rights and copyright violations. A popular 2009 book, *Unhappy China*, claimed that the United States lost its leadership role in the financial crisis and now China must stand up to the West, become a superpower, and lead the world. The book could not have appeared without Beijing's permission. With government approval, Chinese raged when U.S. jets bombed the Chinese embassy in Belgrade in 1999 and when U.S. surveillance ships and planes get near China's coast.

Geography

Peasants in the Cities

Rapid urbanization characterizes the developing world. Unemployed or underemployed rural people flock to cities looking for jobs and a better life. The trend is strong in China, where the urban-rural gap is huge. Historically, 90 percent of Chinese lived in the countryside. In 1978, only 18 percent lived in cities; in 2014, 54 percent did.

Every year, millions of rural Chinese move to cities for the factory jobs that are the basis of China's growth. They ignore the **hukou** residence permits, an ancient control system designed to keep Chinese at their heriditary residence. Now a third of China's urban dwellers—some born in the city—lack an urban hukou and have scant rights to education, health care, housing, and a chance to rise into the middle class. In 2014, Beijing announced that by 2020, it would grant urban hukous to 100 to 200 million Chinese, many of them already living in cities.

Back in the village, discontent simmers. Most peasants are wretchedly poor, with some families living on $1 a day. Remembering the starvation of the Great Leap Forward, many peasants leave the countryside or urge their children to. When peasants go to a city for work—some at 50 yuan ($8) a day in pick-and-shovel construction—they see the vastly better life of the emerging urban middle class—apartments, cars, money to spend—and resent their lowly status.

Peasant mentality—the willingness to work hard for one's family and not ask for much—carries over into China's cities. Many of China's best entrepreneurs fled rural poverty for urban opportunities. They know how to work around official barriers (bribery). Earthy peasant humor and folkways and frugal personal habits are found in cities and industries. Unfortunately, peasant habits such as spitting on the sidewalks and reckless driving have also carried over.

Orderly urbanization is a huge problem for the regime. On the one hand, they know they have to get Chinese out of peasant farming. There is simply not enough land, and ignorant, uneducated peasants do not move China ahead. Unrest grows in rural China as peasants protest seizures of their farmland. In fairness, local tax bases are so skimpy—because land is collectively owned and therefore not taxed—that county officials must lease out land to developers in order to fund local schools and roads. (One solution: Privatize land and tax it, as other countries do.) Leading protesters are often unemployed ex-soldiers. Fearing a large, dispossessed underclass, Beijing is spreading industrialization inland, up the great river valleys and into towns and smaller cities. They aim at the orderly urbanization of another 250 million rural Chinese by constructing huge, new apartment blocks (which few peasants like).

hukou
(sounds like *who cow*) Registered place of residence.

Anti-Japanese feelings are even stronger. Chinese bitterly remember how the Japanese army butchered Chinese civilians, even babies, during World War II. The 1937 Japanese "Rape of Nanjing"—with an estimated 20,000 female victims—is especially remembered. Anti-Japanese protests break out frequently, some with Beijing's connivance to let people blow off steam.

Beijing turns on and off anti-U.S., anti-Japanese, or take-over-Taiwan demonstrations to deflect mass discontent, an old governing technique. These outpourings are tacitly government encouraged but have strong roots in Chinese nationalism, especially against Japan. But once the protests get rolling, the protesters become too eager and use the demonstrations to vent displeasure at the Communist regime. Then the regime gets frightened that antiforeign demonstrations are spinning out of control and abruptly calls them off.

Maoism

China's constitution still proclaims **Maoism**, or Mao Zedong Thought, as Beijing calls it, as one of the bases of modern China, but the regime has let it fade. New high school history books pay little attention to Mao, but a Maoism course is still required in colleges. Mao Thought contains several strands. From traditional China, it takes the Confucian emphasis on thinking right thoughts. Willpower is more important than weaponry in wars and more important than technology in building China. The unleashed forces of the masses, guided by Mao Zedong Thought, can conquer anything. This extreme form of **voluntarism** comes from China's past.

From nationalism, Mao took the emphasis on strengthening and rebuilding China so that it can stand up to its old enemies. The trouble is that traditional and nationalist values partly conflict with each other. Traditional values call for China to ignore the West and its technology, but nationalist values call for China to learn and copy from the West.

Maoism also draws on Mao's "mass line" and guerrilla warfare. According to Maoist doctrine, what the PLA did to beat Jiang's Nationalists, China as a whole must do to advance and become a world leader: Work with the masses, be self-reliant, and use more willpower than technology to overcome obstacles. Mao can be seen as a theorist of guerrilla warfare who continued to apply his principles to governance—with catastrophic results.

In the Great Leap Forward from 1958 to 1961, Mao tried guerrilla warfare tactics on the economy, using raw manual labor plus enthusiasm to industrialize overnight. Engineers, experts, and administrators were bypassed. The Soviets warned Mao it would not work and urged him to follow the Soviet model of building the economy by more conventional means; Mao refused. In 1960, unhappy with Mao's radicalism, the Soviets withdrew their numerous foreign-aid technicians, and the Sino-Soviet split became public.

For the Soviet Communists, the revolution was over; the proletariat triumphed in 1917 and moved Russia into the most advanced stage of history. For Mao, the revolution never ends. Mao held that, at any stage, conservative tendencies block the path to socialism: bureaucratism, elitism, and opportunism. Mao resolved to combat these tendencies with "permanent revolution," periodic upheavals to let the force of the masses surge past the conservative bureaucrats.

Socialism, however, needs lots of bureaucrats—something Max Weber saw long ago—but Mao hated China settling into bureaucratic patterns and was determined to reverse them by instituting permanent upheaval. In the resulting Cultural Revolution from 1966 to 1976, young people were encouraged to criticize, harass, and oust authority. Chaos blanketed China, the economy slumped, and the army took over. After Mao's death, power returned to the bureaucrats.

Mao refused to recognize the unhappy truth that socialism needs a big bureaucracy. By trying to leap directly into a guerrilla socialism without bureaucrats, Mao nearly wrecked China. On balance, Mao Zedong Thought is inherently unworkable, and, in today's China, Mao is quoted little and out of context. Such vague homilies as "Get truth from facts" lets leaders claim they are following Mao even as they repudiate him. Mao's picture is on Tiananmen and all paper currency, but few follow his ideas.

Political Culture

Beijing Rules

A taxi ride in a Chinese city teaches much. (Under no circumstances drive yourself.) Streets are crowded, often jammed. Drivers dodge, weave, force their way, even drive on the wrong side of the street. They nearly run over bicyclists, pedestrians, and three-wheeled cargo motorcycles. A left turn into oncoming traffic is like a video game. But drivers are skilled and usually miss each other by inches. Car drivers yield only grudgingly to big trucks and buses.

Beijing Rules are basically: "There are no rules." Rules on the books are not enforced or even understood, so people do whatever they can get away with. In fairness, this lawless culture is standard throughout the Third World. Poisonous melamine was added to boost the apparent protein content of pet food and milk. China produced toxic toothpaste, lead-painted toys, and defective tires. Some mines and factories use child slave labor. Producers shrug and note that laws and enforcement are so vague and flexible in China that everyone ignores the rules. Only a mass outcry makes authorities stop covering up and go after wrongdoers.

This "no-rules" rule seems to apply to China's laws, government regulation, diplomacy, corruption, commerce, and fake or hazardous products. No one cares if it is illegal; one does whatever it takes to get ahead in business or traffic. Many evade paying personal income tax. The Chinese fighter pilot who clipped a U.S. surveillance plane in 2001 (he died) was flying by Beijing Rules. The massive pirating of foreign DVDs, political science textbooks, and handbag labels are Beijing Rules. Flexible accounting and banking standards are Beijing Rules. Beijing Rules exemplify the lack of civil society, of the usages and interactions that over time build up into polite, predictable behavior. Beijing Rules make China colorful but lawless. Eventually, China will have to evolve some rules.

Something to Believe In

Educated Chinese in the twentieth century had a cause to believe in. At first, it was building a new republic that would not be carved up by foreigners. Then it was in repelling the Japanese. With the Communist takeover, many Chinese believed in Mao's vision of a prosperous, socialist China. After Mao wrecked China with his Great Leap Forward and Cultural Revolution, Deng Xiaoping offered the image of a prosperous, semicapitalist China. After the June 1989 massacre of students in Tiananmen Square, many thinking Chinese fell into despair and now ignore Marx, Mao, and Deng. The Party now has nothing to offer except career advancement for some.

What then do Chinese have to believe in? Making money. A 2013 poll found 71 percent of Chinese respondents said they "measure success by the things I own" (South Koreans 45 percent, Japanese 22, Americans 20, and Swedes 7). Chinese now have few values beyond materialism. Confucian values are erased, bourgeois values never took hold, and Maoist values are discredited. As in Russia after the collapse of communism, China has an "anything goes" mentality in which most are out for themselves with little notion of a common good. This is partly the fault of the CCP's power monopoly: It alone defines the common good, and it fails to do so. Chinese live in a spiritual vacuum, which may be communism's saddest legacy.

Xi Jinping offered a "Chinese dream" of a great-power China. Unlike the individualistic "American dream," Xi's is collectivist and nationalist. China as a whole is to become strong, prosperous, and happy. "Revival," "rejuvenation," and "strong army" are Xi's major themes, which echo a 2010 book by a hawkish PLA colonel, *China Dream*, calling for China to become the world's most powerful country. China's nationalistic and military dream can easily clash with the U.S. "pivot" to Asia.

Guangdong
Southern coastal province, capital Guangzhou.

Pearl River Delta
Major industrial area in *Guangdong*; includes Guangzhou, Shenzhen, and Hong Kong.

As in Russia, civil society is weak in China. As Alexis de Tocqueville observed in *Democracy in America*, civil society is the autonomous associations bigger than the family but smaller than the state—churches, labor unions, business associations, voluntary groups—and the habits and usages that come with them. Such associations, the basis of pluralism and a prerequisite of stable democracy, are starting to appear in China, as shown by the voluntary help after the 2008 Sichuan earthquake. In 2009, environmentalists and community activists got the site of a planned oil refinery moved far away from **Guangdong**'s heavily populated **Pearl River Delta**. A Politburo member and the province's Party chief said the decision "reflects how Guangdong values environmental protection, the ecology, and the opinions of our citizens." It is also a way to head off trouble.

A huge but unknown number of environmental, farming, business, and homeowner groups form spontaneously in China, but the regime largely rejects their lawsuits and jails obstreperous leaders. It takes over and supervises some of the biggest associations, but the key to pluralism is autonomous organizations, those outside of state control. In Communist East Europe, environmental groups were grudgingly allowed because they staked out "safe" issues that did not threaten regime legitimacy. Citizens who were not especially green joined them as a sly way to protest against the regime in general. One suspects the same is at work in China. Optimists argue that Beijing, in cautiously heeding some environmental demands, may be sprouting a little pluralism. Skeptics say they have just become slightly flexible control freaks.

Religion, both old (including Christianity) and new, is growing rapidly despite the arrest, imprisonment, and torture of believers. The sudden rise in the 1990s of a new religion, *Falun Gong*, an offshoot of Buddhism, illustrates what can happen in a spiritual vacuum: Any faith may rush in to fill it. Falun Gong attracted all kinds of Chinese with faith healing and traditional exercises. As in Japan, Buddhism generates numerous variations. Beijing understands that religion can bring upheaval—the Taipings and Boxers in the nineteenth century—and, in 1999, denounced Falun Gong as a brainwashing cult, outlawed it, and arrested thousands of its followers, some of whom died in custody. This is the reaction of a nervous regime.

Some educated Chinese have rediscovered classic liberalism—the philosophy of freedom and small government of Locke, Adam Smith, and Jefferson—that was popular a century ago among Chinese intellectuals. Now young Chinese returning with American MBAs understand the free markets extolled by Hayek and Friedman. This could challenge the regime's state control and lead to democracy, but discussions are low key and among friends. Open advocacy of liberalism could get you in trouble.

Over the decades, Chinese had to mouth slogans and participate in mass campaigns—one year anti-Confucius, the next anticapitalist roaders, then anti-Gang of Four, then anti-"spiritual pollution," then anti-"bourgeois liberalization." Many Chinese, fed up with this nonsense, mentally tune out and ignore politics.

Political Culture

How China Uses Its Past

Mao denounced old China as feudal and reactionary. During the Cultural Revolution, he encouraged Red Guards to "destroy the four olds." Zhou Enlai quietly ordered the army to protect important sites from their rampages. Since Mao's death in 1976, the regime has rediscovered—much as Stalin did—the utility of history: The past, artfully interpreted, makes it easier to rule the present. Beijing now uses old China to deliver lessons for today. More recent horrors, however, such as the Great Leap, Cultural Revolution, and Tiananmen massacre are barred from Chinese books and classes, but educated Chinese know about them.

In 1974—fortunately after the worst of the Cultural Revolution—a peasant digging a well in Shaanxi Province found the terra-cotta soldiers of **Qin** Shihuang, the emperor who first united China in 221 BC. Archaeologists unearthed thousands of fragments—there are more than 8,000 figures in all—and, from them, reconstructed hundreds of the life-size soldiers. Each one is different, modeled on strapping individual soldiers of that day. To protect Qin in the afterlife, all were equipped with weapons (looted very early) and drawn up into companies of pikemen, archers, cavalry, and so on. They were originally painted in lifelike colors. Chinese and foreign tourists now swarm to see them near the city of Xian. The message: China's unity is old and enduring. You got that, **Taiwan**?

Likewise, Beijing's Military Museum (which has its own subway stop) devotes much space to a historical review of all China's dynasties, emphasizing that each had to be very strong in the face of peasant uprisings, breakaway provinces, and Mongol or Manchu invasions. No dynasty enjoyed tranquil times; all had to be prepared. If they weakened, they perished. Attempts to undermine or overthrow the emperor were punished by torture and dismemberment. You got that, intellectuals and troublemakers? Also shown in the Military Museum (but without English captions) is how the heroism of the PLA won the **Korean War**, which China fought to block U.S. aggression. You got that, Americans?

The strongest use of the past is the **Anti-Japanese War** of 1937–1945. Beijing has a separate Anti-Japanese War Museum that stresses the invaders' atrocities. Television series show how China "fought bravely against Japan under the leadership of the Communist Party." With communism no longer a usable ideology, the regime hypes hatred of Japan to

Unearthed in 1974 near Xian in central China, thousands of terra-cotta soldiers of Emperor Qin, who first united China in 221 BC, remind Chinese of the unity and strength of their country.

deflect discontent and hold China together. The regime thunders against Japan getting nuclear weapons or a permanent seat on the UN Security Council, and all Chinese agree. You got that, Tokyo?

Beijing often invokes its **Century of Humiliation** and is dedicated to erasing the humiliations and restoring China to its rightful place in the world. Mao's mausoleum is perfectly on axis with the Meridian Gate of the Forbidden City across Tiananmen Square, just where the old geomancers would have sited it. Mao's continuity with the past he hated is now for all Chinese to see. In 2005, archaeologists unearthed a 4,000-year-old bowl of petrified noodles, proving that China invented pasta. You got that, Italians?

Hidden Anger, Crouching Dissent

There is discontent in China, but it is free floating and unfocused. Chinese are cynical about government, seen as corrupt. Most doubt official statistics. Protests and demonstrations are increasing in China—among rural people, unemployed rust-belt workers, and minority groups. There are tens of thousands of "mass incidents" every year, some of them ending in police gunfire. Most protests are local, unorganized, spontaneous, and related to specific grievances, such as land seizures, failure to pay wages, plant layoffs, and corrupt officials.

The regime crushes protests, jails their leaders, and smothers news reports. Brave souls who publicize corruption and incompetence—journalists, lawyers, medical doctors, and academics—are fired, harassed, and arrested. Until recently, police, without trial, sent troublemakers to camps for brutal "reeducation through labor" for up to four years. News organizations pull their punches by practicing **self-censorship**, a common practice in authoritarian systems. To keep their jobs, they refrain from criticism. The Chinese media—China Central Television (CCTV), for example—look slick and Western but concentrate on good news. Chinese journalists and academics who have become U.S. citizens can tell it like it is.

Brave souls who charged that shoddy school construction led to the deaths of thousands of children in the 2008 Sichuan earthquake were tried—without defense witnesses—for subversion and possessing state secrets, widely used charges. Workers who try to organize labor unions languish in prison. Lawyers who help victims of government neglect—such as instructing how to sue over poison milk—are disbarred and jailed for "tax evasion," something most Chinese could be charged with, but prosecution is selective. Blind self-taught rights lawyer Chen Guangcheng, who protested forced abortions, escaped brutal and extralegal house arrest in 2012 and made it into the U.S. embassy in Beijing. Embarrassed by the negative publicity, the regime let him leave for New York University. A nervous regime, afraid of one blind man, denies and covers up problems with the phrase, "Stability is the overriding priority."

Reasoned criticism comes from Chinese intellectuals, whose boldest effort was "Charter '08," modeled on the Czechoslovak "Charter '77," an important step in the process that led to the overthrow of the Prague Communist regime in 1989. The 2008 Chinese charter said that "freedom is at the core of universal human values" and called on the CCP to give up its

Qin
First dynasty to unify China, 221–206 BC.

Taiwan
Large island off China's southern coast, ruled by Nationalists since 1945.

Korean War
1950–1953 conflict involving North and South Korean, U.S., and Chinese forces.

Anti-Japanese War
Chinese name for World War II in China, 1937–1945.

Century of Humiliation
China's term for its domination by imperialists from the first Opium War to Communist victory, 1839–1949.

self-censorship
The curbing of criticism writers impose on themselves.

Political Culture

Religion in China

Religion is under the surface in China; no one really knows how big it is. Officially, only 10 percent of Chinese are religious, but survey research suggests that some 30 percent are, two-thirds of them Buddhist or Daoist, China's traditional religions.

Buddhism was less important in China than Confucianism and never rooted itself in China as deeply as it did in Tibet, Thailand, or Vietnam. **Daoism** survives in the cult of luck, which still obsesses many Chinese as the way to win money. The number eight, for example, is especially lucky and desirable. Muslims, both the Uighurs of Xinjiang and Chinese Muslims in several pockets throughout China, may total 2 percent.

Some 70 million (5 percent) or more of Chinese are Christians, a number that is growing fast and is possibly higher than the number of CCP members. Exact estimates are difficult because many Chinese Christians attend "home churches" outside of state-registered churches. The Communists (and, long ago, the Boxers) always regarded Christianity as an unwelcome foreign import that missionaries used to subordinate China to the imperialists. Foreign missionary work is prohibited, and the leaders of some home-grown Chinese Protestant sects have been executed.

There has been a Catholic presence for centuries, first brought to China, as to Japan, by brilliant **Jesuits**. The Communists, in the 1950s, ordered the Catholic Church to break with the Vatican and become a state-supervised "patriotic" church, which includes a large cathedral in Beijing. There may be as many as 12 million Catholics in China. The regime did not permit Rome to appoint bishops—the argument against foreign influence again—so ordination of new priests was problematic because Rome does not recognize the ordination of priests by Communist-appointed bishops.

Some Chinese academics note that Protestant Christianity first appeared in northwest Europe and made it capitalist, rich, and strong (a theory advanced a century ago by German sociologist Max Weber). Accordingly, they surmise, it might not be a bad thing for China. On this basis, some Chinese intellectuals could be potential converts to Christianity. They, however, have little or no contact with the broad masses of Chinese and are unlikely to link up with underground churches. Christian intellectuals combined with broad masses of believers could produce a major Christian interest group in China.

The regime, however, fears any alternative organization that could challenge or ignore the Party. If Beijing permitted it, Christianity could spread rapidly in China and help build the missionaries' old dream of a prosperous and democratic Christian China. Chinese need something to believe in, and Chinese society needs the pluralism that comes with religious freedom.

Daoism
From Dao, "the way"; old Chinese religion originally based on nature; earlier spelled *Taoism*.

Jesuit
Society of Jesus; Catholic religious order once active in converting Asians.

monopoly on power in favor of a new democratic constitution in which "the people select their government." Initially signed by 303 Chinese intellectuals, more than 10,000 joined them (many online). Beijing immediately blocked the Charter on the Internet. Dozens of signers lost their jobs or were arrested. Charter '08 may eventually stand alongside the Magna Carta and Declaration of Independence as a document of democracy.

The great hope for Chinese students is to go abroad. Many study English and dream of joining the thousands of Chinese students already in the United States, some of whom do not return to China. The regime, aware of this brain drain, now restricts their numbers. Chinese university graduates are supposed to first work five years before they can apply for graduate study overseas. The great prize: a graduate degree, often an MBA, from a prestigious U.S. university. Some high-ranking Chinese get their children into such programs. President Xi had a daughter (under an assumed name) at Harvard.

Putonghua
"Common language" of China, now standard; earlier called Mandarin.

The Chinese way of handling the latest government crackdown is called *biaotai*, "to express an attitude." They crank out the current line while concealing their true feelings. This leads to what Chinese call *nei jin, wai song*, "repression within, tranquility outside." Everything looks calm, but only because people know they are being watched. Just below the surface, though, repressed anger waits to erupt. Some of this shows up in the constant flow of nasty rumors on the social media about repression, economic incompetence, and the corruption of officials. This has been called a struggle between the Big Lie and Little Whisper: The government tries to fool people with big lies, but the people fight back with little whispers.

"My Father Is Li Gang!"

In October 2010, a drunken young man drove his car fast across Hebei University campus, striking two women students, killing one. Upon arrest, he shouted, "My father is Li Gang!" (the local deputy police chief), as if that would protect him. The official media blocked all word of the incident, but, within days, every student in China knew of it through the new electronic media and was using the phrase to snicker at misuse of power. Eventually, even the official press had to carry the story, and the driver was sentenced to six years. The victim's parents were bought off for an undisclosed amount.

Geography

Region and Language

China illustrates the close connection—and problems—between a country's languages and its regions. All but small countries have regions, often based on language. In some cases, as between Serbs and Albanian-speaking Kosovars, the country splits apart. China is populated mostly by Han Chinese, but they are divided into several languages.

China's rulers have always proclaimed the unity of China, but China has eight main language groups—mutually unintelligible—and hundreds of dialects. (India may be the world's most linguistically complex country.) China's biggest language by far is Mandarin, dialects of which are spoken by 800 million in a broad swath from north to south, but not in the important southern coastal provinces, where 90 million speak some form of the Wu language (including Shanghai) and 70 million speak Cantonese.

Over a century ago, the late Qing dynasty tried to make Mandarin standard and universal, a cause adopted by the Nationalists. The Communist regime has largely succeeded with a modified Beijing Mandarin, **Putonghua**, now the language of government and education and increasingly of urban Chinese. Rural Chinese learn it in school but still speak the local language. A Shanghai professional might speak Shanghainese for daily life but switch to Putonghua to communicate with Chinese from elsewhere and English for international business. Hong Kongers and Macanese still speak Cantonese, although many now learn Putonghua to deal with mainland tourists and businesspeople. In 2012, Hong Kong's new chief executive gave his inaugural speech in Mandarin, something Hong Kongers resented.

Solidarity
Huge Polish labor union that ousted the Communist regime in 1989.

Computers and cell phones now let Chinese protest injustice, so the regime tries to block them. China has 350 million Internet users, more than the U.S. population. A like number use equivalents of Twitter and Facebook, called *weibo* (microblogs), whose speed and ubiquity vex the regime. In 2011, China combined several agencies into the State Internet Information Office, which sometimes shuts down Internet and weibo sites. Tens of thousands of censors supervise China's electronic media, filtering mails for "lewd content" and keywords such as "democracy," "Tiananmen," and "Taiwan," what Chinese call the "Great Firewall," which they leap with freeware and sound-alike words.

The regime jails some bloggers for "subverting state power" and closes hundreds of critical sites (including YouTube), but these can be reached indirectly. However many sites it closes, slippery bloggers open new ones. Cell phones are hard to monitor and can energize and organize local protesters. A text message, very cheap in China, can reach many, simultaneously and anonymously. (Chinese text messages in pinyin.) Beijing periodically closes the Chinese equivalents of Twitter.

China's leaders, jittery over the 2011 "Arab Spring" and 2012 leadership changes, rounded up more suspects than usual. Ai Weiwei, China's top artist, was badly beaten in 2009 and jailed in 2011. One young woman went to jail for sending one sarcastic tweet. People were arrested for strolling in the wrong part of town (it might be a protest demonstration). Most Chinese are apolitical, but some dislike and distrust the regime. They especially resent rich cadres, marked by black Audi A6 cars, a prestige favorite at $61,500 each. Chinese, some 2 million of whom visit Taiwan yearly, see that Taiwanese enjoy four times the income plus democratic freedoms. In an economic downturn, Chinese frustration could boil over again.

A triggering event—such as a recession, police brutality, or egregious corruption—could bring together China's peasants, workers, and students to challenge the regime. Needless to say, the police work hard to prevent a Chinese equivalent of Poland's **Solidarity**. Repression, of course, solves nothing; it merely postpones the day of reckoning. Some scholars see China approaching a "tipping point" in which a minor incident taps heretofore private criticism, which encourages more to voice their discontent in an angry, expanding cascade, such as East Europe experienced in 1989.

A Bourgeois China?

One of the contradictions—a term Marx used for major dysfunctions that rip the system apart—now troubling China is its rapid creation of a middle class, precisely the class that Communists staunchly oppose. Antibourgeois ideology is woven into Marxism. Even as a student, Marx hated the bourgeoisie; he later developed his complex theories to prove that they were doomed. Actually, the *bourgeoisie* was and still is the most successful social class in history. It rose with the modern state and created the modern economy, bringing prosperity, democracy, personal freedom, education, and mass communications. Marxists hate to admit that middle classes do anything good; they are a mere temporary step in the march to a proletarian paradise.

Now China is creating a new middle class at a record-setting rate by expanding its universities. After the Cultural Revolution had closed universities for a decade, the portion of young Chinese attending college shot up from 1.4 percent in 1978 to 25 percent in 2010. Now some

Democracy

Academic Freedom in China

There is some academic freedom in China, but subdued and private. On several sojourns in China, I discovered that whatever American academics are discussing about China, so are Chinese academics. But they keep it among themselves, whereas we publish it.

Liu Xiaobo won the Nobel Peace Prize—China's first Nobel—but was imprisoned and denounced for authoring Charter '08. Many Chinese professors are aware—through the electronic media—and generally supportive of Charter '08 but offer nuanced comments, namely, favoring cautious steps toward democracy but not to federalism, which could rip China apart.

Chinese speak rather freely in private—my experience years ago in Communist East Europe—but mostly face-to-face among trusted friends. Chinese academics lecture on a range of topics, but what is said in the classroom stays in the classroom. Criticism of the regime is sometimes implied, but there are no ringing calls for democracy. Many academics research and write on hot subjects that go as reports to Beijing ministries, but they are not published.

This helps explain the paucity of probing, thought-provoking books and articles from Chinese academics. Few Chinese universities are on the intellectual map. What they publish supports the regime in a ho-hum fashion. That is a pity, because many Chinese academics have important insights, often based on empirical research.

Hong Kong universities, on the other hand, count for tenure and promotion only publication in English-language journals that are refereed. Hong Kong academics assume that publication in a Chinese journal is based on favors and political correctness.

Instead of gaining prestige through publications, the standard Western path, mainland Chinese universities attempt to win it through contacts and connections with foreign universities. If they invite enough foreign guest lecturers, they figure (mistakenly) that the visitors' prestige will rub off on them.

7 million graduate a year (up from 830,000 in 1998). The regime, itself run by engineers, educates massive numbers of engineers and scientists to push China's economic growth. Students who test well get into one of a dozen prestigious universities, most in Beijing or Shanghai. China's Harvard is (and for a century has been) Beijing University (*Beida*); its MIT is the nearby **Qinghua**. China has many lesser institutions with lower standards for admission. A bigger student population can lead to more discontent, especially when graduates have massive debts but few jobs. (Sound familiar?) Ironically, skilled blue-collar workers are now in greater demand and higher paid than college graduates. Higher education does not solve all problems and may have overexpanded in China.

What, exactly, makes a person middle class? A certain level of income? Of education? Of material possessions? There is no standard definition that can be used transnationally, but some of the characteristics of middle class are growing rapidly in China: cars, nice apartments with air conditioners, and even single-family homes in suburban developments. The more important question: Does becoming bourgeois make one interested in politics and in favor of democracy? Or can the regime forever feed the material cravings of the middle class to keep it quiet and disorganized? Virtually all industrializing countries show that, as middle classes grow, they demand responsive political systems and increasingly voice their discontent.

Qinghua
China's top technological university, in Beijing (still often spelled in Wade-Giles *Tsinghua*).

Geography

Ethnic Strife in China

Communists claimed to have solved the "nationalities question" on the basis of equality and brotherhood. It did not work in the Soviet Union or Yugoslavia, and it may not work in China. Chinese, aware of their ancient and proud culture, look down on and mistrust their 55 ethnic minorities (as do Russians). The Uighur areas of Beijing are dangerous, I was warned. Ethnic riots broke out in Tibet in 2008, in Xinjiang in 2009, and in Inner Mongolia in 2011.

These three provinces together form over 40 percent of China's territory but are thinly populated: 3, 20, and 24 million people, respectively. Beijing governs them as "autonomous regions," but they are more like colonies. Han Chinese, seeking economic opportunities, pour into Tibet, Xinjiang, and Inner Mongolia where they are now, respectively, 10, 55, and 79 percent of the populations. Beijing encourages Han settlement to cement the regions into China. (What, by the way, did Americans do in the western part of their continent?)

Tibetans, Uighurs, and Mongolians angrily complain that the Chinese settlers—who are better off and run most businesses—are erasing their languages, cultures, and religions, Buddhism in Tibet and Mongolia and Islam in Xinjiang. The Chinese settlers respond that they build the local economy and boost living standards. Many Tibetans, Uighurs, and Mongolians themselves have migrated from poor rural areas to cities. Not all speak Mandarin. Police and officials—nearly all Han—discriminate against them, and economic growth and jobs go mostly to ethnic Chinese. China, like many countries, has created a poor and angry underclass.

Ethnic conflict was a major factor in ending the Soviet Union. The same could probably not happen in China. Ethnic Russians were a bare majority of the Soviet Union, but Han Chinese are more than 90 percent of China's population. The Soviet Union was in economic decline, but China is growing rapidly. The Soviet Union was a federal system that gave local talent many leading roles. Unitary China keeps power in Han hands. Ethnic unrest in China will simply be crushed, something most Han Chinese approve of.

Proud China

Yale's Harold Lasswell (1902–1978) argued that a nervous regime will try to deflect discontent away from its problems and shortcomings and onto allegedly threatening foreign powers: in a word, nationalism. China's current rulers behave as if they have read Lasswell, cranking up (and then down) anti-U.S. and anti-Japanese campaigns at irregular intervals. Many Chinese are tired of these campaigns and ignore them. The U.S. Congress plays this game too, blaming China for everything from loss of jobs to oil prices. Thirty years earlier, Congress blamed Japan.

How can a regime handle the several and contradictory impulses of Chinese political culture? Uncontrolled, they could be dangerous. Beijing's answer is to cultivate patriotic pride. Almost everything the regime does goes toward demonstrating China's greatness. In 2003, China sent an astronaut into Earth's orbit, the third country to do so. China's motive was the same as the earlier U.S. and Soviet space programs: to show the world that it is a great nation. In 2008, Beijing hosted the Olympics, which China used to showcase how modern and powerful it is.

China is quite open about its aim to become, once again, the leading power in Asia and one of the top world powers. Some suggest that China could supplant the United States. In economics, China has accomplished much. Will China's policy of national pride ease

China through to becoming a normal, prosperous, and calm country? Or could national pride run out of control and turn aggressive and expansionist?

Great Leap Forward
Mao's failed late 1950s effort to industrialize China overnight.

Cultural Revolution
Mao's late 1960s mad effort to break bureaucracy in China.

Patterns of Interaction

7.4   Compare and contrast China's Great Leap Forward and its Cultural Revolution.

Since the Communists came to power in 1949, there have been three major upheavals plus several smaller ones. Among major upheavals are the "agrarian reforms" (that is, execution of landlords and redistribution of land) of the early 1950s, the **Great Leap Forward** from 1958 to 1961, and the **Cultural Revolution** from 1966 to 1976. Smaller upheavals include the brief Hundred Flowers liberalization of 1956, the antirightist campaigns of 1957 and the early 1970s, the crushing of the Gang of Four and their supporters in the late 1970s, and the 1989 repression of alleged "counterrevolutionary rebellion" of prodemocracy students.

The big upheavals and most of the smaller ones can be traced to the same underlying problem: Beijing's leaders, having inherited a poor and backward land, want to make China rich and powerful. Mao Zedong Thought taught that everything is possible: China can leap into the modern age and even beyond it. But the old, stubborn, traditional China does not yield easily; it frustrates the bold plans and tugs the system back toward the previous patterns and problems.

The Great Leap Forward

In 1958, Mao Zedong launched a strange effort to move China ahead: the Great Leap Forward. His belief that progress can be coerced severely damaged China. Vowing to progress "20 years in a day" and "catch up with Great Britain in 15 years," all of China was urged to "walk on two legs" (use all possible means) to industrialize rapidly. It was a self-destructive policy that failed to understand that other countries have industrialized rapidly without coercion.

In the Great Leap, peasants—a majority of Chinese—were enslaved into gigantic communes, some with 100,000 people. They had to eat in communal dining halls, leave their children in nurseries, and even sleep in large dormitories. The communes were ordered to undertake engineering and industrial projects. Relying on "labor-intensive" methods to compensate for lack of capital, millions had to move earth with carry poles to build dams and irrigation works. Backyard blast furnaces were ordered built so that every commune could produce its own iron. The projects were foolish and a waste of labor.

Failure was fast and catastrophic. Peasants—as in Stalin's collectivization drive—were supposed to produce a lot of grain but were allowed none to eat. Local officials lied about record harvests to make themselves look good, so much grain went to the cities and was even exported. As a result, an estimated 36 to 45 million Chinese died of starvation, the twentieth century's worst killing episode. (Cannibalism was reported.) Even Mao had to admit the failure; he resigned as president of the PRC but kept his chairmanship of the CCP. The communes were quietly phased out, broken into "production teams," which were in fact the old villages. Land was then leased back to individual families, in effect returning to private farming. Many rural Chinese never trusted the government again and left for the cities. This massive but quiet opposition underlies much of China's subsequent changes.

Red Guards
Radical Maoist youth who
disrupted China during the
Cultural Revolution.

The Great Proletarian Cultural Revolution

Mao Zedong, although he lost much power during the catastrophic Great Leap Forward, did not give up on pushing China into his desired paths, no matter how much the harm. In the bizarre Great Proletarian Cultural Revolution, an elderly Mao, no longer fully in charge, battled the very structures his new China had created. Mao saw himself combating the growth of bureaucracy; arrogant, comfortable bureaucrats were betraying his egalitarian, peasant-based revolution. He especially hated chief of state Liu Shaoqi, a progrowth pragmatist who was branded a "capitalist roader" and mistreated to death in 1969. The Cultural Revolution was a weakened Mao's effort to make China's revolution permanent and a power struggle over Mao's successor.

Of the many slogans from the Cultural Revolution, "bombard the command post" perhaps best summarizes its character. Mao encouraged young people, who formed local outfits called **Red Guards**, to destroy authority, even the CCP. They did, and China was set back at least a decade. Some of their slogans, many of them quotes from Mao:

- "Put destruction first, and in the process you have construction."
- "Destroy the four olds—old thought, old culture, old customs, old habits."
- "Once all struggle is grasped, miracles are possible."
- "Bombard the command post." (Attack established leaders if they are not revolutionary.)
- "So long as it is revolutionary, no action is a crime."
- "Sweep the great renegade of the working class onto the garbage heap!" (Dump moderate Liu Shaoqi.)
- "Cadres step to the side." (Bypass established authorities.)
- "To rebel is justified."

The Cultural Revolution began with a 1965 Shanghai historical play that some radicals claimed criticized Mao. Mao turned a small literary debate into mass criticism that led to the ouster of several Party officials. Then university and high school students were told to air their grievances against teachers and school administrators. Behind their discontent was a shortage of the kind of jobs the students thought they deserved upon graduation. Some young people saw a chance to cut loose and have fun destroying things.

By the fall of 1966, schools and universities were closed as their students demonstrated, humiliated officials, wrote wall posters, and travelled to "share revolutionary experiences." Some 1.5 to 2 million victims of the Red Guards were killed or committed suicide after physical abuse and psychological degradation. Worried officials set up their own Red Guard groups to protect themselves. Red Guard factions fought each other.

China descended into such chaos that even Mao grew worried and, in early 1967, ordered the army to step in. Soon the PLA effectively ran China, setting up "revolutionary committees," upon which sat PLA officers, Red Guard leaders, and "repentant" officials. By 1969, the worst was over, although, officially, the Cultural Revolution did not end until 1976 when Mao died and the ultraradical Gang of Four (headed by Mao's wife, Jiang Qing) was arrested.

The effects of the Cultural Revolution were terrible. The abilities of millions of bright, energetic young people were squandered. The economy was set back at least ten years. Education, when it resumed, was without standards, and students were chosen for their political attitudes rather than abilities. Moderate and level-headed officials, whom the Red Guards sought to destroy, laid low and pretended to go along with the Cultural Revolution. When it was over, they reasserted themselves and made sure one of their own was in charge: Deng Xiaoping (who, in 1980, posthumously rehabilitated Liu Shaoqi).

state-owned enterprises (SOEs)
Firms still owned by the Chinese government.

And what became of the Red Guards? Seventeen million urban young people were "sent down" to the countryside to "learn from the people" for years of hard farm labor. Eventually, most bribed their way back home to resume their education but carried the bitter experience all their lives. Some former Red Guards, disillusioned with the way they had been used, left for the British colony of Hong Kong or even the United States. A few eventually became capitalist millionaires in China's new market economy. Surveying the combined damage of the Great Leap and Cultural Revolution, some Chinese privately say that Mao lived 20 years too long. If he had died in 1956 instead of 1976, China would have been spared the madness of his declining years.

Chinese Left and Right Politics

The CCP is not completely stable. Left and right factions—both oversimplified labels—have some serious quarrels. The Chinese left tends to be people with positions in the Party, army, bureaucracy, and **state-owned enterprises (SOEs),** much like Soviet *apparatchiks.* Other leftists are from poor areas that feel neglected or are academics who deplore the major inequality that has developed in China. They note that the constitution still says "socialist," and they want more control over the economy to lift up impoverished inland provinces with health insurance and free education for all. Some are nostalgic for Mao and invoke his name and slogans.

The Chinese right includes a wide variety of moderates and liberals, often younger and better educated, plus urban people who were "sent down" during the Cultural Revolution. That would include Xi and Li. Most favor freeing market forces, even for SOEs. They point to the record-setting economic growth that came with private and foreign enterprises and argue that inequalities can be cured by locating industry inland. Liberals hate corrupt cadres and fear they damage legitimacy (correct). Some also seek political democracy and cultural freedom but without disturbing China's "stability." Former Premier Wen several times called for political and market reforms, but the media (including the Internet) swiftly deleted his words. Wen was isolated within the Standing Committee and was ineffectual. Still, (relative) liberal Wen had his supporters, but none on the current Standing Committee stake out liberal positions.

Bo Xilai was a leading figure on the left. A princeling, Politburo member, and populist Party chief of Chongqing, Bo was slated for the Standing Committee until brought down in 2012. Bo promoted "sing red and strike black"—Maoists songs and crackdowns on alleged mafias. His police tortured ordinary businessmen and seized their firms. After his wife poisoned a British business associate, it came out that Bo's family had amassed a fortune, much of it taken overseas. Bo's wife got a suspended death sentence (common in China). Bo was stripped of all positions and given a staged trial in 2013 for corruption. Many read it as political infighting in which the right faction marginalized the left faction.

China's chiefs keep disputes quiet as they balance left and right policies with measures to please both poor inland people and the urban coastal middle class. In the National People's

Congress, right and left debate such issues. A 2007 law on property rights had to be applied cautiously; no one owns land in China, but local authorities control it. City dwellers can get renewable "usage rights" for 40 to 70 years, and farmers can get 30-year leases. The new law makes these rights more secure, something the left does not like, as it seems to overturn socialism and favor the better off. The urban middle class likes the greater security over their apartments and businesses.

As in the old Soviet Union, ideology is often a mask for self-interest. The people who have cushy jobs warn that democracy and liberalization mean "abandoning socialism." If China fully liberalized, their bureaucratic sinecures could end. In analyzing Communist (and many other) systems, take ideology with a grain of salt; follow the jobs.

There are, and always have been, CCP factions behind the scenes, often nasty and back-stabbing. All Communist parties prohibit factions, but all have them. Using factions is one of two ways to gradually introduce democracy into China. The first is to let pluralistic groups form in the society at large and voice their views and demands. The best bet for a smooth transition, however, is to let the factions within the CCP present their views to the citizenry at large. If contested voting among People's Congress factions is allowed, the factions in effect become separate parties but preserve continuity by claiming they are just pursuing "socialism with Chinese characteristics." Gradual change is better than tumultuous change.

Left and Right in Chinese Politics	
Left	**Right**
selectively quote Mao	forget about Mao
keep Party Communist	admit businesspeople
control media closely	freer media, including Internet
help the poor	tolerate inequality for sake of growth
limit the market economy	cautiously expand the market economy
oppose foreign influence	be open to foreign influence
minimize mass input	expand local elections
take over Taiwan	tolerate Taiwan
ideological	pragmatic

Rice-Roots Democracy?

Around 2000, scattered across China, some village-level competitive elections of non-Party members were allowed. Some believe it was the work of liberalizers in the Party introducing democracy. Others say it comes from the bottom up, from villagers' anger at corrupt local officials who demand arbitrary "taxes." In some villages and townships, the Party candidate lost.

But the experiment was brief. Elected village and township chiefs are again controlled by local Party secretaries. But, gradually, local Party secretaries are also chosen by more-open methods among Party members. Since 1999, a few urban neighborhoods have had direct, competitive elections for minor offices. Some Chinese political scientists hope the level of elections will climb to include mayors and provincial and eventually even national office.

A clever regime could slowly expand democratic elections as a way to defuse anger, but if it does not let democracy go all the way to top national offices, it could end up increasing mass anger. The quick introduction of democracy to China, on the other hand, would likely bring tumult. Restive regions like Tibet and Xinjiang could vote for greater autonomy. *Demagogues* would whip up voters with irresponsible promises. Some Chinese scholars warn that Chinese democracy would resemble that of unstable Thailand, a country of demagoguery, breakaway regions, and military takeovers. They may be right.

Rule by Engineers

While *technocrats* are prominent in France and Mexico, the term applies much more to China. Most of the seven members of the Party's Standing Committee are graduate engineers. In most of the world, the term "technocrat" means a high unelected official who governs by economic and financial skills, often the case in France. In China, it refers to officials with engineering backgrounds. To be sure, China's engineers also have a great deal of experience in running ministries and provincial governments. They have also learned economics from advisors and academics with Western (especially U.S.) doctorates.

What does rule by engineers do for China? They are quite bright, and their emphasis on rationality minimizes ideological considerations. They generally allow growth of a market economy, so long as it builds a richer, stronger China, as they are also very nationalistic. They beam with pride at China's economic growth and the world political clout that comes with it.

But technocrats—whether in France, Mexico, China, or even the United States—have a weakness: They expect quick, right answers and pay little or no attention to the human factor and to long-term consequences. They are cool, distant, rational number crunchers. The decisions of distant technocrats, even if they are correct economic decisions, rub citizens the wrong way. America has a painful example of a technocrat in Robert McNamara, Kennedy's and Johnson's brilliant secretary of defense (he had a Harvard MBA), who assured us in 1962 that "every quantitative measurement we have shows we're winning the war" in Vietnam. He overlooked the human factor that the enemy was willing to take enormous casualties to expel the Americans and unify their country. The human factor did not compute, so he missed it.

China's technocrats operate along similar lines: Numbers matter, people do not. The technocrats argue that, at this stage of China's economic takeoff, they are precisely the right people to run things. The quicker they can industrialize China, the sooner they can spread the prosperity. No country has industrialized in an even, fair, and balanced way. The beginnings of capital accumulation are rough in any country, characterized by inequality and bad working conditions. That is why labor unions formed in Western countries.

China, like all Communist countries, has fake official unions (the All-China Federation of Labor Unions), but they do not complain or strike, even over the most wretched and dangerous working conditions. China permits no independent unions and jails workers who try to organize one. Unions just get in the way of rapid growth—an old capitalist argument. Even worse, unions (along with churches) would be organizational alternatives that could rally opposition to Communist rule. In 2010, spontaneous strikes hit foreign-owned factories in Guangdong. Workers, fed up with low wages and forced overtime, shut down several plants. Beijing, frightened of militant worker behavior spreading, leaned on the firms to increase wages 30 to 50 percent. Once workers feel their strength, they form unions. Communists should know that.

Some of China's technocrats pointed out that Japan also industrialized on a top-down basis, first with the Meiji modernizers and then after World War II with *MITI* supervision.

Democracy

A Chinese Way to Democracy?

Political scientist Kate Zhou of the University of Hawaii argues that, belatedly and grudgingly, the Chinese regime gives way to greater freedom. There are no organized movements, she notes, but mass, spontaneous, leaderless waves of disobedience over the decades make the Zhongnanhai retreat from total control. They can't arrest everybody or halt modernization. By focusing on repression, outside observers tend to overlook the real gains Chinese have made.

The Great Leap Forward started the first wave. Peasants, faced with starvation, illegally returned to private farming. With the quiet disobedience of hundreds of millions, the regime had to finally legalize private farming. Next, millions of peasants fled rural poverty for the city, where they lived and worked illegally. The regime could not send all of them back—besides, they were manpower for the fast industrialization of the 1980s—so it let them stay. Local officials could also be bribed.

Some of these peasants in the cities became hustling entrepreneurs; a few grew rich. Local police, at first, busted up their stalls and shops, but the shopkeepers set them back up to supply what the threadbare Communist economy could not. Again the regime gave way, and now, China's streets are lined with small shops and restaurants, and "night markets" (great fun and good bargains) are in every city. The regime could not stop the information (especially the Internet and cell phones) and sexual revolutions, so it lived with them. Zhou makes a good case that Chinese have greatly enlarged their areas of personal freedom. Many mainland academics know and like her book, which has not been translated.

The regime, in the words of Berkeley political scientist Peter Lorentzen, practices "adaptive authoritarianism." The Zhongnanhai responds to discontent by reforms—such as allowing some couples to have two children, abolishing labor camps, and granting more urban hukous—but permits no organized pluralism or criticism. It is doubtful that piecemeal reforms gradually produce democracy. Without parties and interest groups, mass discontent can become explosive and anarchic. Democracy requires preparation—in education, free mass media, unfettered interest groups—that the regime firmly resists. If the Zhongnanhai does not start prepping for democracy soon, China's modernization could jump off the tracks.

China should do the same. But beware of analogies between countries; they can deceive. Meiji central control of Japan's rapid modernization brutally suppressed the common people and paved the way to Japan's aggressive militarism. (Some see parallels between this and China's current industrialization.) MITI influence after the war—and some say MITI was never really that important—took place in a democratic context with few state enterprises that had to be privatized. One point in common: Both Japanese and Chinese banks lent foolishly and recklessly, and both refused for years to admit that they were **insolvent**. The Japanese banks, however, are privately held and accountable to shareholders; most Chinese banks are state owned and accountable only to Beijing. The MITI analogy applies poorly to China.

China's current technocrats must be given credit for moving to correct the imbalances. They recognize that economic unevenness is dangerous and are now spreading investment to the north and west of the country to industrialize China's vast interior. There are now modest welfare programs for the poorest rungs of Chinese society. With the global financial meltdown of 2008–2009, we saw the ability of China's technocrats. By massive stimulus spending, focused on domestic infrastructure and consumption, China kept growing while the West slumped.

insolvent
Owes more than it owns.

Coercion in Reserve

coercion
Government by force.

guanxi
Chinese for connections (do not confuse with Guangxi Province); polite term for corruption.

China's regime retains authority by means of patriotism and performance-based legitimacy—delivering the goods—but keeps ample **coercion** in reserve. China's government spends more on internal security than on its regular armed forces. Beijing keeps discontent and unrest small and local by outlawing organizational alternatives, leaving discontent unfocused and free-floating. The regime takes elaborate precautions against the formation of civil society—especially churches and labor unions—that might provide organizational alternatives.

The Tiananmen area of Beijing is laced with plainclothes police who pounce on incipient protest. Any group that lingers in one spot gets spoken to. Security police remember how Falun Gong used e-mails to quietly organize a large, sudden gathering in Tiananmen Square in 1999. That will not happen again. In 2009, for the massive sixtieth anniversary of the Communist triumph, only a few handpicked citizens were allowed to witness the parade past Tiananmen. Even people who lived on the parade route were ordered to keep away from windows and watch it on television.

The 2008 Olympics were a mixed blessing for China. They showcased the modern face of China, but preparations displaced tens of thousands of farmers and *hutong* (alleyway) dwellers. By law, people who lose their homes must be compensated, but few receive enough. Usually they are just ordered out. No one can own land in China—you lease—so occupancy rights are weak. Beijing feared that dissidents might use the Olympics to make a statement the whole world would see, like the Mexican student protests on the eve of the 1968 Mexico City Olympics, so they arrested critics in advance and banned beggars, poor people, and many cars from the city for the games. Beijing's air cleared up briefly.

Law can powerfully boost civil society. China claims to have rule of law, but it is more "law of the ruler": selective and used to bolster the regime. Suspects deemed to have challenged Party control are quickly convicted and sentenced to harsh terms. The CCP's Central Commission for Discipline Inspection investigates but does not dent corruption. Lawyers defending church and union organizers risk disbarment and arrest. Some go into hiding. A 1989 law is supposed to give citizens the right to sue state agencies, but only a handful succeed. Western freedoms owe much to courageous lawyers who insisted that even the powerful be bound by law. Many Chinese want China to move in this direction.

Trying to Discipline Corruption

Public administration scholar Helena Rene found that corruption really took root in China about 1973, as millions of "sent-down" youths used **guanxi** on local cadres to get back to their homes. Corruption is now deeply entrenched. Chinese officials rig bids, collect bribes, siphon off funds, and throw people off land for favored developers. Many relatives of cadres use their guanxi to make lucrative business deals. Premier Wen's family amassed an estimated $2.7 billion. Vast sums, some of them from sweetheart contracts, are smuggled out every year, often via Hong Kong and Macau, money laundries that Beijing could close but allows because many of the regime's top families use them. By one count, China has 2.7 million dollar millionaires,

Comparison

Equality and Growth

Do big income differentials spur economic growth? Ronald Reagan, George W. Bush, and Margaret Thatcher thought so; under them, incomes in America and Britain grew more unequal. The reasoning: If people can make a lot of money, they will have a greater incentive to work hard and get rich. And rich people invest more. According to this theory, inequality and growth are twins.

Data are not so clear; some even point in the opposite direction. The first column in the table below is the **Gini Index**, a measure of inequality. The lower the Gini, the more equal incomes are. Called the Gini Coefficient in decimal form (.45), it depends on accurate statistics—rare in developing lands—and using the same methodology for each country. Accordingly, Gini studies vary wildly and should be taken as estimates. One put China's Gini at an extremely high 61 rather than 47. A large survey found that, in 2012, the top 5 percent of China's households raked in 23 percent of income and the bottom 5 percent got 0.1 percent, yielding a Gini of 49. The second column shows the estimated per capita GDP growth in 2012. Be careful here, too: Growth numbers bounce around a lot; in 2010, for example, Brazil climbed 7.5 percent. Oil-producing countries like Russia and Nigeria grew because oil prices were high (but Iran did not).

Recent data do not prove that income inequality promotes growth. They don't prove much of anything. China had greater income inequality than the United States and grew rapidly, but unequal Mexico and Brazil grew weakly. The theory that inequality accompanies growth is too simple; many factors make economies grow. Government policies have a lot to do with it. Government—through corruption, high taxes, and state ownership—may discourage private investment. Some cultures have an internalized work ethic or nationalistic pride. Some cultures (China, Japan, Germany) have a strong propensity to save. Americans save little. Savings fund investment, which helps sustain growth, but too much saving can retard consumption. Beware of one-cause theories.

	Gini Index	GDPpc Growth
	Most Recent	*Estimated 2013*
Germany	27	0.5%
France	33	0.2
India	37	4.7
Japan	38	2.0
Britain	40	1.4
Russia	42	1.3
Nigeria	44	6.2
Iran	45	−1.5
United States	45	1.6
China	47	7.6
Mexico	48	1.2
Brazil	52	2.5

SOURCE: UNDP, CIA

many of whom stash their cash abroad, a situation resembling Latin American and Russian "capital flight" to get money to a safe haven.

Factory and mining officials do not enforce safety rules, and hundreds die. In 2008, Chinese babies died from milk poisoned by melamine that made it test higher in protein. Charges of corruption flared after the 2008 Sichuan earthquake. Schools collapsed while nearby apartment buildings stood intact, because the schools were shoddily built with insufficient rebar. Those who complained were arrested. Journalists were kept out of the area. Those who expose corruption can be beaten and jailed for disturbing the "harmonious society" the regime promotes. (Bloomberg's and *The New York Times* websites were blocked for revealing family fortunes.)

Gini Index
Measure of inequality; higher is more unequal.

Democracy

The Tiananmen Massacre

During the early morning of June 4, 1989, more than 100,000 Chinese troops opened fire on a crowd of young demonstrators camped out in Beijing's Tiananmen Square, killing hundreds and injuring thousands. (The regime never released figures, so the numbers can only be estimated.) Much of the killing, including tanks crushing protesters and bicyclists shot at random, took place outside the Square, but the horror went down in history as "Tiananmen."

Tiananmen marked the point at which China's Communist chiefs choked over letting China's 1980s experiment with a partial market economy spill over into political reform, never their intention. The massacre illustrates the danger of halfway reform: It gets people thinking and demanding more. Although Tiananmen is commonly referred to as a "prodemocracy" demonstration, the students had only vague ideas of democracy; they mostly wanted a rigid and corrupt regime to reform, something that could have led to democracy.

Trouble began with the death of the liberal ex-Party chief Hu Yaobang in April 1989. Students gathered to mourn him and protest corruption. On April 18, thousands began to occupy the Square. While the regime pondered how to handle the demonstration, the students organized, gave speeches, and built a Goddess of Democracy statue. Around the country, many sympathized with the demonstrators, and criticism of the regime mounted.

If demonstrations had kept going, the regime would have been in trouble. The Zhongnanhai knew that and struck back. Zhao Ziyang, who succeeded Hu in 1987, went out to talk with the students and took their side. Politburo members already disliked Zhao for revealing their splits to the outside world and immediately ousted him. (Zhao was under house arrest until his death in 2005, and his funeral was nearly secret so as not to give mourners another occasion to demonstrate for freedom. Even funerals are touchy events in China.) Deng Xiaoping, still chair of the powerful Central Military Commission and the real power at age 84, ordered the army to crush the demonstrators. "We do not fear spilling blood," he said.

Troops and tanks poured into Beijing. The soldiers, mostly country boys, felt little in common with the urban students. In one memorable videotaped confrontation, a lone protester blocked a tank column; when the tanks tried to go around him, he quickly stepped in front of them again. It seemed to symbolize the individualism of democracy standing up to the coercion of dictatorship. Many ordinary Beijingers sided with and helped the students. After the bloodbath, thousands were arrested. The top protest figures received sentences of up to 13 years, with shorter sentences for those who "repented." Hundreds were held for years without trial. China's elite decided to keep going with economic change but to keep the lid on political change. The ingredients for new upheavals in China are simmering.

Many Chinese automatically assume that everything in China is corrupt—cadres, business, universities, even sports. Observers see corruption as signs of the regime starting to crack. Official misdeeds drive Chinese to petitions, protests, and riots that could spin out of control. China's top leaders recognize, however, that corruption is so widespread that cleaning it up would cost them precisely the cadres they rely upon to govern. If you jail all your helpers, you will be helpless. Accordingly, prosecutions are selective and political, often aimed at consolidating the top leaders' power by getting rid of competitors. Some innocent cadres are accused of corruption and treated brutally.

The Party claims its Central Commission for Discipline Inspection is effective. Operating outside the legal system, it demotes, expels from the Party, refers to criminal courts, or jails and beats (sometimes to death) cadres suspected of corruption. Officials and heads of state-owned

S-curve

Typical trajectory of economic development.

enterprises can receive death sentences for accumulating millions (most suspended in favor of life imprisonment.) As in Mexico and Nigeria, state oil industries are notoriously corrupt. But a commission cannot clean up corruption that the political-economic system produces anew every year. A regime with great powers and no countervailing checks can easily become corrupt itself. As the Latin phrase asks, "Who will guard the guardians?"

Xi Jinping vowed to clean up corruption and went after some high officials (while leaving others untouched). Xi, however, opposed reformists' calls to make cadres disclose all their assets; that would undermine the basis of China's governance. Singapore shows how tough rules can end systemic corruption; it now ranks as one of the cleanest countries in the world.

What Chinese Quarrel About

7.5   Explain why Beijing wants to "rebalance" China's economy.

The Political Economy of China

For a third of a century, China's economy roughly doubled every seven years, a spectacular rate of 10 percent—sometimes 11—which Premier Wen in 2011 called "unbalanced, uncoordinated, and unsustainable." For 2011–2015, he aimed to lower this to a sustainable but still high 7 percent, approximately its present rate. Even during the 2009 global recession, China's economy grew 8 percent while Western economies declined. China is now the world's second-largest economy (but not per capita) and could become the largest in a few years. It has the world's biggest foreign-currency reserves and is the largest foreign holder of U.S. debt. Urban China shows off its modern downtowns and traffic-clogged streets.

And China did this without following the Japanese economic model, which kept out foreign firms. In contrast, China welcomes foreign investment, technology, and (partial) ownership. All of China's advanced industries are based on foreign investments. Beijing correctly saw this as the speediest way to industrialize.

There are several reasons for China's growth. Unlike Latin America, China has no old dominant class that invests little. With the old class of landowners and capitalists shot or fled, China started capitalism with a clean slate. Chinese are extremely practical and have no cultural or religious inhibitions against rapid modernization and copying from the West. China had cheap labor, plentiful capital, and a regime that pushed economic growth. Chinese workers earn from $200 to $500 a month, lower inland than in the big coastal cities.

China's growth, however, is flagging. Economic growth typically forms an **S-curve**—an elongated S that starts slow at the bottom, climbs rapidly for some decades, and then levels off. There are signs that China, along with several other emerging economies, is nearing the third phase. No economy—neither Germany's nor Japan's—goes upward forever. China used cheap labor combined with imported technology, but its labor costs are no longer so low, and fuel costs for shipping have climbed. China's growth will likely still be good but not what it was. Much Chinese investment was politically influenced, incoherent, short term, and wasted but masked by low labor and capital costs. Eventually, these had to run out.

Contributing to the levelling off of the S-curve is the "Lewis turning point" (named after British economist Arthur Lewis), when a developing country has used up its rural surplus labor, forcing wages up. The Chinese countryside, once seen as an inexhaustible labor source, has begun to run dry after millions moved to urban factories, where they climb to higher-skilled, higher-paying jobs. Chinese manufacturing wages now rise by double-digit percentages annually. Further, China's one-child policy means few new workers. Corporations now shift low-skilled jobs from China to lower-wage countries, such as Vietnam and Indonesia. Notice how some of your recent purchases are from those two countries.

It Only Looks Capitalist

China's streets are lined with small shops and restaurants and sprinkled with hawkers and hustlers. ("You want buy T-shirt? Special price for you.") It looks like a capitalist boomtown and, at the micro level, is indeed one. But of China's 70 largest companies, including banks, 65 are state owned. For example, the Chinese National Overseas Oil Company (CNOOC) and China Aluminum Company (Chinalco) are owned by government ministries. China's SOEs still account for more than half of its GDP. The state is in overall control, and SOE executives, high up in the Party, form a wealthy, powerful lobby to keep it that way.

Other Communist countries have tried mixtures of socialism and capitalism. Tito's Yugoslavia and Gorbachev's Soviet Union suggest that such third-way economies are unstable. They tend to turn more and more into market economies until the regime, afraid of losing control, retightens central supervision and discipline. Seeking faster growth, however, the regime loosens controls again after a while. The economy moves in a zigzag, never finding stability. President Xi urged giving market forces the "decisive role" in the economy, a contradiction to his commitment to keep China under Party control.

Incoherence brings economic errors. Vast sums are invested foolishly, mistakenly, or crookedly. Government control has forced some well-run and rapidly growing firms to make bad business decisions. Peasants fleeing rural unemployment kept labor costs cheap and let developers overbuild. Banks lent generously for modern buildings because they impress everyone, especially foreigners. Builders, all aiming for the top of the rental market, constructed too many glitzy high-rise buildings, which became partially occupied money losers. Shanghai alone has twice as many skyscrapers as New York City. China's building boom is a bubble that could pop.

After years of bad loans to SOEs, Party officials, and just plain crooks, some of China's banks became technically insolvent and had to be bailed out by the state. Beijing requires banks to lend to SOEs, which rarely repay the loans. With weak (but rising) accounting standards, the banks carry on as if they will be repaid, much like Japan's banks did for years. Massive savings and rapid industrial growth mask the underlying problems. There is no requirement to write off nonperforming loans, for that would force banks and SOEs to admit they are bankrupt. Many of the massive loans Beijing orders banks to make are wasteful and nonperforming and create borrowing booms and overinvestment bubbles.

An especially dangerous Chinese problem: "Shadow banks," largely unregulated lenders that fill the gap left by big state banks that serve SOEs and large corporations. The shadow banks perform necessary economic functions—they pay decent dividends and lend to

soft landing
Gradual calming of destabilizing economic shifts.

R & D
Research and development of new technologies.

small- and medium-sized businesses—but many are overextended and could suddenly fail, unleashing a flood of bad debt through China's economy. As in capitalist democracies, banking is the Achilles heel of the Chinese economy.

Virtually all educated professionals, many with U.S. degrees, understand China's economic imbalances—reckless borrowing and stimulus packages, which create bubbles—but most say the regime understands them, too. But views on them diverge. Chinese professionals connected to the establishment claim that the regime knows what it is doing in bringing the situation under control. "We are well governed by very bright technocrats such as economist Li Keqiang," is their message. They note that China's leaders avoided the currency crisis that swept East Asia in 1997–1998 and made a **soft landing** during the 2008–2009 world recession. China's reserves are so huge, they argue, that the government can inject billions into banks to cover their bad loans (many of them to SOEs) and to stimulate the economy, as they did in 2009. All will be well, regime defenders claim.

Those not dependent on state connections, on the other hand, worry that the regime alternately cools an overheated economy (as in 2007) and then reheats it (as in 2009), overshooting both ways. Fearful of damaging China's miracle growth and creating unemployment, the regime lets banks and stock markets rumble on to a crash (as did the U.S. Fed). China's banks, by law, pay very low interest, so urban savers shifted their money to the stock market, which produced a bubble that collapsed in 2007 to half its value. Domestic overborrowing could spin out of control and collapse, skeptics argue.

So far, it must be admitted that China's rulers have managed the economy well, heading off most problems before they got dangerous and coming out of the recession in better shape than Western and Japanese economies. In 2009, Chinese banks tripled lending to pump some $1 trillion into domestic infrastructure and consumption. Home and car sales exploded, exactly what Beijing wanted to fight recession and unemployment. China came out of the recession faster than any other major economy. Then, in a few months, to prevent inflation and bubbles, officials ordered banks to ease back on lending. China's brilliant technocrats performed deftly but set up new imbalances, such as a looming debt bomb.

"Rebalance" China's Economy?

For over three decades, China has been obsessed with exports, and it became the world's biggest exporter. Exports quickly boost growth but, after some years, can overshoot. What does China (and, earlier, Japan) do with all the dollars and euros it has accumulated? They pay for imports—especially oil and raw materials—but China's per capita domestic consumption, as a percentage of GDP, is the lowest of Asia. And if, one day, China exhausts its export advantages—cheap labor and borrowed **R & D** —its growth slows. Greater reliance on domestic consumption helps prevent this. Japan never gave up its high-export model and went into a prolonged slump.

For some years, Chinese have debated "rebalancing" their exports in favor of greater domestic consumption. India and Brazil have a much better balance than China. (The United States is bad the other way—too few exports.) Why shouldn't the hard-working Chinese live better? After all, the purpose of an economy is to look after your own people, not to accumulate foreign exchange without limit.

But China's export giants form a powerful lobby in Beijing. The export-driven model has been good for China, they contend, and good for them; they oppose shifting to domestic consumption. Accordingly, while China's top leaders understand why China must rebalance, in practice, they go slow. China's five-year plan announced in 2011 implements a major boost in consumer spending. One good way to encourage this is to float China's currency, which would incrementally tilt production from exports to domestic consumption.

Should China Float?

East Asia's banking crises in the late 1990s saw some currencies suddenly **devalued**. China's currency problem has been the opposite: its **RMB** was long undervalued. A big, sudden rise in the **yuan**, however, would slow China's exports, so Beijing guarded against it. From 1995 to 2005, partly to avoid the fate of other East Asian currencies, China **pegged** the yuan at ¥8.3 to the dollar. At the time, all applauded, including the United States, for the stabilizing move.

Over time, however, Washington criticized the fixed rate as unfair; it kept the RMB too low and allowed Chinese exports to gain at the expense of U.S. factory jobs. The U.S. Congress thundered that this had to change. Some urged China to **revalue** the yuan by 20 to 30 percent. Most economists say an undervalued yuan is not the root of America's trade problems with China (the low U.S. savings rate is the chief culprit). China, due to its low wages (and high savings rate), is just a super producer, and its cheap goods hold down U.S. inflation. Some rebalancing is inevitable and now under way, as Chinese, with Beijing's approval, learn to consume more.

A country with a trade surplus could let its currency **float** to a higher value, letting the market revalue the currency. But China, like many countries, wants its money cheap to keep its export advantage. To do this, in the 1990s, China began buying massive amounts of U.S. Treasury securities (Japan does the same). This has intertwined the Chinese and U.S. economies in strange ways. Rich America is now deeply indebted to poor China. Chinese purchase of U.S. Treasury notes kept our interest rates low and underwrote our real estate boom. If China were to sell—or simply stop purchasing—U.S. bonds and notes, the dollar would weaken around the world. On the other hand, a sudden major Chinese pullout of the U.S. debt market would also decrease the value of China's huge dollar holdings. To avoid that, China is slowly and quietly diversifying out of the U.S. dollar.

In 2005, Beijing gave in a little and carried out a "controlled managed float" that let the RMB climb 18 percent and then repegged it at a nearly constant ¥6.8 to the dollar. In 2010, worried about U.S. retaliation, Beijing let the yuan gradually rise roughly 6 percent per year until it reached about ¥6 to a dollar, close to its fair value. The RNB is not yet allowed to float freely, as fluctuations would undermine Beijing's domestic economic controls, but it is increasingly used in currency swaps with trading partners, a step to full convertibility.

devalue
To change the worth of a currency downward in relation to other currencies (opposite of *revalue*).

RMB
Renminbi (people's money), official name of China's currency, same as *yuan*.

yuan
China's currency (symbol ¥), officially called RMB, worth about 16 U.S. cents.

peg
To fix one currency at an unchanging rate to another.

revalue
To change the worth of a currency upward in relation to other currencies (opposite of *devalue*).

float
To allow a currency to find its own level based on supply and demand.

Comparison

Big Mac Index

Traditional per capita GDP (GDPpc) figures that use the "market exchange rate" are deceptive because they do not figure in the cost of living in each country. China's GDPpc at exchange rate, for example, is only about $6,900. But exchange rates overvalue or undervalue currencies and change rapidly. To correct for this, economists now calculate GDPpc in **purchasing power parity (PPP)** by measuring what it costs to live in each country. This makes Chinese a lot richer, about $9,800 GDPpc in 2013.

PPP is tricky to calculate because economists must evaluate a market basket of goods and services that is the same in each country. The British news-weekly *The Economist* devised a quick way to approximate PPP: Compare the price of a Big Mac sandwich at the local McDonald's with its U.S. (big-city) price. Because a Big Mac requires the same ingredients, labor, and overhead wherever it is produced, it is actually a mini-market basket that tracks more-complex PPP calculations.

A Big Mac that is more expensive than the U.S. price indicates that the local currency is overvalued, strongly the case in Brazil, a little for the euro (France and Germany). A cheaper Big Mac indicates that the local currency is undervalued, the case in Mexico, India, China, and Russia. Those near the U.S. price suggest that the currency is about right. These Big Mac prices are at exchange-rate prices, not PPP.

	GDPpc at PPP, 2012	Big Mac Price, Jan. 2014
United States	$52,800	4.62
Canada	43,100	5.01
Germany	39,500	4.96
Britain	37,300	4.63
Japan	37,100	2.97
France	35,700	4.96
Russia	18,100	2.62
Mexico	15,600	2.78
Brazil	12,100	5.25
China	9,800	2.74
India (chicken Maharaja Mac)	4,000	1.54

SOURCES: First column CIA, second column *The Economist*.

A Market Economy for China?

Will China become a full market economy? Starting with Deng's reforms in 1978, the Chinese economy grew at amazing rates, but the really big question is whether it can combine a market economy with centralized political control. Several countries tried it, but it proved unstable.

Change came first in the countryside. Collectivized farms were broken up, and families were permitted to go on the "responsibility system," a euphemism for private farming. Peasants lease land from the locality for 30 years, generally renewable. They must deliver a certain quota to the state at set prices but can sell the rest for the best price they can get. They choose their crops, fertilizer, and farm machinery, which they buy at their own expense. Initially, farm production soared, Chinese ate better, and farmers' incomes went up; some even got rich.

By the 1990s, however, things were not going so well in the countryside. Competition held farm prices and profits down, and farm incomes declined. Rural order frequently breaks down now as villagers protest local authorities for taking their lands for development. In 2005, Beijing ended millennia-old taxes on harvests and even offered peasants some financial aid. The regime fears that

purchasing power parity (PPP)
A currency's value taking cost of living into account.

peasant anger could turn into the sort of uprising that has punctuated China's history. Mao based his revolution on the peasantry.

A partly free market was soon allowed in the cities. Faced with unemployment, the regime let individuals open small stores, restaurants, repair shops, and factories. It was even permissible to hire workers, something Marxists used to call capitalist exploitation. But it worked. Individuals produced and sold more and better products than the indifferent state factories and stores. Hole-in-the-wall "department stores" had customers lined up to buy the fashionable clothing and footwear Mao used to scorn. Outdoor markets sold home-produced furniture. Restaurants sprang up on every street.

Starting with the Shenzhen area around Hong Kong, parts of coastal China were declared **Special Economic Zones** (SEZs), open to private and **foreign direct investment (FDI)** that was invited to turn China into a modern, market economy. FDI is extremely important for the developing world. Marxists and nationalists hate and fear it as a form of capitalist takeover, but it is the key to rapid economic growth. Possibly a trillion dollars of FDI poured into China (much of it from Taiwan and Hong Kong) to take advantage of low Chinese wages, and production soared. These private enterprises compete in a world market to make profits, and, since 1978, China's GDP has made it the world's second-largest overall economy (ahead of Japan) and biggest exporter (ahead of Germany). China's economy was 30 times bigger in 2007 than it had been in 1980. In comparison, even profitable SOEs earn much less than private firms; one-third lose money and are propped up by subsidies and loans that will never be repaid. Whether to close weak SOEs and create unemployment is a major question facing Beijing. In 2009, some of the stimulus package went to SOEs and export subsidies, not good long-term investments.

As modern, high-rise boomtowns sprang up on the coast, some Chinese businesspeople became millionaires, and a substantial middle class formed. Most Chinese like the free market and its nice department stores and restaurants but many cadres, who make a good living by supervising a controlled economy, do not. Deng purged or retired the old guard and replaced them with young technocrats who pursued market-based economic growth and called it "socialism with Chinese characteristics." Everyone understands that it means capitalism.

But market economies produce problems of their own and awaken resentments and jealousies. China's leaders worried that the economy could career out of control and attempted to slow it. Then, in the 2008–2009 recession, they worried that it would slow too much. In the longer term, the system needs democracy, but Beijing vows that China will have only one party. What will happen if a destabilizing economic system escapes the bonds of a dictatorial political system? Think of a bucking bronco (China's economy) throwing its rider (the Party). It must be admitted that, so far, China's leaders have met the challenge.

Special Economic Zones
Areas originally on China's southern coast where capitalist economic development was encouraged.

foreign direct investment (FDI)
Foreign firms setting up operations in other countries.

Birth Effects

China's program to limit population growth shows what can go wrong with coercing society into paths the government has decided are desirable. It also illustrates the problem of second- and third-order effects—sometimes called "unforeseen consequences"—namely, how difficult it is to predict the longer-term impacts of a policy.

yuppie
Short for "young urban professional."

In 1980, China started a ferocious program to curb births. Women could have only one child and were fined and lost benefits if they had more. Many women were forced to have abortions, including late-term abortions. The first-order consequence, as might be expected, was to bring down China's rate of population increase, now less than half a percent a year, little higher than Europe and very low for the Third World, much of which grows at 3 percent.

A second-order effect, however, was a large excess of boy over girl babies, both by abortion and female infanticide. About 5 percent of the girls expected to be born from 1979 to 1995 were not born, 10 percent in the 1990s. In 2013, 118 males were born for 100 females (the normal sex ratio is 105 to 100). Cheap ultrasound scans permit selective abortions (as in India). Like many Third World cultures, Chinese value boys above girls, both to work on the farm and to support the parents in old age. So, if they are allowed only one child, many Chinese strongly prefer a son. This is not the case with educated urban Chinese, who welcome daughters.

Third-order effects flow from the second-order effects. The surplus of males over females means that millions of Chinese men will never find brides. Further, the drastic restriction in fertility rates—from 2.29 births per average woman in 1980 to 1.55 in 2014 (the European level)—means that China's retired generation—now much bigger and living much longer, thanks to improved nutrition and health care—will not have nearly enough working Chinese to support it. By 2030, one-fourth of Chinese will be over 65 and there will be only two working Chinese for every retiree. Chinese speak of "4-2-1": four grandparents and two parents supported by only one child, the logical result of the one-child policy. China, still a poor country, will thus face the same problem as rich Europe. China's State Family Planning Commission, which now emphasizes education and contraception, did not consider the second- and third-order consequences.

How can developing areas handle population increases? Economic growth solves the problem without coercion, as young Chinese already demonstrate. They have few children (and welcome daughters). As the economy grows, more people become urban and middle class and decide for themselves to limit their number of children, as countries around the world have done. As more women are educated, they postpone marriage in favor of career, a strong trend among Chinese **yuppies**, who work so long and hard they may not have time for marriage. No rich country has a problem of too many babies (in fact, it is just the opposite), and newly industrializing lands show a dramatic falloff in births. Under demographic pressure, Beijing relaxed the one-child policy in 2013, now allowing couples where one was an only child to have two children.

The Trouble with Markets

The trouble with introducing a market economy into Communist countries—such as Yugoslavia, Hungary, or China—is that it risks running out of control and destabilizing. China has seen major increases in the following:

OVERINVESTMENT Eager to show that they are growing the GDP, local banks and officials keep stuffing low-interest money into dubious projects, leading to overcapacity and unneeded construction, what Japan has done. China has some 65 million apartments and new cities that stand empty.

LIMITED RESOURCES China faces severe shortages in energy, water, and land. Chinese industry is energy inefficient. Some rivers have run dry; others are too polluted to use. China

Democracy

Ten Preliminary Steps to Democracy

The sudden imposition of democracy in China could lead to tumult and breakdown, something Chinese leaders, academics, and journalists understand and discuss. Gradual liberalization over several years, however, could prevent an uncontrolled Soviet-style skid into chaos. The following ideas, already debated in China, could be carried out gradually. The first four are aimed at removing sources of discontent, especially to calm rural anger.

1. *Clear title to land.* China's biggest source of discontent is in the countryside, where farmers can only lease their land. It would be legally complex—who would be entitled to what land?—but letting tillers convert their leases into ownership deeds would provide a badly needed tax base and gradually allow consolidation of plots into bigger, more efficient farms.

2. *No land seizures.* Government should not be allowed to take land for development, a major source of corruption. If developers need land, they should negotiate to buy it from the owners.

3. *Abolish the* hukou *system.* Residence registration, designed to prevent peasants from swarming to the cities, is already being relaxed, with many now receiving urban hukous. China might take that all the way and let everyone change residence as they wish.

4. *Permit lawsuits against corruption.* The Central Commission for Discipline Inspection may refer cases to courts for criminal trial, but this does not catch nearly all the guilty. Individuals need the right to sue corrupt officials in civil cases.

5. *Free churches and unions.* Let them form and act—including strike—without government control. Chinese need something to believe in, which religion can provide. The Communist regime, supposedly based on workers, ought to be embarrassed for having no mechanism to voice working-class demands.

6. *Permit discussion groups within the Party.* This is already happening informally and on functional questions. Communist regimes are based on the fiction that they contain no factions, but this retards change and reform.

7. *Publish the groups' discussions.* Chinese have plenty of online capacity to consider several policy alternatives being debated within the Party, learning that plural views are contentious but necessary, an important step to democracy.

8. *Permit Hong Kong democracy and learn from it.* A democracy movement is growing in Hong Kong that forced Beijing, in 2012, to accept a better Hong Kong chief executive. The British colonialists never allowed democracy in Hong Kong—Beijing told them not to. Democracy in Hong Kong could introduce democratic values to the mainland, just as it did market values.

9. *Allow contested elections within the Party.* Let several factions compete and publish their views. This could split the Party but allow it to happen slowly with people taking sides—in effect, practicing for political choice.

10. *Finally, set up tame parties.* Take a page from the Brazilian generals and permit Party factions, just two at first, to turn themselves into parties that offer somewhat different but not radical viewpoints.

Notice that weakening the Party, free media, and mass elections are not among these points. Introducing them too early would take China down the Gorbachev path to system collapse. They might come a few years later, after the above ten points have been implemented. China will need firm central control to make these reforms work, especially the first point. Beijing, like most regimes, however, is inclined to wait until it is too late.

has 20 percent of the world population but only 7 percent of the world's fresh water. Drought has hit areas of North China.

BUBBLES Too much money chasing too few investments creates speculative asset bubbles—as in China's property and stock markets—which periodically pop. The Shanghai stock exchange index tripled, then collapsed. Millions of Chinese play the market, many recklessly (Chinese love gambling), partly because banks pay very low interest, a form of taxation and subsidy to state industries. Some Chinese buy multiple apartments and gold, speculations that may go bust. Many secretly send their money abroad.

INFLATION China has gone through bouts of inflation, the result of rapid growth and economic mismanagement. With food, energy, and labor costs climbing, inflation is now several percent a year. Beijing orders price freezes in select areas, but these tend to just delay and magnify inflationary pressures. Fear of inflation spurs overinvestment.

INEQUALITY Some individuals and provinces get rich faster than others. With foreign direct investment (FDI), the Special Economic Zones (SEZs) of the coast grew fast while inland provinces lagged. Skilled and educated urban Chinese became a new middle class. Urban Chinese earn much more than rural Chinese.

LABOR ABUSES Especially in poor rural areas, some workers, including children, toil in slave-like conditions, deprived of pay, food, sleep, and the freedom to leave. Local governments do little to stop it, figuring that all that really matters is economic growth. Parents desperately search for their kidnapped children in such factories. Low wages and bad working conditions—especially for miners—push some Chinese workers to form unions; they are jailed. Beijing denies that independent unions exist. Ironically, a Communist regime that turned antilabor and procapitalist has created the basis of a Marxist class struggle.

CORRUPTION Corruption grows at the interface of the private and governmental sectors. Economic liberalization multiplies such interfaces as entrepreneurs need permits from government officials, obtained by under-the-table payments. China has become one of the world's most corrupt countries (but not as bad as Russia). Most Chinese business is based on guanxi.

CRIME With all of the factors listed previously plus weakened social controls, crime grows, along with campaigns to stop it. Firing squads execute thousands each year. China leads the world by far in capital punishment (Iran is second but first per cap). Counterfeiting is widespread; banks check U.S. currency, and businesses check larger yuan bills.

POLLUTION Focused only on economic growth, China has the world's worst environmental problems. Coal burning, lead smelting, and cars poison the air; chemical dumping poisons ground water and rivers; and diseases spread rapidly. Pollution kills perhaps a million Chinese per year, harms children, sparks protests and riots, and slows China's growth. Massive coal use in North China shortens northern Chinese lives an average of 5.5 years compared to southern Chinese. Officials cover up problems and jail activists for revealing them, but every Chinese knows about the terrible pollution just from breathing.

POISONOUS PRODUCTS Unregulated Chinese manufacturing ignores safety. Melamine poisoned Chinese milk and pet food. Toys with lead paint were popular on the U.S. market. Chinese cold medicine and toothpaste contained a chemical used in car antifreeze. Beijing's response was to quickly try and execute the head of their equivalent of our Food and Drug Administration. These problems were discovered only because the products were exported; products for domestic consumption are worse and unnoticed.

How to solve these problems? A start is letting people organize interest groups and bring civil charges to hold officials legally accountable.

A Middle Way for the Middle Kingdom?

The basic supposition of Beijing's recent and current rulers is that there is a middle way between capitalism and communism, between a controlled and a free-market economy, between the Soviet and the American model. (Soviet President Gorbachev tried a middle way, leading to his ouster and Soviet collapse.) By bringing in elements of a market economy while keeping overall control in state hands, they suppose that they have found a middle way. Is there one? Not really, and some observers think that the Chinese elite quietly admit it among themselves.

When a Communist country introduces a bit of market economics—supply and demand, competing producers, profits, family farming, prices finding their own level—the first few years are usually good. Farm output especially grows, and people eat well. Consumer goods become far more available, and people live and dress better. New industries produce clothing and consumer electronics for the world market. Statistically, growth rates shoot up, and it looks like the happy balance: a market economy at the *micro* level to produce consumer goods under the benevolent guidance of a state-run economy at the *macro* level. While consumer goods are

Democracy

Do Markets Lead to Democracy?

Economic liberalization tends to encourage political participation. You cannot just reform the economy, for economic reform generates demands for political reform—namely, democracy. As political scientist Peter Berger put it: "When market economies are successful over a period of time, pressure for democratization inevitably ensues."

A market economy generates a large, educated middle class and interest groups. People start resenting a corrupt government treating them like small children. They want some democratic input. If the regime is intelligent and flexible, it gradually opens up, usually by permitting a critical press, then opposition parties, and, finally, free and fair elections.

Taiwan is a textbook example of this transition from authoritarianism to democracy. Some argue that China will follow a similar path, but there are differences. First, Taiwan is small, making it easier to control. Taiwan's elites, many of them educated in the United States, led the way to democracy in the late 1970s. One of their motives: Show the Americans that Taiwan is a democracy, to win U.S. support against Beijing's demands to take over Taiwan.

The Taiwan model does not fit mainland China. China's elite is still firmly Communist, has no desire for democracy, and is not trying to please the Americans. Much of China's economy is still state controlled. China's leaders are not building capitalism; they are building Chinese power. China's middle class is rapidly growing, but it is tied to the state, which also blocks the growth of civil society, the autonomous groups that underlay pluralist democracy. Calls for democracy are ruthlessly crushed. Do not count on China moving to democracy automatically or peacefully, no matter what its economic growth.

produced by private firms, much of them with FDI, some big industries as well as banking and planning systems are still state owned and under Party control.

After a few years, things start to go wrong. Shortages, distortions, and bottlenecks appear. The private sector keeps bumping into the state sector. Every time it does, there is a "crisis" that can be resolved only by expanding the private sector and shrinking the state sector. After some years of this, there is little socialism left. The Chinese—like the Yugoslavs and Hungarians—found that a little bit of capitalism is like being a little bit pregnant. The choice that Communist regimes faced was difficult. If they went part of the way to a market economy, they experienced a few years of growth followed by dangerous distortions. If they called off the liberal experiment, they returned to the centralized, Stalinist system that was slowly running down, leaving them farther and farther behind the capitalist world. If they went all the way to a market system, they admitted that they had been wrong all these decades.

Another problem cropped up with the financial problems that hit other East Asian lands in 1997: China's banks also loan recklessly and crookedly; the banking system, until recently entirely state owned, faces problems. Some loans are made under government orders to prop up money-losing state industries. The central government itself is deeply in debt from subsidizing too much and collecting too little in taxes. Local governments owe an estimated $2 trillion, all of which Beijing has to cover. A flawed fiscal system threatens China's growth. Like America, China has a ticking debt bomb. The difference is that China has massive reserves to cover its subsidies for some time.

China's reforms were far cleverer than the Soviet Union's and have a much better chance to succeed. First, China permitted private farming. The Soviet Union was still debating private farming when it collapsed. Then China permitted small businesses. Next, China designated SEZs for foreign investment. Missing in China is the political liberalization that blew up in

Geography

The Hong Kong Example

In 1997, Hong Kong, a British colony for 155 years, returned to China. Most of Hong Kong actually consisted of the leased New Territories on the mainland—the source of the colony's water supply—and the lease was up in 1997. Beijing demanded return of the whole colony. Many Hong Kongers feared the mainland takeover; some took their money and fled to Canada.

Beijing guaranteed, under the formula "One Country, Two Systems," that Hong Kong could keep its autonomy for 50 years. In 1999, nearby Macau, after 442 years under Portugal, returned to China on the same basis. Macau, with 11 square miles and three dozen glittering casinos, became the Las Vegas of Asia. Hong Kong and Macau are now "special administrative regions" of China, with internal autonomy. Beijing intends to show Taiwan that it could rejoin the mainland and still keep its political and economic system. Few Taiwanese are buying.

Under Beijing's eye, Hong Kong slowly introduced new laws on "security" and "information" to prevent criticism. Beijing legislation eroded Hong Kong's special status. Critical Hong Kong editors lost their jobs. Corruption grew, as certain cooperative Hong Kongers got special deals. Beijing favors Shanghai as China's financial hub, as it once was before World War II, but Hong Kong, with rule of law, boomed as Asia headquarters for many international banks.

Gorbachev's face. All Beijing's rulers fear becoming China's Gorbachev, so they tolerate no democracy, competing parties, or free press, precisely the reforms that Gorbachev did first. Did the Chinese do it right, sequencing their reforms so as to build an economic basis for democracy before reforming their political system?

World Trade Organization (WTO)
Organization whose 120-plus members open themselves to trade and investment; has quasi-judicial powers.

Some fear that China could destabilize, that its economic reforms without political reforms will malfunction. With increasing corruption and inequality, there is growing mass unrest. So far, the only successful transitions from communism to free-market capitalism have come in Central Europe—Poland, the Czech Republic, and Hungary—where anticommunists completely threw out the communist regimes. Middle-way systems tend to destabilize.

China and the World

China is aggressively purchasing energy, minerals, and farmland worldwide, especially in Africa. Some see a kind of Chinese colonialism, but Beijing sees it as a simple necessity to feed its industries and people and argues that it brings prosperity and development to other lands. If the West can practice globalization, why cannot China? Much African land sits unused, waiting for modern know-how. Northern China, hit by a multiyear drought, cannot grow the grain it used to. South Korea, Saudi Arabia, and other countries make similar deals.

China feels that Westerners discriminate against China. Starting with President Nixon in 1972, we urged China to come into the world market and make money. China did and now has some $4 trillion in foreign reserves—the most of any country—to spend. When U.S., Australian, or other firms are for sale, why cannot China bid? Is America—which continually faults China on trade, currency, and copyright questions—enraging the Chinese dragon? The road to Pearl Harbor was paved with U.S. trade restrictions on Japan, especially on oil.

China's trade and budget surpluses, especially with the United States, also disturb relations. China surpassed Japan to become the largest holder of U.S. debt—$1.5 trillion, more than half of it in U.S. Treasury notes—and worries about them losing value if China sells its mountain of dollars. Thus, China, unless it is willing to take a financial hit, is locked into holding dollars. Increasingly, China uses its own currency in trade deals, slowly approaching currency convertibility. Just as the dollar replaced the weakened British pound as the main world reserve currency after World War II, the *renminbi* could replace a weakened dollar, but for that, the RMB would need to float, something Beijing does not want.

China is now being hit by several destabilizing forces. The easy economic reforms—allowing a capitalist microeconomy—have been accomplished. The tough parts remain: government, banking, and state-industry debts; inefficient agriculture and energy usage; and the need to add millions of new jobs every year. China, like Japan, discovered that exports cannot be the sole basis of an economy.

In 2001, China won membership in the **World Trade Organization (WTO)**, which it had long sought in order to boost China's exports. WTO membership brought new difficulties. Now China has to play fair and allow in foreign products, investments, and companies, even banks. The WTO ruled against China for keeping out imported auto parts, books, movies, and music. Other lands protest China's domination of the world textile and clothing market and invoke WTO provisions to limit imports from China. In 2009, President Obama charged

dumping

Selling goods overseas for less than it costs to produce them.

Taipei

(Pronounced *Type-A*) Capital of Taiwan.

that China was **dumping** tires and steel pipe on the U.S. market and imposed tariffs on them. China reacted angrily, complaining of unfair treatment of its exports. Do not count on increased trade to dissolve frictions among nations.

A big question is whether China could some day seize Taiwan, which Beijing regards as a renegade province. Figuring that time is on its side, Beijing gradually boosts trade, tourism, and increased contacts with **Taipei**. The present Taipei government cultivates calm, even friendly, relations with Beijing. But if Taiwan should ever declare independence—which many Taiwanese wish—Beijing would turn to military means. By a 1979 law, the United States is committed to a peaceful, voluntary reunification. If Beijing applies force or intimidation to Taiwan, how should we react? U.S. military intervention in the Taiwan Strait could quickly escalate into war, even nuclear war. A U.S. trade embargo would not frighten China, which could inflict great economic damage on the United States simply by selling its Treasury notes. China would also take a hit but would not hesitate to do so. Do not underestimate Chinese nationalism.

Tension also flares in cyberspace. Washington was outraged with the 2013 news that PLA Unit 61389, housed in a Shanghai office building, massively hacks the computer sites of U.S. defense-related corporations. China, to be sure, is not alone in hacking other countries, and Beijing fired back that the United States does it too. The difference seems to be that the Chinese chiefly aim at stealing technology, the Americans at penetrating security. Badly needed: an international agreement on hacking before it turns into cyberwarfare.

Until recently, China had not been stable for more than a century and could destabilize again. China, hard to govern in good times, now has a split and uncertain Party, a slowing economy, corrupt officials, weakening central authority, and growing regional disparities. Some observers fear that Beijing is deflecting discontent outward by promoting a defiant nationalism.

China is already the major world economic force and military power of East Asia, having eclipsed Japan. China's military budget is rising sharply. Former Party chief Jiang claimed that by 2020 there would be only two superpowers—China and the United States. One of China's priorities is its navy, which has claimed all of the East and South China Seas and established ports on the Indian Ocean. This worries other Asian countries—India, Japan, the Philippines, Malaysia, Indonesia, and Vietnam. Underlying these policies is China's deep craving for respect for what was once the world's greatest civilization, one that was brought low by Western and Japanese imperialists. How China achieves this recognition will be one of the great chapters of twenty-first century history.

Review Questions

Learning Objective 7.1 Describe China's "bureaucratic empire" and how it compares with Europe's political development, p. 272.

1. Compare the Chinese and Roman empires.
2. What were the *spheres of influence* on China's coasts?

3. How well does Brinton's theory of revolution fit China?

Learning Objective 7.2 Outline the main points of China's current political model, p. 281.

4. How does the Chinese political model differ from the Soviet model?

5. How could China be described as a *cadre*-based system?

6. How did Deng Xiaoping set China on its present course?

7. What is the *hukou* system and why does it have to go?

Learning Objective 7.3 Identify the main sources of discontent in today's China, p. 292.

8. Describe the three layers of Chinese political culture.

9. What is the current "Chinese dream" and why is it potentially dangerous?

10. Argue whether the growth of a Chinese middle class points to democracy.

Learning Objective 7.4 Compare and contrast China's Great Leap Forward and its Cultural Revolution, p. 305.

11. Why did Mao keep wrecking China with his grandiose campaigns?

12. How can there be left and right factions in a single-party dictatorship?

13. Why is corruption such a threat to China's stability?

Learning Objective 7.5 Explain why Beijing wants to "rebalance" China's economy, p. 314.

14. Why is Chinese capitalism deceptive?

15. Why is *foreign direct investment* important for economic growth?

16. What steps could China take to turn democratic?

Key Terms

Further Reference

Beardson, Timothy. *Stumbling Giant: The Threats to China's Future*. New Haven: Yale Univesity Press, 2013.

Brown, Kerry. *The New Emperors: Power and the Princelings in China*. London: I. B. Tauris, 2014.

Callahan, William A. *China Dreams: Twenty Visions of the Future*. New York: Oxford University Press, 2013.

Dikötter, Frank. *The Tragedy of Liberation: A History of the Chinese Revolution*. New York: Bloomsbury, 2013.

Dreyer, June Teufel. *China's Political System: Modernization and Tradition*, 9th ed. New York: Pearson, 2014.

Eimer, David. *The Emperor Far Away: Travels at the Edge of China*. New York: Bloomsbury, 2014.

Fenby, Jonathan. *Tiger Head, Snake Tails: China Today, How It Got There and Where It Is Heading*. New York: Simon & Schuster, 2012.

Fu, Ping. *Bend, Not Break: A Life in Two Worlds*. New York: Penguin, 2012.

Goossaert, Vincent, and David A. Palmer. *The Religious Question in Modern China*. Chicago, IL: University of Chicago Press, 2012.

He, Rowena. *Tiananmen Exiles: Voices of the Struggle for Democracy in China*. New York: Palgrave Macmillan, 2014.

Hillman, Ben. *Power and Patronage: Local State Networks and Party-State Resilience in Rural China*. Stanford, CA: Stanford University Press, 2014.

Hua, Yu. *Boy in the Twilight: Stories of the Hidden China*. New York: Random House, 2014.

Lampton, David M. *Following the Leader: Ruling China, From Deng Xiaoping to Xi Jinping*. Berkeley, CA: University of California Press, 2014.

Lieberthal, Kenneth G., Cheng Li, and Yu Keping, eds. *China's Political Development: Chinese and American Perspectives*. Washington, DC: Brookings, 2014.

Lim, Louisa. *The People's Republic of Amnesia: Tiananmen Revisited*. New York: Oxford University Press, 2014.

Lin, Yifu Justin. *Against the Consensus: Reflections on the Great Recesion*. New York: Cambridge University Press, 2013.

Link, Perry, Richard P. Madsen, and Paul G. Pickowicz, eds. *Restless China*. Lanham, MD: Rowman & Littlefield, 2013.

Nathan, Andrew, J., Larry Diamond, and Marc F. Plattner, eds. *Will China Democratize?* Baltimore, MD: Johns Hopkins University Press, 2013.

Osburg, John. *Anxious Wealth: Money and Morality among China's New Rich*. Stanford, CA: Stanford University Press, 2013.

Osnos, Evan. *Age of Ambition: Chasing Fortune, Truth, and Faith in the New China*. New York: Farrar, Straus & Giroux, 2014.

Pantsov, Alexander V., and Steven I. Levine. *Mao: The Real Story*. New York: Simon & Schuster, 2012.

Rene, Helena K. *China's Sent-Down Generation: Public Administration and the Legacies of Mao's Rustication Program*. Washington, DC: Georgetown University Press, 2013.

Schell, Orville, and John Delury. *Wealth and Power: China's Long March to the Twenty-First Century*. New York: Random House, 2013.

Vogel, Ezra F. *Deng Xiaoping and the Transformation of China*. Cambridge, MA: Harvard University Press, 2011.

Yang Jisheng. *Tombstone: The Great Chinese Famine, 1958–1962*. New York: Farrar, Straus & Giroux, 2012.

Zheng Wang. *Never Forget National Humiliation: Historical Memory in Chinese Politics and Foreign Relations*. New York: Columbia University Press, 2012.

Chapter 8
India

Hindus consider Varanasi, on the banks of the sacred Ganges, a holy city.

 ## Learning Objectives

8.1 Assess how the British put themselves out of a job in modernizing India.

8.2 Compare and contrast India's and Britain's parliamentary systems.

8.3 Explain how India lends itself naturally to pluralism.

8.4 Contrast the aims and supports of India's two main parties.

8.5 Contrast the Indian and Chinese economies.

WHY INDIA MATTERS

Few poor countries are democracies, but India is the massive exception. India is the most complex of our 11 countries, arguably the world's most complex. Its regions, states, castes, and languages trip up simple explanations. India was founded on the Westminster model, but its federalism and parties make it function quite differently from Britain. How can a country with such a diverse and mostly poor population of 1.2 billion not only stay together but still function as a democracy? Many dismissed the Indian economy for years as hopeless, but India is enjoying rapid economic growth, forcing the world to pay attention. Cultural explanations are often given for poverty, but India illustrates that *policy* may better explain economic growth. The big question for the twenty-first century is: Who will win the Asian race, India or China? China is now way ahead, but India's resilient if imperfect democracy may give it the edge in the long run.

Geography

What Are the Developing Areas?

It is hard to put one label on the lands of Asia, Africa, and Latin America, home to five-sixths of the human race. One attempt coined by French writers in the 1950s, *le Tiers Monde* (**Third World**), referred to the majority of humankind that was in neither the Western capitalist First World nor the Communist Second World. It is an awfully broad term that permits few firm generalizations. Critics claim "Third World" is pejorative and should be discarded in favor of "developing areas." Now, after the collapse of communism in East Europe and the ex-Soviet Union, there is no more Second World. Some say the only meaningful dividing line is now "the West and the rest."

The developing areas are mostly poor, but some oil-producing countries are rich, and some lands are industrializing fast. They are mostly nonwhite. Almost all of them were once colonies of a European imperial power. Most of them are hot and closer to the equator than the rich countries, so a few writers call them the Global South. Business calls them "emerging markets." The U.S. State Department and some international banks call them LDCs (less-developed countries). The ones making fast economic progress are called NICs (newly industrializing countries), which a Goldman Sachs economist dubbed the BRICs (Brazil, Russia, India, China). Many show good and even excellent rates of economic growth. Their biggest economic danger: surging food prices.

How to lift up the poor areas is a long and major controversy. Cultural theorists argue that not much

can happen until local cultures turn from passivity and fatalism to a modern mentality of change and self-improvement. Once a country has that, it grows on its own with little foreign aid. Without it, aid matters little. Good governance and policies can change psychologies and cultures, turning previously "passive" peoples into energetic entrepreneurs, as in India.

Liberals generally support foreign-aid programs and loans from international banks, but much of this is skimmed off by corrupt officials. Some see **microcredit** as the way to spark economic growth on a free-enterprise basis. Others counter that tiny startup firms cannot seriously boost economic growth or employ the vast numbers of jobless—major foreign direct investment (FDI) is needed. FDI fuels the growth of many developing countries.

Curiously, natural resources such as oil do little to grow the economy. Some of the poorest countries have abundant natural resources, whereas some growth demons have few or no natural resources (examples: Hong Kong, Singapore, and South Korea). **Petrostates**, which concentrate wealth and power into the hands of a few, have become notorious for thwarting democracy.

One generalization about the developing areas: They are unstable. The political institutions of almost all of these 120-plus countries are weak. Most lack a single, integrated culture and are pulled apart by region and religion. Many are wracked by tensions that can explode in revolutions, coups, and breakaway movements and end in dictatorship. Rule of law is weak or absent. Crime and **corruption** penetrate most Third World political systems. Power holders routinely use their offices to get rich. In some countries, you cannot tell where politics leaves off and crime begins.

Few developing countries have yet made it into the ranks of stable democracies, a characteristic now common of all countries in the West. Some developing lands are unstable democracies; **demagogues** gull unsophisticated voters with deceptive promises and turn themselves into dictators, such as in Venezuela.

Scholars find an imperfect correlation between economics and democracy. Most countries with per capita GDPs above $10,000 (middle-income countries and higher) are able to found stable democracies that do not revert to authoritarianism. Countries with per capita GDPs below $6,000 have trouble establishing and sustaining democracy; they often revert to authoritarianism. India is an amazing exception to the wealth-democracy link. Pakistan is more typical: unstable elected governments alternating with military rule. Some of the countries in this book are in this borderline area. No per capita income guarantees democracy, nor does any doom it; much depends on the size, education levels, and pluralistic organization of the country's middle class and the cleverness of democratic elites. Middle class is the key variable, not GDP.

Impact of the Past

8.1   Assess how the British put themselves out of a job in modernizing India.

India is a very old collection of cultures but a new nation. For much of its history, it was not one country. It has great ethnic and regional diversity, with at least three main geographical areas: the foothills of the Himalayas in the north, the Indo-Ganges Plain across north-central India, and the Peninsula of the south, all homes to very different peoples. Long ago, India was mostly dense forest; now much of it is densely populated.

As in Mesopotamia, Egypt, and China, India's civilization began along a river. From 2500 to 1600 BC, the Harappan culture flourished in northwest India on the Indus River (which now flows through Pakistan). The name India derives from the Indus, called the Sindhu in Sanskrit but pronounced Hindu in Persian. Major cities of Hindustan (Persian for "land of the Hindus") traded with Mesopotamia. Around 1500 BC, Aryan immigrants and conquerors pushed in from Central Asia and built kingdoms ruled by *rajans* (Sanskrit for kings, cognate to *reign, regent, regime, region, roi, rey*) over most of northern India. They made the Ganga (Ganges) a sacred river and a major trade route. With them came the Indo-European language of Sanskrit and four holy books, the Vedas, which form the basis of **Hinduism** and of India's **caste** system. In India, Sanskrit occupies the historical and theological role held by Latin in Europe.

Indian intellectual life flourished. Kautilya, in the fourth century BC, devised a remarkably modern political philosophy. Kautilya, a prime minister and adviser to a king, wrote in *Arthasastra* (*The Principles of Material Well-Being*) that prosperity arises from a well-run kingdom. Like Hobbes, Kautilya posited a state of nature that meant

Third World
Most of Asia, Africa, and Latin America.

microcredit
Very small loans to startup businesses.

petrostate
Country based on oil exports.

corruption
Use of public office for private gain.

demagogue
Manipulative politician who wins votes through impossible promises.

Hinduism
Chief religion of India, polytheistic and based on Vedic scriptures, rebirth, and caste.

caste
Rigid, hereditary social stratum or group.

Geography

Bound India

India is bounded on the north by China, Nepal, and Bhutan;

on the east by Bangladesh and Myanmar (formerly Burma);

on the south by the Indian Ocean; and on the west by Pakistan.

India

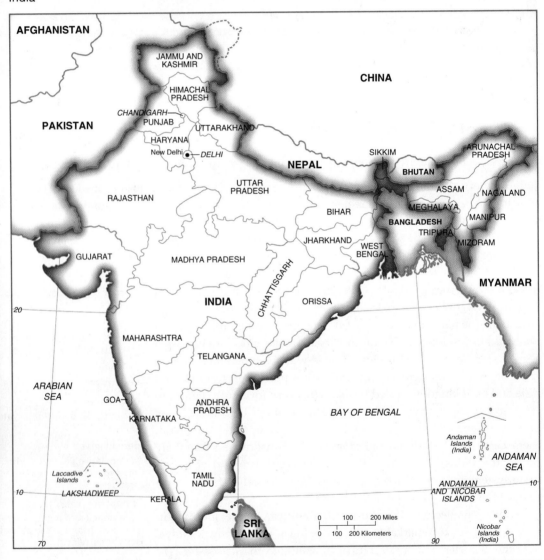

anarchy. Monarchs arose to protect the land and people against anarchy and to ensure their prosperity. Like Machiavelli, Kautilya advised his prince to operate on the basis of pure expediency, doing whatever it took to secure his kingdom domestically and against other kingdoms. Kautilya thus could be said to have founded both political economy and the realist school of statecraft. At about the time of Kautilya, Indian mathematicians devised a system of numbers, later known as "Arabic numerals" because they were transmitted to the West by Arab traders.

Buddhism
Sixth century BC offshoot of Hinduism; seeks enlightenment through meditation and cessation of desire.

sultanate
Muslim state governed by a sultan (holder of power).

In the sixth century BC, however, the Persian Empire conquered northern India, bringing much Persian culture into India. Alexander the Great pushed to the Indus River in 326 BC but died before he could conquer India. Several empires and dynasties followed, mostly concentrated in northern India. The Mauryan Empire (326–184 BC) united most of India. Its great king Ashoka (273–232 BC) was so shocked by the bloodshed of his wars that he embraced **Buddhism** (which originated in India) and turned it into India's dominant faith for a few centuries before it faded to a minority religion. Buddhism is still the main faith in Sri Lanka (formerly Ceylon), Mongolia, Tibet, and Southeast Asia, but not in India. The classic period of India—in some ways like the Han period of China—was the Gupta Empire (320–550 AD) of northern India. China unified early and acquired an indelible nationwide Han culture. India mostly stayed fragmented.

The Arrival of Islam

Islam spread quickly. In 711 AD—the same year Arabs conquered Spain—Arabs took the Sindh region of the lower Indus (now in Pakistan), first bringing Islam to India. More substantial numbers of Muslim Turkic tribes from Afghanistan, fighting from horseback with crossbows, arrived around 1000 AD and set up **sultanates** that rose and fell with new invasions.

Comparison

The Uniqueness Trap

One key question for India and Japan is whether they are countries like other countries or hard to compare. Samuel P. Huntington classified India and Japan as unique, one-of-a-kind civilizations. Many Indian and foreign observers claim that India is a society like no other, the complex intermingling of dozens of peoples and religions. Many say the only way to understand India is through its deep spiritual and religious values, which influence its governance today.

It is the view of this book—and indeed probably the basis of comparative politics—that descriptions of a country as totally unique are unwarranted. Granted,

Indian and Japanese cultures are different from Western political cultures. When you compare, though, you discover that any country's political patterns can be understood. Much of India can be explained by waves of conquest and fragmentation. Much of Japan can be explained by prolonged feudalism. You find that people everywhere are not so different. Both Indian and Japanese politicians take money from interest groups and court voting blocs, just like politicians everywhere. Avoid the uniqueness trap and the related Mystique Mistake, the overly romantic fascination with a supposedly exotic country.

Mughal
From *Mongol*; Muslim conquerors of India; formed empire.

colonialism
Gaining and exploitation of overseas territories, chiefly by Europeans; related to imperialism.

The main Muslim conquest was that of the **Mughals** (sometimes spelled *Moguls*), Muslim tribes of Turkic, Persian, and Mongol origin who swept into India from the north in 1526 equipped with artillery. Akbar the Great (1556–1605) expanded and consolidated the Mughal Empire to include most of northern India. An enlightened emperor, Akbar ordered tolerance of all religions and even held interfaith dialogues. Many of his officials were Hindus. The Mughals used Persian (written in Arabic script) as the administrative language, and it lasted until replaced by English. A Mughal high point is the Persian-influenced Taj Mahal, built by Shah Jahan in the seventeenth century to honor his late wife. The greatest impact of the Mughals, however, was India's Muslim minority of perhaps 25 percent before partition in 1947 (now nearly 15 percent).

The British Takeover

Colonialism means several things. From the legal point of view, a colony lacks sovereignty; ultimate lawmaking authority resides in a distant capital. London controlled the laws governing India, Paris those of Senegal, and Brussels those of the Congo. For the most part, the "natives" were kept politically powerless, as the imperial power deemed them too backward and ignorant, although the British often gave traditional rulers some local responsibilities.

In economics, **colonialism** involved exploitation by the imperial country. The colonies supplied cheap agricultural and mineral raw materials, which the imperial country manufactured into industrial products that it sold back to the colonies. Marxists argue that colonies were captive markets that were kept poor in order to enrich imperialists. Actually, most colonies cost imperial governments more to administer and defend than they earned. Individual firms, to be sure, profited from the colonial trade.

Racially, colonies were governed on the basis of skin color on the principle that "the lowest of the Europeans is higher than the highest of the natives." An English clerk in Calcutta (now Kolkata) was the social better of an Indian professor. A French policeman directing traffic in

Geography

Turbulent Frontiers

UCLA historian John S. Galbraith explained the piecemeal British takeover of India as unplanned but inevitable. London was too distant to run India, and local British governors of the East India Company always faced a "turbulent frontier" at the edge of their holdings: hostile princes, uprisings, and bandit raiders. "Governors continued to try to eliminate the disorderly frontier by annexations, which in turn produced new frontier problems and further expansion," wrote Galbraith in 1960. In this way, the initial British trading posts gradually expanded into coastal colonies, then into whole provinces, and eventually swallowed most of India.

The turbulent frontier theory explains much imperial expansion. Lugard in Nigeria had to take over the turbulent north in 1903. The French in the 1830s never intended to take over all of Algeria, just the seaports to stop piracy. But they had to move inland to protect their positions on the coast. The tsars had to take Siberia and Central Asia to protect Russia. In this way, empires tend to expand until they overexpand.

Algiers was superior to an Algerian doctor. Racism was part of colonialism; it psychologically enabled the imperialists to govern millions of unlike peoples who did not want them there. It also contributed to the rage felt by educated subjects, some of whom became leaders of independence movements: "You treat us like dirt in our own country, but we'll put an end to that!"

maharajah
Sanskrit for "great king"; Hindu prince.

sepoy
Indian soldier in the British Indian Army.

Raj
From Hindi *rule*; British government of India, 1858–1947.

In hindsight, colonialism stands condemned as brutal and evil. But it was the unavoidable outcome of the restless, dynamic West encountering the traditional areas of the globe that were easy pickings. The imperial powers had no right to conquer and govern others; they simply had better guns. Of course, without colonialism, there would be no United States. "Colonial" has a nice sound to Americans, connoting hardy settlers, Thanksgiving, and pretty landscapes. It has a bitter ring for most other peoples. Colonialism left a chip on the shoulders of the developing areas and helps explain lingering anti-West feelings.

As usual in Asia, the first Europeans to arrive were Portuguese, who rounded Africa in 1488 and explored the Indian Ocean. Vasco da Gama reached India in 1498. One Portuguese colony, Goa, on India's west coast, lasted from 1510 to 1961, when India took it over. The English East India Company was chartered in 1600 to trade in spices, cotton, silk, and sugar through company "factories" (actually, warehouses) in coastal enclaves. The Dutch and the French did the same. Mughal emperors and local princes, eager for foreign goods and money, welcomed the European trade. As in North America, colonialism began as money-making enterprises.

The British, under the energetic Robert Clive, beat the Mughals in Bengal in 1757 and ousted the French from their small colony of Pondicherry in 1761 (about the same time they ousted the French from Canada). The British takeover of India was piecemeal, and much of India remained legally in the hands of **maharajahs** in their "princely states," under varying degrees of British supervision. A puppet Mughal emperor still reigned in Delhi. Cornwallis, defeated at Yorktown, became governor-general of India and died there in 1805.

By 1818, most of India was under the control, direct or indirect, of the British East India Company and became a captive market for British industry. Many Indians were schooled in English, which became standard for Indian education and administration in 1835, an important measure for the cultural unification of India. Christian missionary schools attempted to convert Indians, with little success.

The East India Company got a major fright with the massive Sepoy or Indian Mutiny of 1857, which Indians call their First War of Indian Independence. It showed that, just under the surface, Indians deeply resented British rule. The spark was new rifles that had powder and shot packed in paper cartridges. A false rumor spread that these were greased with pig and cow lard. Muslims, who do not eat pork, and Hindus, who do not eat beef, were outraged because they had to tear open the cartridges with their teeth. The **sepoys** shot their British officers, besieged several cities, and killed English civilians. The East India Company's reaction was so ferocious that London dissolved the Company in 1858 and set up "direct rule" under a governor-general, a system called the **Raj**. The Crown had to take over India to save it from the misrule of a giant corporation, a pattern that also appeared in Dutch, French, and Belgian colonialism. You cannot run countries on a purely commercial basis.

subcontinent
Asia south of the Himalayas (India, Pakistan, and Bangladesh); also called South Asia.

India became the most important and lucrative part of the British Empire. To reach it and other colonies in Asia, Britain (along with France) constructed the Suez Canal, which opened in 1869, part of the "imperial lifeline." Cut off from U.S. cotton during the Civil War, Britain increased India's cotton crop but did not allow Indian industry to make cloth. Instead, Indian cotton fed the mills of Lancashire and was sold back to Indians at high prices. Britain destroyed Indian industry. Restoring Indian cloth production became a symbol of Gandhi's independence movement. Gandhi personally spun his own thread in defiance of the British, and a spinning wheel is in the center of India's flag today.

Indian Independence

British rule, while basically exploitive, also did much to modernize India. The English language allowed educated Indians to speak to each other across the entire **subcontinent** and to voice their discontent. Universities created a new intellectual class of lawyers, journalists, and educators, who soon turned critical of their British masters. The railroad and telegraph

Personalities

Gandhi: The Great Soul

Mohandas Gandhi (1869–1948) was an unlikely liberator. A slight, bespectacled man, often in a homespun loincloth, he exuded a quiet charisma that mobilized millions of Indians to press the British to "Quit India!" Gandhi was called *Mahatma* (great soul in Sanskrit) and *Bapu* (father), as he was indeed the father of modern India.

Son of a prime minister of a small principality in Gujarat (in western India) and a devout Hindu mother, Gandhi showed little early intellectual promise but did study law in London. His formative experience was as a lawyer and organizer of downtrodden Indians in South Africa from 1893 to 1914, where he felt racism and repression firsthand. There, in 1908, he wrote his most important work, *Hind Swaraj* (Independent India), which the British tried to suppress. Returning to India, Gandhi turned sharply anti-British after the 1919 Amritsar massacre of 400 Indians at a peaceful meeting. In 1921, Gandhi took command of the Indian National Congress and turned it from an elite debating society into a well-organized mass movement that, after long struggle, persuaded Britain to leave.

Gandhi abjured violence and led the Congress in noncooperation campaigns that ultimately wore down the British. He urged *satyagraha* (soul force) based on *ahimsa* (not injuring any living thing) mixed with Thoreau's civil disobedience. He demanded tolerance for all religions and help for the lowliest, the outcastes. His most famous act was to lead a 250-mile march to the ocean to make salt from seawater to protest the salt tax; 60,000 of his followers were imprisoned.

The British saw Gandhi as a ridiculous but irritating figure and jailed him many times. Gandhi disliked industry and cities and offered a vision of an India of villages, where Indians would retain their spirituality. Such rural idylls mean poverty, with farmers starving on tiny plots.

Ultimately, Gandhi succeeded by delegitimizing British colonial rule. Britain was exhausted after World War II, and India was seething with anger. Besides, how could Britain fight for freedom during the war but deny it to Indians? (Other British colonies such as Nigeria asked the same question.) The Muslim League insisted on a separate Pakistan, and both Hindu and Muslim violence grew. A Hindu fanatic who believed Gandhi was soft on Muslims—he proclaimed them as brother Indians—assassinated him in early 1948. Wishing for precisely the opposite, Gandhi had unleashed terrible violence.

stitched together the disparate country. Before imperialism, there was little Indian nationalism. The British, by modernizing India, got themselves invited to leave.

In 1885, intellectuals founded the Indian National **Congress** (INC) to debate government reforms. It was an elite thing, not radical or aiming for independence. That changed with the return of Gandhi to India; he took over the INC and turned it into a huge, effective mass movement demanding **swaraj**. Indian political stability after independence owes much to the age, size, and organization of the Congress, which subsequently turned into a political party that ruled India for many years.

But the Indian independence movement split in three: (1) the mainstream Congress of Gandhi that sought to represent all Indians, (2) a Muslim movement that feared and fought domination by Hindus, and (3) a Hindu nationalist movement that preached exclusivity and hatred of Muslims. In hindsight, there was probably no way India could have achieved independence without releasing the tensions that British colonial rule had built up.

Congress
Led India's independence movement and later was the dominant party.

swaraj
Swa = self, *raj* = rule; Indian independence.

partition
Divide a country among its communities.

Geography

Partition

In colonial situations, the imperial power can sometimes calm communal tensions (which it may also have created), but when sovereignty—the key question of who is to be the boss—is up for grabs, deadly conflict can emerge, as it did between Hindus and Muslims in India. In such cases, **partition** may be an unhappy but "least bad" solution, one that seldom leads to peace and stability. India's is not the only sad case of partition.

Ireland, 1922 Britain misruled Ireland for seven centuries, putting down several uprisings and ignoring the Irish Potato Famine of the 1840s. Shaken by the 1916 Easter Rising, Britain agreed to an Irish Free State in 1922, but Northern Ireland, with its Protestant majority, stayed British and became the scene of Catholic–Protestant violence.

Palestine, 1948 Britain took Palestine from the Turks in World War I and ruled it under a League of Nations mandate. The Arabs of Palestine rioted against Jewish immigration, which became urgent with the Holocaust. In 1947, an exhausted Britain threw the question to the UN, which devised a partition that looked like a checkerboard. The Jews accepted it; the Arabs rejected it. As Britain pulled out in 1948, Israel proclaimed its independence and has been fighting Arabs ever since.

Cyprus, 1961 Britain took Cyprus from the Turks in 1878, but, after World War II, the Greek Cypriot majority agitated for *enosis* (union) with Greece. Greek guerrillas harassed the British, who agreed to leave in 1961. The Turkish minority, fearful of Greek massacres, demanded *taksim* (partition). In 1974, Turkey invaded and took the northern third of the island, which stays partitioned to this day.

Bosnia, 1992 After Yugoslav dictator Tito died in 1980, Yugoslavia's *republics* turned to independence. Even Bosnian Muslims—a plurality but not a majority of Bosnia—demanded their own country, something that had historically never existed. Amid a terrible three-sided civil war, Serbs and Croats partitioned Bosnia by seizing adjacent portions of it. Bosnia is now effectively a NATO protectorate.

There are no examples of the happy partition of a state with intermingled but hostile peoples. The only argument for it is that trying to hold the country together would be worse. Partition among Shia, Sunni, and Kurds would likely not solve Iraq's problems.

communal
Ethnic or religious communities within a nation.

Muslim League
Organization demanding a separate Muslim Pakistan.

Hindutva
Literally, Hinduness.

Kashmir
Valley near Himalayas contested by India and Pakistan.

There had long been **communal** tensions and sometimes violence between India's Muslims and Hindus. As soon as the INC began agitating for *swaraj*, some of India's Muslim minority started to worry. Muslims and Hindus initially cooperated in the INC, but, in 1906, the **Muslim League** split off and, in 1940, demanded a separate Pakistan for Muslims. Gandhi tried to reassure Muslims that they would be at home in India—177 million still are—but many did not believe it. Exclaimed Muslim League chief Muhammad Ali Jinnah: "Islam is in danger!" The British used the standard line of colonialists everywhere that they alone could keep India together and reasonably calm. Rather blindly, however, they also created much of the tension and did little to prepare India for independence.

In 1925, Hindu nationalists founded the Rashtriya Swayamsevak Sangh (RSS, National Volunteers Union) to make sure **Hindutva** dominated India. Although the RSS for a while worked with Gandhi and the Congress for independence, they, like Jinnah, split from it. An RSS supporter assassinated Gandhi, and the organization was briefly banned. (Current Prime Minister Modi grew up in the RSS.)

In World War II, Japan quickly took Southeast Asia and pushed into eastern India. The British were scared. With only a few British and Anzac troops, they had to rely on Indian soldiers and even officers. (Their best: the Gurkhas, from Nepal.) The Japanese put out the line that they were liberating Asia from the Europeans and Indians should join them. Some did; a former Gandhi lieutenant, Subhash Chandra Bose, went over to the Japanese in World War II along with thousands of captured Indian soldiers. Britain knew it could not keep India forever.

In 1947, Britain sent Lord Mountbatten, who had commanded Allied forces against the Japanese, to negotiate independence. The Muslim League insisted on a separate Pakistan, which meant partition, always an unhappy affair (see box on partition). India's partition was a botched job, hasty and unplanned. Borders were drawn arbitrarily without knowledge of local loyalties. Few anticipated massacres or refugees. The predominantly Muslim areas, on the east and the west, went to Pakistan, the rest to India. In princely states, the maharajah decided. In **Kashmir**, the Hindu maharajah opted for India despite the wishes of a big Muslim Kashmiri majority. The Kashmir quarrel sparked three wars between India and Pakistan and still smolders.

Amid growing violence, India was declared independent at midnight on August 15, 1947. In an orgy of ethnic cleansing, more than 7 million Muslims fled to newly created Pakistan, while a like number of Hindus and Sikhs fled from Pakistan to India. Altogether, the 1947 partition of India led to 14.5 million refugees and half a million deaths. British forces did nothing to stop the violence. Gandhi was horrified at the bloody chaos and soon became a victim himself.

The Key Institutions

8.2 Compare and contrast India's and Britain's parliamentary systems.

India, like Britain, is a parliamentary system: Its cabinet is formed from and staffed by members of parliament. India's constitution defines it as "socialist, secular, and democratic," as its framers, led by Nehru, were caught up in the democratic socialism they had learned as students in Britain. This socialism skewed and retarded Indian economic development but has been partly discarded as India plunged into rapid capitalist growth in the 1990s. Under Gandhi, the Congress movement also insisted on keeping Indian government secular, not tied to any religion. Some Hindu nationalists would like to change that.

president's rule
Delhi's ability to take over state governments.

Instead of a monarch, however, India has a president who, like Germany's weak president, is largely ceremonial. Like the German president, India's is chosen for five-year terms by an electoral college of both houses of parliament plus state legislatures. In 2012, former defense, foreign, and finance minister Pranab Mukherjee, then 76, was elected president with support from the Congress and other parties.

India's Main Prime Ministers			
Prime Minister	**Party**	**Term**	**Remembered for**
Jawaharlal Nehru	INC	1947–1964	Secularism, statism, neutralism
Indira Gandhi	INC	1966–1977, 1980–1984	Authoritarianism, breaking up Pakistan, Emergency
Morarji Desai	Janata	1977–1979	Repudiation of Indira
Rajiv Gandhi	INC	1984–1989	Computers trigger economic liberalization
Atal Bihari Vajpayee	BJP	1996, 1998–2004	Hindu right, nuclear tests, economic growth
Manmohan Singh	INC	2004–2014	Calm, economic growth

The Prime Minister

As in Britain, in India, power is in the hands of the prime minister. Part of the reason India's prime minister (PM) is so powerful is the imprint its first occupant, the brainy Jawaharlal Nehru, put on the office for its first 17 years. Nehru, 20 years younger than Gandhi and also British educated, was the day-to-day administrator of India's independence movement under Gandhi and immediately became prime minister in 1947, serving until he died in office in 1964. Nehru devised and built up India's political institutions, with the prime minister in charge overall, giving the office plentiful economic and political powers that have lasted to this day.

The PM may ask the president to invoke **president's rule**, which gives New Delhi the power to take over a state government in an emergency—such as rioting—and run it directly. The prime minister sets the main government policies and can call new general elections whenever he or she likes within a five-year maximum term. To "form a government," the PM must control a majority of seats in the lower house, which usually requires a coalition. Like presidents in other parliamentary systems, India's president names as prime minister whomever the largest party in parliament designates. Prime ministers need not be the party chief or a member of the lower house, although they usually are. Manmohan Singh was named prime minister in 2004 from the *upper* house, a first in India's history. The conservative and Hindu BJP swept the 2014 elections and made the successful if controversial chief minister of Gujarat state, Narendra Modi, prime minister without a coalition.

India has a very large cabinet appointed by the prime minister from among the parties supporting the government in parliament. The roughly 30-minister cabinets have most ministers named from the lower house and fewer from the upper. The largest party in the coalition, either the BJP or INC, gets most portfolios; smaller parties a few. Below cabinet level, India has another perhaps 40 "ministers of state." In addition to the usual ministries, India has some specialized ministries, such as railways, chemicals, urban development, rural development, mines, heavy industries, small-scale industries, tribal affairs, textiles, power, minority affairs, petroleum, and water resources. Until the 1990s, India had a government-supervised economy requiring many specialized ministries, and this lingers in present-day India. If India turns more to free markets, some of these ministries may disappear. Titles and responsibilities, as usual in parliamentary systems, are routinely shuffled and renamed.

A Bicameral Parliament

India's parliament is bicameral; the upper chamber represents India's states but, as in most bicameral legislatures, is less powerful than the lower house, the Lok Sabha (People's Assembly). The Lok Sabha has 543 elected members and, like Britain's Commons, serves for up to five years, although elections can be called early. Election is by single-member districts, Anglo-American style, with only a plurality needed to win. The president appoints another two members to represent the small Anglo-Indian community, so the total size of the Lok Sabha is 545. Only the Lok Sabha can initiate money bills.

The Rajya Sabha (Council of States) is the upper house, which can have up to 250 members (up to 12 of them distinguished persons appointed by the president) who serve six years. As in the United States before 1913, they are chosen by their state assemblies, one-third every two years. Each state, depending on population, gets from 1 to 31 representatives. If the two houses cannot agree on legislation, they meet and vote jointly. The greater numbers of the Lok Sabha then give it the upper hand.

A Fragmented Party System

Until 1977, all of India's prime ministers were from the Indian National Congress, making India look, for a while, like a dominant-party system, as were Japan and Mexico back then. India's Congress Party played a role similar to Mexico's PRI: a system-founding large party that established order and stabilized a potentially tumultuous system for several decades. Both delivered entitlements for the poor and subsidies, which in the long run hurt growth. Both the INC and PRI became rigid and corrupt, but they invented their respective countries and then stood aside. Every developing country should be so lucky as to have an equivalent founding party.

Since 1977, Congress has lost several elections to right-wing parties whose names have changed over the years—from Janata, to Janata Dal, to the current Bharatiya Janata Party (BJP, Indian People's Party)—espousing both Hindu nationalism and a free-market economy. (*Janata* is Hindi for "people's," the same name taken by several European rightist parties.) The BJP is strongest in the Hindi-speaking areas of north and west India. The *alternation in power* between Congress and the BJP illustrates one of the defining characteristics of democracy that keeps rulers on their toes and responsive to voters.

Political Culture

India's Political Eras

A bit like Mexico, India has undergone wrenching changes, mostly related to conquest, all of which left behind cultures that imperfectly and gradually melded into a distinctly Indian political culture.

Era	Years	Remembered for
Early civilizations	2500–1600 BC	Indus Valley culture
Vedic Age	1500–500 BC	Migration of Aryan speakers
Mauryan Empire	326–184 BC	Ashoka reigns, Buddhism spreads
Gupta Empire	320–550 AD	Classic age of Northern India
Islamic India	711–1526	Piecemeal conquest, Delhi sultanates
Mughals	1526–1757	Large Muslim empire, Taj Mahal
British	1757–1947	Colonial rule, ousted by Gandhi and INC
Independent India	1947–present	Nehru, democracy, accelerating growth

India's party system is far more complex than a simple left–right division. India has gone from a *dominant-party system* under Congress to a fragmented party system that clusters into several "alliances" or "fronts." Dozens of Marxist, caste-based, nationalist, regional, and local parties make it impossible for any one party to win a majority of parliamentary seats. This fragmentation is unusual for an FPTP electoral system, which tends to produce a two-party, or at least a two-plus, system. In Britain and America, it does, but where third parties are territorially concentrated, it can lead to a multiparty system (as it does in Canada). In India, it does so with a vengeance: The Lok Sabha contains more than 30 parties, some with just one seat, looking like the product of a proportional representation electoral system.

But India's fragmented party system pulls together into two big alliances and two smaller fronts, so it is not quite as chaotic as it sounds. The BJP, before the election, agreed on a coalition with about ten smaller parties to form the National Democratic Alliance (NDA), which turned out to be unnecessary. The INC had earlier governed with the United Progressive Alliance (UPA), composed of a similar number of parties. The Communists form a smaller Third Front, and the Dalit-based Samajwadi form a Fourth Front. Instead of the two-plus party systems we saw in Europe, India has a two-plus alliance system: the NDA and UPA plus the Third and Fourth Fronts. The Indian party system permits the existence of dozens of parties but aggregates them into governing coalitions.

Indian Federalism

India is federal rather than unitary, but less federal than Canada, Australia, or Germany. India has 29 states—one just added in 2014 as Telangana split away from Andhra Pradesh—with locally elected legislatures and "chief ministers" as executives. Another seven "union territories" have governments named by "the Centre" (New Delhi). Federalism, as in Germany, is

Democracy

India's 2014 Elections

In the biggest democratic election ever, Indians dumped a worn-out centrist party and gave a majority of parliamentary seats (but not of popular votes) to a rightwing party and leader who promised major reforms and economic growth: Narendra Modi, age 63, of the Bharatya Janata Party (BJP, Indian Peoples Party). The previous general elections were in 2009, so new elections had to be held in 2014.

The BJP, with only 31 percent of the popular vote, took 282 out of 543 Lok Sabha seats, the kind of disproportion that comes with single-member electoral districts where plurality wins ("first past the post," as in Britain and U.S. congressional districts). India's fragmented party system used to require multiparty coalitions to form governments, but the BJP can now govern alone. Dozens of small parties got a few percent of the vote and a few seats.

The Indian National Congress (INC), the party of Gandhi and Nehru which led India to independence and governed most of the time since, suffered from charges of corruption and a slowing economy and got its worst showing ever, only 19 percent of votes and 44 seats, possibly marking the end of the Gandhi dynasty. The lackluster Rahul Gandhi barely kept his seat, but his Italian-born mother, INC chief Sonia Gandhi, withdrew from politics. A new anti-corruption party, Aam Aadmi (Common Man), attracted much publicity but few votes. Much of the anti-corruption vote appears to have gone to the BJP.

The BJP drew heavily from young, educated, urban voters—called an "aspirational class"—connected by the new social media. Business and most newspapers and television networks supported the BJP. Many appreciated Modi's vision of a modern, growth-oriented India. Modi, chief minister (equivalent to governor) of Gujarat state since 2001, had overseen its impressive economic growth. Others liked the BJP's Hindu nationalism. The combination of market economics and traditional religion resemble that of U.S. Republicans. Although played down in the campaign, the BJP is implicitly anti-Muslim.

The logistics of the election were staggering: 814.5 million Indians eligible to vote for 300 parties in 543 constituencies using 1.7 million voting machines in 930,000 polling stations. Voting had to be spread out among constituencies in nine "phases" from April 7 to May 12, to ensure sufficient monitors and security forces for fair voting nationwide. In some states, all constituencies voted in one phase; others, such as mammoth Uttar Pradesh (UP), needed several phases. In some states, adjacent constituencies might vote weeks apart. The 551 million votes cast were a 66 percent turnout, a record for India.

The 2014 Indian elections illustrate what can go wrong when a dominant party—such as Mexico's PRI and India's INC—stays in power too long. It becomes a played-out force, absorbed in itself and convinced it is entitled to govern. It ignores an increasingly educated and critical electorate who no longer accept corrupt misrule and slow economic growth. A time in opposition, though, may force the ousted party to clean up its act, rethink its positions, and eventually return to power, as did the PRI in 2012. The INC could do the same.

especially suitable in large countries or those with cultural and linguistic diversity. India amply qualifies on both counts. In addition to English, spoken by educated Indians, and Hindi, which Delhi pushes as the national language, India's constitution recognizes 22 languages as legal for conducting government business.

The provision of *president's rule*—which has been used more than 100 times—makes India less federal than other federal systems. It may be invoked if a state government lacks a majority in the state legislature or cannot handle major disturbances. (The closest U.S. analogy is the

Geography

India's Languages

India has two main language families, many languages, and myriads of local **dialects**. The largest group is the Indo-European languages, spoken by three-fourths of Indians in a broad swath across northern India. Like Persian, they are related to most European languages. Among them are Sanskrit and **Hindi**. Most educated Indians speak English.

India's constitution, repudiating British colonialism, designated Hindi written in the Devanagari script as the official language of national government but also allowed English to continue in this role. India has 18 official regional languages, meaning state governments may use them. Hindi (and Pakistan's Urdu, which is similar but written in Arabic script) is unrelated to the Dravidian languages of the south, the second major language family, spoken by nearly a quarter of Indians. Educated southerners preferred English as the national language, but, gradually, Hindi has gained ground.

Notice the parallel of India trying to establish Hindi and China trying to establish Mandarin (*Putonghua*) as the national language. France, Germany, Italy, and many other European lands struggled to establish a common language and pronunciation, a process hastened after World War II by television. The process can also go backward. Serbo-Croatian was the standard language of Yugoslavia for most of the twentieth century, but as the country fell apart, Croatian nationalists proclaimed a separate Croat language and Bosnian Muslims a separate Bosnian language. The differences in vocabulary and pronunciation among Serbs, Croats, and Bosniaks are small—they need no interpreters when they meet—but deliberately hyped for political purposes. Language is intensely political.

president's ability to "federalize" the National Guard, as Eisenhower did in 1957 to enforce desegregation in Arkansas.) Indian critics claim president's rule has mostly been used by prime ministers to get rid of political opponents running state governments.

India's Judiciary

An independent judiciary in the developing lands, one that can and does nullify laws and executive moves as unconstitutional, is rare. India's judicial system has helped keep India democratic, even during its turn toward authoritarianism under Indira Gandhi in the 1970s. India's Supreme Court resembles its U.S. counterpart. Its one chief justice and 25 associate justices are appointed by the president and serve until age 65. Parliamentary consent is not required. Major cases concerning the constitution, including disputes between the states and Delhi, are appealed to India's Supreme Court, which has the final word.

Conflict comes from inserting a basically U.S. institution—judicial review by a supreme court—into an otherwise British model of "parliamentary sovereignty." Well, which is supreme in India, the court or the parliament? India has had some heated debates about this, usually when the Supreme Court overturns a piece of legislation. India inherited the British common law, and Indian cases are designated by the plaintiff's and/or defendant's names in italics.

dialect
Mutually intelligible variety of a language.

Hindi
National language of India.

Personalities

Narendra Modi

India's eighteenth prime minister was earlier the longest-serving (2001–2014) chief minister (governor) of Gujarat, India's westernmost state and an economic growth model. The charismatic Modi mixed pro-business efficiency with unapologetic Hindu nationalism. Voters, tired of the drift and slowing economy under Manmohan Singh's Congress government, went for Modi's BJP in 2014.

Born in 1950 to a tea-stall owner, Modi entered a teenage arranged marriage but never cohabited and calls himself single—the better to devote himself to the nation. Like Gandhi, an earlier Gujarati, Modi is a vegetarian and lives simply. He earned a political science degree at Gujarat University and then a master's in it at Delhi University. His real education was in the Hindu-nationalist RSS, which assigned him to its related political party, the BJP, in 1985. In 1998, he was named BJP national secretary. He returned to Gujarat to become governor in 2001, pushing privatization and small government. It worked, and Gujarat tripled its GDP under him.

A major cloud emerged in Modi's leadership when, in 2002, he either encouraged anti-Muslim pogroms in Gujarat or did nothing to stop them. The RSS had always promoted hatred of Muslims. The Gujarat riots appalled many Indians and cost the BJP the national government in the 2004 election. Since then, Pakistani-sponsored terrorism played into the BJP's hands. Modi had earlier been denied visas to enter the United States, a policy reversed under Obama. In 2014, Modi abandoned anti-Muslim rhetoric, but many feared his election would bring tension and violence. Others, especially in the north and in the middle class, voted on Modi's promise of jobs and growth.

Indian Political Culture

8.3   Explain how India lends itself naturally to pluralism.

Similar institutions function quite differently in countries with different political cultures. India is a feast for students of political culture. Its complexity and diversity make one wonder how India can hold together at all, much less get anything done. But these factors may actually support democracy by making pluralism natural and standard. Indians, unlike Russians, did not have to learn about the give and take of conflicting opinions and interests. India was born and remains highly pluralistic, and pluralism is the bedrock of democracy, for one group cannot get a hammerlock on politics and institute authoritarian rule, of which India got a taste in the late 1970s.

Most agree that Indians from all walks of life are talkative and argumentative. Everyone has an opinion and shares it. (The opposite: Japanese, who argue little because of cultural tradition and a lack of interest in politics.) This has given India a free and lively press of some 300 major newspapers with a combined circulation of 160 million. English-language newspapers such as the respected *Times of India* are popular among the educated and upwardly mobile. Any government attempts to curb the Indian press are howled down, which helps keep India democratic.

China Lessons

The Importance of Being Secular

India makes many ponder how such a poor country could stay democratic. One factors is that the Indian National Congress (INC) of Gandhi and Nehru, which founded Indian independence and governed India from 1947 to 1977, was and is a *secular* party with no formal ties to any religion. Nehru, prime minister for India's first 17 years, was firm on secularism.

INC rule was interrupted from 1998 to 2004 and again in 2014 by the electoral victory of the BJP, a party espousing *hindutva* that includes hostility to India's Muslim minority and could spell trouble. Under the British, some Indian Muslims split from the INC and set up the Muslim League to demand a separate Muslim state; Islam and even *Islamism* still threaten Pakistani politics. Generally, secular societies modernize sooner and faster than ones that mix religion and governance. This could be a key factor that let India modernize faster than Pakistan and is a good omen for China.

China, much more so than India, does not have a problem with competing religions. China is completely secular, with neither an official religion nor struggles between religions. Granted, on the peripheries of China, Buddhists and Muslims dislike rule by Han Chinese, but their resentment is more ethnic than religious. Chinese Christians are growing in number—there could be more Christians than CCP members—but they stay out of politics and do not challenge the state.

Religion in India

Some say India is one of the few countries where religion is really alive; for many, faith defines identity. Gandhi was a good Hindu, but Nehru, despite his Brahmin origin, disdained religion. His **secularism**, however, did not dent Indian religiosity. Eighty percent of Indians identify themselves as Hindus. (Nepal and the Indonesian island of Bali are two of the few places outside of India that are also majority Hindu.) Depending on locale, many Indians pay special homage to one deity—the five main Hindu gods are Shiva, Vishnu, Devi, Ganesha, and Surya—in effect creating denominations within Hinduism.

secularism
In India, treating members of all religions equally.

Some Indian Muslims trace their origins back centuries to Persian or Mughal invaders, but more to conversion within India, making India home to the world's third-largest Islamic community (first is Indonesia, second is Pakistan). Upon partition in 1947, the majority of India's Muslims did not move to Pakistan. Some have done well in Indian government, science, and business, but, on average, they are poorer and less literate. Hindu nationalists such as the RSS periodically attack Muslims in murderous riots.

Christians and Sikhs account for around 2 percent each, Buddhists less than 1 percent (but growing), Jains less than half a percent of the population. One of the most interesting religious groups is the Parsis, descendants of the Zoroastrians who fled the Arab conquest of Persia. Although tiny in number, Parsis are prominent in business and own many of India's largest enterprises (the biggest: Tata, famous for steel, cars, airlines, and information technology). In effect, Parsis form another caste.

Political Culture

Indian Passivity?

An American who had been on a church project to help poor rural Indians once told me how difficult it was due to Indian passivity. One incident stood out: When his bus got stuck in sand, the upper-caste people stayed seated while the lower-caste went out to push. My friend was furious and ordered everyone out to push. He exploded: "This country needs either a John D. Rockefeller or a Mao Zedong to get it working!" He meant that India needed disciplined coercion—either in capitalist or communist form—to jolt it out of passivity.

Does India (and the Third World in general) have so much cultural baggage that it cannot escape poverty without coercion? The question is fascinating and important. Cultural theorists blame passivity and fatalism, often rooted in religion, as the key factor. But then how would you explain the excellent economic growth—without coercion—in India in recent years? Indian culture has not changed that much; something else must have changed. The likely factor: Delhi's economic policies.

The difficulty is that you cannot tell whether passivity is the cause or result of culture. Adverse conditions may give rise to a fatalistic religion rather than the other way around. People who have had no opportunities for centuries will naturally appear resigned and passive. You would, too. Change the circumstances, though, and attitudes can quickly follow.

In India, government economic policy in the 1990s shifted from statist and antimarket to capitalist and promarket. Soon, Indian entrepreneurs were making fortunes in information technology (IT), manufacturing, and customer support. (Your last call for help with your computer or satellite dish probably went to Mumbai or Bangalore.) It turns out that Indians are as active and materialistic as anyone.

So are previously passive Chinese, Indonesians, Thais, Brazilians, and Nigerians. Lurking under the surface of many "passive" cultures are latent active attitudes waiting for the right economic context in which to emerge, which is why culture is a poor predictor of economic growth. Cultures are durable but not set in concrete. As the late U.S. Senator Daniel Patrick Moynihan said in a 1986 Harvard lecture: "The central conservative truth is that it is culture, not politics, that determines the success of a society. The central liberal truth is that politics can change a culture and save it from itself."

India's Castes

Much of Indian politics consists of politicians trying to form caste alliances by promising jobs and affirmative action programs. No one knows where India's caste system comes from. The conventional story is that it springs from Hinduism, but it may antedate the ancient Vedas, which portrayed four main castes in descending order of moral worth:

Brahmins—priests, teachers, and philosophers

Kshatriya—warriors and rulers

Vaisya—farmers and traders

Sudra—manual laborers

In addition, there are thousands of *jatis*, social groups originally based on occupation and family names (Gandhi is "greengrocer") that are sometimes considered subcastes. Most Indians stay and marry in the caste in which they are born. Those outside of any castes are literally "outcastes," called untouchables, *Dalits*, and other names. They, too, subdivide into myriad subgroups, some lower than others. Terribly poor, illiterate, and discriminated against, untouchables are the victims of upper-caste and police brutality. Orthodox Brahmins avoid direct contact with Dalits. By living a moral and religious life, however, an untouchable can be reincarnated into a higher caste in the next life. There is also some mobility by stealth, as lower castes change locales and claim they belong to a higher caste.

The caste system also serves this-worldly goals. For the Aryan conquerors, it was an almost perfect device to subjugate and control a large native population. The Aryans could say, "See, we're up here, and you're down there, so keep your place and obey." (Actually, Plato proposed using much the same myth: Citizens would be told they were born with gold, silver, or iron souls, which determined their place in the Republic.) People who believe that the gods have assigned them their status will not complain about poverty or attempt to change it or revolt.

The British made the caste system worse. By listing caste in Indian censuses starting in the late nineteenth century, they hardened vague and flexible notions into firm categories. Some see British emphasis of the caste system as a form of the divide-and-rule tactic practiced by colonialists everywhere: By keeping them divided, you can more easily rule them.

To escape their wretched status, some outcastes convert to another religion—Islam, Christianity, or Buddhism—that preaches equality of souls. Unfortunately, their old untouchable status follows them into the new faith, and they are still not recognized as equals. There are "Christian Dalits" and "Muslim Dalits," showing the stubborn persistence of cultural patterns. Converting to Buddhism is socially and religiously easier, as it is historically an offshoot of Hinduism. Most outcaste Hindus still believe Hinduism is India's good and natural religion, even if it has penalized them in this lifetime. The caste system, by teaching fatalism, could retard India's economic and political growth.

Gandhi called untouchables *Harijan* ("children of God") and denounced the caste system, but Congress's rule did little to eradicate it. The BJP and Hindu nationalists approve of the caste system as part of *Hindutva*. The caste system is fading in urban India (where it still influences marriage choices) but is still strong in the conservative countryside. As a component of religion, the most profound element of any political culture, caste is terribly difficult to cure.

Let us not be too critical of India. Caste systems by other names are found in several countries. Japan's *burakumin*, descended from a feudal outcaste of slaughterers and tanners, are still strongly discriminated against. Much of Latin America is stratified according to how much European blood one has. Until recently, South Africa's *apartheid* system rigidly classified people by race and kept Africans separate and down. And the United States, home of freedom and equality, held blacks to an inferior status—sometimes by Jim Crow laws, sometimes simply by social usage—long after slavery.

Patterns of Interaction

8.4 Contrast the aims and supports of India's two main parties.

Democracy is often conservative because it lets influential groups block changes that would hurt their interests. Landlords, businesspeople, and bureaucrats warp policies to favor themselves, either in parliament or in implementation. Nehru, for example, got a land reform law passed, but landlords, often local Congress Party leaders, used it to get more land for themselves. Indeed, Indian "reform" programs to help poor farmers help mostly rich farmers. In a democracy, one well-placed interest group can subvert the good of the whole. Politicians, wary of offending important groups, hold back from real change, which explains why India changes only slowly and why, in frustration, some supported the authoritarian Indira Gandhi and her "emergency powers" (see upcoming Democracy box). A dictatorship can ignore or, as Stalin used to say, "liquidate" recalcitrant groups.

Corruption and Politics

A major impediment to change in India is its vast bureaucracy, which is considered one of the least efficient and most corrupt in the world. Inheriting British colonial administration, Nehru's socialism amplified it with layers of laws to inhibit capitalism, laws that begged for misuse. Ministers collect millions in kickbacks for government contracts. Bureaucrats get paid for "facilitating" paperwork. Drivers pay off police to use roads and railway clerks for the privilege of buying a ticket. Funds for subsidized food, fuel, schools, or road maintenance "leak" until little is left. Some officials steal from the starving. Precisely the same things happen in Brazil and in

Political Culture

Anticolonial Rage

Many ex-colonial areas harbored resentments against their former masters and the West in general. For this reason, much of the Third World was neutralist during the Cold War, siding with neither the United States nor the Soviet Union. India is a good illustration of anticolonial rage.

Many Indians feel that they are twice the victims of conquest and subjugation, first by Muslims, second by British. Hindus and Muslims have lived together in India for a thousand years, mostly in peace but punctuated by outbursts on both sides. The reign of Mughal Akbar the Great in the sixteenth century was a high point of culture and tolerance in India, much like Moorish rule in Spain. The Taj Mahal, India's signature showpiece, is Islamic architecture built for a Muslim ruler.

But underneath, some historians and psychologists claim, Hindus felt shamed and humiliated. They saw their Muslim conquerors as more manly and warlike than Hindus. Under the surface, Hindus raged. Actually, Hindus can be plenty tough; the legendary Gurkhas, Hindus from Nepal, were Britain's best soldiers. The British in the eighteenth century beat the Mughals and lorded it over Muslims and Hindus, humiliating both.

Colonialism seems almost psychologically calculated to produce rage among its victims. For what it was like to live in an India with the English on top and Indians—even those highly educated—on the bottom, read E. M. Forster's classic *A Passage to India*. The novel claimed that colonialism prevented English and Indians of good will from becoming friends. (Many Indians ignore English novels about India, arguing that they were written from the colonialist viewpoint.)

Gandhi calmed and controlled Indian rage, turning it into nonviolent disobedience that finally wore down British ability to govern India. Not all shared Gandhi's nonviolence; some sided with the Japanese or settled scores with Muslims. After independence, India turned a cold shoulder first to Britain and then to the United States, which was seen as the inheritor of Western arrogance. Many Americans favored India's independence (after all, what was 1776?) but were shocked when Indian intellectuals denounced them as the new imperialists. This rage gave India its neutralist foreign policy that tilted toward the Soviet Union. As the colonial era recedes into the past and the Indian economy grows, the resentment has subsided. Many Indians are now rather pro-American.

many other countries. India is implementing a vast biometric database, called "unique identity" (UID), to deposit cash directly to recipients' bank accounts, bypassing bureaucrats.

Naxalites
Maoist guerrilla fighters in India.

Many Indians want government jobs, not for their mediocre pay but for the chance to take bribes. Of course, they have to pay big bribes to get such jobs. The elite Indian Administrative Service has many able, honest people, but they are more than offset by slothful and corrupt self-seekers. India consistently rates as one of the most corrupt countries in Transparency International's index. Corruption enrages a growing number of Indians and is a permanent political issue, used by whatever party is out of power, and the accusations are true. In 2014, some angry voters supported the new anticorruption Aam Aadmi party.

Indian parties make the corruption problem worse. Indians presume that all politicians are corrupt, and dozens of Lok Sabha members face criminal charges, including murder and rape, but buy elections to shield themselves from prosecution. Once in parliament, many accept bribes of $2 million or more for their vote. Indian politicians form caste alliances by promising jobs and affirmative action programs under the misleading label "social justice." Politicians deliver small payoffs to their followers and live luxuriously themselves. India has been called a "patronage-based democracy," a warped form of democracy. (But notice how most of the presently advanced democracies, including the United States, earlier were also based on patronage.)

India's Fragmented Politics

For many years, the Congress Party called itself leftist, but now parties much farther left have in effect shoved it toward the center. Now that Congress has moved away from state ownership of industry and in favor of market economics —as has Britain's Labour Party—it actually has become a centrist or center-left party. The INC is liberal in the sense of upholding secular values in the face of *Hindutva*.

To the left of Congress are several Marxist and Communist parties, each accusing the others of revising true Marxism. The largest of these is the Communist Party of India (Marxist); the parenthetical identification "Marxist" distinguishes it from the other Communist parties that it deems mistaken and misguided. One such party is the violent Communist Party of India (Maoist), whose followers are called **Naxalites**. Several left parties—including two Communist parties—allied themselves briefly with Congress in the United Progressive Alliance.

India's right is also fragmented. The BJP, much like the U.S. Republicans, combines probusiness, anti–affirmative action, and religion. The strands do not fit together in a long-term way. Business wants stability for economic expansion; upper castes want to roll back job "reservations"; and Hindu rightists want to define India as a Hindu country, even if that leads to violence against Muslims.

Its very fragmentation has prevented India from falling into one-party misrule. From 1989 to 2014, no single party won a majority of Lok Sabha seats, but this changed with the big BJP victory of 2014. If Modi cannot fulfill his grand economic promises, however, India's multiparty cabinets may return. Some worried that the BJP would govern as an intolerant Hindu-nationalist party able to pass any law. In office, the BJP government minimized its anti-Muslim image by pitching its message to middle- and upper-caste Hindus in northern India. Lower-caste Hindus are attracted to other parties that promise them a better economic deal.

Democracy

Indira's "Emergency"

One of the most illuminating episodes of Indian democracy was the decidedly undemocratic "Emergency" of Prime Minister Indira Gandhi in 1975–1977, in which she ruled virtually by decree. The interesting point is that most Indians recoiled from her heavy-handed experiment and voted her out. Indian democracy, temporarily abrogated, ultimately worked.

Trouble started with accusations that Indira Gandhi—who was actually Nehru's daughter married to a Gandhi unrelated to the Mahatma—had unfairly used her powers to ensure election of the Congress Party in 1971. Although nothing serious was proven, India seethed with protest. Thousands of protesters, including top political figures, were arrested.

Indira persuaded President Fakhruddin Ali Ahmed (a Muslim) to declare a "state of emergency" in June 1975. This allowed Indira to use a series of decrees to override civil rights, jail opponents, silence the media, institute massive programs to fight poverty and illiteracy, clear slums, and force vasectomies on thousands of men to control population growth. India started looking a bit like Mao's China. Some, however, said that India needed such centralized power to overcome the institutional and cultural impediments to modernization. A little dictatorship, they argued, can sometimes be a good thing.

Indira's opponents organized a new Janata (People's) party and demanded a general election, which was held in 1977. Janata warned that this was India's last chance to choose between "democracy and dictatorship." In many Third World countries, such elections are rigged and lead to dictatorship, but, in India, they were free and fair. Janata won a majority of Lok Sabha seats, and the INC took a drubbing. Indira and her son Sanjay lost their seats and were arrested on charges that did not stand up in court.

But Indian voters soon grew displeased with Janata's disarray, and, in 1980, they voted Congress back in with a chastened Prime Minister Indira Gandhi promising never to pull another "Emergency" again. Indians twice kicked out politicians they did not like. Indian democracy withstood its greatest challenge and came out stronger. Now, corrupt or ineffective national, state, and local governments are booted out by angry voters.

In India, many jest, "you do not cast your vote, you vote your caste." (By the 2014 elections, caste was receding, as younger Indians now tend to vote their economic interests.) By the same token, Congress now cannot get the votes it once could get, because upper-caste voters have switched to the BJP. India's social fragmentation has prevented its FPTP electoral system from producing a majoritarian parliament. India's complex pluralism has probably saved its democracy, but at the expense of coherence and efficiency.

Violent India

Many think of Indians as saintly Gandhians, but India has plenty of violence. Gang rapes and murder of women are frequent; many claim Indian police do little to stop them. A brutal 2012 rape-murder led to tighter laws and some hangings. Some fear violence could rip India apart. In 1984, Sikh secessionists took over the sacred Golden Temple in Amritsar in the Punjab. Indira Gandhi ordered the Indian army to storm the temple, which killed many innocent Sikh pilgrims. Later that year, two of her Sikh bodyguards shot her in revenge. In return, thousands of Sikhs were killed in New Delhi anti-Sikh riots. Indira's son Rajiv was himself killed by a Tamil suicide bomber in 1991.

Comparison

India, Mexico, and Colombia

India's Naxalite rural rebels resemble Mexico's Zapatistas and Colombia's FARC (*Fuerzas Armadas Revolucionarias de Colombia*) guerrillas. All are Marxist, armed, and intent on overthrowing their respective governments, which they deem to be under the thumb of capitalists and imperialists. All three are decades old and have base areas in remote jungles that make them hard to catch.

India and Colombia have ferocious anti-Marxist paramilitaries who face few legal restraints. The guerrillas and the paramilitaries both engage in criminal activities. In the Third World, crime and politics overlap. Distant countries with different cultures can produce similar problems. The common factors in India, Mexico, and Colombia are rural poverty, vast inequality, Marxist intellectuals who provide leadership, and peripheral areas bypassed by modernization. Once rooted in difficult terrain and isolated villages, such movements are hard to crush and can carry on their wars for decades.

Many call the Naxalites India's greatest security problem, worse than Pakistan-sponsored Muslim terrorists. Formally the Communist Party of India (Maoist), they are named after Naxalbari village in West Bengal where they began in 1967. Some 20,000 of their armed fighters feed off the government's neglect of poor tribal peasants in a "red corridor" down the east side of India. They are growing. Officials count some degree of Naxalism in over a third of India's districts, mostly in jungle areas. Naxalites derail trains and kill several hundred people a year, including Indian soldiers and police and anti-Marxist paramilitaries who hate them.

The Naxalites face the same problem Mao found in China: How can there be a proletarian party when there is scarcely a proletariat? Mao tried to solve it by proclaiming that poor peasants are proletarians, an un-Marxist thing to do, but one copied by the Naxalites. Their stated goal is to "liberate India from the clutches of feudalism and imperialism," the same line as that of their Mexican and Colombian counterparts. Few give any of the three movements much chance of winning, but they surely can disrupt.

In 1992, a Hindu mob pulled down the sixteenth-century Babri Mosque in Ayodhya (in Uttar Pradesh in the north of India), claiming that Muslims had built it on the site of an ancient Hindu temple to the legendary Lord Ram. The BJP state government, based on the Hindu vote, did not stop them. In 2002, a trainload of Hindu pilgrims returning from Ayodhya rampaged against Muslims at a station. Fire broke out on the train, killing 58 passengers. Angry Hindus, led by the RSS, blamed Muslims for the fire. Then Hindu attacks in Gujarat (India's western-most state, bordering Pakistan and the Arabian Sea) killed some 1,000 Muslims while Chief Minister Narendra Modi and police just stood by. Some accuse Modi of ordering the pogrom, for which he has never apologized. Most Indians were shocked that the governing BJP, ideologically tied to the RSS, did nothing to stop the violence. The BJP national government would not declare *president's rule* over the BJP state government in Gujarat. This was one of the reasons Indians voted out the BJP in 2004 and why some feared unrest under Prime Minister Modi.

In 2006, Muslim terrorists bombed seven commuter trains in Mumbai (formerly Bombay), killing 183. Other bombings have been linked to Muslim groups. Until recently, India's Muslims have been largely quiet, but the 2002 Gujarat pogrom against Muslims turned some into Islamist radicals, who get training and bombs in Pakistan. Indian Muslims are under heavy police surveillance, which makes them even angrier. Kashmir, the only Indian state with a Muslim majority, has been an insurgency zone since 1990. Some 500,000 Indian soldiers patrol

Comparison

The Three Economic Sectors

British economist Colin Clark developed the idea that economies can be divided into three sectors. The "primary" sector is agriculture, which appears with the dawn of civilization. Much later came the "secondary" sector, industry, as factories employed more and farming fewer. With mechanization, one farmer could do the work of many. As an economy modernizes, the primary sector shrinks to single digits and the secondary sector declines, too, but the percentage working in services, the "tertiary" sector, grows. Virtually everyone reading this book is aiming for a career in one service or another: teaching, law, government, finance, IT, and other professions that put no dirt under your fingernails.

One way to tell a country's level of development is by comparing the percentage of its workforce in each of the three sectors. A country where most still work the land is less developed than one where most work in factories or services. And where most work in services, it is a more developed or "mature" economy. Rich countries have two-thirds or more of their workforce in the tertiary sector and very few in the primary sector.

Some worry that India has jumped over the middle stage, manufacturing, which heretofore has been the basis of economic development. India has many peasant farmers and an unusual number of service workers, especially in IT; it has relatively few factory workers. China shows a more normal progression as its workforce shifts from farming to manufacturing to services. Which path will be more stable and prosperous in the long run?

	Percentage of Workforce in		
	Agriculture	*Industry*	*Services*
United States	1	20	79
Britain	1	18	80
France	4	24	72
Germany	2	25	74
Japan	4	26	70
Russia	8	27	65
China	35	30	36
India	53	19	28
Mexico	14	23	63
Brazil	16	13	71
Nigeria	70	10	20
Iran	25	31	45

SOURCE: CIA World Factbook

Kashmir looking for 1,000 Kashmiri terrorists. Indian heavy-handedness in shooting stone-throwing youths inflames rather than calms. Some Indian Muslims feel trapped in a hostile land. Hindu nationalists created Muslim unrest, which could unleash massive violence.

The Hill States in the very northeastern part of India, nearly cut off from the rest of India by Bangladesh, are isolated, poor, and populated by ethnic groups and tribes related to Tibetans and Burmese (some of them Christian) who do not feel Indian. Breakaway elements conduct low-level but nearly permanent guerrilla warfare. Many Naga tribes of Nagaland, bordering Myanmar, have been in rebellion since 1947. Migration of poor people from other parts of India sparks violence in the area. Local natives bitterly resent the newcomers for allegedly taking their jobs and crowding them out of their old neighborhoods. Deadly riots break out.

Crime in India is a vast and growing problem, and the police in some states may be a part of it. Backlogged courts and crooked judges make it easy for well-connected criminals to go free. Frustrated, police shoot notorious criminals to save going to trial. They also bash protesters and mistreat suspects, some of them arrested capriciously. *Slumdog Millionaire* accurately portrayed how Indian police handle cases. Many poor people, innocent of any wrongdoing, die in Indian prisons; better-off people, of course, do not. Few policemen are ever held accountable.

What Indians Quarrel About

8.5   **Contrast the Indian and Chinese economies.**

The Political Economy of India

Perceptions of a "New India" and its booming economy get overblown (as do perceptions of China). Led by a large service sector (see box on economic sectors), India's economy has become the world's fourth biggest (and could overtake Japan for third place). The Indian **rupee** is respected (if somewhat weakened). In 2007, India's Tata Steel bought the big Anglo-Dutch Corus group, a symbol of the colonial underdogs now on top of their former imperialist masters.

India, however, like most developing nations, is actually two countries—a small, modern, and prosperous one inside a poor and backward one. India has a new and growing middle class of 100 to 250 million people, depending on who counts as middle class. A third of Indians, however, live below the World Bank poverty line of $1.25 a day, more than two-thirds on less than $2 a day. A third of the globe's poor are Indians. Most Indians live in the countryside, where children are nutritionally and educationally stunted. Half of Indian children are malnourished. Many poor farmers commit suicide each year to escape crushing debts. Public services—schools, medical care, water supply, electricity, highways—lag far behind. Most urban residents live in slums without water or sewers. India's crowded streets are pungent.

As a British colony, India's per capita growth in the first half of the twentieth century averaged zero; that is, population growth offset slow GDP growth. From 1950 to 1980, its per cap grew at an average of only 1.3 percent—what economists joked was a "Hindu rate of growth"—less than half what the rest of the developing areas were averaging. In 1966, Yale economist Charles Lindblom asked, in *Foreign Affairs*, "Has India an Economic Future?" He concluded that it did not because the socialist/statist policies of Prime Minister Nehru discouraged growth. Nehru, who learned socialism at Cambridge, aimed for *swadeshi* (self-reliance) or **autarchy**, which Adam Smith saw was a mistake. Nehru promoted **import substitution** (common in Latin America) and money-losing, state-owned industries, while agriculture was neglected. Bureaucracy throttled growth through a jumble of permits—called in jest a "license *raj*"—that protected Indian firms from foreign competition and told them what and how much to produce.

During the 1980s, however, this Nehru-minded system began to loosen up. Prime Minister Rajiv Gandhi and a new class of young entrepreneurs embraced computers, and information technology took off. The U.S.-funded Green Revolution doubled farm production in the 1970s and 1980s. By 1991, however, India was in economic difficulties and unable to pay what it owed other countries. Economist Manmohan Singh, named finance minister in 1991, immediately opened India to foreign investment and rolled back some controls on business, a small dose of Thatcherite "neo-liberalism" that many countries adopted. The BJP government that took over in 1998 continued and expanded these policies, and India began to boom. From 2003 to 2008, Indian growth averaged 8 percent a year, second only to China. More recently, India's growth slowed to some 4 percent while inflation climbed to 10 percent.

rupee
India's currency (symbol Rs); Rs.65 are worth about $1.

autarchy
Economic self-sufficiency, importing and exporting little.

import substitution
Policy of excluding foreign goods and producing them domestically; means high tariffs.

Comparison

The India–Pakistan Contrast

The sharp differences between India and Pakistan give political scientists a rare chance to examine how similar countries can develop differently. Both were born out of British-ruled India in 1947 but took separate paths. Is it culture or structure that makes the difference? Or some combination of the two?

For half of its history, Pakistan has been ruled by generals; India never has been. Pakistan had military coups in 1958, 1977, and 1999. The first brought 13 years of military rule; the second, 11 years; and the third, 9 years. In between were elected civilian politicians whom the generals overthrew for egregious corruption. Pakistan alternates between democracy and dictatorship, the *praetorianism* common in the developing lands. India, perhaps except for Indira's 1975–1977 Emergency (see previous Democracy box), stayed democratic.

Pakistan's geography was unfavorable; it was founded as two wings separated by a thousand miles of India. In 1971, East Pakistan, complaining of mistreatment by larger and ethnically distinct West Pakistan, fought to become independent Bangladesh. India, to be sure, is threatened by breakaway movements in its peripheral areas, but none of them has succeeded. Pakistan's economy earlier grew faster than India's but is now slower, with a lower per capita GDP than India's. India's big information technology sector has not developed in Pakistan.

Why the difference? The easiest explanation is Pakistan's Islam. Muslim countries seem to have unusual difficulty modernizing, which some blame on the intertwining of Muslim values, especially **sharia**, with politics. Islam was always intended to be a blueprint for governance, not just a religion. Jinnah himself was a secular Muslim (among other things, he drank) and never intended Pakistan to be an Islamic state; he saw it as a place of refuge for India's Muslims but not explicitly religious. Jinnah, however, planted the seeds of Islamism, which blossomed with Pakistani dictator Zia-ul-Haq (1977–1988), who instituted *sharia* as the law of the land in 1984, fanning Islamic fundamentalism. Today, Islamic extremists—still a minority—try to overthrow the government in favor of a Taliban-type Islamist state. They have expanded out of their tribal territories. Bombings and raids are frequent.

But culture does not explain everything; structures also matter. The Indian National Congress was well organized and institutionalized and committed to democracy long before it took power in 1947. The Muslim League was weaker and was unable to turn itself into a durable political party the way Congress did. The beginning of a political system often sets its path for generations.

Few expect Pakistani democracy to endure; many fear it will be overthrown by the army again or by Islamic extremists. Osama bin Laden hid out for years in Pakistan. The Pakistani government, swearing it was fighting terrorism, did not catch him or reveal his whereabouts. Critics think Pakistan never wanted to, as that might trigger an Islamist uprising.

Indian leftists are sceptical about pure capitalism and rally to Harvard's Amartya Sen's call to lift India's miserable nutritional and educational levels for both justice and economic growth. Scrawny, ignorant people are unproductive. A 2013 program lets 800 million poor Indians get 5 kilos (11 pounds) of grain a month each, the world's biggest food subsidy. Conservatives call this a vote-getting populist handout that India cannot afford and adds to already-big deficits and inflation. They argue that first must come market-led economic growth; higher living standards will soon follow. (Does this debate sound familiar?)

sharia
Muslim religious law based on the Koran.

Indian economic growth is still blocked by red tape. Starting or expanding a firm or enforcing contracts requires massive paperwork and cash, making India one of the hardest countries to do business in.

FDI shies away from complexity and uncertainty. Strict labor laws discourage letting a worker go, so companies hire few, leaving surplus manpower untapped. India could boom under further free-market reforms, but many parties resist them.

India is again under pressure to open up wider. Several East Asian economies, especially China, are leaving India behind. If India does not want FDI, others do, and they win. No country likes to fall behind; it means poverty, military weakness, and ridicule. Over the long term, India is likely to further liberalize, but not without a fight. Its massive numbers of unemployed or underemployed could power economic growth at or beyond the Chinese level. Lindblom's 1966 question still hovers over India, but now the answer is yes.

A Secular or Hindu India?

India's constitution specifies that it is secular, but secularism is hard to enforce. Politicians over the years have bent to the demands of religious groups to win their votes, which has resulted in the erosion of secularism and in nasty backlashes from other groups. For example, in the 1985 *Shah Bano* case, a divorced and destitute Muslim woman appealed her claim for alimony to the Indian Supreme Court, which ruled for her under Indian secular law. The Muslim community went into an uproar, claiming that *sharia* must govern family law among Muslims, and *sharia* grants no alimony. Should there be one law for all, or should there be a separate Muslim "personal law"? Prime Minister Rajiv Gandhi pushed through parliament a 1986 law letting Muslims have their way in the matter of divorces. Then the Hindu community was furious, accusing Rajiv of pandering to Muslims for their votes and undermining the secular rule of the Supreme Court. This was one reason that the Hindu-right Janata Dal won the 1989 elections.

The Hindu right constantly tries to redefine India as a Hindu country, much as some U.S. politicians try to define America as a Christian country. RSS *shakhas* (branches) still train hundreds of thousands of uniformed young Hindus in early morning drills, workouts, and games with an anti-Muslim theme. Bengali poet Rabindranath Tagore, who won the 1913 Nobel Prize for literature, wrote India's national anthem in 1911, the generous *Jana Gana Mana* ("The Minds of All People"), but Hindu nationalists want to change it to the angry and narrow *Bande Mataram* ("Hail Motherland").

It is difficult to tell how many Indians are Hindu nationalists. They are a minority but a substantial one. Votes for the BJP do not measure underlying Hindu nationalism because they include voters who like the party's free-market policies or dislike something the Congress Party has done, such as Indira's Emergency or corruption. Horrors like the 2002 Gujarat pogrom can swing Indians back to Congress. Tension with Pakistan over Kashmir or nuclear weapons can raise nationalist sentiment. The question of Hindu-right governments is: Will they pursue militantly anti-Muslim and anti-Pakistan policies?

Quotas and Voters

India's Dalits and lower castes are terribly disadvantaged and have been for centuries. Should they therefore get special treatment—education quotas and job quotas—that expands and lasts indefinitely? Nearly 13 percent of Indians are classified as Dalits, 27 percent as Other Backward Classes, and 10 percent as Advanis (tribal). That makes half of Indians eligible for some form of affirmative action, such as "scheduled" status and "reserved" jobs in the public sector.

Dalit political parties demand this as "social justice." One such party, the Bahujan Samaj Party (BSP), led a coalition that took a majority of seats in the state legislature of huge and poor Uttar Pradesh (UP) in northern India in 2007, eclipsing both Congress and the BJP. The BSP's "Dalit queen," Mayawati (just one name), was UP's chief minister from 2007 to 2012.

Upper-caste critics denounced this as affirmative action run amok, resulting in unfairness to better-qualified applicants. Hatred of the lower-caste quotas rallied many upper-caste voters to the BJP. Notice how the Indian situation parallels America's affirmative action, which pushed many white males to the Republicans.

India's Muslim minority gets little from India's rapid economic growth and falls farther and farther behind Hindus. Their religion does not qualify Muslims for "scheduled" status. If they lag, argue some Hindus, it is because of their rigid religious upbringing and scanty education. Rote memorization of the Koran does not build modern skills. Congress governments are more likely to pay attention to the Muslim gap; BJP claims that making special efforts for Muslims is just pandering to minorities.

Mass or Elite Education?

India's population is now 1.22 billion and growing about 12 million a year; China's, at 1.35 billion, is graying and declining about 3 million a year. India will overtake China in population. An average Indian in 2020 will be 29 years old; an average Chinese will be 37. India faces a demographic bulge (China does not); half of Indians are under 26, and educating them has become an urgent concern. India's schools, especially at the elementary level, are often terrible: no money, no buildings, no teachers. Education in India is largely a state matter—the case in federal systems generally—and some states either do not have the money or spend it on other things. Public schools in India charge fees the very poor cannot afford. Indians who can afford it send their children to private schools. Note the parallel with the very uneven U.S. education systems among its states.

India's top universities, such as the Indian Institutes of Technology (IIT) or of Management (IIM), are excellent, but they train only a small elite. Indian students compete to get into one of the several campuses of the world-class IIT or IIM, which rival their U.S. counterparts. Some graduates go on to start businesses either in India or the United States. India produces more than 350,000 engineers a year, the United States 70,000, explaining why Indians staff many U.S. engineering positions. But India's elite education exists side by side with mass illiteracy. There are not nearly enough jobs for India's many unskilled, poorly educated people at the same time that high-tech job openings go begging, an imbalance that slows India's economic growth.

The problem parallels British education and that of some other countries that educate a small elite superbly while neglecting the needs of the masses. A World Bank study found that the best payoff is in mass education K–12, rather than in higher education for a few. India's literacy rate is 60 percent; China's is 90 percent. Much of Indian grade-school education is rote memory, boring, and (depending on which party has ruled the particular state) heavy on *Hindutva*. Many Muslims are too poor to afford school and accept the free education offered by a *madresa* (Muslim school), where boys memorize the Koran and sayings of the Prophet. Most Indians agree that education requires a massive injection of funds and personnel, but India's budget deficit is already too big.

Foreign Policy: Neutral or Aligned?

During the Cold War, India practiced neutralism between East and West and was proud to be a leader of the Nonaligned Movement along with Nasser's Egypt, Tito's Yugoslavia, and Sukarno's Indonesia. Delhi originally proclaimed "Indians and Chinese are brothers" but changed its tune when pushed back by China in a short border war in 1962. India and the Soviet Union grew close, while Pakistan and the United States favored each other. With the end of the Cold War, India focused its national interests on securing its borders. It worries that an Islamist takeover of Pakistan and Bangladesh could encourage Muslim extremists inside India. India aims to become—and may already be—the regional power of the Indian Ocean; its army and navy are not trivial, and it has enough nuclear weapons for what it calls a "minimum deterrent." China, meanwhile, is constructing a "string of pearls" of friendly seaports in Southeast Asia and the Indian Ocean (in Cambodia, Myanmar, Sri Lanka, and Pakistan) to guard its petroleum lifeline from the Persian Gulf. Tension between the two powers in the Indian Ocean seems inevitable. China still claims that part of the Indian state of Arunachal Pradesh (in the extreme northeast of India) is Southern Tibet and thus part of China.

For half a century, relations between India and the United States were correct but distant. Now they are improved but not nearly an alliance. India pursues respect and good relations in all directions, with no entangling alliances. Delhi's relations with Beijing grow testy as their rivalry mounts. China makes clear that it will be the dominant power in Asia, disquieting some Indian strategic thinkers. Islamist terrorism rattles India, promoting a common stand with Washington. India's economic growth, especially in IT, is linked to the U.S. economy.

Washington perhaps too eagerly courted India and, in 2005, gave India a sweetheart nuclear deal. Washington said, in effect, "You can keep your nuclear weapons, but we'll help you with your peaceful nuclear program." The U.S. offer undermined the Nuclear Nonproliferation Treaty by suggesting that other countries could also have two nuclear tracks, one for weapons and one for power generation. India, worried about China and Pakistan, had been developing nuclear weapons for decades and tested its first in 1974. Washington protested for years, but, in 1998, India exploded five bombs underground and proclaimed itself a nuclear power. The United States no longer protests, demonstrating that nuclear weapons really do bring respect. India welcomes cooperation with the United States but will not follow American-led crusades, especially in Muslim countries, for that would exacerbate India's own Muslim problem.

India's big problem is still Pakistan, for now both nations have nuclear weapons. India and Pakistan were born hostile, and the Kashmir question has caused three wars (1947–1948, 1965, and 1999) between them. By some accounts, they twice considered using nukes. (A fourth war, in 1971, grew out of the breakaway of Bangladesh from Pakistan.) India accuses Pakistan of supporting Kashmiri terrorists, whose bombings have spread beyond Kashmir. India–Pakistan tensions have gone up and down. A peaceful interlude was shattered in 2008 when ten Pakistani terrorist gunmen killed 173 people in Mumbai. Islamabad claimed it had nothing to do with the attack, but the perpetrators received funds and training from Pakistani intelligence.

Pakistan knows that India is both economically and militarily more powerful. Both sides want to settle the Kashmir issue, although this would not guarantee an end to local terrorism. Diplomats suspect that Pakistan would settle for Kashmir's present borders but with a special autonomous status. Top officials and cricket teams exchanged visits, and a rail line across their

Comparison

India's and China's Economies

India's and China's economic development show some similarities but more differences. Both had booms that have slowed and could slow more. Both countries' economies grew so fast that they **overheated** and unleashed instability, which both tried to cool—chiefly by raising interest rates. Stock market bubbles popped and loans turned dud. Delhi and Beijing now seek long-term **sustainable** growth in preference to short-term maximum growth.

In both India and China, growth is concentrated in certain coastal areas, which are more open to foreign commerce, have better infrastructure, and are home to more-sophisticated urban people. Both depend on imported oil, and when oil prices rise, they suffer. In both lands, an urban middle class has emerged. Both push peasants off farmlands to make room for factories and push city dwellers out of simple homes to make way for high-rises (but more so in China). Corruption is huge in both lands.

The two countries, however, pursue different development paths. China's path is labor intensive, using manufacturing with low-cost unskilled labor to export massive amounts of goods. But India's path is more capital intensive, using services such as IT staffed by educated, English-speaking young people. This skews India's growth, however: Only 1 million employees, less than one-quarter of 1 percent of India's labor force, work in IT. India's millions of unskilled workers produce little and cannot get factory jobs; instead, they do piecemeal, temporary work and are essentially unemployed or underemployed. India employs 7 million in manufacturing; China, more than 100 million. As one Indian put it, "We are a back office, and China is a factory." To be sure, India's Mahindra, the world's biggest tractor maker, exports to the United States and China.

China's growth exploded decades ago with Special Economic Zones (SEZs) that lure foreign direct investment (FDI) through tax breaks and better infrastructure. India, still suspicious of FDI, has been slow in setting up SEZs. China has high literacy but lags in training a technological and management elite to run its burgeoning economy. India has neglected mass education in favor of training a gifted few in top institutes.

Whereas China (like Japan) is an export maniac, India focuses on developing its domestic market. Chinese save more of their income than do Indians. China uses domestic savings for growth but short-changes domestic consumption, so Chinese do not live as well as they could. Sixty-four percent of India's GDP goes to domestic consumption—almost the U.S. level—as compared with 58 percent of Europe's, 55 percent of Japan's, and 42 percent of China's. Some economists think that India is wise in doing this, as it partially insulates India from the ups and downs of world markets.

---

border reopened. A 2007 bomb attack on this train—possibly by Muslim Kashmiris—brought greater antiterrorist cooperation between the two countries. If radical Islamists take over Pakistan (see earlier Comparison box on India–Pakistan contrast), hostility could quickly resume.

The Great Asia Wager

overheat
Experience too-rapid economic growth characterized by inflation, factories at full capacity, and excessive borrowing.

sustainable
Can keep going for many years with no major downturns.

In the early 1960s, U.S. ambassador to New Delhi (and Harvard economist) John Kenneth Galbraith called India "a functioning anarchy." Some think it still is. India's GDP grows several percent a year but has lagged well behind China, which started its economic liberalization earlier (1979) and did it more thoroughly. The big question is: Who will become the economically dominant Asian power, India or China? This has strategic as well as economic importance.

The early rounds clearly go to China and its "authoritarian capitalist" model that does not let democracy get in the way. Chinese are more than twice as rich and far better fed, clothed, housed, and educated than Indians. China's great weaknesses, however, are an economy based on overinvestment and its one-party dictatorship. Over the long haul, India's economy and democracy may prove more resilient and adaptable. China will eventually reach a point where the Communist Party has to give way to democratic forces. Are China's leaders clever enough to engineer a peaceful transition, or will it be traumatic, accompanied by instability and economic disruption? India does not have to transition to democracy; it is already there. What India must overcome is its fragmented and chaotic form of democracy.

Review Questions

Learning Objective 8.1 Assess how the British put themselves out of a job in modernizing India, p. 331.

1. Is there a relationship between wealth and democracy? Why?
2. Explain the "turbulent frontier" theory of imperialism.
3. Could India have avoided partition upon independence?

Learning Objective 8.2 Compare and contrast India's and Britain's parliamentary systems, p. 338.

4. Who has the most power in the Indian political system? What is his name?
5. What kind of party system does India now have? Why?
6. What is "president's rule," and does it make India less than federal?

Learning Objective 8.3 Explain how India lends itself naturally to pluralism, p. 344.

7. Why does secularism aid modernization?

8. Is passivity a cause or a result of poverty? What evidence could you use?
9. Explain anticolonial rage and how it lingers.

Learning Objective 8.4 Contrast the aims and supports of India's two main parties, p. 347.

10. Compare India's INC and BJP with their U.S. counterparts.
11. How can India—and many other countries—cut back corruption?
12. Compare rural violence in India, Mexico, and Colombia.

Learning Objective 8.5 Contrast the Indian and Chinese economies, p. 353.

13. Why are the Indian economy and education system often described as skewed?
14. What would you do to boost Indian economic growth?
15. Long-run, who will win the great Asia race, India or China?

Key Terms

autarchy, p. 353
Buddhism, p. 333
caste, p. 331
colonialism, p. 334

communal, p. 338
Congress, p. 337
corruption, p. 331
demagogue, p. 331

dialect, p. 343
Hindi, p. 343
Hinduism, p. 331
Hindutva, p. 338

Further Reference

Bahl, Raghav. *Superpower? The Amazing Race between China's Hare and India's Tortoise*. New York: Penguin, 2010.

Bhagwati, Jagdish, and Arvind Panagariya. *Why Growth Matters: How Economic Growth in India Reduced Poverty and the Lessons for Other Developing Countries*. New York: PublicAffairs, 2013.

Boo, Katherine. *Behind the Beautiful Forevers: Life, Death, and Hope in a Mumbai Undercity*. New York: Random House, 2012.

Chaudhuri, Amit. *Calcutta: Two Years in the City*. New York: Knopf, 2013.

Dalrymple, William. *Nine Lives: In Search of the Sacred in Modern India*. New York: Knopf, 2010.

Das, Gurcharan. *India Grows at Night: A Liberal Case for a Strong State*. New York: Penguin, 2012.

Deb, Siddhartha. *The Beautiful and the Damned: A Portrait of the New India*. New York: HarperCollins, 2011.

Doniger, Wendy. *On Hinduism*. New York: Oxford University Press, 2014.

Doron, Assa, and Robin Jeffrey. *The Great Indian Phone Book: How the Cheap Cell Phone Changes Business, Politics, and Daily Life*. Cambridge, MA: Harvard University Press, 2013.

Eck, Diana. *India: A Sacred Geography*. New York: Crown, 2012.

French, Patrick. *India: A Portrait*. New York: Knopf, 2011.

Ganguly, Sumit, and Rahul Mukherji. *India since 1980*. New York: Cambridge University Press, 2011.

Giridharadas, Anand. *India Calling: An Intimate Portrait of a Nation's Remaking*. New York: Times Books, 2010.

Guha, Ramachandra. *Gandhi Before India*. New York: Knopf, 2014.

Kapur, Akash. *India Becoming: A Portrait of Life in Modern India*. New York: Riverhead, 2012.

Kaviraj, Sudipta. *The Imaginary Institution of India: Politics and Ideas*. New York: Columbia University Press, 2010.

Lelyveld, Joseph. *Great Soul: Mahatma Gandhi and His Struggle with India*. New York: Knopf, 2011.

SarDesai, D. R. *India: The Definitive History*. Boulder, CO: Westview, 2007.

Sen, Amartya, and Jean Drèze. *An Uncertain Glory: India and Its Contradictions*. Princeton, NJ: Princeton University Press, 2013.

Singh, Rani. *Sonia Gandhi: An Extraordinary Life, an Indian Destiny*. New York: Macmillan, 2011.

Stepan, Alfred, Juan J. Linz, and Yogendra Yadav. *Crafting State-Nations: India and Other Multinational Democracies*. Baltimore, MD: Johns Hopkins University Press, 2011.

Tully, Mark. *India: The Road Ahead*. London: Rider, 2011.

Vajpeyi, Ananya. *Righteous Republic: The Political Foundations of Modern India*. Cambridge, MA: Harvard University Press, 2013.

Varshney, Ashutosh. *Battles Half Won: India's Improbable Democracy*. New York: Penguin, 2013.

Chapter 9
Mexico

Mexico's growth shows in the rapid urbanization in Guanajuato in Central Mexico.

 Learning Objectives

9.1 Describe how a revolution can be "institutionalized."

9.2 Evaluate the advantages of a single six-year presidency compared to two four-year terms.

9.3 List the several ideologies Latin America has imported.

9.4 Explain the interpenetration of crime and politics in weak states.

9.5 Evaluate the problems that come with being able to walk from the Third World into the First.

WHY MEXICO MATTERS

Mexico illustrates the interpenetration of crime and politics that characterizes much of the Third World. Mexican democracy is locked in a militarized war against crime with an uncertain outcome. As *narcotraficantes* murder thousands each year, some see Mexico collapsing into a *failed state*, not at all the case. Mexico does, however, illustrate the *weak state*; it cannot control drug cartels, kidnapping, murder, and bribery. This especially bothers Americans, as the Mexico-U.S. border is the only place you can walk from the Third World into the First. We often emphasize Mexico's problems, but Mexico has made considerable progress, becoming a stable democracy and major economy, albeit one with terrible income inequality. We cannot seal off Mexico from the United States, so we had better start paying attention to Mexico's problems and progress.

Impact of the Past

9.1   Describe how a revolution can be "institutionalized."

Roughly 15,000 years ago, hunter-gatherers walked from Asia into North America, probably pursuing game. The Ice Age had lowered the sea level and formed a land bridge across the Bering Strait. (Linguistic and DNA analyses suggest that there were later waves of immigrants.) In a few millennia, these hunter-gatherers spread the length of the Western Hemisphere. Some of them founded civilizations, but several thousand years later than the first civilizations of the Middle East. The domesticated plants and animals that spread from Mesopotamia to Europe and Asia never crossed the Bering Strait. The Americas had few domesticable plants (corn in Mexico and potatoes in Peru) or animals (llamas in Peru), so their civilizations lagged behind Europe's, leaving them easy prey for the greedy Europeans.

Several civilizations rose and fell in Mexico long before the Spaniards arrived. The first, the Olmec, flourished around present-day Veracruz a thousand years before Christ and set the pattern for subsequent **Mesoamerican** civilizations. In the first centuries AD, the Zapotec and Teotihuacán constructed palaces and pyramids that tourists visit today. During the first millennium, the Mayas built a high civilization in the Yucatán. From the tenth to twelfth centuries, the Toltec held sway in Central Mexico until they were destroyed by nomadic invaders, the Aztecs among them.

The Aztecs, or Mexica, who originated in the northwest of Mexico, pushed into the Valley of Mexico around 1300. They made their capital on an island where they had sighted a prophetic eagle with a snake in its beak, later the symbol of Mexico. In 1376, the first Aztec king was crowned. Aztec kings had absolute power and ran their empires through a huge bureaucracy. The Aztecs kept expanding because they needed more land, serfs, and captured warriors to sacrifice to their deities. As a result, subject peoples did not love the Aztecs. The Aztec kingdom was complex and highly developed but not terribly old by the time Columbus sailed.

New Spain

Mesoamerica
Spanish for Middle America; southern Mexico and northern Central America.

Portugal actually started the voyages of discovery, initially aimed at direct access to the wealth (especially spices) of the "Indies" by a route that bypassed the Arab traders and the Moors, whom Spain and

Portugal had just expelled. Spain's Ferdinand and Isabella, aware that Portugal was ahead in opening the Asia trade, accepted Columbus's argument that Spain could reach Asia directly across the Atlantic. (Yes, even then, educated people understood—from the ancient Greeks—that the world was round.) Columbus's 1492 voyage was to be a quick way to catch up with Portugal.

Columbus thought that he had nearly reached India, and he called the inhabitants of Hispaniola "Indians." The name stuck, although some now prefer Native Americans, Amerindians, First Nations (Canada), or *indígenas* (Latin America). The Spaniards charged quickly into the New World for "gold, God, and glory," serving, respectively, the royal treasury, the Catholic Church, and the *conquistadores*, who had just won a struggle of nearly eight centuries to expel the Arabs from Spain. The Spaniards regarded the Indians with the same contempt in which they held the Moors. Indian lives meant nothing to them.

The Aztecs had a big population—their capital was probably larger than any European city at that time—and were well organized into a bureaucratic empire. Why could they not send the Spaniards packing? Several factors doomed the Aztecs. First, the Spaniards brought smallpox with them, against which Native Americans had no immunity. Mexico's population plunged from about 20 million at the time of the conquest to barely 1 million by 1600. Only in 1940 did Mexico regain the population it had under the Aztecs. Next, the Spaniards had steel; their swords sliced up the Aztecs (and later the Incas), and their steel armor protected them. They also had horses and guns, which the Aztecs had never seen before. Many of the peoples the Aztecs had subjugated aided the Spaniards. Finally, the Aztecs had a legend that the white god Quetzalcóatal would return from the east and destroy them.

Initially based in Cuba, Spanish ships explored Mexico's coast and brought back news of fabulous wealth in the interior. Partly at his own expense, Hernán Cortés equipped 11 ships and sailed from Havana in late 1518. After founding the city of Veracruz, he pushed inland with a force of 500

cacique
Originally, Indian chief; local political boss.

Geography

Mexico's Mountains

Mexico's geography is distinctive and helped mold its current politics, which is highly regional. Two mountain chains, the Sierra Madre Oriental on the east and Sierra Madre Occidental on the west, connect at Mexico's narrow neck, forming a kind of Y. Between the Y's two arms is the Mesa Central, an upland that includes the Valley of Mexico with its rich volcanic soil and abundant rainfall. Mexico City, at 7,500 feet elevation (a mile and a half), is one of the world's highest capitals.

As in other mountainous areas (Spain, Colombia, and the Caucasus), mountains make a country hard to unify. With communication slow and difficult, some tribes and ethnic groups live in *patrias chicas* (little countries) outside central control. As the West Virginia motto says, *Montani Semper Liberi* (Mountaineers Are Always Free). Mexico was never well integrated—neither by the Aztecs nor by the Spaniards—and still retains important regional differences and politics. In remote mountain villages, many still speak Indian languages and are in semirevolt against central authority. Mexico's crumpled geography forced any national government to work through and with **caciques**. Current Mexican voting patterns (and cuisine) are still regional.

pre-Columbian
The Americas before Columbus arrived.

creole
Spaniard born in the New World.

Spanish soldiers and several thousand Indians. The Aztec emperor Moctezuma (known to Americans as Montezuma) at first welcomed the Spaniards to his capital of Tenochtitlán, but they soon arrested him, and fighting broke out. Cortés retreated from the city but returned in 1521 after smallpox had killed much of its population. After three weeks of fierce battle, the Spaniards captured and killed the last emperor, Cuauhtémoc. Mexico today celebrates Aztec heroes but no Spanish ones, and many **pre-Columbian** traditions remain in Mexican culture.

On the ruins of Tenochtitlán, the Spaniards built a new capital and called it Mexico. Upon the ruins of the main Aztec temple, they built a huge cathedral. With little resistance, they soon took over most of Southern Mexico. Rich silver mines moved the Spaniards to expand over Central Mexico, but takeover of Northern Mexico, arid and thinly populated, was not completed until about 1600. North of the present U.S.-Mexican border, Spanish occupation was sparse and late—Texas in 1716 and California in 1769—which ultimately led to the Mexico-U.S. war and loss of the vast territories that became the Southwest United States.

To control what they called New Spain, Spain used a Roman institution, *encomiendas*, grants of land and the people who worked on it to Spanish soldiers and settlers. In the feudal manner, the *encomendero* was the lord and master of Indian serfs. At the top of Mexican society were those born in Spain, *peninsulares,* who held all administrative positions as well as a social edge over *criollos* (**creoles**). Persons of mixed parentage, *mestizos*, became artisans and foremen, often in competition with poor Spaniards. The Indians worked the land on the *encomiendas* or stayed in the mountains out of Spanish control. Mexico is still partly stratified along these lines.

The Spanish Habsburgs ran out of heirs; in 1707, a French Bourbon became king. (Spain's present monarch, Juan Carlos, is a Bourbon.) The Spanish Bourbons improved administration by dividing New Spain into 12 *intendencias*, each supervised by a French-style *intendente*, who reported to a central authority. Economic liberalization boosted Mexico's economy, and more Spaniards settled there. Bourbon reforms thus helped wake up Mexico.

Mexican Independence

The late eighteenth century brought new ideas to Spain's and Portugal's Latin American colonies. The Enlightenment and the U.S. and French Revolutions inspired some to seek independence. A parish priest, Miguel Hidalgo, on September 16, 1810, proclaimed Mexico's independence. It got nowhere but is still commemorated as Mexico's Independence Day. Hidalgo led a strange uprising of Indians that presaged the turmoil of the Mexican Revolution a century later. Hidalgo demanded equality of all Mexicans and the redistribution of land to Indians but also fought French-style atheism and for Catholicism. Hidalgo's band ran out of control and massacred Spaniards and creoles. Royalist forces soon captured and executed Hidalgo. Another priest of similar persuasion, José Maria Morelos, in 1814 and 1815, led a widespread guerrilla uprising in Southern Mexico until he, too, was caught and shot. Hidalgo and Morelos are considered revolutionary heroes who founded the populist nationalism still very much alive in Mexican politics. Mexico's states of Hidalgo and Morelos are named after them.

Geography

Bound Mexico

Mexico is bounded on the north by the United States;

on the east by the Gulf of Mexico and the Caribbean;

on the south by Belize and Guatemala;

and on the west by the Pacific.

Geographically, Mexico is considered part of North America. To its south is Central America, consisting of Belize, Guatemala, Honduras, El Salvador, Nicaragua, Costa Rica, and Panama. South America is south of that. Everything south of the United States, including Mexico, is called Latin America.

Mexico

Napoleon's occupation of Spain in 1808 triggered Mexico's independence. Spain's *Cortes* (parliament) passed the liberal 1812 constitution, which Mexico's conservative elite feared would spread French atheism and liberalism into their realm and threaten their privileged status. To preserve it, they declared independence from Spain in 1821. The impulse behind Mexico's independence was conservative, not revolutionary as in the United States. Mexican

caudillo
Military chief or strongman who takes over the government.

independence was an elite thing with no mass participation and no fighting with Spain. Only Brazil's 1822 independence from Portugal was as painless.

Between Monarchy and Republic

Mexico, like Brazil, began as a conservative monarchy, but that lasted only a year and a half (Brazil's lasted until 1889). Immediately, Mexico's elite split into two camps: conservative centralizers and liberal federalists, a split that has never fully healed. For much of the nineteenth century, Mexico, like most of Latin America, was led by **caudillos**.

The key figure in the first decades of the Republic of Mexico was Antonio López de Santa Anna, Mexico's off-and-on president, general, and dictator, who played both sides of every conflict and continually broke his word. Santa Anna's big problem was Texas. To populate huge, empty Texas, Mexico gave American settlers land there in 1821, and they soon outnumbered Mexicans. To discourage further American immigrants—who brought slaves with them— Mexico outlawed slavery in 1828. (Texas was later a slave state and joined the Confederacy.)

By 1833, Texas had some 30,000 American settlers who demanded state's rights to govern themselves (and their slaves) within a Mexican federation. Santa Anna rejected the demand, the Republic of Texas declared independence in 1836, and Santa Anna marched north to reclaim it. He took the Alamo but was captured by the Texans. The United States annexed Texas in 1845, but Mexican and U.S. forces soon clashed, leading to the 1846–1848 war with Mexico. The United States, after occupying Mexico City, took the southwest states and paid Mexico $15 million, leaving Mexico permanently humiliated.

Mexico's brief occupation by France (1861–1867) was strange. Mexican conservatives in Paris convinced the ambitious Napoleon III that he could reconstruct a Catholic monarchy in Mexico to become the base for a French-led "Latin America." The U.S. Civil War gave Napoleon III an opening; he used the pretext of Mexico's big European debts to send French troops to install the Austrian Habsburg Maximilian as his puppet emperor of Mexico. Few Mexicans supported the effort, and it collapsed. With the U.S. Civil War over, the French left, and Maximilian was shot. Paris had supposed that Mexico was more or less like orderly Europe, where rational authority is obeyed. One of the few remnants of the French in Mexico is the word *mariachi*, a musician hired to perform for a *marriage*.

The iconic figure of nineteenth-century Mexican politics was Benito Juárez (1806–1872), who was remarkable on several counts. First, he was born of Indian parents (who died when he was 3) at a time when all power was in creole hands. Educated in law, Juárez rose in state and national politics and became president in 1858. A classic nineteenth-century liberal, Juárez deplored a stagnant Mexico dominated by an old aristocracy and conservative Catholic Church. He wanted to redistribute their lands and institute a market economy, federalism, and separation of church and state. Juárez did not invent Mexican *anticlericalism* but gave it a powerful boost. Conservatives forced Juárez to spend 1853–1855 in New Orleans, and, in the 1860s, the French forced him to withdraw to the U.S.-Mexican border, to a city later renamed after him. Although not long in power, Juárez set standards of modesty and honesty that few other Mexican leaders have met.

Porfirio Díaz (1830–1915) was Juárez's top general, who turned into a harsh dictator. Like Juárez, Díaz was born in the southern state of Oaxaca (pronounced *wha-haw-ka*), but of a mestizo family. Díaz studied law, fought the French, but turned against Juárez. Díaz was "elected" president 17 times between 1877 and 1910 and personally centralized control over all branches of government. With the *positivism* then popular in Latin America, Díaz's top bureaucrats, *los científicos*, pushed economic growth, but profits and land ownership went to a wealthy few and to foreign (mostly U.S.) investors. Debt forced peasants to sell their land and grow poorer. By 1910, perhaps 95 percent of rural Mexican families were landless and eager to follow revolutionaries, who demanded return of the land to the peasants. Díaz's long stay in power, called the *Porfiriato*, offered Mexicans *pan y palo* (bread and bludgeon), prominent in Mexico's governing philosophy ever since.

The Mexican Revolution

Compared with Mexico's complex 1910–1920 upheaval, the Russian and Chinese revolutions are clear. They had only two sides; Mexico's had several, and they changed allegiances during the course of it. Mexico's is one of Latin America's few genuine revolutions. Latin America, to be sure, has had scores of military coups and "palace revolutions," but they were among elites. Mexico and, much later, Cuba and Nicaragua had armies fighting for years to overthrow regimes and replace them with totally different ones. A revolution is seldom caused by just one problem. It takes a series of mutually reinforcing, insoluble problems. Mexico had been storing up its contradictions until they erupted in the Revolution of 1910.

Under the long *Porfiriato*, discontent increased at the unfairness and cruelty of the Díaz regime. Anarchist and socialist ideas arrived from Europe. Juárista liberals who organized clubs, parties, and newspapers were jailed; many fled to the United States. Government troops crushed labor unrest. Influenced by Russian revolutionary Mikhail Bakunin, in 1906, the Mexican group Regeneration published a manifesto calling for one-term presidencies, civil rights, public education, land reform, improved pay and working conditions, and ending the power of the Catholic Church. These eventually became the program of the party that ruled Mexico for most of the twentieth century.

The trigger for the Mexican Revolution was Díaz having the obedient Chamber of Deputies "reelect" him once again. Presidential candidate Francisco Madero, from a wealthy family that owned much of Northern Mexico, proclaimed from San Antonio, Texas, that the election was illegal and urged Mexicans to revolt on November 20, 1910, now celebrated as the start of the Revolution. Madero used his own fortune to supply rebels. Díaz's decrepit

Political Culture

Poor Mexico!

¡Pobre México! Tan lejos de Dios, tan cerca de los Estados Unidos. "Poor Mexico!" exclaimed President Porfirio Díaz. "So far from God, so close to the United States." He voiced the widespread Mexican view that just sharing a long border with us condemns them to be dominated by the powerful United States. Díaz had seen the U.S. invasion of 1846–1847 that robbed Mexico of its northern half in 1848. The sad exclamation shows Mexican resentment of their rich, well-run neighbor, a sentiment found throughout Latin America.

ejido
Land owned in common by villages.

Federalist army fell back, and Díaz resigned and left for Paris. Mexico's Congress proclaimed Madero the new president. If things had stopped there, Mexico would have had another of its many irregular changes of power.

But Federalist general Victoriano Huerta, encouraged by the U.S. ambassador, had President Madero arrested and shot. Huerta assumed the presidency himself, and full-fledged revolution broke out. Angered by the assassination and believing that the United States could put things right in Mexico, President Woodrow Wilson had the U.S. Navy occupy Veracruz in 1914 and sent General Pershing after the bandit and guerrilla chief Pancho Villa in 1916. Wilson announced that the United States "went down to Mexico to serve mankind," but the effort solidified Mexican opposition to U.S. intervention, and U.S. forces had to fight Mexican guerrillas. (Sound familiar?)

Huerta fell in 1914, but at least four armies then battled for control of the country. Two of them were genuinely revolutionary, that of peasant leader Emiliano Zapata in the south and Pancho Villa in the north. The other two, under moderates Venustiano Carranza and Álvaro Obregón, sought to establish a stable order. Their two sides initially collaborated but later bitterly fought each other. Zapata was assassinated in 1919, Carranza in 1920, Villa in 1923, and Obregón in 1928. Revolution is a dangerous business. Mexicans still celebrate the revolutionary tradition of Zapata and Villa.

The Revolution Institutionalized

With the 1917 constitution, Mexican generals and state political bosses started what Peruvian novelist Mario Vargas Llosa called "the perfect dictatorship"—perfect because it was quite thorough but looked like a democracy. Others have called it a series of six-year dictatorships because of limits on the presidential term. It lasted longer than Lenin's handiwork in Russia. The system grew out of a deal between Obregón and Calles.

Obregón became president in 1920 and began to implement rural education and land reform, including the granting of **ejidos** to poor villagers. In 1924, he arranged the election of his collaborator, Plutarco Elías Calles, who, in turn, got Obregón reelected in 1928. But just then, a Catholic fanatic assassinated Obregón, part of the bloody 1927–1929 Cristero Rebellion. Calles had implemented the anticlericalism of the 1917 constitution by banning foreign priests and clerical garb. With the cry "¡Viva Cristo Rey!" ("Long live Christ the King"), militant Catholics rebelled, and government troops crushed them. Mexico's Church–anticlerical split healed only with the election of the conservative and Catholic Vicente Fox in 2000.

Calles, still running things from behind the scenes, decided in 1928 on a law making Mexico's presidency a single, nonrenewable six-year term, something Mexicans had wished for since Díaz kept reelecting himself. To perpetuate his hold on power, in 1929, Calles organized a coalition of state political bosses, generals, union chiefs, and peasant leaders into the National Revolutionary Party (PNR), renamed, in 1946, the Institutional Revolutionary Party (*Partido Revolucionario Institucional*, PRI).

The remarkable politician is one who builds lasting institutions, and Calles founded the institutions that brought stability and led Mexican politics for 71 years. It could not, however, last forever. The Calles system masked contradictions and concentrated power in the presidency. From its 1929 founding until 2000, PRI never lost national elections (which, to be sure, were less than democratic). Still, considering what much of Latin America went through in the twentieth century—numerous military coups—the "soft authoritarianism" of the Mexican system was not bad.

Calles was basically a conservative, and his PNR made only moderate reforms until the 1934 election of Lázaro Cárdenas, who took Mexico on a more radical path by implementing what the Revolution and 1917 constitution had promised. When Calles opposed him, Cárdenas had Calles exiled to California. Cárdenas was of mestizo descent and had little formal

priísmo
Ideology and methods of PRI.

sexenio
From *seis años*; six-year term of Mexico's presidents.

Political Culture

Mexico's Political Eras

Few countries have gone through such radical changes over the centuries as Mexico. Most political cultures develop slowly and gradually, but Mexico's was jerked back and forth by the introduction of new cultures and ideas, which never blended into a coherent whole.

The three phases of **priísmo** summarize the thrust of the presidents of each period. The four **sexenios** of the conservative period mark PRI's turning away from the Revolution and from *Cárdenismo*, giving lip service to labor and peasants but favoring business and stability. The three destabilizing *sexenios* mark the oil boom and government debt plus the 1968

massacre of students in Mexico City and psychological breakdown of President Echeverría.

The desperate phase marks the recognition by Presidents de la Madrid, Salinas, and Zedillo that Mexico's economy was in shambles and the whole system lost legitimacy that it never regained. U.S.-trained economic *technocrats* tried to stabilize it with policies of *austerity* to rein in Mexico's runaway economy, but average Mexicans were hurt. Two political assassinations under Salinas turned many Mexicans against PRI. *Panismo* faced an uphill struggle during its two terms.

Era	Years	Remembered for
Aztec	1325–1521	High civilization, bureaucratic empire, human sacrifice
New Spain	1521–1821	Colonialist exploitation, Catholicism
Empire	1821–1823	Conservative independence
Santa Anna	1830s–1850s	Erratic leadership, lost Texas and U.S. war
Juárez	1850s–1860s	Equality, federalism, anticlericalism
Porfiriato	1877–1911	Dictatorship, economic growth, poverty
Revolution	1910–1920	Complex multisided upheaval
Maximato	1924–1934	Calles, *el jefe máximo,* founds single six-year term and PNR
Cárdenismo	1934–1940	Cárdenas makes PRI leftist and corporatistic; nationalizes oil
Conservative Priísmo	1940–1964	Favors business and foreign investment; crackdown on leftists
Destabilizing Priísmo	1964–1982	Oil, overspending, and inflation spur unrest; massacre of students
Desperate Priísmo	1982–2000	Technocrats calm economy, promote NAFTA, clean up elections; assassinations
Panismo	2000–2012	First non-PRI presidents; attempts free-market reforms; violent crime

corporatism
Direct participation of interest groups in governance.

clientelism
Government favors to groups for their support.

education but joined Carranza in the Revolution, becoming a general in 1920. Cárdenas was one of the PNR's founders and its first president, transforming it from a loose coalition to a cohesive and well-organized nationwide party.

Upon taking office, President Cárdenas implemented a leftist program by nationalizing U.S.-owned oil industries, which he turned into Petróleos Mexicanos (Pemex). In doing this, Cárdenas connected to an old Latin American pattern, statism, which Mexico has been reluctant to shed. Cárdenas carried out massive land redistribution and organized peasants and workers, making their unions constituent groups of the renamed Party of the Mexican Revolution. Cárdenas became a symbol of Mexican nationalist radicalism, something that helped his son, Cuauhtémoc Cárdenas, later head of the leftist Party of Democratic Revolution (*Partido de la Revolución Democrática*, PRD).

Cárdenas also made the party corporatist. **Corporatism**, which brings interest groups directly into parties and parliaments, was riding high at the time. Initially a device of Mussolini's fascism, Brazil's Vargas also adopted corporatism into his New State in 1935. Cárdenas organized the PNR with peasant, labor, military, and "popular" sectors. The last included small businesses and expanded later to include big businesses. He built a large bureaucracy to mediate demands among groups and distribute funds among them, what is called **clientelism**. Initially, Cárdenas's steps seemed to solve the problems of participation, power-sharing, and allocation of resources in chaotic situations. They were, however, not really democratic and over time became rigid and unstable. They were contrived and temporary fixes and left the system saddled with an overlarge bureaucracy.

China Lessons

Founding Parties as Stabilizers

Mexico in the nineteenth century was structurally weak, dominated by figures such as Díaz, who took over repeatedly and governed dictatorially. Amid increasing poverty, Mexico exploded in revolution from 1910 to 1920 and turned into chaos. Calles rescued Mexico from chaos in 1929 by forming a new party from local politicians and army officers. It turned into the PRI and governed—by rigged elections—until ousted in 2000.

The PRI may have been corrupt and unfair, but it stabilized Mexico until modernization and a substantial middle class carried out a peaceful alternation of government. Any comparisons with China? From the fall of the Qing in 1911 to the Communist takeover in 1949, China was chaotic. Provincial warlords moved into the organizational vacuum until Chiang Kai-shek's Nationalists established shaky national rule in the 1930s. Based on superior organization, Mao's Communists won in 1949 and imposed a tight dictatorship. Mao committed self-destructive folly, but his successors produced record-setting stable growth.

PRI, facing mass discontent, loosened up and permitted increasingly fair elections. Now PRI is back in power. Mexicans used to say that PRI was the only party that could run the country; without PRI, chaos could break out. But that was untrue; Mexico practices alternation in power, one hallmark of a democracy. The Chinese Communist Party might take note and reflect that their ultimate triumph would be the stable alternation of power. Founding parties are good, especially those that step aside at the right time.

The Key Institutions

9.2   Evaluate the advantages of a single six-year presidency compared to two four-year
terms.

Obviously, politics depends on power. Power is not necessarily force, which is a subset of
power, a coercive one best used sparingly. Reason: If you use a lot of force, people will hate you
and be eager for your overthrow. You will build little legitimacy. Political power is temporary
unless it is turned into **political institutions**.

Mexico has had plenty of strong leaders who concentrated power, but the power vanished
when they left office. Then the new leader had to amass power into his hands. Political power
must not be too personal. Franco ruled Spain, sometimes by jail and firing squad, from 1939
to his death in 1975. He built what looked like a stable regime, but it was too much based on
his one-man rule and quickly unraveled after his death. Dictators rarely **institutionalize** their
power. Within two years, there was essentially nothing left of the Franco setup.

No country is born with functioning institutions; they have to evolve over time, usually
in a series of accommodations among groups. An institution is not just an impressive building (although often it is housed in one to foster respect) but relationships of power that have
solidified or congealed into understandings—sometimes written into constitutions or statutes,
sometimes just traditions (as in Britain)—about who can do what.

Political scientists speak of Third World governments as "poorly institutionalized," characterized by irregular or extralegal changes of leaders (such as revolutions and coups) and no
clear boundaries as to who can do what. There are no rules; many try to seize power. Long
ago, all countries were like that. We admire British government as "well-institutionalized,"
but, centuries ago, it suffered conquest, massacre, civil war, a royal beheading, a temporary
Commonwealth, and attempts at absolutism. British institutions evolved and did not reach
their modern form until the nineteenth century. Go back far enough and Britain resembled
Mexico. Thanks to several historical factors, Britain institutionalized out of its tumultuous
phase some three centuries ago.

Accordingly, let us not ask too much of countries like Mexico too soon. They are bound to
be messy and chaotic. Mexico did not begin political institutionalization until the 1920s, with
Calles, and has not yet completed the process. (It may be getting close, however, as power now
alternates democratically among Mexico's parties.) Americans often wonder why Mexico cannot be like us—with democracy and rule of law—but Americans, too, spilled rivers of blood,
first for independence, then to hold the country together. And America
is no stranger to gangsters, drug traffickers, and crooks in high places.

The first thing you notice about Mexico's political history is that,
prior to 1924, few Mexican presidents either came to power or left office
in a regular, legal way. Most were installed and/or ousted on an ad
hoc basis by a handful of elites or military coups, sometimes with violence. Mexico has had four constitutions since independence but not
much **constitutionalism**. Once in office, Mexico's presidents observed
few limits on their powers and tended to construct personalistic

political institution
Established and durable
relationships of power and
authority.

institutionalize
To make a political relationship
permanent.

constitutionalism
Degree to which government
limits its powers.

Democracy

Mexico's 2012 Presidential Election

Mexico's 2012 presidential election, although fraught with peril, was its third democratic election in a row. Mexicans again could choose among left, right, and center, something PRI had earlier not allowed. And the election of the PRI after its 12 years in opposition passed the "two-turnover test" that Huntington proposed as the mark of stable democracy. Turnout was 63 percent.

On the left, the populist ex-mayor of Mexico City, Andrés Manuel López Obrador (AMLO) of the PRD, again promised money for the poor and curbs on NAFTA. On the right, Josefina Vázquez Mota of the PAN (*Partido Acción Nacional*), which had won in 2000 and 2006, urged a market economy within NAFTA. She also called López Obrador a radical demagogue like Venezuela's Hugo Chávez. In a reconstituted center, Enrique Peña Nieto (EPN) moved the PRI out of its corrupt one-party rule and won as a fresh new face. The results are in the table below.

Peña Nieto, former governor of the State of Mexico (adjacent to the Federal District), won with only 38 percent of the national vote, but was still 3 million votes ahead of López Obrador, who, as in 2006, cried media bias and demanded a recount and invalidation of the entire election. There were irregularities, but minor ones. López Obrador's supporters finally tired of his messianic rants, and he left to form a new party.

Few demographic factors predicted who would vote for EPN and who for AMLO. The rising, educated Mexican middle class has less party identification, and privatization has broken the PRI hold over workers in state-owned enterprises. Region, however, was still important. Most of the North went PRI. The South, home to statist/socialist thinking, went PRD. Most of the Caribbean-facing states went PAN. Mexicans had tired of the conservative promises of the two previous PAN administrations and the dreadful war with narcotraficantes and tended to the sensible centrism of PRI, which emphasized economic growth. The 2012 election represented a calming of the old radical–conservative ideological polarization.

Peña Nieto took office knowing that most Mexicans voted against him, and he faced a Congress still divided among three parties, which he brought together in a Pact for Mexico, a coalition across party lines in favor of tax reform and the breakup of monopolies, including telecoms and energy. Some suggested that paralyzed Washington could use such a pact.

	Party	Percentage
Enrique Peña Nieto	PRI	38
Andrés Manuel López Obrador	PRD	32
Josefina Vázquez Mota	PAN	25

dictatorships. This is true of much of the developing areas (and now Russia), where politics consists of strong personalities making their own rules.

That changed—but not completely—with the beginning of the single, six-year presidency in 1928 and the 1929 founding of what became the PRI. A contrived stability settled over Mexico for the rest of the century. There were no more upheavals because all the major reins of power—including the military—passed through PRI into the hands of the president. The personality of the president still counted—some, such as Cárdenas, were radical, others were conservative—but the system counted more. Mexico was an example of what political scientists call a *clientelistic* system, in which most major groups have been co-opted into cooperation. They feel they have a stake in the system and minor input into government policy. Peasants get land reforms and *ejidos*, workers get unions, and bureaucrats get jobs.

The Six-Year Presidency

dedazo
From *dedo*, finger; tapped for high office.

Latin America generally has modeled its institutions on the U.S. pattern, preferring presidential to parliamentary systems. Mexico's presidential system, like that of the United States, combines head of state and chief of government. For most of the twentieth century, the Mexican presidency was even more powerful than the U.S. presidency. We must qualify that statement by noting that it was powerful when a PRI president dominated a Congress with a big PRI majority. The 2000 election of Vicente Fox of PAN did not give PAN a majority in the Congress, making Fox much less powerful than his PRI predecessors. Starting in 2000, Mexico tasted the "divided government" that often prevails in the United States, when a president of one party faces a Congress dominated by another. The situation reappeared with Peña Nieto's 2012 election, as his PRI was a minority in both houses of Congress.

Since 1928, Mexico has not deviated from the single, six-year term devised by Calles. Under the long PRI twentieth-century reign, succession was in the hands of the president, who was also party chief. In consultation with past presidents and other PRI leaders, the president would name his successor, who became the party's nominee for the next election. Once nominated, of course, until 2000, no PRI candidate lost, and many won by 90 percent. Presidents would pick their successors—not necessarily well-known persons—with an eye to preserving stability and the power of PRI. The process was called, half in jest, **dedazo**. It may also have included understandings that the new president would not look into corruption. No choice was absolutely predictable, and, once in office, presidents often departed from previous policies. Calles did not know, for example, how far left Cárdenas would veer.

Personalities

Enrique Peña Nieto

Inaugurated for a single six-year term in late 2012, Enrique Peña Nieto was, at age 47, one of Mexico's youngest presidents. He was born in 1966 in a small town in the State of Mexico, 55 miles northeast of Mexico City, to an electrical engineer father with family ties to the PRI. Peña proclaimed his interest in politics in grammar school. He earned a law degree in Mexico City and an MBA in Monterey. His education and wealthy contacts put him in PRI's moderate, pro-business wing, little different from the PAN.

Working his way up in the State of Mexico's PRI organization, Peña won the governorship in 2005 and carried out most of his promises to improve the state's infrastructure in transportation, medical care, and clean water, marking him as a hard-working, can-do executive. He married in 1993 and fathered three children (and another two out of wedlock) before his wife died in 2007. In 2010, he married a *telenovela* (soap opera) actress, Angélica Rivera, boosting his national recognition. The attractive couple did not lack for media coverage, but critics accused him of a wealthy, superficial lifestyle out of touch with ordinary Mexicans.

In office, Peña Nieto moved away from previous PAN president Felipe Calderón's fierce war on drugs, which cost over 10,000 Mexican lives a year. He favors a reduction in violence over shootouts with criminal cartels. Under Peña, violence did subside, but it was hard to tell why—the new, cleaner police of the Fuerza Civil (Civil Force), the capture of Zeta kingpins, or an easing off of pursuit? Peña's greatest challenge was to make competitive Mexico's growth-retarding monopolies and state-owned enterprises, including the badly run Pemex.

dominant-party system
One party is much stronger than all others and stays in office a long time.

Mexico's Legislature

Mexico's bicameral Congress (*Congreso de la Unión*) has been much less important than its presidency. Díaz was famous for putting obedient supporters into the legislature, and PRI did much the same. Legislative elections changed with the 1986 Electoral Reform Law, induced by uproar over PRI's habitual election frauds. Inspired by Germany's *mixed-member* system, Mexico (like Italy) now fills most seats from single-member districts, Anglo-American style, but allocates additional seats based on each party's share of the popular vote—that is, by proportional representation (PR).

Mexico's upper house, the Senate (*Cámara de Senadores*), now has 128 seats and six-year terms. Ninety-six of the seats are filled from single-member districts, 32 by PR. The lower house, the Chamber of Deputies (*Cámara de Diputados*), now has 500 seats with three-year terms. Three-hundred seats are filled by district voting, 200 by PR in five regions of 40 seats each. The 2009 and 2012 elections made PRI the biggest party in both chambers but short of a majority (see upcoming Democracy box).

Comparison

Term Lengths

Some American critics of our two four-year presidential terms say we should consider a single six-year term. The theory here is that presidents are so concerned with reelection that they accomplish little their first term and then do irresponsible things their second term because they do not have to worry about reelection. It is not clear that term lengths cause anything very specific. Both limited and unlimited terms have lent themselves to mistakes and corruption. The table below shows how our 11 countries' terms for chief executives compare.

Remaining too long in office can lead to corruption, but not if chiefs of government must face an informed electorate at regular intervals. Margaret Thatcher served 11 years through three elections until her party dumped her over policy questions and slumping popularity. Term limits in Nigeria, on the other hand, do nothing to curb corruption. A limited term may even encourage officials to grab more sooner. By themselves, term limits do little; it all depends on the institutional and cultural context.

Britain	prime minister	Unlimited terms, each for up to five years (but usually four)
France	president	Two consecutive five-year terms
Germany	chancellor	Unlimited terms, each for up to four years (but sometimes shorter)
Japan	prime minister	Unlimited but usually short
Russia	president	Two consecutive six-year terms (renewable after an interlude)
China	president	Two five-year terms (but this is recent)
India	prime minister	Unlimited terms, each for up to five years
Mexico	president	One six-year term
Brazil	president	Two four-year terms
Nigeria	president	Two four-year terms (barring overthrow)
Iran	president	Two four-year terms (but lifetime Islamist Guide holds real power)

Mexico's Three-Party System

Britain is a "two-plus" party system: two big parties and several small ones. Some countries are "one-plus" or **dominant-party systems**, for they are dominated by parties so strong that they cannot lose, such as Putin's United Russia. Japan, Mexico, and India, under the long reigns, respectively, of the Liberal Democrats, PRI, and Congress Party, used to be dominant-party systems but have since experienced electoral alternation. Mexico is now a three-party system, with PAN on the right, PRD on the left, and PRI in the center.

In a dominant-party system, other parties are legal, but the dominant party is so well organized and has so many resources that challengers seldom have a chance. In some cases, the party founded the country, as the Congress Party under Gandhi did in India. The big parties dominate the media and civil service. Voters know the dominant party is corrupt, but many prefer the stability and prosperity it brings. Many Japanese voters saw the Liberal Democrats in this light. When the dominant party offers neither benefit, as Mexico's PRI discovered, it ceases to be dominant.

PRI, founded by Calles in 1929, is Mexico's oldest party. As its name attests, it billed itself as revolutionary and socialist long after it abandoned such policies. PRI presidents such as Cárdenas and Luis Echeverría Álvarez took leftist, especially anti-U.S., stances, but most have been moderate centrists. Calles and Cárdenas designed the party well, with its four sectors and strong patronage network, but as Mexico gained a large middle class—now roughly half of Mexicans—these sectors became less and less important, making PRI out of date. Some Mexican commentators call the PRI sector chiefs "dinosaurs." PRI regrouped and is still popular in a broad swath across Northern and Central Mexico. PRI staged a rebound in the 2009 and 2012 legislative elections and won the 2012 presidential election.

PAN was founded in 1939 to oppose PRI on religious grounds. PAN was a Catholic reaction to Calles's anticlericalism. Mexico's church–state relations have been bloody at times, and serious Catholics felt martyred by the PRI government. In the 1980s, the modern business

Comparison of Party Systems		
System	**Example**	**Probable Causes**
Two-party	United States	Single-member plurality elections
Two-plus	Britain	Single-member plurality election districts; inherited third party
Multiparty	France	Historical complexity; runoff elections
Two-plus tending to multiparty	Germany	Hybrid single-member and PR elections
Dominant-party (now ended)	Japan	Postwar consolidation; weak opposition; obedient political culture
Dominant-party	Russia	Personality-based consolidation from fragmented system
Single-party	China	Complete control by Communist Party
Fragmented	India	Breakdown of dominant Congress into many state- and caste-based parties
Three-party	Mexico	Long PRI dominance eroded
Two-plus	Brazil	Lula's personality and organizational skills
Two-plus tending to dominant	Nigeria	PDP holds more resources
Nonparty	Iran	Formal parties not permitted

community, which dislikes state-owned industries and economic instability, found PAN a useful vehicle for their interests. The two strands, Catholic and business, coexist uneasily within PAN and could pull it apart. PAN made its best showings in Northern Mexico, where proximity to the United States has contributed to prosperity and a capitalist orientation, although now its strength is along the Caribbean coast. PAN, still dominated by Catholic militants, is not nearly as well organized as PRI. Mexicans' votes for PAN did not indicate that they had become conservative Catholics but that they were fed up with PRI. PAN Presidents Fox and Calderón accomplished little, and voters blamed PAN for the slow economy and the bloody war on drug cartels. As expected, PAN came in third in 2012.

The south of Mexico is the poorest and most radical part of the country, where Zapata, a local boy, is remembered and where the PRD makes its best showing. Cuauhtémoc (the Aztec name won him some votes) Cárdenas, son of the oil nationalizer, might have won the 1988 presidential election if not for PRI rigging. Cárdenas, along with a leftist chunk of PRI, split from PRI in 1988 over its turn to free-market policies. PRI had to split; it had abandoned revolution in favor of business. With some Socialists and Communists, Cárdenas, in 1989, formed the leftist PRD, which claims to be true to the ideals of his father, anticapitalist and anti-United States. With a bickering leadership and much weaker organization than PRI or PAN, PRD, too, has an uphill struggle. The PRD's López Obrador, the former mayor of Mexico City with a messianic view of himself, was initially the leading presidential contender in 2006 and came in second in 2012. Mildly leftist parties have won elections in Argentina, Brazil, Chile, and Venezuela. Mexico could one day elect a PRD president.

Democracy

Mexico's 2012 Legislative Elections

Although not as important as Mexico's presidential elections, its legislative elections are watched as an indicator of who is likely to win the presidency next. In 2009, PRI did surprisingly well, boosting its share of seats in the lower house to nearly half and foreshadowing PRI's 2012 presidential victory. Mexico now uses a mixed-member electoral system inspired by Germany's, with 300 single-member-district seats and 200 PR seats. The Chamber of Deputies results in 2012 are shown below.

The small Greens, Citizens, and Workers parties won a few seats. Six percent "voted blank"—that is, they deposited an unmarked ballot—to show their indifference to all parties. Peña's PRI government never had a majority of seats, so he needed—and sometimes got—votes from other deputies to pass new laws. The radical PRD and conservative PAN together could theoretically outvote PRI in the Congress and produce the sort of executive-legislative deadlock that hamstrung the two PAN *sexenios*, but they dislike each other and have trouble cooperating.

Party	PR Vote	PR Seats	District Seats	Total Seats
PRI	32%	49	163	212 (42%)
PAN	26	62	52	114 (23%)
PRD	18	44	60	104 (21%)

We might call Mexico a "former dominant-party system." The PRI has weakened and now faces **bilateral opposition** —that is, both on its left (PRD) and right (PAN). The key factor in PRI's decline: its corruption and the growth of an educated middle class that no longer stands for it. In some state and local elections, PAN and PRD form tactical alliances to block the hated PRI. The United States is no stranger to dominant-party systems: Most U.S. congressional districts reliably return the same party to Congress, sometimes without opposition.

bilateral opposition
Undermining of centrist governments from both sides.

populist
Claims to be for common people and against elites.

Mexican Federalism

Most countries are unitary systems, but the Western Hemisphere boasts the largest number of the world's federal systems, partly due to the U.S. model and partly due to the sprawling geography of many countries. Argentina, Brazil, Canada, and Mexico are federal systems, some more federal than others. Mexico consists of 31 states and the Federal District (*Distrito Federal*, DF, the equivalent of our D.C.) of Mexico City. Each state has a governor elected for a single six-year term but only a unicameral legislature.

In actuality, Mexican federalism concentrates most power in the center, a bit like Soviet federalism, but this is changing. For most of the twentieth century, PRI presidents handpicked state governors, who then used the office as a tryout for federal positions. As in the United States, many Mexican presidents first served as governors, including President Peña Nieto. The states get much of their revenue from the national government and then dispense it to the municipalities, a food chain that kept subordinate levels of government loyal and obedient. The PRI still wins the most state elections, with the PAN in second place and the PRD third. With most state governments now in different hands than the federal government, the former strong connection between the two levels has eroded. The three-party system makes Mexico more federal. Periodically, federal police and troops intervene against drugs, crime, and insurrection at the state level.

Mexican Political Culture

9.3   List the several ideologies Latin America has imported.

Mexican political culture—and this is true of much of Latin America—is hard to comprehend because it is a dysfunctional pastiche of several cultures and ideologies: Indian passivity, Spanish greed, Catholic authoritarianism, **populist** nationalism, European anticlericalism, liberalism, anarchism, positivism, and socialism. Unsurprisingly, these many strands never blended. Mexico is regionally, socially, and culturally poorly integrated, never forming a coherent whole (see box on Mexico's political eras). Mexican political culture did not grow slowly and locally over time but was imported in waves, mostly from Europe, none of which sank in enough to create a single Mexican political culture. In comparison, most elements of American political culture blend and reinforce each other: freedom, equality, Protestantism, individualism, pragmatism, materialism, market economics, and rule of law (see box). The U.S. creeds that did not easily blend—slavery, Catholicism, and welfarist liberalism—formed America's political divides for several generations.

hacienda
Large country estate with Spanish owner (*hacendado*) and Indian serfs.

mestizaje
Intermingling of Spanish and Indian.

norteamericanos
"North Americans"; U.S. citizens.

Mexico's Indian Heritage

Mexico looks Spanish but, many scholars argue, beneath the surface remains very Native American. Indian cultures and languages still survive in isolated villages. Mexico's cuisine is basically Indian. Mexico's spirituality is a blend of pre-Columbian religions and Spanish Catholicism. The Indians were used to blood sacrifice at the hands of the Aztecs and took easily to the bloody twist of Spanish Catholicism. The Spanish Inquisition traveled to Mexico and even to New Mexico. Because the Spaniards built their great cathedral on the ruins of the main Aztec temple, it is hard to tell if it is a purely Christian or a pre-Christian pilgrimage site.

Most of Mexico's pre-Columbian societies were strongly hierarchical. Those at the base, peasants, were taught to defer to their social superiors. Social class distinctions accompany civilization. (In contrast, the Indians of the present-day United States had no cities and were highly egalitarian.) When the Spanish took over from the Aztecs, Indian peasants were used to being subordinates; most adapted to the forced labor of **haciendas** and silver mines. The Spanish, of course, brought their own feudal society with them and imposed it on the Indians.

One important demographic point about Mexico is that its Spanish conquerors were exclusively males; Spanish women did not arrive until much later. (The English settled whole families in America.) Very quickly, a new class of persons appeared in Mexico, mestizos, those of mixed descent. **Mestizaje** was also a cultural and social factor, contributing to Mexican Catholicism and the beginnings of a middle class between the Spaniards (later creoles) and the Indians.

Latin Americans boast, especially to **norteamericanos**, that they are free of racial prejudice. In Latin America, they say, money and manners count for more than skin color in deciding race. A person with the "right" culture and language is accepted as essentially European. As they say in much of Latin America, "money lightens" (one's skin color). There is some truth to this, but money and life chances tend to come with racial origin in Latin America. Lighter-skinned people have a much better chance of going to a university, entering a profession, making lots of money, and living in a nice house. Mexicans of Indian descent run a high risk of infant death, malnutrition, poverty, and the lowest jobs or unemployment.

Still, Mexico has done a better job historically than the United States in letting at least some nonwhites rise to the top. Juárez, of Indian descent, led Mexico in the mid-nineteenth century. Cárdenas and several other presidents were of mestizo descent. The United States got that sort of racial breakthrough only with Obama's 2008 election. Most of Mexico's top leaders, in the economy and politics, to be sure, have been white, a point true of Latin America generally. Because few Mexicans are of purely European descent, all Mexican politicians celebrate the country's Indian heritage. There are no statues of Cortés in Mexico, and the quincentennial of Columbus's 1492 voyage was little noticed.

Imported Ideologies

Latin America is noted for picking up ideas invented elsewhere, warping them, and then trying to apply them where they do not fit. Some Latin America experts call the continent a *reliquiario*, a place for keeping old relics of saints and pieces of the true cross. Now it is a reliquary for ideas passé in the rest of the world, a sort of remainder sale of dated ideologies, such as the following.

Comparison

Mexico and America as Colonies

The Spanish colonies of the New World resembled the declining feudal system of Europe. Society was rigidly stratified by birth and race into privileged and lower ranks. The Catholic Church, supervised by Rome, tried to calm Mexico's Indians by education and spiritual uplift. Madrid's chief interest in New Spain was the gold and silver it could ship to the royal treasury. For this, Spain set up Mexico (indeed, all of its Latin American holdings) as vast bureaucracies, which plague the region to this day. Latin America was born bureaucratic.

Mexico was Spain's richest colony; its gold and silver funded the giant Habsburg military effort in the Thirty Years War. Under the mistaken doctrine of *mercantilism*, Spain reckoned it was rich, but gold and silver produce neither crops nor manufactured goods. Ironically, as Spain stole the vast wealth of the New World, it grew poorer. The extractive industries impoverished Mexico, too.

The English colonizers arrived in Virginia and New England a century after the Spaniards did in Mexico. By the early seventeenth century, the feudal age was over in England, and the immigrants carried little feudal baggage or bureaucracy. The colonies largely ran themselves. No one expected quick gold or silver, either for themselves or for London. Although the English brought ranks of nobility with them, most settlers were farmers or merchants with an **egalitarian** ethos (exception: Virginia). They concentrated on agricultural production. Their several varieties of Protestantism—none of which had Catholicism's central control—taught hard work, delayed gratification, equality, and individuality. They pushed the Indians westward but did not turn them into serfs.

Samuel Huntington's controversial 2004 book, *Who Are We?*, posited religion as the biggest determinant of political culture. If French, Spanish, or Portuguese Catholics had originally settled the United States, he argued, we would today resemble, respectively, Quebec, Mexico, and Brazil. The fact that we were first settled by Anglo-Protestants has made all the difference.

Liberalism here means the original, nineteenth-century variety that rejected monarchy and opened society to new forces. The United States, with its large middle class, took naturally to this philosophy of freedom, but Latin America, encumbered by inherited social positions, big bureaucracies, and state-owned industries, did not. No middle class, no liberalism. Juárez and Díaz could not make liberalism work in Mexico. Some Latin American countries have recently turned to economic "neoliberalism" by building free markets.

egalitarian
Dedicated to equality.

Positivism proposed that experts should improve society through science. It died out in Europe but caught on in Latin America, especially Brazil, where its motto, "Order and Progress," is in the flag. In Mexico, Díaz's *científicos* typified the positivist spirit, which conflicts with the hands-off philosophy of liberalism.

Socialism in Europe made sense, as Europe had a lot of industry and a large working class that was amenable to unionization and leftist parties, such as Britain's Labour and Germany's Social Democrats. Latin America, however, until recently, had little industry and only a small proletariat; it was precapitalist. No working class, no socialism. Governments such as Mexico's and Brazil's invented and coddled unions to make a contrived working-class base. Some idealists still see socialism as the answer to Mexico's vast poverty, but they offer no successful examples of it. Chile prospered after it overthrew the socialist government of Salvador Allende.

Rural socialism rejects industry in favor of small farms. It proposes returning to a rural idyll of equality and sufficiency based on family farming. Zapata was its hero. It idealizes a past that never existed and cannot be: There is simply not enough land to redistribute to exploding populations. Peasant farming equals poverty. Zapatista guerrillas in Chiapas State in Mexico's south, however, still pursue this romantic vision.

Anarchism is a sort of primitive socialism that argues the end of government will erase class differences. A small political movement, it appeared in the late nineteenth century in Russia and in Spain, where it became anarcho-syndicalism: no government needed because trade unions will run things. Several Mexican revolutionaries were influenced by anarchism.

Anticlericalism, founded by French writer Voltaire, caught on strongly in Spain and then spread to Latin America. Anticlericalists such as Calles claim the Catholic Church has too much political power, favors the rich, and keeps Mexico backward. Catholicism is still popular and powerful, despite the shortage of priests and inroads of evangelical Protestantism.

Fascism, founded by Mussolini and copied by Hitler, briefly influenced some Latin American countries, especially those with many German and Italian immigrants. It combines nationalism, corporatism, and fake socialism under a charismatic leader. Vargas's Brazilian New State drew the quip "fascism with sugar." Perón's Argentina was not as sweet and welcomed Nazi war criminals.

Communism, revolutionary Marxist socialism under Moscow's control, was for decades popular among Latin American intellectuals. It proposed to cure the region's drastic inequality and poverty by a state takeover of production and the end of U.S. exploitation, a permanent and popular theme. Some of Mexico's leading artists, such as Diego Rivera and David Siqueiros, were Communists. Castro's Cuba and Che's icon drew much support until Latin intellectuals noticed that Cuba is a stagnant tyranny. Although largely defunct, Marxism lingers in *dependency theory*.

Latin American intellectuals have been so addicted to one ideology after another that they fail to notice that the rest of the world has already discarded them. Communism, for example,

Democracy

Cautious Democrats

Latin America (except Cuba) turned democratic in the 1980s, but Latins have embraced democracy slowly and cautiously. Like Russians, they expected democracy to bring prosperity; both were slow in coming. More than half of Latin Americans tell pollsters that democracy is always preferable, but a minority still says that an authoritarian government can sometimes be preferable.

Democratic feeling rises and falls with the economy, as most Latins worry about unemployment and poverty. In a downturn, some say a dictatorship that puts food on the table is not so bad. As Brazil boomed, support for democracy firmed up. Mexico's economy took a hit in the 2008–2009 downturn, and so did democratic support. Many Latin Americans perceive all government, democratic or not, as essentially rigged to favor a few powerful interests.

In Mexico, the percentage preferring democracy was 53 in 1996, 59 in 2005, 42 in 2009, and 49 in 2010. During the same period, however, the percentage saying authoritarian rule can be preferable dropped from 23 to 10. Fear of crime rose to the top of Mexicans' agenda. Democracy is not yet fully rooted in Latin American political culture, but authoritarianism has been largely uprooted.

collapsed in East Europe and the Soviet Union and is meaningless in China but still lives in Cuba, which could become the world's last Communist country, the reliquary of Marx's bones.

Patterns of Interaction

9.4 **Explain the interpenetration of crime and politics in weak states.**

Clientelism and Co-optation

How could a society as fractured as Mexico's hold together? Why is it not still mired in civil wars, upheavals, and coups? Clever political leaders, such as Calles and Cárdenas in Mexico, may be able to calm such situations by making sure that important groups have a share not only of seats in parliament but also of favors, such as development projects, rigged contracts, subsidies, or just plain cash. In a clientelistic situation, the elites of each major group strike a bargain to obtain resources and restrain their followers from violence. Most major groups get something; no one group gets everything. *Clientelism* is widely practiced in the Third World (heck, maybe in the First as well), and in the Persian Gulf oil sheikdoms and Nigeria.

Clientelism in Mexico has at least three problems. First, it may be fake, with only small payouts to labor and agrarian sectors, which PRI kept in line with the traditional *pan y palo.* Second, it may exclude important groups. In Mexico, the Catholic Church got no part of the deal, and big businessmen got little until some were co-opted into PRI during World War II. (The Catholic Church and business helped bring PAN to power in 2000.) A third problem is rigidity. The allocation of which group gets how much help and money cannot be frozen; it has to change as society and the economy evolve. Village land held in common is often unproductive. State-owned industries, many headed by PRI "dinosaurs," slow economic growth, but those who benefit fight change. Mexico's giant (1.5 million members) and powerful teachers' union stunts education standards. It controls hiring and firing for teaching jobs, which are often bought. A 2013 constitutional amendment opened the way to better teacher qualifications and took back hiring and firing. The wealthy and corrupt union chief was arrested. Teachers, who had been a PRI constituency, shut down Mexico City in 2013 with massive strikes. At times, militant teachers have turned violent.

Calles and Cárdenas devised a system of **co-optation** that gave the Mexican government control over groups that might otherwise cause them trouble. They promised peasants and workers a good deal but rarely gave them much. When rural and worker unions got demanding, the government crushed them. The large Mexican Workers Confederation, for example, was under the thumb of PRI through its chief, who served 56 years. While professing "socialism," Mexican presidents tolerated no competition from Communists, especially after Stalin had Trotsky assassinated in Mexico in 1940. Even "leftist" presidents such as López Mateos had no trouble arresting Communists and breaking strikes. There was a large element of fakery in PRI governance. Chiefly, they served themselves.

For decades, the Mexican government tried to co-opt students by giving them a nearly free education and then employing them as civil servants. (Saudi Arabia attempts to do the same.) This cannot work forever; there is simply not enough money. Student numbers and

co-optation
To enroll other groups in your cause, rendering them harmless.

discontent grew. Many turned radical and accused PRI of abandoning its commitments to social justice. President Gustavo Díaz Ordaz was obsessed with order and tolerated no criticism. With the 1968 Mexico City Olympics just weeks away, he feared that student protests would mar his picture of a modern, happy Mexico. In October at the Plaza of the Three Cultures in Mexico City, police gunned down as many as 300 student protesters. What PRI could not co-opt, it crushed. Some mark this as a turning point in PRI rule, the point at which it visibly began to destabilize.

Políticos versus Técnicos

Mexican politics, as in much of Latin America, is pulled between two forces, called, in Mexico, *políticos* and *técnicos*, politicians and technicians. The *políticos* are populists seeking elected

Democracy

Elections and Democracy

Americans are given to the notion that elections equal democracy. PRI won 14 presidential elections in a row, illustrating that democracy is more complex than just balloting. Elections are just the visible parts and can mislead foreign election monitors, who see little more than the physical balloting on election day and miss the longer-term and less-visible problems. Monitors are getting better, though, and, in recent years, have called several elections rigged. Few elections in the Third World are completely free and fair. There are several ways to rig them.

Media Dominance The big problem is what happens in the weeks and months before the election. To a considerable extent, he who controls television rules the country, as Putin showed in Russia. A country with one or two government-controlled channels will give much news coverage to the ruling party and little to opposition candidates. Newspapers can suffer distribution problems and shortage of newsprint.

Bribery Poor people are often so desperate for money or jobs that they vote for the party that provides them. Mexico's PRI was notorious for rewarding voters. In the 2000 elections in Yucatán, PRI gave voters thousands of washing machines, no doubt to ensure a clean election.

Ballot Security Voting is supposed to be secret, but there are techniques to figure out who voted how. Actually, just telling people you know how they voted is often enough to scare them into compliance. This is especially a problem in unsophisticated rural areas. If a whole village does not vote for the party in power, it may miss out on next year's road repair hires. Ballot boxes can be stuffed in advance. As they used to say in Chicago, "Vote early and often!"

Ballot Counting Opposition parties may not have enough poll watchers and counters to ensure honest counts. They may be barred from watching. Computers do not necessarily make tabulating votes honest. In the 1988 elections, with Cuauhtémoc Cárdenas mounting a major challenge, Mexico's computers tabulating the vote crashed; when they were back up, PRI won with a bare 50.4 percent. Over the 60 previous years, PRI had never won less than 70 percent. Iran, in 2009, may have not bothered counting the ballots.

In 1990, amid major complaints of PRI fraud, especially from PAN and PRD, the PRI government of Salinas, to its credit, abolished the Federal Electoral Commission, widely believed to be crooked. In its place, the Federal Electoral Institute (IFE), autonomous and supervised by representatives of all parties, greatly cleaned up Mexican voting at all levels. Immediately, non-PRI parties started winning more votes. The IFE demonstrates that Mexico is getting modern and democratic. Recent problems in U.S. voting suggest we could use an IFE.

office; they pay attention to mass needs and demands. As such, they pay little heed to economics and are not averse to running up huge deficits. This pleases the crowd but leads to inflation and out-cries from foreign investors and international banks. Presidents Díaz

peso
Spanish for "weight"; Mexico's currency, worth about 7 U.S. cents.

Ordaz (1964–1970), Echeverría (1970–1976), and López Portillo (1976–1982) typify the *político* approach. They relied too much on Mexico's new oil finds and overspent. Eventually, Mexico's economy crashed.

The *técnicos* (known in much of the world as *technocrats*) try to fix economic instabil-ity. They are more likely to staff appointive positions and worry less about mass demands. Many have studied modern economics in the United States and see a free market and fewer government controls as the path to prosperity. They urge what much of the world calls *neolib-eralism*, the return to Adam Smith's original economic ideas. This confuses Americans, as we call it *conservatism*. In European and Latin American terminology, however, Britain's Margaret Thatcher instituted a neoliberal economic program. In Chile under Pinochet, the "Chicago boys" (who studied neoclassical economics at the University of Chicago) put neoliberalism into practice with good results.

Presidents Miguel de la Madrid Hurtado (1982–1988) and Carlos Salinas de Gortari (1988–1994) gave technocrats a chance to stabilize the fiscal chaos wrought by the overspend-ing of their predecessors. Actually, these fiscal technicians in PRI implemented some of the free-market reforms that PAN also sought. But reforms provided insufficient regulation, and Mexico's newly freed banks made bad and even crooked loans. Mexico's financial sec-tor crashed in 1995. The **peso** lost most of its value against the dollar. (In 1997, Asian banks folded from exactly the same sort of crony capitalism.) The problem is not a lack of bright, well-educated economists. Both PRI and PAN have plenty. The problem is partial economic reforms that provide freedom without rule of law. These tend to set up wild expansion followed by crashes, as the United States saw in 2008.

Mexican Catholicism

The sleeper in Mexican politics has been the Roman Catholic Church. Eight percent of the world's Catholics are Mexicans (less than Brazil). In 2012, 83 percent of Mexicans considered themselves Catholic (down from 96 percent in 1970, as Protestant evangelicals make inroads), many of them quite serious. Since independence, however, the spirit of the Mexican Republic has been secular. The Church was never happy with Mexico's break from Spain and tilted strongly conservative. It was conservative Mexican Catholics who convinced Napoleon III that France could take Mexico. The republic tilted in an anticlerical direction, which became especially pronounced in the 1910–1920 Revolution. Its leaders saw the Church as a bastion of upper-class conservatism and reaction. The 1917 constitution imposed limits on church lands, educational institutions, and religious orders. Detectives ferreted out secret convents and closed them. Priests had to travel in ordinary clothing, without clerical collars. Calles's anti-clericalism provoked the Cristero Rebellion. For much of the twentieth century, the Mexican church was on the defensive.

But the Church never gave up. Through Catholic teachings, lay organizations, schools and universities, and the 1939 founding of PAN, it methodically set the stage for the return

Political Culture

Songs of Drug Dealing

Mexico has long celebrated bandits in folk ballads known as *corridos*. Currently popular are polka-tempo *narcocorridos* that celebrate drug smugglers as romantic daredevils who fight cops and other gangs and die young. Mexicans deplore the drug trade, crime, and insecurity, but, as in most of Latin America, respect for law is not part of the political culture, and few condemn lawbreakers.

Mexicans learn early that the rich and powerful own the police and courts; in defense, the poor learn to evade and ignore the law. It is a logical reaction to an unjust system. Most Mexicans are personally open, honest, and friendly. But they say that obeying a brutal and unfair judicial system is absurd. Everyone knows the police are among the biggest criminals, in the pay of the **narcotraficantes**, who are not arrested or saunter out of prison at will. Police coerce confessions out of suspects, and the courts take that confession as ironclad proof of guilt. Mexican attitudes on law are common throughout the Third World: It is something to be worked around.

of Catholic politics. These are not the politics of a reactionary past but of a modern, business-oriented future. PAN is more Catholic than Italy's postwar Christian Democrats (now the Popular Party), a catchall party that is not very religious.

Crime and Politics

We have mentioned several Mexican interest groups—labor unions, peasant associations, business, the Catholic Church—but Mexico's most powerful interest group is drug cartels. An estimated 450,000 Mexicans make their living off drugs, either cultivating or trafficking. Actually, looking at the world as a whole, crime of all sorts is humankind's biggest economic activity. This is nothing new. Early in human history, the state gave birth to twins—politics, the means of influencing the state, and crime, the means of avoiding the state.

Politics and crime know and understand each other quite well, forming an almost symbiotic relationship, one especially clear in a country such as Mexico. Politics needs money to win elections and pays little attention to the sources of this money (for example, Japanese Liberal Democratic politicians and *yakuza* gangsters). And crime needs the protection of politics to continue its enterprises (for example, the inability of the Russian police to solve assassinations). Corruption occurs at the triple interface of the state, politics, and crime. In a weak state, politics, because it is unrestrained, easily turns violent. Crime, because it has little to fear from the state, ignores state power.

Justice has always been weak in Mexico. Pancho Villa blended banditry and revolution. As we noted, starting with Madero in 1913, assassination of top leaders was common. Assassinations continue in our day. Nosy journalists, zealous prosecutors, candidates, and elected officials are routinely gunned down. No one is safe. A hit on a rival drug lord in 1993 by mistake killed a Mexican cardinal in his vestments. Mexicans were outraged. Frustrated at police corruption, in 2004, a Mexico City mob lynched two cops. In Mexico, rapists, murderers, and kidnappers are rarely arrested, but police beat innocent people until they confess. About 90 percent of Mexico's crimes are not reported; people feel it is useless. As in Russia, the inability of police to solve crimes suggests that they are

narcotraficante
Drug trafficker.

in on the deal. For as little as $85, Mexican cops tip off narcotraficantes about impending busts. Mexican newspapers, whose staffs have been kidnapped and killed, self-censor and minimize news about drug trafficking. Even bloggers have been murdered for their drug coverage.

Two killings in 1994 shocked the world and paved the way to PAN's electoral victories. Luis Donaldo Colosio, PRI's own presidential candidate handpicked by President Salinas, was shot dead at an election rally in Tijuana. Who ordered the hit is unclear. PRI party secretary general José Ruiz Massieu was later shot dead. President Salinas's brother Raúl, who got very rich with drug connections during the *sexenio* of his brother, got 50 years for ordering the killing (but was freed in 2005). Massieu's own brother, a deputy attorney general, was assigned to investigate but resigned, accusing PRI bosses of complicity and coverup. President Salinas, who worked his way up as a brilliant U.S.-educated economist, ended his term in disgrace and went into exile in Ireland. In 2004, the youngest Salinas brother, Enrique, suspected of laundering money in France for Raúl, was strangled in Mexico City. The Salinas family started looking like a mafia.

The killings brought together two trends that had been growing over the years: (1) PRI was stinking more and more, and (2) Mexicans were sufficiently educated to vote out PRI. Calderón vowed to break the *narcotraficantes*. Unable to trust the police, many of whom are in the pay of drug gangs, in 2008, Calderón ordered the Mexican army into open warfare with the heavily armed cartels, much of it in cities on the U.S. border. Since 2006, gang-related deaths have reached 80,000—many of them innocent bystanders and kidnapping victims. Bodies turn up everywhere. Citizens form *autodefensas*, armed vigilante groups that soon turn criminal themselves. Thousands are arrested, even top cartel chiefs, but the war may never end, as the billions made in drug smuggling are irresistible to poor Mexicans, including underpaid police officers. Drug cartels offer *plata o plomo*—silver (payoff) or lead (a bullet)—for cooperation, and once you cooperate, you do not quit. Mexican soldiers leave the army to murder and torture for the cartels. It pays a lot better.

What Mexicans Quarrel About

9.5 **Evaluate the problems that come with being able to walk from the Third World into the First.**

The Political Economy of Mexico

Mexico's economy in some years grows well; in others, not. In a Latin American growth race, in some years, Mexico is ahead of Brazil. Mexico is now hitting the sweet spot where productivity is hight but wages are low. Mexico can truck cheaply to the U.S. market just as high fuel costs for shipping across the Pacific slow Asian manufacturing. Mexico's favorable location delivers ample foreign direct investment (FDI). Mexico exports more manufactured goods than the rest of Latin America combined, much of it to the U.S. market. Chrysler makes Fiat 500s in Mexico for the China market.

Until recently, however, Mexico's population growth—from 16 million in 1935, to 34 million in 1960, to 120 million in 2014—has partly offset economic growth, producing weak gains per capita. Mexico's rate of population growth has more than halved to little more than 1 percent a year, testimony to the power of economic development to solve the population explosion. Middle-class people turn naturally and with no coercion to small families. Mexico's fertility rate in the 1960s was an amazing 7 but now only 2.3, and will soon reach the U.S. rate. Average Mexican lifespans have climbed to 77, nearly the U.S. lifespan.

Mexicans do not quarrel about population, but they do quarrel about how to make an economy that creates jobs for the millions of unemployed and underemployed. PAN wants a free-market economy focused on exports; the PRD wants socialism and a domestic focus. Mexico's state-owned industries grow too slowly to dent unemployment.

The gap between rich and poor in Mexico is large (but narrowing), as it is throughout Latin America. Economists estimate that the top 4 percent of Mexicans own half of Mexico's wealth while 40 percent of Mexicans live below the poverty line, which is not very high. (Brazil has even greater inequality of wealth and incomes.) With no land or jobs, millions of Mexicans stream to the cities, where they live in shanties and eke out a living selling small items or stealing. Some 22 million Mexicans work off the books, in the "informal economy" (black market), and pay no taxes, contributing to Mexico's chronic federal budget deficits. Greater Mexico City, with a population of some 21 million, is one of the biggest cities in the world, with some of the world's worst air pollution.

Poverty is especially stark in the interior south of Mexico, precisely where the Zapatista rebellion started in 1994. Although the Mexican army quickly drove the guerrillas from the towns of Chiapas, they still operate in the mountainous jungles of the region, where they are very hard to catch. Their leader, "Subcomandante Marcos," speaks eloquently and accurately about Mexico's history of exploitation and poverty and about PRI's betrayal of its promises to uplift the poor. Marcos, however, has no feasible program of his own. He imbibes the romanticism of the Revolution, as do many Mexicans.

In addition to its obvious injustice, maldistribution of income has several other negative consequences. Some Mexicans go hungry, and many do not earn even the minimum daily wage of $4.50. Poor people have no money to save, which means insufficient capital for investment and growth. With little domestic capital, Latin American lands depend on foreign capital, which not everyone likes. (Americans also save little, and the same happens: massive inflows of foreign capital, much of it from China and Japan.) The very poor have trouble acquiring the skills to lift themselves into the middle class. Schools are inadequate in rural Mexico and in the vast shantytowns around Mexico's cities. Over the generations, a "culture of poverty" became endemic among Mexico's poor, discouraging them from climbing out. One escape hatch is *el Norte*, sneaking into the United States.

Trying to fight this, under a conservative president in 2002, Mexico instituted its *Oportunidades* program of conditional monthly cash directly to families—especially to mothers—that regularly send their children to school and health clinics. Resembling Brazil's larger *Bolsa Família* program, Oportunidades reduced Mexican poverty levels and boosted education and health levels. One of the best things elieviating Mexico's poverty has been the FDI that recently made the economy boom as Chinese labor costs climbed.

The Pemex Problem

A major Mexican quarrel is over what to do with the nationalized oil firm—some call it a dinosaur—Pemex. The hot question could lead to violence in the streets. Schoolbooks teach that oil is the pillar of Mexican nationhood. Peña, however, proposed changing the constitution's Article 27 to allow badly needed private and foreign partnerships to develop Mexico's energy.

The PRD and AMLO led massive demonstrations against giving away
Mexico's treasure to foreign capitalists with a cry from the 1930s, "The
oil is ours!"

globalization
World becoming one big
capitalist market.

Some change is surely due. Pemex is in decline. Many of its fields are played out, and
it lacks refining capacity. Without reforms allowing foreign and private investment, Mexico
may soon have to *import* refined petroleum products. Although sitting on vast natural gas
fields, Mexico must import much U.S. gas. The Mexican government gets a third of its revenues from Pemex, which hands over 55 percent of its income to the state, starving Pemex of
investment funds. Pemex's bloated 151,000-employee workforce makes it one of least efficient
oil companies in the world. Norway's Statoil produces 78 barrels of oil a day per employee;
Exxon Mobil, 55; and Pemex, only 24. Pemex's unions guard their jobs and resist efficiency
improvements.

Mexico's many young, U.S.-trained economists recognize that state-owned industries are
stagnant, inefficient, and corrupt, especially Pemex. Such people are Panistas or PRI técnicos.
Recent PRI presidents gingerly liberalized Mexico's economy; Peña wishes to go further, and
PAN, further yet. Privatized a little, a lot, or not at all, oil is an unreliable fix for Mexico's economic problems. Some speak of the "petroleum curse" that skews development away from
long-term and balanced growth, concentrates wealth in the hands of a few, and makes the country dependent on the rise and fall of oil prices. When new oilfields were discovered in Mexico's
south in the 1970s, Presidents Echeverría and López Portillo went crazy with spending. For a
while, some Mexicans felt rich, but inflation and the 1995 crash of the peso ended that. Mexico
followed oil sheiks in squandering oil revenues to produce a temporary and unsustainable illu-
sion of wealth. Oil is a kind of drug that induces fantasies of grandeur.

The NAFTA Question

Globalization has been a buzzword for years. Whole books are written either praising it or
denouncing it. We need to ask at least two questions about **globalization**: (1) Does it really
exist? (2) Does it uplift poor countries? Basically, globalization is a big jump up in world
trade patterns that have been building for centuries. World trade increased with Portugal's
and Spain's voyages of discovery and their trade with, respectively, Asia and Latin America.
World trade grew quickly with the steamship and the British Empire, "Victorian globalization."
Recent globalization, aided by instant communication and rapid transport, is distinguished by
its multinational corporations that produce in many lands and sell everywhere.

Globalization never really covered the globe. Wide areas—especially the Middle East
and Africa—were little involved. Globalization extended in a band across North America and
Europe, fell off, and picked up again in East Asia. Some developing countries benefited enor-
mously from free trade, namely the Asian "growth dragons." The 2008–2009 financial crisis
brought renewed protectionism; some argue that deglobalization could take hold.

Latin America played a relatively minor role and was never sure about globalization,
because it had just begun to enjoy its benefits. Brazil, thanks to massive food and raw materials exports, became one of the high-growth BRICs. Some critics cite Latin America's uneven
economic growth as proof that globalization either does not work at all or at least does not
work in Latin America, where a rigid class structure stifles growth. China zoomed along at 10
percent growth per year; only since 2004 has Latin America reached 5 percent. Leftists point out

NAFTA
1994 North American Free Trade Agreement among the United States, Canada, and Mexico.

that Latin America's gaps between rich and poor stifle growth and produce the leftist electoral victories in Argentina, Brazil, Chile, Bolivia, and Venezuela.

NAFTA (the 1994 North American Free Trade Agreement) was both hailed and feared. American fearmongers said U.S. jobs would make a "vast sucking sound" as they drained down to Mexico. Nothing of the sort happened; U.S. employment reached record heights in the late 1990s. Canadian and Mexican nationalists feared that the U.S. economy would dominate their two countries. Free-market optimists foresaw economic growth for all.

Since NAFTA came into effect, merchandise trade among the three NAFTA partners has more than tripled. Trade between Mexico and the United States has more than quadrupled. Mexican wages in manufacturing are one-tenth U.S. wages and now little higher than China's rapidly rising wages. Thanks to cheap and fast shipping to the U.S. market, foreign firms set up new factories in Mexico, making it the world leader in exports of refrigerators and wide-screen TVs.

Much of Mexican politics still revolves around NAFTA. The left, including PRD people, want to either scrap the whole thing or seriously modify it. PAN is solidly for NAFTA; Vicente Fox exemplified and celebrated globalization as Mexico's way out of poverty. PRI negotiated and ratified NAFTA but had some doubts, now largely overcome. To reap more benefits from NAFTA, Mexico must undertake radical domestic economic reforms—increasing competition, lowering energy costs, and investing more in education, which is badly underfunded.

Drugs: A Mexican or U.S. Problem?

Mexico grows marijuana and manufactures methamphetamines, but most cocaine and heroin for the U.S. market originates in Colombia, Peru, and Bolivia, transiting through Mexico, whose long U.S. border makes smuggling relatively easy. By air, trucks, boats, tunnels, or "mules," drugs pour into an eager U.S. market, and firearms from U.S. gun shops pour back into Mexico. For every kilo found, many more get through. An estimated 80 to 90 percent of drugs consumed in the United States come from or through Mexico.

Drugs are both a Mexican and a U.S. problem. For Mexico, drugs have brought crime into the highest levels of power. Mexico's police, judicial system, and army have all been corrupted by drug money. Even President Salinas had a brother in the drug trade. In 2005, a spy for a drug cartel was found in President Fox's office. One of the characteristics of the weak state is its penetration by crime. In Mexico, crime and politics depend on each other; drug money helps politicians, and politicians help traffickers—a difficult cycle to break. Many Mexicans have concluded that stopping drugs is impossible; it might be better to legalize them to break the power of the cartels. With far less money to be made in drugs, they figure, the violence would subside. Drugs are mostly a U.S. problem, they argue, but Mexicans pay the heaviest costs in lives and security. About half of U.S. convicts are in for drugs. The expense for prisons has persuaded 15 U.S. states to decriminalize pot, and half of Americans approve.

The U.S. drug market is indeed lucrative—tens of billions of dollars per year. If no Americans took illicit drugs, a wide layer of Latin American crime would disappear. But there are drug users in every walk of life in the United States. They might consider that the *narcotraficantes* murder thousands and harm the stability and growth of several Latin American lands.

Drugs finance the decades-long guerrilla war in Colombia. Catching traffickers and checking border crossings has little impact on overall U.S. drug consumption. The profits from feeding the U.S. drug market are so great that many gladly join.

remittance
Money sent home.

Illegal or Undocumented?

We call them "illegal immigrants"; Mexicans call them "undocumented workers." An estimated 11 million are in the United States. The Mexican-U.S. border is the only place on earth you can walk from the Third World into the First. For the millions of Mexicans who have made the risky walk, they merely relocated to the northern portion of their republic that the United States seized in 1848. Many die every year, but few worry about breaking the law. The U.S. Border Patrol, at times, arrested more than 1 million a year and sent them back. Many immediately tried again. Probably more than 1 million a year got through, a flow that drastically declined as U.S. jobs dried up during the long recession and tighter enforcement in U.S. hiring.

The problem of the *indocumentados* parallels the drug problem. There is both a push and a pull. Unemployment and poverty push Mexicans to leave, and jobs and the opportunity to give their families a decent life pull. And Americans do hire Mexicans (and others from farther south) with little thought to their immigration status. Many businesses, especially in the U.S. Southwest, depend on cheap Mexican labor. "Heck, he gave me a Social Security number," say employers. (True, but it's the same number used by dozens of illegals.) Few U.S. families could afford household help—maids and gardeners—if they had to hire Americans. Tough laws in several U.S. states against undocumented farmworkers left crops to rot in the field; Americans simply refused to do the backbreaking labor.

Again, this is not really a Mexican problem; it's an American problem. The Mexican government, as a humanitarian service, puts out a comic book showing how to survive the dangers and deserts when crossing the border. Mexico wants a better deal from the U.S. administration: to accept more immigrants, as either legal or temporary immigrants, and grant amnesty to illegals already here. Americans do not want a flood of Hispanic immigrants, but employers in clothing, manufacturing, construction, meatpacking, and agriculture like the cheap labor and make campaign contributions. Their payoff: U.S. investigators are chronically shorthanded in enforcing laws against hiring illegals. Illegal immigration divides the U.S. Republican Party; conservative voters want it ended whereas moneyed interests want it reformed. The issue moves U.S. Hispanics to vote Democratic, possibly for generations.

Going to the United States has been both an escape valve for Mexican unemployment and a source of **remittances** from those working here, who send back over $20 billion a year. Much Third World development depends on remittances, which are the best form of foreign aid because they bypass corrupt officials and go right to families for raising children and starting businesses. The best thing we could do for Mexico's development is to make remittances safe and cheap.

Modern Mexico?

For some decades, Mexico, compared with most of Latin America, was a model of growth and prosperity. Recently, Mexico has again eclipsed Brazil as the "Latin tiger," rivaling the Asian growth dragons. Per cap, Mexicans are richer than Brazilians. With the right policies, Mexico might surge ahead even faster. State-sanctioned monopolies block competition. Huge poverty exists side by side with enormous wealth. The world's richest individual is Carlos Slim, a Mexican (of Lebanese descent) who owns 70 percent of Mexico's mobile phone network (which the Peña administration tried to make competitive). Education, starved of funding, is weak. Mexico collects roughly half as much in taxes as a percentage of GDP compared to its peer middle-income countries.

What is the right policy for growth? The record of the postwar world shows one combination: low wages and good productivity. When labor costs (including taxes, pensions, and hourly wages) lag behind productivity growth, you can produce more at lower cost and earn a share of the world market. Labor costs rise over time. The trick is to keep productivity rising faster. You do this by technology (meaning more capital investment) and higher worker skills (meaning better education). The models for the combination of low wages and high productivity: postwar Germany, Japan and, more recently, China. Mexico is now in this position.

The twin impediments to Mexico's continued rapid growth are crime and corruption. The late Milton Friedman, winner of a Nobel Prize in economics, long extolled the free market as the basis of economic growth. Asked late in life if he still thought so, he said he now realized it is not; the real basis, he said, is rule of law. He might have been speaking of Mexico.

Review Questions

Learning Objective 9.1 Describe how a revolution can be "institutionalized", p. 362.

1. How did Spanish colonialism influence Latin America's subsequent development?
2. Was Mexico's independence a revolutionary or a conservative act?
3. Why could Calles be described as a founding genius?

Learning Objective 9.2 Evaluate the advantages of a single six-year presidency compared to two four-year terms, p. 371.

4. Which parties now alternate in power in Mexico?
5. Describe Mexico's electoral system. Which country inspired it?
6. What kind of party system did Mexico used to have? What system does it have now?

Learning Objective 9.3 List the several ideologies Latin America has imported, p. 377.

7. Which ideologies have had an impact in Latin America?

8. Contrast Latin American and U.S. attitudes on race.
9. Contrast Spanish colonialism in Latin America with English in North America.

Learning Objective 9.4 Explain the interpenetration of crime and politics in weak states, p. 381.

10. Explain *clientelism*, giving examples from Mexico.
11. Use Mexico to explain why elections do not equal democracy.
12. Does the interpenetration of crime and politics describe Mexico?

Learning Objective 9.5 Evaluate the problems that come with being able to walk from the Third World into the First, p. 385.

13. How has Mexico's economy done in recent years?
14. Should Mexico privatize Pemex? Why is this impossible?
15. Are drugs a Mexican or a U.S. problem?

Key Terms

bilateral opposition, p. 377

cacique, p. 363

caudillo, p. 366

clientelism, p. 370

constitutionalism, p. 371

co-optation, p. 381

Corporatism, p. 370

creole, p. 364

dedazo, p. 373

dominant-party system, p. 375

egalitarian, p. 379

ejido, p. 368

globalization, p. 387

hacienda, p. 378

institutionalize, p. 371

Mesoamerica, p. 362

mestizaje, p. 378

NAFTA, p. 388

narcotraficante, p. 384

norteamericano, p. 378

peso, p. 383

political institution, p. 371

populist, p. 377

pre-Columbian, p. 364

priísmo, p. 369

remittance, p. 389

sexenio, p. 369

Further Reference

Ai Camp, Roderic. *Mexico: What Everyone Needs to Know*. New York: Oxford University Press, 2011.

Babb, Sarah. *Managing Mexico: Economists from Nationalism to Neoliberalism*. New York: Routledge, 2001.

Brading, David. *Mexican Phoenix, Our Lady of Guadalupe: Image and Tradition across Five Centuries*. New York: Cambridge University Press, 2001.

Campbell, Howard. *Drug War Zone: Frontline Dispatches from the Streets of El Paso and Juárez*. Austin, TX: University of Texas Press, 2010.

Castañeda, Jorge. *Mañana Forever? Mexico and the Mexicans*. New York: Knopf, 2011.

Dawson, Alexander. *First World Dreams: Mexico since 1989*. New York: Palgrave, 2006.

Domínguez, Jorge I., and Rafael Fernández de Castro. *United States and Mexico: Between Partnership and Conflict*, 2nd ed. New York: Routledge, 2009.

Grayson, George W. *Mexico: Narco-Violence and a Failed State?* Edison, NJ: Transaction, 2009.

Grillo, Ioan. *El Narco: Inside Mexico's Criminal Insurgency*. New York: Bloomsbury, 2012.

Krauze, Enrique. *Mexico: Biography of Power: A History of Modern Mexico, 1810–1996*. New York: HarperCollins, 1997.

_____. *Redeemers: Ideas and Power in Latin America*. New York: HarperCollins, 2011.

Le Clézio, J. M. G. *The Mexican Dream: Or, the Interrupted Thought of Amerindian Civilizations*. Chicago: University of Chicago Press, 2009.

Mann, Charles C. *1493: Uncovering the New World Columbus Created*. New York: Knopf, 2011.

O'Neil, Shannon K. *Two Nations Indivisible: Mexico, the United States, and the Road Ahead*. New York: Oxford University Press, 2013.

Preston, Julia, and Samuel Dillon. *Opening Mexico: The Making of a Democracy*. New York: Farrar, Strauss & Giroux, 2004.

Shirk, David A. *Mexico's New Politics: The PAN and Democratic Change*. Boulder, CO: Lynne Rienner, 2005.

Tuckman, Jo. *Mexico: Democracy Interrupted*. New Haven, CT: Yale University Press, 2012.

Youngers, Coletta A., and Eileen Rosin, eds. *Drugs and Democracy in Latin America: The Impact of U.S. Policy*. Boulder, CO: Lynne Rienner, 2004.

Chapter 10
Brazil

The sun comes up over Rio de Janeiro's landmark Sugarloaf.

Learning Objectives

10.1 Compare and contrast Brazil's colonization with those of other Latin American countries.

10.2 Explain how Brazil managed to stabilize its tumultuous politics.

10.3 Explain why Latin Americans are cautious about democracy.

10.4 Describe Brazil's mobilization-demobilization cycle.

10.5 Evaluate the Brazilian economic miracle.

WHY BRAZIL MATTERS

Brazil, Latin America's giant, offers hopeful lessons on democracy and prosperity. After a tumultuous century, Brazil arrived at both and now sets standards for the rest of Latin America. Earlier editions of this book offered Brazil as an example of **praetorianism**—a tendency for the military to take over government—but Brazil has modernized out of it. (Nigeria is a current example of praetorianism.) Brazil is now an example of modernization theory, the idea that economic growth produces a large, educated middle class that is ready for democracy. After years of snarling between radicals and authoritarian generals, Brazil (and Chile) has settled into a civil contest between center-left and center-right, like much of Europe. Brazil may at last be achieving its motto: *Ordem e Progresso*.

Impact of the Past

10.1   **Compare and contrast Brazil's colonization with those of other Latin American countries.**

Portugal and Spain wanted the same thing: direct access to the wealth (especially spices) of the "Indies," bypassing the Arab traders and the Moors, whom they had just expelled. Portugal took the lead, slowly exploring down the west coast of Africa in order to go around it. Portuguese navigators rounded the Cape of Good Hope in 1488 and quickly crossed the Indian Ocean to set up trading posts as far away as Japan. Spain started much later but, thanks to Columbus, tried due west, across the Atlantic, to reach the Indies. Accordingly, Portugal focused on Asia, not the New World.

In 1494, before South America was even discovered, the Treaty of Tordesillas (mediated by the pope) gave Portugal any possible lands to the east of a meridian 370 leagues west of Portugal's Cape Verde Islands. Pedro Alvares Cabral discovered Brazil in 1500 and took formal possession of it for the king of Portugal. Subsequent Portuguese settlements pushed their control farther westward to give Brazil its present borders.

The Portuguese Difference

The Spanish charged quickly into Latin America for its gold and silver. The Portuguese did nothing for 30 years; they were busy with the Asia trade, and Brazil offered no easy riches. It did have a red wood for making dye; from its brazed color came the name Brazil (*Brasil* in Portuguese). Only when the French started to settle there in 1530 did the Portuguese Crown take an interest. Ordering the French expelled, Dom João (King John) III parceled out the coastline into 15 *capitanías*, or royal grants, which he gave to wealthy Portuguese willing to finance settlement. The original capitanías, like the 13 English colonies in North America, gave initial shape to Brazil's present-day states and its later federalism. Growth in the capitanías, however, was slow and spotty. Portugal's population at that time was only around one million, and few were eager to emigrate.

Economic life centered on sugar, for which Europe had recently acquired a taste. Growing sugarcane requires lots of labor. The Indians of Brazil were few in number and made poor slaves; used to a life of casual hunting, many refused to work. The Portuguese found their answer in African slaves. From the sixteenth

praetorianism
Tendency for military takeovers.

through the nineteenth centuries, of the 10.7 million Africans shipped across the Atlantic, 4.9 million went to Brazil (about 600,000 went to the United States), chiefly for the sugarcane fields. Interbreeding among the three population groups—Indians, blacks, and Portuguese—was rife, producing Brazil's complex racial mixture. The Portuguese always prided themselves on being nonracist, and this attitude, in public anyway, carries over into present-day Brazil.

Other Portuguese attitudes distinguish Brazil from the former Spanish colonies of Latin America. Portuguese are historically less inclined to violence and bloodshed than Spaniards: "In a Portuguese bullfight, we don't kill the bull." In comparison, Brazil's junta killed nearly 500 leftists; Argentina's junta, some 30,000; Chile's 3,000; and little Guatemala's, 200,000. Flexibility and compromise are more valued in Brazilian politics than in Brazil's Spanish-speaking neighbors.

Painless Independence

Brazil's independence from Portugal also contrasts with the Spanish colonies' long struggles. Slowly, Brazil grew in population and importance. When the Netherlands made Pernambuco (now Recife) a Dutch colony in the mid-seventeenth century, Portuguese, blacks, and Indians together struggled to expel them and, in the process, began to think of themselves as Brazilians. In the 1690s, gold was discovered in what became the state of Minas Gerais (General Mines). A gold rush and, later, a diamond rush boosted Brazil's population. Economic activity shifted from the sugar-growing region of the Northeast to the South and stayed there. To this day, Brazil's economy centers in the more temperate climes of the south, while the drought-stricken Northeast has become an impoverished area.

By the late eighteenth century, Brazil was richer than Portugal, and thoughts of independence flickered in Brazil, inspired, as throughout Latin America, by the U.S. and French Revolutions. Brazilian independence, like Mexico's, came about partly because of Napoleon. In sealing off the Continent from Britain, Napoleon took Portugal in 1807, and the royal court in Lisbon, at British prodding, sailed for Brazil. Dom João VI was welcomed in Rio de Janeiro, which he ordered cleaned, beautified, and turned into a true capital. In 1815, Brazil was raised in rank from colony to kingdom within the Portuguese empire.

In 1821, Dom João VI returned to Lisbon and gave his son, Dom Pedro, then age 23, some parting advice: If Brazilian independence became inevitable, he should lead it. This pragmatic Portuguese flexibility contrasts with Spanish obduracy. The next year, Dom Pedro proclaimed Brazil independent, and Portugal did not resist.

From Empire to Republic

Brazil was a monarchy from 1822 to 1889, another point of contrast with the rest of Latin America. Dom Pedro I proved an inept ruler; the army turned against him, and he abdicated in 1831 while his Brazilian-born son was still a child. Under a **regency**, power was dispersed among the various states; an 1834 act set up states' rights and introduced de facto federalism.

Politics became a series of quarrels among the states and the rich land-owning families that ran them. The instability was so serious that it led to agreement in 1840 to declare Dom Pedro II—only 14 years old—of age to rule.

regency
Council that runs state until king comes of age.

Geography

Bound Brazil

Brazil is bounded on the north by Venezuela, Guyana, Suriname, and French Guiana;

on the east by the Atlantic Ocean;

on the south by Uruguay, Argentina, and Paraguay;

and on the west by Bolivia, Peru, and Colombia.

Bounding Brazil labels most of South America. Only Chile and Ecuador do not border Brazil. What is the difference between *South America* and *Latin America*? South America is the continent south of Panama. Latin America is everything south of the U.S. border with Mexico.

Brazil

Old Republic
Brazil's first republic, 1889–1930;
rigged democracy.

coronéis
"Colonels," Brazilian state-level
political bosses.

Positivism
Philosophy of applying scientific
method to social problems and
gradually improving society.

Dom Pedro II was beloved for his calm, tolerant manner and concern for Brazil. He did not, however, do much. Basing his rule on big plantation owners (*fazendeiros*), Pedro let things drift while he exercised the "moderating power" of the liberal 1824 constitution in appointing and dismissing ministers. But the Brazilian economy changed. The large landowners mattered less, while vigorous businessmen and bankers gained importance. The growing modern element resented the conservative monarchy and favored a republic. One big question Pedro II left untouched was slavery. Under British pressure, importation of new slaves ended in the 1850s, but slavery continued, deemed humane and necessary by Pedro's landowning supporters. (After the U.S. Civil War, some 10,000 Confederates moved to Brazil, where they felt at home.) Finally, his daughter, Princess Isabel, acting as regent while he was in Europe, signed an abolition bill in 1888, making Brazil one of the last countries to emancipate its slaves.

By now, wide sectors of the Brazilian population were disgusted with monarchy. Intellectuals, businesspeople, and army officers, imbued with Positivist philosophy (see Political Culture box below), wanted modernization. In 1889, a military coup ended the monarchy and introduced a republic without firing a shot.

The Old Republic

The relative stability conferred by Brazil's Portuguese heritage—bloodless independence and nineteenth-century monarchy—wore off during the **Old Republic**. Revolts, rigged elections, and military intervention marked this period. Brazil's 1891 constitution was modeled after the United States', but **coronéis** and the military held power. The presidency alternated between the political bosses of two of the most important states, São Paulo and Minas Gerais.

Grumbling increased during the Old Republic. More sectors of the population saw that their interests were unheeded by the conservative political bosses. Idealistic army officers revolted in 1922 and 1924, believing they could save the republic. The Brazilian army

Political Culture

"Order and Progress"

French philosopher Auguste Comte (1798–1857) developed the doctrine of **Positivism**. With its slogan of "Order and Progress," this optimistic philosophy held that humanity can and will progress by rejecting theology and abstract speculation in favor of the scientific study of nature and of society. Positivism advocates a building-blocks approach of empirical observation and data gathering. By assembling the blocks, society can be analyzed, predicted, and then improved, not in a revolutionary way, but gradually and under the supervision of humanitarian specialists. Said Comte: "Progress is the development of order."

Comtean Positivism launched modern social science (and still holds sway in psychology) and took root especially in Brazil. By the 1880s, many Brazilian army officers had been instructed in Positivism by mathematics professor Benjamin Constant Magalhães, who taught in the national military academy. With the 1889 republic, Positivists put their motto onto the Brazilian flag, where it remains to this day: *Ordem e Progresso*.

at this time was liberal or even radical. Many officers were imbued with Positivism and opposed conservative politicians, who seemed to block progress. To this day, the Brazilian military sees itself as a progressive force.

What finally destroyed the Old Republic was the Depression and the collapse of coffee prices, a crop that Brazil depended upon. Further, in 1930, the old Paulista-Mineiro combination split, and a crafty politician from Rio Grande do Sul—the home of many maverick politicians—took advantage of it to run for the presidency. Getúlio Vargas claimed that the election results had been rigged against him (entirely plausible) and, with help from the military and amid great popular acclaim, took over the presidency in Rio in October 1930.

mobilize
To bring new sectors of the population into political participation.

autogolpe
"Self-coup," top executive seizes more power.

Estado Nôvo
"New State," Vargas's corporatistic welfare state.

Vargas's "New State"

Latin American populist strongmen (*caudillos* in Spanish, *caudilhos* in Portuguese) are hard to label, for they appear to be both leftist and rightist. After their takeover, they often win elections by big margins. They expand the economy by statist means (see Comparison box at the end of chapter). They claim to be for the people and institute many welfare measures. They create a labor movement and give it a privileged status that is long remembered among the working class. But they concentrate power in themselves, treat opponents brutally, and are no more democratic than the old political bosses they overthrew. They may support the interests of existing elites, such as keeping coffee prices high. And they are very much for "order."

Some called such figures as Vargas of Brazil and Perón of Argentina fascists, but "authoritarian populist" is probably more accurate. These *demagogues*, rather than building ideological parties, **mobilized** the masses with their personal appeal. During the 1930s and 1940s, however, when fascism in Europe was having its day, they threw in some fascistic rhetoric. Vargas, like Perón, looked after the working class by instituting an eight-hour workday, minimum wages, paid vacations, and collective bargaining. Labor did not have to fight for its rights; Vargas handed them over long before there was an organized labor movement to make demands. He also founded the *Partido Trabalhista Brasileiro* (Brazilian Labor Party, PTB for short, not to be confused with the current PT). The result, as in much of Latin America, is a weak labor movement that constantly seeks the protection of a paternalistic state.

Vargas's 1934 constitution brought in a *corporatist* element—one-fifth of the legislature directly represented professional and trade groups—on the pattern of Italy and Portugal. The constitution also limited the president to a single four-year term. By 1937, however, Vargas decided to stay president and carried out a coup against his own regime, what is called in Latin America an **autogolpe**. Vargas proclaimed himself president, but this time there was no legislature to limit his powers. He called his regime the **Estado Nôvo**; his critics called it "fascism with sugar." There was material progress—industry, highways, public health, social welfare—but there was also a loss of freedom. The United States got along well with Vargas, for he did not curb U.S. investments.

The military, however, alarmed at Vargas's populistic dictatorship, forced him to resign in 1945. By then, Vargas had become a hero to many Brazilians, who continued to support his

PTB. In both Brazil and Argentina, the working masses longed for the return of their respective dictators and reelected them to office—Vargas in 1950 and Perón in 1946 and 1973. Once mobilized by a populistic dictator, the masses may prefer such rulers and their statism to democracy and free markets.

The Rise and Fall of Jango Goulart

The reelected Vargas was a poor president; corruption and inflation soared. Many Brazilians, including top military officers, demanded that he resign in 1954. Instead, he committed suicide, blaming reactionary international (that is, U.S.) and domestic forces for blocking his good works. One of Vargas's appointments had particularly angered the military. Vargas named a neighbor from Rio Grande do Sul, the radical João (Jango) Goulart, as labor minister, but the military forced him to resign in 1954.

Goulart, however, continued to head the PTB and, in 1955, helped moderate Juscelino Kubitschek win the presidency with Goulart as vice president. Kubitschek mobilized into his Social Democratic Party (PSD) the old political class of state and local elites who had dominated Brazil before Vargas. Kubitschek tried to focus Brazilians' energies on developing the interior; he pushed construction of Brasilia, which became the capital in 1960. Heedless of economic problems, Kubitschek promoted industrialization and allowed inflation to soar.

Brazil's working classes responded to populist appeals and, in 1960, elected president Jânio Quadros, who promised major reforms; Goulart was vice president. An unstable alcoholic, Quadros resigned after just seven months. Now Goulart, the very man the military forced out in 1954, was in line for the presidency.

The Brazilian army started talking about a coup, but a compromise was worked out: Goulart could be president but with the powers of that office greatly curtailed. Goulart accepted but played a waiting game. As the economy got worse—inflation climbed to 100 percent a year by 1964—he knew the Brazilian masses, by now mobilized and seething with demands for radical change, would support him in a leftward course. In a January 1963 plebiscite, Brazilians voted five to one to restore full powers to the president so he could deal with the economic chaos. Goulart now veered farther left and called for "Basic Reforms": land redistribution, nationalizing the oil industry, enfranchising illiterates, legalizing the Communist Party, and turning the legislature, which had blocked his schemes, into a "congress composed of peasants, workers, sergeants, and nationalist officers."

Brazilian society—like France and Germany in earlier decades—split into leftist and conservative wings with little middle ground. Conservatives, including most middle-class Brazilians, were horrified at Goulart and his appointment of Marxists to high positions. The United States saw Goulart as another Castro, cut off financial aid, and stepped up covert activity to destabilize the Goulart government. Brazil seemed to be on the verge of revolution. What finally brought Goulart down was his challenge to the armed forces. Goulart publicly supported some mutinous sailors, which Brazil's generals saw as undermining their military discipline and command structure. On March 31, 1964, with scarcely a shot, the generals put an end to Brazil's tumultuous democracy; they ruled for 21 years.

Realizing they could not govern with a heavy hand forever, in the 1970s, the generals began to carry out a *descompressão* (decompression) and then *abertura* (opening up). Gradually

China Lessons

Decompression

China might consider Brazil's transition, one of the most intelligent of the modern era. The generals who ruled Brazil from 1964 to 1985 implemented a controlled *descompressão* (decompression) that gradually allowed freer media and two moderate parties to debate some matters in parliament, provided they did not attack the ruling junta.

The two parties were, to be sure, somewhat artificial, but they served a useful purpose in gradually opening up to a free and democratic multiparty system after the generals. By the time Lula's Workers' Party (PT) won free elections in 2002, it was no longer so radical and did not alarm Brazil's military. Brazil showed that an incremental, measured decompression is the best way to transition to democracy.

and with some backsliding, they permitted media criticism, two tame political parties, and partly free elections. The concept of tame parties is interesting. Dictators generally hate political parties, blaming them for the country's ills (sometimes deservedly). But they find they cannot govern without some connection to the masses, so they often allow a regime-supporting party, as Franco did in Spain with his National Movement. The Brazilian generals were more clever, permitting two tame parties, one a total creature of the regime, the Renovating Alliance (*Aliança Renovadora Nacional*, ARENA), the other a tame opposition, the Brazilian Democratic Movement (*Movimento Democrático Brasileiro*, MDB). Brazilian critics called the MDB the "Party of Yes" and the ARENA the "Party of Yes, Sir!" Nonetheless, these essentially fake parties helped Brazil transition to democracy.

The Key Institutions

10.2 **Explain how Brazil managed to stabilize its tumultuous politics.**

The Struggle to Stabilize

The handover of political power to civilians in Brazil was scary. Much could have gone wrong, leading to a new military takeover. Brazil inherited some defective basic institutions that stymied the best intentions, leaving the country stuck in old quarrels that were not overcome by Brazil's 1988 constitution. The Old Republic echoes in the free-spending powers of Brazil's states and their governors. Vargas's New State echoes in the state-owned industries and employee protections. Free-market Brazilians, such as former President Fernando Henrique Cardoso (1995–2002), try to overcome these roadblocks. Leftist Brazilians, such as President Luis Inácio Lula da Silva (2003–2010), try to retain the Vargas pattern.

Much of the criticism focuses on Brazil's 1988 constitution, the country's seventh since independence. Its aims and general structure are fine, but its details seem designed to trip up needed reforms. Like most modern constitutions, Brazil's includes numerous social and

fiscal
Related to taxes and public spending.

economic rights—a 40-hour work week, medical and retirement plans, minimum wages, a 12 percent interest ceiling on loans, the right to strike, Indian rights, and environmental protection. Such details have no place in a constitution. But the writers of new constitutions, especially in developing lands, are often idealistic and think they can right all wrongs by mandating fixes in the constitution.

The problem with guaranteeing such rights is that they create expectations and demands that cannot possibly be met by a struggling economy, and this deepens popular discontent. Such details also fail to distinguish between a constitution and *statutes*. Even worse, Brazil's constitution allows national referendums—called "popular vetoes" and "popular initiatives"—to voice these discontents. California, with its myriad initiatives on each ballot, trips itself up with hyperdemocratic nonsense, but, in Brazil, the consequences can be more serious. Another potentially disruptive feature of Brazil's constitution: Minimum voting age is now 16.

Brazilian states and municipalities are more independent and less responsible than their U.S. counterparts; they get federal revenue and run up big debts. (U.S. states have to stand nearly on their own **fiscally** and cannot run deficit budgets.) After great effort, Cardoso got a fiscal responsibility law to limit states' spending and debts. Brazilian states and cities are also overstaffed with patronage civil servants who retire young on good pensions, producing massive public sector overspending. Trimming their pensions is a major reform effort.

Congress and the Presidency

The 1988 Brazilian constitution is basically presidential; that is, a powerful president is directly elected. The Congress, fragmented into many weak parties, has difficulty in passing badly needed reforms. Until a 1997 constitutional amendment, Brazilian presidents could be elected for just one five-year term; now they can be elected to two four-year terms but (as in Russia) return to run after an interval out of office. In 1993, a plebiscite decided to keep the presidential system—Brazil's tradition since 1889 and the pattern throughout Latin America—rather than go to a parliamentary system with a prime minister as chief executive.

Brazil's parliament, the National Congress, is bicameral. The lower house, the Chamber of Deputies, has 513 members, each elected for four-year terms based on a type of proportional representation that left it fragmented into 15 parties, some of them dead set against reforms (like Russia's Duma before Putin). The largest party is Lula's PT, but it has only 88 of the seats. Brazil's 26 states (plus the Federal District of Brasilia) have from 8 to 70 deputies, depending on population. This overrepresents the rural, less populous states and is unfair to the big, economic powerhouse states such as São Paulo.

For elections to the Chamber of Deputies, each state is a multimember PR district. Voters can either pick a party or write in the names of their preferred candidates. This system, known technically as "open-list proportional representation," lets candidates of the same party compete against each other, one of the flaws of the old Japanese electoral system. For the Senate, each of Brazil's 26 states, and the federal district, sends three senators to the upper house, whose 81 members are elected for eight-year terms by British-style FPTP. One-third of the Senate is elected in one election, the other two-thirds in the next. For many in both chambers, party matters little; candidates tend to run on personality, contributing to the weakness of Brazil's parties. Reform of this system could reduce the absurd number of parties and build coherent ones.

Democracy

Brazil's 2014 Presidential Elections

Worldwide, voters are fed up with corruption. Also worldwide, state-owned oil companies tend to be corrupt (see Mexico's Pemex). In Brazil's 2014 election, a corruption scandal involving Brazil's Petrobras almost cost the incumbent president re-election.

The first round on October 5, 2014, featured 11 parties, most of them with leftist names. Dilma Rousseff of the Workers' Party (PT), Lula's designated successor, led on the first round with 42 percent. Challenger Aécio Neves of the more-conservative Social Democratic Party (PSDB) got 34 percent. Turnout was 76 percent, boosted by mandatory voting for those 18 to 70, a law not all Brazilians observe.

When a plane crash killed the Socialist (PSB) presidential candidate in August, Marina Silva stepped into that role. A real outsider—a poor, nonwhite Protestant environmentalist from the Amazon—Silva attracted Brazilians looking for a clean alternative to the PT and PSD but won only 21 percent on the first round and was eliminated.

In a nasty campaign, a big Brazilian magazine charged that the PT skims Petrobras income for the party and its politicians. Though the PSDB is hardly clean, Rousseff's lead eroded, and in the runoff October 26 she edged Neves only 52-48 percent.

Policy differences between the PT and PSDB were not as great as their candidates' backgrounds. Rousseff had joined the revolutionary underground and was arrested and tortured. Neves, born into a Minas Gerais political family, had served under the generals. Both vowed to boost Brazil's slowing economy, but Neves wanted further liberalization, especially of the labor market, whereas Rousseff promised to protect workers and the poor.

The 2014 Brazilian election resembled those of most advanced democracies, a contest between center-left and center-right parties, with the middle classes and business tending center-right, the poorer (plus many intellectuals) tending left. Marina Silva's brief surge showed that corruption could push Brazilians to an outsider in 2018.

The military presidents of Brazil were extremely powerful, their civilian successors much less so. Their power to initiate needed reforms is restricted by Congress on one side and state governors on the other. Members of Brazil's Congress, essentially the representatives of their states and their powerful interest groups, generally want to spend more, especially on their clients. They pay little attention to the budget deficits this creates, which in turn lead quickly to inflation. All their incentives push them to spend.

President Cardoso fought inflation by curbing government spending. By background, Lula and Rousseff were inclined to boost government spending, although, in practice, they balanced that with fiscal responsibility. Reforms to curb spending have rough going in the fragmented Congress. Few think of the good of the whole, only of their favored interest group. Some state governors simply ignore Brasilia's decrees to balance their budgets, trim the bureaucracy, and stop borrowing. Brazilian politicians—like those of the French Fourth Republic—are good at blocking but not at building.

A Deceptive Party System

You can't tell a Brazilian party by its name. Of the 11 parties that ran candidates in 2014, four had "workers" and another six had "social" in their name. That would seem to slant Brazilian politics to the left. But some parties with leftish names are center-right or even

Personalities

Lula: "I Changed. Brazil Changed."

On his fourth try, Luiz Inácio Lula da Silva won the 2002 presidential election on the (French-style) second round. (His nickname, "Lula," was so popular that he added it to his given names.) Lula was Brazil's first working-class president; all previous presidents represented Brazil's elites. Several of Lula's cabinet ministers were also raised in poverty. The 2002 election marked a major step in Brazilian democracy; for the first time, poor Brazilians entered politics. Lula won reelection on the second round in 2006.

Born in 1945 in the impoverished Northeast, the seventh of eight children of farm laborers, Lula went hungry and lived in a shack. Lula's father soon left for São Paulo, where he started another family, a common pattern in Brazil. At age 7, Lula rode on a truck to a São Paulo **favela** with his mother, whom he helped support by selling candy and shining shoes. With only four years of schooling—he is the least educated president of Brazil—Lula became a lathe operator. His first wife died in childbirth because they could not afford medical care. Recalling his childhood, Lula wanted to "guarantee each Brazilian one plate of food a day."

An older brother, a Communist (later tortured by the military regime), urged Lula to become a union organizer, and, in 1975, Lula was elected president of a metalworker's union. A charismatic speaker, Lula led a series of strikes that undermined the generals' government. Lula was jailed but freed in 1980 and founded the Workers' Party (PT). Originally strongly leftist, by 2002, the PT had moderated, although Lula could still crank out anticapitalist slogans and wear a red star on his lapel. Lula switched from jeans to coat and tie and said: "I changed. Brazil changed." In office, it became clear how much he had changed.

Lula adopted the free-market policies of his predecessor, the PSDB's Cardoso. "Creating jobs is going to be my obsession," said Lula as he took office. But in addition to fighting inflation and attracting capital, he emphasized help for the poor, including his *Bolsa Família*. Initially, Brazil's currency dropped as investors hung back in fear of socialist experiments, but Lula reassured them by naming respected economists and businesspeople to top jobs. Soon, Brazil boomed, and Lula became widely respected, even among conservatives.

favela
Brazilian shantytown, found in most cities.

inchoate
Not yet organized, incoherent.

conservative. Brazil's parties and their members change quickly. Like Japan's, they are founded, merged, renamed, and split so fast that it is hard to keep up with them. Many Brazilians disdain parties; they see them as corrupt and irresponsible. Elected representatives often switch parties, some more than once, depending on the deals they get from the new party. These are the marks of an **inchoate** party system in which the poorly institutionalized parties are simply personalistic vehicles to get their leaders elected. (Putin created such a party in Russia.)

Parties with clear programs or coherent policies are new and few in Brazil but, if Brazil continues to modernize, may become dominant. The Brazilian pattern has been for leaders to set up a party with a nice name, use it to get elected, and then grab government resources (jobs, contracts, loans, kickbacks) to keep themselves in power and get rich. Fernando Alfonso Collor de Mello, for example, created his own National Reconstruction Party to win the presidency in 1989, but his party soon faded. He did not care, for he was then able to enrich himself and his friends. About to be impeached for corruption, he resigned in 1992 but got elected senator in 2002 on a party with "worker" in its name. He has belonged to a total of six parties.

Settling into a stable, meaningful party system is one of the best things Brazilian democracy could do for itself, and it may be underway. Lula's presidency produced a center-left "Lulista" grouping in Congress that generally supported his legislation. Now, several parties do the same for Dilma Rousseff. On the other side, an informal "center-right" coalition opposes her policies. Brazil's electoral system permits or even encourages numerous small, personalistic parties; changing it could accelerate the tendency to coalesce into a two-bloc system.

With the *abertura* of the 1980s, several socialist or workers' parties sprang up. The main party of the left, the Workers' Party (*Partido dos Trabalhadores*, PT), led by charismatic union organizer Lula da Silva, won the presidency and largest number of congressional seats in 2002 and 2010. (The PT is unrelated to Vargas's old PTB, whose name was taken over by his niece, but it is a small center-right party.) The tame party of the generals, the MDB, turned itself into the Party of the MDB (PMDB), a catchall party renowned for corruption. It became part of the Lulista coalition.

In opposition, Cardoso's Brazilian Social Democratic Party (*Partido da Social Democracia Brasileira*, PSDB) was formed in 1988 from a variety of centrist and reformist deputies. Cardoso won the presidential elections in 1994 and 1998, but his less colorful successor, José Serra, lost to Lula in 2002 and to Dilma Rousseff in 2010. The uncharismatic Aécio Neves lost to her in 2014. What's missing in Brazil is a clear-cut conservative party, or one that admits it is conservative. The closest is perhaps the Democrats, a vague descendant of the generals' ARENA. Brazilian parties like to sound leftist; it wins votes.

The Military as Political Institution

As in much of the Third World, Brazil's political institutions are weak. Unlike Europe, with its well-established parliaments, parties, and bureaucracies, Brazil's political institutions are barely capable of handling the demands of mass politics in an orderly way. When the political system gets stuck or chaotic, the army is often the only institution capable of governing. Direct military rule ended in 1985, but if things get tumultuous again, another military takeover is possible.

The Brazilian military has intervened in politics many times: at the birth and through the life of the Old Republic, at first in support of Vargas and then against him; at the establishment of reasonably democratic regimes at the end of the two Vargas periods; and in 1964. Prior to 1964, however, the Brazilian military never tried to stay in power. They saw themselves the way Dom Pedro II had seen his role—that of a "moderating power" to restrain politicians from excesses. Step in when need be, set things right, then step out was the Brazilian military pattern.

By 1964, both the Brazilian military attitude and the nation's situation had changed. Brazilian officers, partly thanks to U.S. guidance, had redefined their mission from defending Brazil against external enemies to guarding it against internal threats, especially communism. In the Superior War College, the ESG (see box below), top officers studied politics, economics, psychology, and counterinsurgency.

Thus higher Brazilian military officers, technically highly trained and newly motivated toward a more active role in their country's politics, were ready to upset a long-held (especially by Americans) view that truly professional military officers do not engage in coups. Looking around, the Brazilian officers found—almost like a case study—a Brazil that was sliding

Comparison

Brazil's School for Praetorians

A school facing a luxurious Rio beach does not seem a likely spot for a powerful political institution, but, in Brazil, virtually the entire ruling class of the military period (1964–1985) emerged from the Superior War College (*Escola Superior de Guerra*, ESG). Founded in 1949 on the model of the U.S. National War College (which trains midcareer officers for higher command), by the 1960s, the ESG had shifted its emphasis from external to internal security. Still influenced by the old Positivism—which, in fact, had been spread in the nineteenth century through Brazil's military academy—ESG students came to the conclusion that only Brazil's rapid economic development would save it from chaos and communism.

The ESG trained not only the best colonels but top civilians as well. Government administrators, private industrialists, and leading professional people tended to outnumber ESG's military students. The ESG drew its 90 students a year from key areas of the political and economic power structure: banking, mass communications, education, and industry. ESG's graduates returned to their branches imbued with the authoritarian developmentalist doctrines they learned at the school. In civilian-ruled Brazil, ESG graduates are not so influential, although many are still in high positions.

The ESG actually resembles a French *grande école*, such as the Polytechnique or ENA, which gives French policy making cohesion and continuity. "We don't actually make government policy," said a senior Brazilian officer on the ESG staff. "The great contribution of the school has been to establish an elite of people who can think in the same language and who have learned the team approach to planning here." The French could not have said it better. The United States has no equivalent to the ESG. Should it?

rapidly to the left. The Brazilian army chose to intervene, and it did so precisely because it was professionally trained to prevent revolution. This time, the officers were determined to stay in power, block the return of divisive politics, and modernize their potentially rich country in an organized, rational manner.

For two decades, Brazil was governed by a succession of generals, each chosen by a small group of generals. The Brazilian military did not rule the country directly, as if it were an army camp. Rather, they structured the political system so that only a military officer or a civilian who cooperated with the military could attain executive office. Once named president, a Brazilian general usually retired from active service and seldom wore his uniform.

Brazil's military regime was not just military, and that may be why it lasted so long. The Brazilian military had close ties to civilian bankers, educators, industrialists, and governmental administrators, many of whom trained together in the Superior War College in Rio. The weakness of most military regimes is their isolation and lack of contact with civilian elites. Unable to run the complexities of economy, society, and diplomacy without skilled civilians, military regimes often blunder badly and then decide to give up power and responsibility.

Brazil's generals avoided this kind of isolation by partially integrating themselves with conservative civilian elites who held views and values close to the military's. Brazil's "military" regime was actually a civilian-military network of authoritarian developmentalists who controlled most of Brazil's economic, political, and military structures. In public, the government looked civilian, and most executive positions were occupied by civilian technocrats.

Can an army be a political institution? Historically, the evidence is against the military holding power permanently. The Myanmar (formerly Burma) army set a record, (mis)ruling from 1962 to 2011. Armies are clumsy tools to govern with. After some years, military regimes tend to return power to civilians, or turn into civilian regimes themselves, or get overthrown in a new military coup. The first is what happened in Brazil in the early 1980s.

A Lack of Institutions

The underlying reason that Brazil got its military governments was the lack of sturdy institutions that could handle the influx of newly mobilized sectors of the population and their demands. In the absence of firm, well-established parties and parliaments, demagogic populists aroused both the masses and the military. The military won, and, as we shall see, the masses lost. The trouble was that the Brazilian military did not found durable institutions either.

One of the principal functions of political institutions is winning and channeling mass loyalty to the system. The chief mechanism for doing this is political parties. Without loyalty, mere technical arrangements, even if they work well in promoting economic growth, become more and more isolated from the population they rule. Franco's Spain supervised an economic boom, but there was little positive feeling among Spaniards for the Franco institutions. After his death in 1975, those institutions were dismantled with scarcely a protest.

By stunting the growth of political institutions, the Brazilian military did great harm to the country. The world was delighted to see Brazil escape from its cycle of weak civilian institutions overthrown by clumsy military regimes, which in turn gave way to weak civilian administrations again. Could there be another coup? In previous decades, one heard muttering from top officers, but Brazil's economic growth has given it a per capita GDP of $12,000 and moved it

Personalities

Dilma Rousseff, Brazil's First Woman President

Dilma Rousseff is not Latin America's first woman president—Argentina and Chile each had one earlier— but it is still highly unusual. She is the daughter of a Bulgarian Communist who settled and married in Brazil before World War II. Dilma was born in 1947 into a comfortable household but turned to far-left politics in high school during a time of Brazilian radicalism, which the military coup ended in 1964.

Going underground, Dilma worked with armed revolutionary groups and was arrested and tortured (one of thousands) in 1970 but released at the end of 1972. Twice married, both times to leftists, she gave birth to her only child in 1976 and now has a grandson. She earned a degree in economics in 1977 and worked in local administration. In a parallel with Lula,

her ideology evolved from Marxist to moderate and pragmatic. She identifies herself as Catholic and is not against market economics. A member of Lula's PT, she became his energy minister and then chief of staff.

Winning the presidency in late 2010 on the second round, Rousseff basically continued Lula's policies in coalition with the PMBD. A very bright detail person but not a grandstander, she strove to keep the economy growing while cleaning up corruption. Her first year in office, she fired seven of her ministers for corruption, and Brazilians loved it. In 2012, when unemployment dropped below 6 percent, Rousseff's approval topped 70 percent, a record high. But then a major economic slump set in, making her fight for reelection in 2014.

into the ranks of the middle-income countries, which tend to be stable democracies. Lula's successful presidency and the peaceful election of Rousseff indicate Brazil has modernized out of praetorianism.

Brazilian Political Culture

10.3 Explain why Latin Americans are cautious about democracy.

The Easygoing Image

Both Brazilians and resident foreigners describe Brazilians as easygoing people, seldom angry or violent, largely indifferent to politics, and unlikely to rise in revolt. The image of laid-back Brazilians may have been overdone; an economy cannot expand at several percentage points a year without people working hard. Brazilians are emotional; they laugh, joke, and embrace in public. They love children—possibly, some suggest, because the infant mortality rate is high—and tend to spoil their offspring, especially the boys. This creates a male-centered society in which men, but not women, may indulge themselves.

Many of the Portuguese who settled Brazil either were minor noblemen or pretended they were. They brought with them antiwork attitudes and looked down on entrepreneurial activities. Many of the more vigorous business and government people have been of non-Portuguese origin (German, Italian, Japanese, and East European). Avoidance of work is common throughout the middle classes in Latin America (and in much of the Middle East); educated people would rather become bureaucrats than entrepreneurs. Hustle and vigor for a long time were weak in Latin American capitalism (no longer the case), a point sometimes offered as an explanation of both tardy growth and penetration by U.S. capital. If local capital won't do it, American capital will.

Brazilian Racism

Easygoing Brazilian attitudes on race help keep society calm and stable. Half of Brazilians define themselves as black or brown. Brazil has the largest African-descended population outside of Africa. Precise classification is complex and difficult, however, because of the spectrum of skin colors and the Latin American tendency to let culture decide race. Throughout the continent, a person with the right education, manners, and money is considered "European" with little regard to skin color. Brazilians have more than 300 words to distinguish racial combinations. In law and in public, no Brazilians are racists. Walking down the street, one Brazilian feels as good as another.

But their society is structured along racial lines, although few white Brazilians admit it. Life chances are related to skin color. While there are plenty of poor white Brazilians, their odds of becoming middle class, healthy, and educated are greater than those of black Brazilians. Recent economic growth has boosted incomes and living standards of most Brazilians, but black and brown Brazilians, on average, still earn less than half as much as whites. The Brazilian economic and political elite are white, even ex-radicals such as Lula and Rousseff. Brazil's Congress is a sea of white faces. The standard explanation is that black Brazilians lack the education to achieve higher status. One might ask: Why, after many generations, do they still lack the education?

Some blacks move upward, but many are blocked by unstated preferences to hire whites. A famous handful succeed in entertainment and sports. The world's greatest (and highest-paid) soccer star, Pelé, was black. Even he encountered discrimination early in his career and, as Cardoso's minister of sports, was the only black in an all-white cabinet. Intermarriage is perfectly legal, but whites frown upon it. Brazil's mass media rarely discuss problems of race. Brazil, by minimizing race into a nonissue, has been more clever than the United States, where barely covert racism still influences politics. Increasingly, Brazil's blacks are not fooled by invisible barriers and demand U.S.-style affirmative action programs, which the 2010 Racial Equality Statute started in university admissions. As in the United States, Brazil's left favors greater racial equality.

Brazil's Poor: Passive or Explosive?

Do poor people turn naturally to social revolution, or are they too busy staying alive to bother with political questions? Brazil was a test of some of the long-standing debates about why people revolt. The answers depend not just on people being poor—most Brazilians through history have been poor—but on the context in which poor (and not-so-poor) people find themselves.

In the dry, overpopulated Northeast, some starve. Many rural poor, hoping to improve their condition, flood into the favelas, where some do find work while others eke out a precarious living from peddling or crime. But rich Brazilians—a rapidly increasing class—live sumptuously. For most of the military era, there was little open class resentment. First and most important, the Brazilian underclass was deprived of its leadership and organizational alternatives. The radical parties and leaders of the Goulart period were, respectively, outlawed and exiled or had their political rights annulled, *cassado* in Portuguese. Anyone caught trying to form a radical opposition got into bad trouble—"disappeared" to torture or death.

The strong economic growth of the 1970s gave people hope and thus dampened protests, but the economic downturns in the 1980s, 1990s, and 2010s dimmed hope. In response, angry crowds looted supermarkets, set cars ablaze, and attacked police. Brazil's riots sent chilling warning signs to other countries. People who have just begun to taste the good life turn bitter when it is yanked away from them. In the last century, about 45 percent of Brazilians were below the (rather low) poverty line, and 30 percent lived in absolute poverty (under $1.25 a day). Brazil had practically no unemployment compensation, welfare benefits, or food stamps. When Brazilians have no money for food, they starve or steal. Traditionally, Brazilians shrugged off their impoverished class as a normal thing that could not be helped. With the prospect of social breakdown and violence, however, some took notice and supported workable welfare measures.

An echo of this breakdown appeared with the big-city riots of 2013 and 2014, triggered by a nine-cent increase in São Paulo bus fares that quickly spread nationwide when police brutally attacked protestors. The underlying cause was a sharp economic downturn on top of European-level taxes (36 percent of GDP) but lousy public services, especially healthcare and education. Nearly half of Brazilians name lack of medical care as their biggest problem. Many also resented rising prices, inequality, corruption, and spending billions on soccer stadiums for the 2014 World Cup, a show-off project that did little for most Brazilians. The riots demonstrated how leaders disconnect from mass needs until violence gets their attention.

The arousal of Brazil's poor from passive to active came at the time Brazil was democratizing and forming parties, some of them with radical leadership. The explosive potential continues with the feeling among the large lower-middle class—known in Brazil as *Classe C*, a big step up from *Classes D* and *E*—that they are left behind as great wealth concentrates at the top. Classe C people, now half of Brazilians, are more likely to revolt than those at the bottom. People of limited means, eager to improve their tenuous positions, become sparkplugs for mass unrest. Some analysts see the simultaneous outpourings of mass discontent in Brazil, Turkey, Egypt, and elsewhere as uprisings of middle classes angered by inequality and corruption.

Brazil seems to be making it through the difficulties of democratization. Now, with the economy slowing, the unevenness of rewards may destabilize politics. People, whether poor or middle class, are not automatically passive or active but can become either, depending on the situation. In a severe economic downturn, Brazilian radicals could again attempt to mobilize mass discontent, and the military might feel forced to intervene again.

Uneven Democratic Attitudes

Brazil's economic stabilization builds democratic attitudes; economic downturns worsen them. Roughly half of Brazilians, in relatively prosperous years, tell pollsters that democracy is the best form of government, but this falls to roughly a third in bad times. The riots of 2013 and 2014, it should be noted, came during a sharp falloff in economic growth.

Over the long run, however, declining percentages say an authoritarian government can sometimes be preferable. Only a few percent of Brazilians say they could trust most people,

Geography

Shantytowns

Most developing countries have shantytowns, vast tracts of squatter housing that surround and interpenetrate the cities, called *barrios coloniales* in Spanish (one of many terms) and *favelas* in Portuguese. Starting as just shacks, over time, some turn into modest homes. Few occupants own the land under their dwellings, so they have no legal claim to them and cannot use them as collateral for loans. Peruvian economist Hernando de Soto claims that just giving shanty owners legal title would yield loans and rapid economic growth.

Brazil's poor are sometimes called *marginals*. Many of them huddle in favelas. Some *favelados* hold regular jobs, others sell pop on the beach, and some steal. Crime bosses hold sway in the favelas. Brazil's crime rates are astronomical. Heavily armed police periodically "pacify" favela drug gangs, with only partial success. Rio's murder rate declined, but drug lords still hold sway, sometimes with police protection. There is no place for the marginals to go, and few care about them.

Politically, they are on the margin, too. Unorganized and too busy just trying to get food, favelados can riot when faced with starvation. Brazilian sociologists point out that, however wretched life seems in the favelas, it is worse in the countryside. Moving to a favela for many is a step up, for there they have access to better education and health services and may even find a job. And, thanks to the low rent and cheap labor, small businesses and a new middle class grow in the favelas.

the lowest of Latin America. The "trust" question is important, for without widespread trust, you cannot build democracy or an economy. Especially weak is confidence in anything political, such as the president, Congress, or parties, feelings widespread in Latin America. Only the church enjoys great confidence.

personalismo
Politics by strong, showoff personalities.

machismo
Strutting, exaggerated masculinity.

Some Brazilians, especially the middle class and educated, are convinced democrats. Others, especially poorer and working-class people, are interested in little besides jobs and are willing to support whatever will put food on the table, democratic or not. This is typical of the Third World—and even much of the First. Commitment to democratic values is stronger among those higher up on the socioeconomic ladder, people who do not have to worry about eating. The poor often prefer an authoritarian populist.

In many countries—including the United States—commitment to democratic values falls off as one moves down the socioeconomic ladder. The irony here is that democracy—a system that is supposed to be based on the broad masses of people—receives its strongest support from better-off, educated people. This does not mean that democracy is impossible in Brazil—or elsewhere in the developing world—but it takes time and effort. Part of the impulse for Brazil's democratization came from the educated upper-middle class, a group that was relatively small but strategically positioned to make its voice heard. Brazil makes us aware that democracy—or indeed any kind of political system—is usually the work of the few mobilizing the many.

Much of Latin America abandoned statism and socialism. Free markets, international trade, and foreign investment no longer looked bad; they started taking on positive connotations. The new attitude spread unevenly in Latin America, with uneven results. The recent economic downturn briefly revitalized dependency theory (see below) this time focused on **globalization**. Fortunately, Lula left Brazil's burgeoning market economy largely alone, and it boomed, based heavily on exports of food and raw materials to other developing lands, especially to China. When China's demand for raw materials slowed, however, much of the developing world suffered as exports fell.

Political Culture

Personalismo and Machismo

Latin American politicians, including Brazilians, frequently rely on **personalismo** in politics rather than on clear thinking, party programs, or patient organizing. Most Latin Americans like to be perceived as having a strong personality, the men especially as *macho*, leading to **machismo**. Latin American leaders, civilian or military, traditionally combine personalismo and machismo in varying degrees. They figure it is the only way to gain mass respect.

The Brazilian generals, given the way in which they were selected for power, tended to downplay these qualities. With the return of civilian politics, however, personalismo and machismo reappeared in Brazilian politics. Both Collor de Mello and Lula exuded personalismo. A sign of Brazilians' maturity was the election of Dilma Rousseff, Brazil's first woman president, who won largely on being Lula's successor, not on personality.

dependency theory
Radical theory that rich countries exploit and impoverish poor countries.

Dependency Theory

During the Cold War, part of Latin American political culture was the fashionable leftist view that the region's poverty was the result of exploitation by wicked capitalists, especially by *norteamericanos*. After World War II, radicals worked this up into what they called **dependency theory**, a theory that the Third World is economically dependent on the capital, products, and policies of the First World, especially the United States. (One book portrayed a U.S. "shark" feeding on Latin American "sardines.")

Only by getting out from under the control of U.S. corporations—which dictated what Latin American lands would produce (bananas and coffee) and what they would consume (Chevrolets and Coca-Cola)—would Latin America eliminate poverty. Accordingly, leftists praise radical regimes such as Cuba, Nicaragua, and, currently, Venezuela because they broke their dependency on the Yankees and instituted independent economic development aimed at benefitting their own peoples (that often did not).

Dependency theory contains several disputes. It is a type of Marxist theory, but some orthodox Marxists dislike it. Marx saw class conflict *within* a country as the key to its economic and political development. Many Latin American critics blame their continent's poverty on its "predatory class structure," in which a few rich families own everything and there is not much of an industrial proletariat. Latin America's problem, in their view, is that it is still saddled with a feudal social structure. Marx had little to say about relations among countries. Lenin made that leap with his claim that the imperialist countries have redone the globe to suit themselves by exploiting colonies. Dependency theory partakes more of Lenin than of Marx. Dependency theorists name Vargas of Brazil, Cárdenas of Mexico, and Chávez of Venezuela as heroes who tried to break *dependencia*.

By the 1990s, many dependency theorists came to doubt the theory. Brazilian President Fernando Henrique Cardoso (1995–2002), for example, had been a radical sociologist and promoter of dependency theory, but, by the 1980s, he had abandoned it. A famous Latin American saying: "If you are not a Communist when you're 20, you have no heart. If you're still a Communist when you're 40, you have no head." Aging wises you up.

The demise of Communist regimes in East Europe and the Soviet Union—and the lingering death of Cuban socialism—made many ask if "socialism" really worked. Peruvian economist Hernando de Soto pointed out that the most effective and dynamic sector of Latin economies is the black market. Why? Every other sector is choked into stagnation by government controls. The solution: Get rid of the controls and go to a free market. The economic success of markets in several Latin American countries—with Brazil in the lead—made many appreciate market systems and foreign trade.

Patterns of Interaction

10.4 Describe Brazil's mobilization-demobilization cycle.

An Elite Game

Politics in Brazil has historically been largely a game for elites: big landowners, bankers and industrialists, and top bureaucrats and military people. Many did not welcome mass participation in politics. The stakes of the game are political power, patronage jobs, and the control of funds that come with them. The rules of the game are that none of the players gets seriously hurt or threatened and that nobody mobilizes the Brazilian masses in an angry way, for that would destroy the game's fragile balance and hurt them all.

Accordingly, Vargas, himself a wealthy rancher, was an acceptable player when he supported coffee prices for the growers, but when he started to mobilize poor Brazilians, he had to be ousted. Kubitschek was a good player who looked after his elite friends and deflected potential discontent with his grandiose plans to open Brazil's interior. Goulart, also a wealthy rancher, was a very bad player: He threatened all the elites and mobilized the masses at a furious rate. The PT's Lula, an antielite labor union radical, mobilized Brazil's working class in a way that frightened many of Brazil's elites. He was such a pragmatic moderate in office, though, that they calmed down and accepted him. Besides, many were becoming very rich.

Until recently, Brazil's political history has been the same elite game: Dom Pedro with his fazendeiro friends, the Old Republic with its Paulista-Mineiro alternation, and the military technocracy with its industrial and bureaucratic clientele. Since Vargas, however, the political mobilization of the masses has been a recurring threat to the game. Periodically, a populist who did not like the elite's fixed rules was tempted to reach out to Brazil's masses, both to secure his own power and to help the downtrodden. Seeing the threat, Brazil's elites, through the military, remove it and try to demobilize the masses. Mobilization and demobilization can be seen as a cycle.

The Mobilization-Demobilization Cycle

Scholars of the developing countries in general and Brazil in particular often focus on "political mobilization." Mobilization means the masses waking up, becoming aware, and, often, becoming angry. Prior to the beginning of mass political mobilization in a country, few participate in politics, and decisions are made by traditional elites, such as Brazil's big landowners and political bosses. This has been termed *whig democracy*, and it is standard in the opening decades of democratic development, as in the pre-Jackson United States. Democracies typically start with participation limited to the better off; then some social stimulus, such as economic growth, brings new sectors of the population (in Brazil, the urban working class) to political awareness; they are "mobilized" and start participating in politics with new demands. The Brazilian electorate shot up from fewer than a quarter-million voters before 1930 to 14 million in the early 1960s.

The problem with Brazil and other developing countries is that weak institutions are not able to handle the influx of new participants and their demands. Well-organized, strong political parties can channel, moderate, and calm mass demands in a constructive way. But Brazilian parties were little more than personalistic vehicles to get their chiefs into power. The chiefs, such as Vargas and Goulart, used their parties in a demagogic way to get support from the newly mobilized and politically unsophisticated masses by promising them quick economic improvement. Society's more conservative elements—the better off, who often have close ties to the military—view this process with horror. The military sees it as "chaos" and may end it by a military coup, the story of many Latin American countries. Thus mobilization, which could be the start of democratization, can lead to authoritarian takeovers. (Any resemblance to Egypt?)

The 1964 military takeover in Brazil ended one phase of what might be termed a mobilization-demobilization cycle (as did Chile's military coup in 1973). The generals had grown to hate civilian politics, especially political parties and their demagogic leaders. We can, to

disinflation
Bringing down the rate of inflation (not the same as *deflation*, an overall decline in prices).

a degree, understand their hatred. As guardians of Brazil's unity and security, they witnessed their beloved republic falling into the hands of irresponsible crowd-pleasers.

Typically, the military tries the only solution they know: demobilization and **disinflation**. Blaming disruptive political activity, they ban most parties, handpick political leaders, and permit only rigged elections. Initially, things do calm down. Some people are thankful that the army has stepped in to put an end to extremist politics and empty promises. Mass rallies, loud demands, and radical leaders disappear—the latter sometimes physically.

But the problems are not solved. The demands—although no longer whipped up by politicians—are still present and growing. As the economy grows, more people come to live in cities, and the pent-up demands for change increase. To repress such demands, the regime turns to the police-state brutality of arbitrary arrests and torture. Once people are awakened or mobilized, they can never be fully demobilized, even by massive doses of coercion. The trick is to channel their needs and demands along moderate, constructive paths. Lula did this brilliantly.

Much of Brazilian politics, from the arrival of Vargas in 1930 to Lula's election in 2002, can be summarized in the "mobilization-demobilization cycle" shown below. The cycle was probably unavoidable, a logical outgrowth of mobilization and its tendency to feed demagoguery. Some developing lands are still caught up in this cycle, but Brazil seems to have modernized out of it (as has Chile). China—by rapidly growing the economy while drastically holding down political participation—is a great experiment to see if this cycle can be avoided. What Brazil can teach China is how to execute a "decompression" over many years in which the regime gradually relaxes controls, frees the media, stops arresting dissidents, and finally holds reasonably free elections. If Brazil can do it, so can China.

mobilization → demagoguery → military → demobilization → decompression → democracy
(inflation) (disinflation)

The Inflation Connection

Inflation is a political problem the world over, especially in Latin America, where regimes may fall over the rate of inflation. Inflation may also be seen as part of the mobilization-demobilization cycle. In Brazil, inflation in currency corresponds to the inflation in promises made by politicians seeking mass support. Current economic problems threaten to unleash Brazilian inflation again.

Controlling inflation is an unhappy task. By restricting credit and cutting the amount of money being printed, an austerity policy can lower the inflation rate, but at a cost of high unemployment, slow economic growth, and disappointed hopes. Latin American inflation cutters are often conservative authoritarians, sometimes military officers, who can pursue disinflation without regard to mass desires. As in much of Latin America, the Brazilian military in effect said to Brazilians: "We don't care how much it hurts. The sooner inflation ends, the better we'll all be. Take the bitter medicine now before inflation wrecks the entire economy." When Cardoso made Brazilians swallow this bitter medicine just after his reelection in late 1998, his popularity fell.

Encouraging inflation, on the other hand, is easy; regimes can do it in a fit of absentmindedness. Politicians, wanting to make everybody happy, let the national mint's printing presses run to finance government projects. This is the way Kubitschek built Brasilia. Inflation tends to feed on itself and get out of hand, and soon, people cannot make ends meet. Conservative businesspeople and bankers become convinced that the politicians have gone insane. The military, whose fixed salaries are eroded by the galloping inflation, seethes in jealous rage and starts planning a coup to save both the republic and its own incomes.

real
(plural, **reís**; symbol, R$) Brazil's currency, worth about 45 U.S. cents.

IMF
International Monetary Fund, grants loans to promote economic stability.

When the military does take power, its disinflationary measures correspond to the political demobilization they also try to enforce. Under the military, this consisted of controls on wages but not on prices, with the result that lower-class Brazilians had to work like dogs to keep up with food prices while some speculators enjoyed an economic boom. Civilian regimes may try to do the opposite, with equally bad results.

Although the Brazilian generals had excellent economic planners, they did not end inflation, which by 1984 reached 223 percent, double what it was in 1964 when the military seized power. This extremely embarrassing fact undermined regime support among the businesspeople and bankers who had welcomed the 1964 takeover. One reason Brazil turned democratic was that the military proved as inept as civilians in controlling inflation.

Until recently, Brazil suffered seemingly incurable inflation, sometimes at more than 50 percent a month. At times, the government froze wages and prices and took other drastic steps. "Prices, starting tomorrow, are halted," said the economy minister in 1991. But prices

Democracy

The Economy Connection

Lula da Silva, Brazil's first leftist-populist president since 1964, made many worry about Brazil's stability. Some feared that Lula would repudiate Brazil's huge foreign debts and choke off economic growth with grandiose welfare schemes. He didn't.

Outgoing President Cardoso of the center-right Social Democratic party had done a good job, but Brazil, in 2002, was in recession, and average Brazilians had grown poorer as unemployment climbed. As in much of the world, candidates win or lose based on the economy. In 1994, as finance minister, Cardoso had authored the "Real Plan" that introduced a new currency, the **real** (royal), and drastically reduced Brazil's runaway inflation. (One *real* was then worth 2.75×10^{15} of the *cruzeiros* of 30 years earlier. When you have to use astronomical notation, you know you have hyperinflation.) Brazil has had

ten currencies since its colonial days, starting with the Portuguese real. The typical cycle was to let the currency inflate until it was worthless, then replace it with a new currency, which again inflated until it was worthless.... Cardoso stopped the madness of weakening currency and beat Lula twice, in 1994 and 1998, but constitutionally could not run a third time. His party's candidate in 2002, José Serra, was lackluster and tarred with corruption.

Lula, on the other hand, was a charismatic populist with socialist ideas to help the poor and working class at the expense of the rich and foreign companies, ideas that resonated well during the economic downturn. But Lula reassured the **IMF** and nervous investors that he would not default on Brazil's massive loans, for, without foreign investment, Brazil couldn't deliver on his promises.

Democracy

The Demagoguery Tendency

Demagogue has the same root as *democrat*—*demos*, the people—but demagogues use issues in a manipulative and self-serving way to erase democracy. The populist demagogue, or "rabble rouser," whips up poor or frightened masses with promises of jobs, welfare, or law and order, and, once in office, becomes dictatorial.

Every society has demagogues—Louisiana's Huey Long or France's Le Pen—but they attract crowds chiefly in times of stress, such as high unemployment, growing crime, or national humiliation. Then, their arguments—often rants—start gaining audiences. Brazil went through a series of demagogues, including Vargas and Goulart. Some thought Lula had all the makings of a demagogue, but he was quite levelheaded and pragmatic.

Demagoguery is especially strong in poor countries that are only recently democratic, such as much of the developing areas today. Desperate people confuse democracy with prosperity, and the demagogue helps in this confusion: "The people cry out for bread, and I shall give them bread!" When the country reaches middle-income levels and has a large, educated middle class, demagoguery fades; few people swallow the deceptive promises. The rapid growth of the middle class in most of Latin America firmed up its democratic governance.

Latin America has been fertile ground for demagoguery, now in Venezuela, where Hugo Chávez—a former paratroop officer who earlier attempted a coup—was elected president and reelected with the line that Venezuela has lots of oil but has been robbed by the United States (see the discussion of dependency theory), rich Venezuelans, and corrupt officials. Most Venezuelans are below the poverty line. Chávez's "Bolivarian" revolution took over industry and redistributed wealth to try to end poverty. But Venezuela was not that rich, and, under Chávez, its economy declined, making him angrier and more extreme. Increasingly, Venezuela resembled Cuba.

disobeyed. The effort to control wages and prices was the fifth in five years; none worked. Finally, in 1994, Cardoso's Real Plan worked.

For decades, Brazil's problem was an overlarge state sector that had to be propped up with big subsidies, which were provided by simply printing more money. In the early 1990s, Brazil's Central Bank increased the nation's money supply severalfold each year, producing a hyperinflation of several *thousand* percent a year. To turn off the printing presses, though, would have meant shutting down a large part of the Brazilian economy, resulting in even more unemployment. Unions warned they would not stand for it. Wage-and-price freezes, experience from many countries shows, simply do not work for more than a few months. They are instituted in desperation when the real cures would hurt too many politically influential groups.

The Corruption Connection

One of the characteristics of developing countries is their massive corruption. Throughout Latin America, officials expect *la mordida* (the bite) for contracts, licenses, and other favors. Some argue that corruption is part of Latin American political culture. Perhaps, but it grows at the interface of the public and private sectors. Latin America, with its large state sectors and regulated economies, is thus especially fertile ground for corruption. The solution? Cut the state sector back. Where this was done, in Chile, corruption also diminished.

The interesting thing about Brazil (and many other countries) is that the public is increasingly fed up with corruption, especially in high places. Presidents and prime ministers are now routinely hounded from office when citizens—thanks to improved education and new media— come to understand how corrupt their rulers are. What they got away with in years past, they no longer can. Mass discontent over corruption boils up in Russia, China, India, Mexico, Brazil, Nigeria, Iran, and other countries. In Tunisia, Egypt, and Ukraine, it led to revolution.

constructive bankruptcy
Economic theory that weak firms should fold to make way for new enterprises.

This new public concern is a very good sign, an indication of growing political maturity. Stealing from the starving is no longer acceptable. Brazilian politicians have looted their country long enough; let them now face angry citizens. The danger here is that if Brazilians start to think that democracy equals corruption, the way is open for a coup. Brazil's top general warned Congress to clean up its act: "Beware the anger of the legions," the exact words once used by Rome's Praetorian Guard. In 2010, Brazil's Congress passed legislation disqualifying corrupt politicians from office for eight years. At that time, more than a hundred deputies faced charges of stealing public money but were protected by congressional immunity. Brazil is getting cleaner.

Resurgent Interest Groups

For most of the life of the military regime, the Brazilian government continued the corporatist model that Vargas had borrowed from Italy and Portugal. Under corporatism, interest groups are controlled or coordinated by the government. With the *abertura* of the 1980s, Brazil's interest groups emerged with a life of their own once again.

After the 1964 takeover, the military abolished the big union that Goulart had fostered and placed all labor unions under direct government control. Particularly drastic was the control of rural unions, whose impoverished and militant farmworkers threatened the property of the conservative landowning allies of the military government. Union leaders were henceforth handpicked to make sure they would cooperate with the new order and not lead workers in excessive wage demands or strikes.

While this arrangement held down wages, prices rose until workers could stand it no longer. New unions and leaders outside government control emerged as a major force. The largest and most radical Brazilian union, the United Confederation of Workers (CUT), is tied to the PT of Lula and Rousseff. CUT is especially strong in São Paulo and has struck against many big industries there. The military does not like CUT. The tamer General Confederation of Workers (CGT) is tied to the large but corrupt PMBD.

Many businesspeople had welcomed the 1964 coup only to find that the military technocrats would sometimes ride roughshod over their interests in the name of economic rationality. The theory of **constructive bankruptcy** let weak Brazilian firms go under rather than subsidize them with tariff protection against foreign competition. Now businesses generally want sound money and an end to government economic controls and restrictions. Other groups, such as students and farmers, also voice their discontent. Opposition to the rule of the generals developed across a broad front of conservative and radical Brazilians. The most interesting group, however, was the Catholic Church, a force to be reckoned with in the world's largest Catholic country.

Second Vatican Council
Series of meetings that modernized the Roman Catholic Church and turned it to problems of poverty; also called Vatican II.

The Church as Opposition

The Roman Catholic Church was the only large Brazilian group that maintained its autonomy and was in a position to criticize the military regime. Typically, in Catholic countries, the church has been conservative and has favored conservative regimes. In France, Spain, and Italy, the long fight between clericalism and anticlericalism split society into two camps.

Brazil never had this kind of split. With the 1891 republican constitution, modeled after the U.S. constitution, the Brazilian church consented to disestablishment—that is, to losing its special privileges as church and state were separated. Brazil settled this important and divisive issue quickly and early, leaving the church as an independent force.

Still, in social and economic outlook, the Brazilian Catholic Church was pretty conservative, urging the faithful to save their souls rather than to reform and improve society. With the **Second Vatican Council** of 1962–1965, this conservative attitude changed, and many church people, especially younger ones, adopted the "theology of liberation," which put the church on the side of the poor and oppressed. In some Latin American countries, young priests actually became guerrilla fighters trying to overthrow what they regarded as wicked and reactionary regimes.

In the late 1960s, Brazilian church leaders denounced the regime for "fascist doctrines" and for arresting and torturing priests and nuns accused of harboring political fugitives. During the 1970s, the Brazilian church developed a strong stand for human rights and against Brazil's terrible poverty. Strikers often held meetings and sought refuge from police clubs in churches. As a whole, the Brazilian Catholic Church was the most activist in Latin America, to the chagrin of the Vatican, which ordered priests out of direct political actions.

In 1980, John Paul II visited Brazil and was visibly moved by what he saw in the favelas. In a Rio slum, he called to Brazil's rich: "Look around a bit. Does it not wound your heart? Do you not feel remorse of conscience because of your riches and abundance?" In 2013, Pope Francis, the first Latin American pope, visited Brazil and, amid a massive welcome, echoed this sentiment. In his native Argentina, Francis had been especially active in helping the poor. But both popes stopped short of endorsing active church involvement in politics. Church people should provide charity and guide spiritually but not politically. In Brazil, this middle road is hard to tread because concern for the poor tends to radicalize people.

Under the democratic regime, the Brazilian church continued to support the poor. Some Brazilian church people did not hear the Vatican's order to steer clear of radical politics. They argued that, to save the souls of the poor, the church must also help feed them, something Pope Francis agreed with. Many Catholics supported Lula. In the poverty-stricken Northeast, priests keep reminding the government of its land reform program while they support the militant *Movimento Sem Terra* (Movement of Those Without Land). Landlords charge that priests and nuns encourage the poor to illegally occupy private farms. Some priests receive death threats. Brazil, however, is becoming less Catholic; one Brazilian in five has turned to evangelical Protestantism, a trend throughout Latin America that will likely alter the political culture.

What Brazilians Quarrel About

10.5 **Evaluate the Brazilian economic miracle.**

The Political Economy of Brazil

Brazil enjoyed the best economic growth of its history in the first decade of the twenty-first century—rising from 5 percent a year to 7.5 percent—to become the world's eighth-largest economy. In line with Latin America's rapidly expanding middle class in this decade, more than 30 million Brazilians exited poverty. During the second decade, however, inflation climbed and growth slumped, partly because China was no longer buying so many raw materials.

Especially important was the opening up of vast tracts of the Amazon rainforest to mechanized, scientific farming, supported by agricultural research institutes' efforts to match seeds to soils. Brazil turned into one of the world's biggest food exporters, especially strong in soybeans, first planted by Japanese immigrants. Now China buys six million tons of soybeans a year from Brazil. China is now Brazil's biggest trading partner, ahead of the United States. A major new undersea oil field off Brazil's coast promises to become one of the world's biggest.

Thanks to economic growth, unemployment fell to its lowest recorded levels. Pay climbed rapidly as workers with skills could shop around for jobs. In some sectors, the minimum wage became irrelevant. Incomes of black Brazilians rose some 40 percent in a decade. Instead of depending on foreign capital, Brazil now raises much of its own and holds billions in U.S. bonds.

There were some problems. Many Brazilian workers lack the reading and math skills to take better jobs, a factor limiting Brazil's growth. Consumers went on a buying spree, and banks lent too freely, resulting in inflation. Foreign investors, eager to get in on Brazil's economic growth, bid up the value of the real until it became much too strong and hurt Brazilian exports. Brazil, like several other countries, tried to hold down the value of its currency, even imposing a tax on foreign capital flooding into the country. Some propose tougher Brazilian controls on lending and investing to ensure sustained, long-term growth.

Brazil has experienced two economic miracles, one under the generals and the recent one. From 1968 to 1974, under the military, Brazil's annual growth rate averaged 10 percent, equal to Japanese rates at the time. A series of very bright economic *technocrats* used state-owned banks and industries to make Brazil a major producer of food, shoes, steel, aluminum, and cars. This earlier Brazilian miracle, however, was based on foreign rather than Brazilian capital investment and on cheap imported oil. Brazilian capitalists, instead of reinvesting their money in industrial growth, preferred to spend it, speculate with it, or stash it abroad. Capital flight is common in Latin America and now in Russia and China. For new capital investment, Brazilian firms got government or foreign loans. This was one of the reasons Brazil accumulated one of the Third World's largest public debts, over $250 billion.

In the 1980s, however, the cheap foreign loans and oil dried up, turning the boom into a declining GDP a decade later. From 1980 to 1993, Brazil's GDP grew at an annual average of only 1.5 percent. Per capita GDP (which takes into account population growth) declined an average of half a percent per year. Brazilians grew poorer at the very time democracy was being reintroduced, making many wonder if the cycle of military takeover was ready to start over.

At this same time, fortunately, a major turnaround began. Under the generals and their technocratic helpers, some 60 percent of Brazil's industry had been in government hands—including mines, petroleum, and electricity. The majority of loans came from government banks, giving the state the power to determine what got built and where. In the 1980s, Latin American intellectuals were starting to see state-owned industries and government supervision of the economy as mistaken paths.

President Collor began selling off steel and petroleum industries. Cardoso took it farther and privatized (by auction) state-owned telecommunication, electricity, mines, railroads, banking, and other industries. He also cut Brazil's nationalistic restrictions on foreign ownership, drastically trimmed the number of bureaucrats and their pensions, and reined in state-level banks, which loan recklessly to friends of governors. Lula did not reverse privatization and happily reaped its rewards. These presidents faced strong opposition every step of the way, for every one of these measures meant rich, powerful interests giving up their cushy deals.

The freeing up of Brazil's red-tape economy is analogous to economic reform efforts undertaken in Russia and Japan. Many see what needs to be done for the long-term good of the country, but those who will be hurt by the reforms block them. From 1996 to 2002, due in large part to global currency collapses, Brazil had only weak economic growth. In the following years, however, it boomed—like China and India, with only a slight slowdown during the 2008–2009 recession—but a few years later slumped back down, something Brazilians desperately want to reverse. The project can be seen as a long pushback against statism and dependency theory. Over the years, businesspeople and economists increasingly pointed to Brazil's large state sector and red-tape controls on the economy. Brazil, they noted, had not really been a free-market country relying on private initiative.

Statism—where the government is the number-one capitalist—can both accomplish big projects and make big mistakes. Some projects that Brazil poured money into were prestigious but money losers. For example, the government invested heavily in nuclear power in a country where hydroelectricity was just beginning. (Hydro now generates 80 percent of Brazil's power, with more on the way from the giant Belo Monte dam.) The nuclear program was a waste—but it made Brazil look like an advanced country—and, by 1980, it was curtailed. Government loans were sometimes extended foolishly, too. The interest on these loans was so low, and Brazil's inflation so high, that the credits amounted to free money, which the borrower could immediately loan out at high interest. Why work for a living when you can just shift some paper around? The subsidized loans from the government, however, ultimately came from working Brazilians in the form of inflation. Brazil's cheap government loans were another reason the rich got richer and the poor got poorer.

State control produced other distortions in the economy. Brazil's Vargas-era labor laws, designed to coddle and co-opt unions, specify a minimum wage and make it hard and expensive to let workers go in a downturn, a hindrance to economic growth. There were so many laws and regulations—many of them still on the books—that businesses had to employ red-tape specialists called *despachantes* (expediters) to jog the bureaucracy into giving a license or allowing a price change. Many despachantes were related to the bureaucrats they dealt with; some were former bureaucrats themselves. The Brazilian word for getting around a regulation is *jeito*, literally "knack," meaning having someone who can fix it for you. The whole system fed corruption. Cleaning out obsolete laws could deepen and strengthen Brazil's economy.

Leftists used to point to dependency as the root of Brazil's problem, whereas businesspeople pointed to state controls. Actually, the two views complement each other. State control does stunt domestic capital formation, and this makes Brazil dependent on foreign capital.

Bolsa Família
"Family Allowance," 2004 Brazilian welfare program.

Cure one and you cure the other. Instead of a vigorous private sector of local businesses, the Brazilian economy was, until recently, divided between the foreign multinationals and the state. Brazilians tended to attach themselves to one of the two. The cure for statism is privatization, which Brazil undertook during the 1990s. Most of the purchasers were foreign (especially U.S.) multinationals. Promarketeers cheered, arguing that the sales bring new investment, competition, and economic growth. Leftists objected, claiming that Brazil was giving foreign capitalists its wealth.

Brazil's Lula years were great, but, by the time Dilma Rousseff took office at the start of 2011, the economy was overheating (as was China's). How to cool it down but keep Brazil growing became her giant challenge. Inflation is growing, but raising bank interest rates to stem it attracts ever more foreign money, making the real much too strong; it doubled in recent years. These were warning signs of a bubble, something that Brazil had experienced before. When the bubble popped under Rousseff —and it had to pop, no matter who was president—it inflicted pain. One looming problem that will inflict more pain: a giant bill from overly generous pensions. Rousseff was much less popular than Lula, who was lucky to come in at the start of the boom.

How to Fight Poverty?

Another weakness of the Brazilian economy is that Brazil has one of the most unequal income distributions in the world—a Gini Index of 52, the highest of our 11 countries (although China, if accurate figures were known, could be higher). Brazil's top fifth rakes in some 20 times more than the bottom fifth. One Brazilian in four is below the poverty line, many more not much above it, even with the Bolsa Família. Until recently, per capita income in the Northeast was lower than in Bangladesh. The "Brazilian miracle" overlooked these people.

In 2004, Lula combined three smaller programs into the **Bolsa Família**, welfare payments to 12 million poor families for basic sustenance. The Bolsa is conditional: Kids must get vaccinated and be in school. (Graduation rates jumped.) Poor families get 22 reís (about $9) per child per month for up to three children. "Citizen Cards" are mailed to mothers and used like debit cards. Typically, an allowance of R$58 (about $23 U.S.) goes to rural families making around R$50 (about $20 U.S.) a month, the difference between eating and not eating. Critics fumed that it would go for alcohol or create welfare dependency, but the Bolsa was considered a success and model for other Latin American countries. (Mexico has a similar *Oportunidades* program.) One catch: The Bolsa began during a time of major economic growth, so it is hard to disentangle its effects from those of overall job improvements.

Those urging caution about welfare measures point out that Brazil contains two economies, a First World economy that is modern and productive and a Third World one that is traditional and unproductive. Actually, most Third World countries have First World sectors within them. In Brazil, the contrast is stark. But, argue moderates, the gap cannot be bridged overnight. Brazil must first build up its modern sector until it gradually takes over the whole

Comparison

The Addiction of Statism

The Old Regime in France started *statism*, the idea that the government should supervise the economy and own much industry, and it spread throughout much of the world. Regimes intent on rapid change—the Bolsheviks in Russia, Atatürk in Turkey, Perón in Argentina, and Vargas in Brazil—embraced statism as a seemingly logical solution to their problems of backwardness. Statism caught on like an addiction in Latin America: Once you had a little state supervision, you soon wanted more. Have a social or economic problem? A new government program, industry, or regulation can solve it.

Statism's basic premises have long been examined and found wanting. Adam Smith concluded long ago that state intervention merely gets in the way of economic growth. State-owned industries often become monopolistic, uncompetitive, graft ridden, inefficient, and money losing. Many have to be propped up with state subsidies, money that comes from citizens' pockets. But once established, statist structures resist reform. Politicians, fearful of unemployment and of appearing pro-American or procapitalist, hesitate to privatize inefficient and crooked state enterprises. Even conservative Mexican presidents could not privatize the inefficient state oil monopoly, Pemex. Only in our day have wide areas of Latin America, starting with Chile, kicked the habit and turned to the free market. Privatizing Brazil's state-owned industry—including the state-run oil firm Petrobras—was a major issue. Brazilian leftists—people far to the left of Lula and Dilma Rousseff—still hate privatization and try to block it.

---

hyperurbanization
Overconcentration of populations into cities.

country. To simply redistribute income to marginals, who produce little, would be economic folly. The trick is to keep the economy growing so as to absorb the marginals and turn them into producers and consumers, something that has been happening.

The Population Problem

Brazil, like most developing areas, has seen a hefty population increase. The Catholic Church, of course, forbids artificial birth control, and the military regime thought a growing population fueled economic growth. Accordingly, in Brazil, until the 1970s, there was no emphasis on slowing population growth, and Brazil's population is now 203 million, half under age 30. The good news is that Brazil's fertility rate, like much of the Third World, has plummeted since 1970, when a Brazilian woman had an average of 5.8 children, to 1.8 in 2013, below the U.S. level. This showed the impact of birth control, television, and economic downturn. Brazil's popular TV soaps now show small, affluent families with only one or two children, and this has become a national norm.

As usual, it is poor people, especially peasants, who have the most children. The Northeast, where families are large, is a reservoir of marginal Brazilians, millions of whom pour into the cities of the South—as the 7-year-old Lula did. The result is **hyperurbanization**, common throughout the Third World, where cities are surrounded by huge slum belts created by peasants who can no longer live off the land. Nearly 90 percent of Brazilians live in cities, an absurd situation for a big, empty country. São Paulo, with 20 million inhabitants, is among the world's largest cities.

The rural immigrants to the cities settle in favelas. With little education—until recently, a majority of Brazilians did not finish primary school—or job skills, many do not find regular work. Those who do usually travel hours to and from their jobs. With prices rising, many get poorer and abandon their children to live on the streets. Poverty plus widespread gun ownership gives Brazil murder rates among the world's highest—twice as high as Mexico's. Rich Brazilians travel by armor-plated cars or helicopters to avoid kidnapping, a common crime.

Brazilian citizens and police, fed up with crime, turn to extralegal remedies. Unofficial "death squads" of off-duty police officers execute criminal suspects in the favelas or streets. Some young purse and wallet snatchers are beaten to death on the spot. Police shoot street kids as they sleep on the assumption they are petty criminals. And the police may be worse than the criminals; some set up roadblocks to shake down and even shoot motorists. Some gun down landless peasants. Police kill an average of 2,000 unarmed citizens a year, but officers are rarely convicted of anything. Photojournalists are warned to take no pictures of police in action. Seventy percent of Brazilians say they distrust the police.

Stable Democracy?

In the 1970s, almost all of Latin America was under some form of dictatorship, but, by 1990, almost all of Latin America had returned to democratic, civilian rule (exception: Cuba). Democracy may be contagious in Latin America, but it is also unstable. Will Brazil's democracy—or any of the others—last? Latin America's problems are incredible: unsteady

Geography

Developing the Amazon Region

The vast Amazon rainforest produces a considerable fraction of the world's oxygen and contains much of its biodiversity. But a lot of Brazil's economic growth depends on developing the Amazon basin. Some claim deforestation does more harm than good.

The first to be harmed are Brazil's Indians, pushed back until they face extinction. Brazil's constitution guarantees Indians rights to traditional rainforest lands, but, in practice, the need of farmers, ranchers, and miners for ever more territory has made enforcement spotty at best.

Of the 270 tribes of Brazilian Indians found at the beginning of the twentieth century, 90 have disappeared altogether, and others are slipping fast. Particularly vicious have been gold miners, who readily invade Indian reserves and kill them with guns and dynamite or by using mercury (for isolating gold particles). More intent on development and jobs, few Brazilians worry much about Indians, who are now militantly demanding their rights and tribal areas.

Brazilian agribusiness and government planners—together dubbed the "ruralistas"—say that controls on development hold back economic growth. Environmentalists, on the other hand, warn that the Amazon rainforest—already 18 percent deforested—is near a tipping point, ready to slide into *savanna* and lose biodiversity. Brazil's current Forest Code calls for keeping 80 percent of Amazon properties as forest, but this is widely evaded.

A parallel problem is the huge Belo Monte hydroelectric dam on the Xingu River in the state of Pará in the north, due to open in 2015. Power blackouts are frequent, and Brazil badly needs the electricity, but the dam will flood 120,000 acres and displace 20,000 to 40,000 people. A former energy minister, President Rousseff strongly favors the dam.

economic growth, unemployment, bloated state sectors, military establishments accustomed to intervening in politics, and a lack of seasoned political institutions such as parties and parliaments. The democratic wave of the 1970s and 1980s washed back in Ecuador, Venezuela, and Bolivia, leaving them only partly democratic. Interestingly, after leftist Ollanta Humala was elected president of Peru in 2011, he said he would opt for the Brazilian path of a market economy with welfare measures rather than the statist/socialist path of Venezuela's Chávez.

Eventually, Latin America will be democratic. The region has a bigger middle class, the bearers of democracy. Better educated and informed, they no longer swallow demagogic promises. Many are now aware of the dangers of statism and inflation. Markets work, and trade between countries benefits all. Even Cuba may become democratic. Brazilians used to joke, "Brazil is the country of the future and always will be." Now the future has arrived, and Brazil led the way.

Review Questions

Learning Objective 10.1 Compare and contrast Brazil's colonization with those of other Latin American countries, p. 393.

1. What political attitudes did Portuguese colonization bequeath Brazil?
2. Explain *Positivism* and how it became rooted in Brazil.
3. Was Vargas's New State really fascistic?

Learning Objective 10.2 Explain how Brazil managed to stabilize its tumultuous politics, p. 399.

4. What could China learn from Brazil's "decompression"?
5. Compare and contrast Lula and Dilma as Brazil's presidents.
6. Why are Brazilian party names deceptive?

Learning Objective 10.3 Explain why Latin Americans are cautious about democracy, p. 406.

7. How does Brazil handle the racial question?

8. Why are shantytowns a hallmark of the developing lands?
9. What is dependency theory, and why did it become rooted in Latin America?

Learning Objective 10.4 Describe Brazil's mobilization-demobilization cycle, p. 410.

10. Why did Brazil, until recently, have *praetorianism*? Is it now cured?
11. Why does *demagoguery* often appear in developing countries?
12. What is the likely political impact of today's Catholicism on Latin America?

Learning Objective 10.5 Evaluate the Brazilian economic miracle, p. 417.

13. Was Brazil's economy heavily statist? Is it still?
14. Describe Brazil's *bolsa família*. Does it work?
15. Should the Amazon basin be developed or left alone?

Key Terms

autogolpe, p. 397
Bolsa Família, p. 419
constructive bankruptcy, p. 415
coroneís, p. 396
dependency theory, p. 410
disinflation, p. 412
Estado Nôvo, p. 397
favela, p. 402

fiscal, p. 400
globalization, p. 409
hyperurbanization, p. 420
IMF, p. 413
inchoate, p. 402
machismo, p. 409
mobilize, p. 397
Old Republic, p. 396

personalismo, p. 409
Positivism, p. 396
praetorianism, p. 393
real, p. 413
regency, p. 394
Second Vatican Council,
 p. 416

Further Reference

Bourne, Richard. *Lula of Brazil: The Story So Far.* Berkeley, CA: University of California Press, 2008.

Brainerd, Lael, and Leonard Martinez Diez, eds. *Brazil as an Economic Superpower? Understanding Brazil's Changing Role in the Global Economy.* Washington, DC: Brookings, 2009.

Cardoso, Fernando Henrique. *The Accidental President of Brazil: A Memoir.* New York: PublicAffairs, 2006.

Diamond, Larry, Jonathan Hartlyn, Juan J. Linz, and Seymour Martin Lipset, eds. *Democracy in Developing Countries: Latin America,* 2nd ed. Boulder, CO: Lynne Rienner, 1999.

Fishlow, Albert. *Brazil since 1985.* Washington, DC: Brookings, 2011.

Garzón, Juan Carlos. *Mafia & Co.: The Criminal Networks in Mexico, Brazil, and Colombia.* Washington, DC: Wilson Center, 2010. [Available at www.wilsoncenter.org/ publication/mafia-co]

Gordon, Lincoln. *Brazil's Second Chance: En Route toward the First World.* Washington, DC: Brookings, 2001.

Kingstone, Peter R., and Timothy J. Power, eds. *Democratic Brazil Revisited.* Pittsburgh, PA: University of Pittsburgh Press, 2008.

Levine, Robert M. *The History of Brazil.* New York: Palgrave, 2003.

Power, Timothy J., and Matthew M. Taylor, eds. *Corruption and Democracy in Brazil: The Struggle for Accountability.* Notre Dame, IN: University of Notre Dame Press, 2011.

Roett, Riordan. *The New Brazil.* Washington, DC: Brookings, 2010.

Rohter, Larry. *Brazil on the Rise: The Story of a Country Transformed.* New York: Palgrave, 2010.

Skidmore, Thomas F. *Brazil: Five Centuries of Change.* New York: Oxford University Press, 1999.

Teixeira, Carlos Gustavo Poggio. *Brazil, the United States, and the South American Subsystem: Regional Politics and the Absent Empire.* Lanham, MD: Lexington, 2012.

Chapter 11
Nigeria

Street markets, like this one in the capital Abuja, show Nigeria's commercial hustle.

 ## Learning Objectives

11.1 Describe the impact of European colonialism on Africa.

11.2 Explain why Third World elections are so problematic.

11.3 Illustrate the ways Nigeria shows political fragmentation.

11.4 Characterize the praetorian tendency in some lands.

11.5 Explain why plentiful oil works against political and economic development.

WHY NIGERIA MATTERS

Nigeria is important but could fall apart. It has the largest economy and population in Africa—one-fifth of Africans south of the Sahara are Nigerians—but they are split between Muslims and Christians. It produces—or could produce—a tenth of the world's oil, making it a major oil-exporting country and oil supplier to the United States, but violence disrupts Nigeria's oil output. We often treat Nigeria as little more than a gas station, like we did the Persian Gulf, but such places turn into zones of chaos and conflict, like Nigeria is doing now. Nigeria has much influence in Africa and, along with South Africa, has led peace-keeping operations in several African countries. Nigeria is also attempting, for the third time, to establish democracy in a deteriorating situation that could explode into violence or military coup at any time. The key to stabilizing Nigeria's shaky democracy: wise use of its oil revenues, much of which now disappear into corruption.

Impact of the Past

11.1   Describe the impact of European colonialism on Africa.

Nigeria, like Mexico, had civilizations long before the Europeans came. The Nok culture, which was adept at grain farming and iron smelting, created an inland kingdom around the time of Christ, at the southern end of the trade route from North Africa. Starting in the eleventh century AD, the Yoruba built a series of city-states in the southwest, under a king in the city of Ife. Only the Igbo (also known as Ibo) appear to have been stateless; they lived in egalitarian, self-contained villages in the southeast. There was never a single kingdom of Nigeria.

Islam, from the Sudan region, arrived in the Sahel of northern Nigeria in the ninth century AD and converted the Hausa and Fulani peoples, now known as the Hausa-Fulani. The Borno kingdom and later Songhai empire were seats of Islamic learning and culture. Islam also meant that Nigeria, in modern times, is split between a Muslim north and a largely Christian south, the source of much conflict today.

The Coming of the Europeans

Nigeria, like Mexico and Brazil, was launched by the voyages of discovery. Portuguese naviga-tors, in their effort to round Africa, were the first Europeans to reach, in 1471, what was much later called Nigeria. The Portuguese began a pattern later followed by other Europeans. They did not venture far inland—climate and disease made that unpleasant—but set up trading forts along the African coast.

They soon found their chief item of trade: slaves. Slavery had always been practiced in Africa; most slaves were used locally, but some were sent to North Africa. Starting with the Portuguese, local African chiefs, by raiding and kidnapping, delivered slaves to the Europeans' slave forts on the coast, which became known as the "slave coast." Portugal's colony of Brazil and Spain's colony of Cuba needed labor for their sugarcane fields. England's American colo-nies needed labor for their cotton and tobacco fields. From the 1530s to the 1850s, Portuguese, Spanish, French, English, and, later, Americans shipped more than 10 million Africans across the Atlantic, chiefly to Brazil (which took several times as many as the United States did). Due to this brutal trade, many Americans, Brazilians, and Cubans are of Yoruba or Igbo ancestry.

Nigeria

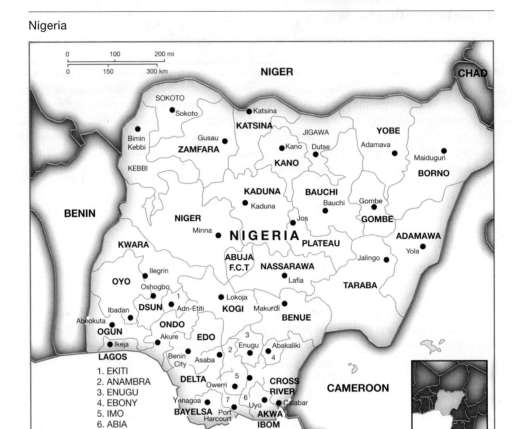

An Islamic **jihad** from 1804 to 1808 in the northern region was little noticed by Europe but contributed to Nigeria's current difficulties. Islamic scholars, in a familiar pattern, found the Muslim kingdoms there insufficiently pure and demanded their overthrow. That done, they set up what was known as the Sokoto **Caliphate**, a single political system much more powerful than any other in the region and one motivated by Islamic fundamentalism. In less than a century, it collided with British colonialism.

Scottish explorer Mungo Park, often wracked with fever, surveyed the Niger River from 1795 to 1806, when he drowned while trying to canoe down it. Few ventured after him until quinine was developed for use against malaria in the 1850s. Christian missionaries arrived to convert the Yoruba, Igbo, and others, setting up missionary posts on the coast. Missionaries were often the advance element of imperial expansion, as protecting them soon required a military presence.

jihad
Arabic for "struggle"; also Muslim holy war.

caliphate
Islamic dynasty.

Britain's suppression of the slave trade was the first step that led to the establishment of Nigeria. Under pressure from British Christians, Parliament, in 1807, outlawed the shipping of slaves (but not slavery itself, which Parliament ended in the British Empire in 1834). To enforce the ban, the Royal Navy stationed a squadron in the Gulf of Guinea. And to replace the slave trade, Britain encouraged trade in palm oil, used (even today) for soaps and lubricants. An example of unforeseen consequences, the move stimulated the capture of more slaves, who were needed to produce and transport the palm oil. To suppress this internal trade, Britain first shelled Lagos, the Yorubas' island capital, in 1851 and then annexed it in 1861.

Geography

The Geography of Imperialism

We understand much about the developing areas by knowing who their former imperial masters were. Who set up the borders (most of them artificial), languages, legal codes, transportation lines, and styles of governance? Notice how few non-European lands stayed free of imperial rule: Afghanistan, Ethiopia, Japan, Thailand, and Turkey. China and Iran were reduced to semicolonial status. It is easier to enumerate the countries that were never colonies than list those that were.

Much has been written about Europe's imperial impulse. Marxists see it as a race for riches. Lenin theorized that capitalism needs colonial markets to prolong its faltering economies and that World War I was an imperialist competition to gain colonies. This economic theory of imperialism has many holes. Overall, administering and defending colonies cost the imperial powers more than they gained. West Europe's richest countries never had colonies, but its poorest, Portugal, was drained by colonial expenses. Private interests, to be sure, profited from the colonial trade.

Strategists see imperialism as a race for security: "If we don't take it, someone else will." Spain, Britain, France, and others competed for colonies out of fear that they would be at a strategic disadvantage if they had none. A "contagion" or "copy-cat factor" was also at work: Colonies brought prestige. Only powers with colonies were respected. This helps explain the U.S. push for colonies in 1898. Roughly, the following accounts for who had what.

Spain, starting with Columbus, had most of Latin America (almost all of it lost in the 1820s) and the Philippines (lost to the United States in 1898). After stealing tons of New World gold and silver, Spain ended up one of Europe's poorest countries.

Portugal's was the first and last colonial empire. In the fifteenth century, Portuguese navigators, seeking access to Asia, worked their way down the coast of Africa, setting up colonies as they went. Portugal claimed Brazil in 1500 and held it until independence in 1822. Portugal kept Goa until India took it in 1961; Angola, Mozambique, and Guinea-Bissau in Africa until 1975; East Timor until invaded by Indonesia in 1975; and Macau (near Hong Kong) until 1999, when it was ceded back to China.

Britain's was the biggest empire—"The sun never sets on the British Empire"—and included Canada, Australia, New Zealand, India (which then included Pakistan and Bangladesh), Sri Lanka, Burma, Malaya, South Yemen, much of Africa below the Sahara (including Kenya, South Africa, and Nigeria), and Hong Kong, plus temporary rule of Egypt, Palestine, Jordan, and Iraq.

France's was the second-biggest empire. It held Vietnam, Laos, Cambodia, most of North and Equatorial Africa, and bits of the Caribbean and South Pacific. France and Britain gave up their colonies, beginning in 1947 and finishing in 1964. After France gave independence to its African colonies in the early 1960s, it grew richer.

The Netherlands held the rich Dutch East Indies (now Indonesia) from the seventeenth century to 1949 and South Africa's Cape area in the eighteenth century, plus specks in the Caribbean. Indonesia's instability owes much to Dutch misrule. South Africa's Afrikaners, who long dominated the country, still speak a Dutch-based language, Afrikaans.

Belgium brutally exploited the vast Congo from 1885 to 1960, initially as the personal property of King Leopold. Conditions—described in Joseph Conrad's

Heart of Darkness—were so horrid that the Belgian government had to take it over.

Germany, a latecomer in 1885, got some leftover pieces of Africa (Tanganyika, Namibia, Cameroon) and half of Samoa but lost them all at the close of World War I.

Italy, another latecomer, took Somalia in 1889, Eritrea in 1890, and Libya from the Ottomans in 1912 but lost everything in World War II.

The Ottoman Turkish Empire took the Balkans in the late fourteenth century and held a bit of it until the early twentieth. They also took the Middle East in the sixteenth century until they were pushed out by Britain in World War I. Imperialism was not solely a European thing.

Japan took Taiwan in 1895, Korea in 1910, and Manchuria in 1931 but lost them all in 1945.

The United States, let us not forget, had an empire, too. In 1898, America took the Philippines (independent since 1946), Puerto Rico, Hawaii, and Guam, as well as part of Samoa in 1899.

The Scramble for Africa

The Niger (from the Latin for *black*) River, the greatest river of West Africa, rises far to the west, in Guinea, only 150 miles from the Atlantic, and makes a 2,600-mile semicircle, at first north through Mali, then turning south through Niger and finally Nigeria. During the nineteenth century, trade along the Niger, much of it in cocoa, grew more profitable. In response to calls from missionaries, a Scottish captain made monthly steamboat runs up the lower reaches of the Niger.

British businessman George Goldie, the "father of Nigeria," set up the United Africa Company in 1879 and turned it into the chartered Royal Niger Company in 1886, after the Berlin Conference (see the "Boundaries in Africa" box) had carved up Africa and assigned borders to European imperial powers. The conference stated, however, that no power could claim what it did not occupy, setting off a race to turn vague claims into colonies. This "scramble for Africa" prompted the British to grab Nigeria before the French could.

In 1894, real British colonialism took shape with the arrival of Fredrick Lugard, one of a remarkable handful of energetic Englishmen who dedicated their lives to the British colonial service and the vision of a British Empire that brought peace and prosperity to the world. To do this, they often used their new Maxim gun on the Africans, as Lugard did in many colonial battles around the world. Lugard consolidated the areas of the Yoruba and Igbo—who fought a guerrilla war against him—into two British protectorates and, in 1900, moved into the Muslim north with a military force. By 1903, he had captured Kano and Sokoto to form the Protectorate of Northern Nigeria. In 1914, Sir Frederick (he was knighted) combined Southern and Northern Nigeria into nearly its present form under a governor-general in Lagos. (A piece of the German-ruled Cameroon was added on the east after World War I.) In classic imperialist fashion, Lugard invented Nigeria, and his wife, a journalist, invented the name Nigeria.

indirect rule

British colonial governance through native hereditary rulers.

divide and rule

Roman and British imperial ruling method of setting subjects against each other.

Lugard used two British colonialist styles, the twin policies of **indirect rule** and **divide and rule**. With only a few hundred white men, the British ran colonies as vast as India by working with and through local chiefs and princes, who were bought off with titles and honors. France practiced a much more direct rule and was reluctant to turn over local responsibilities to Africans. Accordingly, France needed thousands of Frenchmen to staff its colonies. The British were far more efficient.

Divide and rule is an old technique of the Roman Empire: *divide et impera* in Latin. Its logic: "If you keep them divided, you can easily rule them. United, they could throw you out." Under this policy, colonialist

officials emphasized the distinctiveness of cultures, powers, and territories of existing tribes to set them against each other. There were always tribes in Africa, but the Europeans hyped tribalism to facilitate their rule. The often murderous tribalism found today owes something to colonialist manipulations.

Colonialism, however, is a wasting asset. The more you organize and educate the local citizens, the more they want to rule themselves. Missionary activity produced a growing number of educated Africans, some through college level. In the 1920s, especially in the British colonies of Africa, intellectuals developed **pan-Africanism** to liberate the continent from European domination. They argued that, without the imperialists to divide them, Africans of all tribes could get along in a united Africa. The British strategy for handling growing political claims from Africans was to cede them local and partial political power in small steps. In 1914, the British established a Nigerian Legislative Council in Lagos and enlarged it with elected members in 1922. It had limited powers and did not include the north. Actually, Britain pursued fairly enlightened colonial policies that may have prevented the worst violence during and after independence. The Belgians, on the other hand, gave the Congolese nothing, trained them for nothing, and prepared them for nothing. Result: When Belgium, after some riots, hastily granted the Congo independence in 1960, it erupted into civil war and is still strife torn.

Independence

World War II weakened the European empires both materially and psychologically. They could no longer afford or justify ruling distant, unlike peoples. Decolonization came first as a trickle and then as a flood: India and Pakistan in 1947; Israel (formerly Palestine) in 1948; Indonesia (the Dutch East Indies) in 1949; Ghana (the Gold Coast) in 1957; then 17 countries in 1960, mostly British and French colonies in Africa. Where there were many European settlers—Algeria, Kenya, and Rhodesia—decolonization was long, hard, and violent, as the settlers tried to keep their privileged status. Where there were few settlers—West Africa in general, including Ghana, Sierra Leone, and Nigeria—decolonization was easy. By the mid-1960s, all of the old African colonies had been liquidated except for Portugal's Angola, Mozambique, and Guinea-Bissau. The first European empire was also the last. In 1975, Lisbon, too, gave way. After white-ruled Rhodesia became black-ruled Zimbabwe in 1980, South Africa was the last white-ruled country in Africa, and this ended in 1994 with the election of a black government under Nelson Mandela. Africa returned to African hands.

Aiming at independence, the first Nigerian political party was founded in 1923. Herbert Macaulay, grandson of a prominent African Christian minister, founded the Nigerian National Democratic Party. Macaulay, whom the British fought, is now called the father of Nigerian independence. The Nigerian Youth Movement was founded as a nationwide party in 1934. Macaulay and Nnamdi Azikiwe ("Zik"), a U.S.-educated Igbo, brought together more than 40 groups in 1944 to form the National Council of Nigeria and the Cameroons (NCNC). World War II, in which Nigerian soldiers served in the British army, made subject

Geography

Bound Niger

Bounding Niger (a former French colony easy to confuse with Nigeria) teaches us more African geography than bounding Nigeria.

Niger is bounded on the north by Algeria and Libya;

on the east by Chad;

on the south by Nigeria (a former British colony) and Benin;

and on the west by Burkina Faso (formerly Upper Volta) and Mali.

Niger

peoples ask what the struggle against fascism meant when they still lived under authoritarian colonial regimes. The British had no good answer. By now, many Nigerians were calling for independence.

The British strategy was to give way piecemeal. In 1947, they set up a federal system—the only plausible solution to Nigeria's regional differences—with Northern, Western, and Eastern

Geography

Boundaries in Africa

The boundaries of Africa are especially artificial. Notice how several of Africa's borders are straight lines, a sure sign of artificiality. Many of the ones for Central Africa were drawn up at a conference in Berlin in 1885, the great "carve-up" of Africa to settle overlapping claims of imperial powers.

The British envisioned owning a band of Africa running the entire length of the continent, "from Cairo to the Cape." After pushing the Germans out of Tanganyika in World War I, they achieved this. Their competitors, the French, turned a great swath of Africa running east–west across the continent's great bulge into French West Africa and French Equatorial Africa. Portuguese, Germans, and Belgians took smaller pieces of Africa.

The imperialist-imposed artificial boundaries cut through tribes and forced together unworkable combinations of tribes. A river in Africa is a poor border because, typically, people of the same tribe live along both banks. In 1963, however, with most of Africa independent, the new Organization of African Unity (renamed African Union in 2002) decided not to change the Berlin borders and even put them in its charter. The new leaders were afraid both of unleashing chaos and of losing their governing jobs. Best to leave these artificial borders alone, they figured. In Africa, the imperialists' land grabs became permanent boundaries.

regions, corresponding, respectively, to the three largest ethnic groups, the Hausa-Fulani, the Yoruba, and the Igbo. (Nigeria is now divided into many much smaller states.) In 1951, the British set up a national House of Representatives, but it fell apart over the question of who represented what, a harbinger of today's Nigerian fragmentation. In 1954, the British made the Nigerian federation self-governing, with a Muslim prime minister from the north. Western and Eastern regions got internal self-government, the Eastern under Azikiwe and the NCNC and the Western under Chief Obafemi Awolowo, a lawyer who founded the Action Group, a party for Yoruba. Parties in Africa tend to form along tribal lines.

Nigeria's big problem was clear: how to make the huge Muslim Northern province and the two mostly Christian Southern provinces into one Nigeria. They do not go together easily or naturally. The chief party of the north was the People's Congress, which was always wary that the mostly Christian Eastern and Western peoples and parties would dominate. Muslims do not like being ruled by non-Muslims. A parallel happened earlier in India, where, in 1906, the Muslim League split off from the Indian National Congress and eventually got a separate Pakistan in 1947.

Britain left Nigeria with a federal constitution and a prime minister that looked pretty good on paper. As in India, the British political position in Nigeria had become impossible to sustain; Britain had to leave and planned it for years. On October 1, 1960, Nigeria became independent. It had been a formal colony less than 60 years but had experienced European imperialism for much longer. The imperialists take much blame for Nigeria's troubles. They deranged it with a massive slave trade, took it over at gunpoint, cobbled together an artificial country composed of tribes who disliked each other, and then left. Thus, it was not surprising that Nigeria, weak from the start, collapsed into military dictatorships. Nigeria is not unique; it is the story of many nations created by imperialists (example: Iraq).

Geography

Bound Kenya

Kenya is bounded on the north by Sudan and Ethiopia;

on the east by Somalia and the Indian Ocean;

on the south by Tanzania;

and on the west by Uganda.

Kenya

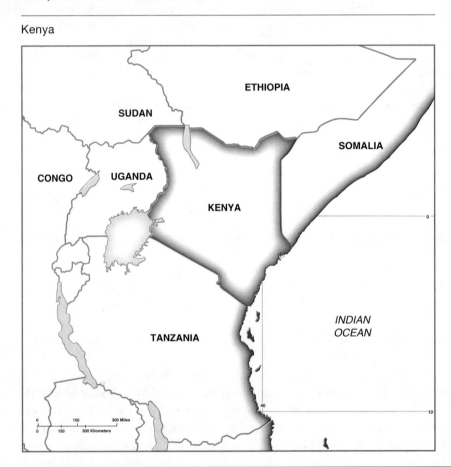

The Key Institutions

11.2 Explain why Third World elections are so problematic.

In the first half-century of independent Nigeria, civilians ruled little more than a third of the time. The other two-thirds of the time, the military ruled, under six different generals, some more brutal and greedy than others. The current period of civilian rule, starting in 1999, is the longest one. We hope it will continue but must be forever mindful that Nigeria is still an

Geography

Sahara, Sahel, Savanna

African geography can be looked at as climate bands running east to west. The northernmost of these bands, the Sahara, is very dry, and the south, close to the equator, is very rainy. The Sahara was not always a desert, but, about 5,000 years ago, its **desiccation** began, making it difficult to traverse and leaving **sub-Saharan** Africa semi-isolated.

Traders, raiders, and Muslim armies occasionally crossed from North Africa into the **Sahel**, which includes northern Nigeria. With uncertain rainfall, the Sahel can be used for little more than cattle grazing, so human populations are thin. The Sahara has been expanding southward as the Sahel gets drier. Some blame global warming, others ice ages, and still others increasing populations of cattle growers for drawing too much water from its very limited **aquifer**.

South of the Sahel are Africa's vast **savannas**, characterized by hot, wet summers and hot, dry winters. Much of Nigeria, indeed much of Africa, is savanna. Here rainfall permits farming. Only the south of Nigeria, along the coast of the Gulf of Guinea, has the lush rainforest that some suppose covers most of Africa. Actually, this region of year-round rainfall occupies only the equatorial band of Africa.

A focus on Europe may cause us to overlook one of the most basic physical determinants of a politico-economic system. Rainfall in Europe is generally sufficient and predictable, but, in much of the world, it is not. There is plenty of land in the world; water for humans and crops is the limiting factor. More than one billion humans do not have clean drinking water, a number that is growing rapidly. With water tables dropping rapidly, many warn that water supplies will soon reach dangerous levels in wide areas. Massive industrial pollution makes matters worse.

Irrigation and conservation can compensate for lack of rain, but they require a high degree of human organization and governmental supervision. This may explain why high civilizations arose early in China and Iran. Large desert or semidesert areas of our developing countries—China, India, Mexico, Brazil, Nigeria, and Iran—limit development.

---

unstable country with strong tendencies to fall apart. When breakup threatens, the military takes over.

From British to U.S. Model

The British set up Nigeria on the Westminster model, with a prime minister as chief of government, but the 1979 constitution, now somewhat modified, turned Nigeria into a U.S.-style presidential system, and for a good reason. The British system depends on one party winning a majority of seats in Commons, which almost always happens in Britain. But if the legislature is fragmented into many parties, as it was in Nigeria's earlier years, the government must form multiparty coalitions and can "fall" easily on votes of no confidence.

A U.S.-type presidential system avoids this, as the president can govern with or without majority support in the legislature. Presidents stay until the end of their terms and cannot easily be ousted. Nigeria's president, like the U.S. president, combines head of state with chief of government for a maximum of two 4-year terms. Olusegun Obasanjo, the first president of Nigeria's Fourth Republic, which emerged after dictator Sani Abacha died, tried to change

desiccation
Drying out.

sub-Saharan
Africa south of the Sahara.

Sahel
Narrow band south of Sahara; arid but not yet desert.

aquifer
Underground water-bearing layer.

savanna
Tropical grasslands south of *Sahel*.

Personalities

Good Luck, Jonathan!

Goodluck Jonathan, a southern Christian of the Ijaw tribe, was an accidental president. In 2007, in a badly flawed election, Jonathan became vice president to Umaru Yar'Adua, also of the powerful People's Democratic Party (PDP). Jonathan took over when Yar'Adua, nice but indecisive and ill, died in 2010 from kidney failure. Jonathan had been acting president for a year and was elected on his own in 2011, Nigeria's third civilian president in a row.

But northerners, in 2010, resented a Christian taking over early and felt he should not run in 2011 but make way for a Muslim, a charge they repeated for the 2015 elections. They felt they were getting short-changed because an unwritten deal inside the PDP was to alternate the presidency every two terms (eight years) between a northern Muslim and a southern Christian. The PDP claims to speak for all Nigerians but is mainly a Christian party. Complaining of Jonathan's heavy handedness, mostly northern members split off to form a New PDP, possibly dooming PDP rule.

Jonathan was born in 1957 in a remote village in the Niger Delta into a family of canoe builders. His parents invested everything they could in their son's education, and Jonathan earned a PhD in zoology but entered politics in the PDP. When the governor of oil-rich Bayelsa state was arrested for corruption—not rare in Nigeria—in 2005, Jonathan moved up from deputy governor to governor.

The Nigerian setup resembles Mexico's *dedazo*, where one PRI president picked his successor. Nigeria's previous president, Olusegun Obasanjo, after two terms, picked the little-known Yar'Adua to succeed him in 2007 and added Jonathan as vice presidential candidate for balance. Obasanjo had tried to change the constitution to serve a third term, but the legislature rejected the move, fearing dictatorship. Senators received bribes of up to $400,000 to vote for it. Some suggest that Obasanjo, who remained PDP chairman, picked two weak, unknown figures to be his puppets.

Jonathan is intelligent, but many punned that he needed lots of luck. He kept promising to end Nigeria's chronic corruption and misrule, but, like every Nigerian president, achieved little in the face of powerful and rich interests. Nigeria needs drastic oil and fiscal reforms, but they require tough leadership, and Jonathan dislikes confrontation. He was increasingly perceived as weak and ineffectual, the very charges his predecessor faced.

Jonathan attempted to calm things—especially in his home Delta region—by spreading around oil revenues, the tried and true method of every Nigerian president. Unfortunately, such payouts confirm and deepen the corruption. His very election as a southern Christian tended to fuel violent Islamism in Northern Nigeria, which Jonathan seemed unable to stop.

the constitution so he could have a third term. Parliament was suspicious of his motives and blocked the effort, a victory for democracy. He left office on schedule in 2007.

Nigerian Federalism

Nigerian federalism also resembles the U.S. variety but is dysfunctional. Nigeria's rulers, some of them military dictators, progressively increased the number of states, from 12 to 19 to 31 to the present 36. Every few years, the map of Nigeria is redrawn to calm Nigeria's many ethnic groups, who often feel trapped in a state dominated by another group. When they turn violent, Nigeria carves out a new state for them, a process that some fear is a slow slide to disintegration. India also creates new states, but at a much slower rate.

Political Culture

Nigeria's Political Eras

Nigeria is badly fragmented and lacks a unifying political culture. Consciousness focuses on religions, tribes, and regions. The brief British colonial period gave some Nigerians a modern education and a semblance of unity among Nigeria's elites but was not nearly enough to psychologically unify Nigeria as a nation. Nigeria's elites mostly know each other, but they look out more for their tribes than for Nigeria as a whole, as the tribes are their supporters.

Era	Years	Remembered for
Slave Trade	1530–1820	Massive export of humans
Precolonial	1820–1894	Suppression of slave trade; British explorers and missionaries
Colonial	1894–1960	By 1914, Lugard consolidates regions into one colony named Nigeria
Independence	1960–1963	Commonwealth member, falls apart
First Republic	1963–1966	Becomes a republic
Military Rule	1966–1979	Coups, Biafra War
Second Republic	1979–1983	Presidential system, corrupt civilian rule
Babangida	1983–1993	Long military dictatorship
Third Republic	1993	Abortive transition to democracy
Abacha	1993–1998	Cruel and corrupt military dictatorship
Fourth Republic	1999–	Another attempt at democracy

In 1991, the military dictator Ibrahim Babangida (1985–1993) moved the capital from its old colonial location of Lagos, on the coast, to Abuja, in the precise center of the country. The move resembled Brazil's shift of capital from Rio de Janeiro to Brasilia in 1960 to open up the interior. The purpose of the move in Nigeria was to take the capital out of Yoruba hands and put it in more-neutral territory. Abuja is now designated the Federal Capital Territory, rather like the District of Columbia. Like Brasilia, Abuja is in the middle of nowhere and has been costly and inefficient.

Nigeria's 36 states and their governors have considerable autonomy but few financial resources, requiring them to depend on federal handouts. Each governor names one federal cabinet minister, producing an overlarge cabinet. Many complain, however, that Nigerian federalism is less than genuine, because Abuja still controls oil revenues and dispenses them to state governors as bribes to keep them in line. Most governors are reputed to be corrupt. Nigeria's federal government either cannot or will not deliver much in basic services such as road maintenance, electricity, or schools, so state governments are left with the tasks, which most do poorly. Islamist groups in the north move into the vacuum by providing many basic services, thereby gaining adherents. Northern Nigeria's states are now under **sharia**, which Muslims claim is the only way to clean up corruption. There is nothing the center can do to stop the use of *sharia* without triggering a major revolt in the north.

sharia
Muslim religious law.

The National Assembly

The U.S. model is again evident in Nigeria's legislative branch, the bicameral National Assembly, which meets in Abuja. The Senate has 109 seats; each of the 36 states has 3 Senate seats, plus 1 for the Federal Capital Territory. The House of Representatives has 360 seats, 10 for each state, each representing a single-member district. Both houses are elected for four-year terms at the same time. Nigerian Assembly members' base salary is $189,500 a year—more than the $174,000 of U.S. congresspersons—but some pocket as much as $2 million a year.

The Nigerian setup departs from its U.S. model because its states each get 10 seats regardless of population. It would be like the United States having two Senates. Nigeria feels it must do this to appease smaller ethnic groups with their own states. Overrepresenting the smaller states, however, creates resentment in the more populous states because it leaves them underrepresented. The U.S. solution—a Senate to represent states on the basis of equality and a House to represent districts on the basis of population—strikes us as a good compromise, but we do not have Nigeria's touchy ethnic situation. The danger in Nigeria is hyperfederalism, a system that tries too hard to represent ethnic groups. It seems to work for a while but can lead to the country falling apart, as it did in Yugoslavia.

Nigeria's Parties

Nigeria's big Peoples Democratic Party (PDP) bills itself as a centrist party representing all Nigerians but is perceived as a basically Christian party, strongest in the south. In 2013, a New PDP split off to represent northerners, including 22 of the PDP's senators. The PDP was developed as the personalistic vehicle of former president Obasanjo. The smaller Congress for Progressive Change (CPC) gets its strongest following from northern Muslims; some of its leaders earlier supported the brutal dictatorship of Sani Abacha (1993–1998) and got rich during that time. The Action Congress of Nigeria (ACN) is basically a Yoruba party that joined with the CPC and two other opposition parties to run as the All Progressives Congress (APC) for the 2015 elections. If the APC can hang together, enough Nigerians are fed up with unfulfilled PDP promises to seriously boost the new party. Many other smaller parties, some of them militant northern Muslim parties, win one or two seats in the House.

Nigeria's party system has evolved from many parties—nearly one per tribe—first into a "two-plus" party system and now perhaps into a dominant-party system, a bit like Mexico's PRI. The PDP is a well-funded and well-organized nationwide party and draws votes from all ethnic groups, including many Muslims. It also rigs elections. The big question: Could the PDP become Nigeria's PRI? Whatever negative things one might say about Mexico's formerly dominant party, it got Mexico out of chaos and held it together during times of rapid change and modernization. The PRI analogy, however, poorly fits Nigeria, as few northern Muslims support the PDP; some vote for regionalist and Islamist parties. Mexico has troublesome regions, but none with different religions. Nigeria parallels Iraq in its fragmentation. Like Iraq, Nigeria has three major ethnic regions that British imperialists forced into a single artificial state. Suggestions to let Nigeria and Iraq fall apart into their three main components overlook the bloodshed that would accompany such breakups.

Democracy

Nigeria's 2011 Elections

As expected, interim President Goodluck Jonathan of the PDP won election in 2011 with 59 percent of the vote. Muhammadu Buhari, a former military dictator, won 32 percent. Unfortunately, the election neatly split Nigeria in two, with the PDP carrying the Christian south and Buhari's Congress for Progressive Change (CPC) carrying the Muslim north. Violence immediately erupted in the north, killing at least 500, most of them Christians.

The 2011 Nigerian presidential elections, the fourth since the last military dictator, were a big improvement over those of 2007, which were fraudulent and rigged by registration only for favored parties, missing ballots, stuffed boxes, intimidation, and violence. Parties simply hired armed local gangs to make sure their bosses won. The PDP won with two-thirds of the vote in 2007, but no one believed this number.

The 2011 legislative elections resembled those of 2007. Again, the National Electoral Commission could not post the results for the House of Representatives and Senate for months. The PDP, although weakened, still held the most House and Senate seats, with the CPC second and the Action Congress of Nigeria (ACN) a weak third. Although not totally clean, remember that the PRI ruled Mexico like this for decades, but, eventually, Mexico grew into democracy. Perhaps we should get used to less-than-fair elections in a country's early stages of building democracy.

Nigerian Political Culture

11.3 Illustrate the ways Nigeria shows political fragmentation.

Nigerian Fragmentation

Half of Nigerians are Muslim; another 40 percent are Christian, and 10 percent practice indigenous faiths—for example, the Yoruba religion. Nigeria is also ethnically fragmented. Of Nigeria's approximately 350 ethnic groups, these are the largest: Hausa-Fulani, 29 percent; Yoruba, 21 percent; Igbo, 18 percent; and Ijaw, 10 percent. Mexico has regionalism, but Nigeria's problem is far worse, and the country tends to fragment along religious, ethnic, and regional lines. It has been called "the patchwork country." Eastern, Western, and Northern regions have trouble living together and exist within Nigeria only because the British colonialists set up an artificial country.

The north is especially different—poor (with half the south's average income), isolated, traditional, Muslim, and discontent. With much lower literacy, few skilled people, and endemic terrorism, it cannot attract investment and is in decline. The north has never liked being ruled by Christians, either British or southern Nigerians, and feels Abuja starves it of oil funds. If they had to be in a single country, the northerners always sought to be its rulers. Islam has been the chief religion in Northern Nigeria for a millennium and, like Islam elsewhere in Africa, is spreading south through vigorous proselytizing. African Muslims argue that Islam is the natural religion for Africa because it pays no attention to skin color and has deep roots in Africa, whereas Christianity is a recent arrival brought by Europeans with an implicit racism. Many Northern Nigerians especially disliked President Obasanjo for being a born-again Christian who supported the U.S. war on terror.

Islam can be rigid and intolerant. Some Nigerian Muslim clerics insist on a strictly religious education of Arabic, memorizing the Koran, and a Muslim dress code, including the *hijab* for women. Those who deviate may be arrested. Muslim preachers insist on Islamic purity, sometimes for all of Nigeria. In the north, a strong fundamentalist movement has now made *sharia* state law. This has the potential to rip federal Nigeria apart, because it means states can override national laws. (Note the similarity to the U.S. "nullification" question that preceded the Civil War: Did states have the right to nullify federal laws?) But there is essentially nothing Abuja can do about it.

Sharia can be harsh, for example, punishing adulterous women (but rarely men) by stoning them to death and thieves by chopping off their hands. The penalties, however, apply only to Muslims, not to Christians, producing a bifurcated legal system. A country with two very different legal systems is a house that cannot stand. Some say compromise might be possible—*sharia* for family law in the north, Nigerian secular law for everything else—but Islamists insist that *sharia* is God's law and must not be mixed with other legal systems. (India has a parallel problem with *sharia* law.)

The fundamentalist Islamic Movement of Nigeria—dubbed the "Black Taliban"—has al Qaeda and Iranian ties. Clerics in the north denounced a World Health Organization project to immunize all children against polio, claiming that it was to sterilize Muslim children. Vaccinations were stopped in three northern states, and polio cases climbed. Muslims took offense at the 2002 Miss World pageant, which was to be held in Abuja. Riots broke out, and the pageant was hastily relocated to London. The smallest incident touches off violence by Muslim militants, and thousands are killed.

One growing militant sect demanding *sharia* law, Boko Haram ("Western education is sinful"), responsible for some 10,000 deaths, has created a virtual civil war in Northern Nigeria. In 2013, President Jonathan declared a state of emergency in three states in Nigeria's northeast corner, authorizing brutal police and military retaliation against what he calls terrorism. Unfortunately, the heavy-handed tactics generate more Boko Haram recruits. Boko Haram and its more violent offshoot Ansaru get arms, explosives, and training from Al Qaeda in the Islamic Maghreb (AQIM). The northern Nigerian underwear bomber got Al Qaeda training. Suicide bombers hit churches, police posts, and even Abuja, Nigeria's capital. They oppose any education for women and kidnap schoolgirls. U.S. counterterrorist officials now closely scrutinize Northern Nigeria as a major center of terrorist recruitment and fund-raising. The young Christmas 2009 "underwear bomber" who tried to blow up a jetliner over Detroit was from a wealthy northern Muslim family.

Other parts of Nigeria also present problems. The worst was the bitter Biafra War of 1967–1969, in which the Igbo of eastern Nigeria attempted to break away with their own country, Biafra. In the Niger Delta, well-armed Ijaw and Itsekiri tribesmen fight government soldiers for control of the oil terminals, a struggle that can erupt into full-scale war at any time.

To put things into perspective, though, we might consider what happened in tiny Rwanda, a former Belgian colony east of the Congo. Belgium played classic divide and rule by setting up one tribe, the Tutsis, to be aristocratic masters and another tribe, the Hutus, to be underlings. After the Belgians left in 1962, Hutu-Tutsi fighting and massacres became intermittent and exploded in 1994 as Hutu *genocidaires* massacred an estimated 800,000. (The nonfiction film *Hotel Rwanda* offers a glimpse of the horror.) The conflict spilled over into eastern Congo, where it took an estimated 1.7 million lives, most from starvation and disease. The combined Rwanda-Congo death toll of 2.5 million is the world's highest wartime killings since World War II. Nigeria has not had anything that bad, but it could.

The Igbo and Biafra

Nigeria's prime example of interethnic violence is what happened with the Igbo people of southeastern Nigeria in the late 1960s. British explorers and colonial officials noted long ago that the Igbo lacked the cities and culture of the Yoruba of the southwest or the Hausa-Fulani of the north. The Igbo people, who lived in scattered villages in the rainforest and Niger Delta, seemed rather primitive in comparison. But the Igbo harbored a competitive and hustling culture that was not noticed until later. Under the British, they eagerly took to Christianity and to self-advancement through business, education, the civil service, and the military. They also scattered throughout Nigeria; Igbo merchants dominated much of the commercial life of Northern Nigeria, where they were despised for both their wealth and their religion. Some observers called them the "Jews of Nigeria" because they were hard working, dispersed, better off, and of a different faith. The Igbo were the most modern and educated Nigerians but were culturally at odds with more-traditional Nigerians.

Independent Nigeria started destabilizing almost immediately; unrest and disorder broke out early and often. In response to the fraudulent elections of October 1965, in January 1966, a group of army officers, mainly Igbo, attempted a coup. Prime Minister Abubakar Tafawa Balewa, a northern Muslim, was assassinated. General Johnson Aguiyi-Ironsi, an Igbo, took over with a plan to save Nigeria by turning it from a federal to a unitary system. Especially to the Muslims of the north, this looked like an Igbo conspiracy to seize the entire country. In July 1966, another coup, under Colonel Yakubu Gowon, a Christian from a small tribe in the center of Nigeria, the Anga, overthrew Ironsi, who was killed.

Nigeria's ethnic pot boiled over. In October 1966, murderous riots against Igbo merchants and their families in the north killed some 20,000 and sent perhaps a million Igbos streaming back to Igboland. After some futile efforts to hold Nigeria together, a consultative assembly of three eastern states, knowing that they had Nigeria's oilfields, authorized an Igbo colonel, Odumegwu Ojukwu, to set up a separate country. On May 30, 1967, Ojukwu proclaimed the Republic of Biafra. The federal government also knew where the oil was and therefore had to get back the breakaway area. Much of the Biafra War was about oil. At first, the Biafran army did well, almost reaching Lagos, until the Nigerian army under Gowon threw them back. For two painful years, the Biafra fighters held out, improvising munitions within a shrinking perimeter, until they finally collapsed in December 1969. Igbo deaths, mostly from starvation, are estimated at half a million.

Gowon was actually quite magnanimous in victory and brought back the eastern states into Nigeria as equals within the federation, which he had divided into 12 states. It helped that he was from a small tribe that posed no threat to other ethnic groups. The oil boom that soon followed in the 1970s brought some jobs and a bit of prosperity. Gowon was overthrown by a coup in 1975 by Brigadier Murtala Ramat Mohammed, a Hausa Muslim from the north, who was himself assassinated in 1976. The Biafra War serves as a reminder of just how ethnically fragile Nigeria is and how risky it is to be a Nigerian head of state.

Geography

Bound the Democratic Republic of Congo

The Democratic Republic of Congo (formerly Zaire, earlier the Belgian Congo) is bounded

on the north by the Central African Republic and Sudan;

on the east by Uganda, Rwanda, Burundi, and Tanzania;

on the south by Zambia and Angola;

and on the west by the Atlantic, the Angolan exclave of Cabinda, and (the formerly French) Congo-Brazzaville.

Democratic Republic of the Congo

The Trouble with Nigeria

cleft
In Huntington's theory, a country split by two civilizations.

torn
In Huntington's theory, a country with a Westernizing elite but traditional masses.

cross-cutting cleavages
Multiple splits in society that make group loyalties overlap.

Nigeria has no shortage of intelligent, educated people. Two-thirds of Nigerians are literate (but far more in the south than in the north), not bad for a still-poor developing country. Nigeria has considerable numbers of college graduates, some from British or U.S. universities. Many of its army officers were trained in British military academies.

Nigeria, in the theory of Samuel Huntington, is **cleft**; that is, it is split between two cultures, Islam and Christianity, displaying what he calls "intercivilizational disunity." The two cultures rarely live peacefully within one country. Muslims especially tend to break away from such countries. Upon independence in 1947, Muslim Pakistan split from India, which has a big Hindu majority. In Yugoslavia, Muslims in Bosnia and Kosovo refused to be ruled by Serbs. The Muslim Central Asian republics of the Soviet Union separated from it in late 1991. In 1974, Muslim Turks broke away the north of Cyprus from the Christian Greeks, who held the reins of government. In a parallel with Nigeria, Christians in the south of Sudan—where oilfields are being developed—broke away from the Muslims of the north. (Do not confuse "cleft countries" in Huntington's terms with **torn** countries, such as Turkey and Mexico, whose leaders wish to make them modern and Western despite traditionalist resistance.)

Nigeria is not unique in this regard. Most of the coastal nations of West Africa have a Muslim interior and a Christian coastal region. The reason: Islam came by land from the north and from Sudan; Christianity came by ship from Europe. East Africa, on the other hand, has a Muslim coast and a heavily Christian interior, as in Kenya and Tanzania. Some countries with the two faiths manage to get along tolerably well if they can keep religion in the personal sphere and have adherents of the two faiths dispersed enough to make it hard for either to claim a special area as theirs. The overlap of religion with politics, though, can easily produce breakaway movements.

Political scientists have long celebrated *pluralism* as the basis of modern government and democracy. This is true but only within limits. There must be widespread agreement among groups not to take things too far and to live within certain rules and bounds. Lebanon and Nigeria have plenty of interactions among their many groups, but rules to limit the interactions are weak, so they turn competitive and violent, and the country breaks down. Pluralism without restraint and overarching national values leads to civil war.

Cross-Cutting Cleavages

One of the puzzles of highly pluralistic or multiethnic societies is why they hold together. Why do they not break down into civil strife? One explanation, offered by the German sociologist Georg Simmel early in the twentieth century, is that successful pluralistic societies develop **cross-cutting cleavages**. They are divided, of course, but they are divided along several axes, not just one. When these divisions, or cleavages, cut across one another, they actually stabilize political life.

In Switzerland, for example, the cleavages of French-speaking or German-speaking, Catholic or Protestant, and working class or middle class give rise to eight possible combinations (for example, German-speaking, Protestant, middle class). But any combination has at least one attribute in common with six of the other seven combinations (for example,

cumulative
Reinforcing one another.

French-speaking, Protestant, working class). Because most Swiss have something in common with other Swiss, goes the theory, they moderate their conflicts.

Where cleavages do not cross-cut but instead are **cumulative**, dangerous divisions grow. A horrible case is ex-Yugoslavia, where all Croats are Catholic and all Serbs are Eastern Orthodox. The one cross-cutting cleavage that might have helped hold the country together—working class versus middle class—had been outlawed by the Communists. The several nationalities of Yugoslavia had little in common.

Many of Africa's troubles stem from an absence of cross-cutting cleavages. Tribe counts most, and, in Nigeria, this is usually reinforced by religion. Nigeria does, however, have some cross-cutting cleavages. Not all Nigerian Muslims, for example, are Hausa-Fulani of the north; some are Yoruba in the southwest, and others are Ijaw in the Delta. Social class may also cut across tribal lines, as when a Yoruba businessman knows he has much in common with an Igbo businessman. Nigeria, indeed all of Africa, needs more such connections across tribal lines.

Democrats without Democracy

Most Nigerians want democracy but are bitterly dissatisfied with the present Nigerian government. Amidst corruption, rigged elections, ethnic strife, and poverty, a majority of Nigerians express dissatisfaction with the way democracy works in Nigeria. They expect elections to be unfair and are seldom disappointed. Just wanting democracy does not necessarily make it happen. The problem is not that insufficient numbers of Nigerians understand and desire democracy; there are more than enough educated Nigerians who do. If they were not divided by tribe and religion, Nigerians might have achieved stable democracy. Freedom House rates Nigeria 4.5, "partly free," better than Russia (which earns a not-free 5.5). The terrible dilemma for Nigerian democrats is that they know that whenever Nigeria attempts democracy—as it is doing now—it can easily fail amid tribal and religious animosities, corruption, and military power grabs. Still, most Nigerians have not given up on democracy.

Patterns of Interaction

11.4 Characterize the praetorian tendency in some lands.

Mexico is a weak state, characterized by the penetration of crime into politics. Nigeria is even weaker but is not yet a *failed state* such as Somalia or Afghanistan, where national government effectively ceased. Some classify Nigeria as a "fragile" state, a term suggesting that it could fail. Nigeria, however, has a central government and a strong incentive for most of Nigeria's elites to keep the country intact: graft from the lush oil revenues. If Nigeria falls apart, only the Niger Delta would have the oil. This was one of the roots of the Biafra War.

Crime is astronomical in Nigeria, the world's worst country for kidnapping (second: Mexico). Even university students go into crime. Secret student fraternities, to make sure they pass their courses, intimidate professors by burning their cars and even kidnapping their children. Some then become gangster cults, murdering members of rival cults and selling their services to politicians, thugs, and militants trying to seize the Niger Delta. Nigeria has become

Geography

The Niger Delta

The delta of the Niger River is one of the main features of West Africa's coast and a place where two problems overlap: (1) It produces a fair fraction of the world's oil, and (2) it is the home of several angry tribes, angry over their share of the oil revenue. Violence in the Delta takes more than a thousand lives a year and can explode anytime into civil war. If it does, the world will experience another oil shortfall and price jump.

Royal Dutch Shell first exported oil in 1958 from the Niger Delta around Port Harcourt, now capital of Rivers state, but major oilfields came on line in the 1970s, just as oil prices were quadrupling. Several oil companies, including Shell and Chevron, built major operations there that make billions but pollute soil and water, leaving local people to sicken and die young. Parts of the Delta, burned black and smoldering with oil fires, look like scenes from Dante's *Inferno*. (Some pollution, to be sure, comes from locals puncturing the pipelines to steal fuel.) Many fishermen and farmers lost their livelihood, and few got jobs in the oil industry. Their poverty feeds ethnic tensions in the Delta, home of many tribes. Ken Saro-Wiwa, a writer and environmental activist from the small Ogoni tribe in the oil region, was hanged (along with eight others) in 1995 on trumped-up murder charges. His real crime was calling attention to the ecological damage uncontrolled oil pumping had done to his people. In 2009, Shell, never admitting complicity in the case, paid the Ogoni people $15.5 million in a New York court settlement.

Well-armed Delta gangs (they buy their weapons from Nigerian soldiers) under an umbrella organization, the Movement for the Emancipation of the Niger Delta (MEND), seek "self-determination"—that is, control of the oil. The oil companies try to buy them off with protection money. MEND says it seeks compensation for the massive environmental damage, but its stealing of oil from the pipelines and kidnapping of foreign oil workers looks a lot like banditry. As much as a fifth of Nigeria's oil is stolen, about $1 billion a month. For an unemployed young man in the Niger Delta, as in Mexico, joining a gang is not a bad job. Equipped with speedboats and automatic weapons, gangs can outshoot and outmaneuver the Nigerian army. Theft and sabotage have cut Nigeria's oil exports so that it is now behind Angola as Africa's largest oil producer. The oil companies do more and more drilling offshore for security and profit reasons.

The government, fearing loss of most of Nigeria's revenue if the Delta slides into chaos and disruption, tries both carrots and sticks to calm things. It steps up tough police and military measures, which force thousands to flee and deepen local resentments. A 2009 amnesty—turn in your weapon and get paid $13 per day—attracted some but not all gunmen. Billions of dollars of Nigeria's oil revenues are transferred annually to the Delta, to little effect. A civil war in the Niger Delta could cut the world's oil supply by several percent, enough to induce a global recession.

famous for Internet scams that get you to reveal your bank account numbers. For many, crime is a good job, the only one they can get.

praetorianism
Tendency for military takeovers.

The Praetorian Tendency

As the Roman Empire ossified and crumbled, the emperor's bodyguard, the Praetorian Guard, came to play a powerful role, making and unmaking emperors, some of them their own officers. Political scientists now use the term **praetorianism** to describe a situation where the military feels it must take over the government in order to save the country from chaos. It tends to be recurrent.

Praetorianism is not just a problem of power-hungry generals but reflects deep conflict in the whole society. In praetorian societies, it is not only the generals who want to take power

patronage

Giving government jobs to political supporters.

but many other groups as well: Students, labor unions, revolutionaries, and demagogic politicians would like to seize the state machinery. Institutional constraints and balances have broken down; nobody plays by the rules. In such situations of chaos and breakdown, it is the army among the many power contenders that is best equipped to seize power, so praetorianism usually means military takeover, the case in Nigeria.

Weak states often experience repeated military coups, which indicate that the normal institutions of government—parliaments, parties, and presidents—have too little legitimacy and authority to keep control in times of stress. Most coups are easy and involve little fighting, because the government has no mass support. Let us count Nigeria's military coups (see table at end of this section).

The best of the lot was Obasanjo, who, in 1979, turned power over to a civilian government but then got democratically elected as president of Nigeria from 1999 to 2007. The worst was Sani Abacha, a cruel supercrook who, with his family to help him, looted at least $3 billion of Nigerian oil money and stashed it in Swiss, British, and U.S. banks. Oil revenues give a great incentive for Nigerian generals to think about coups. Another cause of Nigeria's coups is apparent: disputes among ethnic groups, a reflection of Nigeria's fractured political culture. Northern Muslims, especially, bristle at rule by southern Christians and vice versa.

Nigeria still seethes with poverty and violence and could experience another coup. Praetorianism tends to become a self-reinfecting illness, endemic in the Third World. A country that has had one coup will likely have others. Bolivia has had dozens of coups since independence. Brazil last had a coup in 1964 and was ruled by generals until 1985. Mexico, during the nineteenth century, was praetorian, but Calles ended this trend by bringing Mexico's main political forces into one party, the PRI. Nigeria's problem is that it has not yet developed the equivalent of PRI, a dominant nationwide party.

The praetorian tendency raises the question: If these countries slide so easily into military rule, why do they ever slide out? Why do military dictators ever leave power? The material rewards from control over natural resources should be ample incentives to stay in office forever. The means for keeping power are well known and widely practiced in the Third World: **patronage** and *clientelism*. Mobutu seized power in a 1965 coup and ruled and robbed the Congo (which he renamed Zaire) until 1997, with the flimsy cover story that he was the only one who could keep the country together. His real strength was the patronage and clientelistic networks he developed. Sani Abacha of Nigeria set up similar networks and died in office of a heart attack in 1998, what Nigerians called the "coup from heaven."

Year	Ousted	Installed
1966 (Jan.)	Balewa (Hausa) killed	Ironsi (Igbo)
1966 (July)	Ironsi killed	Gowon (Anga)
1975	Gowon deposed	Mohammed (Hausa)
1976	Mohammed killed	Obasanjo (Yoruba)
1983	Shagari (Fulani) deposed	Buhari (Hausa)
1985	Buhari deposed	Babangida (Gwari)
1993	Babangida deposed	Abacha (Hausa)

Geography

Bound Guinea

Guinea, a former French colony in West Africa not to be confused with Guyana in South America, is bounded

on the north by Guinea-Bissau, Senegal, and Mali;

on the east by the Ivory Coast;

on the south by Liberia and Sierra Leone;

and on the west by the Atlantic Ocean.

Guinea

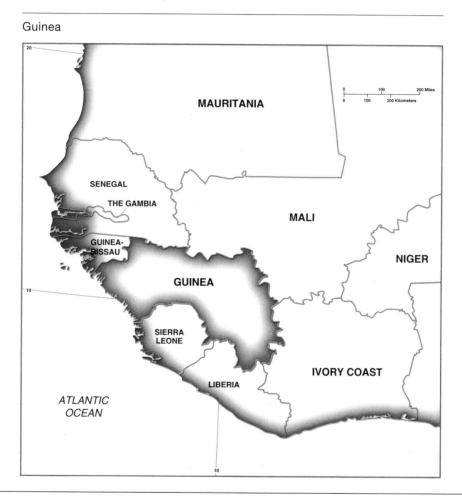

But other forces work against permanent military government. Military officers overthrow governments that have little legitimacy, but the military regime then has even less legitimacy. The military rulers know they are unpopular. A few heads of military regimes may be genuine patriots and professional soldiers who recognize that military government soon turns rotten. Obasanjo, for example, handed power over to a civilian government in 1979. The Brazilian generals who seized power in 1964 boasted how they would end inflation and modernize the

Brazilian economy. By the 1980s, they were embarrassed as their economic miracle stalled; they left power voluntarily in 1985.

A more persuasive motive for dictators to leave is their recognition that an angry mob or their own officers could overthrow them. Every general who has seized power in a coup knows that there are several other generals waiting to do the same. With no legitimacy to rely on, the dictator may, for a time, buy support with pieces of graft, but, sooner or later, those bought off ask, "Why settle for a piece?" Praetorian systems are rife with conspiracies and corruption. The dictator may sense when the time has come to flee with his life and his off-shore bank accounts.

What Nigerians Quarrel About

11.5   Explain why plentiful oil works against political and economic development.

The Political Economy of Nigeria

Many observers, both Nigerian and foreign, conclude that predatory governance has made Nigerians poorer. Thanks to the big runup in oil prices, Nigeria's GDP growth has been several percent a year, but this is meaningless because most of it goes to a handful of already rich people in the right positions. Even as GDP has grown, Nigerian living standards have been declining for decades. Inequality is extreme and getting worse. An estimated 80 percent of Nigeria's oil revenues go to 1 percent of the population. There is not much of a middle class in Nigeria. If a large, educated middle class is necessary for democracy, Nigeria's democratic future is problematic.

Little petroleum income goes to investments that give Nigerians jobs and raise their abysmal living standards. No Nigerian oil refinery works like it should; fuel must be imported (as in Iran). Unemployment, always high, got higher in the global economic slowdown of 2008–2009. Population, growing at 2.5 percent a year with a fertility rate of 5.3 (it was 6.8 in 1975), could reach 300 million by 2040. Forty percent of Nigerians are under 15 and receive little education from a decaying public school system.

Oil wealth is a poor foundation for economic growth. Upon independence in 1960, Nigeria had roughly the same per capita GDP as several East Asian countries. Fifty years later, these Asian lands are many times richer than Nigeria. Political scientists and economists have sought explanations at several levels for this growing gap. These divide into two great camps: (1) explanations from the physical and material world and (2) explanations from the cultural and psychological realm. The two, of course, are not exclusive; it is likely that one feeds into the other in a continual loop.

One standard explanation—that the poor countries have few natural resources—does not hold up. Nigeria and Indonesia have great mineral wealth but are poor. Japan, South Korea, Taiwan, Hong Kong, and Singapore have almost no natural resources and are rich. There may even be an inverse relationship between natural resources and prosperity. Oil often becomes a curse, its revenues a prize for corruption. With few natural resources, Asian Rimland countries

Democracy

The Developmentalist Impulse

In the late 1950s, the Cold War refocused from Europe to the Third World. Academics and the U.S. government became fascinated with the developing areas, where the big showdown with communism was to come.

Many universities offered "area studies" of Southeast Asia, Africa, Latin America, and every other part of the globe. Political scientists were much too optimistic in supposing that the Third World would achieve stable democracy and economic growth. Some developing countries, mainly on the rim of Asia, did achieve both, but few academics predicted these success stories in advance. As Princeton economist Paul Krugman points out, no one has successfully predicted the next country or region of rapid economic growth; it always surprises us.

The academics' poor predictions grew out of the pervasive American fear that the Soviets would take over most of the developing areas. Cuba and the 1962 Missile Crisis were frightening warnings. Kennedy's advisors wrote urgently that either we develop the newly independent lands or the Communists would. These countries were undergoing shaky, vulnerable transitions, but U.S. help could guide them through and put them on the path to free-market democracy. This came to be called **developmentalism**. The Kennedy administration responded with the Agency for International Development (AID), the Peace Corps, and Vietnam.

The State Department's AID, the CIA, and the Ford Foundation funded studies on implementing developmentalist strategies, and academics won grants and built theories to support the strategies. Improving communications was touted as an important technique. But Third World countries developed along the lines of their own internal logic, not ours. Some received lots of U.S. money and advice and declined or stagnated. Others received little and prospered.

The theories underestimated the impact of culture by assuming that all peoples are ready for good governance and development. The corruption factor was almost totally overlooked. In an echo of the 1960s, recent alarms urged us to democratize the Middle East before radical Islam took it over. Review the mistaken assumptions of the developmentalist impulse of the 1960s before you sign up.

---

had to get clever, competitive, and productive. It is not natural resources but incentivized humans that really matter.

developmentalism
Early 1960s theory that America could develop Third World lands.

Another culprit is imperialism, but it too does not provide a complete explanation. In some countries, there was a great deal of imperialist exploitation; others, where there was not much to exploit, were left largely alone. The imperialists did not do nearly enough to get their colonies ready for independence. They should have provided more education and training.

Colonialism does not explain success stories in some ex-colonies. Consider what Hong Kong and Singapore had working against them. Both had been British colonies for more than a century. Both are very small with zero natural resources; they were economically important only for their locations. Both were occupied by the Japanese in World War II. That should predict poverty, but now both are thriving economies at the First World level.

In explaining such apparent anomalies, cultural factors loom large. Some cultures take quickly to economic development; others do not. Those who believe that the future can be formed by one's own activities generally do well. Fatalism, on the other hand, keeps people

strategic variable
Factor you can change that makes a big improvement.

policy
The specific choices governments make.

passive; all is God's will. Cultures that instill discipline and a work ethic can grow rapidly. So far, the winners in this cultural race seem to be the Confucian-influenced lands of East Asia, although few predicted their growth. Indeed, some decades ago, scholars attributed Asia's *backwardness* to its Confucian heritage. In the right circumstances, as in India, a seemingly sleepy culture can wake up and produce an economic miracle. In Nigeria, the Igbo are an example of this; what was latent in their culture became manifest under the British. Do not write off Africa as forever poor. Cultures change.

Some social scientists seek a **strategic variable**, and that is usually in the area of **policy**, a regime's decisions, laws, and programs that may either encourage or retard growth. Governments have two types of economic policy tools: macroeconomic and microeconomic. Some economists urge governments to get the macroeconomy, sometimes called "the fundamentals," in order—little public debt, plentiful savings, low inflation, sufficient investment capital—and then stand back and let the market do its stuff. The German "economic miracle" followed this pattern. Third World technocrats—who are now as prominent in Nigeria as they are in Mexico—tend, however, to get into the microeconomy by choosing which industries to foster or phase out. Postwar Japan used considerable microeconomic management (as well as getting its fundamentals right).

Nigeria shows signs of both macroeconomic and microeconomic mismanagement. The president and ministers often propose major reforms and crackdowns on corruption, but little comes of them. The politicians and commercial interests who benefit from the present rip-off system block any change or investigation that hurts them. Nigeria's inflation, debt, and unemployment indicate poor choices at the macro level. And the oil industry, in Nigeria as in Mexico, is a constant temptation for microeconomic meddling. Leaving it to market forces would likely produce the best growth. In both countries, that is improbable. Economic rationality often conflicts with political expediency.

The impact of a given policy is hard to judge in advance; you have to see how it works out. Generous public spending (a macroeconomic policy) may keep Nigeria's state governments compliant but unleash inflation, currently around 20 percent a year in Nigeria. Nigeria subsidizes fuel prices to keep them low, and Nigerians riot at any suggestion of ending the cushy deal. Nigerian subsidies for fuel (a microeconomic policy) mean there is less to sell on the world market. Nigeria's technocrats understand that the subsidies must be cut, but the politicians don't dare.

The Corruption Factor

Since independence in 1960, Nigerian officials have stolen some $400 billion of the country's oil revenues, and none have been publicly tried for corruption, suggesting that officials fear what might come out in a trial. Little petroleum money reaches ordinary Nigerians, who stay terribly poor. This is one reason per capita GDP numbers—like all averages—often deceive. Yes, Nigerian oil earns the country a lot, but very few people benefit from the earnings. British economist P. T. Bauer coined the term *kleptocracy* (rule by thieves) to describe countries like Nigeria.

China Lessons

The Danger of Corruption

Nigeria ranks as one of the most corrupt countries in the world, worse than China or Russia. Billions of dollars in oil revenues pour into Nigeria but are skimmed off into private pockets, leaving most Nigerians poorer. Rich Nigerians could not care less. In much of the world, enriching one's family is what matters, not one's nation. Nigerian governors take their ample salaries as a starting point for more rapid enrichment, easy when there is a lot of oil revenue around.

Corruption can become so extreme that it damages legitimacy. One of the heartening developments of recent years is that corruption, until recently barely mentioned or shrugged off, has now become a hot political topic. Worldwide, people are fed up with corruption and vote against corrupt regimes. Part of the Arab Spring focused on the corruption of regimes in Tunisia, Egypt, Libya, and Syria. Special favors for friends and benefactors are hard to conceal in the digital age. The revolt against corruption can often be a positive thing for democracy. As in China, as Nigerians gain education, they are less willing to tolerate corruption.

Corruption is China's Achilles' heel, the main cause of cynical attitudes. Most Chinese are highly patriotic and appreciate their growing living standards, but this makes them more aware that power is abused for personal gain. The Zhongnanhai knows all this—academic researchers continually send public opinion survey results to Beijing ministries—but is reluctant to mount a full-scale anti-corruption campaign against the very cadres it needs to run China, a parallel to Nigeria's problem: "How can I run this place without payoffs?" The message to Beijing (and several other regimes), even warned by Xi Jinping: Kill corruption before it kills you.

Nigeria's Economic and Financial Crimes Commission (EFCC) charges hundreds of officials with corruption, but critics say that the EFCC uses corruption charges as political weapons to make disfavored candidates ineligible for election. President Obasanjo charged his vice president, Atiku Abubakar, with misusing a $125 million oil fund. Abubakar countered that Obasanjo was out to get him for leaving the PDP and joining an opposition party, which several did to protest Obasanjo's dictatorial tendencies. The head of the EFCC was booted out in 2008 when he started investigating former state governors, and the EFCC lost credibility. In Nigeria, one cannot tell genuine from political charges of corruption. Chances are that both accuser and accused are corrupt.

The corruption factor trips up the best-laid plans for the developing countries. In addition to the obvious unfairness and injustice, it siphons investment capital into private pockets and away from development. Corruption can be divided into petty and grand. The petty is the small demands for cash—called "dash" or "sweetbread" in West Africa. A friend of mine once flew into Lagos (then the capital of Nigeria) on an assignment for the World Bank. An airport health officer stopped him, saying his inoculation record (often required for travel in the tropics) was missing a stamp (it wasn't), but he could fix it for $20. My friend refused, arguing that he was there to help Nigeria. A higher official came and urged him to pay: "You are a rich man, and he is a poor man." My friend finally paid. Such holdups are still standard at Lagos airport and show the logic of petty corruption. Any time you need a stamp, permit,

Comparison

Corruption International

Corruption is nearly everywhere, according to Transparency International (TI), a Berlin-based organization that polls businesspeople on their perceptions of having to pay off government officials. TI ranks countries on a hundred-point scale, 100 being totally clean, 1 totally corrupt. Some of their 2013 Corruption Perceptions Index (CPI) findings are shown in the table. Notice that Russia, Iran, and Nigeria virtually tie each other and that the United States, Chile, and France are almost the same.

TI founder Peter Eigen was a World Bank official in charge of loans to East Africa but concluded that so much was skimmed off in graft that the loans did little good. To call attention to the massive problem—and to put pressure on governments for **transparency** in their financial dealings—he formed TI in 1993. A poor TI ranking chastises a corrupt country, hopefully pushing it to get clean.

Some scholars doubt the validity of the CPI (not to be confused with the U.S. Consumer Price Index), because it is just a compilation of subjective perceptions. It may miss secret transfers at the very highest levels. Rankings change from year to year—depending on which businesspeople are interviewed—and countries often trade positions on the TI rankings even though little in their behavior has changed. That weakness is built into TI's methodology, but there is no other way to measure corruption, even approximately. Corruption (along with drugs and crime) does not show up in GDP calculations, and crooked officials do not list "earnings from kickbacks" on their income tax. TI's CPI is the best measure we have. The big question is: Will TI's efforts over time increase rule of law and boost economic growth?

Denmark	91
Singapore	86
Canada	81
Germany	78
Britain	76
Japan	74
United States	73
Chile	71
France	71
Italy	43
Brazil	42
South Africa	42
China	40
India	38
Mexico	34
Russia	28
Iran	25
Nigeria	25
Iraq	16
Afghanistan	8

SOURCE: Transparency International

transparency

Exchanges of money open to public scrutiny. (Opposite: opacity.)

license, or help from the police—even driving or parking a car—in the Third World, be prepared to pay sweetbread, tea money, *la mordida*, or *baksheesh*. It is a normal part of daily life. In Nigeria, police set up roadblocks and demand 15 cents per car.

Some see petty corruption as an unofficial welfare system to redistribute wealth from the better off to the poor, but it seldom goes to the truly needy and does not spare those with little money. Petty corruption is the demands of underpaid policemen and bureaucrats who are in a position to help or hurt. The historical root of Third World corruption is a less-developed country acquiring a large bureaucracy before it is ready for one. Spain set up Latin America with a giant bureaucracy to supervise its extractive economy, and it has been

the source of corruption ever since. One solution is to pay civil ser- **kickback**
vants more, but developing countries can seldom afford to. Another   Bribe paid to government
is to cut the number of regulations and the bureaucrats needed to   official for a contract.
enforce them. Chile got a lot less corrupt after it did both.

Petty corruption is a minor annoyance compared with grand corruption, the use of official positions to grab money wholesale—called "eating" in much of Africa. Grand corruption depends on international ties, such as oil contracts and banks that launder money. Petty corruption stays inside the country, but if the money goes into overseas accounts, you can be sure it is the grand variety. (The governor of oil-rich Bayelsa state stashed millions abroad and was arrested in Britain in 2005 but slipped out disguised as a woman. Back in Nigeria, he enjoyed immunity as a governor.) Transparency International's CPI (see box on previous page) does not distinguish between the two levels. A country could theoretically have grand corruption at the highest levels and still have an honest civil service, but, more typically, one is a reflection of the other. If a postal clerk steals your stamps, chances are the minister of communications is stealing much larger amounts. Grand corruption does far more damage than petty corruption, for it eats capital that should go for economic growth, health, and education. It is a major factor in keeping the Third World poor.

Grand corruption is not simply a matter of crooks in government but of foreign businesses willing to pay them—usually by **kickbacks**—for profitable contracts. Many corporations that would never bribe in their home countries reckon it is normal in the Third World: If they do not kick back, a competing firm that does will get the contract. There is no quick, simple cure for corruption, which often feels as if it is rooted in the soil. Some countries have developed an ethos of clean administration, but this may take centuries. A nobleman developed the Swedish civil service in the seventeenth century and hired other aristocrats, thereby stamping the Swedish bureaucracy with traditions of honor and service. But change can come quicker. Singapore, a new country (independent only in 1965), applied draconian penalties to produce clean administration in a region with much corruption. It also became rich. With enough will at the top, it can be done.

Nigeria's pervasive corruption drains it of development, education, and infrastructure funds, but those who would clean it up should be warned: Corruption may be the only thing that holds Nigeria together. The president's ability to direct oil revenues to cooperative ministers and state governors keeps them on board. A thorough cleanup could take away their incentives to cooperate. Governors, especially in the Muslim north, might decide that they get nothing worthwhile from Abuja and depart the federation, leading to civil war.

Oil and Democracy

There is an unhappy correlation between petroleum wealth and nondemocratic government. One of the few democratic oil-producing countries is Norway, but it has many other industries and a long history of democracy. Note how this book's four major oil-producing countries—Russia, Mexico, Nigeria, and Iran—are (or recently were) nondemocratic. Russia attempted democracy but slid back to authoritarianism. Mexico is coming out of a long period of one-party domination. Nigeria, at this moment, has an elected government but, for most of its history, did not. And Iran overthrew one tyrant but got worse ones.

Oil also fosters corruption. Nigerian politics works through a series of payoffs to state governors—most of them PDP—and other officials to keep them in line. They do not like to lose their lucrative positions and will do whatever it takes to keep them, including violence against opponents. Like Iran, Nigeria is a member of *OPEC,* which assigns quotas to member states to keep oil production down and oil prices up. The good thing about Nigeria here is that it is one of the easiest OPEC members to bribe to get officials to (secretly) produce above Nigeria's quota. Millions of barrels of oil are pumped into offshore tankers without paying fees or taxes, something that could not happen without the complicity of officials. None of this builds democracy, however.

What is it about oil that works against democracy? True, it produces vast wealth, but the wealth is terribly concentrated and seldom benefits the whole society. Oil becomes the great prize of politics in that country, for the person who controls the oil monopolizes power. One of Putin's main efforts (successful) was to bring back Russia's petroleum and natural gas production into state hands. The oil industry employs relatively few, and its wealth is squandered in corruption, overlarge bureaucracies, showcase projects, and rewards for supporters of the regime. The oil bonanza lets rulers avoid investing in infrastructure, industry, and other long-term growth mechanisms.

Democracy

Corporate Social Responsibility

A current business buzzword is "corporate social responsibility" (CSR). According to CSR doctrine, large firms must recognize that they owe more than profits to shareholders; they owe fairness and justice to "stakeholders"—their workers, the community, and the environment. Now, most corporations' annual reports trumpet their CSR activities, although critics charge they are little more than public relations.

Nigeria offers a good example of CSR—or lack of it—in action. Oil companies make immense profits from the Niger Delta, but their pollution has ruined much of it for farming and fishing, the traditional economic activities. Most agree that the oil companies have a responsibility for the immense environmental damage. The oil companies pay the Nigerian government some $30 billion to $40 billion a year in taxes and royalties, but much of it disappears into private pockets; little gets back to the Delta. Trying to practice CSR, the oil companies have also given millions to the Niger Delta Development Commission, but it too is corrupt and inefficient. The companies, aware of the poverty and resentment, also build health clinics in the Delta, but many of them are either empty (because the government will not staff them) or are burned down by neighboring tribes who are jealous that they did not get a clinic.

There is no way CSR can deliver help to poor Nigerians; it will always get skimmed. The best thing would be to get the Nigerian government to adopt accountability and transparency standards, but the oil companies have no leverage for this. Said one Chevron executive in Nigeria: "It's very difficult for the private sector to replace government. It's not our role." Some economists argue that corporations should just produce income, out of which come wages and taxes. Stakeholders have real grievances, but they must act through democratic governments to obtain pollution laws, fair wages, public health, and so on. These things need force of law, not corporate generosity. CSR is unlikely to solve vast problems of poverty and corruption.

The petrostates' impressive incomes have netted them little that can be sustained after the oil runs out. When that happens, the elites will still have their secret overseas bank accounts to live well forever. Some Nigerian politicians have London penthouses. A few wealthy Nigerians live in luxury, but some 60 percent, many of them subsistence farmers, live in **absolute poverty**. Nigeria, loaded with oil and natural gas, generates a small fraction of the electricity it needs and is plagued by power blackouts. Far too few power plants have been built, so Nigerians who can afford it have their own generators, making Nigeria the world's largest market for private generators.

absolute poverty
Living on $1.25 a day or less.

What to do with the oil has thus become one of Nigeria's most difficult political problems: how to make sure oil serves the long-term good of all Nigerians. Most Nigerian oil is produced through joint ventures between foreign firms and the Nigerian National Petroleum Corporation (NNPC), which gets most of the revenues. Like Mexico's Pemex, the NNPC is notoriously corrupt. Most presidents try to reform the oil industry to clean up corruption, but key groups, including state governors, block their efforts. Some are tempted to nationalize all Nigerian oil production, but that would simply concentrate more wealth and encourage more corruption. Privatizing Nigeria's oil might help, but only if it were total—that is, with oil companies able to buy the oilfields outright. No Nigerian government will do that, as it would eliminate the kickbacks that come from leases. The stated reason for rejecting any such sales, as in Mexico, will always be: "What? Sell Nigeria's sacred patrimony to greedy foreign capitalists? Never!" Nationalism cloaks corruption.

One possibility is a joint Nigerian–international board of supervisors (perhaps staffed by Danes and Singaporeans) with power of oversight and audit. Such a board would make Nigeria's oil deals transparent and take them out of government hands. The oil revenues should not go to Nigeria's federal treasury, where they could be disbursed to favored officials, but into an internationally supervised bank to make loans for infrastructure, education, and founding and expanding valid enterprises. Microloans have been effective in encouraging thousands of start-up businesses—sometimes just one woman with a sewing machine—at low cost in developing areas. If done well and honestly, oil could give Nigeria a growing economy that would use but not depend on petroleum.

Africa's economies have improved in recent decades. Life expectancy, literacy, girls in school, and many other indicators have climbed. We sometimes forget that there are African success stories. Senegal and Botswana are examples of positive development. Effective leadership, sound policies, and the promotion of a national political culture make a difference. Remember, we used to write off Asia as hopeless.

Review Questions

Learning Objective 11.1 Describe the impact of European colonialism on Africa, p. 425.

1. Outline the main colonial empires circa 1900.
2. How did the British invent Nigeria?
3. Explain *divide and rule* and how it impacted Africa later.

Learning Objective 11.2 Explain why Third World elections are so problematic, p. 432.

4. Why has Nigeria had mostly military governments?
5. Can federalism actually worsen Nigeria's fragmentation?

6. Could Nigeria develop a dominant-party system? What prevents it?

Learning Objective 11.3 Illustrate the ways Nigeria shows political fragmentation, p. 437.

7. Can Nigeria's Christian-Muslim *cleft* be healed?
8. Explain Nigeria's Biafra War.
9. Can a deeply fragmented society sustain stable democracy?

Learning Objective 11.4 Characterize the praetorian tendency in some lands, p. 442.

10. Is Nigeria a *failed state*? Why or why not?

11. Why have there been so many military takeovers in Nigeria?
12. Why do *praetorians* ever give up power?

Learning Objective 11.5 Explain why plentiful oil works against political and economic development, p. 446.

13. Why are Nigeria's GDPpc figures meaningless?
14. Why does oil work against democracy in Nigeria?
15. Why is corruption so deeply rooted in some countries?

Key Terms

absolute poverty, p. 453
aquifer, p. 433
caliphate, p. 426
cleft, p. 441
cross-cutting cleavages, p. 441
cumulative, p. 442
desiccation, p. 433
developmentalism, p. 447

divide and rule, p. 428
indirect rule, p. 428
jihad, p. 426
kickback, p. 451
pan-Africanism, p. 429
patronage, p. 444
policy, p. 448
praetorianism, p. 443

Sahel, p. 433
savanna, p. 433
sharia, p. 435
strategic variable, p. 448
sub-Saharan, p. 433
torn, p. 441
transparency, p. 450

Further Reference

Achebe, Chinua. *There Was a Country: A Personal History of Biafra.* New York: Penguin, 2012.

Apter, Andrew H. *The Pan-African Nation: Oil and the Spectacle of Culture in Nigeria.* Chicago: University of Chicago Press, 2005.

Bah, Abu Bakarr. *Breakdowns and Reconstruction: Democracy, the Nation-State, and Ethnicity in Nigeria.* Blue Ridge Summit, PA: Lexington Books, 2005.

Campbell, John. *Nigeria: Dancing on the Brink.* Lanham, MD: Rowman & Littlefield, 2011.

Collier, Paul. *Wars, Guns, and Votes: Democracy in Dangerous Places.* New York: HarperCollins, 2009.

Cunliffe-Jones, Peter. *My Nigeria: Five Decades of Independence.* New York: Palgrave, 2010.

Howe, Herbert M. *Ambiguous Order: Military Forces in African States.* Boulder, CO: Lynne Rienner, 2004.

Kenny, Charles. *Getting Better: Why Global Development Is Succeeding—And How We Can Improve the World Even More.* New York: Basic Books, 2011.

Larémont, Ricardo René, ed. *Borders, Nationalism, and the African State.* Boulder, CO: Lynne Rienner, 2005.

Lewis, Peter M. *Growing Apart: Oil, Politics, and Economic Change in Indonesia and Nigeria.* Ann Arbor, MI: University of Michigan Press, 2007.

Meagher, Kate. *Identity Economics: Social Networks and the Informal Economy in Nigeria.* Woodbridge, UK: James Currey, 2010.

Okonjo-Iweala, Ngozi. *Reforming the Unreformable: Lessons from Nigeria.* Cambridge, MA: MIT Press, 2012.

Paden, John N. *Faith and Politics in Nigeria: Nigeria as a Pivotal State in the Muslim World.* Washington, DC: U.S. Institute of Peace, 2008.

Peel, Michael. *A Swamp Full of Dollars: Pipelines and Paramilitaries of Nigeria's Oil Frontier.* London: I. B. Tauris, 2009.

Soyinka, Wole. *You Must Set Forth at Dawn.* New York: Random House, 2006.

Young, Crawford. *The Postcolonial State in Africa: Fifty Years of Independence, 1960–2010.* Madison, WI: University of Wisconsin Press, 2012.

Chapter 12
Iran

Persian domes inspired architecture far and wide, even in Russia.

 ## Learning Objectives

12.1 Compare and contrast Iran with its neighboring countries.

12.2 Outline the difficulties of a theocratic political system.

12.3 Demonstrate the relationship between Islam and modernization.

12.4 Apply Brinton's theory of revolution to Iran's Islamic Revolution.

12.5 Evaluate the possibilities of Iran turning into a democracy.

WHY IRAN MATTERS

Iran helps us understand why it is so difficult to turn the Middle East toward democracy. The region, caught between Islam and modernization, seethes with resentment. Although Iran differs from its Arab neighbors in language (Persian) and religion (the Shia branch of Islam), several share the problem of sudden oil wealth destabilizing traditional political arrangements. There was no way the Middle East could have moved smoothly from monarchy to democracy. Can it now? Iran, having gone through one major revolution in 1979, could experience another. Iran's 2013 elections revealed how much Iranians want change, and Iran's clerical establishment shows signs of listening to them. Is Iran's Islamic Republic, one of the world's few theocracies, a stable and durable answer to the problem of modernizing Muslim lands? If not, what is?

Impact of the Past

12.1 **Compare and contrast Iran with its neighboring countries.**

Much of Iran is an arid plateau around 4,000 feet above sea level. Some areas are rainless desert; some get sufficient rain only for sparse sheep pasture. In this part of the world, irrigation made civilization possible, and whatever disrupted waterworks had devastating consequences. Persia's location made it an important trade route between East and West, one of the links between the Middle East and Asia. Persia thus became a crossroads of civilizations and one of the earliest of the great civilizations.

The trouble with being a crossroads is that your country becomes a target for conquest. Indo-European-speaking invaders took over Persia about the fifteenth century BC and laid the basis for subsequent Persian culture. Their most famous kings: Cyrus and Darius in the sixth century BC. The invasions never ceased, though: the Greeks under Alexander in the third and fourth centuries BC, the Arab Islamic conquest in the seventh century AD, Turkish tribes in the eleventh century, Mongols in the thirteenth century, and many others. The repeated pattern was one of conquest, the founding of a new dynasty, and its falling apart as quarrelsome heirs broke it into petty kingdoms. This fragmentation set up the country for easy conquest again.

Iran, known for most of history as Persia (it was officially renamed only in 1935), resembles China. Both are heirs to ancient and magnificent civilizations that, partly at the hands of outsiders, fell into "the sleep of nations." When Iran awoke, it was far behind the West, which, like China, Iran views as an adversary. If and how Iran will move into modernity is one of our major questions.

Although it does not look or sound like it, Persian (*Farsi*) is a member of the broad Indo-European family of languages; the neighboring Arabic and Turkic are not. Today, Farsi is the mother tongue of about half of Iranians. Another fifth speak Persian-related languages (such as Kurdish). A quarter speak a Turkic language, and some areas speak Arabic and other tongues. The non-Farsi speakers occupy the Iranian periphery and have, at times, been discontent with rule by Persians. In Iranian politics today, to be descended from one of the non-Persian minorities is sometimes held against politicians.

The Arab Conquest

Allah's prophet Muhammad died in Arabia in 632, but his new faith spread like wildfire. **Islam** means "submission" (to God's will), and this was to be hastened by the sword. Islam arrived soon in Iran by military conquest. The remnant of the Sassanid Empire, already exhausted by

Geography

Bound Iran

Iran is bounded on the north by Armenia, Azerbaijan, the Caspian Sea, and Turkmenistan; on the east by Afghanistan and Pakistan;

on the south by the Gulf of Oman and the Persian Gulf;

and on the west by Iraq and Turkey.

Iran

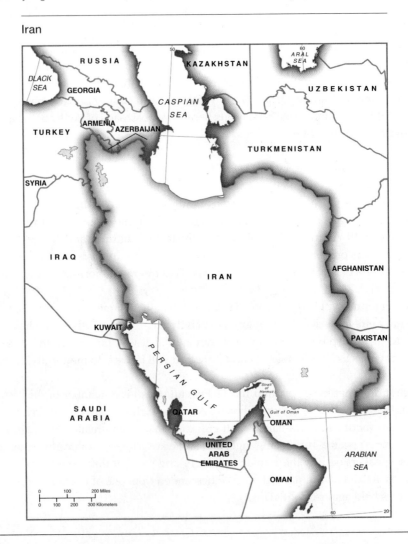

centuries of warfare with Byzantium, was easily beaten by the Arabs at Qadisiya in 637, and, within two centuries, Persia was mostly Muslim. Adherents of the old religion, Zoroastrianism, fled to India where, today, they are a small, prosperous minority known as *Parsis*.

The Arab conquest was a major break with the past. In contrast to the sharp social stratification of Persian tradition, Islam taught that all Muslims were, at least in a spiritual sense, equal. Persia adopted the Arabic script, and many Arab words enriched Persian. Persian culture flowed the other way, too, as the Arabs copied Persian architecture and civil administration. For centuries, Persia was swallowed up by the Arab empires, but, in 1055, the Seljuk Turks invaded from Central Asia and conquered most of the Middle East. As usual, their rule soon fell apart into many small states, easy prey for Genghis Khan, the Mongol "World Conqueror" whose horde thundered in from the east in 1219. One of his descendants who ruled Persia embraced Islam at the end of that century. This is part of a pattern Iranians are proud of: "We may be conquered," they say, "but the conqueror ends up adopting our superior culture and becomes one of us."

The coming of the Safavid dynasty in 1501 boosted development of a distinctly Iranian identity. The Safavids practiced a minority version of Islam called **Shia** (see next Geography box) and decreed it Persia's state religion. Most of their subjects switched from **Sunni** Islam and are Shias to this day. Neighboring Sunni powers immediately attacked Safavid Persia, but this enabled the new regime to consolidate its control and develop an Islam with Persian characteristics.

Islam
Religion founded by Muhammad.

Shia
Minority branch of Islam.

Sunni
Mainstream Islam.

Majlis
Arabic for assembly; Iran's parliament.

Western Penetration

It is too simple to say Western cultural, economic, and colonial penetration brought down the great Persian empire. Safavid Persia was attacked from several directions, mostly by neighboring Muslim powers: the Ottoman Turks from the west, Uzbeks from the north, and Afghans from the east. In fighting the Ottomans, Safavid rulers made common cause with the early Portuguese, Dutch, and English sea traders in the late sixteenth and early seventeenth centuries. As previously in the region's history, the outsiders were able to invade because the local kingdoms had weakened themselves in wars, a pattern that continues in our day.

In 1722, Afghan invaders ended the Safavid dynasty, but no one was able to govern the whole country. After much chaos, in 1795, the Qajar clan emerged victorious and founded a dynasty. Owing to Persian weakness, Britain and Russia became dominant in Persia, the Russians pushing in from the north, the British from India. Although never a colony, Persia, like China, slid into semicolonial status, with much of its political and economic life dependent on imperial designs, something Persians strongly resented. A particularly vexatious example was an 1890 treaty giving British traders a monopoly on tobacco sales in Persia. Muslim clerics led mass hatred of the British tobacco concession, and the treaty was repealed.

At this same time, liberal, Western ideas of government seeped into Persia, some brought, as in China, by Christian missionaries (who made very few Persian converts). The Constitutional Revolution of 1906–1907 (in which an American supporter of the uprising was killed) brought Persia's first constitution and first elected parliament, the **Majlis**. The struggles over the tobacco

shah
Persian for king.

modernizing tyrant
Dictator who pushes a country ahead.

concession and constitution were led by a combination of two forces: liberals who hated the monarchy and wanted Western-type institutions and Muslim clerics who also disliked the monarchy but wanted a stronger role for Islam. This same combination brought down the **Shah** in 1979; now these two strands have turned against each other over the future of Iran.

At almost exactly the same time—1905 in Russia, 1906 in Persia—corrupt and weak monarchies promised somewhat-democratic constitutions in the face of popular uprisings. Both monarchies, dedicated to autocratic power and hating democracy, only pretended to deliver, a prescription for increasing mass discontent. A new shah inherited the throne in 1907 and shut down the Majlis with his Russian-trained Cossack bodyguard unit. Mass protest forced the last Qajar shah to flee to Russia in 1909; he tried to return in 1911 but was forced back even though Russian troops occupied Tehran. The 1907 Anglo-Russian treaty had already cut Persia in two, with a Russian sphere of influence in the north and a British one in the south. Before World War I, the British discovered Persia's oilfields and began their exploitation. During the war, Persia was nominally neutral, but its strategic location turned it into a zone of contention and chaos. Neighboring Turkey allied with Germany, and Russia and Britain allied with each other. Russian, British, and German agents tried to tilt Persia their way.

The First Pahlavi

As is often the case when a country degenerates into chaos, military officers see themselves as saviors of the nation—the *praetorianism* that still lurks in Nigeria. In 1921, an illiterate cavalry officer, Reza Khan, commander of the Cossack brigade, seized power and, in 1925, had himself crowned shah, the founder of the short-lived (1925–1979) Pahlavi dynasty. The nationalistic Reza took the pre-Islamic surname Pahlavi and told the world to call the country by its true name, Iran, from the word *aryan*, indicating the country's Indo-European roots. (Nazi ideologists also loved the word aryan, which they claimed indicated genetic superiority. Indeed, the ancient Persian Zoroastrians preached racial purity.)

Like Atatürk, Reza Shah was determined to modernize his country (see Comparison box below). His achievements were impressive. He molded an effective Iranian army and used it to suppress tribal revolts and unify Iran. He created a modern, European-type civil service and a national bank. He replaced traditional and Islamic courts with civil courts operating under Western codes of justice. In 1935, he founded Iran's first Western-style university. Under state supervision and fueled by oil revenues, Iran's economy grew. Also like Atatürk, Reza Shah ordered his countrymen to adopt Western dress and women to stop wearing the veil. But Reza also kept the press and Majlis closely obedient. Critics and dissidents often died in jail. Reza Shah was a classic **modernizing tyrant**.

World War II put Iran in the same situation as World War I had. It was just too strategic to leave alone. Iran was a major oil producer and conduit for U.S. supplies to the desperate Soviet Union. As before, the Russians took over in the north and the British (later the Americans) in the south. Both agreed to clear out six months after the war ended. In September 1941, the British exiled Reza Shah, who tilted toward Germany, to South Africa, where he died in 1944. Before he left, he abdicated in favor of his son, Muhammad Reza Pahlavi.

The Americans and British left Iran in 1945; the Soviets did not, and some propose that this incident marked the start of the Cold War. Stalin claimed that Azerbaijan, a Soviet *republic* in the Caucasus, was

containment
U.S. Cold War policy of blocking expansion of communism.

entitled by ethnic right to merge with the Azeris of northern Iran and refused to withdraw Soviet forces. Stalin set up puppet Communist Azeri and Kurdish governments there. In 1946, U.S. President Truman delivered some harsh words, Iran's prime minister promised Stalin an oil deal, and Stalin pulled out. Then the Majlis canceled the oil deal.

The Last Pahlavi

Oil determined much of Iran's twentieth-century history. Oil was the great prize for the British, Hitler, Stalin, and the United States. Who should own and profit from Iran's oil—foreigners, the Iranian government, or Iranians as a whole? Major oil deposits were first discovered in Iran in 1908 and developed under a British concession, the Anglo-Persian (later Anglo-Iranian) Oil Company (AIOC). Persia got little from the oil deal, and Persians came to hate this rich foreign company in their midst, one that wrote its own rules. Reza Shah ended the lopsided concession in 1932 and forced the AIOC to pay higher royalties.

The AIOC still rankled Iranians, who voted in the radical nationalist Prime Minister Muhammad Mossadeq in the early 1950s. With support from Iranian nationalists, liberals, and leftists, Mossadeq nationalized AIOC holdings. Amid growing turmoil and what some feared was a tilt to the Soviet Union, young Shah Muhammad Reza Pahlavi fled the country in 1953. The British urged Washington to do something, and President Eisenhower, as part of the U.S. **containment** policy, had the CIA destabilize the Tehran government. It was easy: The CIA's Kermit Roosevelt arrived with $1 million in a suitcase, rented a pro-Shah mob, and encouraged a coup. Mossadeq was out, the Shah flew back and was restored, and the United States won a battle in the Cold War. Washington thought it had solved the Iran problem, but, a quarter century later, Iran fell into the hands of America haters far worse than Mossadeq.

Like his father, the Shah became a modernizing tyrant, promoting what he called his "White Revolution" from above (as opposed to a red revolution from below). Under the Shah, Iran had excellent relations with the United States. President Nixon touted the Shah as our pillar of stability in the Persian Gulf. We were his source of technology and military hardware. Some 100,000 Iranian students came to U.S. universities, and 45,000 American businesspeople and consultants surged into Iran for lucrative contracts. (This point demonstrates that person-to-person contacts do not always lead to good relations between countries.)

The United States was much too close to the Shah, supporting him unstintingly and unquestioningly. The Shah was Western educated and anti-Communist and was rapidly modernizing Iran; he was our kind of guy. Iranian unrest and opposition went unnoticed by the U.S. embassy. Elaborate Iranian public relations portrayed Iran in a rosy light in the U.S. media. Under Nixon, U.S. arms makers sold Iran massive quantities of weapons. We failed to see that Iran and the Shah were two different things and that our unqualified backing of the Shah was alienating many Iranians. We ignored how the Shah governed by means of a dreaded secret police, the SAVAK. We failed to call a tyrant a tyrant. Only when the Islamic Revolution broke out did we learn what Iranians really thought about the Shah. We were so obsessed by communism penetrating from the north that we could not imagine a bitter, hostile Islamic revolution coming from within Iran.

Comparison

Atatürk and Reza Shah

During the 1920s, two strong personalities in adjacent Middle Eastern lands attempted to modernize their countries from above in the face of much traditional and Islamic reluctance. Kemal Atatürk in Turkey and Reza Shah in Iran were only partly successful. Both were nationalistic military officers and Muslims but **secular** in outlook; both wished to separate **mosque** and state.

In economics, both were *statists* and made the government the number-one investor and owner of major industries. Both pushed education, the improved status of women, and Western clothing. As such, both aroused traditionalist opposition led by Muslim clerics. Both ordered "You will be modern!" but religious forces opposed their reforms and continue to do so to this day.

Their big difference: Atatürk ended the **Ottoman** monarchy and firmly supported a republican form of government in Turkey. He pushed his reforms piecemeal through parliament, which often opposed him. Reza Shah rejected republicanism and parliaments as too messy; he insisted on an authoritarian monarchy as the only way to modernize his unruly country, as did his son. Although Turkey has had several coups since Atatürk, it has not been ripped apart by revolution. Atatürk built some political institutions; the Pahlavi shahs built none.

secular
Nonreligious.

mosque
Muslim house of worship.

Ottoman
Turkish imperial dynasty, fourteenth to twentieth centuries.

OPEC
Cartel of oil-rich countries designed to boost petroleum prices.

mullah
Muslim cleric.

What undermined the Shah's rule? Too much oil money went to his head. With the 1973 Arab-Israeli war, oil producers worldwide got the chance to do what they had long wished: boost the price of oil and take over oil operations from foreign companies. The Shah, one of the prime movers of the Organization of Petroleum Exporting Countries (**OPEC**), gleefully did both. What Mossadeq started, the Shah finished. World oil prices quadrupled. Awash with cash, the Shah went mad with vast, expensive schemes. The state spent oil revenues for the greater glory of Iran and its army, not for the Iranian people, creating resentment that hastened the Islamic Revolution. Oil led to turmoil.

The sudden new wealth caused great disruption. The Shah promoted education, but as Iranians became more educated, they could see that the Shah was a tyrant. Some people got rich fast while most stayed poor. Corruption grew worse than ever. Millions flocked from the countryside to the cities where, rootless and confused, they turned to the only institution they understood—the mosque. In their rush to modernize, the Pahlavis alienated the Muslim clergy. Not only did the Shah undermine the traditional cultural values of Islam, he seized land owned by religious foundations and distributed it to peasants as part of his White Revolution. The **mullahs** also hated the influx of American culture, with its alcohol and sex. Many Iranians saw the Shah's huge military expenditures—at the end, an incredible 17 percent of Iran's GDP—as a waste of money. As Alexis de Tocqueville noted in his study of the French Revolution, economic growth hastens revolution.

One of Iran's religious authorities, **Ayatollah** Khomeini, criticized the Shah and incurred his wrath. The Shah had Khomeini exiled to Iraq in 1964 and then forced him to leave Iraq in 1978. France allowed Khomeini to live in a Paris suburb, from which his recorded messages were telephoned to cassette recorders in Iran to be duplicated and distributed through mosques nationwide. Cheap cassettes bypassed the Shah's control of Iran's media and helped bring him down.

ayatollah
"Sign of God"; top Shia religious leader.

In the late 1970s, matters came to a head. The Shah's overambitious plans had made Iran a debtor nation. Discontent from both secular intellectuals and Islamic clerics bubbled up. And, most dangerous, President Jimmy Carter made human rights a U.S. foreign policy goal. As part of this, the Shah's dictatorship came under criticism in Washington. Shaken, the Shah began to relax his grip, and that is precisely when all hell broke loose. As de Tocqueville observed, the worst time in the life of a bad government is when it begins to mend its ways. Compounding his error, Carter showed his support for the Shah by exchanging visits, proof to Iranians that we backed a hated tyrant. In 1977, Carter and the Shah had to retreat into the White House from the lawn to escape the tear gas that drifted over from the anti-Shah protest (mostly by Iranian students) in Lafayette Park.

By late 1978, the Shah, facing huge demonstrations and (unknown to Washington) dying of cancer, was finished. Shooting into the crowds of protesters just made them angrier. The ancient Persian game of chess ends with a checkmate, a corruption of the Farsi *shah mat* ("the king is trapped"). On January 16, 1979, the last Pahlavi left Iran. *Shah mat.*

Geography

Sunni and Shia

More than 80 percent of the world's Muslims practice the mainstream branch of Islam, called Sunni (from *sunna*, the word of the Prophet). A minority branch (of 100 million) called Shia is scattered unevenly throughout the Muslim world.

The two split early over who was the true successor (*caliph*) of Muhammad. Shias claim the Prophet's cousin and son-in-law, Ali, has the title, but he was assassinated in 661. Shia means followers or partisans; hence, Shias are the followers of Ali. When Ali's son, Hussein, attempted to claim the title, his forces were beaten at Karbala in present-day Iraq (now a Shia shrine) in 680, and Hussein was betrayed and tortured to death. This gave Shia a fixation on martyrdom; some of their holidays feature self-flagellation.

Shia also developed a messianic concept that was lacking in Sunni. Shias in Iran hold that the line of succession passed through a series of 12 *imams* (religious leaders), of whom Ali was the first. The twelfth imam disappeared in 873 but is to return one day to "fill the world with justice." He is referred to as the Hidden Imam and the Expected One.

Shias are no more "fundamentalist" than other Muslims who also interpret the Koran strictly. Although the origin and basic tenets of the two branches are identical, Sunnis regard Shias as extremist, mystical, and crazy. Some 60 percent of Iraqis are Shia, but only in Iran is Shia the state religion. With their underdog status elsewhere, some Shias rebel (with Iranian money and guidance), as in Lebanon, southern Iraq, eastern Arabia, and Bahrain. Shia imparts a peculiar twist to Iranians, giving them the feeling of being isolated but right, beset by enemies on all sides, and willing to martyr themselves for their cause.

The Key Institutions

12.2 Outline the difficulties of a theocratic political system.

A Theocracy

Two-and-a-half millennia of monarchy ended in Iran with a 1979 referendum, carefully supervised by the Khomeini forces, that introduced the Islamic Republic of Iran and a new constitution. As in most countries, the offices of head of state and head of government are split. But instead of a figurehead monarch (as in Britain) or weak president (as in Germany), Iran's leading religious figure is far more powerful than its president, who does much day-to-day administration but under the sharp limits laid down by the religious chief. That makes Iran a **theocracy** and a dysfunctional political system whose two leaders can be at odds.

Theocracy is rare and tends not to last. Even in ancient times, priests filled supporting rather than executive roles. Russia's tsar, officially head of both church and state, was far over on the state side; he wore military garb, not priestly. Iran (plus Afghanistan and Sudan) attempted a theocratic system. For centuries, Persia's Shia clerics, reasoning that only God can ultimately govern, avoided and ignored politics, an attitude called *quietism*. They did not like any shah but practiced a kind of separation of mosque and state. Khomeini's radical design overturned all this; now clerics must rule an "Islamic republic." Murmurings of returning to quietism can now be heard from some Iranian theologians unhappy with the corruption and power-seeking of the clerical establishment.

Khomeini developed the principle of the **velayat-e faqih**, rule of the Islamic jurist. In the Khomeini constitution, the leading Islamic jurist, the *faqih*, serves for life. "Jurist" means a legal scholar steeped in Islamic, specifically Shia, religious law. (The closest Western equivalent is **canon law**. In medieval Europe, canon lawyers were among the leading intellectual and political figures.) Allegedly, the *faqih*, also known as the "Spiritual Guide" and "Supreme Leader," can use the Koran and Islamic commentaries to decide all issues, even those having nothing to do with religion. (An **Islamist** would likely say everything is connected with religion.)

Khomeini (1902–1989), the first and founding *faqih*, was nearly all-powerful. Successors are chosen by an Assembly of Experts of 86 Muslim clerics elected every eight years, who are supposed to choose from among the purest and most learned Islamic jurists. The man they elect (Islam permits no women religious leaders) is not necessarily an ayatollah, the highest of Shia jurists. In 1989, the Experts chose Ali Khamenei, a *hojatollah*, the rank just below, but he was immediately promoted to ayatollah. Khamenei, expected to serve for life, lacks Khomeini's (do not confuse the two names) charisma and Islamic authority but is still the real power. Downplaying his role in day-to-day politics, from behind the scenes, Khamenei names the heads of all major state and religious organizations and can declare war. He controls the judiciary, armed forces, security police, intelligence agencies, radio, and television. He is much more powerful than Iran's president and holds a veto over presidential appointments. Seeing 2009 street protests as a threat to his rule, Khamenei abandoned neutrality and made a rare public

theocracy
Rule by priests.

velayat-e faqih
"Guardianship of the Islamic jurist"; theocratic system devised by Khomeini.

canon law
Internal laws of the Roman Catholic Church.

Islamist
Someone who uses Islam in a political way.

appearance to declare the blatantly rigged election fair and finished and to threaten punishment for protesters.

Below the Supreme Leader is an ordinary president, who is elected, but from a very short list of only those approved by the strange Council of Guardians, and may serve two four-year terms. In 1997, almost by accident, a relatively liberal cleric, Muhammad Khatami, was elected president, but every move he made to reform the system was blocked by the Supreme Leader. Khatami filled two terms but accomplished nothing. Mahmoud Ahmadinejad was elected (but not fairly) in 2005 and reelected in a fake landslide in 2009. In 2011, a power struggle broke out between Khamenei and the ambitious Ahmadinejad. Hassan Rouhani, a moderate cleric, was elected in 2013 with vague promises to liberalize and improve relations with the United States. He, too, accomplished little.

Iran's Legislature

Iran's unicameral (one-house) legislature, the Islamic Consultative Assembly (*Majlis*), sometimes disagrees with presidents and blocks their proposals. Some of the Majlis's 290 deputies fear a president getting too much power or liberalizing too much. Members are elected for four-year terms from 265 single-member districts, like Britain and the U.S. Congress. Minimum voting age is 18 (raised from 16). Additional seats are reserved for non-Muslim deputies: five each for Assyrian Christians, Jews, and Zoroastrians; two for Armenian Christians; none for Baha'is. The Speaker of parliament is a major position. The constitution guarantees MPs immunity from arrest, but the conservative judiciary still jails MPs who call too loudly for reforms.

Electoral balloting, except in 2009, is generally free and fair, but permission to run is stringently controlled. The Council of Guardians must approve all candidates, and they disqualify thousands who might be critical. Open liberals are thus discouraged from even trying to run. The low-turnout 2012 parliamentary elections gave the Majlis to Ahmadinejad's radicals because no openly liberal candidates were allowed, and not many Iranians bothered to vote.

More powerful than the Majlis is the Council of Guardians, a strange institution combining features of an upper house, a supreme court, an electoral commission, and a religious inquisition. Its 12 members serve six years each, half of them changed every three years. The *faqih* chooses six Islamic clerics; Iran's supreme court (the High Council of Justice) names another six, all Islamic lawyers, who are approved by the Majlis.

The Council examines each Majlis bill to make sure it does not violate Islamic principles. If a majority decides it does, the bill is returned to the Majlis to be corrected. Without Council approval, a bill is, in effect, vetoed. All bills aiming at reform are blocked in this way. To settle conflicts between the Majlis and the Council, an "Expediency Council" appointed by the Leader has become like another legislature. In 2005, the Expediency Council was given additional powers to oversee the president. Iran's conservative religious establishment had grown mistrustful of the ambitious Ahmadinejad.

More important, the Council of Guardians scrutinizes all candidates and has the power to disqualify them without explanation. The Council scratches a large fraction of Majlis and presidential candidates, including a top Ahmedinejad advisor in 2013, indicating the conservative clerics' displeasure at the rambunctious president. In 2002, President Khatami and the Majlis had tried to take this power away from the Council of Guardians, but the Council vetoed the

Geography

Cruising the Persian Gulf

The countries bordering the Persian Gulf contain most of the world's proven petroleum reserves. Some of you may do military service in the Gulf, so start learning the geography now. Imagine you are on an aircraft carrier making a clockwise circle around the Gulf. Upon entering the Strait of Hormuz, which countries do you pass to port?

Oman, United Arab Emirates, Qatar, Saudi Arabia, Bahrain (an island), Kuwait, Iraq, and Iran.

bills. The Council of Guardians thus makes the Iranian system unreformable. If there is ever to be serious change in Iran, the Council of Guardians will have to go.

Emerging Parties?

Parties are not illegal under Iran's constitution, but the government does not allow them; only individual candidates run. Even Khomeini dissolved his own Islamic Republic Party in 1984. Lack of party labels makes Iranian elections less than free, for, without them, voters cannot discern who stands for what. Because voters have no *party IDs*, Iranian elections are often decided by late *swings* that come from out of nowhere. It is difficult to count how many seats each of the several "tendencies" control; they have to be estimated. In practice, candidates are linked with informal parties and political tendencies called "fronts" or "coalitions." Eventually, these may turn into legal parties. Observers see four main political groupings plus many factions and individual viewpoints.

Radicals, the most extreme supporters of the Islamic Revolution—such as former President Ahmadinejad—preach a populist line of help for the poor and hatred of the United States. They claimed to adhere to Khomeini's original design for an Islamic republic but ended up disobeying Iran's current Spiritual Guide, who slapped down Ahmadinejad. In 2013, his United Principlist Front disappeared, and radicals are now marginalized.

Conservatives, calmer and generally older than the radicals, want a nonfanatic Islamic Republic with economic growth. In 2012, they ran as several fronts and won 60 percent of the vote and 182 seats. Iran's politics is now largely a debate among conservatives over how much to loosen up. Current President Rouhani is described as a moderate conservative.

Reformists tend to cluster in the educated middle class. They favor privatization of state enterprises, less Islamic supervision of society, elections open to most candidates, fewer powers for the Council of Guardians, and dialogue with the United States. In the late 1990s, they held a majority in the Majlis, but the Council of Guardians now disqualifies most of their candidates. In 2012, they ran as three coalitions and won a total of 36 percent of the votes and 75 seats.

Liberals would go further. Popular among Iranian students, they emphasize democracy and civil rights and want totally free elections and an end to all social controls imposed by the Islamists. In economics, however, they are a mixed bag, ranging from free marketers to socialists. Knowing the Council of Guardians would reject them, few liberals even try to run for office. Both reformists and liberals keep quiet in public but voice their complaints among friends. They joined forces in 2013 to vote in Rouhani as president.

Democracy

Iran's Half-fair 2013 Presidential Election

Hopes stirred with Iran's June 2013 presidential election, which seemed to offer a chance to curb rigid Islamic rule, liberalize a bit, and improve the sagging economy. Hassan Rouhani, age 64, won 51 percent of the first-round vote in a field of six because Iranians ready for change had no one else to support. (In second place, the mayor of Tehran got 17 percent.) Rouhani was not really a liberal—they are not allowed to run—but more a moderate and pragmatist. Turnout was a hefty 73 percent.

The possibility of change was enough to energize Iranian liberals and others who dislike the rigid and corrupt system. Many Iranians, not allowed to vote for liberal or reformist candidates, had been ignoring elections, but the mild-mannered Rouhani came across on televised debates as more liberal than the other five. Iranians read into him reformist qualities he never had and never delivered. The crowd created a hero for itself.

Rouhani followed in the footsteps of fellow-cleric Muhammad Khatami, who won in a surprise landslide in 1997. Unknown before the election, Khatami hinted at reform and suddenly became a symbol of change. When no liberals are allowed to run, Iranians turn to the least-bad candidate as a form of protest. In the 2005 election, Ahmadinejad got the votes of poor and less-educated Iranians, who believed his demagogic promises of welfare. By 2013, however, many of Ahmadinejad's supporters, disgusted by the feeble economy and repression, went to Rouhani.

The 2013 election was not completely democratic, but it was much better than 2009. The Council of Guardians in both elections screened out hundreds of candidates deemed liberal or insufficiently Islamic. Only a few were allowed to run. But in 2009, balloting was rigged, and critical newspapers were closed.

Iran's religious hard-liners backed Ahmadinejad. Iran elects presidents in a French-style two rounds. If no one gets a majority in the first round, a runoff between the two biggest winners is held two weeks later. In 2005, Ahmadinejad won the second round 62 to 36 percent, with a low turnout, as many Iranians knew the fix was in.

Just before the 2009 election, Ahmadinejad was behind in polls, but, within four hours of the polls closing, officials announced that the ballots had been counted—with amazing speed, considering the record 85 percent turnout—and that Ahmadinejad had won on the first round with an improbable 63 percent, so no runoff was necessary. Mexico's PRI in its heyday could not have done it better.

Iranians were not fooled and turned out massively in 2009, connected by the Internet, Facebook, and Twitter, to protest the electoral fraud. "Where is my vote?" their placards asked. Police and the **Basij** militia ruthlessly broke up their rallies, killing more than 30 and jailing thousands. There were reports of torture and rape (both male and female) in prison. A woman student was shot by a sniper on a Tehran street and instantly became a martyr. Hundreds of critics were given show trials in which some "confessed" their crimes on television. Most Iranians knew better, and the regime lost legitimacy.

In 2013, by contrast, the regime seemed to understand that it could not repeat 2009, so it allowed—possibly even set up—the moderate Rouhani to win in fair balloting from among a hand-picked field. There were celebrations instead of protests, and many hoped that Rouhani would deliver on reforms. He didn't. As before, Ayatollah Khamenei was in charge and was uninterested in change.

Some of the regime's sharpest critics were leaders of the 1979 revolution who now do not like its authoritarianism and seek separation of mosque and state. Hundreds of clerics, some of them senior figures of Shia Islam, now denounce repression and demand reform, without which, they warn, there could be another revolution. A few clerics

Basij

Persian for "mobilization"; Iranian volunteer paramilitary force.

called Supreme Leader Khamenei a dictator and urged him to resign. Iran's clerical establishment began to splinter. President Rouhani tries to bridge the conservative and reformist wings of Iran's Shia establishment so as to preserve overall clerical rule.

Iran could be described as a political system waiting to be free. The potential is there, but institutional changes would have to be made. First, the power of the Leader would have to be reduced to that of a purely spiritual guide with few or no temporal powers. Next, the Council of Guardians would have to be abolished. With these two changes, Iran's institutions could quickly turn it into a democracy, with a real executive president, a critical Majlis, multiparty elections, and a free press. Iran has the greatest democratic potential of any Persian Gulf country.

Personalities

Hassan Rouhani

Hassan Rouhani emerged from a string of important positions in the very heart of Iran's Islamic Republic to win the 2013 presidential election on the first round. Although little in his past pointed to it, he billed himself as a moderate and reformist. Many Iranians who voted for him were disappointed with how little he reformed the system, especially in human rights.

Born Hassan Feridon, he changed his name to Rouhani, meaning "spiritual." Son of a spice merchant, he was born in 1948 in a small town in northern Iran not far from Tehran. Aiming to be a mullah from childhood, his early education was largely clerical, but he added a law degree from Tehran University in 1972. As a teenager, he joined the anti-Shah Islamist movement and was arrested many times by SAVAK.

An early supporter of Ayatollah Khomeini, he was elected to the majlis in 1980 and served there 20 years, becoming head of the defense and foreign affairs committees and of national broadcasting. During the long Iran–Iraq war, he held several executive positions, including head of air defense. He long served on Iran's National Security Council, Expediency Council, and Assembly of Experts. In 1999, he was eager to crack down on student protesters. Rouhani even headed Iran's nuclear negotiating team for two years and knows the issues well.

So far, Rouhani sounds like a rigid Islamist revolutionary. But something may have changed him, possibly his years in the 1990s at Scotland's Glasgow Caledonian University earning a masters and doctorate in law. His 1999 thesis: "The Flexibility of Sharia with Reference to the Iranian Experience." Rouhani did not like the 2005 election of Mahmoud Ahmadinejad and resigned many of his positions, an indication of the split between traditional conservative Iranian clerics and young radicals.

Rouhani speaks fluent English and Arabic and cautiously entered into negotiations aimed at lifting U.S. and EU sanctions by settling the nuclear issue. He knows Iran's economy is in bad shape and that the only way to improve it is through foreign trade, now largely blocked. He probably also knows that Israel is not bluffing in its readiness to end Iran's nuclear program. It was hard to tell if Rouhani would open Iran to international inspections of possible nuclear-weapons sites. The U.S. message to Tehran: You can have nukes or you can have trade; you can't have both.

Many Iranians, especially young people, are fed up with the Islamic restrictions on their lives and the weak economy. Rouhani, however, was either unable or unwilling to implement promised reforms, and citizen bitterness grew. He began to resemble the earlier self-proclaimed moderate reformer, the ineffective Mohammad Khatami, president from 1997 to 2005. Without some timely reforms, Iran could explode again.

Iranian Political Culture

12.3 **Demonstrate the relationship between Islam and modernization.**

Many Iranians and others in developing lands do not want their traditional culture replaced by Western culture. "We want to be modern," say many Third Worlders, "but not like you. We'll do it our way, based on our values and our religion." Whether you can be a modern, high-tech society while preserving your old culture is a key question today. Will efforts to combine old and new cultures work or lead to chaos? In some cases, like Japan, it has worked. For Islamic nations, so far, it has not. The key factor may be the flexibility and adaptability of the traditional culture, which is very high in the case of Japan. Japan learned to be modern but still distinctly Japanese. Can Muslim countries do the equivalent?

Beneath all the comings and goings of conquerors and kingdoms, Persian society kept its traditions for centuries. As in China, dynastic changes did not disturb most of the population, poor farmers and shepherds, many of them still tribal in organization. Iranian traditional society was stable and conservative. Islam, the mosque, the mullah, and the **Koran** gave solace and meaning to the lives of most Persians. People were poor but passive.

Then came modernization—mostly under foreign pressure—starting late in the nineteenth century, expanding with the development of petroleum, and accelerating under the two Pahlavi shahs. According to what political scientists call *modernization theory*, a number of things happen more or less simultaneously. First, the economy changes, from simple farming to natural resource extraction to manufacturing and services. Along with this comes urbanization, the movement of people from the country to the cities. Education levels rise; most people become literate, and some go to college. People consume more mass media—at first newspapers, then radio, and finally television—until many are aware of what is going on in their country and in the world. A large middle class emerges and, with them, interest groups. People now want to participate in politics; they resent being treated like children. Modernization, in this optimistic theory, leads gradually to democracy, but this process is not smooth, automatic, or guaranteed.

It was long supposed that *secularization* comes with modernization, and both Atatürk and the Pahlavis had tough showdowns with the mullahs. But Iran's Islamic Revolution and other religious revivals now make us question the inevitability of secularization. Under certain conditions—when things change too fast, when the economy slows and unemployment grows, and when modernization repudiates traditional values—people may return to religion with renewed fervor. If their world seems to be falling apart, church or mosque gives stability and meaning to life. This is as true of the present-day United States as it is of Turkey. In the Muslim world, many intellectuals first passionately embraced modernizing creeds of socialism and nationalism, only to despair and return to Islam. (Some intellectuals are now interested in free-market capitalism, which had been unpopular because it was associated with the West.)

The time of modernization is a risky one in the life of a nation. If the old elite understand the changes that are bubbling through their society, they will gradually allow democratization in a way that does not destabilize the system. A corrupt and rigid elite, on the other hand, that is convinced the masses are not ready for democracy (and never will be), blocks political reforms until there is a tremendous head of steam.

Koran
Muslim holy book.

Islamism
Islam turned into political ideology.

Then, no longer able to withstand the pressure, the elite suddenly gives way, chaos breaks out, and it ends in tyranny. If the old elite had reformed sooner and gradually, they might have lowered the pressure and eased the transition to democracy. Brazil and Taiwan are examples of a favorable transition from dictatorship to democracy. Iran under the Shah is a negative example.

The Shah was arrogant, believing that he alone would uplift Iran. He foresaw no democratic future for Iran and cultivated few sectors of the population to support him. When the end came, few Iranians did support him. Indeed, the Shah scorned democracy in general, viewing it as a chaotic system that got in its own way, a view as ancient as the Persian empire, which believed that, under one ruler, it would surely beat a quarrelsome collection of Greek city states. (Wrong!) The Shah supposed that Iran, under his enlightened despotism, would soon surpass the decadent West. Asked why he did not relinquish some of his personal power and become a symbolic monarch, like the king of Sweden, the Shah replied that he would—just as soon as Iranians became like Swedes.

The answer to this overly simple view is that, yes, when your people are poor and ignorant, absolute rule is one of your few alternatives. Such a country is far from ready for democracy. But after considerable modernization—which the Shah himself had implemented—Iran became a different country, one characterized by the changes discussed earlier. An educated middle class resents one-man rule; the bigger this class, the more resentment builds. By modernizing, the Shah sawed off the tree limb on which he was sitting. He modernized Iran until it no longer tolerated him.

Islam as a Political Ideology

Some object to the term "Islamic fundamentalism." Fundamentalism was coined in the early twentieth century to describe U.S. Bible Belt Protestants. It stands for inerrancy of Scripture: The Bible means what it says and is not open to interpretation. But that is the way virtually all Muslims view the Koran, so Muslims are automatically fundamentalists. Some thinkers propose we call it *Islamic integralism* instead, indicating a move to integrate the Koran and sharia with government. Integralism, too, is borrowed, from a Catholic movement early in the twentieth century whose adherents sought to live a Christlike existence.

The Sunni movement for returning to the pure Islam of the founders is *salafiyya*, which has been around for centuries in several forms. It is not part of Shia Islam; *salafis*, in fact, despise Shia. The Wahhabi Islam of Saudi Arabia, the Afghan Taliban, and ISIS are *salafi*.

Ayatollah Khomeini developed an interesting ideology that resonated with many Iranians. Traditionally, Shia Islam disdained politics, waiting for the return of the Twelfth Imam to rule (see box below). Khomeini and his followers, departing from this old tradition, decided that, while they wait, the top Shia religious leaders should also assume political power. Called by some **Islamism**, it was not only religious but also social, economic, and nationalistic.

The Shah and his regime, said Khomeini, had both abandoned Islam and turned away from economic and social justice. They allowed the rich and corrupt to live in Westernized luxury while most struggled in poverty. They sold out Iran to the Americans, exchanging the people's oil for U.S. weapons. Tens of thousands of Americans lived in Iran, corrupting Iran's youth with their "unclean" morals. By returning to the Koran, as interpreted by the

Political Culture

Is Islam Antimodern?

Most Middle East experts deny that there is anything inherent in Islamic doctrine that keeps Muslim societies from modernizing. Looking at cases, though, one finds no Islamic countries that have fully modernized. Under Atatürk, Turkey made great strides between the two wars, but an Islamic party has undone some of his reforms. In Huntington's terms, Turkey is a *torn* country, pulled between Western and Islamic cultures. Recently, Malaysia, half of whose people are Muslim, has scored rapid economic progress. Generally, though, Islam coincides with backwardness, at least as we define it. Some Muslim countries are rich, but only because oil has brought them outside revenues.

By itself, Islam probably does not cause backwardness. The Koran prohibits loaning money at interest, but there are ways to work around that. Islamic civilization was, for centuries, far ahead of Christian Europe in science, philosophy, medicine, sanitation, architecture, steelmaking, and much more. Translations from the Arabic taught Europe classic Greek thought, especially Aristotle, which helped trigger the Renaissance and Europe's modernization. A millennium ago, you would hear Muslims concluding that Christianity was keeping Europe backward.

But Islamic civilization faltered, and European civilization modernized. By the sixteenth century, when European merchant ships arrived in the Persian Gulf, the West was ahead of Islam. Why? According to some scholars, early Islam permitted independent interpretations of the Koran (*ijtihad*), but, between the ninth and eleventh centuries, this was replaced by a single, orthodox interpretation (*taqlid*), and, as a result, intellectual life atrophied. Islam has never had a reformation.

The Mongol invaders of the thirteenth century massacred the inhabitants of Baghdad and destroyed the region's irrigation systems, something that the Arab empire never recovered from. (The Mongols' impact on Russia was also devastating.) Possibly because of this, Islam turned to mysticism. Instead of an open, flexible, and tolerant faith that was fascinated by learning and science, Islam turned sullen and rigid. When the Portuguese opened up a direct trade route between Europe and Asia, bypassing Islamic middlemen, trade through the Middle East declined sharply and so did the region's economy.

Islam has a structural problem in its combination of religion and government, which makes it difficult to split mosque and state. Those who try to do so (such as Atatürk) are resisted. Even today, many Muslims want *sharia* to be the law of the land. This creates hostility between secular modernizers and religious traditionalists, who compete for political power, a destructive tug-of-war that blocks progress. Egypt had an ugly showdown in 2013 between the two groups.

A major factor was the domination by European (chiefly British) imperialists starting in the nineteenth century. This created the same resentment we saw in China, the resentment of a proud civilization brought low by unwelcome foreigners: "You push in here with your guns, your railroads, and your commerce and act superior to us. Well, culturally and morally, we are superior to you, and, eventually, we'll kick you out and show you." With this comes hatred of anything Western and therefore opposition to modernity, because accepting modernity means admitting that the West is superior. Islam teaches that it is superior to all other civilizations and will eventually triumph worldwide. Devout Muslims do not like ideas to the contrary.

If Islamic countries do not discard their cultural antipathy to modernity—which need not be a total imitation of the West—their progress will be slow and often reversed. Millions of Muslims living in the West are modern and still Islamic. Ideas for religious modernization are already afoot in Islam with, ironically, Iranian intellectuals in the lead. Eventually, we could see societies that are both modern and Muslim. One of the best ways to promote this: Educate women, which is precisely what is happening in Iran.

mullahs, Iranians would not only cleanse themselves spiritually but also build a just society of equals. The mighty would be brought low and the poor raised up by welfare benefits administered by mosques and Islamic associations. Like communism, Islamism preaches leveling of class differences but through the mosque and mullahs rather than through the Party and *apparatchiks*.

Islamism is thus a catchall ideology, offering an answer to most things that made Iranians discontent. It is a potent mix, but can it work? Probably not. Over time, its several strands will fall apart, and its factions will quarrel. Islamism's chief problem is economics (as we shall consider in greater detail later). As Islamism recedes as a viable ideology, look for the reemergence of other ideologies in Iran.

Democracy and Authority

Observers, both Iranian and Western, estimate that only a minority of Iranians support the current regime and that rule by the mullahs could be overturned. Even if reformists someday prevail, could Iranians establish a stable democracy, or was the Shah right—do Iranians need a strong hand to govern them? There were two impulses behind the 1979 revolution: secularist intellectuals seeking democracy and Islamists seeking theocracy. The secular democrats, always a minority, threw in with the more numerous Islamists, figuring that they would oust the Shah and then the secularists, being better educated, would lead. But the Islamists, better organized and knowing exactly what they wanted, used the secular democrats and then dumped them (and, in some cases, shot them). Many secular democrats fled to other countries. Learning too late what was happening to them, some democratic supporters of the Revolution put out the slogan: "In the dawn of freedom, there is no freedom."

But these secular democrats did not disappear; they laid low and, outwardly, went along with the Islamic Revolution. To have opposed it openly could have earned them the firing squad. Among them are the smartest and best-educated people in Iran, the very people needed to make the economy grow. With Iran's economic decline, many lost their jobs and became private consultants and specialists, working out of their apartments. More than 2 million Iranians have left since 1979, chiefly for the United States and Canada. Many Iranians speak scathingly in private of the oppression and economic foolishness of the regime. These people are not anti-Islam; they just don't want to be ruled by mullahs. In 2013, such people came out enthusiastically for Rouhani, who seemed to be extending an olive branch to them.

These people believe Iranians are capable of democracy. They argue that the anti-Shah revolution was hijacked by the Islamists but that its original impulse was for democracy, not theocracy, and this impulse still remains. Especially now that people have tasted the economic decline, corruption, and general ineptitude of the mullahs, they are ready for democracy. If the regime ever opens up, the secular democrats will go public to demand open elections with all parties eligible. For now, they stay quiet and aim their TV satellite dishes to pick up critical views from the large (800,000) Iranian community in the United States.

Iranian Nationalism

Nationalism, always strong in Iran, is coming back. Some analysts hold that Iran, today, is more motivated by nationalism than by religious fervor. Iran, like China, strives to increase its power

Political Culture

Are Iranians Religious Fanatics?

Only a minority of Iranians are Muslim fanatics. Not even the supposed Islamic fundamentalists are necessarily fanatic. Many Iranians are perfectly aware that religion is a political tool and are fed up with it. Massive regime propaganda depicts the United States as the "Great Satan," but most Iranians are very friendly to the few Americans who visit. Some have been in the United States or have relatives there. Many remember that when Iran was allied with America, Iraq did not dare invade. Iran was the only Muslim country where tens of thousands spontaneously showed sympathy with Americans after 9/11. Do not confuse regime propaganda with the attitudes of ordinary citizens.

Ironically, Iranians pointed to the Taliban government of neighboring Afghanistan as *salafi* extremists. The Taliban were overthrown in 2001 but are now fighting to come back. Far stricter than Iranian Islamists, the Taliban confine women to the home and require all men to grow beards. Why the conflict with Iran? Like most Afghans, the Taliban are Sunni and attack the Shia minority, some 1.5 million of whom fled to Iran. The Taliban killed Iranian intelligence agents who were aiding Afghan Shias. In 2014, Tehran scathingly denounced the salafi ISIS as non-Islamic. Dangerous stuff, this religious extremism.

and prestige. Ahmadinejad attempted to fuse Shia Islam with Iranian nationalism, something conservatives called "deviant."

hajj
Muslim pilgrimage to Mecca.

Islam was imposed on Persia by Arab swords, and Iranians, to this day, harbor folk memories of seventh-century massacres by crude, barbaric invaders. Iranians do not like Arabs and look down on them as culturally inferior and lacking staying power. By adopting Shia, Iranians were and are proud to distinguish themselves from their mostly Sunni neighbors. The Iranian message: "We are actually the best Muslims and should lead the Islamic world." Accordingly, not far under the surface of Iranian thought is Persian nationalism, affirming the greatness of their ancient civilization, which antedates Islam by a millennium.

The Shah especially stressed Persian nationalism in his drive to modernize Iran. The Shah was Muslim and had himself photographed during religious devotion, such as during his **hajj**, a pilgrimage required of all Muslims who can afford it once in their lifetime. But the Shah's true spirit was secular and nationalistic: to rebuild the glory of ancient Persia in a modern Iran. If Islam got in the way, it was to be pushed aside. The Shah was relatively tolerant of non-Muslim faiths; Baha'is (a universalistic and liberal offshoot of Islam), Jews, and Christians were unharmed. Since the Islamic Revolution, non-Muslims have been treated harshly, especially the 300,000 Baha'is, Iran's largest minority religion, who are regarded as dangerous heretics. For centuries, Iran's sense of its unique Persianness coexisted uneasily with its Islam. The Shah's modernization program brought the two strands into open conflict.

The Islamic Revolution of 1979 did not totally repudiate the nationalist strand of Iranian thought. It put the stress on the religious side of Persianness, but the long and horrible war with Iraq from 1980 to 1988 brought out the regime's Persian nationalism. Iranians were fighting not only for their faith but for their country and against Iraq, a savage, upstart Arab country that did not even exist until the British invented it in the 1920s. Iran celebrates two types of holidays: Persian and Muslim. The Persian holidays are all happy, such as New

Democracy

Iran's Angry Students

In the late 1970s, Iranian students, most of them leftists, battled to overturn the old regime. Now Iran's students—whose numbers have exploded to 2 million—again demonstrate for civil rights. Many students are outspoken liberals and push for pluralism, a free press, and free elections. They also worry about the serious lack of jobs for graduates. Most students backed Rouhani in 2013. Police have, at times, raided campuses to arrest student protesters. (The Shah did the same.)

Every year, hard-line courts—especially the Revolutionary Court—close liberal newspapers and block Web sites. Between 2,000 and 4,000 Iranian editors, writers, professors, public opinion pollsters, student leaders, and politicians are in jail. (Rouhani quietly set some of them free.) Some of them fought in the 1979 Revolution and in the long war against Iraq. At least a hundred dissidents were mysteriously killed. Iran, per capita, is the world's death penalty leader. When Ahmadinejad spoke at a Tehran university, students chanted "death to the dictator," which led to an angry regime crackdown on students and professors on many campuses.

Could students and intellectuals one day lead the way to democracy? By themselves, probably not. They are not allowed to organize and lack ties to the broad masses of Iranians, who are just beginning to show open discontent. But in the 2013 election, students began to organize and join with other groups to criticize the clericalist regime. In many countries, students have been the sparkplugs of revolution.

Year (*Noruz*). The Islamic holidays are mostly mournful, such as the day of remembrance of the martyrdom of Hussein at Karbala, during which young Shia men beat themselves until they bleed.

Patterns of Interaction

12.4 Apply Brinton's theory of revolution to Iran's Islamic Revolution.

Religion as a Political Tool

Manipulate, use, discard. This is how Khomeini's forces treated those who helped them win the Revolution. Like turbaned Bolsheviks, the Islamists in the late 1970s hijacked the Iranian Revolution as it unfolded. First, they captured the growing discontent with the Shah and his regime. By offering themselves as a plausible and effective front organization, they enlisted all manner of anti-Shah groups under their banner—the democratically inclined parties of the National Front, the Iran Freedom Movement, the Marxist (and Soviet-connected) Tudeh Party, and Islamic guerrilla movements. They had these groups do their dirty work for them and then got rid of them, sometimes by firing squad. The flowering of democratic, Islamic, secular, and socialist parties that accompanied the Shah's overthrow was crushed within three years. As an example of revolutionary technique, Lenin would have admired their skill and ruthlessness.

In doing all this, the Islamists used their religion much as the Bolsheviks used Marxism: as a tool, a recruiting and mobilizing device, a means of gaining authority and obedience, and a way to seize and consolidate power. They were, of course, serious about Islam, but, in a revolutionary situation, the instrumental uses of their faith predominated over the devotional. If you want to seize state power, you cannot be otherworldly; you must be very shrewd and practical. There is nothing "crazy" about the Islamists who run Iran; they make calm and rational decisions calculated to benefit themselves. In our eyes, to be sure, some look crazy.

After some time immersed in politics, the power side takes over, and the original religious (or ideological) side takes a back seat. As with the Bolsheviks, this soon leads to opportunism and cynicism among the politically involved and, ultimately, to regime decay. The ruling group turns into a self-serving new class. This is why regimes that base themselves on ideology or religion (Islamism combines both) have finite life spans. After a while, everyone notices the power and greed of the ruling class, and mass disillusion sets in; the regime loses legitimacy. This is happening in Iran. Iran's Islamic Revolution is burning out.

An example of this was the seizure of the U.S. embassy in Tehran by student militants in November 1979, which brought American cries of outrage and a complete break in relations. The embassy takeover and holding of 52 American officials for 444 days indeed broke every rule in the diplomatic book and seemed to prove that mad fanatics governed Iran.

A closer look reveals the incident as a domestic Iranian power play, cynically manipulated by the Khomeini forces. The ayatollah wished to complete the Islamic Revolution and get rid of the moderate prime minister he had appointed early in 1979, Mehdi Bazargan. The admission of the ailing Shah to the United States for cancer treatment stirred mass rage in Iran. The revolutionaries claimed that medical help for the Shah proved that the United States still supported the ousted regime. Student militants invaded and took over the U.S. embassy, probably not intending to stay. The embassy had already been reduced to a skeleton staff. No shots were fired; the U.S. Marine guards were ordered not to shoot. The American hostages were treated harshly, but none was killed. The militants published classified embassy documents (pieced together from the shredder) purporting to show how dastardly the Americans were. Khomeini took advantage of the chaotic situation. He let the students occupy the embassy, got rid of all moderates in the government, prevented U.S. interference (as there had been in 1953), and carried the revolution to a frenzied high point.

The Islamic activists whipped up anti-American hysteria ("Death to USA!") to consolidate their hold on the country. Humiliated and powerless, Bazargan resigned. Anyone opposed to the embassy takeover was fired or worse. One foreign-ministry official (who had dropped out of Georgetown University to promote revolution) helped some U.S. diplomats escape via the Canadian embassy. He was tried and shot. Khomeini's followers seemed to enjoy watching President Carter squirm, especially after the aborted U.S. rescue mission in April 1980. Carter's apparent weakness on Iran hurt him in the 1980 election, which he lost to Reagan.

At that point, the holding of U.S. diplomats had exhausted its utility for Khomeini. Knowing Reagan was not averse to military measures, Tehran released the diplomats just as he was inaugurated. The militants who had seized and held the Americans had also served their purpose. Considered unreliable, some were arrested and executed. Others were sent to the front in the war with Iraq, where they died in the fighting. As French revolutionary Danton observed (just before his execution), the revolution devours its children.

Moderates	Islamists
calm the Islamic Revolution	maintain the Revolution
shift power to Majlis	preserve power of faqih
permit some parties	ban non-Islamic parties
free press	censored press
permit Western women's attire	Islamic attire only (veil)
improve relations with West	keep distant from West
dialogue with America	hate America
open nuclear programs to inspection	continue nuclear programs without inspection
liberalize economy	keep economy statist

Moderates and Islamists in Iran

Much of Iranian politics takes place in the largely unseen clash between conservative moderates and radical Islamists. You have to look closely for differences between the two. Both are conservative, but in different ways—the former calm and pragmatic, the latter pugnacious and revolutionary. Both are strongly Muslim and support the Islamic Revolution, but the conservatives are not interested in spreading it beyond Iran. The conservatives are more open to a free market; the radicals want state controls. Regime change may come from the struggle between Iran's militants and moderates, not from any outside—including U.S.—pressures.

After the 1986 Iran-Contra fiasco, in which White House aides attempted to secretly sell U.S. missiles to Iranian "moderates," the term "Iranian moderate" disappeared from Washington's vocabulary. The U.S. officials fell for a sucker play by Iranian revolutionaries, who set up the deal and then leaked word that the United States was trading with Iran, illegal under U.S. law. The incident embarrassed the Reagan administration.

Conservative moderates want to preserve the Islamic Republic but think that the radicals are reckless and dangerous. Presidents Hashemi Rafsanjani (1989–1997), Mohammad Khatami (1997–2005), and Hassan Rouhani (2013–), all clerics, are such moderates. Iranian conservatives prefer to quietly exercise their influence in the religious hierarchy but, after the 2009 rigged election, publicly denounced Ahmadinejad, especially as he relied more and more on the Revolutionary Guards and less and less on the clergy. The alienation of Iran's conservatives from Ahmadinejad's government spelled serious trouble for him, as the conservatives had the ear of the Supreme Leader.

The militant Islamists such as President Ahmadinejad (2005–2013) want a truly Islamic republic, although few of them are clerics. Anything else means giving in to Iran's enemies—the West in general, the United States in particular—with eventual loss of Iran's independence, culture, and religion. They block any liberalizing reforms, close newspapers, fire ministers who stray, and put political critics on trial. The arrest of visiting Iranian-American academics and journalists for alleged espionage was a radical attempt to scuttle any improvement in U.S.-Iranian relations.

Ahmedinejad's radical Islamists tried to control the Islamic Revolutionary Guards (*Pasdaran*). Originally formed in 1979 to support Khomeini, the Guards took many casualties in the war with Iraq and now, with 125,000 members, are separate from and higher than the

Political Culture

Does Islam Discriminate Against Women?

Iran is one of the better Muslim countries in the treatment of women. Unlike the Arab kingdoms on the southern shore of the Gulf, Iranian women drive cars, go to school, work outside the home, and participate in politics. Iranian women are now more than 60 percent of Iran's university students. (The U.S. percentage is similar. Any ideas why?) But, in Iran, there are still tough restrictions on dress, contact with males, and travel. An Iranian girl can be forced into marriage at age 13 and divorced whenever the husband wishes.

Devout Muslims swear that women are deeply honored in their societies, but their place is in the home and nowhere else. Women are kept at a subservient status in most Islamic countries; often they get little education, cannot drive a car, and their testimony is worth half of men's in courts of law. But such discrimination does not always come from the Koran. In some Muslim countries (not Iran), such customs as

the seclusion of women, the veil, and female genital mutilation are pre-Islamic and were absorbed by Islam (much as Europeans adopted, for Christmas, the pagan worship of trees). These non-Koranic imports can therefore be discarded with no harm to the faith, maintain Muslim feminists, who are increasingly speaking out and organizing. If they succeed, they will greatly modernize their societies. The widespread education of Iranian women predicts social and legal change.

One feminist voice is that of 2003 Nobel Peace Prize winner Shirin Ebadi, a lawyer and regime opponent who defends women's rights and cites the Koran to show that Islam should not discriminate against women. (She now lives in London.) Many Iranian women share this view and protest for their rights; some are arrested, tried, and imprisoned. Iran is becoming the birthplace of Islamic feminism.

regular armed forces, rather like the Nazi Waffen SS. They have their own army, navy, and air force, get the best weapons, run industries, dominate the defense and intelligence ministries, and supervise Iran's nuclear program. Former Pasdaran hold about a third of Majlis seats. President Ahmadinejad, a Pasdaran in the war with Iraq, placed many in high positions and relied on them. Conservative critics, including clerics, opposed Ahmadinejad's use of the Pasdaran. Ayatollah Khamenei reasserted control of the Pasdaran, denying Ahmadinejad an important power base.

Another radical support is the Basij, an Islamist militia subordinate to the Pasdaran with branches in most mosques. Basij membership, according to dubious official figures, is 10 million but is probably closer to 1 million. Ahmadinejad was a *basiji*, and they supported him. Decreed by Ayatollah Khomeini in 1979 to enforce the revolution and supervise morals and women's attire, Basij toughs helped crush protests after the rigged 2009 election. If the Revolutionary Guard is the SS, the Basij are the SA (Storm Troopers). Basij presence on the streets diminished when Rouhani took office.

Recent Iranian opinion has trended against the radicals. Reformists and conservatives beat Ahmadinejad supporters for seats on municipal councils and in the Majlis in 2008. Pragmatic conservatives seem to control the Assembly of Experts, which chooses the next Supreme Leader. Populist Ahmadinejad would likely have lost a fair election in 2009. Moderate Rouhani, clearly with Ayatollah Khamenei's approval, won in 2013.

On the fringe, both inside and outside the country, are Iranians who want to get rid of the whole Islamic Revolution. They stand no chance. A few monarchists wish to restore the son of the last Pahlavi, born in 1960 and now living in the West, to the throne—a quixotic venture. The times are against monarchy; every decade, there are fewer and fewer ruling (as opposed to figurehead) monarchs.

On the other side, some Marxist-type revolutionaries, the Mujahedin-e Khalq (Fighters for the People), who earlier worked with the Islamists to overthrow the Shah, now try to overthrow the Islamists. Among them are some of the young militants who seized the U.S. embassy. Subsequently, it is estimated that more than 10,000 Mujahedin were executed by the Khomeini forces. Their survivors were sheltered in and sponsored by Saddam Hussein's Iraq, which invaded and massacred Iranians (sometimes with poison gas) during the 1980s, so few Iranians support the Mujahedin. Even Washington now considers them a crazy cult.

The Revolution Burns Out

Iran could be used to update Crane Brinton's classic 1938 theory of revolution. The Shah's regime loses its legitimacy. Antiregime groups form, rioting breaks out, and the Shah leaves. Initially, moderates take power, but ruthless Islamists soon dump them and drive the revolution to a frenzied high. But this burns itself out; eventually, a *Thermidor*, or calming down, arrives. It was almost as if Iranians had read Brinton and gone through his stages—although the last may have happened without a clear-cut Thermidor. Instead, it may have been a low-key, rolling Thermidor marked by Khatami's election in 1997.

No revolution lasts forever. In Iran, we can see an effort to become stable and normal, which is opposed by Islamic radicals. But time is probably on the side of the normalizers. Many mullahs have corrupted themselves; some do not go out in clerical garb. Mullahs run the *bonyads*, foundations originally set up to redistribute the wealth of the Shah and his supporters. These *bonyads* now control billions of dollars and much of Iran's industry. They are supposed to be run for the good of all, a sort of Islamic socialism, but, in practice, they have made their mullahs rich, powerful, and corrupt while their industries are run poorly. As Lord Acton observed, power corrupts.

Aware of power's tendency to corrupt, many Iranians want the mullahs to return to the mosque and get out of government and the economy. Many mullahs also wish it, as now they see that running a country ruins their reputation and their spiritual mission and clouds the future of the Islamic Republic. Chant Iranian demonstrators: "The mullahs live like kings, while the people are reduced to poverty." Another factor is that, now, most Iranians were born after the Shah and have no personal commitment to the Islamic Revolution. They want jobs and more freedom, and they can vote at age 18.

Will there be a point at which we can say that the Iranian Revolution is finally over? The reestablishment of diplomatic ties between the United States and Iran—something many Iranians want to happen soon—would indicate that point had passed some time earlier. There were hopes of this reestablishment of diplomatic ties under former President Khatami, but he was blocked by conservative forces. President Ahmadinejad was bitterly hostile. President Rouhani started a "dialogue" with Washington over Iran's nuclear program in 2013. If that leads to international inspection of Iran's nuclear sites, U.S.-Iran relations could be restored.

Comparison

Is Saudi Arabia Next?

The 9/11 attacks suggested that the Kingdom, as Saudis call their country, is quietly lurching toward instability. Fifteen of the 19 hijackers were Saudis. Al Qaeda terrorists set off bombs in the Kingdom. Islamists such as Osama bin Laden, son of a Saudi billionaire, represent forces similar to those that overthrew the Shah in Iran. The Saudi regime fears this and tries to buy off threats and deflect discontent by funding extremist religious schools (many in Pakistan) and minimizing Islamist recruitment.

The House of Saud conquered the country in the 1920s based on the austere Wahhabi creed of salafi Islam and is highly vulnerable for the same reasons as the Shah of Iran. Saudi Arabia is less democratic than Iran is now, and the legitimacy of the royal family has eroded amid charges of abandoning Wahhabism in favor of Western pleasures. The Saudi throne passes among brothers, not sons, so all Saudi kings have been sons of founder Abdulaziz. But now they are elderly, and succession must go to a new generation. Of the 5,000 Saudi princes, more than 500 are eligible to become king, an invitation for a succession struggle.

Oil created some very rich Saudis, including the princes, but left many poor Saudis far behind. Oil revenues allow the regime to buy loyalty with subsidies for millions of Saudis. But oil prices fluctuate, and the population exploded from 7 million in 1980 to 30 million now, cutting per capita Saudi income in half. Half of Saudis are under 25. Cushy jobs no longer await young Saudis; many are unemployed and discontent. Shia Saudis from the oil-producing Eastern Province carry out bombings (with Iranian backing), including on U.S. targets.

News from the Kingdom is rigorously censored—nothing negative is allowed—and, until 9/11, Washington never criticized "our good friends," the House of Saud. It was the same way we treated the Shah. After 9/11, some U.S. analysts called Saudi Arabia a false friend and supplier of money and personnel for Islamist terrorism. Hundreds of young Saudis crossed into Iraq for jihad against the Americans and Shia. A succession struggle over the new king could destabilize the Kingdom. It may be too late to do anything to prevent a Saudi revolution. Reforms can hasten revolution, as we saw in Iran.

Controlled moves to democracy, such as the following, might stabilize the Kingdom.

- Allow some moderate opposition parties and let them criticize in a constructive way. Make sure there are several parties (some conservative, some liberal, none radical) to divide public discontent.

- Permit a semifree press along the same lines as parties: limited criticism only.

- Crush and suppress Islamists. Do not ease up on them. These people are out to destroy you, and if they take over, they will not be moderate or democratic.

- Become a constitutional monarchy by separating the offices of king and prime minister, gradually giving more power to the prime minister and letting the king assume symbolic duties.

- Hold legislative elections, but among parties ranging from conservative to moderate. Gradually, you can let other parties participate.

- Have the new legislature redistribute wealth in the form of heavy taxes on the rich, especially on members of the royal family, who must be seen taking a financial hit. This is to defuse mass anger over the royals' great and unfair wealth.

- Do not automatically follow U.S. policy in the region, as that delegitimizes your regime. Limit any American presence; it is a cultural irritant and natural fodder for Islamic extremists. (Saudi leaders did not support our 2003 invasion of Iraq and had U.S. troops leave. They are not stupid.)

- Crack down on corruption, especially among the highest officials and princes. Show that you mean business here and that the crackdown will be permanent.

Have we learned anything from Iran? Would any of this work to head off a revolution? Maybe, but it would require the willingness of the House of Saud to cut its own wealth and power, something that ruling classes rarely do. But if Saudi Arabia cannot transition to some kind of democracy, revolution and then U.S. military involvement is likely. The Persian Gulf and its oil tend to drag the United States in.

China Lessons

Deflecting Discontent

In the late 1930s, Yale's Harold Lasswell argued that worried regimes hype foreign threats to deflect discontent from domestic problems, something now also happening in Iran and China. Some Iran specialists argue that the insecure Tehran regime *needs* hatred of the United States to keep itself in power. No outstretched hand of U.S. friendship will alter this. Chinese nationalism was aimed successively against the British, then the Japanese, and now the Americans. Periodically, Beijing cranks up mass hatred of Japan and the United States but cranks it back down when it threatens to get out of control.

This deflection of discontent may work for a while but then fade amid the regime's corruption and ineptitude. The people cannot be fooled forever. The real danger is that hatred locks the country into collision courses with outside powers that lead to diplomatic and commercial isolation, arms races, and even war, a risk run by both China and Iran. The lesson: Don't whip up nationalist fury against foreigners; you may not be able to turn it off.

What Iranians Quarrel About

12.5   Evaluate the possibilities of Iran turning into a democracy.

The Political Economy of Iran

Iran has changed rapidly, partly under the Shah and partly under the Islamic Revolution. The countryside has received schools, electricity, health care, and tractors. Infant mortality, a key measure of health care, fell from 169 per 1,000 births in 1960 to 40 in 2013. Average life expectancy jumped 20 years, from 50 to 70. Literacy has climbed from less than half to 85 percent.

The Iranian economy was hurt by revolution, war, sanctions, and mismanagement. Although total oil income has increased, only recently has per capita GDP recovered to pre-1979 levels. Iran depends almost totally on oil; pistachios and carpets are trivial exports. When oil prices fall, Iran is in trouble (as are Russia and Nigeria). There is now growth, but inflation, unemployment, and poverty are high. Iran needs some 1.5 million new jobs a year. Pay is low, so people hold two and three jobs to make ends meet. Many jobs and business dealings, as in Russia, are off the books. The oil industry, still the pride and basis of the Iranian economy, lacks replacement parts and up-to-date technology. U.S. and EU sanctions have kept most oil companies from cooperating with Iran, whose oil production has dropped. The *bonyads* are run badly and corruptly, something Iranians have known for many years.

Until recently, Iranians got an expensive welfare floor (including subsidized food, electricity, and gasoline), costing Tehran some $100 billion a year. Iran's great source of revenue (its petroleum connection with the West) was meanwhile damaged, creating budget deficits and inflation. In 2011, Ahmadinejad was forced to drastically cut the subsidies, angering many Iranians. Then, in 2014, Rouhani had to do the same. Gasoline prices nearly doubled, again angering citizens. Iran has to import much of its gasoline to sell at a loss because it lacks refining

Geography

How Many Iranians?

Islam traditionally frowns on family planning: The more babies, the better. After the revolution, Iran's mullahs urged women to produce a generation of Muslim militants; subsidized food helped feed them. Iran's rate of population growth averaged 3.5 percent a year during the 1980s, one of the world's highest. Despite the murderous war with Iraq, since the 1979 Revolution, Iran's population has doubled.

By the early 1990s, though, the government, realizing that it could not subsidize or employ the vast numbers of young Iranians—most Iranians were born after the Revolution—reversed the high-births policy.

Amid economic decline, families now can afford fewer children. Clinics offer all manner of contraception free of charge (but not abortions). Women agents go door to door to promote family planning. Food and other family aid decreases after a family has three children. One Muslim cleric even issued a **fatwa** in favor of smaller families. From an average 7 births per woman over her life in 1986, the fertility rate plunged to 1.9 in 2013, lower than in the United States. By 2013, the rate of population growth was a moderate 1.24 percent. The turnaround on births is an indication that the revolution is over.

capacity (like Nigeria). Motorists, used to cheap gas, raged when gas prices quadrupled in late 2010. Subsidies create costly and dangerous distortions, but cutting them can spark riots and even revolution.

fatwa
Ruling by Islamic jurist.

The Islamic Revolution did not dismantle the Shah's *statist* economy. The state still controls 60 percent of Iran's economy (biggest part: the oil industry). The *bonyads* control another 10 to 20 percent. Only about 20 percent of Iran's economy is in private hands. Theoretically, foreigners can invest in Iran, but most are scared off by the many and tangled limits and regulations. Investors must pay numerous bribes. Iran's is not a free-market economy. The big question: Should it become one?

Opposing arguments show up in Majlis debates over economic policy, which have become thinly disguised battles over the future of strict Islamic rule. As we have considered, Islamism is a surrogate socialism; it blends Islamic correctness with collectivist economics. In the minds of many Islamists, socialism is the logical extension of Islam, for Islam preaches equality and leveling of class differences. Thus, they claim, Islam is the true and only path to a just society of equal citizens, where no one is either rich or poor. What the Marxists, Socialists, and Communists talked about, they say, we can deliver.

Most moderates respond that socialism and/or statism is not the way to go, that they just keep Iran poor and backward. The collapse of the Soviet system demonstrates that socialism does not work, and the decline of Iran's economy demonstrates that statism does not work. Besides, they note, there is no Koranic basis for government control of the economy. It is perfectly feasible to combine free-market capitalism with the alms-giving required of Muslims and achieve social justice. If we keep declining economically, moderates also worry, we will never be able to build a first-class army and so will be vulnerable to hostile outside forces. And if our towering unemployment problem is not solved soon, the Islamic republic could end. The best and quickest way to solve these problems is the free market. State ownership of major industries, especially petroleum, is what the Shah tried, and we certainly do not want to follow in his footsteps. Such are the arguments of Iranian moderates. Notice that rejection of the Islamic Revolution is not one of their points.

The Veiled Debate on Islam

Iran will always be a Muslim country, but what kind of Islam will it have? A moderate kind that keeps out of most direct political involvement or a militant kind that seeks to guide society by political means? Judging by the votes of 1997, 2001, 2009, and 2013, most Iranians prefer the moderate path.

Because the Council of Guardians bars openly liberal candidates, public debate on the religion question is muted. No one risks being branded "anti-Islamic." Still, one can infer that such a debate is taking place. One of the stand-ins for a discussion of Islam in public life is the debate on what kind of clothing is permissible, especially for women. Even for men, though, blue jeans were frowned upon, partly because they represent American culture. Liberals say they do not; jeans are simply a comfortable and international garment with no political connotations.

Before the Islamic Revolution, urban and educated Iranian women dressed as fashionably as European women. Then, suddenly, they could not use makeup and had to wear the veil and *chador*, the single-piece head-to-toe garment designed to cover feminine attractiveness. Devout Muslims, including many women, say this attire is better than Western clothing as it eliminates

Geography

Strategic Waterways

These are mostly narrow choke points connecting two bodies of water. Hostile control of them causes worldwide discomfort or fear. Notice that several of these main ones are in the Middle East:

Turkish Straits (Dardanelles and Bosporus), connecting the Black and Mediterranean Seas

Suez Canal, connecting the Mediterranean and Red Seas

Bab al Mandab, connecting the Red Sea and Indian Ocean

Strait of Hormuz, connecting the Persian Gulf and Indian Ocean, through which a sixth of the world's oil exports pass, mostly for Asia

Strait of Gibraltar, connecting the Atlantic and the Mediterranean

English Channel, connecting the Atlantic Ocean and North Sea

Skagerrak, connecting the Baltic and North Seas

North Cape, dividing the Atlantic from the Barents Sea

Cape of Good Hope, where the Atlantic and Indian Oceans meet off the southern tip of Africa

Strait of Malacca, connecting the Indian Ocean and South China Sea, East Asia's oil lifeline

Korea (Tsushima) Strait, connecting the East China Sea and Sea of Japan

Panama Canal, connecting the Atlantic and Pacific Oceans

You are the captain of a small tanker that has just loaded oil in Kuwait for delivery in Umea, Sweden. Which bodies of water—including seas, oceans, straits, and canals—do you pass through? (Note: Supertankers are too big for Suez; they have to go around Africa. But small tankers still pass through Suez.)

lust, vanity, and distinctions of wealth. (Some U.S. schools come to similar conclusions about school uniforms.) Western clothes and makeup are the first steps toward debauchery and prostitution, Islamists argue.

But, in subtle ways, urban Iranian women dress in a manner that pushes to the limit of the permissible in public (and, in private, dress as they wish). The veil and *chador* are no longer mandatory on the street, so long as a woman is dressed very modestly without makeup and with hair and forehead covered by a kerchief. Women still risk Islamic morals police stopping them on the street and sending them home or to jail. Young people suspected of having a good time may be beaten by Basij. Such restrictions are some of the most obnoxious features of the Islamic regime and have alienated young urban and educated Iranians.

Iran as a Regional Power

Iran made no secret of its drive to become the Persian Gulf's dominant power, but this is increasingly unlikely. Much of what Iran does internationally is aimed at increasing its power and prestige. "We are rapidly becoming a superpower," claimed Ahmadinejad—an exaggeration, although Iran is already the top regional power. Tehran sees itself as the leader of the entire Islamic world and tries to spread its revolutionary influence. Sunnis, however, resent and fear Iran; they despise Shias. This is the limiting factor in Iran's dream of regional dominance. Indeed, Al Qaeda and ISIS urge that Shias be killed as heretics. In Syria and Iraq, Sunnis and Shias fight a murderous civil war.

Thanks to the 2003 U.S. invasion of Iraq, Iran is now the most influential power in Iraq, where Shias, long a suppressed 60 percent of the population, now rule. The Sunni Arabs of central Iraq, only about 20 percent, traditionally monopolized political power. Many of the main Shia shrines are in southern Iraq, where Khomeini was exiled in 1964. Upon taking power in Tehran, Khomeini's agents propagandized Iraqi Shias and urged them to join the Islamic Revolution. This was one of the irritants—but hardly a sufficient excuse—for Iraqi dictator Saddam Hussein to invade Iran in 1980. Baghdad's Shia regime heeds Tehran's wishes, and Iranian arms move freely into and across Iraq into Syria to enable Iran ally Bashar al-Assad to crush the majority-Sunni uprising. This contributes to a region-wide Sunni-Shia showdown, nullifying Iran's ambitions to lead Islam.

Iran works through its Shia brethren in Iraq, Lebanon, Kuwait, Bahrain, Afghanistan, and Saudi Arabia. It is the main support for Bashar al-Assad's Syrian regime, whose Alawites are an offshoot of Shia. Iran supplies funds and munitions to dangerous movements and is on the U.S. State Department's list of countries sponsoring terrorism. It proclaims its leading role in destroying Israel, which it depicts as a polluter of Islamic holy ground (Jerusalem is also sacred to Muslims) and outpost of Western imperialism. Under the Shah, Tehran had good (but informal) relations with Israel and quietly sold it most of its oil. Iran's Islamic Revolution totally changed that, and Iran funds Lebanon's Hezbollah (Party of God), which provoked a nasty one-month war with Israel in the summer of 2006. In this way, Iran claims leadership in the struggle against Israel, but Sunnis no longer pay attention to this boast.

Iran isolated itself, not only creating U.S. hostility but angering the Sunni-ruled lands of the Persian Gulf. Iran's stonewalling on its nuclear program alienated Britain, France, and Germany, which had sought a diplomatic solution to ensure that Iran does not build nuclear

Political Culture

The United States and Iran

A culture gap hinders Americans and Iranians from understanding each other. We have not been clever in dealing with the Iranian Revolution. Part religious, part nationalistic, part cultural, and part antityranny, it defied our predictions and efforts to tame it. When we tried to deal with "Iranian moderates" in 1986, we got humiliated. When we tilted toward Iraq in its war against Iran, we supported a bloody dictator (Saddam Hussein) whom we twice fought ourselves. In 1988, a U.S. destroyer mistook an Iranian jetliner for an attacking fighter, shot it down with a missile, and killed all 290 people aboard. Iran, and indeed the whole Persian Gulf, is a tar baby: Once you punch it, you get stuck worse and worse.

But if we are calm and clever, things may work out. Iranian radicals are marginalized, and Tehran hints at improving U.S. relations. Many Iranians want contact and dialogue with the United States. In the long term, Iran needs us. We can provide the petroleum technology and other means to modernize Iran. U.S. attempts to encourage "regime change" in Iran, however, are counterproductive. American broadcasts, funds, and contacts in support of Iranian critics are the kiss of death, allowing the regime to portray them as traitors and U.S. stooges.

Anthropologists point out that when two Iranian *bazaaris* quarrel, by long tradition, they simply shun and ignore each other for some years. Gradually, the quarrel fades, and they cautiously reestablish relations with each other. After a while, the quarrel is forgotten. It is a civilized way to handle a quarrel. We might take a leaf from Persian folkway in dealing with Iran.

Iranians do not understand American culture. Americans are, in many ways, the opposite of Iranians; we are direct, unsubtle, and prone to violence: cowboys. Americans like guns and military solutions, even though most see America as good and trying to do good in the world. We are poorly informed about the Gulf region. Few Americans know as much about Iran as the student who has just read this chapter. To win mass support, some presidents use simplified rhetoric—"axis of evil"—and notice only later that it sets back efforts to improve U.S.-Iranian relations (desired by two-thirds of Iranians). Loose talk about knocking out Iran's nuclear facilities makes matters worse, leading to Iranian counterthreats and increased support for the regime.

Iranians must watch their rhetoric, too. The mass chanting of *Marg bar Amrika!* ("Death to America!") sounds like a direct threat. Do Iranians really want to kill us? If not, they'd better stop saying so. After 9/11, these things are taken very seriously. Most Americans agree on the U.S. commitment to making sure that the oil of the Persian Gulf flows. No amount of bombings can persuade Washington to abandon this policy. And a U.S.-led international sanctions campaign inflicts serious damage on an Iranian economy already weakened by mismanagement.

If Iran wants calm, it must stop sponsoring or encouraging terrorism or funding and arming Shia parties in other lands, such as Hezbollah in Lebanon. Developing nuclear weapons provokes rather than deters the United States. Iran might turn to its own tradition and simply shun America. And when Tehran is ready to resume contact and economic growth, it could let Washington know in a public way. Eventually, relations will thaw. America and Iran were friends once and can be again. Angry moves on either side could lead to a war neither wants.

weapons. Tehran says it seeks only nuclear power generation—in a country with massive oil and natural gas reserves—but no one trusts it. In 2006, the International Atomic Energy Agency (IAEA) referred the matter to the UN, where the Security Council solidly supported nuclear inspections of Iran. Iran's isolation harms its economic growth and requires it to maintain armed forces it cannot afford.

Many Iranians dislike being isolated. They want to avoid conflict and improve relations with the West, even with America. Meddling in other countries, they argue, brings nothing but trouble and could even lead to war. The radicals want to keep up the militant foreign policies, no matter what they cost the country. Iran has been both the victim and practitioner of terrorism. Antiregime forces, particularly the nutty Mujahedin-e Khalq, assassinated several Iranian leaders, including one prime minister. Iranian hit squads in Europe took out several regime opponents. Iran's great foreign policy problem is that, by expanding its power and influence, it created enemies.

Do Revolutions End Badly?

Edmund Burke was right: Revolution brings in its wake tyranny far worse than that of the regime it toppled. Iran is a good example: The Shah was a dictator, but rule of the mullahs is worse. Only in America did revolution lead to the establishment of a just, stable democracy—and the American Revolution was a very special, limited one, aimed more at independence than at overturning society. Recent history is littered with failed revolutions: fascist, communist, and now Islamist. The few remaining Communist countries that still celebrate and base their legitimacy on an alleged revolution, Cuba and North Korea, are hungry and isolated. Communist China and Vietnam, by joining in world trade, have prospered.

Why do revolutions end badly? Several writers have attempted to answer this question. Burke argued that the destruction of all institutional and political restraints leaves people confused and ripe for dictatorial rule. François Furet wrote, along similar lines, that the French Revolution unleashed such chaotic forces that it had to "skid out of control." Crane Brinton wrote that revolutions fall into the hands of their most ruthless element, who then proceed to wreck everything until they are replaced in a Thermidor. And Hannah Arendt wrote that revolution goes astray when revolutionists try to solve the "Social Question" (how to bring down the rich and lift up the poor); to do this, they must institute a tyranny. It is interesting to note that all of these writers were, to some extent, conservatives. Radicals and leftists often refuse to admit when revolutions end badly; if something goes wrong, they tend to blame individuals for "betraying" the revolution.

The unhappy revolution is something that Iranians ponder. Although few want a return of the Pahlavis, many Iranians know that the Islamic Revolution has turned out wrong. At least, under the Shah, there was economic growth, however unfairly distributed, and modernization. Now there is economic stagnation and unemployment. Some Iranians live in greater poverty than before. Certain mullahs and their friends, those in charge of the *bonyads*, do well, however. Given a chance, most Iranians would throw these rascals out. The mullahs and their security and judicial forces try to make sure this never happens. They have some bases of support—more than the Shah had—among the religious and the poor who have benefited from Islamic handouts.

Iran may now be coming out of a stalemate between moderate and militant forces. Eventually, change will come to Iran; the status quo is unsustainable. Stonewalling by fanatic Islamists increases the danger of political violence, fueled by millions of angry, unemployed young Iranian males. What can the United States do? U.S. threats just play into the hands of hard-liners, but the right combination of firmness (over Iran's uranium enrichment efforts) and carrots (trade) could start a dialogue. Time and economic difficulties will calm the Iranian revolution. I am convinced that Iran will one day be free and Iran and the United States will be friends again.

Geography

Bound Israel

Israel is bounded on the north by Lebanon; on the east by Syria and Jordan; on the south by Egypt; and on the west by the Mediterranean Sea.

Israel

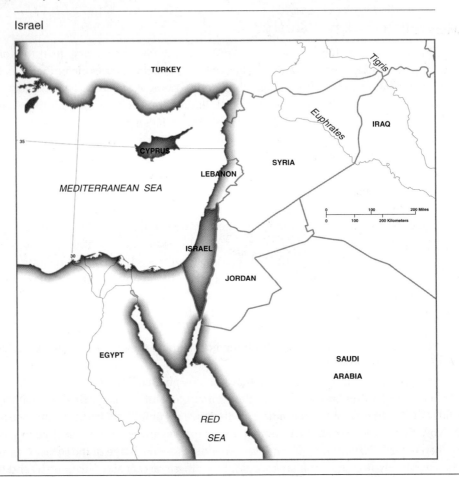

Review Questions

Learning Objective 12.1 Compare and contrast Iran with its neighboring countries, p. 457.

1. What has geography contributed to Iran's development?
2. How does Iran differ from Arab countries?
3. What is a *modernizing tyrant*? Why do they fail?

Learning Objective 12.2 Outline the difficulties of a theocratic political system, p. 464.

4. Explain Iran's dual executive. Who is more powerful?
5. How are Iran's elections "half-fair"?
6. Has President Rouhani really been able to change Iran?

Learning Objective 12.3 Demonstrate the relationship between Islam and modernization, p. 469.

7. Does modernization always bring secularization?
8. Is Islam inherently anti-modern?
9. How has Islam been turned into a political ideology?

Learning Objective 12.4 Apply Brinton's theory of revolution to Iran's Islamic Revolution, p. 474.

10. How would you explain the power struggle in Iran?

11. How do Iranian conservatives and Islamists differ from each other?
12. Could Saudi Arabia experience an Islamic revolution?

Learning Objective 12.5 Evaluate the possibilities of Iran turning into a democracy, p. 480.

13. How have America and Iran misunderstood each other?
14. Should the United States be militarily involved in the Persian Gulf region?
15. Do all revolutions end badly? Why?

Key Terms

ayatollah, p. 463
Basij, p. 467
canon law, p. 464
containment, p. 461
fatwa, p. 481
hajj, p. 473
Islam, p. 458
Islamism, p. 470

Islamist, p. 464
Koran, p. 469
Majlis, p. 459
modernizing tyrant, p. 460
mosque, p. 462
mullah, p. 462
OPEC, p. 462
Ottoman, p. 462

secular, p. 462
shah, p. 460
Shia, p. 459
Sunni, p. 459
theocracy, p. 464
velayat-e faqih, p. 464

Further Reference

Abrahamian, Ervand. *A History of Modern Iran.* New York: Cambridge University Press, 2008.

Adib-Moghaddam, Arshin. *Iran in World Politics: The Question of the Islamic Republic.* New York: Columbia University Press, 2008.

Afary, Janet. *Sexual Politics in Modern Iran.* New York: Cambridge University Press, 2009.

Amanat, Abbas. *Apocalyptic Islam and Iranian Shi'ism.* London: J. B. Tauris, 2009.

Axworthy, Michael. *Revolutionary Iran: A History of the Islamic Republic.* New York: Oxford University Press, 2013.

Azimi, Fakhreddin. *The Quest for Democracy in Iran: A Century of Struggle against Authoritarian Rule.* Cambridge, MA: Harvard University Press, 2008.

Bellaigue, Christopher de. *The Struggle for Iran.* New York: New York Review, 2008.

Buchan, James. *Days of God: The Revolution in Iran and Its Consequences.* New York: Simon & Schuster, 2013.

Esfandiari, Haleh. *My Prison, My Home: One Woman's Story of Captivity in Iran.* New York: HarperCollins, 2009.

Kamrava, Mehran. *Iran's Intellectual Revolution.* New York: Cambridge University Press, 2008.

Khosravi, Shahram. *Young and Defiant in Tehran.* Philadelphia: University of Pennsylvania Press, 2008.

Leverett, Flynt, and Hillary Mann Leverett. *Going to Tehran: Why the United States Must Come to Terms With the Islamic Republic of Iran.*New York: Holt, 2013.

Majd, Hooman. *The Ayatollah Begs to Differ: The Paradox of Modern Iran.* New York: Doubleday, 2008.

Milani, Abbas. *The Shah.* New York: Palgrave, 2011.

Peterson, Scott. *Let the Swords Encircle Me: Iran—A Journey Behind the Headlines.* New York: Simon & Schuster, 2010.

Polk, William R. *Understanding Iran: Everything You Need to Know, from Persia to the Islamic Republic, from Cyrus to Ahmadinejad.* New York: Palgrave, 2009.

Riefer-Flanagan, Barbara Ann. *Evolving Iran: An Introduction to Politics and Problems in the Islamic Republic.* Washington, DC: Georgetown University Press, 2013.

Sadjadpour, Karim. *Reading Khamenei: The World View of Iran's Most Powerful Leader.* Washington, DC: Carnegie Endowment, 2008.

Sedghi, Himdeh. *Women and Politics in Iran: Veiling, Unveiling, and Reveiling.* New York: Cambridge University Press, 2007.

Slavin, Barbara. *Bitter Friends, Bosom Enemies: Iran, the U.S., and the Twisted Path to Confrontation.* New York: St. Martin's, 2008.

Taheri, Amir. *The Persian Night: Iran under the Khomeinist Revolution.* New York: Encounter, 2009.

Takeyh, Ray. *Guardians of the Revolution: Iran and the World in the Age of the Ayatollahs.* New York: Oxford University Press, 2009.

Wright, Robin, ed. *The Iran Primer: Power, Politics, and U.S. Policy.* Washington, DC: Institute of Peace, 2010.

Epilogue
Lessons of Eleven Countries

1. *States* often precede and create *nations*. Countries are rather artificial, the constructs of governments instilling a common culture over many generations. A working, effective government is the crux of nationhood; those without one are *failed states.*

2. The modern state has existed only about half a millennium and is not necessarily the last word in political organization. The emergence of the *European Union* suggests a new entity beyond the nation-state.

3. Most *boundaries* are artificial. Where one country ends and another begins is a political decision, often contested. The expansion and contraction of Germany is an example of how fluid some boundaries can be.

4. Most countries have *core areas*, often where the state began and still home to the country's capital. Outside of these core areas, in the *periphery*, regionalism and resentment at being governed by a distant capital often grow. Thus peripheral areas often vote differently than core areas.

5. The past is alive and well in current politics, forming a country's political institutions, culture, and quarrels. The past is especially lively in the resentments of aggrieved people—for example, among regions and social groups that feel they have been shortchanged.

6. War can wreck political systems. War, said Marx, is the midwife of revolution. Several of our countries have undergone total system change as a result of war.

7. Economic growth is destabilizing, especially rapid growth. Economic growth and change bring new people into politics, some of them bitterly discontent. Do not think economic growth solves political problems; it often makes them worse. Democracy should follow economic growth to head off systemic upheaval.

8. A system that cannot change to meet new challenges is doomed. Wise rulers make gradual and incremental reforms to avoid sudden and radical changes. Rulers who wait to reform until revolution is nigh may actually fuel it by offering concessions. All regimes tend to petrify; the good ones stay flexible.

9. Solid, time-tested *institutions* that people believe in are a bulwark of political stability. No political leader, however clever, has pulled functioning institutions out of a hat. They require time, intelligence, and continual modification.

10. Constitutions rarely work the way they are intended and written. Many factors modify the working of *constitutions*: popular attitudes, usages that change over time, powerful parties and interest groups, and behind-the-scenes deals.

11. Everywhere, *parliaments* are in decline. Some have become little more than ritual, under such tight executive and/or party control that they have lost their autonomy. As governance becomes more complex and technical, power flows to bureaucrats and experts.

12. Everywhere, *bureaucracies* are in the ascendancy. In some systems, the permanent civil service is already the most powerful institution. Bureaucrats tend to see themselves as the indispensable saviors of their countries. No country fully controls its bureaucracies.

13. Multiparty systems tend to be less stable than two-party systems. Much depends on other factors, such as the rules for forming a cabinet or choosing the executive. Reforms can stabilize *multiparty* systems so that their behavior is not much different from that of two-party systems.

14. Electoral system helps determine *party system*. Single-member districts with a simple plurality required to win tend to produce *two-party systems*, because third parties have difficulty surviving in such systems. *Proportional representation* tends to produce many parties.

15. There are no longer purely *federal* or purely *unitary* systems. Instead, the trend is for federations to grant more and more power to the center, while unitary systems set up regional governments and devolve some powers to them.

16. Most cabinets consist of about 20 ministers. By American standards, many cabinets are large and their portfolios rather specialized. In most countries (but not the United States), ministries are added, deleted, combined, or renamed as the prime minister sees fit; the legislature automatically goes along.

17. In some ways, *prime ministers* in parliamentary systems are more powerful than *presidents* in presidential systems. If they have an assured and disciplined majority in parliament, prime ministers can get most of what they want with no deadlock between executive and legislative. Prime ministers who rely on *coalitions*, of course, are weaker.

18. Most people, most of the time, are not much interested in politics. As you go down the socioeconomic ladder, you usually find less interest in political participation. More-educated people participate more. Mass participation in politics tends to be simple and episodic, such as voting every few years.

19. Corruption is a huge worldwide problem that grows where the public and private sectors meet. It undermines democracy, legitimacy, and the economy. Cleaning it up is difficult, as many influential people benefit from it.

20. Political culture is as much a reflection of government performance as it is a determinant of the workings of government. *Political culture* can be taught, intentionally or inadvertently, by a regime. Countries with a cynical, untrusting political culture have usually earned it with decades of misrule. By the same token, a democratic regime that does a good job over many years firms up democratic attitudes.

21. Social class is only one factor in establishing political orientations. Often, other factors, such as religion and region, are more important. Usually, these three—*class, religion,* and *region* in varying combinations—explain most of party identification and voting behavior.

22. Religion is important in politics. In Iran, the two merge. More typical are political parties based on religion, as in Nigeria and India, or religiosity (degree of religious feeling), as in France and the United States.

23. Political systems are rarely totally ideological, but neither are they totally pragmatic. Parties and regimes usually talk some *ideology* to justify themselves, but rulers tend to *pragmatism* in making decisions. Ideology as window dressing is a common political device.

24. Every country has its *elites*, the few people with great influence. Party, labor, business, military, or even religious elites may play leading roles in different countries. Elites pay

attention to politics, usually battling for the groups they lead. Elites rather than masses are the true political animals.

25. Elites, especially intellectual elites, create and articulate political ideas (ideologies, reform movements, media commentary), something the masses rarely do. Elite attitudes tend to be more democratic than mass attitudes.

26. Education is the gateway to elite status. Except in revolutionary regimes, most elites now have university educations. Some countries—Britain, France, Japan—have elite universities that produce much of the leadership. Educational opportunity is never totally equal or fair; the middle class usually benefits most from it.

27. Much of politics consists of competition and bargaining among elites. Occasionally, elites, to gain leverage on competing elites, refer questions to the masses in elections or referendums and call it democracy. Of all the political interactions discussed in this book, notice how relatively few of them involve mass participation.

28. Mass politics is easier to study than elite politics. With *mass politics*—parties, elections, voter alignments, public opinion—political scientists can get accurate, quantified data. Because much of elite politics is out of the public eye, we have to resort to fragmentary anecdotal and journalistic data. This means that some of the most crucial political interactions are hard to discern and even harder to document.

29. Democracy grows when elites open their decisions and deals to public scrutiny and approval. Typically, bargains are struck among elites and then presented to parliament and the public. Much legislative and electoral behavior is in ratifying decisions made earlier among elites.

30. Politicians are endlessly opportunistic. Most will do whatever it takes to get, keep, or enhance their power. To this end, they will change their views and policies. This is not necessarily deplorable, however; it lets democracy work by making politicians bend to the popular will.

31. Politicians are addicted to money. They need it for election campaigns and, sometimes, to enrich themselves. Countries with very different institutions and political cultures have similar scandals over fund-raising.

32. Parties are balancing acts. Most parties combine several groups, factions, and wings. Some *parties* split apart over personal and ideological differences. To keep the party together, politicians dispense favors, jobs, and promises to faction leaders. This holds for both democratic and authoritarian parties.

33. Once the army has taken power, it will probably do so again. Democracy and reformism are often short-lived phenomena between periods of military rule. Countries can mature out of *praetorianism* with economic growth, increased education, and stable governance, as Brazil did.

34. Most of humanity lives in the developing areas, or *Third World*, roughly defined as Asia, Africa, the Middle East, and Latin America. Some countries are progressing to prosperity and democracy; others, encumbered by institutional, ideological, and cultural rigidity, are not.

35. The Third World is trying to get into the First World. A big and uniform issue for the rich world is the foreign workers—Pakistanis in Britain, Algerians in France, Turks in Germany, Mexicans in America—who come for jobs and then stay. Given the differential rates of birth and economic gaps between First and Third Worlds, migration is bound to increase.

36. Within developing countries, people are flocking to cities. Overpopulation and few jobs in the countryside push people to cities, where many live in *shantytowns*. The Third World already has some of the globe's biggest cities, most surrounded by shantytowns.

37. Racism can be found nearly everywhere. Most nations deny it, but discrimination based on skin color, religion, or ethnic group is widespread. When searching for racism, look to see what a country does, not what it says. Underdog racial and ethnic groups are locked out of economic and political power.

38. Cutting *welfare* benefits and subsidies is extremely difficult; recipients take them as a right and protest angrily. Conservatives dislike the welfare state, but they seldom do much about it. Once a benefit has been extended, it is almost impossible to withdraw it. The most that conservatives can do is to restrain expansion of the welfare system.

39. Likewise, cutting state sectors of an economy is difficult. Most countries have state ownership, control, or guidance over the economy (the United States has relatively little). In countries as diverse as Russia, India, Mexico, Nigeria, and Iran, those who have something to lose oppose ending *statism*. Many governments talk about privatization but delay doing it.

40. Much of what people and politicians quarrel about is economic. Some economists claim that economics is the content of politics. There are important political conflicts that are not directly economic, such as questions of region, religion, and personality. Still, most of the time, people argue over who should get what. Study economics.

41. Countries tend to follow global trends in economics. Statism surrendered to market economics worldwide, which recently restored some state supervision. To fight recession and unemployment in the 2008–2009 downturn, most countries used similar policies of stimulus spending and bank bailouts.

42. Democracy depends a great deal on economic development. Poor countries rarely sustain democracy. Middle-income and richer countries are mostly democracies. The likely reason: Economic growth generates a large, educated, pluralistic, and moderate middle class that insists on political rights. Mexico and Brazil are examples. China could eventually follow them.

43. Oil blocks democracy. Regimes that rely on oil exports—such as Russia, Nigeria, and Iran—concentrate great wealth in the hands of rulers who resist reforms, competing parties, and free elections. Oil is a curse.

44. Unemployment is a problem everywhere and one few governments solve. Worldwide, there is a struggle for jobs, ranging from difficult in West Europe to desperate in the developing areas.

45. Many political issues are insoluble. They are the surfacing of long-growing economic and social problems that cannot be "fixed" by government policy. Time and underlying economic and social change may gradually dissolve the problems. Politics has been overrated as a way to cure problems. Often, the best that politics can do is to keep things stable until time can do its work.

46. Things get more political, not less. As government takes on more tasks, what were previously private transactions become political interactions, with all the quarreling that entails. No country ever runs out of political problems. As soon as one is solved, new ones appear, usually over the administration of the problem-solving mechanism.

47. Party positions are broadly similar across nations. Rightist parties seek to cut taxes, welfare, and regulations. Many also oppose immigration, bailouts, and affirmative action.

Leftist parties support government economic activism such as redistribution, higher minimum wages, and welfare benefits to lift up the poor.

48. Everywhere, governments are paralyzed, unable to tackle the big problems they all face. Europe and Japan cannot jolt their economies into growth, the developing areas cannot cure corruption, and the United States has a gridlocked Congress. Prolonged paralysis can lead to systemic upheaval.

49. Whenever you look closely at political phenomena, you find they are more complicated than you first thought. You discover exceptions, nuances, and differentiations that you did not notice at first. You can modify and sometimes refute generalizations—including the ones offered here—by digging into them more deeply.

50. Ultimately, in studying other countries, we are studying ourselves. Neither our country nor we as citizens are a great deal different from other countries and peoples. When you compare politics, be sure to include your own system.

Glossary

Following are some frequently used words or technical terms from the field of comparative politics. Each is defined here in its political sense. The country where the term originated or is most commonly used is given where appropriate, but often the word is now used worldwide.

absolute poverty   Living on $1.25 a day or less.

absolutism   Royal dictatorship that bypasses nobles.

alienated   Psychologically distant and hostile.

Allies   World War II anti-Axis military coalition.

alternation in power   The electoral overturn of one party by another.

analogy   Taking one example as the model for another.

anarchism   Radical ideology seeking to overthrow all conventional forms of government.

ancien régime   French for old regime, the monarchy that preceded the Revolution.

Anti-Japanese War   Chinese name for World War II in China, 1937–1945.

anticlerical   Wants to get the Roman Catholic Church out of politics.

apparatchik   "Man of the apparatus"; full-time CPSU functionary.

aquifer   Underground water-bearing layer.

aristocrat   Person of inherited noble rank.

asset stripping   Selling off firm's property and raw materials for short-term profit.

austerity   Government cutting expenditures to balance budget; economic belt-tightening.

autarchy   Economic self-sufficiency, importing and exporting little.

authoritarian   Nondemocratic or dictatorial politics.

authoritarianism   Dictatorial rejection of democracy, but milder than *totalitarianism*.

authority   Political leaders' ability to be obeyed.

autocracy   Absolute rule of one person in a centralized state.

autogolpe   "Self-coup," top executive seizes more power.

autonomous region   Soviet-style home area for ethnic minority.

ayatollah   "Sign of God"; top Shia religious leader.

baccalauréat   French high school exam and diploma.

backbencher   Ordinary MP with no executive responsibility.

bailout   Emergency loan to prevent a collapse.

Basij   Persian for "mobilization"; Iranian volunteer paramilitary force.

Bastille   Old and nearly unused Paris jail, the storming of which heralded the French Revolution in 1789.

Beida   Short name for Beijing University, long China's best (equivalent to Japan's *Todai*).

Berlin airlift   U.S.–British supply of West Berlin by air in 1948–1949.

Berlin Republic   Reunified Germany, since 1990, with the capital in Berlin.

bilateral opposition   Undermining of centrist governments from both sides.

bimodal   Two-peaked distribution.

Bolsa Família   "Family Allowance," 2004 Brazilian welfare program.

Bolshevik   "Majority" in Russian; early name for Soviet Communist Party.

Bonn Republic   West Germany, 1949–1990, with the capital in Bonn.

Bourbon   French dynasty before the Revolution.

bourgeois   Middle class.

Boxer   Chinese antiforeigner rebellion in 1900.

Buddhism   Sixth century BC offshoot of Hinduism; seeks enlightenment through meditation and cessation of desire.

Bundes-   German prefix for "federal."

Bundesrat   Literally, federal council; upper chamber of German parliament, represents states.

Bundestag   Lower house of German parliament.

bureaucratized   Heavily controlled by civil servants.

by-election   Special election for a vacant seat in Parliament.

cabinet   Top executives (ministers) of a government.

cacique   Originally, Indian chief; local political boss.

cadre   Communist member serving as an official; Chinese: *gànbù*.

caesaropapism   Combining the top civil ruler (caesar) with the top spiritual ruler (pope), as in Russia's tsars.

caliphate   Islamic dynasty.

canon law   Internal laws of the Roman Catholic Church.

capital goods   Implements used to make other things.

Cartesian   After French philosopher René Descartes, philosophical analysis based on pure reason without empirical reference.

caste   Rigid, hereditary social stratum or group.

catchall   Nonideological parties that welcome all.

Caucasus   Mountainous region between Black and Caspian seas.

caudillo   Military chief or strongman who takes over the government.

causality   Proving that one thing causes another.

Celts   Pre-Roman inhabitants of Europe.

censure   Legislative condemnation of executive.

center   In federal systems, the powers of the nation's capital.

center-peaked   Distribution with most people in the middle, a bell-shaped curve.

center-seeking   Parties trying to win a big centrist vote with moderate programs.

center-periphery tension   Resentment in outlying areas of rule by the nation's capital.

Central Asia   Region between Caspian Sea and China.

Central Committee   Large, next-to-top governing body of most Communist parties.

central office   London headquarters of British political party.

Century of Humiliation   China's term for its domination by imperialists from the first Opium War to Communist victory, 1839–1949.

chancellor   German prime minister.

charisma   Pronounced "kar-isma"; Greek for gift; political drawing power.

chauvinism   After Napoleonic soldier named Chauvin; fervent, prideful nationalism.

civility   Good manners in politics.

civil society   Associations larger than the family but not part of government, and the pluralistic values that come with them.

class voting   Tendency of classes to vote for parties that represent them.

cleft   In Huntington's theory, a country split by two civilizations.

clientelism   Government favors to groups for their support.

co-optation   To enroll other groups in your cause, rendering them harmless.

coalition   Multiparty alliance to form government.

coercion   Government by force.

cohabitation   French president forced to name premier of opposing party.

Cold War   Period of armed tension and competition between the United States and the Soviet Union, approximately 1947–1989.

colonialism   Gaining and exploitation of overseas territories, chiefly by Europeans; related to imperialism.

Comecon   Trading organization of Communist countries, now defunct.

Comintern   Short for Communist International; the world's Communist parties under Moscow's control.

Common Agricultural Program (CAP)   EU farm subsidies, the biggest part of the EU budget.

Common Law   System of judge-made law developed in England.

Commons   Lower house of Parliament; the elected, important chamber.

Commonwealth   A republic; also organization of countries that were once British colonies.

communal   Ethnic or religious communities within a nation.

communism   Economic theories of Marx combined with organization of Lenin.

comparative politics   Subfield of political science focused on interactions *within* other countries.

compartmentalization   Mentally separating and isolating problems.

Confucianism   Chinese philosophy of social and political stability based on family, hierarchy, and manners.

Congress   Led India's independence movement and later was the dominant party.

consensus   Agreement among all constituent groups.

conservatism   Desire to preserve or return to old ways.

conservatism   Ideology of preserving existing institutions and usages.

Constantinople   Capital of Byzantium, conquered by Turks in 1453.

constituency   The district or population that elects a legislator.

constitution   Written organization of a country's institutions.

constitutional monarchy   King with limited powers.

constitutionalism   Degree to which government limits its powers.

constructed   Deliberately created but widely accepted as natural.

constructive bankruptcy   Economic theory that weak firms should fold to make way for new enterprises.

constructive no-confidence   Parliament must vote in a new cabinet when it ousts the current one.

consumer goods   Things people use, such as food, clothing, and housing.

consumption   Buying things.

containment   U.S. Cold War policy of blocking expansion of communism.

contradiction   In Marxism, deep, opposing forces that can rip the system apart (modern term: *dysfunction*).

core   Region where the state originated.

coronéis   "Colonels," Brazilian state-level political bosses.

corporatism   Direct participation of interest groups in governance.

corruption   Use of public office for private gain.

counterculture   Rejects conventional values, as in the 1960s.

coup d'état   Military takeover of a government.

CPSU   Communist Party of the Soviet Union.

creole   Spaniard born in the New World.

cross-cutting cleavages   Multiple splits in society that make group loyalties overlap.

Crown   The British government.

cult of personality   Personal glorification of a dictator.

Cultural Revolution   Mao's late 1960s mad effort to break bureaucracy in China.

cumulative   Reinforcing one another.

current account balance   A country's exports minus its imports.

cynical   Untrusting; holding belief that political system is wrong and corrupt.

Cyrillic   Greek-based alphabet of Eastern Slavic languages.

Daoism   From Dao, "the way"; old Chinese religion originally based on nature; earlier spelled *Taoism*.

deadlock   U.S. tendency for executive and legislature, especially when of opposing parties, to block each other.

dealignment   Voters losing identification with any party.

debt   Sum total of government *deficits* over many years.

decolonization   Granting of independence to colonies.

dedazo   From *dedo*, finger; tapped for high office.

default   Country announces that it cannot pay back a loan.

deficit   Government spends more in a given year than it takes in.

deflation   Decrease in prices; opposite of inflation.

deindustrialization   Decline of heavy industry.

demagogue   Manipulative politician who wins votes through impossible promises.

democracy   Political system of mass participation, competitive elections, and human and civil rights.

demography   Study of population growth.

denazification   Purging Nazi officials from public life.

département   Department; French first-order civil division, equivalent to British county.

dependency theory   Radical theory that rich countries exploit and impoverish poor countries.

deputy   Member of French and many other parliaments.

desiccation   Drying out.

deutsche Mark   German currency from 1948 to 2002.

devalue   To change the worth of a currency downward in relation to other currencies (opposite of *revalue*).

developmentalism   Early 1960s theory that America could develop Third World lands.

devolution   Central government turns some powers over to regions.

dialect   Mutually intelligible variety of a language.

Diet   Name of some parliaments, such as Japan's and Finland's.

dignified   In Bagehot's terms, symbolic or decorative offices.

dirigiste   Bureaucrats directing industry; closely connected to French statism.

discontinuity   A break and new direction in the expected course of events.

disinflation   Bringing down the rate of inflation (not the same as *deflation*, an overall decline in prices).

divide and rule   Roman and British imperial ruling method of setting subjects against each other.

Dolchstoss   German for "stab in the back."

dominant-party system   One party is much stronger than all others and stays in office a long time.

Duma   Russia's national parliament.

dumping   Selling goods overseas for less than it costs to produce them.

dynastic cycle   Rise, maturity, and fall of an imperial family.

dysanalogy   Showing that one example is a poor model for another.

Ecole Nationale d'Administration (ENA)   France's school for top bureaucrats.

efficient   In Bagehot's terms, working, political offices.

egalitarian   Dedicated to equality.

ejido   Land owned in common by villages.

electoral franchise   Right to vote.

elites   Those few persons with great influence.

Elysée   Presidential palace in Paris, equivalent to U.S. White House.

Enlightenment   Eighteenth-century philosophical movement advocating reason and tolerance.

entitlements   Spending programs citizens are automatically entitled to, such as Social Security.

Estado Nôvo   "New State," Vargas's corporatistic welfare state.

Estates-General   Old, unused French parliament.

ethnicity   Cultural characteristics differentiating one group from another.

euro (symbol: €)   Currency for most of Europe since 2002; worth around $1.25.

Eurocommunism   1970s move by Italian Communists away from Stalinism and toward democracy.

European Central Bank   Supervises interest rates, money supply, and inflation in the euro area, like the U.S. Fed.

European Union (EU)   Quasi-federation of most European states; began in 1957 as the Common Market or European Community (EC).

eurozone   The 19 (out of 28) EU countries that use the euro currency.

Events of May   Euphemism for riots and upheaval of May 1968.

excess liquidity   Too much money floating around.

Exchequer   Britain's treasury minister.

exclave   Part of country separated from main territory.

extraterritoriality   Privilege of Europeans in colonial situations to have their own laws and courts.

extreme multipartism   Too many parties in parliament.

failed state   Collapse of sovereignty; essentially, no national governing power.

fake state   Artificial country that splits apart or is absorbed.

fatwa   Ruling by Islamic jurist.

favela   Brazilian shantytown, found in most cities.

Federal Constitutional Court   Germany's top court, equivalent to U.S. Supreme Court.

Federal Republic of Germany   Previously West Germany, now all of Germany.

federalism   System in which component areas have considerable autonomy.

fertility rate   How many children an average woman bears.

feudalism   Political system of power dispersed and balanced between king and nobles.

fiefdom   Land king grants to nobles in exchange for support.

Final Solution   Nazi program to exterminate Jews.

first-order civil divisions   Main territorial units within countries, such as departments in France.

fiscal   Related to taxes and public spending.

Five-Year Plans   Stalin's forced industrialization of the Soviet Union, starting in 1928.

flash party   One that quickly rises and falls.

flight capital   Money that the owner sends out of the country for fear of losing it.

float   To allow a currency to find its own level based on supply and demand.

Forbidden City   Emperor's walled palace complex in Beijing.

foreign direct investment (FDI)   Foreign firms setting up operations in other countries.

Four Tigers   South Korea, Taiwan, Hong Kong, and Singapore.

Free French   De Gaulle's World War II government in exile.

fusion of powers   Connection of executive and legislative branches in parliamentary systems; opposite of U.S. *separation of powers*.

gaijin   Literally, "outside person"; foreigner. (Japanese suffix "jin" means person, thus Nihon-jin and America-jin.)

Gang of Four   Mao's ultraradical helpers, arrested in 1976.

Gastarbeiter   "Guest workers"; temporary labor allowed into Germany.

GDP   Gross domestic product; sum total of goods and services produced in a country in one year.

general election   Nationwide vote for all MPs.

general will   Rousseau's theory of what the whole community wants.

generalization   Process of finding repeated examples and patterns.

genocide   Murder of an entire people.

gensek   Russian abbreviation for "general secretary"; powerful CPSU chief.

geomancy   Divinely correct positioning of structures.

geopolitics   Influence of geography on politics and use of geography for strategic ends.

Gini Index   Measure of inequality; higher is more unequal.

glasnost   Gorbachev's policy of media openness.

globalization   World becoming one big capitalist market.

Gosplan   Soviet central economic planning agency.

government   A particular cabinet, what Americans call "the administration."

grand coalition   A government of two largest parties with only minor parties in opposition.

grande école   French for "great school"; an elite, specialized college.

Grands Corps   Top bureaucrats of France.

Great Leap Forward   Mao's failed late 1950s effort to industrialize China overnight.

Greens   Environmentalist party.

Grundgesetz   Basic Law; Germany's constitution.

Guangdong   Southern coastal province, capital Guangzhou.

guanxi   Chinese for connections (do not confuse with Guangxi Province); polite term for corruption.

guilt   Deeply internalized feeling of personal responsibility and moral failure.

Gulag   The Soviet central prisons administration.

Habsburg   Catholic dynasty that once ruled Austria-Hungary, Spain, Latin America, and the Netherlands.

hacienda   Large country estate with Spanish owner (*hacendado*) and Indian serfs.

hajj   Muslim pilgrimage to Mecca.

Han   Early dynasty, 206 BC to 220 AD, that solidified China's unity and culture. Ethnic meaning: main people of China.

hard currency   Noninflating, recognized currencies used in international dealings, such as dollars and euros.

Hindi   National language of India.

Hinduism   Chief religion of India, polytheistic and based on Vedic scriptures, rebirth, and caste.

Hindutva   Literally, Hinduness.

Holocaust   Nazi genocide of Europe's Jews during World War II.

home rule   Giving a region some autonomy to govern itself.

hooliganism   Violent and destructive behavior.

hukou   (sounds like *who cow*) Registered place of residence.

hung parliament   One in which no party has a majority of seats; requires a *coalition*.

hyperinflation   Very rapid inflation, more than 50 percent a month.

hyperurbanization   Overconcentration of populations into cities.

ideal–typical   Distilling social characteristics into one example.

ideology   Belief system to improve society.

IMF   International Monetary Fund, grants loans to promote economic stability.

immobilisme   Government inability to solve big problems.

imperialism   Powerful countries turning other lands into colonies.

import substitution   Policy of excluding foreign goods and producing them domestically; means high tariffs.

inchoate   Not yet organized, incoherent.

indicative planning   Government suggestions to industry to expand in certain areas.

indirect rule   British colonial governance through native hereditary rulers.

infant mortality rate   Number of live newborns who die in their first year, per thousand; standard measure of nation's health.

inflation   Increase in most prices.

informal economy   Off-the-books transactions to avoid taxes and regulations.

input-output table   Spreadsheet for economy of entire nation.

insolvent   Owes more than it owns.

Inspection   Short for General Finance Inspection; very top of French bureaucracy, with powers to investigate all branches.

institution   Established rules and relationships of power.

institutionalize   To make a political relationship permanent.

intendants   French provincial administrators, answerable only to Paris; early version of *prefects*.

interest group   Association aimed at getting favorable policies.

interested member MP known to represent an interest group.

interior ministry In Europe, department in charge of homeland security and national police.

international relations (IR) Politics *among* countries.

iron triangle Interlocking of politicians, bureaucrats, and businesspeople to promote the flow of funds among them.

Islam Religion founded by Muhammad.

Islamism Islam turned into political ideology.

Islamist Someone who uses Islam in a political way.

Jesuit Society of Jesus; Catholic religious order once active in converting Asians.

jihad Arabic for "struggle"; also Muslim holy war.

junior minister MP with executive responsibilities below cabinet rank.

Junker (Pronounced *YOON care*) From *junge Herren,* young gentlemen; Prussian nobility.

jus sanguinis Latin for "right of blood"; citizenship based on descent.

jus soli Latin for "right of soil"; citizenship given to those born in the country.

Kaiser German for Caesar; emperor.

Kashmir Valley near Himalayas contested by India and Pakistan.

kickback Bribe paid to government official for a contract.

kleptocracy Rule by thieves.

knighthood Lowest rank of nobility, carries the title "Sir."

Koran Muslim holy book.

Korean War 1950–1953 conflict involving North and South Korean, U.S., and Chinese forces.

kow-tow Literally, "head to the ground"; to kneel and bow deeply.

Kremlinology Noting personnel changes to analyze Communist regimes.

Kulturkampf Culture struggle, specifically Bismarck's with the Catholic Church.

labor-force rigidities Unwillingness of workers to take or change jobs.

"La Marseillaise" French national anthem.

Land Germany's first-order civil division, equivalent to U.S. state; plural *Länder*.

Landtag German state legislature.

Lebensraum German for "living space" for an entire nation. (Note: All German nouns are capitalized.)

legitimacy Mass perception that regime's rule is rightful.

liberal European and Latin American for free society and free economy. (Note: much different than U.S. meaning.)

liberal democracy Combines tolerance and freedoms (liberalism) with mass participation (democracy).

Liberal Democrats (LDP) Japan's long-dominant party, a *catchall*.

Lords Upper house of Parliament; now much less important than Commons.

lycée French academic high school.

machismo Strutting, exaggerated masculinity.

Machtpolitik Power politics (cognate to "might").

macroeconomy Big picture of a nation's economy, including GDP size and growth, productivity, interest rates, and inflation.

Maginot Line Supposedly unbreachable French defenses facing Germany before World War II.

Magna Carta 1215 agreement to preserve rights of English nobles.

maharajah Sanskrit for "great king"; Hindu prince.

Majlis Arabic for assembly; Iran's parliament.

majoritarian Electoral system that encourages dominance of one party in a parliament, as in Britain and the United States.

Malthusian Malthus's theory that population growth outstrips food supply.

Manchu Last imperial dynasty of China, 1644–1912; also known as *Qing*.

Manchukuo Japanese puppet state in Manchuria.

Mandarin High civil servant of imperial China; now main language of China.

Mandate of Heaven Old Chinese expression for legitimacy.

Maoism Extreme form of communism, featuring guerrilla warfare and periodic upheavals.

Marshall Plan Massive U.S. financial aid for European recovery.

Marxist Socialist theories of Karl Marx.

mass Most people; those without influence.

mass line Mao's theory of peasant-based revolution for China.

Medef French business association.

Meiji Period of Japan's rapid modernization, starting in 1868.

meritocracy Promotion by brains and ability rather than heredity.

Mesoamerica Spanish for Middle America; southern Mexico and northern Central America.

mestizaje Intermingling of Spanish and Indian.

METI Japan's powerful Ministry of Economy, Trade, and Industry (formerly MITI).

Metternichian system Contrived conservative system that tried to restore pre-Napoleon European monarchy and stability.

microcredit Very small loans to startup businesses.

microeconomy Close-up picture of individual markets, including product design and pricing, efficiency, and costs.

middle class Professionals or those paid salaries, typically more affluent and more educated.

Middle Kingdom China's traditional and current name for itself, "in the middle of the heavens" (translation of *Zhōngguó*).

middle way Supposed blend of capitalism and socialism; also called "third way."

Midi French for "noon"; the South of France.

Ming Chinese dynasty between Mongols and Manchus, 1368–1644.

minister Head of a major department (ministry) of government.

Mitbestimmung "Codetermination"; unions participating in company decisions.

Mitteleuropa Central Europe.

mixed monarchy King balanced by nobles.

mixed-member (MM) Electoral system combining single-member districts with proportional representation.

mobilize To bring new sectors of the population into political participation.

Modell Deutschland German economic model.

modernizing tyrant Dictator who pushes a country ahead.

monetarism Friedman's theory that the rate of growth of money supply governs much economic development.

money politics Lavish use of funds to win elections.

Mongol Central Asian tribes combined by Genghis Khan; ruled China as the Yuan dynasty in the thirteenth and fourteenth centuries.

mosque Muslim house of worship.

MP Member of Parliament.

Mughal From *Mongol*; Muslim conquerors of India; formed empire.

mullah Muslim cleric.

multiculturalism Preservation of diverse languages and traditions within one country; in German, *Multikulti*.

Muslim Follower of Islam; also adjective of *Islam*.

Muslim League Organization demanding a separate Muslim Pakistan.

NAFTA 1994 North American Free Trade Agreement among the United States, Canada, and Mexico.

narcotraficante Drug trafficker.

Narodniki From Russian for "people," *narod*; radical populist agitators of late nineteenth-century Russia.

nation Cultural element of country; people psychologically bound to one another.

National Assembly France's parliament.

National Front French anti-immigrant and anti-EU party.

nationalism Belief in greatness and unity of one's country and hatred of rule by foreigners.

Nationalist Chiang Kai-shek's party that unified China in the late 1920s, abbreviated KMT.

nationalization Government takeover of an industry.

Naxalites Maoist guerrilla fighters in India.

neo-Gaullist Chirac's revival of Gaullist party, now called Union for a Popular Movement (UMP).

neoliberalism Revival of free-market economics, exemplified by Thatcher.

New Economic Policy (NEP) Lenin's economic policy that allowed private activity, 1921–1928.

nomenklatura List of sensitive positions and people eligible to fill them, the Soviet elite.

nonaggression pact Treaty to not attack each other, specifically the 1939 treaty between Hitler and Stalin.

nonperforming loan One that is not being repaid.

norteamericanos "North Americans"; U.S. citizens.

North Caucasus Mountainous region north of Georgia and Azerbaijan, including Chechnya.

Old Republic Brazil's first republic, 1889–1930; rigged democracy.

oligarchy Rule by a few.

OPEC Cartel of oil-rich countries designed to boost petroleum prices.

Open Door U.S. policy of protecting China.

Opium Wars Nineteenth-century British (and French) campaigns to keep China open to opium imports.

opportunist Unprincipled person out for himself or herself.

opposition   Parties in Parliament that are not in the cabinet.

Orangemen   After William of Orange (symbol of Netherlands royal house), Northern Irish Protestants.

Ossi   Informal name for East German.

Ostpolitik   Literally "east policy"; Brandt's building of relations with East Europe, including East Germany.

Ottoman   Turkish imperial dynasty, fourteenth to twentieth centuries.

output affect   Attachment to a system based on its providing material abundance.

overheat   Experience too-rapid economic growth characterized by inflation, factories at full capacity, and excessive borrowing.

Palais Bourbon   Paris house of French National Assembly.

pan-Africanism   Movement to unite all of Africa.

paramilitary   National police force organized and equipped like a light army, such as the French CRS.

paranoia   Unreasonable suspicion of others.

Paris Commune   Citizen takeover of Paris government during 1870–1871 German siege.

parliament   National assembly that considers and enacts laws.

Parliament   When capitalized, Britain's legislature, now usually meaning the House of Commons.

particularism   Region's sense of its difference.

partition   Divide a country among its communities.

party identification   Psychological attachment of a voter to a political party.

party image   Electorate's perception of a given party.

party list   In PR elections, party's ranking of its candidates; voters pick one list as their ballot.

patronage   Giving government jobs to political supporters.

Pearl River Delta   Major industrial area in *Guangdong*; includes Guangzhou, Shenzhen, and Hong Kong.

peerage   A lord or lady, higher than knighthood.

peg   To fix one currency at an unchanging rate to another.

per capita   GDP divided by population, giving approximate level of well-being.

perestroika   Russian for "restructuring"; Gorbachev's proposals to reform the Soviet economy.

periphery   Nation's outlying regions.

permanent secretary   Highest civil servant who runs a ministry, under a nominal minister.

personalismo   Politics by strong, showoff personalities.

peso   Spanish for "weight"; Mexico's currency, worth about 7 U.S. cents.

petit bourgeois   Small shopkeeper.

petrostate   Country based on oil exports.

pinyin   Literally, "spell sound"; current system of transliterating Chinese.

plebiscite   Referendum; mass vote for issue rather than for candidates.

pluralism   Autonomous interaction of social groups with themselves and with government.

pluralistic stagnation   Theory that out-of-control interest groups produce policy logjams.

plurality   Largest quantity, even if less than a majority.

polarized pluralism   A multiparty system of two extremist blocs with little in the center.

policy   The specific choices governments make.

Politburo   "Political bureau"; small, top governing body of most Communist parties.

political culture   Values and attitudes of citizens regarding politics and society.

political economy   Mutual influence of politics and economy; what government should do in the economy.

political generation   Theory that age groups are marked by the great events of their young adulthood.

political geography   How territory and politics influence each other.

political institution   Established and durable relationships of power and authority.

Popular Front   Coalition government of all leftist and liberal parties in France and Spain in the 1930s.

populist   Claims to be for common people and against elites.

pork barrel   Government projects that narrowly benefit legislators' constituencies.

portfolio   Minister's assigned ministry.

Positivism   Philosophy of applying scientific method to social problems and gradually improving society.

postmaterialism   Theory that modern culture has moved beyond getting and spending.

power   Ability of A to get B to do what A wants.

praetorianism   Tendency for military takeovers.

pragmatic   Without ideological considerations; based on practicality.

pre-Columbian   The Americas before Columbus arrived.

precedent   Legal reasoning based on previous cases.

prefect   French *préfet*; top administrator of department.

prefecture   First-order Japanese civil division; like French department.

premier   French for prime minister.

president   Elected head of state, not necessarily powerful.

president's rule   Delhi's ability to take over state governments.

priísmo   Ideology and methods of PRI.

prime minister   Chief of government in parliamentary systems.

privatism   Concerned only with one's personal life; unsocial.

privatization   Government sells off *nationalized* industries to private business.

production   Making things.

productivity   Efficiency with which things are made.

proletariat   According to Marx, class of industrial workers.

proportional representation (PR)   Electoral system of multimember districts with seats awarded by the percentage that parties win.

protectionism   Keeping out imports via tariffs and regulations in order to help domestic producers.

Prussia   Powerful North German state; capital Berlin.

public finances   What a government takes in, what it spends, and how it makes up the difference.

public school   In Britain, a private boarding school, equivalent to a U.S. prep school.

purchasing power parity (PPP)   A currency's value taking cost of living into account.

purge   Stalin's "cleansing" of suspicious elements by firing squad.

Putonghua   "Common language" of China, now standard; earlier called Mandarin.

Qin   First dynasty to unify China, 221–206 B.C.

Qinghua   China's top technological university, in Beijing (still often spelled in Wade-Giles *Tsinghua*).

quarrels   As used here, important, long-term political issues.

quasi-federal   Part-way federal.

Question Hour   Time reserved in Commons for MPs to query ministers.

R & D   Research and development of new technologies.

Raj   From Hindi *rule*; British government of India, 1858–1947.

rational choice   Theory that people rationally pursue their advantage in voting and policies.

reactionary   Seeking to go back to old ways; extremely conservative.

real   (plural, **reís**; symbol, R$) Brazil's currency, worth about 45 U.S. cents.

Realpolitik   Politics of realism.

recession   A shrinking economy, indicated by falling GDP.

Rechtsstaat   Literally, state of laws; government based on written rules and rights.

Red Guards   Radical Maoist youth who disrupted China during the *Cultural Revolution*.

redistribution   Taxing the better off to help the worse off.

referendum   Vote on an issue rather than for an office.

Reform Acts   Series of laws expanding the British electoral franchise.

regency   Council that runs state until king comes of age.

Reich   German for empire.

Reichstag   Pre-Hitler German parliament; its building now houses the *Bundestag*.

reification   Taking theory as reality; from Latin *res*, thing.

Reign of Terror   Robespierre's 1793–1794 rule by guillotine.

remittance   Money sent home.

reparations   Payment for war damages.

republic   Country not headed by a monarch.

republic   First-order civil division of Communist federal systems, equivalent to U.S. states.

republican   In its original sense, supporter of movement to end monarchy.

Résistance   World War II French underground anti-German movement.

revalue   To change the worth of a currency upward in relation to other currencies (opposite of *devalue*).

revisionism   Rethinking an ideology or reinterpreting history.

Rhodes Scholarship   Founded by South African millionaire; sends top foreign students to Oxford.

RMB   *Renminbi* (people's money), official name of China's currency, same as *yuan*.

romanticism   Hearkening to an ideal world or mythical past.

rule of anticipated reactions   Friedrich's theory that politicians plan their moves so as not to anger the public.

rump state   Leftover portions of a country after dismemberment.

runaway system Influential people use their resources to amass more resources.

rupee India's currency (symbol Rs); Rs65 are worth about $1.

S-curve Typical trajectory of economic development.

safe seat Constituency where voting has long favored a given party.

Sahel Narrow band south of Sahara; arid but not yet desert.

savanna Tropical grasslands south of *Sahel*.

scandal Corrupt practice publicized by news media.

seat Membership in a legislature.

Second Vatican Council Series of meetings that modernized the Roman Catholic Church and turned it to problems of poverty; also called Vatican II.

secular Nonreligious.

secularism In India, treating members of all religions equally.

secularization Diminishment of role of religion in government and society.

self-censorship The curbing of criticism writers impose on themselves.

semipresidential System with features of both presidential and parliamentary systems.

sepoy Indian soldier in the British Indian Army.

sexenio From *seis años*; six-year term of Mexico's presidents.

shadow cabinet Leaders of the *opposition* who aim to become the next cabinet.

shah Persian for king.

shame Feeling of having behaved incorrectly and of having violated group norms.

sharia Muslim religious law based on the Koran.

Shia Minority branch of Islam.

Shinto Japan's original religion; the worship of nature, of one's ancestors, and of Japan.

shock therapy Sudden replacement of socialist economy by market economy.

shogun Feudal Japanese military ruler.

Siberia That part of Russia east of the Ural Mountains.

siloviki "Strong men"; security officials who now control Russia (singular *silovik*).

single-member district Sends one representative to Parliament.

Slavophiles Nineteenth-century Russians who wished to develop Russia along native, non-Western lines; also known as "Russophiles."

slush fund Secret, unbudgeted, and unaccountable money used by politicians.

social class Layer or section of population of similar income and status.

social costs Taxes for medical, unemployment, and pension benefits.

socialize To teach political culture, often informally.

soft landing Gradual calming of destabilizing economic shifts.

soft money In U.S. politics, funds given to parties and other groups rather than to candidates in order to skirt restrictions.

Solidarity Huge Polish labor union that ousted the Communist regime in 1989.

sovereignty Last word in law in a given territory; being boss on your own turf.

soziale Marktwirtschaft "Social market economy"; Germany's postwar capitalism aimed at reconstruction and welfare.

SPD German Social Democratic Party.

Special Economic Zones Areas originally on China's southern coast where capitalist economic development was encouraged.

sphere of influence Semicolonial area under control of major power.

Stalinist Brutal central control over Communist parties.

state Institutional or governmental element of country.

State Duma Lower house of Russia's parliament.

state of nature Humans before civilization.

state-owned enterprises (SOEs) Firms still owned by the Chinese government.

statism Idea that a strong government should run things, especially major industries.

statute Ordinary law, usually for a specific problem.

steady-state A system that preserves itself with little change.

strategic variable Factor you can change that makes a big improvement.

structure Institutions of government such as constitution, laws, and branches.

structured access Permanent openness of bureaucracy to interest-group demands.

sub-Saharan Africa south of the Sahara.

subcontinent Asia south of the Himalayas (India, Pakistan, and Bangladesh); also called South Asia.

subject Originally, a subject of the Crown; now means British citizen.

subsidy Government economic aid to individual or business.

sultanate Muslim state governed by a sultan (holder of power).

Sunni Mainstream Islam.

support ratio Number working compared to number retired.

sustainable Can keep going for many years with no major downturns.

swaraj *Swa* = self, *raj* = rule; Indian independence.

symbol Political artifact that stirs mass emotions.

system affect Attachment to a system for its own sake.

Taipei (Pronounced *Type-A*) Capital of Taiwan.

Taiping Religion-based rebellion in nineteenth-century China.

Taiwan Large island off China's southern coast, ruled by Nationalists since 1945.

Tatar Mongol-origin tribes who ruled Russia for centuries. (*Not* Tartar.)

technocrat Official, usually unelected, who governs by virtue of economic skills.

the Continent British term for mainland Europe.

theocracy Rule by priests.

theory Firm generalization supported by evidence.

Thermidor Revolutionary month when Robespierre fell; a calming down after a revolutionary high.

Third World Most of Asia, Africa, and Latin America.

Thirty Years War 1618–1648 Habsburg attempt to conquer and catholicize Europe.

threshold clause In PR systems, minimum percentage party must win to get any seats.

Tiananmen Gate of Heavenly Peace, Beijing's main square.

Tibet Himalayan region of China with distinct language and culture.

Tokugawa Dynasty of *shoguns* who ruled Japan from 1603 to 1868; also known as the Edo Period.

Tories Faction of Parliament that became Conservative Party.

torn In Huntington's theory, a country with a Westernizing elite but traditional masses.

totalitarianism Attempts to totally control society, as under Stalin and Hitler.

trade surplus Exporting more than you import.

Trades Union Congress (TUC) British labor federation, equivalent to the U.S. AFL-CIO.

transparency Exchanges of money open to public scrutiny. (Opposite: *opacity*).

Treasury British ministry that supervises economic policies and budgets of other ministries.

treaty ports Areas of China coast run by European powers.

Trotskyist Marxist but anti-Stalinist, follower of Leon Trotsky.

tsar From "caesar"; Russia's emperor; sometimes spelled old Polish style, *czar*.

turnout Percentage of those eligible who vote in a given election.

tutelle French for tutelage; bureaucratic guidance.

"two-plus" party system Two big parties and several small ones.

tyranny Coercive rule, usually by one person.

Uighur Muslim, Turkic-speaking Chinese ethnic group, bordering ex-Soviet Central Asia.

Ukraine From Slavic for "borderland"; country south of Russia.

unilinear Progressing evenly and always upward.

unimodal Single-peaked distribution.

unit labor costs What it costs to manufacture the same item in different countries.

unit veto Ability of one component to block laws or changes.

unitary System that centralizes power in the capital with little autonomy for component areas.

value-added taxes (VAT) Large, hidden national sales taxes used throughout Europe.

variable Factor that changes and is related to other factors.

velayat-e faqih "Guardianship of the Islamic jurist"; theocratic system devised by Khomeini.

Versailles Palaces and park on outskirts of Paris begun by Louis XIV.

Versailles Treaty 1919 treaty ending World War I.

Vichy Nazi puppet regime that ran France during World War II.

volatile Rises and falls quickly.

voluntarism Belief that human will can change the world.

vote of no-confidence Parliamentary vote to oust prime minister.

wage restraint Unions holding back on compensation demands.

walking-around money Politicians' relatively small payments to buy votes.

war communism   Temporary strict socialism in Russia, 1918–1921.

warlord   General who ran province after collapse of empire in 1911.

Warsaw Pact   Soviet-led alliance of Communist countries, now defunct.

weak state   One unable to govern effectively; corrupt and crime ridden.

Weimar Republic   1919–1933 democratic German republic.

welfare state   Political system that redistributes income from rich to poor, standard in West Europe.

Weltanschauung   Literally "world view"; parties offering firm, narrow ideologies.

Wessi   Informal name for West German.

Westernizers   Nineteenth-century Russians who wished to copy the West.

Westminster   Parliament building.

Westphalia   Treaty ending the Thirty Years War.

Whigs   Faction of Parliament that became Liberal Party.

whip   Parliamentary party leader who makes sure members obey the party in voting.

Whitehall   Main British government offices.

Wirtschaftswunder   German for "economic miracle."

working class   Those paid an hourly wage, typically less affluent and less educated.

World Trade Organization (WTO)   Organization whose 120-plus members open themselves to trade and investment; has quasi-judicial powers.

write off   Lender admits that a *nonperforming loan* will never be repaid.

xenophobia   Fear and hatred of foreigners.

Xinjiang   China's northwesternmost region, home of *Uighurs*.

¥   Symbol for yen (and Chinese *yuan*); Japan's currency; worth about ¥100 to $1.

yuan   China's currency (symbol ¥), officially called RMB, worth about 16 U.S. cents.

yuppie   Short for "young urban professional."

zemstvo   Local parliament in old Russia.

Zhongnanhai   Walled compound for China's top leaders next to Forbidden City in Beijing.

Zionism   Jewish nationalist movement that founded Israel.

Photo Credits

Photos on the following pages are courtesy of Michael G. Roskin:

Chapter 1   page 1, page 17;
Chapter 2   page 25, page 31;
Chapter 3   page 74,
Chapter 4   page127, page 174,
Chapter 5   page 182,
Chapter 6   page 220,
Chapter 7   page 271, page 275, page 298,
Chapter 10   page 392, and
Chapter 12   page 456.

Additional photo credits are as follows:

Chapter 8   page 329: dzain/Fotolia
Chapter 9   page 361: emattil/Fotolia
Chapter 11   page 424: Amar and Isabelle Guillen-Guillen Photo LLC/Alamy

Index